the Unofficial Guide® to

the Best RV and Tent Campgrounds in Florida & the Southeast

Alabama, Florida, Georgia, Kentucky, Louisiana, Mississippi, North Carolina, South Carolina & Tennessee

Other Titles in the Unofficial Guide
Best RV and Tent Campgrounds Series

California & the West

Great Lakes States

Mid-Atlantic States

The Northeast

Northwest & Central Plains

Southwest & South Central Plains

U.S.A.

Other Unofficial Guides

the Unofficial Guide® to

the Best RV and Tent Campgrounds in the Florida & the Southeast

1st Edition

Alabama, Florida, Georgia, Kentucky, Louisiana,
Mississippi, North Carolina, South Carolina & Tennessee

Grace Walton with Trish Riley

Hungry Minds™

Best-Selling Books • Digital Downloads • e-Books • Answer Networks • e-Newsletters
Branded Web Sites • e-Learning

New York, NY • Indianapolis, IN • Cleveland, OH

For Ben Walton, the travelin' toddler
— Grace Walton

For my Dad, Joe Riley, for his enthusiasm for the project
—Trish Riley

Please note that prices fluctuate in the course of time, and travel information changes under the impact of many factors that influence the travel industry. We therefore suggest that you write or call ahead for confirmation when making your travel plans. Every effort has been made to ensure the accuracy of information throughout this book and the contents of this publication are believed correct at the time of printing. Nevertheless, the publishers cannot accept responsibility for errors or omissions or for changes in details given in this guide or for the consequences of any reliance on the information provided by the same. Assessments of attractions and so forth are based upon the author's own experience and therefore, descriptions given in this guide necessarily contain an element of subjective opinion, which may not reflect the publisher's opinion or dictate a reader's own experience on another occasion. Readers are invited to write to the publisher with ideas, comments, and suggestions for future editions.

Your safety is important to us, so we encourage you to stay alert and be aware of your surroundings. Keep a close eye on cameras, purses, and wallets, all favorite targets of thieves and pickpockets.

Published by Hungry Minds, Inc.
909 Third Avenue
New York, NY 10022

Produced by Menasha Ridge Press
COVER DESIGN BY MICHAEL J. FREELAND
INTERIOR DESIGN BY MICHELE LASEAU

Unofficial Guide is a registered trademark of Hungry Minds, Inc.

ISBN 0-7645-6251-7

ISSN 1536-9692

Manufactured in the United States of America

10 9 8 7 6 5 4 3 2 1

Contents

Acknowledgments

I am deeply grateful for the mentorship of my uncle, Bob Sehlinger. A million thanks to Dawn Charlton, whose tireless efforts helped make this book a reality. Thanks also to the Menasha Ridge Press editorial staff, including Holly Brown Cross, Russell Helms, Chris Mohney, Nathan Lott, Marie Hillen, Annie Long, Bud Zehmer, and Molly Merkle.

Four brave little indians accompanied me on the road: my sweet son, Ben Walton; my mom, Mary Whetsell, my step-mom Anne Pogue; and my brother, Aaron Bergner. The following people showered Ben with affection while I worked: his grandparents Bonnie Walton, Steve Walton Sr., and Chuck and Mary Whetsell; his father Steve Walton Jr.; and family friends Jennie Zehmer and Nora Montague.

Friends, family, and colleagues let me crash on their couches and raid their refrigerators. Thanks are in order for Jackie and Bill Ralston, Trent Sehlinger and Sara Manoucheri, Thomas Peake, Jeremy Englert, Johnny Molloy, Joseph Poole, and Mrs. Ila Brown.

Data intensive projects often require a small army of researchers. I'm thankful for the efforts of Shannon Dobbs, Lanette Milligan, Katie Pittenger, Monica Ssenkoloto, Melinda McChesney, Chris Pappas, Julia Folk, Megan Rogala, Sharon Adams, Jack Wright, and Wendy Dorr.

—*Grace Walton*
(author of Alabama, Georgia, Louisiana, Kentucky,
Mississippi, North Carolina, South Carolina, and Tennessee)

The experience of researching this book was greatly enriched by several people, whose efforts I'd like to acknowledge. Thanks to my daughter Rachel, for her preciousness, patience, and pleasant traveling attitude; to my son Bud for his culinary skills and companionship; to my husband Jim Wurster for his cheery chauffering, for his willingness and ability to find the flow and go with it, and for his acceptance and pleasure in joining me on these explorations. Thanks to our terrors Teddi (a Yorkie) and Christie (a Jack Russell) for their love of adventure—they were clearly the most depressed when the long, long ride was over. Thanks to Mom, Trudy Riley, for editorial support, and to Nathan Lott, my editor at Menasha Ridge Press who was most pleasant to work with. Thanks to Kelli Harms and Sheila Davis at Winnebago Industries for arranging a beautiful 2002 Rialta for our Florida tour, and to local dealer Larry Johnson of Palm Truck and RV Centers of Fort Lauderdale and salesman Ken Perry, whose experiences provided us with invaluable advice. Thanks to Jeff Beddow, formerly with the Recreational Vehicle Industry Association, for his assistance and information. Thanks to Brandy Henley, formerly of Visit Florida, for her help in providing information and guides of Florida campgrounds, and to Pat Striska of the Florida Association of RV Parks and Campgrounds. Thanks to friends Jon Farley, and Hal and Joann Wulff for sharing RV tips, camping experiences, and destination recommendations.

We were thrilled for the opportunity to tour this great and amazing state, and although we were worn and tired when we finally returned home after several weeks, we know that we would do it again in a moment. In fact, we're already trying to figure out how we'll manage to make the next road trip!

—*Trish Riley*
(author of Florida)

the Unofficial Guide® to

the Best RV and Tent
Campgrounds in
the Southeast

Introduction

Why Unofficial?

The material in this guide has not been edited or in any way reviewed by the campgrounds profiled. In this "unofficial" guide we represent and serve you, the consumer. By way of contrast with other campground directories, no ads were sold to campgrounds, and no campground paid to be included. Through our independence, we're able to offer you the sort of objective information necessary to select a campground efficiently and with confidence.

Why Another Guide to Campgrounds?

We developed *The Unofficial Guide to the Best RV and Tent Campgrounds in Florida and the Southeast* because we recognized that campers are as discriminating about their choice of campgrounds as most travelers are about their choice of hotels. As a camper, you don't want to stay in every campground along your route. Rather, you prefer to camp only in the best. A comprehensive directory with limited information on each campground listed does little to help you narrow your choices. What you need is a reference that tells you straight out which campgrounds are the best, and that supplies detailed information, collected by independent inspectors, that differentiates those campgrounds from all of the also-rans. This is exactly what *The Unofficial Guide to the Best RV and Tent Campgrounds* delivers.

The Choice Is All Yours

Life is short, and life is about choices. You can stay in a gravel lot, elbow to elbow with other campers, with tractor-trailers roaring by just beyond the fence, or with this guide, you can spend the night in a roomy, shaded site, overlooking a sparkling blue lake. The choice is yours.

The authors of this guide have combed the Southeastern states inspecting and comparing hundreds of campgrounds. Their objective was to create a hit parade of the very best, so that no matter where you travel, you'll never have to spend another night in a dumpy, gravel lot.

The best campgrounds in each state are described in detail in individual profiles so you'll know exactly what to expect. In addition to the fully profiled campgrounds, we provide a Supplemental Directory of Campgrounds that lists hundreds of additional properties that are quite adequate, but that didn't make the cut for the top 350 in the guide. Thus, no matter where you are, you'll have plenty of campgrounds to choose from. None of the campgrounds appearing in this guide, whether fully profiled or in the supplemental list, paid to be included. Rather, each earned its place by offering a superior product. Period.

Letters, Comments, and Questions from Readers

Many who use the Unofficial Guides write to us with questions, comments, and reports of their camping experiences. We appreciate all such input, both positive and critical. Readers' comments are frequently incorporated into revised editions of the Unofficial Guides and have contributed immeasurably to their improvement. Please write to:

The Unofficial Guide to the Best RV and Tent Campgrounds
P.O. Box 43673
Birmingham, AL 35243
UnofficialGuides@menasharidge.com

For letters sent through the mail, please put your return address on both your letter and envelope; the two sometimes become separated. Also include your phone number and email address if you are available for a possible interview.

How to Use This Guide

Using this guide is quick and easy. We begin with this introduction followed by "Campground Awards," a list of the best campgrounds for RVers, tenters, families, and more. Then we profile the best 350 campgrounds in the southeastern states. Next is a supplemental list of hundreds of additional campgrounds including details about prices, hookups, and more. Bringing up the rear is an alphabetical index of all campgrounds included in the guide.

Both the profiled section and the supplemental directory are ordered alphabetically, first by state and then by city. To see what campgrounds are available:

- Find the section covering the state in question.
- Within that section, look up the city alphabetically.
- Under the city, look up the campgrounds alphabetically.

You can choose and locate campgrounds in four different ways.

1. **Use the Map**   If a city appears with a black, solid bullet on our map, at least one of our profiled or listed campgrounds will be located there. The converse is also the case: if the city has a hollow, outlined bullet, you can assume that we do not cover any campgrounds in that city.

2. **Check the Campground Profiles**   In the section where we profile campgrounds, look up any city where you hope to find a campground. If the city isn't listed, it means we do not profile any campgrounds there.

3. **Check the Supplemental Directory of Campgrounds**   Check for the same city in the supplemental listings.

4. **Use the Index**   If you want to see if a specific campground is profiled or listed in the guide, look up the name of the campground in the alphabetical index at the back of the book.

When looking up campgrounds, remember that the best campgrounds are found in the profiled section; always check there first before turning to the Supplemental Directory of Campgrounds.

Understanding the Profiles

Each profile has seven important sections:

Campground Name, Address, and Contact Information   In addition to the street address, we also provide phone and fax numbers as well as website and email addresses.

Ratings   Using the familiar one- to five-star rating with five stars being best, we offer one overall rating for RV campers and a second overall rating for tent campers. The overall rating for each type of camper is based on a rough weighted average of the following eight individually rated categories:

Category	Weight
Beauty	15%
Site Privacy	10%
Site Spaciousness	10%
Quiet	15%
Security	13%
Cleanliness/upkeep	13%
Insect Control	10%
Facilities	14%

Beauty   This rates the natural setting of the campground in terms of its visual appeal. The highest ratings are reserved for campgrounds where the beauty of the campground can be enjoyed and appreciated both at individual campsites and at the campground's public areas. Views, vistas, landscaping, and foliage are likewise taken into consideration.

Site Privacy   This category rates the extent to which the campsites are set apart and/or in some way buffered (usually by trees and shrubs) from adjacent or nearby campsites. The farther campsites are from one another the better. This rating also reflects how busy the access road to the campsites is in terms of traffic. Campgrounds that arrange their sites on a number of cul-de-sacs, for example, will offer quieter sites than a campground where the sites are situated off of a busy loop or along a heavily traveled access road.

Site Spaciousness   This rates the size of the campsite. Generally, the larger the better.

Quiet   This rating indicates the relative quietness of the campground. There are three key considerations. The first is where the campground is located. Campgrounds situated along busy highways or in cities or towns are usually noisier, for example, than rural or wilderness campgrounds removed from major thoroughfares. The second consideration relates to how noise is managed at the campground. Does the campground forbid playing of radios or enforce a "quiet time" after a certain hour? Is there someone on site at night to respond to complaints about other campers being loud or unruly at a late hour? Finally, the rating considers the extent to which trees, shrubs, and the natural topography serve to muffle noise within the campground.

Security   This rating reflects the extent (if any) to which management monitors the campground during the day and night. Physical security is also included in this rating: Is the campground fenced? Is the campground gated? If so, is the gate manned? Generally, a campground located in a city or along a busy road is more exposed to thieves or vandals than a more remote campground, and should more actively supervise access.

Cleanliness This rates the cleanliness, serviceability, and state of repair of the campground, including grounds, sites, and facilities.

Insect Control This rating addresses questions regarding insect and pest control. Does management spray or take other steps to control the presence of mosquitoes and other insect pests? Does the campground drain efficiently following a rain? Are garbage and sewage properly collected and disposed of?

Facilities This rates the overall variety and quality of facilities to include bath house/toilets, swimming pool, retail shops, docks, pavilions, playgrounds, etc. If the quality of respective facilities vary considerably within a given campground, inconsistencies are explained in the prose description of the campground.

Campground Description This is an informative, consumer-oriented description of the campground. It includes what makes the campground special or unique and what differentiates it from other area campgrounds. The description may additionally include the following:

- The general layout of the campground.
- Where the campground is located relative to an easily referenced city or highway.
- The general setting (wilderness, rural, or urban).
- Description of the campsites including most and least desirable sites.
- Prevailing weather considerations and best time to visit.
- Mention of any unusual, exceptional, or deficient facilities.
- Security considerations, if any (gates that are locked at night, accessibility of campground to non-campers, etc.).

Basics Key information about the campground including:

- *Operated By* Who owns and/or operates the campground.
- *Open* Dates or seasons the campground is open.
- *Site Assignment* How sites are most commonly obtained (first-come, first served; reservations accepted; reservations only; assigned on check-in, etc. Deposit and refund policy.
- *Registration* Where the camper registers on arrival. Information on how and where to register after normal business hours (late arrival).
- *Fee* Cost of a standard campsite for one night for RV sites and tent sites respectively. Forms of payment accepted. Uses the following abbreviations for credit cards: V = VISA, AE = American Express, MC = MasterCard, D = Discover, CB = Carte Blanche, and DC = Diner's Club International.
- *Parking* Usual entry will be "At campsite" or "On road," though some campgrounds have a central parking lot from which tent campers must carry their gear to their campsite.

Facilities   This is a brief data presentation that provides information on the availability of specific facilities and services.

- *Number of RV Sites* Any site where RVs are permitted.

- *Number of Tent-Only Sites* Sites set aside specifically for tent camping, including pop-up tent trailers.

- *Hookups* Possible hookups include electric, water, sewer, cable TV, phone, and Internet connection. Electrical hookups vary from campground to campground. Where electrical hookups are available, the amperage available is stated parenthetically, for example: "Hookups: Electric (20 amps), water."

- *Each Site* List of equipment such as grill, picnic table, lantern pole, fire pit, water faucet, electrical outlet, etc., provided at each campsite.

- *Dump station, laundry, pay phone, restrooms and showers, fuel, propane, RV service, general store, vending, playground* Are these items or services available on site? Their respective fields indicate the answer.

- *Internal Roads* Indicates the road type (gravel, paved, dirt), and condition.

- *Market* Location and distance of closest supermarket or large grocery store.

- *Restaurant* Location and distance of closest restaurant.

- *Other* Boat ramp, dining pavilion, miniature golf, tennis court, lounge, etc.

- *Activities* Activities available at the campground or in the area.

- *Nearby Attractions* Can be natural or manmade.

- *Additional Information* The best sources to call for general information on area activities and attractions. Sources include local or area chambers of commerce, tourist bureaus, visitors and convention authorities, forest service, etc.

Restrictions   Any restrictions that apply, including:

- *Pets* Conditions under which pets are allowed or not.

- *Fires* Campground rules for fires and fire safety.

- *Alcoholic Beverages* Campground rules regarding the consumption of alcoholic beverages.

- *Vehicle Maximum Length* Length in feet of the maximum size vehicle the campground can accommodate.

- *Other* Any other rules or restrictions, to include minimum and maximum stays; age or group size restrictions; areas off-limits to vehicular traffic; security constraints such as locking the main gate during the night; etc.

How to Get There   Clear and specific directions, including mileage and landmarks, for finding the campground.

Supplemental Directory of Campgrounds

If you're looking for a campground within the territory covered in this guide and can't find a profiled campground that is close or convenient to your route, check the Supplemental Directory of Campgrounds. This directory of hundreds of additional campgrounds is organized alphabetically by state and city name. Each entry provides the campground's name, address, reservations phone, fax, website, number sites, average fee per night, and hookups available. .

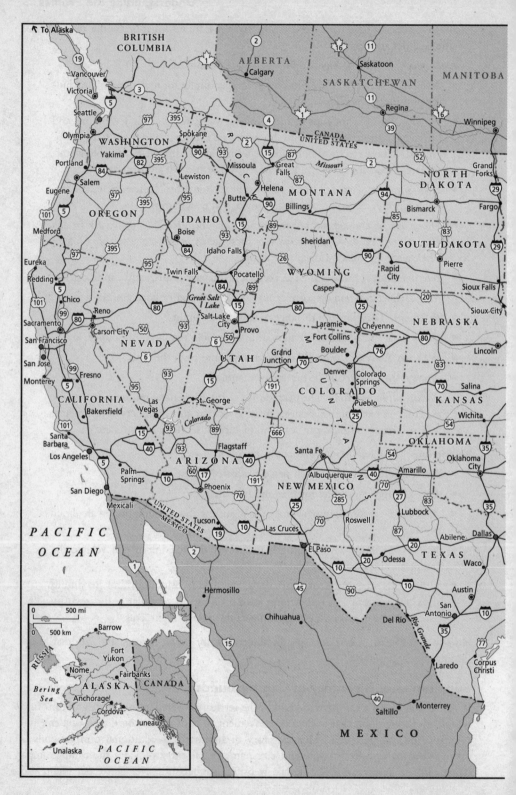

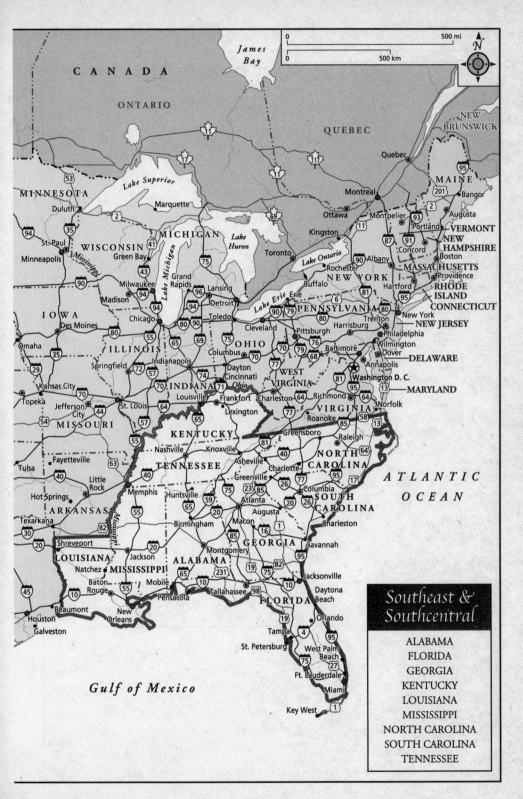

Southeast & Southcentral

ALABAMA
FLORIDA
GEORGIA
KENTUCKY
LOUISIANA
MISSISSIPPI
NORTH CAROLINA
SOUTH CAROLINA
TENNESSEE

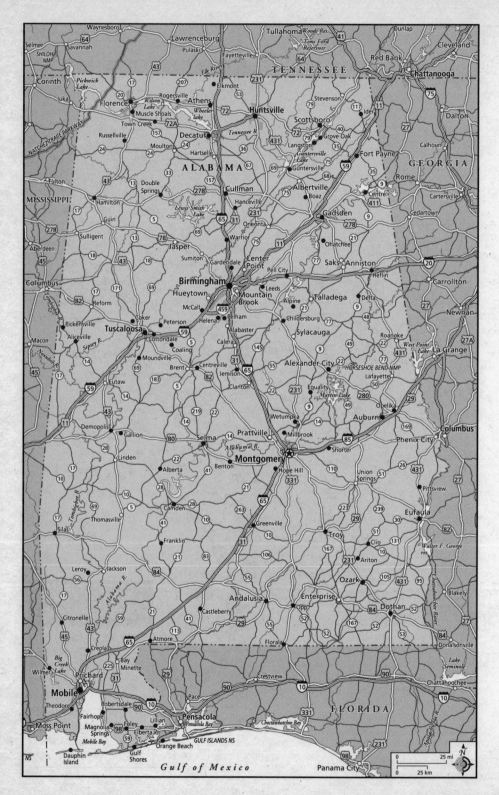

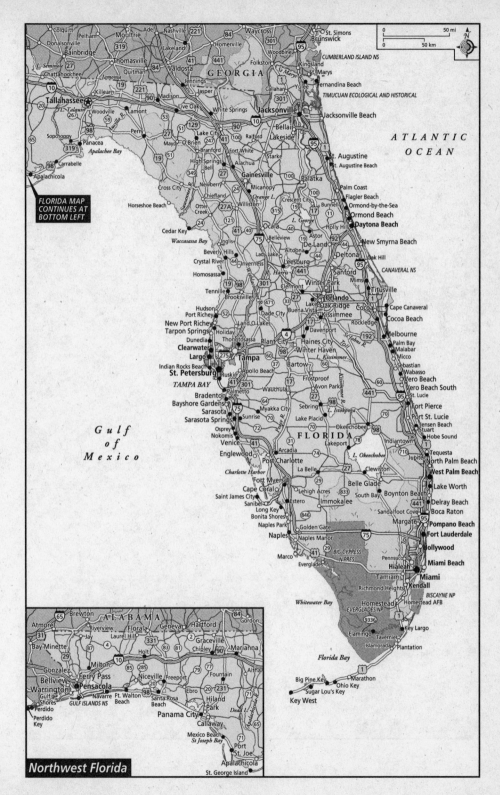

Northwest Florida

9

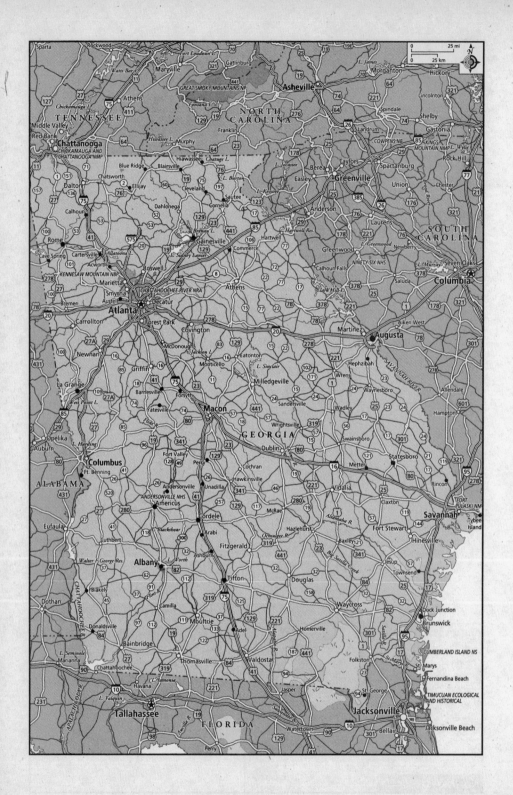

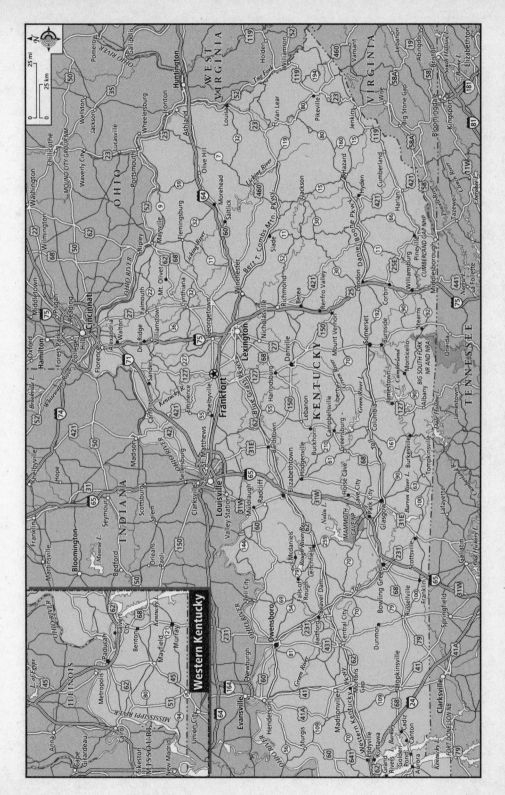

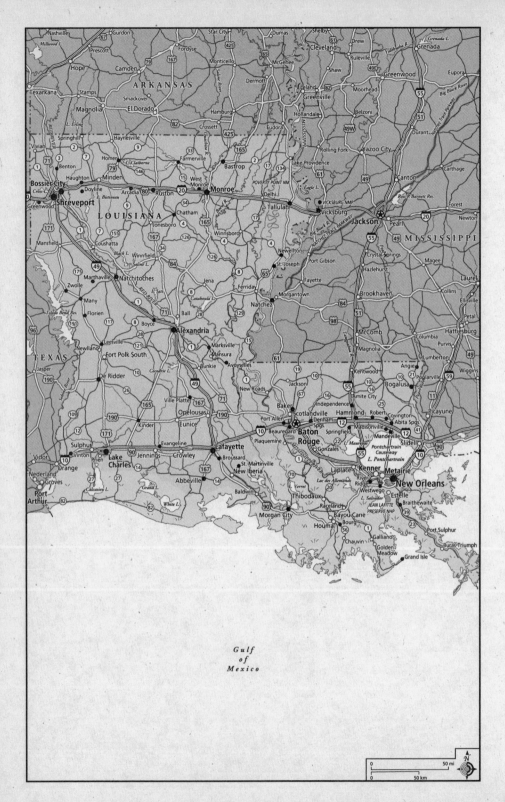

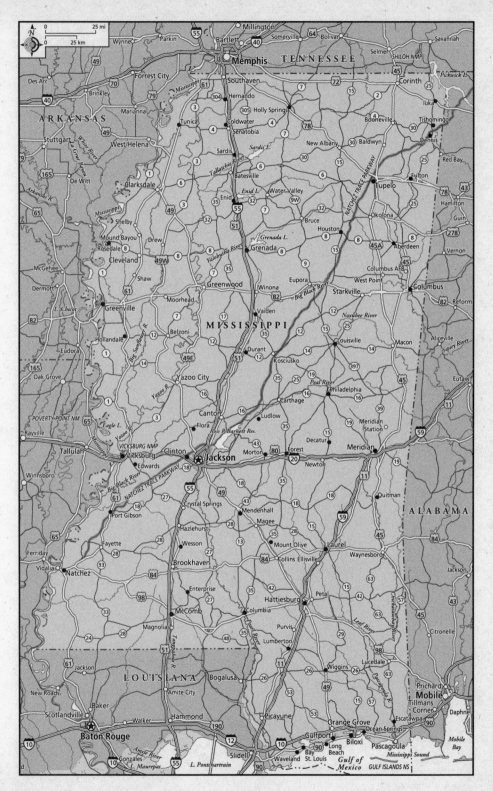

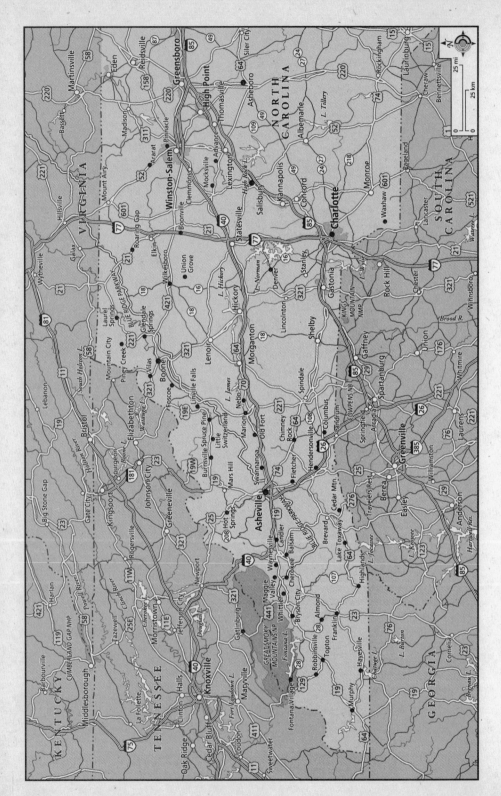

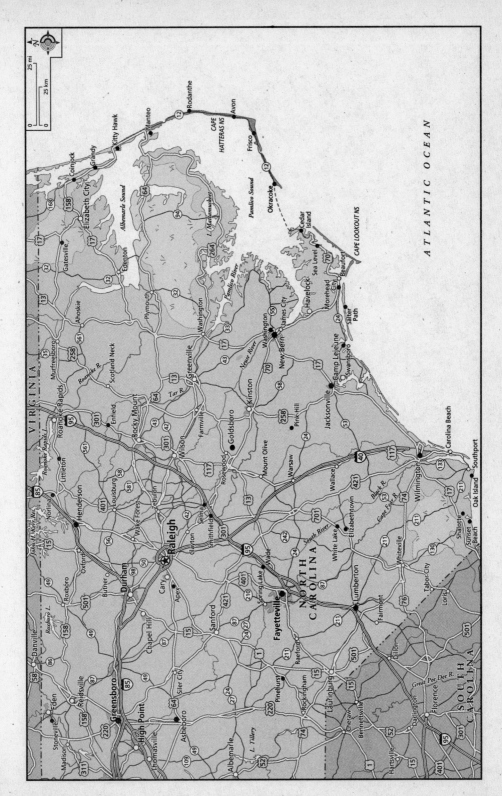

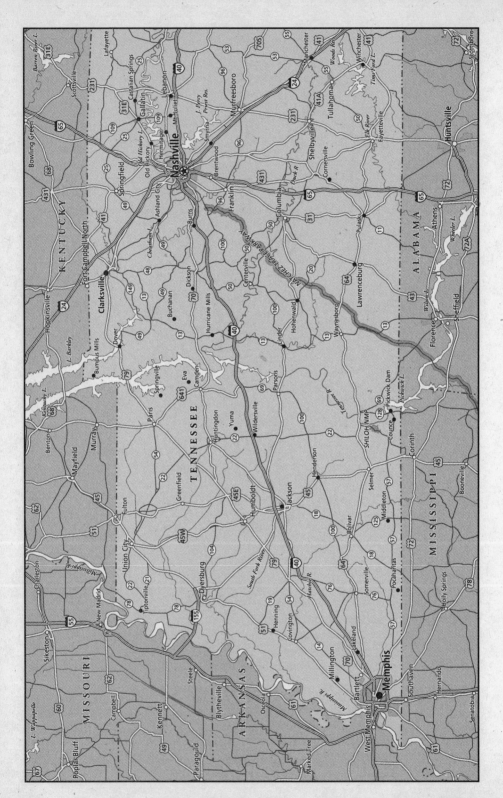

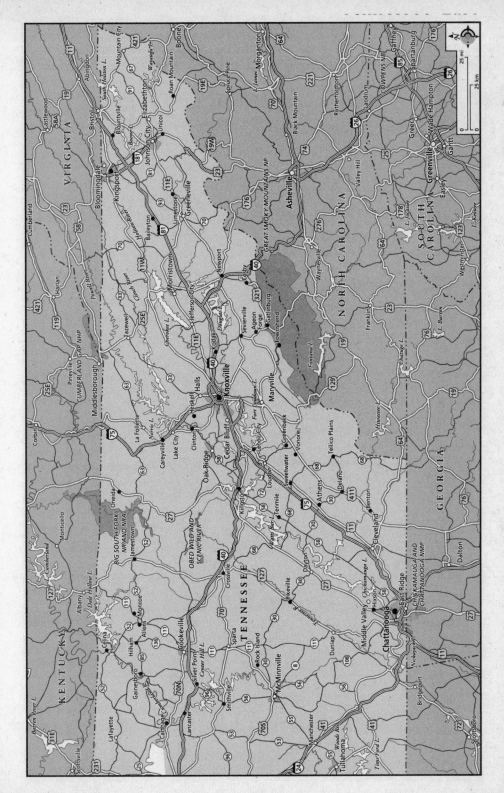

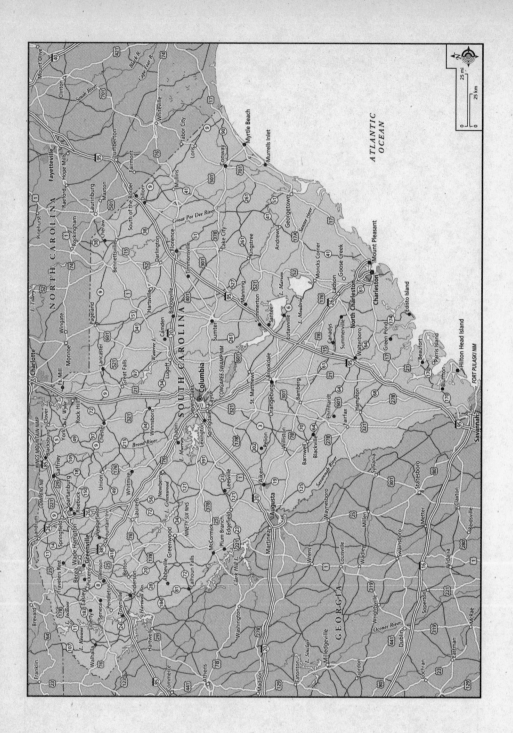

Campground Awards

ALABAMA

Best RV Camping
Clear Creek Recreation Area, Jasper
DeSoto State Park, Fort Payne
Joe Wheeler State Park, Rogersville
Sherling Lake, Greenville

Best Tent Camping
Buck's Pocket State Park, Grove Oak
Clear Creek Recreation Area, Jasper
De Soto State Park, Fort Payne
Joe Wheeler State Park, Rogersville

Most Beautiful Campgrounds
Buck's Pocket State Park, Grove Oak
Clear Creek Recreation Area, Jasper
De Soto State Park, Fort Payne
Joe Wheeler State Park, Rogersville
Sherling Lake, Greenville

Most Private Campsites
Clear Creek Recreation Area, Jasper

Most Spacious Campsites
Clear Creek Recreation Area, Jasper
De Soto State Park, Fort Payne

Quietest Campgrounds
Buck's Pocket State Park, Grove Oak
Clear Creek Recreation Area, Jasper
Sherling Lake, Greenville

Most Secure Campgrounds
Clear Creek Recreation Area, Jasper
Corinth Recreation Area, Double Springs
De Soto State Park, Fort Payne
Joe Wheeler State Park, Rogersville

Pickensville Recreation Area, Aliceville Lake, Pickensville
Sherling Lake, Greenville
Wind Creek State Park, Alexander City

Cleanest Campgrounds
Clear Creek Recreation Area, Jasper
Sherling Lake, Greenville

Best Campground Facilities
Gulf State Park, Gulf Shores
Joe Wheeler State Park, Rogersville
Lake Guntersville State Park, Guntersville
Lakepoint Resort State Park, Eufaula
Little Mountain Marina Resort, Guntersville/Langston
Noccalula Falls Park and Campground, Gadsden
Oak Mountain State Park, Birmingham/Pelham

Best Rural, Farm, or Ranch Settings
Noccalula Falls Park and Campground, Gadsden

Best Urban and Suburban Settings
Doc's RV Park, Gulf Shores
Gulf Breeze Resort, Gulf Shores
KOA Birmingham South, Birmingham/Pelham
McCalla/Tannehill KOA Kampground, McCalla
Perdido Bay KOA, Lillian

Best Mountain Settings
Buck's Pocket State Park, Grove Oak
De Soto State Park, Fort Payne
Monte Sano State Park, Huntsville
Oak Mountain State Park, Birmingham/Pelham

ALABAMA (continued)

Best Waterfront Settings
Joe Wheeler State Park, Rogersville
Lake Guntersville State Park, Guntersville
Lake Lurleen State Park, Coker
Lakepoint Resort State Park, Eufaula
Little Mountain Marina Resort,
  Guntersville/Langston
Old Lock 16 Park, Holt Lake, Peterson
Pickensville Recreation Area, Aliceville Lake,
  Pickensville
Prairie Creek Campground, Woodruff Lake,
  Benton
Wind Creek State Park, Alexander City

Most Romantic Campgrounds
Clear Crek Recreation Area, Jasper
De Soto State Park, Fort Payne
Joe Wheeler State Park, Rogersville
Sherling Lake, Greenville

Best Family-Oriented Campgrounds
De Soto Caverns, Childersburg
Escatawpa Hollow Campground, Wilmer
Gulf State Park, Gulf Shores
Noccalula Falls Park and Campground, Gadsden

FLORIDA

Best RV Camping
Camelot RV Park, Malabar
Emerald Coast RV Beach Resort, Panama City
  Beach
Florida Caverns State Park, Marianna
Lion Country Safari KOA, West Palm Beach
Nettles Island, Jensen Beach
Outdoor Resorts of Chokoluskee, Outdoor
  Resorts of Chokoluskee
Rock Crusher Canyon RV and Music Park, Crystal
  River
Top Sail Hill Preserve State Park: Gregory E.
  Moore RV Resort, Santa Rosa Beach
Travelers Campground, Alachua
Yogi Bear's Jellystone Park Camp Resorts,
  Madison

Best Tent Camping
Anastasia State Park, St. Augustine
Blackwater River State Park, Holt
Falling Waters State Recreation Area, Chipley
Florida Caverns State Park, Marianna
Grayton Beach State Recreation Area, Santa Rosa
  Beach
Highlands Hammock State Park, Sebring
Hillsborough River State Park, Thonotosassa
  (Tampa)
Jonathan Dickinson State Park, Hobe Sound
Ocala National Forest—Alexander Springs,
  Altoona
Paynes Prairie State Preserve, Micanopy
Spirit of the Suwannee Music Park, Live Oak

Most Beautiful Campgrounds
Anastasia State Park, St. Augustine
Blackwater River State Park, Holt

Dr. Julian G. Bruce St. George Island State Park,
  St. George Island
Falling Waters State Recreation Area, Chipley
Florida Caverns State Park, Marianna
Fort Clinch State Park, Fernandina Beach, Amelia
  Island
Grayton Beach State Recreation Area, Santa Rosa
  Beach
Highlands Hammock State Park, Sebring
Hillsborough River State Park, Thonotosassa
  (Tampa)
Jonathan Dickinson State Park, Hobe Sound
Koreshan State Historic Site, Estero
Myaka River State Park, Sarasota
Ocala National Forest—Alexander Springs,
  Altoona
Paynes Prairie State Preserve, Micanopy
Spirit of the Suwannee Music Park, Live Oak

Most Private Campsites
Blackwater River State Park, Holt

Most Spacious Campsites
Craig's RV Park, Inc., Arcadia
Rock Crusher Canyon RV and Music Park,
  Crystal River
Spirit of the Suwannee Music Park, Live Oak

Quietest Campgrounds
Big Cypress State Preserve, Clewiston
Blackwater River State Park, Holt
Chokoluskee Island Park and Campground,
  Chokoluskee
Craig's RV Park, Inc., Arcadia
Dr. Julian G. Bruce St. George Island State Park,
  St. George Island
Falling Waters State Recreation Area, Chipley

FLORIDA (continued)

Quietest Campgrounds (continued)
Florida Caverns State Park, Marianna

Grayton Beach State Recreation Area, Santa Rosa Beach

Hillsborough River State Park, Thonotosassa (Tampa)

Jonathan Dickinson State Park, Hobe Sound

Myaka River State Park, Sarasota

Rock Crusher Canyon RV and Music Park, Crystal River

Steinhatchee RV Refuge, Tennille

Most Secure Campgrounds
Anastasia State Park, St. Augustine

Arrowhead RV Park, Marianna

Bayside Pensacola—Perdido Bay Kampground Resort, Lillian, AL (Pensacola, FL)

Camelot RV Park, Malabar

Craig's RV Park, Inc., Arcadia

Disney's Fort Wilderness Resort and Campground, Lake Buena Vista

Dr. Julian G. Bruce St. George Island State Park, St. George Island

Emerald Coast RV Beach Resort, Panama City Beach

Falling Waters State Recreation Area, Chipley

Florida Caverns State Park, Marianna

Fort Clinch State Park, Fernandina Beach, Amelia Island

Fort Myers Pine Island KOA, St. James City

Gamble Rogers Memorial State Recreation Area, Flagler Beach

Grayton Beach State Recreation Area, Santa Rosa Beach

High Springs Campground, High Springs

Highlands Hammock State Park, Sebring

Hillsborough River State Park, Thonotosassa (Tampa)

John Pennekamp Coral Reef State Park, Key Largo

Jonathan Dickinson State Park, Hobe Sound

Key Largo Kampground, Key Largo

Koreshan State Historic Site, Estero

Lazy K RV Park, Palm Bay

Lion Country Safari KOA, West Palm Beach

Miami/Everglades KOA Kampground, Miami

Myaka River State Park, Sarasota

Nettles Island, Jensen Beach

Ocala National Forest—Alexander Springs, Altoona

Paynes Prairie State Preserve, Micanopy

Rock Crusher Canyon RV and Music Park, Crystal River

San Carlos RV Park, Fort Myers Beach

Sebastian Inlet State Recreation Area, Melbourne Beach

Spirit of the Suwannee Music Park, Live Oak

Sunshine Key Fun Resort, Ohio Key

Tallahassee RV Park, Tallahassee

Top Sail Hill Preserve State Park: Gregory E. Moore RV Resort, Santa Rosa Beach

Zachary Taylor Camping Resort, Okeechobee

Cleanest Campgrounds
Bayside Pensacola—Perdido Bay Kampground Resort, Lillian, AL (Pensacola, FL)

Beverly Beach Camptown RV Resort, Flagler Beach/Beverly Beach

Blackwater River State Park, Holt

Camelot RV Park, Malabar

Cedar Key RV Park, Cedar Key

Craig's RV Park, Inc., Arcadia

Disney's Fort Wilderness Resort and Campground, Lake Buena Vista

Dr. Julian G. Bruce St. George Island State Park, St. George Island

Emerald Coast RV Beach Resort, Panama City Beach

Falling Waters State Recreation Area, Chipley

Florida Caverns State Park, Marianna

Fort Myers Pine Island KOA, St. James City

Gamble Rogers Memorial State Recreation Area, Flagler Beach

Grayton Beach State Recreation Area, Santa Rosa Beach

Highlands Hammock State Park, Sebring

John Pennekamp Coral Reef State Park, Key Largo

Koreshan State Historic Site, Estero

Lion Country Safari KOA, West Palm Beach

Markham Park, Sunrise

Miami/Everglades KOA Kampground, Miami

Nettles Island, Jensen Beach

Ocala National Forest—Alexander Springs, Altoona

Outdoor Resorts of Chokoluskee, Outdoor Resorts of Chokoluskee

Paradise Island Resort—formerly Buglewood RV Resort, Fort Lauderdale

Paynes Prairie State Preserve, Micanopy

Rock Crusher Canyon RV and Music Park, Crystal River

Sebastian Inlet State Recreation Area, Melbourne Beach

Sunshine Key Fun Resort, Ohio Key

Tallahassee RV Park, Tallahassee

Top Sail Hill Preserve State Park: Gregory E. Moore RV Resort, Santa Rosa Beach

FLORIDA (continued)

Cleanest Campgrounds (continued)
Yogi Bear's Jellystone Park Camp Resorts, Madison

Zachary Taylor Camping Resort, Okeechobee

Best Campground Facilities
Anastasia State Park, St. Augustine

Bayside Pensacola—Perdido Bay Kampground Resort, Lillian, AL (Pensacola, FL)

Beverly Beach Camptown RV Resort, Flagler Beach/Beverly Beach

Camelot RV Park, Malabar

Craig's RV Park, Inc., Arcadia

Disney's Fort Wilderness Resort and Campground, Lake Buena Vista

Dr. Julian G. Bruce St. George Island State Park, St. George Island

Emerald Coast RV Beach Resort, Panama City Beach

Florida Caverns State Park, Marianna

Fort Clinch State Park, Fernandina Beach, Amelia Island

Fort Myers Pine Island KOA, St. James City

Grayton Beach State Recreation Area, Santa Rosa Beach

John Pennekamp Coral Reef State Park, Key Largo

Jonathan Dickinson State Park, Hobe Sound

Koreshan State Historic Site, Estero

Lion Country Safari KOA, West Palm Beach

Markham Park, Sunrise

Nettles Island, Jensen Beach

Ocala National Forest—Alexander Springs, Altoona

Paradise Island Resort—formerly Buglewood RV Resort, Fort Lauderdale

Sebastian Inlet State Recreation Area, Melbourne Beach

Spirit of the Suwannee Music Park, Live Oak

Sunshine Key Fun Resort, Ohio Key

Top Sail Hill Preserve State Park: Gregory E. Moore RV Resort, Santa Rosa Beach

Yogi Bear's Jellystone Park Camp Resorts, Madison

Zachary Taylor Camping Resort, Okeechobee

Most Romantic Campgrounds
Blackwater River State Park, Holt

Best Swimming Pools
Florida Caverns State Park, Marianna

Nettles Island, Jensen Beach

Ocala National Forest—Alexander Springs, Altoona

Outdoor Resorts of Chokoluskee, Outdoor Resorts of Chokoluskee

San Carlos RV Park, Fort Myers Beach

GEORGIA

Best RV Camping
Chestnut Ridge Campground, Flowery Branch

Doll Mountain Campground, Ellijay

Payne's Creek, Hartwell

Shoal Creek, Buford

Skidaway Island State Park, Savannah

Stephen Foster State Park, Fargo

Woodring Branch Campground, Chatsworth

Best Tent Camping
Chestnut Ridge Campground, Flowery Branch

Cloudland Canyon State Park, Rising Fawn

Doll Mountain Campground, Ellijay

Lake Blue Ridge Campground, Blue Ridge

Payne's Creek, Hartwell

Rabun Beach Campground, Clayton

Shoal Creek, Buford

Skidaway Island State Park, Savannah

Stephen Foster State Park, Fargo

Woodring Branch Campground, Chatsworth

Most Beautiful Campgrounds
Bald Ridge, Cumming

Blanton Creek Park, Fortson

Blythe Island Regional Park, Brunswick

Chestnut Ridge Campground, Flowery Branch

Cloudland Canyon State Park, Rising Fawn

Crooked River State Park, St. Mary's

Doll Mountain Campground, Ellijay

Fort McAllister State Historic Park, Richmond Hill

General Coffee State Park, Nicholls

Georgia Veterans Memorial State Park, Cordele

Hard Labor Creek State Park, Rutledge

Lake Blue Ridge Campground, Blue Ridge

Lake Lanier Islands, Lake Lanier Islands

Little Ocmulgee State Park, McRae

Mistletoe State Park, Appling

Payne's Creek, Hartwell

Rabun Beach Campground, Clayton

Shoal Creek, Buford

Skidaway Island State Park, Savannah

GEORGIA (continued)

Most Beautiful Campgrounds (continued)
Stephen Foster State Park, Fargo
Unicoi State Park, Helen
Vogel State Park, Blairsville
Watsadler, Hartwell
Woodring Branch Campground, Chatsworth

Most Private Campsites
Chestnut Ridge Campground, Flowery Branch
Cloudland Canyon State Park, Rising Fawn
Doll Mountain Campground, Ellijay
Indian Springs State Park, Jackson
Lake Blue Ridge Campground, Blue Ridge
Payne's Creek, Hartwell
Rabun Beach Campground, Clayton
Shoal Creek, Buford
Skidaway Island State Park, Savannah
Stephen Foster State Park, Fargo
Woodring Branch Campground, Chatsworth

Most Spacious Campsites
Bald Ridge, Cumming
Blythe Island Regional Park, Brunswick
Chestnut Ridge Campground, Flowery Branch
Cloudland Canyon State Park, Rising Fawn
Crooked River State Park, St. Mary's
Doll Mountain Campground, Ellijay
Fort McAllister State Historic Park, Richmond Hill
General Coffee State Park, Nicholls
Georgia Veterans Memorial State Park, Cordele
Indian Springs State Park, Jackson
Lake Blue Ridge Campground, Blue Ridge
Payne's Creek, Hartwell
Rabun Beach Campground, Clayton
Shoal Creek, Buford
Skidaway Island State Park, Savannah
Stephen Foster State Park, Fargo
Woodring Branch Campground, Chatsworth

Quietest Campgrounds
Blanton Creek Park, Fortson
Blythe Island Regional Park, Brunswick
Chestnut Ridge Campground, Flowery Branch
Crooked River State Park, St. Mary's
Doll Mountain Campground, Ellijay
Eagles Roost Campground, Lake Park
Fort McAllister State Historic Park, Richmond Hill
General Coffee State Park, Nicholls
Lake Blue Ridge Campground, Blue Ridge
Rabun Beach Campground, Clayton
Shoal Creek, Buford

Skidaway Island State Park, Savannah
Stephen Foster State Park, Fargo
Woodring Branch Campground, Chatsworth

Most Secure Campgrounds
Bald Ridge, Cumming
Blanton Creek Park, Fortson
Bobby Brown State Park, Elberton
Chestnut Ridge Campground, Flowery Branch
Cloudland Canyon State Park, Rising Fawn
Elijah Creek State Park, Lincolnton
Lake Blue Ridge Campground, Blue Ridge
Lake Lanier Islands, Lake Lanier Islands
Mistletoe State Park, Appling
Old Salem, Greensboro
Parks Ferry, Greensboro
Payne's Creek, Hartwell
Red Top Mountain State Park, Cartersville
Shoal Creek, Buford
Stephen Foster State Park, Fargo
Tugaloo State Park, Lavonia
Woodring Branch Campground, Chatsworth

Cleanest Campgrounds
Bald Ridge, Cumming
Brookwood RV Resort Park, Marietta
Chestnut Ridge Campground, Flowery Branch
Eagles Roost Campground, Lake Park
Forsyth KOA Campground, Forsyth
Shoal Creek, Buford
Stephen Foster State Park, Fargo

Best Campground Facilities
F. D. Roosevelt State Park, Pine Mountain
General Coffee State Park, Nicholls
Georgia Veterans Memorial State Park, Cordele
Hard Labor Creek State Park, Rutledge
Lake Lanier Islands, Lake Lanier Islands
Little Ocmulgee State Park, McRae
Stone Mountain Family Campground, Stone Mountain
The Parks at Chehaw, Albany

Best Rural, Farm, or Ranch Settings
General Coffee State Park, Nicholls
The Parks at Chehaw, Albany

Best Urban and Suburban Settings
Atlanta South KOA RV Resort, McDonough
Brookwood RV Resort Park, Marietta
Fair Harbor RV Park & Campground, Perry
KOA Atlanta North, Kennesaw

GEORGIA (continued)

Best Urban and Suburban Settings
(continued)
- KOA Chattanooga South, Ringgold
- KOA Savannah South, Richmond Hill
- Stone Mountain Family Campground, Stone Mountain
- The Pottery Campgrounds, Commerce
- Twin Oaks RV Park, Perry

Best Mountain Settings
- Cloudland Canyon State Park, Rising Fawn
- Doll Mountain Campground, Ellijay
- Lake Blue Ridge Campground, Blue Ridge
- Moccasin Creek State Park, Clarksville
- Rabun Beach Campground, Clayton
- Unicoi State Park, Helen
- Vogel State Park, Blairsville

Best Waterfront Settings
- Bald Ridge, Cumming
- Blanton Creek Park, Fortson
- Chestnut Ridge Campground, Flowery Branch
- Crooked River State Park, St. Mary's
- Doll Mountain Campground, Ellijay
- Elijah Creek State Park, Lincolnton
- Georgia Veterans Memorial State Park, Cordele
- Hart State Park, Hartwell
- Lake Blue Ridge Campground, Blue Ridge
- Lake Lanier Islands, Lake Lanier Islands
- Mistletoe State Park, Appling
- Payne's Creek, Hartwell

- Red Top Mountain State Park, Cartersville
- Shoal Creek, Buford
- Watsadler, Hartwell
- Woodring Branch Campground, Chatsworth

Most Romantic Campgrounds
- Bald Ridge, Cumming
- Blythe Island Regional Park, Brunswick
- Chestnut Ridge Campground, Flowery Branch
- Cloudland Canyon State Park, Rising Fawn
- Crooked River State Park, St. Mary's
- Doll Mountain Campground, Ellijay
- Fort McAllister State Historic Park, Richmond Hill
- General Coffee State Park, Nicholls
- Georgia Veterans Memorial State Park, Cordele
- Lake Blue Ridge Campground, Blue Ridge
- Payne's Creek, Hartwell
- Rabun Beach Campground, Clayton
- Shoal Creek, Buford
- Skidaway Island State Park, Savannah
- Stephen Foster State Park, Fargo
- Woodring Branch Campground, Chatsworth

Best Family-Oriented Campgrounds
- Elijah Creek State Park, Lincolnton
- General Coffee State Park, Nicholls
- Lake Lanier Islands, Lake Lanier Islands
- Stone Mountain Family Campground, Stone Mountain
- The Parks at Cheaha, Albany

KENTUCKY

Best RV Camping
- Cumberland Gap National Historical Park, Middlesboro
- Mammoth Cave National Park, Mammoth Cave
- Twin Knobs Recreation Area, Morehead

Best Tent Camping
- Cumberland Gap National Historical Park, Middlesboro
- Mammoth Cave National Park, Mammoth Cave
- Twin Knobs Recreation Area, Morehead

Most Beautiful Campgrounds
- Breaks Interstate Park, Elkhorn City
- Carr Creek State Park, Sassafras

- Cumberland Gap National Historical Park, Middlesboro
- Dale Holow Lake SP, Bow
- Lake Barkley State Resort Park, Cadiz
- Mammoth Cave National Park, Mammoth Cave
- Twin Knobs Recreation Area, Morehead

Most Private Campsites
- Cumberland Gap National Historical Park, Middlesboro
- Twin Knobs Recreation Area, Morehead

Most Spacious Campsites
- Cumberland Gap National Historical Park, Middlesboro

KENTUCKY (continued)

Most Spacious Campsites (continued)
Mammoth Cave National Park, Mammoth Cave
Twin Knobs Recreation Area, Morehead

Quietest Campgrounds
Cumberland Gap National Historical Park,
  Middlesboro
Pennyrile Forest SPR, Dawson Springs
Twin Knobs Recreation Area, Morehead

Most Secure Campgrounds
Barren River Lake State Park, Lucas
Big Bone Lick State Park, Union
Dale Holow Lake State Park, Bow
Mammoth Cave National Park, Mammoth Cave
Rough River Dam SRP, Falls of Rough
The Narrows, Barren River Lake, Scottsville
Twin Knobs Recreation Area, Morehead

Cleanest Campgrounds
Dale Holow Lake State Park, Bow
Mammoth Cave National Park, Mammoth Cave

Best Campground Facilities
Barren River Lake State Park, Lucas
Greenbo Lake State Resort Park, Greenup
Kenlake State Resort Park, Hardin
Kincaid Lake State Park, Falmouth
Lake Barkley State Resort Park, Cadiz
Lake Cumberland SRP, Jamestown
Pennyrile Forest SPR, Dawson Springs

Best Rural, Farm, or Ranch Settings
Kentucky Horse Park Campground, Lexington

Best Urban and Suburban Settings
Bowling Green, KY KOA Kampground, Bowling
Green

Cincinnati South KOA, Cincinnati
John James Audubon State Park, Henderson
KOA Louisville South, Shepherdsville

Best Mountain Settings
Breaks Interstate Park, Elkhorn City
Carr Creek State Park, Sassafras
Cumberland Gap National Historical Park,
  Middlesboro

Best Waterfront Settings
General Butler SRP, Carrollton
Kenlake State Resort Park, Hardin
Lake Barkley State Resort Park, Cadiz
The Narrows, Barren River Lake, Scottsville
Twin Knobs Recreation Area, Morehead

Most Romantic Campgrounds
Cumberland Gap National Historical Park,
  Middlesboro
Mammoth Cave National Park, Mammoth Cave
Twin Knobs Recreation Area, Morehead

Best Family-Oriented Campgrounds
Kentucky Horse Park Campground, Lexington
Levi Jackson Wilderness Road State Park Camp-
  ground, London
Yogi Bear's Jellystone Park, Cave City

Best Swimming Pools
Carr Creek State Park, Sassafras
Fort Boonesborough State Park, Richmond
KOA Louisville South, Shepherdsville
Levi Jackson Wilderness Road State Park
  Campground, London

LOUISIANA

Best RV Camping
Chicot State Park, Ville Platte
Kincaid Lake Recreation Area, Kisatchie National
  Forest, Gardner
North Toledo Bend State Park, Zwolle

Best Tent Camping
Chicot State Park, Ville Platte
Kincaid Lake Recreation Area, Kisatchie National
  Forest, Gardner
North Toledo Bend State Park, Zwolle

Most Beautiful Campgrounds
Caney Creek Lake State Park, Chatham
Caney Lakes Recreation Area, Kisatchie National
  Forest, Minden
Chicot State Park, Ville Platte
Kincaid Lake Recreation Area, Kisatchie National
  Forest, Gardner
Lake Bistineau State Park, Doyline
Lake Bruin State Park, St. Joseph
Lake Claiborne State Park, Homer

LOUISIANA (continued)

Most Beautiful Campgrounds
(continued)

Lake D'Arbonne State Park, Farmerville
Lake Fausse Pointe State Park, St. Martinville
North Toledo Bend State Park, Zwolle
Tickfaw State Park, Springfield

Most Private Campsites

Caney Lakes Recreation Area, Kisatchie National Forest, Minden
Chicot State Park, Ville Platte
North Toledo Bend State Park, Zwolle

Most Spacious Campsites

Caney Creek Lake State Park, Chatham
Caney Lakes Recreation Area, Kisatchie National Forest, Minden
Chicot State Park, Ville Platte
Fontainebleau State Park, Mandeville
Kincaid Lake Recreation Area, Kisatchie National Forest, Gardner
Lake Bistineau State Park, Doyline
Lake Fausse Pointe State Park, St. Martinville
North Toledo Bend State Park, Zwolle
Tickfaw State Park, Springfield

Quietest Campgrounds

Caney Lakes Recreation Area, Kisatchie National Forest, Minden
Chicot State Park, Ville Platte
Kincaid Lake Recreation Area, Kisatchie National Forest, Gardner
Lake Bistineau State Park, Doyline
Lake Fausse Pointe State Park, St. Martinville
North Toledo Bend State Park, Zwolle
Tickfaw State Park, Springfield

Most Secure Campgrounds

Caney Creek Lake State Park, Chatham
Chicot State Park, Ville Platte
Grand Isle State Park, Grand Isle
Lake Claiborne State Park, Homer
Lake D'Arbonne State Park, Farmerville
Lake Fausse Pointe State Park, St. Martinville
Tickfaw State Park, Springfield

Cleanest Campgrounds

Caney Creek Lake State Park, Chatham
Grand Casino Coushatta Luxury RV Resort at Red Shoes Park, Kinder

Kincaid Lake Recreation Area, Kisatchie National Forest, Gardner
Lake D'Arbonne State Park, Farmerville
North Toledo Bend State Park, Zwolle

Best Urban and Suburban Settings

Bayou Segnette State Park, Westwego
KOA Kampground Lafayette, Lafayette
KOA Kampground Shreveport-Bossier, Shreveport
KOA Kampground, New Orleans West, River Ridge
Land-O-Pines, Covington
New Orleans/Hammond KOA Kampground, Hammond
Yogi Bear's Jellystone Park, Robert

Best Waterfront Settings

Caney Creek Lake State Park, Chatham
Caney Lakes Recreation Area, Kisatchie National Forest, Minden
Lake Bistineau State Park, Doyline
Lake Bruin State Park, St. Joseph
Lake Claiborne State Park, Homer
Lake D'Arbonne State Park, Farmerville
Lake Fausse Pointe State Park, St. Martinville

Most Romantic Campgrounds

Caney Creek Lake State Park, Chatham
Caney Lakes Recreation Area, Kisatchie National Forest, Minden
Chicot State Park, Ville Platte
Kincaid Lake Recreation Area, Kisatchie National Forest, Gardner
Lake Bistineau State Park, Doyline
Lake Claiborne State Park, Homer
Lake D'Arbonne State Park, Farmerville
Lake Fausse Pointe State Park, St. Martinville
North Toledo Bend State Park, Zwolle
Tickfaw State Park, Springfield

Best Family-Oriented Campgrounds

Yogi Bear's Jellystone Park, Robert

MISSISSIPPI

Best RV Camping
Roosevelt State Park, Morton
South Abutment Campground, Arkabutla Lake, Hernando

Best Tent Camping
Roosevelt State Park, Morton
South Abutment Campground, Arkabutla Lake, Hernando

Most Beautiful Campgrounds
DeWayne Hayes Campground, Columbus
Piney Grove Campground, Dennis
Roosevelt State Park, Morton
South Abutment Campground, Arkabutla Lake, Hernando
Twitley Branch Camping Area, Okatibee Lake, Meridian
Whitten Park Campground (formerly called Fulton Campground), Fulton

Most Private Campsites
Roosevelt State Park, Morton
South Abutment Campground, Arkabutla Lake, Hernando

Most Spacious Campsites
DeWayne Hayes Campground, Columbus
Piney Grove Campground, Dennis
Roosevelt State Park, Morton
South Abutment Campground, Arkabutla Lake, Hernando
Town Creek Campground, Columbus

Quietest Campgrounds
Roosevelt State Park, Morton
South Abutment Campground, Arkabutla Lake, Hernando
Town Creek Campground, Columbus
Whitten Park Campground (formerly called Fulton Campground), Fulton

Most Secure Campgrounds
Blue Bluff, Aberdeen
DeWayne Hayes Campground, Columbus
Piney Grove Campground, Dennis
South Abutment Campground, Arkabutla Lake, Hernando
Twitley Branch Camping Area, Okatibee Lake, Meridian
Whitten Park Campground (formerly called Fulton Campground), Fulton

Cleanest Campgrounds
Piney Grove Campground, Dennis
South Abutment Campground, Arkabutla Lake, Hernando
Town Creek Campground, Columbus
Wallace Creek Campground Enid Lake, Enid
Whitten Park Campground (formerly called Fulton Campground), Fulton

Best Campground Facilities
LeFleur's Bluff State Park, Jackson
Percy Quinn State Park, McComb
Roosevelt State Park, Morton

Best Urban and Suburban Settings
Baywood Campground–RV Park, Gulfport
LeFleur's Bluff State Park, Jackson
Magnolia RV Park, Vicksburg
Mazalea Travel Park, Biloxi
Parker's Landing, Biloxi
Plantation Park, Natchez
Timberlake Campground and RV Park, Jackson

Best Waterfront Settings
Blue Bluff, Aberdeen
DeWayne Hayes Campground, Columbus
Paul B. Johnson State Park, Hattiesburg
Piney Grove Campground, Dennis
Roosevelt State Park, Morton
South Abutment Campground, Arkabutla Lake, Hernando
Town Creek Campground, Columbus
Twitley Branch Camping Area, Okatibee Lake, Meridian
Wallace Creek Campground, Enid Lake, Enid
Whitten Park Campground (formerly called Fulton Campground), Fulton

Most Romantic Campgrounds
Piney Grove Campground, Dennis
Roosevelt State Park, Morton
South Abutment Campground, Arkabutla Lake, Hernando
Whitten Park Campground (formerly called Fulton Campground), Fulton

Best Family-Oriented Campgrounds
Buccaneer State Park, Waveland

NORTH CAROLINA

Best RV Camping
Bear Den Campground, Spruce Pine
Hanging Rock State Park, Danbury
Hibernia, Henderson
Holly Point State Recreational Area, Wake Forest

Best Tent Camping
Bandits Roost Park, W. Kerr Scott Reservoir,
   Wilkesboro
Bear Den Campground, Spruce Pine
Hanging Rock State Park, Danbury
Hibernia, Henderson
Holly Point State Recreational Area, Wake Forest

Most Beautiful Campgrounds
Bandits Roost Park, W. Kerr Scott Reservoir,
   Wilkesboro
Bear Den Campground, Spruce Pine
Carolina Beach State Park, Carolina Beach
Hanging Rock State Park, Danbury
Hibernia, Henderson
High Rock Lake Marina and Campground,
   Southmont
Holly Point State Recreational Area, Wake Forest
Moonshine Creek Campground, Balsam
Morrow Mountain State Park, Albemarle
Ocracoke, Cape Hatteras
Oregon Inlet, Cape Hatteras
Standing Indian, Franklin
The Heritage, Whispering Pines
Travel Resorts of America, Jackson Springs

Most Private Campsites
Bear Den Campground, Spruce Pine
Carolina Beach State Park, Carolina Beach
Crosswinds Campground, Jordan Lake State
   Recreation Area, Apex
Hanging Rock State Park, Danbury
Hibernia, Henderson
Holly Point State Recreational Area, Wake Forest
Poplar Point Campground, Jordan Lake State
   Recreation Area, Apex

Most Spacious Campsites
Bandits Roost Park, W. Kerr Scott Reservoir,
   Wilkesboro
Carolina Beach State Park, Carolina Beach
Crosswinds Campground, Jordan Lake State
   Recreation Area, Apex
Hanging Rock State Park, Danbury
Hibernia, Henderson
Holly Point State Recreational Area, Wake Forest

Poplar Point Campground, Jordan Lake State
   Recreation Area, Apex
Standing Indian, Franklin

Quietest Campgrounds
Bandits Roost Park, W. Kerr Scott Reservoir,
   Wilkesboro
Bear Den Campground, Spruce Pine
Hanging Rock State Park, Danbury
Hibernia, Henderson
Holly Point State Recreational Area, Wake Forest
Ocracoke, Cape Hatteras
Travel Resorts of America, Jackson Springs

Most Secure Campgrounds
Bandits Roost Park, W. Kerr Scott Reservoir,
   Wilkesboro
Bear Den Campground, Spruce Pine
Cherokee KOA, Cherokee
Crosswinds Campground, Jordan Lake State
   Recreation Area, Apex
Hanging Rock State Park, Danbury
Hatteras Sands, Cape Hatteras
Holiday Trav-L-Park Resort, Emerald Isle
Linville Falls Campground, Linville Falls
Ocracoke, Cape Hatteras
Poplar Point Campground, Jordan Lake State
   Recreation Area, Apex
Stone Mountain State Park, Roaring Gap

Cleanest Campgrounds
Bandits Roost Park, W. Kerr Scott Reservoir,
   Wilkesboro
Bear Den Campground, Spruce Pine
Country Woods, Franklin
Doughton Campground, Asheville
Hanging Rock State Park, Danbury
Hibernia, Henderson
Holiday Trav-L-Park Resort, Emerald Isle
Linville Falls Campground, Linville Falls
Morrow Mountain State Park, Albemarle
Stone Mountain State Park, Roaring Gap
Travel Resorts of America, Jackson Springs

Best Campground Facilities
Holiday Trav-L-Park Resort, Emerald Isle

Best Urban and Suburban Settings
Carolina Beach State Park, Carolina Beach
Carowinds, Charlotte
Holiday Trav-L-Park Resort, Emerald Isle
Water's Edge RV Park, Newport

NORTH CAROLINA (continued)

Best Mountain Settings

Bear Den Campground, Spruce Pine

Country Woods, Franklin

Doughton Campground, Asheville

Great Smoky Mountains National Park Smokemont Campground, Cherokee

Hanging Dog, Murphy

Hanging Rock State Park, Danbury

Hidden Valley Campground and Waterpark, Marion

Moonshine Creek Campground, Balsam

Morrow Mountain State Park, Albemarle

Singing Waters Camping Resort, Tuckasegee

Standing Indian, Franklin

Steel Creek Park, Morganton

Stone Mountain State Park, Roaring Gap

Best Waterfront Settings

Bandits Roost Park, W. Kerr Scott Reservoir, Wilkesboro

Crosswinds Campground, Jordan Lake State Recreation Area, Apex

Hibernia Campground, Kerr Lake State Recreation Area, Henderson

High Rock Lake Marina and Campground, Southmont

Holly Point State Recreational Area, Falls Lake, Wake Forest

Morrow Mountain State Park, Albemarle

Poplar Point Campground, Jordan Lake State Recreation Area, Apex

Most Romantic Campgrounds

Bear Den Campground, Spruce Pine

Carolina Beach State Park, Carolina Beach

Hanging Rock State Park, Danbury

Hibernia Campground, Kerr Lake State Recreation Area, Henderson

Holly Point State Recreational Area, Falls Lake, Wake Forest

Standing Indian, Franklin

Best Family-Oriented Campgrounds

Bear Den Campground, Spruce Pine

Camp Hatteras, Waves

Cape Hatteras KOA Kampgound, Rodanthe

Holiday Trav-L-Park Resort, Emerald Isle

Steel Creek Park, Morganton

Yogi in the Smokies, Cherokee

SOUTH CAROLINA

Best RV Camping

Calhoun Falls State Park, Calhoun Falls

Modoc Campground, J. Strom Thurmond Lake, Modoc

Best Tent Camping

Calhoun Falls State Park, Calhoun Falls

Modoc Campground, J. Strom Thurmond Lake, Modoc

Most Beautiful Campgrounds

Baker Creek State Park, McCormick

Calhoun Falls State Park, Calhoun Falls

Edisto Beach State Park, Edisto Island

Hamilton Branch State Park, J. Strom Thurmond Reservoir, Plum Branch

Hunting Island State Park, Hunting Island

Lake Greenwood State Recreation Area, Ninety-Six

Lake Hartwell State Park, Fair Play

Lake Wateree State Recreation Area, Winnsboro

Modoc Campground, J. Strom Thurmond Lake, Modoc

Oconee State Park, Mountain Rest

Santee State Park, Santee

Springfield Campground, Hartwell Lake, Anderson

Most Private Campsites

Calhoun Falls State Park, Calhoun Falls

Lake Wateree State Recreation Area, Winnsboro

Modoc Campground, J. Strom Thurmond Lake, Modoc

Most Spacious Campsites

Calhoun Falls State Park, Calhoun Falls

Hamilton Branch State Park, J. Strom Thurmond Reservoir, Plum Branch

Lake Hartwell State Park, Fair Play

Modoc Campground, J. Strom Thurmond Lake, Modoc

Springfield Campground, Hartwell Lake, Anderson

Quietest Campgrounds

Calhoun Falls State Park, Calhoun Falls

Lake Wateree State Recreation Area, Winnsboro

Modoc Campground, J. Strom Thurmond Lake, Modoc

Oconee State Park, Mountain Rest

Sesquicentennial State Park, Columbia

CAMPGROUND AWARDS: South Carolina

SOUTH CAROLINA (continued)

Most Secure Campgrounds
Dreher Island State Park, Chapin
Huntington Beach State Park, Murrells Inlet
Kings Mountain State Park, Blacksburg
Lake Greenwood State Recreation Area, Ninety-Six
Lake Wateree State Recreation Area, Winnsboro
Lakewood Camping Resort, Myrtle Beach
Modoc Campground, J. Strom Thurmond Lake, Modoc
Myrtle Beach State Park, Myrtle Beach
Myrtle Beach Travel Park, Myrtle Beach
Ocean Lakes Family Campground, Myrtle Beach
Rocks Pond Campground and Marina, Eutawville
Sesquicentennial State Park, Columbia
Springfield Campground, Hartwell Lake, Anderson

Cleanest Campgrounds
Calhoun Falls State Park, Calhoun Falls

Best Campground Facilities
Kings Mountain State Park, Blacksburg
Lakewood Camping Resort, Myrtle Beach
Myrtle Beach Travel Park, Myrtle Beach
Ocean Lakes Family Campground, Myrtle Beach

Best Rural, Farm, or Ranch Settings
Kings Mountain State Park, Blacksburg

Best Urban and Suburban Settings
Barefoot Camping Resort, Myrtle Beach
Cunningham RV Park, Spartanburg
Lakewood Camping Resort, Myrtle Beach
Mt. Pleasant/Charleston KOA, Charleston/Mt. Pleasant
Myrtle Beach State Park, Myrtle Beach
Myrtle Beach Travel Park, Myrtle Beach
Ocean Lakes Family Campground, Myrtle Beach
Sesquicentennial State Park, Columbia

Best Mountain Settings
Oconee State Park, Mountain Rest
Table Rock State Park, Pickens

Best Waterfront Settings
Baker Creek State Park, McCormick
Calhoun Falls State Park, Calhoun Falls
Dreher Island State Park, Chapin
Lake Greenwood State Recreation Area, Ninety-Six
Lake Hartwell State Park, Fair Play
Lake Wateree State Recreation Area, Winnsboro
Modoc Campground, J. Strom Thurmond Lake, Modoc
Oconee State Park, Mountain Rest
Santee State Park, Santee
Springfield Campground, Hartwell Lake, Anderson

Most Romantic Campgrounds
Calhoun Falls State Park, Calhoun Falls
Hamilton Branch State Park, J. Strom Thurmond Reservoir, Plum Branch
Lake Hartwell State Park, Fair Play
Lake Wateree State Recreation Area, Winnsboro
Modoc Campground, J. Strom Thurmond Lake, Modoc
Oconee State Park, Mountain Rest
Springfield Campground, Hartwell Lake, Anderson

Best Family-Oriented Campgrounds
Hunting Island State Park, Hunting Island
Kings Mountain State Park, Blacksburg
Lakewood Camping Resort, Myrtle Beach
Myrtle Beach State Park, Myrtle Beach
Myrtle Beach Travel Park, Myrtle Beach
Ocean Lakes Family Campground, Myrtle Beach

Best Swimming Pools
River Plantation RV Park, Sevierville
Standing Stone State Park, Hilham
Twin Creek RV Resort, Gatlinburg
Valley KOA Kampground, Pulaski

TENNESSEE

Best RV Camping

Elkmont Campground, Great Smoky Mountains National Park, Gatlinburg

Fall Creek Falls State Park, Pikeville

Harrison Bay State Park, Chattanooga

Outdoor Resorts of America, Gatlinburg

Best Tent Camping

Chilhowee Campground, Cherokee National Forest, Benton

Cosby Campground, Great Smoky Mountains National Park, Cosby

Fall Creek Falls State Park, Pikeville

Harrison Bay State Park, Chattanooga

Indian Boundary Campground, Cherokee National Forest, Tellico Plains

Little Oak Campground, Cherokee National Forest, Unicoi

Most Beautiful Campgrounds

Cheatham Lake Lock A Campground, Ashland City

Chilhowee Campground, Cherokee National Forest, Benton

Cumberland Mountain State Park, Crossville

David Crockett State Park, Lawrenceburg

Indian Boundary Campground, Cherokee National Forest, Tellico Plains

Little Oak Campground, Cherokee National Forest, Unicoi

Outdoor Resorts of America, Gatlinburg

Piney Campground, Land Between the Lakes, Dover

Most Private Campsites

Fall Creek Falls State Park, Pikeville

Indian Boundary Campground, Cherokee National Forest, Tellico Plains

Little Oak Campground, Cherokee National Forest, Unicoi

Old Stone Fort State Archaeological Area, Manchester

Rock Island State Park, Rock Island

Most Spacious Campsites

Bandy Creek Campground, Big South Fork National River and Recreation Area, Oneida

Cheatham Lake Lock A Campground, Ashland City

Chilhowee Campground, Cherokee National Forest, Benton

Fall Creek Falls State Park, Pikeville

Harrison Bay State Park, Chattanooga

Indian Boundary Campground, Cherokee National Forest, Tellico Plains

Little Oak Campground, Cherokee National Forest, Unicoi

Old Stone Fort State Archaeological Area, Manchester

Quietest Campgrounds

Chilhowee Campground, Cherokee National Forest, Benton

Fall Creek Falls State Park, Pikeville

Little Oak Campground, Cherokee National Forest, Unicoi

Outdoor Resorts of America, Gatlinburg

Pickett State Park, Jamestown

Rock Island State Park, Rock Island

Standing Stone State Park, Hilham

Most Secure Campgrounds

Cheatham Lake Lock A Campground, Ashland City

Chilhowee Campground, Cherokee National Forest, Benton

Cumberland Mountain State Park, Crossville

David Crockett State Park, Lawrenceburg

Indian Boundary Campground, Cherokee National Forest, Tellico Plains

Little Oak Campground, Cherokee National Forest, Unicoi

Outdoor Resorts of America, Gatlinburg

Piney Campground, Land Between the Lakes, Dover

Cleanest Campgrounds

Cheatham Lake Lock A Campground, Ashland City

Little Oak Campground, Cherokee National Forest, Unicoi

Outdoor Resorts of America, Gatlinburg

Piney Campground, Land Between the Lakes, Dover

Reelfoot Lake State Park, South Campground, Tiptonville

Twin Creek RV Resort, Gatlinburg

Best Campground Facilities

Chickasaw State Park, Henderson

Cumberland Mountain State Park, Crossville

Fall Creek Falls State Park, Pikeville

Harrison Bay State Park, Chattanooga

Montgomery Bell State Park, Burns

TENNESSEE (continued)

Best Campground Facilities

(continued)

Paris Landing State Resort Park, Buchanan

Pin Oak Campground, Natchez Trace State Resort Park, Wildersville

Piney Campground, Land Between the Lakes, Dover

Tims Ford State Park, Winchester

Warrior's Path State Park, Kingsport

Yogi Bear's Jellystone Park, Gatlinburg

Best Rural, Farm, or Ranch Settings

Loretta Lynn Dude Ranch, Hurricane Mills

Best Urban and Suburban Settings

Holiday Trav-L-Park of Chattanooga, Chattanooga

Manchester KOA, Manchester

Memphis-Graceland KOA, Memphis

Nashville KOA Kampground, Nashville

T.O. Fuller State Park, Memphis

Best Mountain Settings

Bandy Creek Campground, Big South Fork National River and Recreation Area, Oneida

Cades Cove Campground, Great Smoky Mountains National Park, Townesnd

Chilhowee Campground, Cherokee National Forest, Benton

Cosby Campground, Great Smoky Mountains National Park, Cosby

Elkmont Campground, Great Smoky Mountains National Park, Gatlinburg

Indian Boundary Campground, Cherokee National Forest, Tellico Plains

Little Oak Campground, Cherokee National Forest, Unicoi

Little River Village, Townsend

Outdoor Resorts of America, Gatlinburg

Tremont Hills Campground, Townsend

Twin Creek RV Resort, Gatlinburg

Yogi Bear's Jellystone Park, Gatlinburg

Best Waterfront Settings

Cheatham Lake Lock A Campground, Ashland City

Harrison Bay State Park, Chattanooga

Indian Boundary Campground, Cherokee National Forest, Tellico Plains

Little Oak Campground, Cherokee National Forest, Unicoi

Little River Village, Townsend

Pin Oak Campground, Natchez Trace State Resort Park, Wildersville

Piney Campground, Land Between the Lakes, Dover

Reelfoot Lake State Park, South Campground, Tiptonville

Tremont Hills Campground, Townsend

Warrior's Path State Park, Kingsport

Most Romantic Campgrounds

Chilhowee Campground, Cherokee National Forest, Benton

Fall Creek Falls State Park, Pikeville

Harrison Bay State Park, Chattanooga

Indian Boundary Campground, Cherokee National Forest, Tellico Plains

Little Oak Campground, Cherokee National Forest, Unicoi

Best Family-Oriented Campgrounds

Loretta Lynn Dude Ranch, Hurricane Mills

Yogi Bear's Jellystone Park, Gatlinburg

Best Swimming Pools

River Plantation RV Park, Sevierville

Standing Stone State Park, Hilham

Twin Creek RV Resort, Gatlinburg

Valley KOA Kampground, Pulaski

Alabama

Called the "Cradle of the Confederacy," Alabama is steeped in Civil War history. Fascinating tours include Montgomery, the first capitol of the Confederacy. It was during the Battle of Mobile Bay that Admiral Farragut exclaimed "Damn the torpedoes! Full speed ahead!"

At the **USS Alabama Battleships Memorial Park** in Mobile, visitors can explore the park's namesake as well as over 20 other World War II–ships, aircraft, and weapons.

The Civil Rights movement thrust Alabama into the national media spotlight in the 1950s and 1960s. Defining events included the 1955 Montgomery Bus Boycott and the historic Selma to Montgomery March. Gain a deeper understanding of the movement at the **Birmingham Civil Rights Institute.** Across the street is the Sixteenth St. Baptist Church, site of the 1963 bombing that killed four little girls.

Natives call Alabama "The Beautiful," and we agree. Its northeast corner lies at the southernmost terminus of the **Appalachian Mountain range.** Quaint mountain towns such as Mentone offer rich fall foliage and excellent craft and antique shopping. **Little River Canyon** in Fort Payne is one of the deepest gorges east of the Mississippi. Four national forests and numerous lakes throughout the state provide enthusiasts with plenty of hunting and fishing.

Alabama's Gulf Coast region is home to moss-covered oak trees and white sand beaches. Orange Beach is known for top-notch saltwater fishing. The **Alabama Coastal Birding Trail** dots **Mobile Bay** with spots for viewing both wading and shore birds.

Golf is the feather in Alabama's outdoor cap. Anchoring Alabama's golf offerings are the eight facilities of the **Robert Trent Jones Golf Trail.** The trail lures golfers from all over the world with its championship courses and country club amenities. Other public, state park, and resort courses are open to visitors.

NASCAR racing fans are familiar with the **Talladega Superspeedway,** home of the Diehard 500 in April and the Winston 500 in October. Combination tickets for year-round track tours and admission to the **International Motorsports Hall of Fame** are available.

Other Alabama destinations include: The **U.S. Space and Rocket Center, VisionLand** theme park, **Mother Angelica's Eternal Word Television Network,** the **Alabama Jazz Hall of Fame, Birmingham Museum of Art, Sloss Furnaces National Historic Landmark, De Soto Caverns, Heart of Dixie Railroad Museum, Alabama Shakespeare Festival, Mercedes-Benz Visitor's Center, Hank Williams Sr. Boyhood Home and Museum, The Dauphin Island Sea Lab,** and numerous historic homes and plantations.

ALEXANDER CITY
Wind Creek State Park

4325 AL Hwy. 128, Alexander City 35010. T: (256) 329-0845; F: (256) 234-4870; www.dcnr.state.al.us/parks; windcreekstpk@mind-spring.com.

🚐 ★★★★   ⛺ ★★★★

Beauty: ★★★★   Site Privacy: ★★
Spaciousness: ★★★   Quiet: ★★★
Security: ★★★★★   Cleanliness: ★★★★
Insect Control: ★★★   Facilities: ★★★★

On the shores of 40,000-acre Lake Martin in east central Alabama, Wind Creek State Park is an excellent choice for families. Children will enjoy the large playground and variety of natural and recreational programs. Campers with lakefront sites are allowed to swim and dock boats right at the sites. Fishermen will find catfish, crappie and bluegill as well as largemouth, salt water striped, white and hybrid bass. Wind Creek State Park is not the top choice for peace and quiet as it is full of children and boats. The park should be assiduously avoided on holiday weekends. Security is outstanding at this gated and extremely remote park. The campground at Wind Creek State Park is laid out in 5 main sections including a primitive overflow area. The large, flat, grid-like section B is nicely shaded by a stand of loblolly and longleaf pine. Section C includes sites on an open peninsula with unobscured views of Lake Martin. Sites C190, C191 and C192 are the prettiest in spite of their complete lack of privacy. Other attractive lakefront sites are found in Section D. Section E contains a few sites with lake views and a modicum of privacy (try E32, E33, E34, E36, E38, or E30). All the sites at Wind Creek State Park are small compared to other Alabama state parks. While some sites are extremely shady, the open sites tend to have better views of the lake. The back-in, paved parking spaces are in various states of repair and disrepair and may be peppered with pine straw, gravel or grass. However, the bathhouses here are in excellent condition—large and clean with no frills.

BASICS

Operated By: Alabama State Parks. **Open:** All year. **Site Assignment:** First come, first served; Alabama State Park reservations system. **Registra-**tion: Main entrance, open 24 hours in-season; night registration available in winter. **Fee:** $16 for RV camping, $14 for tent camping, $3 additional for sewer or waterfront sites, fee includes 4 people, $2 for each additional person, limit 8 people per site. **Parking:** Limit 2 cars per site, overflow parking available.

FACILITIES

Number of Multipurpose Sites: 642. **Hookups:** Water, electric (30, 50 amps), 235 sites w/ sewer. **Each Site:** Picnic table, grill. **Dump Station:** Yes. **Laundry:** Yes. **Pay Phone:** Yes. **Rest Rooms and Showers:** Yes. **Fuel:** No. **Propane:** No. **Internal Roads:** Paved. **RV Service:** 8 mi. northeast in Alexander City. **Market:** 8 mi. northeast in Alexander City. **Restaurant:** 8 mi. northeast in Alexander City. **General Store:** Camp store. **Vending:** Yes. **Swimming Pool:** No. **Playground:** Yes. **Other:** Marina, boat launches, 210-ft. fishing pier, picnic pavilions. **Activities:** Hiking trails, fishing, lake swimming, boating (limited boat rentals), waterskiing, organized summer activities, volleyball, horseshoes. **Nearby Attractions:** Lake Martin, Horseshoe Bend Military Park, Charles E. Bailey Sportsplex. **Additional Information:** Alexander City Chamber of Commerce, (256) 234-3461.

RESTRICTIONS

Pets: Leash only. **Fires:** Allowed. **Alcoholic Beverages:** At site only. **Vehicle Maximum Length:** 50 ft. **Other:** 2 week max. stay on the same site.

TO GET THERE

From Montgomery, take US Hwy. 231 north for 9 mi. At Wetumpka, turn right onto AL Hwy. 170 and go east for 10 mi. At Eclectic follow signs to AL Hwy. 63 north. Follow Hwy. 63 for 18 mi. until you see park signs. Turn right onto AL Hwy. 128 and travel east 5 mi. to the park. From Birmingham, take US Hwy. 280 east to Alexander City. Turn right onto AL Hwy. 63 and go south for 7 mi. Turn left onto Hwy. 128 and go east 5 mi.

ALPINE
Logan Landing RV Resort and Campground

1036 Paul Bear Bryant Blvd., Alpine 35014. T: (256) 268-0045; sites.netscape.net/sambo12h/loganlanding.

 ★★★   ★★★

Beauty: ★★★   Site Privacy: ★★★
Spaciousness: ★★★   Quiet: ★★★
Security: ★★★★   Cleanliness: ★★★
Insect Control: ★★★   Facilities: ★★★

Attractive and clean with friendly owners, Logan Landing is a good choice if you plan on spending a few days in the area. The campground offers boating and other activities and drive times are short to Logan Martin Lake, De Soto Caverns, and Talladega Superspeedway. Cheaha State Park can be reached in less than one hour. Because this is a popular recreation area, summer weekends are busy. By all means avoid the two biggest race weekends at Talladega Superspeedway—the Die Hard 500 in Apr. and the Winston 500 in Oct. If you want to stay here on a race weekend, make advance reservations. Two camping areas are situated next to a small private lake. Section A contains no lakefront sites and may be preferred by tent campers because the sites are wooded. We prefer section B for RVs because sites are generally larger and more level. Even-numbered sites 58–80 have lake-views but little shade. As you move away from the lake in Section B, sites become shadier. Each of the mid-sized sites in section B has gravel parking and a cement patio. Section C is unattractive. The variety of tree species in the campground includes some dogwood. Of the 145 campsites, only a few are pull-throughs. With its remote location in Alpine, Alabama and gated entrance, this campground has very good security.

BASICS

Operated By: Keith Bell. **Open:** All year. **Site Assignment:** First come, first served; reservations accepted for holiday weekends & Talladega Superspeedway race weekends. **Registration:** Guard house. **Fee:** $18 for sites w/ full hookup, $15 for sites w/ water & electric, $10 primitive, fee includes 2 adults, $5 per extra person. **Parking:** At sites.

FACILITIES

Number of RV Sites: 0. **Number of Tent-Only Sites:** 45. **Number of Multipurpose Sites:** 145. **Hookups:** Water, electric (30, 50, 80 amps), some sewer. **Each Site:** Picnic table, grill, fire ring, tent pads. **Dump Station:** Yes. **Laundry:** Yes. **Pay Phone:** Yes. **Rest Rooms and Showers:** Yes. **Fuel:** No. **Propane:** No. **Internal Roads:** Gravel. **RV Service:** 6 mi. north in Pell City. **Market:** 11 mi. north in Pell City. **Restaurant:** 6 mi. north in Pell City. **General Store:** 11 mi. north in Pell City. **Vending:** Beverages only. **Swimming Pool:** Yes. **Playground:** Yes. **Other:** Private lake, boat ramp, paddle boats, canoes, pontoons, pavilion, rental trailers. **Activities:** Fishing, croquet, horseshoes, Lake Logan Martin swimming beach, Bingo Fridays, live music, volleyball, hot dog cookout Saturdays. **Nearby Attractions:** Talladega Superspeedway (NASCAR), De Soto Caverns, Davey Allison Park, Kymulga Grist Mill & Covered Bridge, Cheaha State Park. **Additional Information:** Talladega Chamber of Commerce, (256) 362-9075.

RESTRICTIONS

Pets: Leash only. **Fires:** In fire ring, grill only. **Alcoholic Beverages:** At site only. **Vehicle Maximum Length:** 50 ft.

TO GET THERE

From I-20, take Exit 158 at Pell City. Go south on US Hwy. 231 for 9.5 mi. Turn left onto CR 54 and drive across Logan Martin Dam. Go straight through the first stop sign, cross the railroad tracks, and then turn left at the second stop sign onto CR 207. Go 1 mi. and turn left onto Paul Bear Bryant Blvd. The campground entrance is 1 mi. ahead on the right.

BENTON

Prairie Creek Campground, Woodruff Lake

8493 US Hwy. 80 West, Hayneville 36040. T: (334) 872-9554; F: (334) 875-1603; www.reserveusa.com.

🚐 ★★★★   ⛺ ★★★★

Beauty: ★★★★   Site Privacy: ★★★★
Spaciousness: ★★★★   Quiet: ★★★★
Security: ★★★★   Cleanliness: ★★★★
Insect Control: ★★★   Facilities: ★★★

Prairie Creek is typical of the top quality campgrounds managed by the Army Corps of Engineers. Sites are extremely spacious and most have uncluttered views of the Alabama River. Spanish moss-laden oak trees provide shade and privacy. Two of the three camping areas, Beaver Point and Eagles Roost, are newer and feature paved back-in parking. The older Whitetail Bluff camping area contains pull-throughs but is now used for overflow camping. At Beaver Point, sites 56–62 are reserved for tent campers. RV campers will not be disappointed with any of the waterfront sites, 27–51. Since so many sites are excellent, choose your site based on proximity to facilities. The campgrounds located on the Alabama River Lake system are all extremely remote. Prairie Creek makes a great summer destination as it only fills to capacity on the busiest holiday weekends. Gates lock at night making the park extremely safe. Prairie Creek is located six miles from Holy Ground Battlefield Park, site of 1813–1814 clashes between the Creek Indians and the U.S. Army, led by General Andrew Jackson. Today, Holy Ground Battlefield Park is a day-use only recreation area with swimming beach, boat launch, playground, bathhouse, picnic shelters, multi-purpose court, hiking trails and observation deck. Day-use fees are waived for Prairie Creek campground guests.

BASICS
Operated By: US Army Corps of Engineers. **Open:** All year. **Site Assignment:** First come, first served; 60% of sites are available for reservations, accepted through the National Recreation Reservation Service (NRRS) at **(877) 444-6777** or www.reserveusa.com. Reservations can be made up to 240 days in advance, full payment required upon making reservation; credit card preferred (V, MC, D, AE), or pay by money order if at least 21 days in advance of arrival. $10 fee for cancellation or change of site or dates. Cancellation within three days of arrival charged first night, no-show charged $20 plus first night. **Registration:** Gatehouse or night access lane. **Fee:** $14 for waterfront multipurpose sites; $12 for other multipurpose sites, $10 for tent sites. **Parking:** At sites, overflow parking available.

FACILITIES
Number of RV Sites: 0. **Number of Tent-Only Sites:** 7. **Number of Multipurpose Sites:** 55. **Hookups:** Water, electric (50 amps). **Each Site:** Picnic tables, grills, fire rings, tent pad at tent sites. **Dump Station:** Yes. **Laundry:** Yes. **Pay Phone:** Yes. **Rest Rooms and Showers:** Yes. **Fuel:** No. **Propane:** No. **Internal Roads:** Paved. **RV Service:** 20 mi. west in Selma. **Market:** 20 mi. west in Selma. **Restaurant:** 10 mi. southeast in Lowndesboro. **General Store:** 20 mi. west in Selma. **Vending:** No. **Swimming Pool:** No. **Playground:** Yes. **Other:** Courtesy docks, boat ramp, fish cleaning area, picnic shelters, sports court, scenic overlooks. **Activities:** Swimming, boating, waterskiing, hiking, hunting. **Nearby Attractions:** Brown Chapel

A.M.E. Church & King Monument, Cahawba, National Voting Rights Museum & Institute, Old Depot Museum, Old Live Oak Cemetery Tour, Smitherman Historic Building. **Additional Information:** Selma/Dallas County Chamber of Commerce, (334) 875-7241.

RESTRICTIONS
Pets: Leash only. **Fires:** Fire rings only. **Alcoholic Beverages:** Allowed. **Vehicle Maximum Length:** 50 ft. **Other:** Limit 3 vehicles per site.

TO GET THERE
From Montgomery, take US Hwy. 80 west for 25 mi. Turn right on CR 29 and follow the signs.

BIRMINGHAM

KOA Birmingham South

222 Hwy. 33, Pelham 35124. T: (205) 664-8832 or (800) KOA-4788 for reservations; F: (205) 620-1103.

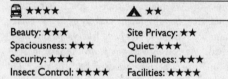

🚐 ★★★★	▲ ★★
Beauty: ★★★	Site Privacy: ★★
Spaciousness: ★★★	Quiet: ★★★
Security: ★★★	Cleanliness: ★★★
Insect Control: ★★★★	Facilities: ★★★★

Though not as attractive as nearby Oak Mountain State Park, KOA Birmingham South is tidy and offers comfortably spaced sites. Campers sometimes prefer the aesthetically bland sites at KOA to the state park because sites are level and hookups include cable television. The KOA may also be quieter, as many of the campers here are retirees. Back-in sites numbered B-8 through B-30 are the shadiest, prettiest, and the most popular. If you prefer an open pull-through site, choose from sites numbered I–36. All roads and RV parking spots are paved.

BASICS
Operated By: KOA. **Open:** All year. **Site Assignment:** First come, first served; reservations accepted. **Registration:** Campground office. **Fee:** $25 water & electric, $20 tent, fee includes 2 people; extra charge for sewer, a/c, electric heat or 50 amp hookup. **Parking:** 2 vehicles per site, plus overflow lot.

FACILITIES
Number of RV Sites: 116. **Number of Tent-Only Sites:** 6. **Number of Multipurpose Sites:** None. **Hookups:** Water, electric (30, 50 amps),

sewer. **Each Site:** Picnic table, paved area, grill on request. **Dump Station:** Yes. **Laundry:** Yes. **Pay Phone:** Yes. **Rest Rooms and Showers:** Yes. **Fuel:** No. **Propane:** Yes. **Internal Roads:** Some gravel, majority Paved. **RV Service:** 15 mi. **Market:** 1 mi. in Pelham. **Restaurant:** 0.5 mi. in Pelham. **General Store:** Camp store, Wal-Mart 2 mi. south in Pelham. **Vending:** Beverages only. **Swimming Pool:** Yes. **Playground:** Yes. **Other:** Gift shop, hot tub, covered pavilion. **Activities:** Game room, horseshoes, basketball, clubhouse w/ television. **Nearby Attractions:** Oak Mountain State Park (golf, fishing, horseback riding, boating, hiking), Birmingham Zoo & Botanical Gardens, Galleria Mall. **Additional Information:** Birmingham CVB, (800) 458-8085; Hoover Chamber of Commerce, (205) 988-5672.

RESTRICTIONS

Pets: Leash only. **Fires:** At tent sites only. **Alcoholic Beverages:** At site only. **Vehicle Maximum Length:** 50 ft.

TO GET THERE

From I-65, take Exit 242, then Hwy. 152 west, then right on Hwy. 33, campground 1 block on the right.

BIRMINGHAM

Oak Mountain State Park

P.O. Box 278, Pelham 35124. T: (205) 620-2524; F: (205) 620-2531; www.dcnr.state.al.us/parks.

🚐 ★★★★	🔺 ★★★★
Beauty: ★★★	Site Privacy: ★★★
Spaciousness: ★★★	Quiet: ★★★★
Security: ★★★	Cleanliness: ★★★
Insect Control: ★★★	Facilities: ★★★★★

While reasonably attractive, Oak Mountain State park doesn't boast the most gorgeous campground in the state. The camp sites are a little ghostly—we could tell that they used to be lovely. Sites are situated in two main areas, within which site shape, size and privacy vary immensely. Area A contains 71 sites, 24 of which have full hookups. Area A is prettier, shadier and more woodsy than B, which has 72 sites crammed into half the space of A. In fact, most of area B is downright unattractive, with the exception of tent sites B6, B8, B64, and B65. All RV parking is on untidy gravel and both areas

have back-in and pull-through parking. Oak Mountain is exceptional for its proximity to Birmingham. It's a good place to stay while visiting Birmingham and it's also the favored outdoor playground for the city's natives. This means that hiking, mountain biking and other activities may not provide the solitude we would expect at other parks. Still, the park's broad offering of activities and its proximity to a number of restaurants and attractions make it a good choice for a visit. Security at Oak Mountain is fair. The back gate is never manned, but both gates are locked at night. Avoid Oak Mountain State Park like the plague on holiday weekends and during the hotter summer months.

BASICS

Operated By: Alabama State Parks. **Open:** All year. **Site Assignment:** Reservations required for weekends & holidays, 2-night min. stay weekends, 3-night min. stay holiday weekends (Memorial Day, Labor Day, & 4th of July). **Registration:** Country store. **Fee:** $17 for sites w/ full hookups, $15 for sites w/ water & electric, $11 for tent sites, fee includes 3 people, $2.22 per extra person, senior discount over 65. **Parking:** Limit 2 cars per site.

FACILITIES

Number of RV Sites: 0. **Number of Tent-Only Sites:** 60. **Number of Multipurpose Sites:** 85. **Hookups:** Water, electric (30 amps), sewer. **Each Site:** Picnic table, grill, fire ring, lantern pole. **Dump Station:** Yes. **Laundry:** Yes. **Pay Phone:** Yes. **Rest Rooms and Showers:** Yes. **Fuel:** No. **Propane:** No. **Internal Roads:** Paved & gravel. **RV Service:** 2 mi. southwest. **Market:** 3 mi. southwest in Pelham. **Restaurant:** 3 mi. southwest in Pelham. **General Store:** Wal-Mart 6 mi. east in Inverness. **Vending:** Beverages only. **Swimming Pool:** No. **Playground:** Yes. **Other:** Boat ramp, lake beach, snack bar, petting zoo, information center, stables, marina, boat rental (no gasoline boats allowed on lake), tennis courts, BMX track, picnic area, Alabama Wildlife Rescue Center, 18-hole golf course, sports fields, picnic shelters & pavilions, conference center. **Activities:** Horseback riding, hiking, mountain biking, fishing. **Nearby Attractions:** VisionLand, Birmingham Zoo & Botanical Gardens, Birmingham Museum of Art, Alabama Jazz Hall of Fame, Birmingham Civil Rights Institute, Sloss Furnaces, Galleria Shopping Mall. **Additional Information:** Birmingham CVB, (205) 458-8001; Hoover Chamber of Commerce, (205) 988-5672.

RESTRICTIONS

Pets: Leash only. **Fires:** In grills, fire rings only. **Alcoholic Beverages:** At site only. **Vehicle Maximum Length:** 56 ft. **Other:** 14-day stay limit.

TO GET THERE

From I-65, take Exit 246 and go west on US Hwy. 119. Take an immediate left onto State Park Rd. Drive for 3.5 mi. to a 4-way stop. Turn left onto Findlay Dr. The main park gate is ahead. Go 5.5 mi. past the gate to Campground Rd. and turn left.

CAMDEN

Roland Cooper State Park

285 Deer Run Dr., Camden 36726. T: (334) 682-4838; F: (334) 682-4050; www.dcnr.state.al.us/parks.

🚐 ★★★   ▲ ★★★

Beauty: ★★★	Site Privacy: ★★★
Spaciousness: ★★★	Quiet: ★★★
Security: ★★★	Cleanliness: ★★★
Insect Control: ★★	Facilities: ★★★★

Golf and fishing are the primary draws at Roland Cooper State Park. Created by a dam on the Alabama River, 22,000-acre Dannelly Reservoir is home to numerous fish species, as well as beaver, waterfowl and American alligator. The nine-hole golf course is a bargain; greens fees are only $9 for 9 holes and $13 for eighteen holes. Here, the woodlands are dominated by pine. The majority of the campsites enjoy the shade of a mature stand of loblolly pine. A bit of privacy is provided by the trees, but none of the sites are entirely secluded. Most of the sites are situated on one loop and feature paved, back-in parking. Sites 22, 24 and 28 are pull-through sites, with views of the reservoir and gravel parking. In the primitive tent camping area, site number 10 has a nice view of the water. Site size is comfortable but not exceptional. Roland Cooper's rural location and gates that lock at night make it fairly secure. Avoid this park in July and Aug. when summer heat crescendos. Also avoid Memorial Day, 4th of July and Labor Day, when crowds are at a maximum.

BASICS

Operated By: Alabama State Parks. **Open:** All year. **Site Assignment:** Reservations accepted; no credit cards accepted; cancellation w/ 24-hour notice; sites are first come, first served. **Registration:** Entrance office. **Fee:** $15. **Parking:** Limit 3 vehicles per site, overflow parking available.

FACILITIES

Number of RV Sites: 0. **Number of Tent-Only Sites:** 10. **Number of Multipurpose Sites:** 47. **Hookups:** 30 w/ electric & sewer, all w/ water. **Each Site:** Picnic table, grill, fire ring. **Dump Station:** Yes. **Laundry:** Yes. **Pay Phone:** Yes. **Rest Rooms and Showers:** Yes. **Fuel:** No. **Propane:** No. **Internal Roads:** Paved. **RV Service:** 75 mi. northeast in Montgomery. **Market:** Camp store. **Restaurant:** 5 mi. south in Camden. **General Store:** 5 mi. south in Camden. **Vending:** No. **Swimming Pool:** No. **Playground:** Yes. **Other:** Clubhouse, picnic pavilion, 9-hole golf course, driving range, boat ramps, fish cleaning area. **Activities:** Golf, fishing, boating, swimming, walking trails. **Nearby Attractions:** Bridgeport Beach, Dale Masonic Lodge, Wilcox Female Institute. **Additional Information:** Wilcox Development Council (334) 682-4929.

RESTRICTIONS

Pets: Leash only. **Fires:** In fire rings, grills only. **Alcoholic Beverages:** At site only. **Vehicle Maximum Length:** No limit.

TO GET THERE

From I-65, take Exit 128. Drive west on Alabama Hwy. 10 for 40 mi. At Camden, turn right onto Alabama Hwy. 41 and drive north for 4 mi. The park is on the left.

CHILDERSBURG

De Soto Caverns

5181 De Soto Caverns Parkway, Childersburg 35044. T: (256) 378-7252; F: (256) 378-3678; www.desotocavernspark.com; awm3@mindspring.com.

🚐 ★★★   ▲ ★★★

Beauty: ★★★★	Site Privacy: ★★
Spaciousness: ★★	Quiet: ★★★
Security: ★★	Cleanliness: ★★★★
Insect Control: ★★★	Facilities: ★★★★

This small, privately owned campground is clean and attractive. Part of a complex that includes De Soto Caverns and a small amusement park, the campground is sandwiched into the front corner of the property. Because some sites are only a few feet from the amusement park, quiet afternoon naps may be out of the question when the park is busy. The triangular campground offers compact sites which are well shaded by pine trees. Parking is mainly back-in with a few pull-throughs, and patchy grass invading the gravel. Sites 2 and 3 are furthest away from 76 making them the quietest at night. Big rigs should avoid this tight, hilly campground altogether (opt for one of the sprawling campgrounds along Logan Martin Lake). Less than 60 miles from Birmingham, this kitschy-but-fun park will be appreciated by children especially. The Great-Onyx Cavern is the venue for a Laser Light Show and the amusement park includes a fishin' hole, gem panning and more. Keep in mind that there is no snack bar at the park. Count on driving about 5 miles to Childersburg if you're not cooking at your site. Security is poor here. There is no gate and the campground is visible from 76. Cave touring is a delightful summer time activity. Just steer clear of visits during holiday weekends and big event weekends at Talladega Superspeedway.

BASICS

Operated By: The Mathis Family. **Open:** All year. **Site Assignment:** First come, first served; reservations accepted for holidays & Talladega Superspeedway race weekends only; full deposit required; one week cancellation policy. **Registration:** Gift shop or night registration. **Fee:** $20 for full hookups, $15 for tent camping, 4 person max., $2 per extra person. **Parking:** At site, overflow parking available.

FACILITIES

Number of RV Sites: 0. **Number of Tent-Only Sites:** 3. **Number of Multipurpose Sites:** 16. **Hookups:** Water, electric, sewer. **Each Site:** Picnic table, grill, some fire rings. **Dump Station:** Yes. **Laundry:** No. **Pay Phone:** Yes. **Rest Rooms and Showers:** Yes. **Fuel:** No. **Propane:** No. **Internal Roads:** Gravel. **RV Service:** 5 mi. southwest in Childersburg. **Market:** 5 mi. southwest in Childersburg. **Restaurant:** 5 mi. southwest in Childersburg. **General Store:** Camp Store, Wal-Mart 15 mi. south in Sylacauga. **Vending:** Yes. **Swimming Pool:** No. **Playground:** Yes. **Other:** Caverns, climbing wall, amusement park. **Activities:** Mazes, mini-golf, pedal boats, go-carts, gem stone panning, laser light show. **Nearby Attractions:** Talladega Superspeedway, Kymulga Grist Mill & Covered Bridge, Bryant's Vineyard, Blue Bell Creameries. **Additional Information:** Childersburg Chamber of Commerce, (256) 378-5482, Talladega Chamber of Commerce, (256) 362-9075.

RESTRICTIONS

Pets: Leash only. **Fires:** Allowed. **Alcoholic Beverages:** Not allowed. **Vehicle Maximum Length:** No limit.

TO GET THERE

From US Hwy. 280 in Childersburg, drive northeast on AL Hwy. 76 (De Soto Caverns Parkway) for 5 mi. The entrance is on the left.

COKER

Lake Lurleen State Park

Rte. 1 Box 479, Coker 35452. T: (205) 339-1558; www.dcnr.state.al.us/parks.

RV: ★★★★ Tent: ★★★★

Beauty: ★★★★	Site Privacy: ★★★
Spaciousness: ★★★★	Quiet: ★★★
Security: ★★★★	Cleanliness: ★★★
Insect Control: ★★	Facilities: ★★★

Named after Alabama's only woman governor, Lurleen Burns Wallace, this lake is popular with fishermen. The 250-acre lake is stocked with bream, catfish, crappie and largemouth and striped bass. Rather not fish? Swim, hike or canoe. Located 12 miles northwest of Tuscaloosa, this park stays busy all summer so we recommend weekday, spring, or fall visits. Four camping areas (A-D) offer nice sized sites. Most have paved back-in parking. A few sites have gravel parking. Section B is devoted to RV campers and contains 8 pull-through sites. Sites B33–B39 (odd numbers) feature wooden decks overlooking Lake Lurleen. In Section A, lakefront sites A2–A14 (even numbers) offer lovely views. While most sites have some shady trees, sites A15 and A16 are exceptionally shady and secluded. In spite of Lake Lurleen's proximity to Tuscaloosa, it feels remote. Gates lock at night making the park extremely secure.

BASICS

Operated By: Alabama State Parks. **Open:** All year. **Site Assignment:** Reservations accepted w/ one night deposit; sites are first come, first served. **Registration:** Entrance station. **Fee:** $14 (MC, V, check, or cash). **Parking:** 2 vehicles per site.

FACILITIES

Number of Multipurpose Sites: 91. **Hookups:** Water, electric (30, 50 amps), 35 sites w/ sewer. **Each Site:** Picnic table, grill. **Dump Station:** Yes. **Laundry:** No. **Pay Phone:** Yes. **Rest Rooms and Showers:** Yes. **Fuel:** No. **Propane:** No. **Internal Roads:** Paved. **RV Service:** 15 mi. south in Tuscaloosa. **Market:** Camp store. **Restaurant:** 7 mi. east in Northport. **General Store:** 7 mi. east in Northport. **Vending:** Yes. **Swimming Pool:** No. **Playground:** Yes. **Other:** Boat ramps, fishing pier, marina, boat rentals, amphitheater, picnic area, group picnic shelters, swimming beach, beach snack stand, nature center, sports field. **Activities:** Fishing, boating, hiking, swimming. **Nearby Attractions:** Paul "Bear" Bryant Museum, Alabama Museum of Natural History, Moundville Indian Archeological Park, Mercedes Benz Visitor Center, Denny Chimes, Gorgas House, Children's Hands-On Museum, Kentuck Art Center, University of Alabama Arboretum. **Additional Information:** West Alabama Chamber of Commerce (205) 758-7588; Tuscaloosa CVB (800) 538-8696.

RESTRICTIONS

Pets: Leash only. **Fires:** In fire pits only. **Alcoholic Beverages:** Site only, Not allowed at beach. **Vehicle Maximum Length:** No limit. **Other:** No ATVs or horses allowed.

TO GET THERE

From I-59, take Exit 71-B in Tuscaloosa. Go north on I-359 for 5 mi. Turn left onto US Hwy. 82 (McFarland Blvd.) and drive west for 5 mi. Turn right onto CR 21 and drive north for 4.5 mi. The park entrance is on the right.

DELTA

Cheaha State Park

Hwy. 281, 2141 Bunker Loop, Delta 36258. T: (256) 488-5111; F: (256) 488-5885; www.dcnr.state.al.us/parks; csparks@wrldnet.net.

🚐 ★★★★	🛖 ★★★★
Beauty: ★★★★	Site Privacy: ★★★
Spaciousness: ★★★★	Quiet: ★★★
Security: ★★★	Cleanliness: ★★★
Insect Control: ★★★★	Facilities: ★★★★

With an elevation of 2407 feet, Mt. Cheaha is the highest point in the state of Alabama. Park guests can enjoy the gorgeous mountain view from atop the observation tower. The camp-grounds are also very attractive, with very spacious sites and a variety of shady hardwood species. Site privacy varies, with dense foliage buffering some sites from their neighbors. There are two campgrounds at Cheaha, Number 1, "Upper", and Number 2, "Lower". Campground Number 1 features mostly back-in parking, but there are a few spacious pull-throughs. Parking spots are an amalgamation of dirt and gravel. In campground Number 1, sites 4 and 5 are extremely private and wooded. Large pull-throughs include 30, 31, 34, 35, and 36. Of these, 34 is the shadiest. In campground Number 2, sites 56 and 57 have a gorgeous view. Most sites in Number 2 are pull-throughs. The popularity of Cheaha's campgrounds can sometimes detract from their beauty. The campgrounds are fairly well maintained, but the potties and trash bins sometimes need more attention than they get. Security is fair at this rural state park. We got the idea that gates may or may not go down at night. This Appalachian park stays cooler than most of Alabama during the summer. Nonetheless, we recommend avoiding Cheaha on summer weekends when the park's beauty and myriad activities attract the masses.

BASICS

Operated By: Alabama State Parks. **Open:** All year. **Site Assignment:** First come, first served; reservations accepted w/ first night's fee in advance; no refunds allowed although date of stay can be changed. **Registration:** Country store. **Fee:** $17 multipurpose sites, $11 primitive sites, 15% discount for handicapped or 62 & over. **Parking:** Site, limit 2 vehicles per site.

FACILITIES

Number of RV Sites: 0. **Number of Tent-Only Sites:** Primitive tent area. **Number of Multipurpose Sites:** 73. **Hookups:** Water, electric (30 amps), sewer. **Each Site:** Picnic table, grill. **Dump Station:** No. **Laundry:** Yes. **Pay Phone:** Yes. **Rest Rooms and Showers:** Yes. **Fuel:** Yes. **Propane:** No. **Internal Roads:** Paved. **RV Service:** 25 mi. east in Oxford. **Market:** 25 mi. east in Oxford. **Restaurant:** In park. **General Store:** Wal-Mart 25 mi. east in Oxford. **Vending:** Beverages only. **Swimming Pool:** Yes. **Playground:** Yes. **Other:** Observation tower, CCC Museum, picnic & play area, sandy swimming beach. **Activities:** Fishing, pedal boat rental, hiking, mountain biking. **Nearby**

Attractions: Anniston Museum of Natural History, Birmingham & Gadsden attractions. **Additional Information:** Inquire at campground.

RESTRICTIONS

Pets: Leash only. **Fires:** Allowed. **Alcoholic Beverages:** At site only. **Vehicle Maximum Length:** 40 ft. **Other:** 14-day stay limit.

TO GET THERE

From I-20 take Exit 191. Go south on US Hwy. 431 for 5 mi. Turn right onto State Hwy. 281 and go south. This runs into the park.

DOUBLE SPRINGS
Corinth Recreation Area

P.O. Box 278, Double Springs 35553. T: (205) 489-5111; www.reserveusa.com.

🚐 ★★★★   ⛺ ★★★★

Beauty: ★★★★   Site Privacy: ★★★
Spaciousness: ★★★★   Quiet: ★★★★
Security: ★★★★★   Cleanliness: ★★★★
Insect Control: ★★★★★ Facilities: ★★★

Located 28 miles from the hiking and equestrian trails at Sipsey Wilderness Area, Corinth Recreation Area offers 52 campsites with full hookups. Sites are attractive, spacious and heavily wooded. Dense brush between sites provides privacy. The campground is laid out in two main loops plus a group camp loop. The Yellow Hammer loop is much prettier than the Firefly loop. All parking is paved. While most of the parking is back-in style, there are five huge pull-through sites. Pull through sites 17 and 19 are lovely and very private. Although the bathhouses in Bankhead National Forest are small, they are some of the tidiest in the state. Security is excellent at Corinth; the campground is extremely remote and gated at all times. Day-use facilities at Corinth are minimal, so the atmosphere is usually incredibly laid back. This tranquil campground rarely fills up, so it's a good bet for a summer weekend (if you can stand the heat).

BASICS

Operated By: Cradle of Forestry in America Interpretive Assoc. **Open:** Mar. 20–Oct. 31. **Site Assignment:** First come, first served; some loops reservable through National Recreation Reservation System (877) 444-6777. **Registration:** Gatehouse. **Fee:** $20 RV, $10 tent, fee includes 1 vehicle

per site, $3 per extra vehicle. **Parking:** At site; wheels must be on pavement.

FACILITIES

Number of RV Sites: 0. **Number of Tent-Only Sites:** 8. **Number of Multipurpose Sites:** 50 (RV). **Hookups:** Water, electric (50 amps), sewer. **Each Site:** Picnic table, fire ring, grill, lantern post, tent pad. **Dump Station:** Yes. **Laundry:** No. **Pay Phone:** Yes. **Rest Rooms and Showers:** Yes. **Fuel:** No. **Propane:** No. **Internal Roads:** Paved. **RV Service:** 35 mi. east in Cullman. **Market:** 5 mi. northwest in Double Springs. **Restaurant:** 5 mi. northwest in Double Springs. **General Store:** 5 mi. northwest in Double Springs. **Vending:** No. **Swimming Pool:** No. **Playground:** No. **Other:** Boat launch, swimming beach, paddle boat rental, group picnic shelter. **Activities:** Fishing, swimming, hiking. **Nearby Attractions:** William B. Bankhead National Forest, Looney's Entertainment & Riverboat, Ave Maria Grotto in Cullman. **Additional Information:** Cullman Area Chamber of Commerce, (800) 313-5114.

RESTRICTIONS

Pets: Leash only. **Fires:** Fire rings only. **Alcoholic Beverages:** Not Allowed. **Vehicle Maximum Length:** 50 ft. **Other:** 14-day stay limit.

TO GET THERE

From I-65, take Exit 308 at Cullman. Go west on US Hwy. 278 for approximately 30 mi. Turn left and drive south on CR 57 for 3 mi. to the park entrance.

EUFAULA
Lakepoint Resort State Park

P.O. Box 267, Eufaula 36072. T: (334) 687-8011 or (800) 544-5253; F: (334) 687-3273; www.dcnr.state.al.us/parks; lakepointstld@mindspring.com.

🚐 ★★★★   ⛺ ★★★★

Beauty: ★★★★   Site Privacy: ★★
Spaciousness: ★★★   Quiet: ★★★
Security: ★★★★   Cleanliness: ★★★★
Insect Control: ★★★   Facilities: ★★★★★

Hide your carrots. Lakepoint Resort Sate Park campgrounds are full of bunny rabbits. The flat campground is situated along Lake Eufaula, home to beaver and American alligator. Four camping areas provide over 500 sites. Of these areas, the Clark Loop, with sites along the lake, is the most attractive. Clark has only water and electric hookups, and is the best choice for tent campers. Even-numbered sites 20–42 have the prettiest views. RV campers should head for the Deer Court area, which has full hookups, and both back-in and pull-through sites. All parking is paved and ground cover consists of grass and pine straw. Site size varies, but sites are generally comfortable. Most sites are nicely wooded with a variety of tree species, some adorned with Spanish moss. None are very secluded. With excellent resort amenities, Lakepoint Resort State Park is a good choice for active families and couples, making its remote location worth the drive. Gated at all times, campground security is excellent. This park becomes chaotic on holiday weekends and should also be avoided in July and Aug. when it's bound to be unbearably hot and humid.

BASICS

Operated By: Alabama State Parks Conservation Dept. **Open:** All year, except Thanksgiving & Christmas. **Site Assignment:** First come, first served; reservations accepted through Conservation Dept. or directly, one night deposit, 7-day cancellation notice; 3-night min. on holidays. **Registration:** Camp store, night registration available. **Fee:** $17 for sites w/ sewer, $15 for sites w/ water & electric, fees include 4 people, $1.10 per extra person. **Parking:** 2 cars per site, overflow parking available.

FACILITIES

Number of Multipurpose Sites: 190. **Hookups:** Water, electric (30 amps), 80 sites w/ sewer. **Each Site:** Picnic table, grill. **Dump Station:** Yes. **Laundry:** Yes. **Pay Phone:** Yes. **Rest Rooms and Showers:** Yes. **Fuel:** Boat fuel. **Propane:** Yes. **Internal Roads:** Paved. **RV Service:** 40 mi. north in Columbus, GA. **Market:** 6 mi. south in Eufaula. **Restaurant:** In park. **General Store:** Camp store. **Vending:** Yes. **Swimming Pool:** No. **Playground:** Yes. **Other:** Marina, Boat launches, swimming beach, picnic area, sports field, information/nature center, RV storage, tennis courts, volleyball courts, basketball courts, lodge, 18-hole golf course, lounge, resort motel, video arcade. **Activities:** Fishing, pontoon boat rental, hiking, tennis courts, lodge, 18-hole golf. **Nearby Attractions:** Downtown Eufaula, antebellum homes, walking & driving tours, antique shopping. **Additional Information:** Eufaula Chamber of Commerce, (334) 687-6664.

RESTRICTIONS

Pets: Leash. **Fires:** In grills, fire rings only. **Alcoholic Beverages:** At site only. **Vehicle Maximum Length:** 60 ft.

TO GET THERE

From Columbus, GA, take US Hwy. 431 south for approximately 50 mi. Go past the intersection of US Hwy. 431 and AL Hwy. 165. The park entrance is the next left.

FORT PAYNE

De Soto State Park

265 County Rd. 951, Fort Payne 35967. T: (800) 568-8840 State Park or (800) 760-4089 Camp Store; F: (256) 845-8286; www.dcnr.state.al.us/parks; desotostpk@mindspring.com.

🚐 ★★★★★	🏕 ★★★★★
Beauty: ★★★★★	Site Privacy: ★★★★
Spaciousness: ★★★★★	Quiet: ★★★
Security: ★★★★★	Cleanliness: ★★★★
Insect Control: ★★★	Facilities: ★★★★

Situated about half way between De Soto Falls and Little River Canyon, De Soto State Park has a rugged ambience even though it's less than 10 miles northeast of Fort Payne. Sometimes referred to as "The Grand Canyon of the East," Little River Canyon has drops of up to 600 feet. Hardcore outdoorsfolk climb the canyon's sandstone bluffs and paddle the Little River's Class III-V White Water. The campground at De Soto State Park is laid out in two loops, each with its own playground and rest rooms. Sites are nicely spaced and the campground is heavily wooded with a variety of hardwoods and pines, making site size outstanding and site privacy excellent. RV parking spaces are gravel. Of the 78 campsites, 10 are pull-throughs. Since all of the sites are nice, choose your site based on proximity to (or distance from) playgrounds and rest rooms. RV campers may want to procure one of the 20 sites with full hookups. Gorgeous sites make this one of the most popular campgrounds in the state, so visit in the spring to avoid the masses. If you don't mind the constant crowds, visit for fall "leaf-peeping" in Sept. and Oct. Security at De Soto State Park is excellent; at night the gate must be opened with a "key card".

BASICS

Operated By: Alabama State Parks. **Open:** All year. **Site Assignment:** Reservations required. **Registration:** Country store. **Fee:** $17 water, electric, & sewer (4 people); $14 water & electric (4 people); $8 primitive (2 people); $3 per extra person; 8 people max.; children under 6 free. **Parking:** At site, limit 2 cars per site.

FACILITIES

Number of RV Sites: 78. **Number of Tent-Only Sites:** 50 acres open camp area (approximately 40 tents). **Number of Multipurpose Sites:** 78 (RV sites). **Hookups:** Water, 58 w/ electric (30 amps), 20 w/ electric (30 amps) & sewer. **Each Site:** Picnic table, grill, fire ring. **Dump Station:** Yes. **Laundry:** Yes. **Pay Phone:** Yes. **Rest Rooms and Showers:** Yes. **Fuel:** No. **Propane:** Yes. **Internal Roads:** Paved. **RV Service:** 35 mi. west in Rainsville. **Market:** Convenience 3 mi., grocery 7 mi. southwest in Fort Payne. **Restaurant:** In park. **General Store:** Convenience 3 mi., Wal-Mart 10 mi. southwest in Fort Payne. **Vending:** Yes. **Swimming Pool:** Yes. **Playground:** Yes. **Other:** Boat launch (7 mi.), nature trails, tennis courts, volleyball court, sports equipment, picnic & play area, lodge, country store. **Activities:** Whitewater paddling (class I-IV), rock climbing, hiking. **Nearby Attractions:** Little River Canyon National Preserve, Mentone crafts & antiques, Depot Museum, Cloudmont Ski & Golf Resort, various waterfalls. **Additional Information:** Fort Payne Chamber of Commerce, (256) 845-2741; Gadsden Chamber of Commerce, (256) 543-3472.

RESTRICTIONS

Pets: Leash only. **Fires:** Grills & fire rings only. **Alcoholic Beverages:** Not allowed. **Vehicle Maximum Length:** 50 ft. **Other:** 14-day stay limit.

TO GET THERE

From I-59, take Fort Payne Exit 218 and drive northeast on AL Hwy. 35. Drive 8 mi. to the top of Lookout Mountain. At the flashing caution light, turn left onto CR 89 and drive 5 mi. to the park entrance.

GADSDEN
Noccalula Falls Park and Campground

P.O. Box 267, Gadsden 35902. T: (256) 543-7412; www.rvcampground.com/al/noccalulafalls.

🚐 ★★★★   ⛺ ★★★★

Beauty: ★★★★　　　Site Privacy: ★★
Spaciousness: ★★★　Quiet: ★★★
Security: ★★★★　　 Cleanliness: ★★★
Insect Control: ★★★★ Facilities: ★★★★★

This city-owned park will be a big hit with the young'uns. The historic Pioneer Homestead consists of over 50 structures which have been preserved by the city of Gadsden. Buildings such as the blacksmith shop and the loom house contain tools typically used by early Appalachian pioneers. Children will also dig the passenger train, animal park, and mini-golf. Adults will appreciate the urban location, with shopping and choice of restaurants found within six miles of the park. Everybody will enjoy the park's centerpiece, 90-foot Noccalula Falls. The campground is attractive, with plenty of back-in sites and a handful of pull-throughs. A few sites have gravel parking, but most are paved. Here, site size varies greatly, with most sites being comfortably sized. The majority enjoy the shade of tall pine trees. But with little foliage between sites, privacy is poor. The prettiest sites (A19–A38) overlook the large bluff that leads down to Black Creek. Security is good at Noccalula Falls. Gates remain open throughout the night, but rangers patrol the park 24 hours a day. Avoid Gadsden in the hotter summer months. Avoid this park completely on holidays. School groups are more likely to visit the Pioneer Village on weekdays in Apr. and May. Call ahead if you would like to avoid them.

BASICS

Operated By: City of Gadsden. **Open:** All year. **Site Assignment:** First come, first served. **Registration:** Camp office. **Fee:** $23 for sites w/ full hookups, $17 for sites w/ water & electricity, seventh night is free, 10% senior discount. **Parking:** At site.

FACILITIES

Number of RV Sites: 83. **Number of Tent-Only Sites:** 47 (additional primitive tent area for large groups only). **Hookups:** 14 RV sites w/ water, electric (30, 50 amps), sewer & cable TV; 13 RV sites w/ water, electric (30, 50 amps), & sewer; 56 RV sites w/ water & electric (30, 50 amps); 47 tent sites w/ water & electric (30, 50 amps). **Each Site:** Picnic table, grill. **Dump Station:** Yes. **Laundry:** Yes.

Pay Phone: Yes. **Rest Rooms and Showers:** Yes. **Fuel:** No. **Propane:** No. **Internal Roads:** Gravel. **RV Service:** 5 mi. east in Gadsden. **Market:** 1mi. south in Gadsden. **Restaurant:** In park. **General Store:** Country store in park; Wal-Mart, K-Mart & Lowe's 10 mi. south in Gadsden. **Vending:** No. **Swimming Pool:** Yes. **Playground:** Yes. **Other:** Botanical gardens, Noccalula Falls, Pioneer Village, animal park, passenger train, picnic pavilions, souvenir shop, concession stand, rec hall, information center. **Activities:** Hiking, carpet golf , swimming, nature & history study. **Nearby Attractions:** Inquire at campground. **Additional Information:** Inquire at campground.

RESTRICTIONS

Pets: Leash only. **Fires:** Allowed. **Alcoholic Beverages:** Not allowed. **Vehicle Maximum Length:** No limit.

TO GET THERE

From I-59 take Exit 188 onto AL Hwy. 211 (Noccalula Rd.). Go south 3.5 mi. to the first light and turn right. The park entrance is ahead.

GREENVILLE
Sherling Lake

P.O. Box 158, Greenville 36037. T: (800) 810-5253; F: (334) 382-7031; www.sherlinglake@alaweb.com; sherlinglake@alaweb.com.

🚐 ★★★★★   ▲ ★★★★

Beauty: ★★★★★	Site Privacy: ★★★★
Spaciousness: ★★★★	Quiet: ★★★★★
Security: ★★★★★	Cleanliness: ★★★★★
Insect Control: ★★★★	Facilities: ★★★★

The city of Greenville operates this impeccably manicured campground. The tidy landscaping includes native azaleas and dogwoods with intermittent shade provided by tall pines. The park encompasses two fishing lakes, stocked with catfish, bluegill, brim, bass, and crappie. For golfers, 27-hole Cambrian Ridge (part of the Robert Trent Jones Golf Trail) is adjacent to Sherling Lake. Nearly deserted in the spring and fall, this campground is an excellent choice for golfers. For families, the playground is one of the nicest we've seen. The majority of the campsites are situated near the "Top Lake". All sites have ample paved parking and there are plenty of large pull-through sites. Folks with large campers should consider 1, 14, 18, and 25–41. Although all sites at Sherling Lake are spacious, back-in sites often feel a bit more secluded. Though most every site enjoys some shade, none are completely secluded by greenery. Sherling Lake is only three miles from Greenville, providing easy access to shopping and restaurants. The park fills to capacity on holidays and during coastal hurricane evacuations. The rest of the time it's an oasis of tranquility. Gates lock at night making security excellent.

BASICS

Operated By: City of Greenville. **Open:** All year. **Site Assignment:** First come, first served; reservations accepted, no deposit required. **Registration:** Office, late-comers register the next morning. **Fee:** $19 developed site for up to 4 people, $12 per tent in primitive area, Good Sam discount available. **Parking:** Limit 1 car per site, overflow parking available.

FACILITIES

Number of RV Sites: 0. **Number of Tent-Only Sites:** Primitive area holds up to 25 tent sites. **Number of Multipurpose Sites:** 41. **Hookups:** Water, electricity (30, 50 amps), sewer. **Each Site:** Picnic table, shelter, fire ring, grill; primitive area includes some tables, fire rings & grills. **Dump Station:** Yes. **Laundry:** No. **Pay Phone:** Yes. **Rest Rooms and Showers:** Yes. **Fuel:** No. **Propane:** No. **Internal Roads:** Paved. **RV Service:** 3.5 mi. south in Greenville. **Market:** 3.5 mi. south in Greenville. **Restaurant:** 3.5 mi. south in Greenville. **General Store:** Snack shop. **Vending:** Yes. **Swimming Pool:** No. **Playground:** Yes. **Other:** Boat launches, picnic pavilions, small meeting room. **Activities:** Fishing lakes, boat rentals, walking trail. **Nearby Attractions:** Adjacent to Cambrian Ridge Robert Trent Jones 18-hole golf course, Historic Greenville, Preesters Pecan Factory & Outlet. **Additional Information:** Greenville Chamber of Commerce, (334) 382-3251.

RESTRICTIONS

Pets: Leash. **Fires:** In grills, fire rings only. **Alcoholic Beverages:** At site only. **Vehicle Maximum Length:** 45 ft.

TO GET THERE

From I-65, take Exit 130 and head northwest on State Hwy. 185 for 1.5 mi. At State Hwy. 263, turn left and continue another 1.5 mi. The park entrance is on the left.

GROVE OAK
Buck's Pocket State Park

393 County Rd. 174, Grove Oak 35975. T: (256) 659-2000; F: (256) 659-2000; www.dcnr.state.al.us/parks.

🚐 ★★★★　　　🅰 ★★★★★

Beauty: ★★★★★　　Site Privacy: ★★★
Spaciousness: ★★★　　Quiet: ★★★★★
Security: ★★★★　　Cleanliness: ★★★★
Insect Control: ★★★★　　Facilities: ★★★★

2,000-acre Buck's Pocket State park is exceedingly beautiful and not heavily visited. Built around the 400-foot deep Buck's Pocket Canyon and featuring five moderately difficult hiking trails, the park is appreciated by day hikers. Fishermen can access Lake Guntersville at Morgan Cove, seven miles from the park. We were very impressed with the quiet campground that lies in the flat valley of the canyon. Completely shaded by a stand of hardwood trees, the campground features sights adjacent to lovely boulder-lined Little South Sauty Creek. Campsites are not huge, but this campground rarely fills to capacity so you'll have plenty of elbow room. While internal roads are paved, sites offer back-in gravel parking. If you are looking for solitude, head for secluded site Number 17. At 900 feet above sea level, this little "pocket" of the southern Appalachians stays cooler than most of Alabama during the hot summer months. Visit Buck's Pocket comfortably during spring, summer, or fall. The park is very remote with poor signage. It is equipped with gates, but as one local said, "there ain't no need to lock 'em!"

BASICS

Operated By: Alabama State Parks. **Open:** All year. **Site Assignment:** First come, first served; reservations accepted for holiday weekends. **Registration:** Park office. **Fee:** $15 full hookups, $14 water & electric, fee includes 8 people, $1 per extra person. **Parking:** At sites.

FACILITIES

Number of RV Sites: 36. **Number of Tent-Only Sites:** 4. **Number of Multipurpose Sites:** 36 (RV sites). **Hookups:** 6 w/ water, electric (50 amps), & sewer; 30 w/ water & electric (50 amps). **Each Site:** Picnic table, grill, fire ring, tent pad at tent sites. **Dump Station:** Yes. **Laundry:** Yes. **Pay Phone:** Yes. **Rest Rooms and Showers:** Yes. **Fuel:** No. **Propane:** No. **Internal Roads:** Paved. **RV Service:** 12 mi. east in Rainsville. **Market:** Convenience store 3 mi. south, Grocery 10 mi. south in Geraldine. **Restaurant:** 10 mi. south in Geraldine. **General Store:** 10 mi. south in Geraldine. **Vending:** Yes. **Swimming Pool:** No. **Playground:** Yes. **Other:** Boat launch, observation overlook, picnic area. **Activities:** Hiking & walking trails, fishing, boating. **Nearby Attractions:** Cathedral Caverns, Huntsville Space Museum, Lake Guntersville State Park, TVA Guntersville Dam, Depot Museum. **Additional Information:** Guntersville Chamber of Commerce, (256) 582-3612.

RESTRICTIONS

Pets: Leash only. **Fires:** In fire rings & grills only. **Alcoholic Beverages:** Not allowed. **Vehicle Maximum Length:** No limit. **Other:** 14-day stay limit.

TO GET THERE

From I-59, take Exit 218 at Fort Payne. Go north on State Hwy. 35 for 7 mi. At Rainsville, turn left and drive south on State Hwy. 75 for 4 mi. At Fyffe, turn right on CR 50, and go 8 mi. Watch carefully for park signs. Turn right onto CR 19 and right again onto CR 556, then left onto CR 73. The park is on the right.

GULF SHORES
Doc's RV Park

17595 State 180/Fort Morgan Rd., Gulf Shores 36542. T: (334) 968-4511; F: (334) 968-1109; www.docsrvpark.com; docsrvpark@gulftel.com.

🚐 ★★★　　　🅰 n/a

Beauty: ★★★　　Site Privacy: ★★
Spaciousness: ★★★　　Quiet: ★★★
Security: ★★★　　Cleanliness: ★★★
Insect Control: ★★★★　　Facilities: ★★★

When we visited Gulf Shores, Doc's RV Park was the quietest in town. Three miles from the beach and within easy distances to restaurants and shopping, Doc's isn't far from touristy hustle and bustle. Campsites at Doc's are built around an elliptical grassy park area. So even though sites are narrow, campers enjoy a view of the grass. Most sites have a little shade provided by trees on the periphery of the park. All sites have back-in, gravel parking which looks a little untidy in some places. The shadiest sites are numbers 46–30. If you want an open site, there are plenty to choose from. Doc's is popular with snowbirds in the winter and popular with families in the summer. For optimal peace and quiet, visit in Spring or Fall. Doc's is in a quiet Gulf Shores neighborhood, but there is no gate. Security is fair, so guard your valuables.

BASICS

Operated By: Roton & Bear. **Open:** All year. **Site Assignment:** Reservations recommended & accepted w/ deposit; 1-week cancellation notice required, 1 month in winter. **Registration:** Clubhouse, self-register at night. **Fee:** $24 in summertime, $21 in wintertime (good for 4 people); 2-day weekend min., 3-day holiday min.; Good Sam discount available. **Parking:** At site, limit 2 cars per site.

FACILITIES

Number of RV Sites: 75. **Number of Tent-Only Sites:** 0. **Number of Multipurpose Sites:** None. **Hookups:** Water, electric (30, 50 amps), cable, sewer. **Each Site:** Picnic table. **Dump Station:** Yes. **Laundry:** Yes. **Pay Phone:** Yes. **Rest Rooms and Showers:** Yes. **Fuel:** No. **Propane:** Yes. **Internal Roads:** Paved. RV Service: 10 mi. north in Foley. **Market:** 2 mi. in Gulf Shores. **Restaurant:** 2 mi. in Gulf Shores. **General Store:** 0.5 mi. in Gulf Shores, Wal-Mart 10 mi. north in Foley. **Vending:** Beverages only. **Swimming Pool:** Yes. **Playground:** Yes. **Other:** Clubhouse, fire grills in central location, RV storage. **Activities:** Volleyball, horseshoes, weekly campground gatherings in winter. **Nearby Attractions:** 3 mi. from the beach, outlet shopping, Bellingrath Gardens, boat tours, USS Alabama Battleship Memorial Park. **Additional Information:** Alabama Gulf Coast CVB, (800) 745-7263.

RESTRICTIONS

Pets: Welcome, on leash only. **Fires:** Grills only. **Alcoholic Beverages:** Allowed. **Vehicle Maximum Length:** No limit.

TO GET THERE

From I-10, take Exit 44 onto Hwy. 59 south. Continue past the junction with Hwy. 98 another 9.5 mi. Turn west on State Hwy. 180/Fort Morgan Rd. and the park entrance will be 2 mi. down on the right. Web-site also has map and directions.

GULF SHORES
Gulf Breeze Resort

19800 Oak Rd. West, Gulf Shores 36542. T: (251) 968-8884; F: (251) 968-8462; www.ehodges.com; wakefieldent@mindspring.com.

🚐 ★★★　　　🅰 n/a

Beauty: ★★★　　　Site Privacy: ★★
Spaciousness: ★★★　Quiet: ★★★
Security: ★★　　　　Cleanliness: ★★★
Insect Control: ★★★★　Facilities: ★★★★

Gulf Breeze Resort offers extensive and well-maintained recreational facilities. It also boasts the nicest bathhouses in Gulf Shores and the tidiest landscaping. Even though the resort feels like it's off the beaten path, it's close to numerous restaurants and tourist attractions. The nearest beach is just four miles away. The campground is laid out in a giant grid and includes both back-in and pull-through spaces. Most of the spaces are paved although a few have gravel parking. Site size is average and very few sites have any shade. The nicest sites are 46–51, which are adjacent to the small fishing pond. Sites 164 and 171 overlook another small pond and are also attractive. This suburban resort is popular with snow-birds in the winter and popular with families in the summer, so it's almost always busy. Avoid visits during spring break, holiday weekends, and sweltering July and Aug. There is no gate at Gulf Breeze so protect your valuables.

BASICS

Operated By: Wakefield Enterprises. **Open:** All year. **Site Assignment:** First come, first served; reservations accepted w/ one night deposit; 48-hour cancellation required, $2 cancellation fee if paid by credit card. **Registration:** Office, no late registration—check in next day by 10 a.m. **Fee:** $22 for 4 people, $2 per extra person up to 8. **Parking:** At site, limit 2 cars per site, overflow parking available.

FACILITIES

Number of RV Sites: 226. **Number of Tent-Only Sites:** 0. **Hookups:** Water, electric (30, 50 amps), sewer, cable TV, 6 overflow sites have water, electricity only. **Each Site:** Picnic table, concrete patios, some w/ concrete pads. **Dump Station:** No. **Laundry:** Yes. **Pay Phone:** Yes. **Rest Rooms and Showers:** Yes. **Fuel:** No. **Propane:** No.

Internal Roads: Paved. **RV Service:** On call. **Market:** 3 mi. in Gulf Shores. **Restaurant:** 3 mi. in Gulf Shores. **General Store:** 0.25 mi., 5 mi. to Wal-Mart. **Vending:** Yes. **Swimming Pool:** Yes. **Playground:** Yes. **Other:** Pavilion, clubhouse for rent, indoor pool, outdoor pool, children's pool. **Activities:** Fishing lake, paddle boat rental, basketball, horseshoes, shuffleboard, 18-hole mini-golf, hot tub. **Nearby Attractions:** Gulf Shores beaches, Waterville USA, Bellingrath Gardens, Dauphin Island Sea Lab, Fort Conde Museum, USS Alabama Battleship Memorial Park, Mobile & Pensacola attractions. **Additional Information:** Alabama Gulf Coast CVB, (800) 745-7263.

RESTRICTIONS

Pets: Leash only, clean-up enforced. **Fires:** Not allowed. **Alcoholic Beverages:** At site only. **Vehicle Maximum Length:** No limit.

TO GET THERE

From I-10, take Exit 44 (Loxley/Foley/Gulf Shores). Drive south on Hwy. 59 and go through Foley. Exit at CR 6 and turn right. The park is 1.5 blocks on the left.

GULF SHORES
Gulf State Park

22050 Campground Rd., Gulf Shores 36542. T: (334) 948-7275; F: (334) 948-4570; www.dcnr.state.al.us/parks.

🚐 ★★★★	⛺ ★★★★
Beauty: ★★★★	Site Privacy: ★★★
Spaciousness: ★★★	Quiet: ★★★
Security: ★★★★	Cleanliness: ★★★★
Insect Control: ★★	Facilities: ★★★★★

Unfortunately, the large campground at Gulf State Park offers no campsites within walking distances of the beach. However, the campground is very attractive and perennially popular with families; don't expect any solitude here during the summer months. Site size is acceptable but the bustling atmosphere makes the campground feel crowded. 185 sites offer back-in parking and 25 offer pull-through parking. Parking areas may be paved, gravel or packed sand. Many of the sites are shady and a few offer views of small Middle Lake. Tent sites offer soft sand tent pads. Of those with lake views, sites 17–39 are the most picturesque. Unless you really want a pull-through, avoid the noisy, highly trafficked sites along the main road. Located just a few miles from the tourist town of Gulf Shores, campers have easy access to excellent dining and other tourist attractions. Amenities within the park are also outstanding, including the state's largest fishing pier (825 feet), an 18-hole golf course, and two-and-a-half miles of white sand beach. The gates at Gulf Shores State Park campground are locked at night and the entrance is manned all day, making security excellent.

BASICS

Operated By: Alabama State Parks. **Open:** All year. **Site Assignment:** First come, first served; roughly half of the sites are available for reservation w/ a one-night, non-refundable deposit. **Registration:** Park entrance. **Fee:** $12–$16. **Parking:** At site, limit 2 vehicles per site.

FACILITIES

Number of Multipurpose Sites: 210. **Hookups:** Electric (15, 30 amps), water, sewer. **Each Site:** Picnic table, grill. **Dump Station:** Yes. **Laundry:** Yes. **Pay Phone:** Yes. **Rest Rooms and Showers:** Yes. **Fuel:** No. **Propane:** No. **Internal Roads:** Paved. **RV Service:** No. **Market:** 3 mi. in Gulf Shores. **Restaurant:** In park. **General Store:** 3 mi. in Gulf Shores. **Vending:** Beverages only. **Swimming Pool:** No. **Playground:** Yes. **Other:** Tennis courts, fishing pier, golf course, game room, bicycle rental, beach pavilion, boat ramp, nature center, resort hotel & conference center, picnic area. **Activities:** Swimming, hiking, fishing, golf. **Nearby Attractions:** Alabama Gulf Coast Zoo, Gulf Shores Beach, Dauphin Island Sea Lab, Adventure Island, Bellingrath Gardens & Home, Biophilia Nature Center & Native Nursery, Gulf Coast Museum of Science, Gulf Coast Amusement Park, Mobile Bay Ferry, Pirate Island Adventure Golf, USS Alabama Battleship Memorial Park, Wildland Expeditions, Waterville USA. **Additional Information:** Alabama Gulf Coast Visitor Information, (800) 745-7263.

RESTRICTIONS

Pets: On leash only. **Fires:** In grills & designated bonfire areas. **Alcoholic Beverages:** At site only. **Vehicle Maximum Length:** No limit.

TO GET THERE

At the intersection of State Hwy. 59 and State Hwy. 182 (Beach Rd.), turn left. Drive east on State Hwy. 182 for 3.5 mi. Pass Gulf State Park

Resort Hotel and take the next left onto CR 2. Campground is on the right.

GUNTERSVILLE
Lake Guntersville State Park

1155 Lodge Dr., Guntersville 35976-9126. T: (256) 571-5455; F: (256) 571-9043; www.dcnr.state.al.us/parks.

🚐 ★★★★   ▲ ★★★

Beauty: ★★★★   Site Privacy: ★★
Spaciousness: ★★★   Quiet: ★★
Security: ★★★   Cleanliness: ★★★
Insect Control: ★★★★   Facilities: ★★★★★

Lake Guntersville Sate Park is really lovely, but the campgrounds are often way too crowded for our tastes. Set in a beautiful stand of tall pines, the huge campground (with over 300 sites) stays full for much of the summer. If you don't mind spending your vacation with an entire village of new friends and neighbors, you may enjoy this park. Here you will find paved back-in sites with very little privacy. Sites are small compared to other Alabama State parks. The campground is laid out in eight grid-like areas (A–F). Tent campers should head for Area A, especially sites 16 and 17. RV campers should try to land a lakeside site in Area D or G. Sites G9, G11, G12, G13, G24, and G36 are among the most attractive. Area E should be avoided as it abuts the picnic pavilion and experiences heavy traffic. Families wishing to camp right next to the playground should head for C51–C59. Lake Guntersville State Park offers plenty of amenities and activities, but their pride and joy is the American bald eagles who winter there. The campground is gated and guarded, but security isn't fantastic because of the number of folks on the campground. We recommend visiting Lake Guntersville in spring or fall to avoid the crowds.

BASICS
Operated By: Alabama State Parks. **Open:** All year. **Site Assignment:** First come, first served; about half of the sites can be reserved; 3 night min. weekends & holidays, one night deposit. **Registration:** Camp store, no late registration. **Fee:** $17 for up to 4 people. **Parking:** At site.

FACILITIES
Number of Multipurpose Sites: 320. **Hookups:** Water, electric (30 amps), sewer. **Each Site:** Picnic table, grill, fire ring. **Dump Station:** Yes. **Laundry:** Yes. **Pay Phone:** Yes. **Rest Rooms and Showers:** Yes. **Fuel:** No. **Propane:** No. **Internal Roads:** Paved. **RV Service:** Inquire at campground. **Market:** 7.5 mi. southwest in Guntersville. **Restaurant:** In park. **General Store:** Camp store, Wal-Mart 15 mi. southwest in Guntersville. **Vending:** Yes. **Swimming Pool:** No. **Playground:** Yes. **Other:** Beach, nature center, art gallery, 18-hole golf course, RV storage, activity building, fishing piers, picnic pavilion, 31 mi. of hiking trails. **Activities:** Swimming, fishing, boating, hiking, tennis. **Nearby Attractions:** American Bald Eagles Convention Center, Cathedral Caverns, Buck's Pocket State Park, Guntersville Museum & Cultural Center. **Additional Information:** Guntersville Chamber of Commerce, (256) 582-3612.

RESTRICTIONS
Pets: Leash only. **Fires:** Fire rings only. **Alcoholic Beverages:** At site only. **Vehicle Maximum Length:** No limit. **Other:** 14-day stay limit Apr.–Oct.

TO GET THERE
From I-59, take the Gadsden exit and go north on US Hwy. 431 for approximately 38 mi. At Guntersville, turn right onto AL Hwy. 227 and go northeast for 7 mi. The park entrance is on the left.

GUNTERSVILLE/LANGSTON
Little Mountain Marina Resort

1001 Murphy Hill Rd., Langston 35755. T: (256) 582-8211; F: (256) 582-6344; www.ehodges.com; wakefieldent@mindspring.com.

🚐 ★★★★   ▲ n/a

Beauty: ★★★   Site Privacy: ★★
Spaciousness: ★★★   Quiet: ★★
Security: ★★★★   Cleanliness: ★★★
Insect Control: ★★★★   Facilities: ★★★★★

Little Mountain Resort is noteworthy for its modern amenities rather than its natural beauty. Located on Guntersville Lake, the resort caters to active families and large groups. For fishing and boating enthusiasts, there's a boat launch, marina, fishing pier and two covered piers containing a total of 86 boat slips. Land amenities include a 500-seat great hall as well as multiple swimming pools and other activities. The gigantic campground is a no-frills affair with mid-sized sites. There are no barriers to provide privacy between sites. Back-in gravel parking is the rule and no tent camping is allowed. The prettiest sites are numbers 110–119 and 110A–119A, which are adjacent to the lake and have power and water only. The nicest sites with full hookups and views of the lake are 18–20, 27–29, 36, 37, 120, and 121. Avoid sites in the 200s and 300s, which have unattractive views of the boat and RV storage areas. Some sites are completely open while others provide plenty of shade. In spite of Little Mountain's extremely remote location, you may feel like you've arrived in Lower Manhattan once you're here. We recommend weekday visits in the summertime, or visits in spring or autumn. The guard house is staffed 24 hours a day, making security good.

BASICS

Operated By: Earl & Elke Hodges. **Open:** All year. **Site Assignment:** First come, first served; 2-night min. for reservations; cancellation penalty is first night's fee on holidays. **Registration:** Guard house. **Fee:** $20, fee includes 4 people, $2 per extra person. **Parking:** Limit 2 vehicles per site.

FACILITIES

Number of RV Sites: 343. **Number of Tent-Only Sites:** 0. **Hookups:** 309 w/ sewer, water & electric (30, 50 amps); 34 w/ water & electric. **Each Site:** Picnic table, concrete patio, grill (at full hookup sites only). **Dump Station:** No. **Laundry:** Yes. **Pay Phone:** Yes. **Rest Rooms and Showers:** Yes. **Fuel:** No. **Propane:** Exchange only. **Internal Roads:** Gravel. **RV Service:** Mechanic On call. **Market:** 1 mi. **Restaurant:** 6 mi. south in Guntersville. **General Store:** Country store 0.5 mi., Wal-Mart 15 mi. south in Guntersville. **Vending:** Yes. **Swimming Pool:** Yes. **Playground:** Yes. **Other:** Marina, boat launch, 86-slip covered pier, fishing pier, indoor & outdoor pools, spa, sauna, game room, club house w/ great hall, exercise room, library, TV/card room, Florida room, dining room, chapel, activity pavilion. **Activities:** Tennis, shuffleboard, basketball, horseshoes, mini-golf, fishing, boating, swimming. **Nearby Attractions:** Cathedral Caverns, Huntsville Space Museum, Lake Guntersville State Park, TVA Guntersville Dam,

Depot Museum. **Additional Information:** Guntersville Chamber of Commerce, (256) 582-3612.

RESTRICTIONS

Pets: Leash only. **Fires:** In grill only. **Alcoholic Beverages:** At site only. **Vehicle Maximum Length:** 40 ft.

TO GET THERE

From I-59, take Exit 218 at Fort Payne. Go northwest on AL Hwy. 35 for 7 mi. to Rainsville. Turn left and drive south on AL Hwy. 75 for 18 mi. At AL Hwy. 227 turn right and drive north for 10 mi. Turn right onto Old Hwy. 227 and go 0.5 mi. Then, turn left onto Murphy Hill Rd. and go 0.5 mi.

HUNTSVILLE
Monte Sano State Park

5105 Nolen Ave., Huntsville 35801. T: (256) 534-3757; F: (256) 539-7069; www.dcnr.state.al.us/parks.

🚐 ★★★★	🗢 ★★★★
Beauty: ★★★★	Site Privacy: ★★★★
Spaciousness: ★★★★	Quiet: ★★★★
Security: ★★★★	Cleanliness: ★★★★
Insect Control: ★★★★	Facilities: ★★★★

This flat campground on top of Monte Sano features lovely hardwoods with foliage between all campsites. In some instances, sites are very secluded by dense foliage. Site size is ample, and parking is mostly back-in. Four pull-throughs (numbers 14, 30, 62, and 82) are extremely large. Parking spaces are fine gravel. The prettiest sites are odd numbers 49–61 and only have water and electric hookups. Avoid sites 31–44, as they parallel a noisy road. The campground is laid out in two loops, each having its own bathhouse. With over 32 miles of trails, Monte Sano is a hiker's haven. This suburban park lies just outside of Huntsville city limits and is popular with the locals. Monte Sano Mountain has an elevation of approximately 1,500 feet, and stays about five degrees Fahrenheit cooler than Huntsville proper, making the park a fine summer destination. The park gates lock at night, but its suburban location necessitates caution with your valuables.

BASICS

Operated By: Alabama State Parks. **Open:** All year. **Site Assignment:** First come, first served; no reservations taken. **Registration:** Camp store, night registration available. **Fee:** $16 for sites w/ full hookups, $15 for sites w/ water & electric, $10 for primitive tent sites. **Parking:** At site, overflow parking available.

FACILITIES

Number of RV Sites: 0. **Number of Tent-Only Sites:** 20. **Number of Multipurpose Sites:** 89. **Hookups:** Water, electric (30 amps), sewer. **Each Site:** Picnic table, fire ring, grill. **Dump Station:** Yes. **Laundry:** Yes. **Pay Phone:** Yes. **Rest Rooms and Showers:** Yes. **Fuel:** No. **Propane:** No. **Internal Roads:** Paved. **RV Service:** 8 mi. south in Huntsville. **Market:** 6 mi. south in Huntsville. **Restaurant:** 6 mi. south in Huntsville. **General Store:** Inquire at campground. **Vending:** Yes. **Swimming Pool:** No. **Playground:** Yes. **Other:** Japanese Gardens, 32 mi. of hiking trials, planetarium, camp store, amphitheater w/ summertime film series. **Activities:** Hiking, walking. **Nearby Attractions:** Huntsville: U.S. Space & Rocket Center, Huntsville Museum of Art, Twickenham Historic District, Alabama Constitution Village, Cathedral Caverns, Children's Museum, Alabama State Black Archives Research Center & Museum. **Additional Information:** Huntsville CVB, (800) SPACE-4-U.

RESTRICTIONS

Pets: Leash only. **Fires:** Fire rings only. **Alcoholic Beverages:** Not allowed. **Vehicle Maximum Length:** No limit. **Other:** 14-night stay-limit.

TO GET THERE

From I-65, take Exit 340 and go east on I-565 to Huntsville. From I -565 take Exit 17 and go east on Governor's Dr. Go through Huntsville and turn left onto Monte Sano Blvd. At the top of the Mountain, turn right onto Nolen St. The park entrance is ahead.

JASPER
Clear Creek Recreation Area

8079 Fall City Rd., Jasper 35501. T: (205) 384-4792.

🚐 ★★★★★	⛺ ★★★★★
Beauty: ★★★★★	Site Privacy: ★★★★★
Spaciousness: ★★★★★	Quiet: ★★★★★
Security: ★★★★★	Cleanliness: ★★★★★
Insect Control: ★★★★	Facilities: ★★★

In the heart of William B. Bankhead National Forest, Clear Creek offers incredibly spacious sites with majestic views of Lake Lewis Smith. The campground is incredibly remote and quiet,

with a dense understory providing an additional noise barrier between campsites. Each site enjoys the cooling shade of mature trees. Parking is paved, and there are both back-in and pull-through spaces. Double sites are available for large families or small groups. Tent campers should head for picturesque lakefront sites 47, 49, and 51. For RV campers, we like a number of sites, including 5, 8, 17, 18, 51, 53, 55, 81, and 82. Site 53 is a pull-through with water view. Facilities here are nice, particularly the swimming beach. Bankhead National Forest and nearby Sipsey Wilderness (35 miles from campground) offer hiking galore. Security is excellent—the park is gated at all times. Visit in late spring, early summer, and fall. Avoid holiday weekends.

BASICS

Operated By: Cradle of Forestry in America Interpretive Assoc. **Open:** Mar. 20–Oct. 31. **Site Assignment:** First come, first served. **Registration:** Gatehouse 7 a.m.–9 p.m. Sunday–Thursday, 7 a.m.–10 p.m. Friday & Saturday; no late registration. **Fee:** $17.85–$18.90 single (up to 6 people, 2 vehicles plus RV or tent); $27.30–$31.50 double (up to 12 people, 4 vehicles plus RV or tent); Golden Age/Access discounts available. **Parking:** Limited space at sites, all wheels must be on pavement.

FACILITIES

Number of RV Sites: 102. **Number of Tent-Only Sites:** 2 group sites. **Number of Multipurpose Sites:** 102 (RV). **Hookups:** Water, electricity (30 amps). **Each Site:** Picnic table, grill, fire ring, lantern post, tent pad. **Dump Station:** Yes. **Laundry:** No. **Pay Phone:** Yes. **Rest Rooms and Showers:** Yes. **Fuel:** No. **Propane:** No. **Internal Roads:** Paved. **RV Service:** 15 mi. in Jasper. **Market:** 15 mi. in Jasper. **Restaurant:** 5 mi. west. **General Store:** 5 mi. south. **Vending:** No. **Swimming Pool:** No. **Playground:** Yes. **Other:** Boat launch. **Activities:** Lake beach, basketball, hiking, mountain biking, fishing, Interpretive programs, wildlife education. **Nearby Attractions:** Arrowhead & Twin Lakes golf, Walker County Lake, Rickwood Caverns State Park, William B. Bankhead National Forest, Smith Lake. **Additional Information:** Walker County Chamber of Commerce, (888) 384-4571.

RESTRICTIONS

Pets: Leash. **Fires:** Fire rings only. **Alcoholic Beverages:** Not allowed. **Vehicle Maximum Length:** Varies up to 50 ft. **Other:** 14-day max. stay.

To Get There

From I-65, take Hwy. 78 west 41 mi. to Jasper, then Hwy. 195 north 8 mi. Turn right on CR 27, which dead ends at 5 mi. at the park entrance.

LILLIAN
Perdido Bay KOA

33951 Spinnaker Dr., Lillian 36549. T: (334) 961-1717; F: (334) 961-1717; www.koa.com; perdidokoa@gulftel.com.

🚐 ★★★   ▲ ★★

Beauty: ★★★	Site Privacy: ★★
Spaciousness: ★★★	Quiet: ★★★
Security: ★★★	Cleanliness: ★★★
Insect Control: ★★★★	Facilities: ★★★

This KOA is situated on Perdido Bay, within 30 miles of Alabama's Gulf Coast. Though crabbing, fishing and dolphin watching are favored activities here, the campground is equipped with all the other amenities we expect from a KOA. The rectangular campground features rows of back-in and pull-through campsites. Parking areas are amoebic in shape and comprised of patchy sand, grass, and dirt. Sites are mid-sized and most afford no seclusion from neighbors. All sites are at least partially shaded by pine trees, with the shadiest sites on row F (F1–F14). Unfortunately, none of the RV sites are near the water. Tent campers should opt for a Kamping Kabin on the water's edge—the alternative is a noisy site adjacent to CR 99. Security is fair at this campground. There is no gate but the park is fairly remote. We recommend visiting Perdido Bay in the spring or fall, when the weather is mild.

Basics

Operated By: Denise Valentyne. **Open:** All year. **Site Assignment:** Often assigned; reservations recommended; credit card deposit required for reservation; one day's notice required for full refund. **Registration:** Office & store. **Fee:** $19–$25 (cash, checks, V, MC, DISC). **Parking:** 1 vehicle per site, overflow parking available.

Facilities

Number of RV Sites: 100. **Number of Tent-Only Sites:** 6. **Number of Multipurpose Sites:** 100 (RV sites). **Hookups:** Water, electric (30, 50 amps), some sewer. **Each Site:** Picnic table. **Dump Station:** Yes. **Laundry:** Yes. **Pay Phone:** Yes. **Rest Rooms and Showers:** Yes. **Fuel:** No. **Propane:** Yes. **Internal Roads:** Paved & dirt. **RV Service:** Yes. **Market:** Camp store. **Restaurant:** 1.5 mi. north in Lillian. **General Store:** 8 mi. east in Myrtle Grove, FL. **Vending:** No. **Swimming Pool:** Yes. **Playground:** Yes. **Other:** Hot tub, fishing pier, boat launch, RV storage, fax service. **Activities:** Basketball, horseshoes, shuffleboard, fishing, crabbing, beaches. **Nearby Attractions:** Naval Air Museum, Bellingrath Gardens in Theodore, Gulf Shores beaches, Old Mobile. **Additional Information:** Mobile Convention & Visitor Corporation, (800) 5-MOBILE; Alabama Gulf Coast CVB, (800) 745-SAND.

Restrictions

Pets: Leash only. **Fires:** Allowed at tent sites w/ water hookups. **Alcoholic Beverages:** At site only. **Vehicle Maximum Length:** No limit.

To Get There

From Pensacola, take Hwy. 98 West 15 mi. to Lillian, on the Alabama state line. From Mobile, take Hwy. 98 East 40 mi. to Lillian. At Lillian, turn south onto Spinnaker Dr. and go 2 mi. The campground entrance is on the left.

McCALLA
McCalla/Tannehill KOA Kampground

22191 Hwy. 216, McCalla 35111. T: (205) 477-4778.

🚐 ★★★   ▲ ★★

Beauty: ★★★	Site Privacy: ★★
Spaciousness: ★★★	Quiet: ★★★
Security: ★★	Cleanliness: ★★★
Insect Control: ★★★	Facilities: ★★★

This suburban campground is a perfectly acceptable place to stay while visiting Birmingham and Tuscaloosa County. The park is located about halfway between downtown Birmingham and the Mercedes-Benz Plant and Visitor Center in Vance (approximately 12 miles to each). With all of the amenities folks expect at KOAs, this is a relaxing place to be after a day in the city. With the exception of untidy gravel and grass, this park is well kept and reasonably attractive. The campground is laid out in two sections divided by the pool, store, and other facilities. Site size is ample, especially when compared to sites at other KOA campgrounds. Sites numbering in the 60s and 70s are shaded by a variety of tree species. A few sites are completely open. Roads and parking spaces are gravel and almost all sites are pull-throughs. KOA McCalla is less than a quarter mile from I-59 and has no security gate, so protect your valuables. Avoid visits in July and Aug., when heat and humidity can be unbelievable in this part of Alabama.

BASICS

Operated By: Andy Thompson & Judy Bogol. **Open:** All year. **Site Assignment:** First come, first served; reservations recommended; cancel w/ 24-hour notice or charge of 1st night. **Registration:** Camp office. **Fee:** $26 (50 amp), $23 full hookup (30 amp), $18 tent. **Parking:** 2 vehicles per site.

FACILITIES

Number of RV Sites: 42. **Number of Tent-Only Sites:** 8 (4 primitive, 4 w/ water & electricity). **Number of Multipurpose Sites:** None. **Hookups:** Water, electric (30, 50 amps), sewer, cable TV. **Each Site:** Picnic table, fire ring. **Dump Station:** Yes. **Laundry:** Yes. **Pay Phone:** Yes. **Rest Rooms and Showers:** Yes. **Fuel:** No. **Propane:** Yes. **Internal Roads:** Gravel. **RV Service:** 15 mi. **Market:** 8 mi. **Restaurant:** 0.75 mi. **General Store:** Camp store, 0.75 mi. **Vending:** No. **Swimming Pool:** Yes. **Playground:** Yes. **Other:** Lighted pavilion w/ kitchen, RV storage. **Activities:** Horseshoes, badminton, volleyball, basketball, game room. **Nearby Attractions:** VisionLand, Tannehill State Park, Mercedes Benz Plant & Visitor's Center, Birmingham Zoo & Botanical Gardens, Birmingham Museum of Art, McWane Center w/ IMAX theater. **Additional Information:** Tuscaloosa CVB, (800) 538-8696; Greater Birmingham CVB, (800) 458-8085.

RESTRICTIONS

Pets: Leash only. **Fires:** In grills, fire rings only. **Alcoholic Beverages:** At site only. **Vehicle Maximum Length:** No limit.

TO GET THERE

From I-20/59, take Exit 100. Go 500 yards west on CR 20 to the park entrance.

MOBILE

Chickasabogue Park and Campground

760 Aldock Rd., Mobile 36613. T: (334) 574-2267; F: (334) 574-0541; www.mobilecounty.org-park; rjones@mobile-county.net.

🚐 ★★★★	🏕 ★★★★
Beauty: ★★★★	Site Privacy: ★★★★
Spaciousness: ★★★★	Quiet: ★★★★
Security: ★★★	Cleanliness: ★★★
Insect Control: ★★	Facilities: ★★★

Operated by the Mobile County Commission, Chickasabogue Park campground includes 47 incredibly spacious sites. Most of the sites are pull-throughs, with plenty of shade and privacy provided by magnolia and post and live oak complete with Spanish moss. These surprisingly lovely sites have gravel parking. Tent campers should head for sites 40–47. RV campers should try sites 1–13, which are commodious, private and attractive pull-throughs. The campground includes a group camp and three other areas. The washhouses are nothing to write home about. Bring your own Lysol. This suburban park offers plenty of outdoor activities including an 18-hole disc golf course. Gates are not locked at night, but rangers patrol hourly, making security acceptable. The Mobile Bay should be avoided in July and Aug. when heat and humidity can be unbearable.

BASICS

Operated By: Mobile County Commission. **Open:** All year. **Site Assignment:** First come, first served; reservations accepted w/ first night's fee deposit by check or credit card. **Registration:** Camp store, Security Guard after hours. **Fee:** $18 for sites w/ full hookups, $15 for sites w/ water & electric, $19 for tent sites; fee includes four people, $1 per extra person. **Parking:** At site.

FACILITIES

Number of RV Sites: 47. **Number of Tent-Only Sites:**. **Number of Multipurpose Sites:** 21. **Hookups:** Water, electric (50, 30 amps), 26 sites w/ sewer. **Each Site:** Picnic table, fire ring, grill. **Dump Station:** Yes. **Laundry:** Yes. **Pay Phone:** Yes. **Rest Rooms and Showers:** Yes. **Fuel:** No. **Propane:** No. **Internal Roads:** Paved. **RV Service:** 5 mi. north in Saraland. **Market:** 5 mi. north in Saraland. **Restaurant:** 5 mi. north in Saraland. **General Store:** Camp store in park, Wal-mart 5 mi. north in Saraland. **Vending:** Yes. **Swimming Pool:** No. **Playground:** Yes. **Other:** Canoe rentals, boat ramp, 18-hole disc golf course, picnic area, sports field, nature center. **Activities:** Boating, hiking, biking. **Nearby Attractions:** USS Alabama,

Dauphin Island Sea Lab, Mobile attractions. **Additional Information:** Mobile Convention & Visitors Corporation, (800) 5-MOBILE.

<u>RESTRICTIONS</u>

Pets: Leash only. **Fires:** In grills & fire rings only. **Alcoholic Beverages:** At site only. **Vehicle Maximum Length:** No limit. **Other:** 2-week max. stay in summertime.

<u>TO GET THERE</u>

From I-65 take Exit 13. If coming from the north, cross State Hwy. 158 (Industrial Rd.) and then turn left onto State Hwy. 213 South (Shelton beach Rd.). If coming from the south, turn left onto State Hwy. 158 (Industrial Rd.) and then left again onto State Hwy. 213 South. Go south on State hwy. 213 for 2 mi. At the first flashing light turn left onto Whistler St. Take the second left onto Aldock Rd. Go 1 mi. to the park entrance.

PELL CITY
Lakeside Landing

4600 Martin St. South, Cropwell 35054. T: (205) 525-5701; F: (205) 525-5423; www.loganmartinguide.com.

🚐 ★★★   ▲ ★★

Beauty: ★★	Site Privacy: ★★
Spaciousness: ★★	Quiet: ★★
Security: ★★	Cleanliness: ★★★
Insect Control: ★★	Facilities: ★★★

This park's location is its saving grace. On the banks of Logan Martin Lake, the park maintains boat launches, fishing piers, and a swimming area. Area attractions include the Talladega Superspeedway and De Soto Caverns. Campers hoping to enjoy the beauty of nature will have to leave Lakeside Landing. We suggest a drive to Pell City Lakeside Park where you'll find walking trails, picnic facilities, and boating and fishing facilities in a more natural setting. The huge campground at Lakeside Landing won't win any beauty contests, but it is clean and well equipped. There are back-in and pull-through sites that once featured paved parking. Now the parking areas are an untidy jumble of pavement, gravel and grass. The campground is almost completely tree-less and sites are on the small side. We hope you like your neighbors because you'll be able to hear them hic-

cup. Lakefront sites 174–193 are the most attractive. Some of these lakefront sites have a few shady trees. Avoid Lakeside Landing during summer holidays and major events at Talladega Superspeedway. If you want to camp here on a race weekend, make your reservations 6 to 12 months in advance. Security here is fair; the campground is located just outside Pell City and there are no gates, but the area is well patrolled at night.

<u>BASICS</u>

Operated By: Mark & Cindy Bagley. **Open:** All year, except Christmas. **Site Assignment:** No reservations accepted, except race weekends (Apr. & Oct.). **Registration:** Camp store. **Fee:** $18, $16.20 w/ Good Sam discount. **Parking:** At site, overflow parking available.

<u>FACILITIES</u>

Number of Multipurpose Sites: 215. **Hookups:** Water, electric (50 amps), sewer. **Each Site:** Picnic table, grill. **Dump Station:** Yes. **Laundry:** Yes. **Pay Phone:** Yes. **Rest Rooms and Showers:** Yes. **Fuel:** Yes. **Propane:** Yes. **Internal Roads:** Paved. **RV Service:** 0.75 mi. **Market:** Camp store, supermarket 3 mi. north in Pell City. **Restaurant:** 0.75 mi. north in Pell City. **General Store:** Camp store, K-Mart 3 mi. north in Pell City. **Vending:** Beverages only. **Swimming Pool:** No. **Playground:** No. **Other:** Boat launch, fishing piers, RV storage, snack bar, picnic area, beach on Lake Logan Martin, meeting hall. **Activities:** Fishing, swimming. **Nearby Attractions:** Talladega Superspeedway (NASCAR), De Soto Caverns, Kymulga Grist Mill & Covered Bridge. **Additional Information:** Pell City Chamber of Commerce, (205) 338-3377; Greater Birmingham CVB, (800) 458-8085.

<u>RESTRICTIONS</u>

Pets: Leash only. **Fires:** Allowed. **Alcoholic Beverages:** Allowed. **Vehicle Maximum Length:** No limit. **Other:** No RV storage at sites.

<u>TO GET THERE</u>

From I-20, take Exit 155B at Pell City/Asheville. Go 6 mi. south on Hwy. 231. The campground is on the left.

PETERSON
Old Lock 16 Park, Holt Lake

P.O. Box 295, Peterson 35478. T: (205) 553-9373; www.reserveusa.com.

🚐 ★★★★   ▲ ★★★★

Beauty: ★★★★   Site Privacy: ★★★
Spaciousness: ★★★★   Quiet: ★★★★
Security: ★★★★   Cleanliness: ★★★★
Insect Control: ★★★   Facilities: ★★★

Old Lock 16 Park on Holt Lake will include 36 tranquil sites when construction is completed in 2002. When we visited, eight attractive sites had been completed. Every site is situated on the water and features paved back-in parking. Sites are larger than average and nicely spaced, making them quiet. There are a few shade trees, but not enough greenery to provide privacy between sites. At press time, we could not tell which sites would be the nicest.

BASICS

Operated By: US Army Corps of Engineers.
Open: All year. **Site Assignment:** First come, first served; reservations accepted through the National Recreation Reservation Service (NRRS) at (877) 444-6777 or www.reserveusa.com. Reservations can be made up to 240 days in advance, full payment required upon making reservation; credit card preferred (V, MC, D, AE), or pay by money order if at least 21 days in advance of arrival. $10 fee for cancellation or change of site or dates. Cancellation within three days of arrival charged first night, no-show charged $20 plus first night. **Registration:** Gatehouse. **Fee:** $14. **Parking:** At site, limit 3 vehicles per site.

FACILITIES

Number of RV Sites: 0. **Number of Tent-Only Sites:** 2. **Number of Multipurpose Sites:** 36. **Hookups:** Water, electric (50 amps). **Each Site:** Picnic table, grill, fire ring, lantern post, some decks. **Dump Station:** Yes. **Laundry:** Yes. **Pay Phone:** Yes. **Rest Rooms and Showers:** Yes. **Fuel:** No. **Propane:** No. **Internal Roads:** Paved. **RV Service:** 35 mi. west in Tuscaloosa. **Market:** Country store 2.5 mi.; Grocery 25 mi. east in Hueytown. **Restaurant:** 10 mi. north in Oak Grove. **General Store:** 25 mi. east in Hueytown. **Vending:** Beverages only. **Swimming Pool:** No. **Playground:** Yes. **Other:** Boat ramp, swimming beach, picnic shelter. **Activities:** Fishing, boating, hiking in area. **Nearby Attractions:** VisionLand, Mercedes-Benz Visitor Center, Birmingham & Tuscaloosa attractions. **Additional Information:** Tuscaloosa CVB, (800) 538-8696; Greater Birmingham CVB, (800) 458-8085.

RESTRICTIONS

Pets: Leash only. **Fires:** In grills & fire rings only. **Alcoholic Beverages:** Not allowed. **Vehicle**

Maximum Length: No limit. **Other:** 14-day stay limit.

TO GET THERE

From I-59, take the Brookwood exit onto CR 59 and go north approximately 5 mi. to AL Hwy. 216. Turn right and drive east for 2.5 mi. Then turn left back onto CR 59 and go north 18 mi. Turn left onto Lock 17 Rd. and go north. After 2 mi. (at Lock 17 Grocery) the road veers to the left. Continue 2.5 mi. north to the campground entrance.

PICKENSVILLE

Pickensville Recreation Area, Aliceville Lake

61 Camping Rd., Carrollton 35447. T: (205) 373-6328; F: (205) 373-8309; www.reserveusa.com; janalie.m.graham@sam.usace.army.mil.

🚐 ★★★★   ⛺ ★★★★

Beauty: ★★★★   Site Privacy: ★★★★
Spaciousness: ★★★★   Quiet: ★★★★
Security: ★★★★★   Cleanliness: ★★★★
Insect Control: ★★   Facilities: ★★★

The necessity of a waterway connecting the Tennessee River to Mobile Bay was noted as far back as 1770, when the Marquis de Montcalm made a report to King Louis XV. Since before Alabama attained statehood, governors have asked Congress to fund such a project. Finally completed in 1985, the Tennessee-Tombigbee Waterway currently flows [haha] south from the Tennessee River. Aliceville Lake is now one of many recreation destinations along the Tenn-Tom. Straddling the Alabama-Mississippi border, the lake provides fishing, swimming, and other activities. The Pickensville campground consists of 176 sites laid out in 3 loops and two spurs. Though mostly flat, the campground is very attractive. Sites are shaded by a variety of tree species and the water's edge is graced with lovely Cypress trees. All roads and parking spaces are paved. Most of the sites offer back-in parking and a good deal of privacy. Eight pull-through sites are gigantic, but lacking in privacy. Riverside sites, numbered 105–138, have the nicest views of the water. Built next to a cypress-lined creek, sites 49–61 are also very pretty. Security at Pickensville Campground is outstanding, with 24-

hour gate attendance. We recommend avoiding this area in July and Aug. when insects, heat and humidity can be oppressive.

BASICS
Operated By: US Army Corps of Engineers. **Open:** All year. **Site Assignment:** First come, first served; reservations accepted through the National Recreation Reservation Service (NRRS) at (877) 444-6777 or www.reserveusa.com. Reservations can be made up to 240 days in advance, full payment required upon making reservation; credit card preferred (V, MC, D, AE), or pay by money order if at least 21 days in advance of arrival. $10 fee for cancellation or change of site or dates. Cancellation within three days of arrival charged first night, no-show charged $20 plus first night. **Registration:** Gatehouse. **Fee:** $14–$18 (cash, check, V, MC, D, AE). **Parking:** 2 large, 4 small vehicles per site, additional charge for more vehicles.

FACILITIES
Number of Multipurpose Sites: 176. **Hookups:** Water, electric (30, 50 amps), some sewer. **Each Site:** Picnic table, grill, fire ring, lantern post, concrete pads. **Dump Station:** Yes. **Laundry:** Yes. **Pay Phone:** Yes. **Rest Rooms and Showers:** Yes. **Fuel:** No. **Propane:** No. **Internal Roads:** Paved. **RV Service:** 25 mi. north in Columbus, MS. **Market:** 15 mi. southeast in Aliceville. **Restaurant:** 3 mi. east in Pickensville. **General Store:** 3 mi. east in Pickensville. **Vending:** Beverages only. **Swimming Pool:** No. **Playground:** Yes. **Other:** Boat launch, fish cleaning station, picnic shelters, group campfire ring, game courts, swimming beach, wildlife viewing area. **Activities:** Fishing, tennis, volleyball, basketball, boating, walking trails. **Nearby Attractions:** Antebellum Visitors Center in Pickensville, US Snag Boat Montgomery, Aliceville Museum & Cultural Arts Center w/ German POW Camp, attractions in Columbus, MS. **Additional Information:** Aliceville Chamber of Commerce, (205) 373-2820.

RESTRICTIONS
Pets: On leash only, not allowed on beach. **Fires:** Fire rings, grills only. **Alcoholic Beverages:** Not allowed. **Vehicle Maximum Length:** No limit. **Other:** Title 36 policies apply.

TO GET THERE
From Tuscaloosa, take US Hwy. 82 west 20 mi. to Alabama Hwy. 86. Go southwest 24 mi. to Pickensville. Continue 3 mi. west to the Recreation Area. From Columbus, MS take MS 69, which becomes AL 14, to Pickensville. Turn right onto Hwy. 86, and go 3 mi. west to the Recreation Area. The entrance is on the right.

ROGERSVILLE
Joe Wheeler State Park

201 McLean Dr., Rogersville 35652. T: (256) 247-1184; F: (256) 247-1449; www.dcnr.state.al.us/parks, joewheelerstpk.home.mindspring.com; joewheelerstpk@mindspring.com.

🚐 ★★★★★   ⛺ ★★★★★

Beauty: ★★★★★	Site Privacy: ★★★★
Spaciousness: ★★★★	Quiet: ★★★
Security: ★★★★★	Cleanliness: ★★★★
Insect Control: ★★★	Facilities: ★★★★★

Straddling Wheeler Lake, and connected by a bridge over Wheeler Dam, Joe Wheeler State Park is a favorite among fishermen. A variety of fish species is found in the lake. Two boat launches serve Wheeler Lake and a third provides access to adjoining Wilson Lake. A marina store augments the fishing experience with fuel and supplies. Joe Wheeler State Park provides a variety of activities on land as well as facilities for large groups. The campground is laid out in three loops with 116 improved sites, and one loop with primitive sites. Site size is ample but not outstanding. Parking is paved and most sites are back-in. The prettiest sites, 9, 10, 22, 24, and 26, have partial views of Lake Wheeler. The campground is surrounded by lovely thick woods, which provide shade at most sites but very little privacy between sites. The tent camping area consists of a nicely wooded loop of gravel road surrounded by trash cans and fire rings. Like many exceedingly attractive tent areas, there are no designated sites. This remote state park is gated and guarded, making security outstanding. Avoid late summer heat and humidity at Joe Wheeler State Park; plan a visit in spring, early summer, or fall.

BASICS
Operated By: Alabama State Parks. **Open:** All year. **Site Assignment:** First come, first served. **Registration:** Campground office; Security will register late-comers. **Fee:** $16 for improved sites, $10 for primitive sites; fee includes 4 people; $2 each additional person, $5 for 2nd tent. **Parking:** At sites, limit 2 cars per site.

FACILITIES

Number of RV Sites: 0. **Number of Tent-Only Sites:** 50 (primitive). **Number of Multipurpose Sites:** 116. **Hookups:** Water, electric (20, 30 amps), sewer. **Each Site:** Picnic table, grill. **Dump Station:** Yes. **Laundry:** Yes. **Pay Phone:** Yes. **Rest Rooms and Showers:** Yes. **Fuel:** Boat fuel. **Propane:** No. **Internal Roads:** Paved. **RV Service:** 15 mi. west toward Florence. **Market:** 4 mi. east in Rogersville. **Restaurant:** In park. **General Store:** Camp store. **Vending:** Yes. **Swimming Pool:** No. **Playground:** Yes. **Other:** Marina, boat ramps, boat fuel, sandy beach, 18-hole golf course, group meeting room & lodge, resort lodge, picnic pavilions. **Activities:** Boating (rentals available), swimming, hiking trails, day-use tennis, basketball. **Nearby Attractions:** Athens, W.C. Handy birthplace Museum & Library in Florence, Civil War Walking Trail, Cook's Natural Science Museum, Oakville Indian Park & Museum. **Additional Information:** Decatur/Morgan County CVB, (256) 350-2028.

RESTRICTIONS

Pets: Leash only. **Fires:** In grills & fire rings only. **Alcoholic Beverages:** Not allowed. **Vehicle Maximum Length:** 50 ft. **Other:** 2-week stay limit.

TO GET THERE

From I-65, take Hwy. 72 west for 22 mi. The Park entrance will be on the left 2 mi. west of Rogersville. The campground is 3 mi. inside the park.

WILMER

Escatawpa Hollow Campground

15551 Moffett Rd., Wilmer 36587. T: (334) 649-4233; F: (334) 649-1235; yerfdogjw@gateway.net.

🚐 ★★★★	⛺ ★★★★
Beauty: ★★★★	Site Privacy: ★★★
Spaciousness: ★★★	Quiet: ★★★
Security: ★★★★	Cleanliness: ★★★
Insect Control: ★★★	Facilities: ★★★★

If your kids are the strong-swimming adventurous types, they will delight in the river and woods at Escatawpa Hollow. In the vernacular of youth, "this place is cool!" Because of its popularity with gregarious families, this campground is anything but quiet on summer weekends. The picturesque private campground is situated on the bank of the Escatawpa River near the Alabama-Mississippi border. An exceptionally clean blackwater river, here the Escatawpa is lined with white sand beach, creating a delightful swimming area. The bream, catfish, and bass in the river are purported to be the best-tasting in the state (if you can catch them). Paddlers enjoy the mellow flat water of the Escatawpa. Boat rental and shuttle arrangements are available at the campground.

BASICS

Operated By: Larry & Janice Godfrey. **Open:** All year. **Site Assignment:** First come, first served; reservations accepted; deposit required on holidays; 2-day notice for refund. **Registration:** Office. **Fee:** $10–$15. **Parking:** 2 vehicles per site, overflow parking available.

FACILITIES

Number of RV Sites: 0. **Number of Tent-Only Sites:** 15. **Number of Multipurpose Sites:** 22. **Hookups:** Water, electric (20, 30 amps). **Each Site:** Picnic table, grill. **Dump Station:** Yes. **Laundry:** No. **Pay Phone:** No. **Rest Rooms and Showers:** Yes. **Fuel:** No. **Propane:** No. **Internal Roads:** Gravel & dirt. **RV Service:** 15 mi. southeast in Mobile. **Market:** 4 mi. east in Wilmer. **Restaurant:** 4 mi. east in Wilmer. **General Store:** 19 mi. southeast in Mobile. **Vending:** No. **Swimming Pool:** No. **Playground:** No. **Other:** Canoe & tube rentals, canoe trips including shuttle service (reservations required), walking trails, rope swings. **Activities:** River swimming, canoeing, kayaking, fishing. **Nearby Attractions:** Bellingrath Gardens in Theodore, Robert Trent Jones Golf Trail, USS Alabama, Mobile attractions. **Additional Information:** Mobile Convention & Visitors Corporation, (800) 5-MOBILE

RESTRICTIONS

Pets: In RV sites only, on leash only. **Fires:** At tent sites only. **Alcoholic Beverages:** Not allowed. **Vehicle Maximum Length:** 35 ft. **Other:** Tent sites max. 1-week stay, read all warnings concerning river swimming.

TO GET THERE

From I-65, take exit 5B at Moffett Rd. and US Hwy. 98. Go 22 mi. west on US Hwy. 98 to the 0-mi. marker at the Mississippi state line. The park entrance is on the left.

Florida

You may think of Florida as the home of Mickey Mouse, roller coasters, and long, long lines. Or maybe the Sunshine State inspires dreams of endless surf and all-night parties on glittery South Beach. You'd be right, but you'd also be missing out on about 54,000 other unique square miles. Although much of Florida's 1,197 miles of coastline is obscured by high-rise condos, there is still a wealth of undiscovered beauty and charm behind the glamorous façade, along the back roads and quiet coastal towns. Perhaps you've visited the Space Coast, the Treasure Coast, and the Gold Coast, but next time you come to Florida, take time to explore with us the Undiscovered Coast, the Forgotten Coast, the Nature Coast, the Emerald Coast, the First Coast, and the Interior.

Join us for a tour of US 19/98 along the **Gulf Coast** through **Pasco County** and north to the **Nature Coast,** a beautiful, wonderful old road through the countryside where road signs warn of bear habitats and others offer such Florida cracker staples as churches, guns and palm readers, boiled peanuts, fresh scallops, and oysters. We'll take I-10 antiquing across the top to the **First Coast,** and stop by **Amelia Island** for succulent copper shrimp. We'll canoe the rivers that course through the central part of the state, and kayak the east and west shorelines, scuba-dive and snorkel the coral reef in the south. We'll take an airboat ride into the depths of the **Everglades** and sample gator tail, frog legs, and swamp cabbage along with a little Indian fry bread. Let's amble around the 700 square miles of **Lake Okeechobee,** buying juicy mangoes and crisp okra from local farmers who've been here all their lives. When we're done with all that, we'll hit the beach. We'll dig for shark's teeth and tales of pirates, and we'll be on the lookout for giant sea turtles, dolphins, and manatees. Come along, we'll have a great time.

Campers need to remember that summertime is swelter time in our fair state, when temperatures can soar into the 90s and higher. Afternoon rains help to cool the air, but the heat can be brutal for those who haven't acclimated to it. Bugs are worse in summertime, especially at night. Mosquitoes and No-See-Ums, too small to see and tiny enough to pass through window screens, are the most annoying. Bug sprays and citronella candles will help, but there will be times when the only solution is to seek shelter. Some folks prefer Florida in the wintertime, when bugs and temperatures are more moderate; but expect to encounter more crowds then, too. No need to let a little nature scare you off—be prepared and you can count on an adventure you'll never forget.

Cinderella's Castle is truly a sight to behold, but just wait until you've had the chance to see the untouched wonders of nature still waiting here in Florida for you to discover. Come explore our treasure.

The following facilities accept payment in checks or cash only:

Cedar Key RV Park, Cedar Key

High Springs Campground, High Springs

Campground Profiles

ALACHUA

Travelers Campground

17701 April Blvd., Alachua 32615. T: (386) 462-2505;
GreenCamper1@juno.com.

🚐 ★★★★★   ⛺ ★★

Beauty: ★★★	Site Privacy: ★★
Spaciousness: ★★	Quiet: ★★★★
Security: ★★★	Cleanliness: ★★★★
Insect Control: ★★★★	Facilities: ★★★★

Designed for travelers as its name implies, this campground is super convenient to the highway, clean and quick to get in and out of. Although some larger sites occupy a friendly hill graced with tall trees, most overnighters are placed in the back lot, six rows of seven drive-through sites. Privacy is not an option. The new shower house is impeccably clean, and further renovations are underway to provide phone hookups and updated electricity. New roads are slated to follow. The perimeter of the campground houses the owners menagerie, which includes a single horse, donkeys, an emu, a pink pig, chickens and chicks, albino peacocks, goats, and an aviary with macaws and other exotic birds. A quiet rec hall hosts occasional dinners, and guests can check e-mail while doing laundry—there is an Internet connection in the laundry room for laptop hookups.

BASICS

Operated By: Owners Harold & Linda. **Open:** All year. **Site Assignment:** First come, first served; also reservations. **Registration:** Office. **Fee:** $22; cash or checks only. **Parking:** Yes.

FACILITIES

Number of RV Sites: 100. **Number of Tent-Only Sites:** 50. **Hookups:** Water, electric (20, 30, 50 amps), sewer, cable TV. **Each Site:** Picnic table on request. **Dump Station:** Yes. **Laundry:** Yes. **Pay Phone:** Yes. **Rest Rooms and Showers:** Yes. **Fuel:** No. **Propane:** Yes. **Internal Roads:** Some paved, some smooth dirt and lime-rock, all in good condition. **RV Service:** Referral. **Market:** 1.5 mi. east on US 441. **Restaurant:** 2 mi. east on US 441. **General Store:** Yes. **Vending:** No. **Swimming Pool:** Yes. **Playground:** Yes. **Other:** Rec hall, horseshoes, shuffleboard, field for golf and ballgames. **Activities:** Monthly pot-luck dinner. **Nearby Attractions:** Freshwater springs offer tubing and canoeing; Antique mall in Micanopy, University of Florida in Gainesville. **Additional Information:** Alachua County CVB, (352) 374-5260.

RESTRICTIONS

Pets: On leash only. **Fires:** Grills only. **Alcoholic Beverages:** Yes, but not openly displayed. **Vehicle Maximum Length:** None.

TO GET THERE

I-75 Exit 78 at US 441 east 200 ft. to April Blvd. (on north side of road next to Waffle House), north 1 mi. to campground on right.

ALTOONA

Ocala National Forest— Alexander Springs

49525 CR 445, Altoona 32702. T: (352) 669-3522; F: (353) 669-0600; www.CampRRM.com; RRMFL@Atlantic.net.

🚐 ★★★   ⛺ ★★★★★

Beauty: ★★★★★	Site Privacy: ★★★
Spaciousness: ★★★	Quiet: ★★★
Security: ★★★★★	Cleanliness: ★★★★★
Insect Control: ★★★	Facilities: ★★★★★

If you're in the mood to take a break from luxury camping for a dip into the wild side, the Ocala National Forest is a great place for the adventure. Rangers report finding bear droppings and paw prints on the beaches in the mornings, and say that a mama bear and her cubs have been known to reside nearby. Sightings are frequent along CR 445 leading to the Alexander Springs Recreation Area—you may want to cruise a bit more slowly than the 55 mph speed limit allows. Other creatures include alligators in the springs (yes, the place is crowded with swimmers), wild hogs, and deer. Osprey and American bald eagles can be seen above. Camping is confined to four loops, each site shielded by a rim of brush and trees offering a little privacy, but paths cross through the back of some sites to the bath houses (some brand new), so you might get to know your neighbors. The nights are so quiet, you'll probably get to hear the giggles of other scouts and campers even if you don't get to meet them—even generators must be silenced during the night. But if you get a little sweaty at night, you'll be instantly refreshed if you take a dip in the perpetually 70° water that replenishes itself at the rate of 70 million gallons a day.

BASICS

Operated By: Recreation Resource Management for the US Government. **Open:** All year. **Site Assignment:** First come, first served. **Registration:** Park office. **Fee:** $15; MC,V for bills of $20 or more. **Parking:** Yes.

FACILITIES

Number of RV Sites: 67. **Number of Tent-Only Sites:** 0. **Hookups:** None. **Each Site:** Picnic table, grill, lantern pole. **Dump Station:** Yes. **Laundry:** No. **Pay Phone:** Yes. **Rest Rooms and Showers:** Yes. **Fuel:** No. **Propane:** No. **Internal Roads:** Paved in good condition. **RV Service:** Referral. **Market:** 3 mi. south on Hwy. 445 to convenience market, 6 mi. north on Hwy. 445 to supermarket in Astor. **Restaurant:** 6 mi. north on Hwy. 445 to Astor. **General Store:** Yes. **Vending:** Yes. **Swimming Pool:** Freshwater-spring swimming area w/ beach. **Playground:** No. **Other:** Hiking and biking trails, canoe launch. **Activities:** Hiking, biking, swimming, fishing, canoeing. **Nearby Attractions:** National Forest surrounds recreation area. **Additional Information:** Ocala National Forest Visitors Center, (352) 669-7495.

RESTRICTIONS

Pets: On leash only, designated areas. **Fires:** Grill only. **Alcoholic Beverages:** Not allowed. **Vehicle Maximum Length:** 35 ft. **Other:** Gate closes at 8 p.m.; quiet time 10 p.m.–6 a.m.

TO GET THERE

From US 441, 6 mi. north on Hwy. 19 to CR 445, 6 mi. north to entrance on left.

ARCADIA

Craig's RV Park, Inc.

7895 NE Hwy. 17, Arcadia 34266. T: (863) 494-1820 or (877) 750-5129; F: (863) 494-1079; www.craigsrv.com; Craigsrv@desoto.net.

🚐 ★★★★   ⛺ ★★★

Beauty: ★★★	Site Privacy: ★★★★
Spaciousness: ★★★★★	Quiet: ★★★★★
Security: ★★★★★	Cleanliness: ★★★★★
Insect Control: ★★★★★	Facilities: ★★★★★

Tucked into Florida's beautiful countryside, Arcadia is a rural town surrounded by a long-standing agricultural community. The scenic Peace River meanders through the cattle ranches, forests, and swamps without a trace of commercial interference for miles on end. The river is very popular for canoeists who pack a few-days-worth of supplies and camp along its banks. The practice is allowed by the ranch owners, but you're at your own risk—the territory is rich with alligators and other wildlife. Craig's RV Park is conveniently situated, with river access just three miles away, and it provides a peaceful place for those seeking the country atmosphere but who still love country fun, such as the bluegrass festivals and informal music nights. Laid out like a suburban neighborhood, sites are tightly packed though spacious, with more trees on the north side of the park than on the south, and a few dozen pull-through sites as well. One great feature is the private bathrooms and showers, but campers must pay 25 cents for 6 minutes of water, thanks to some vandals who once left the taps running and drained the water supply. The camp is run very professionally and kept immaculate by its family owners.

BASICS

Operated By: Owners Vicky &. Allen Wickey &. Sara &. Victor Craig. **Open:** All year. **Site Assignment:** Reservations accepted, $20 deposit required, refundable up to 24 hours in advance w/ 10% service charge. **Registration:** Office. **Fee:** $20; M, V, D. **Parking:** Yes.

FACILITIES

Number of RV Sites: 356. **Number of Tent-Only Sites:** 0. **Hookups:** Water, electric (20, 30, 50 amps), sewer. **Each Site:** Concrete pad. **Dump Station:** Yes. **Laundry:** Yes. **Pay Phone:** Yes. **Rest Rooms and Showers:** Yes. **Fuel:** No. **Propane:** Yes. **Internal Roads:** Paved in good condition. **RV Service:** Referral. **Market:** 9 mi. south to Arcadia, convenience mart 2 mi. south. **Restaurant:** 9 mi. south to Arcadia. **General Store:** Yes. **Vending:** Yes. **Swimming Pool:** Yes. **Playground:** No. **Other:** Shuffleboard, bocci court, horseshoes, game room w/ pool tables, golf driving range. **Activities:** Monthly calendar of events Nov.–Apr. includes bingo, live music, bluegrass festivals in Nov. & Mar., shuffleboard, bocci & horseshoe tournaments. **Nearby Attractions:** Peace River canoe ramp 3 mi. south, antique shops in Arcadia. **Additional Information:** DeSoto County Chamber of Commerce, (863) 494-4033.

RESTRICTIONS

Pets: On leash & in designated areas only, proof of insurance policy for dogs over 30 lbs. required. **Fires:** In grill or designated campfire areas only. **Alcoholic Beverages:** On individual sites only. **Vehicle Maximum Length:** 45 ft., call ahead for availability.

TO GET THERE

I-75 Exit 29/Hwy. 17 north 32 mi. to campground

ARCADIA
Peace River Campground

2998 NW Hwy. 70, Arcadia 34266. T: (863) 494-9693 or (800) 559-4011; F: (863) 494-9110; www.peacerivercampground.com; George@peacerivercampground.com.

🚐 ★★★★   ⛺ ★★★★

Beauty: ★★★★   Site Privacy: ★★★
Spaciousness: ★★★★   Quiet: ★★★★
Security: ★★★★   Cleanliness: ★★★★
Insect Control: ★★   Facilities: ★★★★

This wonderfully rustic and wooded campground might let you forget you're in a campground at all—almost. The shady camp overlooks the Peace River, and the campground has become home to a fossil museum, thanks to the excavation of the bones of three mammoths from the riverbed. Sharks teeth continue to be a popular find for those who like to wade in the scenic river waters and sift through the sands along the bottom and shorelines. The laid-back, peaceful campground hosts an interesting group each year—The Ruckus Society gathers here in the spring to train peaceful demonstrators in the techniques of getting attention without getting in trouble. Lots of wildlife live in the surrounding environs, including alligators, bobcats, deer, grey foxes, even the occasional panther passes through. There are a few pull-through sites among the trees, and although there is plenty of room and plenty of trees, there are not specific site buffers in many cases.

BASICS

Operated By: Owners George & Johnny Lempenau. **Open:** All year. **Site Assignment:** Reservations accepted, $50 deposit plus 3-night min. stay required for holidays. **Registration:** Office. **Fee:** $25 May–Sept., $32 Oct.–Apr. **Parking:** Yes.

FACILITIES

Number of RV Sites: 182. **Number of Tent-Only Sites:** 0. **Hookups:** Water, electric (20, 30, 50 amps), sewer. **Each Site:** Picnic table. **Dump Station:** Yes. **Laundry:** Yes. **Pay Phone:** Yes. **Rest Rooms and Showers:** Yes. **Fuel:** No. **Propane:** Yes. **Internal Roads:** Crushed shell in good condition. **RV Service:** Referral. **Market:** 4 mi. east to Arcadia. **Restaurant:** 4 mi. east to Arcadia. **General Store:** Yes. **Vending:** Yes. **Swimming Pool:** Yes. **Playground:** Yes. **Other:** Boat ramp, video room w/ pool tables, shuffleboard, horseshoes, fishing pond, miniature animal farm, snowbird dance hall, computers. **Activities:** Canoeing, fishing, fossil hunting. **Nearby Attractions:** Peace River, antique shops in Arcadia. **Additional Information:** DeSoto County Chamber of Commerce, (863) 494-4033.

RESTRICTIONS

Pets: Leash only. **Fires:** Yes. **Alcoholic Beverages:** Allowed. **Vehicle Maximum Length:** None.

TO GET THERE

I-75 Exit 29/Hwy. 17, 22 mi. east to Hwy. 70, north/left 4 mi. to campground.

CEDAR KEY
Cedar Key RV Park

P.O. Box 268, Cedar Key 32625. T: (352) 543-5150.

★★★★   🔺 ★★★

Beauty: ★★★   Site Privacy: ★
Spaciousness: ★★   Quiet: ★★★
Security: ★★★★   Cleanliness: ★★★★★
Insect Control: ★★   Facilities: ★★★

A rustic trailer park on an out-of-the-way island that seems to be just beginning to commercialize —find it quickly before this waterfront property has been consumed by the ubiquitous ocean-front condominiums, which have gone up on both sides already. This low-key park may not offer a wide range of amenities—no rec room, modem, or laundry, but the rest room is immaculate and refreshingly private. Although the park itself is unspectacular, the location is unbeatable, with a few prime sites overlooking the shore on a slight bluff with steps leading down to a long dock for fishing and boating. Price listed reflect choice waterfront location—the other sites are packed unceremoniously together without buffers or charm—incomparable to the pleasure of an unobstructed view of the Gulf of Mexico. Don't miss it.

BASICS

Operated By: Shirley Gulley, manager. **Open:** All year. **Site Assignment:** By phone, deposits accepted by mail. **Registration:** Park office. **Fee:** $22; cash or checks only. **Parking:** Yes.

FACILITIES

Number of RV Sites: 30. **Number of Tent-Only Sites:** 4 (beachfront, not divided into sites). **Hookups:** Electric (30 amps), water, sewer, cable TV. **Each Site:** Picnic table. **Dump Station:** No. **Laundry:** No. **Pay Phone:** Yes. **Rest Rooms and Showers:** Yes. **Fuel:** No. **Propane:** No. **Internal Roads:** Gravel in good condition. **RV Service:** No. **Market:** 3 blocks south, 3 blocks east to downtown Cedar Key. **Restaurant:** 3 blocks south. **General Store:** No. **Vending:** No. **Swimming Pool:** No. **Playground:** No. **Other:** Fishing pier. **Activities:** Fishing, crabbing, clamming, bird-watching. **Nearby Attractions:** State Museum & County Museum. **Additional Information:** Cedar Key Chamber of Commerce, (352) 543-5600, www.cedarkey.org.

RESTRICTIONS

Pets: On leash only. **Fires:** In grill only. **Alcoholic Beverages:** Allowed. **Vehicle Maximum Length:** 35 ft. **Other:** Office closes at 8 p.m.

TO GET THERE

From I-75 in Gainesville Exit Hwy. 24, 70 mi. west to Cedar Key, (24 mi. west on Hwy. 24 past US 19/98), right on 6th St. to G St., right to campground at 7th St.

CHIPLEY

Falling Waters State Recreation Area

1130 State Park Rd., Chipley 32428. T: (850) 638-6130; www.myflorida.com.

 ★★★   🔺 ★★★★★

Beauty: ★★★★★   Site Privacy: ★★★★
Spaciousness: ★★★★   Quiet: ★★★★★
Security: ★★★★★   Cleanliness: ★★★★★
Insect Control: ★★★★★   Facilities: ★★★★

Falling Waters State Recreation Area boasts an unusually high elevation for Florida—and that's a great advantage during mosquito season when larvae thrive in puddles and lakes. The campground itself is particularly high within the park, which adds to the interest of the area. Once a camper has made the slow climb to the top of the hill, campsites form a single small circle around central rest rooms and a playground for kids. The quiet, wooded setting is peaceful and friendly. Seven of the 24 sites are pull-through half circles.

BASICS

Operated By: Florida Dept. of Environmental Protection, Division of Recreation & Parks. **Open:** All year. **Site Assignment:** First come, first served; reservations accepted w/ 1-night deposit, refundable w/ up to 24 hours advance notice. **Registration:** Office. **Fee:** $8 Nov.–Feb., $10 Mar.–Oct.; MC, V. **Parking:** Yes.

FACILITIES

Number of RV Sites: 24. **Number of Tent-Only Sites:** 0. **Hookups:** Water, electric. **Each Site:** Picnic table, grill. **Dump Station:** Yes. **Laundry:** No. **Pay Phone:** Yes. **Rest Rooms and Showers:** Yes. **Fuel:** No. **Propane:** No. **Internal Roads:** Paved in good condition. **RV Service:** Referral. **Market:** 3 mi. north on 77A to supermarket. **Restaurant:** 3 mi. north on 77A. **General Store:** No. **Vending:** Yes. **Swimming Pool:** No (Lake). **Playground:** Yes. **Other:** Lake, hiking trails, sinkholes, waterfall, amphitheater. **Activities:** Hiking, swimming, fishing. **Nearby Attractions:** Florida Caverns State Park. **Additional Information:** Washington County Chamber of Commerce, (850) 638-4157, www.washcomall.com.

RESTRICTIONS

Pets: On leash only, proof of vaccinations required. **Fires:** In grill only. **Alcoholic Beverages:** Not allowed. **Vehicle Maximum Length:** 45 ft. **Other:** No firearms, no fireworks, quiet time 11 p.m.

TO GET THERE

Exit I-10 or Hwy. 90 at Chipley, 3 mi. south of town on Hwy. 77A.

CHOKOLUSKEE

Chokoluskee Island Park and Campground

P.O. Box 430, Chokoluskee 34138. T: (941) 695-2414; F: (941) 695-3033; chokislpark@aol.com.

🚐 ★★★   ▲ ★★

Beauty: ★★   Site Privacy: ★★
Spaciousness: ★★   Quiet: ★★★★★
Security: ★★★★   Cleanliness: ★★★★
Insect Control: ★★   Facilities: ★★★

Rustic like the entire community of Chokoluskee, this park has the advantage of a boat dock right on the Ten Thousand Islands, which form a sort of barrier between coastline and the Florida Bay. Fishers—and that's who most like to come to this town—love the easy access. This town is best known as the home of stone crabs, because this is where the practice of harvesting the crabs claws, then tossing them back to sea to grow a new claw for next year's harvest. Fresh stone crabs, boiled in garlic or raw, are available all over town during the season Oct. 15 to May 15. The park is really a fish camp, home to some live-ins and rental trailers, but also offers sites to travelers. Although there are some nice, tall mature palms and trees throughout the park, the sites are crowded quite close together. Not what most of us might consider a vacation paradise, but quite possibly the most beautiful place in Florida to watch the sunset, especially if you love to fish.

BASICS

Operated By: Managers Ray & Sheilah Strobel. **Open:** All year. **Site Assignment:** Reservations

accepted, deposit of 1-night stay. **Registration:** Office. **Fee:** $18 June–Oct., $26 Nov.–May; M, V, AE. **Parking:** Yes.

FACILITIES

Number of RV Sites: 20. **Number of Tent-Only Sites:** 0. **Hookups:** Water, electric (30 amps), sewer. **Each Site:** Picnic Table. **Dump Station:** Yes. **Laundry:** Yes. **Pay Phone:** Yes. **Rest Rooms and Showers:** Yes. **Fuel:** No. **Propane:** Yes. **Internal Roads:** Paved in good condition. **RV Service:** Referral. **Market:** 1 block east. **Restaurant:** 1 block east. **General Store:** Yes. **Vending:** Yes. **Swimming Pool:** No. **Playground:** No. **Other:** Boat ramp, shuffleboard, horseshoes, marina. **Activities:** Fishing trips. **Nearby Attractions:** Florida Bay (for fishing & exploring), Ten Thousand Islands (for canoeing), Ted Smallwood's Historic Store, Everglades National Park. **Additional Information:** Everglades Area Chamber of Commerce, (800) 914-6355, www.florida-everglades.com.

RESTRICTIONS

Pets: Leash only. **Fires:** Grill only. **Alcoholic Beverages:** Allowed. **Vehicle Maximum Length:** 28 ft. **Other:** Quiet time 10 p.m.–8 a.m.

TO GET THERE

US 41 east approximately 22 mi. from Naples (approximately 75 mi. west from Miami) to US 29, south 8 mi. to DeMere St., right past the Church of God, then left to the park on right.

CLERMONT

Clerbrook Golf and RV Resort

20005 US Hwy. 27, Clermont 34711. T: (352) 394-6165; F: (352) 394-8251; www.n1floridacamping.lu; ClerbrookResort@aol.com.

🚐 ★★★   ▲ n/a

Beauty: ★★★   Site Privacy: ★
Spaciousness: ★   Quiet: ★★
Security: ★★★★   Cleanliness: ★★★★
Insect Control: ★★★★   Facilities: ★★★★

This large mobile-home community is a golfer's paradise in Florida's heartland. The three residential sections offer rental and permanent RVs, cabins and family tents, with those on the perimeter more spacious and scenic than those in the interior of each section. Trees and a wildlife conservation area surround Clerbrook, and the golf course provides a lovely rolling landscape in the center of the community, restful to the eyes and mind. Three large clubhouses, ball fields, stocked fishing ponds, whirlpool spas, and three swimming pools promise fun for those less interested in golf, which is clearly the main activity in this locale. Overnight travelers are bunked into a large, grassy parking area with pull-throughs. that lack trees and privacy but have hookups and picnic tables. The community is accessed through a manned security gate closing at 11 p.m.

BASICS

Operated By: Florida Mobile Home Camping. **Open:** All year. **Site Assignment:** Reservations accepted, deposit required. **Registration:** Office. **Fee:** $18, MC, V, D. **Parking:** Yes.

FACILITIES

Number of RV Sites: 1250. **Number of Tent-Only Sites:** 0. **Hookups:** Electric (30, 50 amps), water, sewer, phone, modem, cable TV. **Each Site:** Picnic table. **Dump Station:** Yes. **Laundry:** Yes. **Pay Phone:** Yes. **Rest Rooms and Showers:** Yes. **Fuel:** No. **Propane:** Yes. **Internal Roads:** Paved in good condition. **RV Service:** No. **Market:** 6 mi. southwest in Clermont. **Restaurant:** 6 mi. southwest in Clermont. **General Store:** Yes. **Vending:** Yes. **Swimming Pool:** Yes. **Playground:** Yes. **Other:** 18-hole golf course, rec room, softball field, whirlpool. **Activities:** Golf, horseshoes, shuffleboard, fishing, winter recreation program. **Nearby Attractions:** Disney World & Orlando 45 min. east on Florida Turnpike. **Additional Information:** Lake County CVB, (352) 429-3673, (800) 798-1071.

RESTRICTIONS

Pets: On leash only. **Fires:** Grill only. **Alcoholic Beverages:** Allowed. **Vehicle Maximum Length:** None.

TO GET THERE

Florida Turnpike Exit 285, south on US 27 1.5 mi. to Clerbrook on right.

CLEWISTON
Big Cypress State Preserve

HC Box 54A, Clewiston 33440. T: (863) 983-1330 or (800) 437-4102; F: (863) 983-3122; www.semi-letribe.com/campground.

 ★★★   ★★★

Beauty: ★★★	Site Privacy: ★★★
Spaciousness: ★★★★	Quiet: ★★★★★
Security: ★★★★	Cleanliness: ★★★
Insect Control: ★★	Facilities: ★★★

If you're looking for wilderness in the Everglades, you've found it here in the Big Cypress National Preserve and the Big Cypress Seminole Indian Reservation. And if you think the glades are just a big swamp, you'll be pleasantly surprised to find that there is plenty of high ground, thickly forested with flora, including water oak trees, sabal palms, and shrubbery. The large park also has abundant hibiscus flowers and a pretty pond and garden area.

BASICS

Operated By: Seminole Indian Reservation. **Open:** All year. **Site Assignment:** Reservations accepted, $50 credit card deposit, at least 30-day cancellation. **Registration:** Park office. **Fee:** $22. **Parking:** Yes.

FACILITIES

Number of RV Sites: 110. **Number of Tent-Only Sites:** Primitive camping area. **Hookups:** Water, electric (20, 50 amps), sewer, phone. **Each Site:** Picnic table, grill. **Dump Station:** Yes. **Laundry:** Yes. **Pay Phone:** Yes. **Rest Rooms and Showers:** Yes. **Fuel:** No. **Propane:** Yes. **Internal Roads:** Paved & gravel in good condition. **RV Service:** Referral. **Market:** 2 mi. southeast on CR 833. **Restaurant:** 3 mi. west on Safari Rd. **General Store:** Yes. **Vending:** Yes. **Swimming Pool:** Yes. **Playground:** Yes. **Other:** Rec hall, mini-golf, shuffleboard, basketball, horseshoes. **Activities:** Fishing, swimming, boating, safari air boat & swamp buggy rides. **Nearby Attractions:** Boat ramp, Lake Okeechobee, Billie Swamp Safari Wildlife Park, a Seminole Indian park featuring airboat rides, eco-tours, a restaurant w/ authentic Indian food plus animals including the Florida panther; Ah-Tah-Thi-Ki Museum w/ exhibits depicting the history of the Seminole Indians in Florida. **Additional Information:** Big Cypress National Preserve, (941) 695-2000.

RESTRICTIONS

Pets: On leash only, max. 2 pets per rig. **Fires:** In grill or designated area only. **Alcoholic Beverages:** Not allowed. **Vehicle Maximum Length:** 36 ft. **Other:** No firearms or fireworks, quiet time 11 p.m.–8 a.m.

To Get There

I-75 (Alligator Alley between Fort Lauderdale and Naples) Exit 14 at mile marker 49 onto Snake Rd., north 19 mi. to park.

CRYSTAL RIVER

Rock Crusher Canyon RV and Music Park

275 South Rock Crusher Rd., Crystal River 34429. T: (352) 795-3870; www.rccrvpark.com; information@rccrvpark.com.

🚐 ★★★★★   ▲ ★★★

Beauty: ★★★★	Site Privacy: ★★★
Spaciousness: ★★★★★	Quiet: ★★★★★
Security: ★★★★★	Cleanliness: ★★★★★
Insect Control: ★★★	Facilities: ★★★

This hidden new RV paradise of rolling green hills with shaded, level, grassy sites is like an oasis on Florida's west central coast. Once you've found it, though, you're not likely to forget it for future travels, especially if you're a music lover. The park offers regular concerts with famous vintage and country headliners like Glen Campbell, the Tommy Dorsey Orchestra, and The Ink Spots. The top-rated park features individual rest room/showers, wide sites with plenty of bushes and trees providing privacy, and the unusual bonus of several elevations. The park also offers a fitness center, country store, pool, country store, and clubhouse. It's easy to see how this park has received top ratings from industry experts.

Basics

Operated By: Private operator. **Open:** All year. **Site Assignment:** Reservations accepted, 1-night deposit required except for special events, which require multi-night stays & non-refundable tickets. **Registration:** Park office. **Fee:** $35. **Parking:** Yes.

Facilities

Number of RV Sites: 398. **Number of Tent-Only Sites:** 0. **Hookups:** Water, electric (50 amps), sewer, cable TV, phone. **Each Site:** Picnic table. **Dump Station:** Yes. **Laundry:** Yes. **Pay Phone:** Yes. **Rest Rooms and Showers:** Yes. **Fuel:** No. **Propane:** Yes. **Internal Roads:** Paved in good condition. **RV Service:** Referral. **Market:** 2.5 mi. west to Crystal River/Hwy. 19. **Restaurant:** 2.5 mi. west to Crystal River/Hwy. 19. **General Store:** Yes. **Vending:** Yes. **Swimming Pool:** Yes. **Play-ground:** Yes. **Other:** Amphitheater, lakes, shuffleboard, horseshoes, fitness center. **Activities:** Country music & bluegrass concerts & festivals, fishing. **Nearby Attractions:** Crystal River Springs, Homosassa Springs (home to manatees), Weeki Wachee Springs, mermaid amusement park. **Additional Information:** Nature Coast Tourism Development, Inc. & Welcome Center, (352) 564-9197, www.crystalriver-ecotours.com.

Restrictions

Pets: On leash only. **Fires:** Designated areas only. **Alcoholic Beverages:** Allowed. **Vehicle Maximum Length:** None. **Other:** Quiet hours 11 p.m.–7:30 a.m.

To Get There

From Hwy. 19/Crystal River, turn east on Venable Rd. (by the Home Depot store), 2.3 mi. to Rock Crusher Rd., right/south to entrance on the left.

ESTERO

Koreshan State Historic Site

P.O. Box 7, Estero 33928. T: (941) 992-0311; F: (941) 992-1607; www.myflorida.com.

🚐 ★★★★   ▲ ★★★★

Beauty: ★★★★★	Site Privacy: ★★★★
Spaciousness: ★★★★	Quiet: ★★★★
Security: ★★★★★	Cleanliness: ★★★★★
Insect Control: ★★★	Facilities: ★★★★★

This small, unassuming park with the somewhat daunting name (the 'e' in Koreshan is pronounced as a short vowel like 'eh') offers a fascinating glimpse into a tiny but powerful piece of history. The site is the preserved settlement of a religious sect founded in 1894 by New York doctor Cyrus Teed, who called himself by the Biblical name Koresh. Teed believed in immortality, therefore the sect practiced celibacy. Teed died in 1908, but not before establishing the settlement of a few hundred followers which included a group kitchen, machine shop, and cultural arts hall, where several paintings are still displayed. One depicts Teed's vision of the world, an inverted Earth with Heaven in its center. The buildings and their well-preserved contents make it clear that the group was well educated, musical, and artistic. The gardens they created of bamboo, monkey trees, pineapple, citrus, and mangoes still stand, although the last of the sect members expired in the early 1960s, leaving the settlement to the state for preservation. Campers will enjoy the long loops of very private sites surrounded by an abundance of trees, in close proximity to the Estero River, a prime site for canoeing (rentals available); swimming is prohibited, perhaps because of alligators.

BASICS

Operated By: Florida Dept. of Environmental Protection, Division of Recreation & Park. **Open:** All year. **Site Assignment:** Reservations accepted up to 11 months in advance, 1-night deposit, refundable up to 24 hours in advance. **Registration:** Office. **Fee:** $14.11 May–Nov., $20.70 Dec.–Apr. **Parking:** Yes.

FACILITIES

Number of RV Sites: 50. **Number of Tent-Only Sites:** 10. **Hookups:** Water, electric (30 amps). **Each Site:** Picnic table, fire ring. **Dump Station:** Yes. **Laundry:** Yes. **Pay Phone:** Yes. **Rest Rooms and Showers:** Yes. **Fuel:** No. **Propane:** No. **Internal Roads:** Paved & crushed shell in good condition. **RV Service:** Referral. **Market:** 0.25 mi. across US Hwy. 41. **Restaurant:** 0.25 mi. across US Hwy. 41. **General Store:** No, but in future plans. **Vending:** Yes. **Swimming Pool:** No. **Playground:** Yes. **Other:** Beach, volleyball court, boat launch, historic settlement. **Activities:** Fishing, canoeing (rentals available). **Nearby Attractions:** Corkscrew Swamp Sanctuary, an Audubon Society nature preserve; Everglades Wonder Gardens in Bonita Springs; Dog Racing Track in Bonita Springs; beach; Mound Key Archaeological State Park, an adjacent island; Edison Ford estate in Fort Myers. **Additional Information:** Lee Island Coast CVB, (800) 237-6444, www.leeislandcoast.com.

RESTRICTIONS

Pets: On leash only, proof of vaccinations required, not allowed in buildings or canoes. **Fires:** In grill or fire ring only. **Alcoholic Beverages:** After hours only. **Vehicle Maximum Length:** 45 ft. **Other:** No firearms or fireworks.

TO GET THERE

I-75 Exit 19, Estero onto Corkscrew Rd., 2 mi. west to Koreshan State Historic Site just 0.3 mi. west of US 41.

FERNANDINA BEACH, AMELIA ISLAND

N A

Fort Clinch State Park

2601 Atlantic Ave., Fernandina Beach 32034. T: (904) 277-7274; F: (904) 277-7225; www.myflorida.com.

🚐 ★★★★ ▲ ★★★★

Beauty: ★★★★★ Site Privacy: ★★★
Spaciousness: ★★★★ Quiet: ★★★★
Security: ★★★★★ Cleanliness: ★★★★
Insect Control: ★★★ Facilities: ★★★★★

How does watching the sunset from the riverfront or the beach sound? It's not unlikely that you might see dolphins jumping in the surf, and even possible you might catch sight of the elusive right whales that come to calve in the offshore waters. Train your binoculars on Cumberland Island across the channel and you just might see the wild horses that still live there, left over from the island's days of glory as home to Carnegies and Rockefellers. The campgrounds at Fort Clinch State Park provide shoreside benches to enjoy the view. Campsites are all back-in, but fairly spacious, with a path through the woods behind sites at the river campground leading to the beach—watch out for huge wolf spiders that weave webs among the trees! Take time for a tour of historic Fort Clinch itself, built for the Civil War but never used in battle; the place is fully equipped as a living-history exhibit, with touchable replicas so kids—and adults—can really feel what military life in the late 1800s must have been like. While you're on the island, be sure to sample the delicious local copper shrimp that makes the region famous.

BASICS

Operated By: Florida Dept. of Environmental Protection, Division of Recreation & Parks. **Open:** All year. **Site Assignment:** First come, first served, reservations accepted w/ 1-day deposit, refundable up to 24 hours in advance. **Registration:** Ranger Station. **Fee:** $19; MC, V, D. **Parking:** Yes.

FACILITIES

Number of RV Sites: 54. **Number of Tent-Only Sites:** 6. **Hookups:** Water, electric. **Each Site:** Picnic table, fire ring. **Dump Station:** Yes. **Laundry:** Yes. **Pay Phone:** Yes. **Rest Rooms and Showers:** Yes. **Fuel:** No. **Propane:** No. **Internal**

Roads: Paved in good condition. **RV Service:** Referral. **Market:** 1.4 mi. south from main gate on Atlantic Blvd. (A1A). **Restaurant:** 0.25 mi. south on Atlantic Blvd., continuing 1.5 mi. **General Store:** Yes, firewood & souvenirs. **Vending:** Yes. **Swimming Pool:** No. **Playground:** Yes. **Other:** Civil War era Fort Clinch, beach, pier, river, forest. **Activities:** Tours of historic fort, Civil War reenactments (first weekend of each month), Civil War encampment (first weekend in May), guided nature hikes (9 a.m. Saturdays), kids fishing clinic (June), Memorial & Veterans Day observations. **Nearby Attractions:** Historic town of Fernandina Beach. **Additional Information:** Amelia Island Tourist Development Council, (800) 2-AMELIA, www.ameli-aisland.org.

RESTRICTIONS

Pets: On leash and in designated areas only, proof of vaccinations required; no pets on beach, in buildings, or on boardwalks. **Fires:** In grill only. **Alcoholic Beverages:** Not allowed. **Vehicle Maximum Length:** 50 ft. or more. **Other:** No firearms or fireworks; do not damage or disturb dunes, nature, or wildlife, digging prohibited; quiet time 11 p.m.–7 a.m.

TO GET THERE

Exit I-95 north of Jacksonville onto A1A, east 14 mi. to Fernandina Beach, right on Atlantic Ave. 3 mi. to park.

FLAGLER BEACH

Gamble Rogers Memorial State Recreation Area

3100 South A1A, Flagler Beach 32136. T: (386) 517-2086; F: (386) 517-2088; www.myflorida.com.

🚐 ★★★★　　🏕 ★★★★

Beauty: ★★★★	Site Privacy: ★★
Spaciousness: ★★	Quiet: ★★★★
Security: ★★★★★	Cleanliness: ★★★★★
Insect Control: ★★★	Facilities: ★★★★

This park was named for troubadour Gamble Rogers, a Floridian who drowned off Flagler Beach while saving another man from drowning in the mid-1980s. The campground, on the beach-side, or east of A1A, is a small, gated facility with closely packed sandy sites shielded from the ocean by a bushy barrier of sea oats. Boardwalk paths lead to the beach, but there is no

ocean view for campers. Sites have slight bushy buffers, but no trees to break the ocean breezes. The rest of the park is on the west side of A1A—a thin strip of native land bordered by the highway and the Intracoastal Waterway. The park office displays an interesting but sad collection of road-kill collected from the highway—a skunk, ruby-throated hummingbird, luna moth, rattlesnake, and a dozen or so other snakes. All victims of progress, reminding visitors to drive carefully.

BASICS

Operated By: Florida Dept. of Environmental Protection, Division of Recreation & Parks. **Open:** All year. **Site Assignment:** Reservations accepted up to 11 months in advance, 1-night deposit refundable up to 24 hours in advance. **Registration:** Park office (across Hwy. A1A from the beach campground). **Fee:** $19; M, V, D. **Parking:** Yes.

FACILITIES

Number of RV Sites: 24. **Number of Tent-Only Sites:** 8. **Hookups:** Water, electric (30 amps). **Each Site:** Picnic table, ground grill. **Dump Station:** Yes. **Laundry:** No. **Pay Phone:** Yes. **Rest Rooms and Showers:** Yes. **Fuel:** No. **Propane:** No. **Internal Roads:** Sand roads in good condition. **RV Service:** Referral. **Market:** 3 mi. north on A1A. **Restaurant:** 3 mi. north on A1A. **General Store:** No. **Vending:** No. **Swimming Pool:** No (beach). **Playground:** No. **Other:** Sand box, boat ramp, nature trails. **Activities:** Swimming, fish, boating, hiking.

RESTRICTIONS

Pets: Leash only, not in buildings or on beach. **Fires:** Grill/fire ring only. **Alcoholic Beverages:** Not allowed. **Vehicle Maximum Length:** 46 ft.—call ahead to ensure availability.

TO GET THERE

Exit I-95 at SR 100, 6 mi. east to Hwy. A1A, 3 mi. south to park.

FLAGLER BEACH/ BEVERLY BEACH

Beverly Beach Camptown RV Resort

P.O. Box 1048, Flagler Beach 32136. T: (904) 439-3111 or (800) 255-2706; F: (904) 439-6555; .

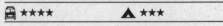

🚐 ★★★★　　🏕 ★★★

Beauty: ★★★★   Site Privacy: ★
Spaciousness: ★   Quiet: ★★
Security: ★★★★   Cleanliness: ★★★★★
Insect Control: ★★★★   Facilities: ★★★★★

We're generally not impressed with camp-grounds that look like parking lots, but this one's directly on the beach—campers pull right up to the seawall, so they can literally wake up and watch the sun rise over the ocean without leaving their beds. That's pretty hard to beat, even without trees and wall-to-wall neighbors. The campground also offers a few tent sites right on the beach. Beverly Beach Camptown has a well-stocked store, too, with everything from souvenirs to beer and wine, plus a small restaurant in case you're tired of cooking. But the best bonus here—at least for those who like to travel with their pets—is that leashed dogs are allowed on the beach, an unusual treat for our furry friends.

BASICS

Operated By: Manager Karen Siefken. **Open:** All year. **Site Assignment:** Reservations accepted w/ credit card guarantee—recommended on holidays and during Daytona special events. **Registration:** Office. **Fee:** $37 Oct.–Jan., $41 Feb.–Sept.; M, V, D. **Parking:** Yes.

FACILITIES

Number of RV Sites: 127. **Number of Tent-Only Sites:** 5. **Hookups:** Water, electric (30, 50 amps), sewer, cable TV. **Each Site:** Picnic table. **Dump Station:** Yes. **Laundry:** Yes. **Pay Phone:** Yes. **Rest Rooms and Showers:** Yes. **Fuel:** No. **Propane:** No. **Internal Roads:** Paved, in good condition. **RV Service:** Referral. **Market:** On site or 4 mi. south on A1A. **Restaurant:** On site for breakfast & lunch or 4 mi. south on A1A. **General Store:** Yes. **Vending:** No. **Swimming Pool:** No (beach). **Playground:** No. **Other:** Beach, meeting room & café. **Activities:** Swimming, fishing, boogie board surfing. **Nearby Attractions:** Daytona Beach 20 mi. south. **Additional Information:** Flagler Beach Chamber of Commerce, (800) 298-0995 www.flaglercounty.com/fbcc.

RESTRICTIONS

Pets: On leash only. **Fires:** Allowed on beach when weather permitting. **Alcoholic Beverages:** Allowed. **Vehicle Maximum Length:** 40 ft.

TO GET THERE

I-95 Exit 91, 3.5 mi. east on SR 100 to A1A, 3 mi. north to campground.

FORT LAUDERDALE

Paradise Island Resort
(Formerly Buglewood RV Resort)

2121 NW 29th Ct., Fort Lauderdale 33311-2175.
T: (954) 485-1150; (800) 487-7395; buglewood.com; buglewood@aol.com.

🚐 ★★★   ⛺ n/a

Beauty: ★★   Site Privacy: ★★
Spaciousness: ★★   Quiet: ★★★★
Security: ★★★★   Cleanliness: ★★★★★
Insect Control: ★★★   Facilities: ★★★★★

Paradise Island Resort is a quaint, peaceful oasis smack in the middle of downtown Fort Lauderdale, just a few minutes from beaches, restaurants, and the historic arts and science district. Popular with snowbirds who visit during the winter months from the northern states and Canada for 24 years, Paradise Island has a strong sense of community demonstrated by the heavily attended petanque (a Canadian game similar to bocci) tournaments during the winter and several dog-walkers out in the early evenings. Shade trees provide a cool breeze. Named a Good Sam Club, Paradise Island Resort is a pleasant park for RVers just passing through and for those looking to stay for awhile. There are 19 pull-through sites and most are 20 feet long, with some as long as 55 feet. Although less-savory areas abut the community, Paradise Island is surrounded by a six-foot hedge and maintains a security system with a night attendant who reports minimal disturbances. It is well-lit, gated park with regular police patrols.

BASICS

Operated By: Managers Bill & Karen Price. **Open:** All year. **Site Assignment:** Reservations required in winter, $10 deposit for 1 night. **Registration:** Office. **Registration:** Office. **Fee:** $36 Nov.–May; $29 May–Nov.; MC, V, D, AE. **Parking:** Yes.

FACILITIES

Number of RV Sites: 232. **Number of Tent-Only Sites:** 0. **Hookups:** Electric (30, 50 amps), water, sewer, phone. **Each Site:** Full hookups,. **Dump Station:** No. **Laundry:** Yes. **Pay Phone:** Yes. **Rest Rooms and Showers:** Yes. **Fuel:** No. **Propane:** No. **Internal Roads:** Paved, in good condition. **RV Service:** Mechanic on call. **Market:** Groceries 3 mi. east on Oakland Park Blvd., pharmacy next door to campground to the north. **Restaurant:** Several within walking distance. **General Store:** Yes. **Vending:** Yes, plus free ice at pool area. **Swimming Pool:** Yes. **Playground:** No. **Other:** Clubhouse w/ full kitchen & 2 rec halls. **Activities:** Horseshoes, shuffleboard, petanque tournaments, billiards; planned activities during the winter include monthly dinners w/ music, holiday parties, live entertainment. **Nearby Attractions:** Fort Lauderdale beach 6 mi. east on Oakland Park Blvd., the Swap Shop flea market about 5 mi. west on Sunrise Blvd., an Indian Casino & Bingo hall north approximately 5 mi. in Coconut Creek. Car rentals available through the office. **Additional Information:** Greater Fort Lauderdale CVB, (800) 231-SUNNY, www.sunny.org.

RESTRICTIONS

Pets: On leash only, small pets preferred. **Fires:** In grill only, portable grills available at pool area. **Alcoholic Beverages:** Allowed. **Vehicle Maximum Length:** 45 ft.

TO GET THERE

Exit I-95 in Fort Lauderdale at Oakland Park Blvd, Exit 31, Oakland Park west about a mile to NW 21'st. Ave., turn south to campground entrance on right.

FORT MYERS BEACH
San Carlos RV Park

18701 San Carlos Blvd., Fort Myers Beach 33931. T: (941) 466-3133; F: (941) 466-3133; www.gocampingamerica.com/sancarlos; sancarrv@aol.com.

🚐 ★★★   ▲ ★

Beauty: ★★★	Site Privacy: ★★
Spaciousness: ★★	Quiet: ★★★
Security: ★★★★★	Cleanliness: ★★★★
Insect Control: ★★★	Facilities: ★★★★

Although a bit crowded, this RV park has been family owned for 20 years and is clearly a favorite among its guests—and likely has been for years. The owners live on-site, and 19 of the park's mobile-home units are available as efficiency rentals. A small plot of land jutting out into the back bay waters of Hurricane Bay off the Gulf of Mexico, the park provides a quiet, unassuming means of being a tourist without feeling trapped by a circus of attractions. Fishers can appreciate the boat docks and marina, and tenters will appreciate the waterfront sites. Swimming in the bay is discouraged, however, because of the sharp barnacles clinging to the rocks covering the ocean floor. Luckily, Fort Myers Beach is just a mile away.

BASICS

Operated By: Owner Vernon Underwood & family. **Open:** All year. **Site Assignment:** Reservations accepted, 1-night deposit required, refundable up to 24 hours in advance. **Registration:** Office. **Fee:** $25 May–Oct., $26 Nov.–Dec. 14, $32.50 Dec. 15–Apr. **Parking:** Yes.

FACILITIES

Number of RV Sites: 145. **Number of Tent-Only Sites:** 0. **Hookups:** Water, electric (20, 30 amps), sewer. **Each Site:** Picnic table, concrete pad. **Dump Station:** Yes. **Laundry:** Yes. **Pay Phone:** Yes. **Rest Rooms and Showers:** Yes. **Fuel:** No. **Propane:** No. **Internal Roads:** Paved in good condition. **RV Service:** Referral. **Market:** 1.5 mi. north, convenience mart 2 blocks south. **Restaurant:** 2–4 blocks north & south. **General Store:** Yes. **Vending:** Yes. **Swimming Pool:** Yes (w/ Jacuzzi). **Playground:** No. **Other:** Rec hall, shuffleboard, horseshoes, boat dock & marina, kayak & paddleboat rentals. **Activities:** Shuffleboard & horseshoe tournaments, potluck dinners, holiday parties, arts & crafts, all during winter season. **Nearby Attractions:** Beach, Sanibel & Captiva islands, dog race track in Bonita Springs, Edison & Ford homes in Fort Myers. **Additional Information:** Lee Island Coast CVB, (800) 237-6444, www.leeislandcoast.com.

RESTRICTIONS

Pets: No pit bulls or rottweilers, max. 2 pets per site, kept on 4-ft. leash. **Fires:** In grill only. **Alcoholic Beverages:** Allowed. **Vehicle Maximum Length:** 40 ft., call ahead for availability. **Other:** No firearms, no feeding wildlife, quiet hours 10 p.m.–8 a.m., pool closes at dusk.

TO GET THERE

I-75 Exit 21/Daniels Pkwy., west 5.5 mi. to Summerlin Rd., left/west 5.5 mi. to San Carlos Blvd., left/south 1.5 mi. to park on left.

HIGH SPRINGS
High Springs Campground

24004 NW Old Bellamy Rd., High Springs 32643.
T: (386) 454-1688; HSCamping@aol.com.

🚐 ★★★   ⛺ ★★

Beauty: ★★★   Site Privacy: ★★
Spaciousness: ★★   Quiet: ★★★
Security: ★★★★★   Cleanliness: ★★★★
Insect Control: ★★★★   Facilities: ★★★★

There's a pleasant country atmosphere at this small, quiet, older campground that's right off the highway. The camping and playground areas are shaded with tall trees, although the sites themselves are not particularly wooded nor private. With some pull-through sites and grass underfoot, this makes a pleasant place to stop for a night or for a few days. Rustic and far from fancy, High Springs offers a laid-back feeling for those anxious to escape the city bustle. But real life is only a few clicks away—Internet access is available in the laundry room. Even Fido can relax here—well-mannered dogs are welcome to go without leashes so long as they remain on best behavior and under their master's control. A popular spot for campers in town to canoe, tube, or swim the area springs as well as those planning to attend the annual Gator National Drag races in Gainesville the third weekend of Mar.

BASICS

Operated By: Jason Outler, manager; Linda McDonald, owner. **Open:** All year. **Site Assignment:** Reservations accepted, 50% deposit for holidays or special events, refundable w/ 7-day notice. **Registration:** Campground office. **Fee:** $18; cash or check only. **Parking:** Yes.

FACILITIES

Number of RV Sites: 48. **Number of Tent-Only Sites:** 5. **Hookups:** Water, electric (30 amps.), sewer. **Each Site:** Picnic table, fire rings. **Dump Station:** Yes. **Laundry:** Yes. **Pay Phone:** Free. **Rest Rooms and Showers:** Yes. **Fuel:** No. **Propane:** No. **Internal Roads:** Paved, in good condition. **RV Service:** Referral. **Market:** South 4 mi. on Hwy. 236 to US 441, right 1 mi. to supermarket on right. **Restaurant:** South 4 mi. on Hwy. 236 to High Springs. **General Store:** Ice only. **Vending:** Yes. **Swimming Pool:** Yes. **Playground:** Yes. **Activities:** Inquire at campground. **Nearby**

Attractions: Fresh water springs nearby (driving distance) at Ichnetucknee Springs & Santa Fe River. **Additional Information:** Alachua County CVB, (352) 374-5260.

RESTRICTIONS

Pets: On leash if necessary. **Fires:** In fire rings unless restriction in effect. **Alcoholic Beverages:** Allowed. **Vehicle Maximum Length:** None.

TO GET THERE

I-75 Exit 79 at Hwy. 236 (just north of Gainesville), west to entrance at Old Bellamy Rd., north 1,000 ft. to campground.

HOBE SOUND
Jonathan Dickinson State Park

16450 SE Federal Hwy., Hobe Sound 33455. T: (561)546-2771; www.myflorida.com.

🚐 ★★★★   ⛺ ★★★★★

Beauty: ★★★★★   Site Privacy: ★★★★
Spaciousness: ★★★★   Quiet: ★★★★★
Security: ★★★★★   Cleanliness: ★★★★
Insect Control: ★★★   Facilities: ★★★★★

Frequently cited as one of the best camping opportunities in South Florida, Jonathan Dickinson State Park offers a range of ecosystems to study and enjoy, from the Loxahatchee River, Florida's first federally designated Wild and Scenic River (which protects the river from future development and restructuring), to the pine scrub, cypress swamp, and pine flatwoods laced with hiking, biking, and nature trails. Try to visit Trapper Nelson's place on the Loxahatchee—the restored homesite of a Florida pioneer trapper who died in 1968 under mysterious circumstances. Boat tours are offered Wednesday–Sunday. The park offers two campgrounds for RVers plus primitive trail camping areas for backpackers. The Pine Grove campground near the park entrance just off US 1 is the largest and provides both small and large sites. Most offer bushy buffers and shade cover from the many tall pine trees throughout the campground. Groups may appreciate the conference building and campfire circle at Pine Grove. The river campground, named for its proximity to the Loxahatchee River that runs along the western border of the park, has less tall trees but more native bushy vegetation, which provides greater privacy at each site but little shade. There are no pull-through sites at either campground.

BASICS

Operated By: Florida Dept. of Environmental Protection, Division of Recreation & Parks. **Open:** All year. **Site Assignment:** Reservations accepted, deposit required (call for amount). **Registration:** Park office. **Fee:** $14–$20; M, V, D, AE. **Parking:** Yes.

FACILITIES

Number of RV Sites: 120. **Number of Tent-Only Sites:** 10. **Hookups:** Water, electric (30 amps). **Each Site:** Picnic table, grill. **Dump Station:** Yes. **Laundry:** No. **Pay Phone:** Yes. **Rest Rooms and Showers:** Yes. **Fuel:** No. **Propane:** No. **Internal Roads:** Paved, in good condition. **RV Service:** Referral. **Market:** 3–5 mi. north or south on US 1. **Restaurant:** 3–5 mi. north or south on US 1. **General Store:** Yes. **Vending:** Yes. **Swimming Pool:** No. **Playground:** Yes. **Other:** Boat dock, hiking trails, observation tower, paved & off-road bike trails, nature trails. **Activities:** Hiking, boating (rentals available include motorboats, canoes, & kayaks), fishing, biking, bird & nature study, boat tours. **Nearby Attractions:** Beaches. **Additional Information:** Hobe Sound Chamber of Commerce, (561) 546-4724.

RESTRICTIONS

Pets: On leash & in designated areas only, proof of rabies vaccination required. **Fires:** In grill only. **Alcoholic Beverages:** After hours only. **Vehicle Maximum Length:** 35 ft. **Other:** No firearms or fireworks.

TO GET THERE

Exit I-95 at SR 708 (Hobe Sound Exit), east to US 1, south to park.

HOLT

Blackwater River State Park

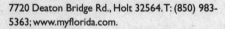

7720 Deaton Bridge Rd., Holt 32564. T: (850) 983-5363; www.myflorida.com.

🚐 ★★★★	⛺ ★★★★★
Beauty: ★★★★★	Site Privacy: ★★★★★
Spaciousness: ★★★★	Quiet: ★★★★★
Security: ★★★	Cleanliness: ★★★★★
Insect Control: ★★	Facilities: ★★★★

Amazingly remote, this campground entrance was unmanned when we arrived, with self–sign in instructions based on the honor system.

Campers were advised to revisit the camp office between 5 and 7 p.m. to register and pay for the campsite. Sites around the two circles were all back-in or pull-in sites, but quite large, with generous buffers. Although peaceful and quiet, the campground was nearly full, and even more visitors were found at the rivers edge—Blackwater River is said to be one of the cleanest, most pristine rivers in the world. Happy groups of canoeists, swimmers, kayakers, and tubing enthusiasts frolicked in the cold, fresh, dark water as it wound its way through the park, dotted with wide, white-sand shores. Bobcats and deer are said to be common in this section of state forest. This one is clearly a Florida treasure. Pack the cooler and plan to stay a few days to enjoy the wilderness.

BASICS

Operated By: Florida Dept. of Environmental Protection, Division of Recreation & Parks. **Open:** All year. **Site Assignment:** First come, first served self-select. **Registration:** Office. **Fee:** $10; M, V, D. **Parking:** Yes.

FACILITIES

Number of RV Sites: 30. **Number of Tent-Only Sites:** 0. **Hookups:** Water, electric. **Each Site:** Picnic table, fire ring, clothesline poles. **Dump Station:** Yes. **Laundry:** No. **Pay Phone:** Yes. **Rest Rooms and Showers:** Yes. **Fuel:** No. **Propane:** No. **Internal Roads:** Paved, in good condition. **RV Service:** No. **Market:** 2 mi. south on Deaton Bridge Rd. **Restaurant:** 3 mi. south to Hwy. 90. **General Store:** No. **Vending:** No. **Swimming Pool:** No (River). **Playground:** No. **Other:** Picnic pavilions, hiking trails & boardwalks, river. **Activities:** Fishing, hiking, swimming, canoeing & kayaking. **Nearby Attractions:** Blackwater Canoe Outpost—rents canoes & tubes. **Additional Information:** Main Street Milton, (850) 623-2339, www.srcchamber.com; Pensacola Convention & Visitor Center, (800) 87401234, www.visitpensacola.com.

RESTRICTIONS

Pets: On leash only, not allowed at riverside pavilions, beaches, or in river. **Fires:** In grill only. **Alcoholic Beverages:** Not allowed. **Vehicle Maximum Length:** 45 ft. **Other:** No firearms or intoxicants.

TO GET THERE

Exit Hwy. 90 at Harold onto Deaton Bridge Rd., north 3 mi. to park.

JENSEN BEACH

Nettles Island

9803 S. Ocean Dr., Jensen Beach 34957. T: (561) (229) 1300; F: (561) 229-1304; www.vnirealty.com; Bev@vnirealty.com.

🚐 ★★★★★   ▲ n/a

Beauty: ★★   Site Privacy: ★
Spaciousness: ★   Quiet: ★★★
Security: ★★★★★   Cleanliness: ★★★★★
Insect Control: ★★★★★   Facilities: ★★★★★

Quite different from most of the RV parks we've visited, Nettle's Island is very popular with retirees who want Florida's great lifestyle at a high value. Nettle's Island is wall-to-wall, privately owned sites, some available as rentals, others available for travelers and snow birds. It is a complete village unto itself, with streets and nicely landscaped grassy lawns on the perimeter sites. Nettle's Island includes a recreational section of property across the road, directly on the beach, with pool and cabana club. Fisher's delight.

BASICS

Operated By: VNI Realty. **Open:** All year. **Site Assignment:** Reservations necessary Jan.–Mar., full payment due 30 days before arrival. **Registration:** Office. **Fee:** $39–$44 (waterfront) Dec.–Apr., $30–$35 May–Nov. **Parking:** Yes.

FACILITIES

Number of RV Sites: 1589. **Number of Tent-Only Sites:** 0. **Hookups:** Water, electric (50 amps), cable TV, phone. **Each Site:** Varies—some tables, grills. **Dump Station:** No. **Laundry:** Yes. **Pay Phone:** Yes. **Rest Rooms and Showers:** Yes. **Fuel:** Yes. **Propane:** Yes. **Internal Roads:** Paved, in good condition. **RV Service:** Referral. **Market:** On site. **Restaurant:** On site. **General Store:** Yes. **Vending:** Yes. **Swimming Pool:** Yes (2). **Playground:** Yes. **Other:** Mini-golf, volleyball & tennis courts, jacuzzi, sauna, gas station, bank, hair salon, marina, clothing store. **Activities:** Fishing off sites, off bridges, in the ocean. **Nearby Attractions:** Ocean. **Additional Information:** Jensen Beach Chamber of Commerce, (561) 334-3444, www.jensenchamber.com.

RESTRICTIONS

Pets: On leash only. **Fires:** In grill only (not provided). **Alcoholic Beverages:** Allowed. **Vehicle Maximum Length:** None. **Other:** No tents or pop-ups–full hookups only.

TO GET THERE

Exit I-95 66 at Fort Pierce (Orange Ave.), east to US 1, north 0.5 mi. to A1A, east across Indian River (Fort Pierce Bridge to Hutchinson Island) then continue south on A1A about 14 mi. to Nettles Island.

KEY LARGO

John Pennekamp Coral Reef State Park

P.O. Box 1560, Key Largo 33037. T: (305) 451-1202; F: (305) 853-3555; www.myflorida.com.

🚐 ★★★★   ▲ ★★★★

Beauty: ★★★★   Site Privacy: ★★
Spaciousness: ★★★   Quiet: ★★★★
Security: ★★★★★   Cleanliness: ★★★★★
Insect Control: ★★★   Facilities: ★★★★★

Boasting numerous awards as one of the best parks and campgrounds in the state, John Pennekamp Coral Reef State Park offers several unique treats thanks to its location in the Florida Keys, just minutes from Miami. The first undersea park in the nation, 178 square miles of this park extend into the Atlantic Ocean, including a portion of the only coral reef in the country. Park management takes advantage of the prime location to offer boat tours for snorkelers, scuba divers, and scenic viewers—glass-bottom boat rides are also offered daily. Equipment and instruction are available. All RV campsites are back-in only, and many are waterfront but don't afford a view because the camping area is surrounded by protected mangrove trees, revered around the world for their erosion protection and their root system (which can get a little smelly at times) which provides nutrients for the tiniest sea creatures forming the foundation of the food chain.

BASICS

Operated By: Florida Dept. of Environmental Protection, Division of Recreation & Parks. **Open:** All year. **Site Assignment:** Reservations recommended, accepted up to 11 months in advance, 1-night deposit required, refundable up to 24 hours in advance. **Registration:** Park office. **Fee:** $29. **Parking:** Yes.

FACILITIES

Number of RV Sites: 41. **Number of Tent-Only Sites:** 6. **Hookups:** Water, electric. **Each Site:** Picnic table, grill. **Dump Station:** Yes. **Laundry:** No. **Pay Phone:** Yes. **Rest Rooms and Showers:** Yes. **Fuel:** No. **Propane:** No. **Internal Roads:** Paved & gravel, in good condition. **RV Service:** Referral. **Market:** 1 mi. south or north of the campground entrance. **Restaurant:** 1 mi. north or south of the campground entrance. **General Store:** Yes. **Vending:** Yes. **Swimming Pool:** No. **Playground:** Yes. **Other:** Coral reef, nature trails, canoe trails, scuba & snorkel boat tours. **Activities:** Swimming, fishing, boating, scuba, snorkeling. **Nearby Attractions:** Florida Keys Wild Bird Center, Tavernier; Key West (100 mi. south). **Additional Information:** Key Largo Chamber of Commerce, (800) 822-1088, www.keylargo.org.

RESTRICTIONS

Pets: No. **Fires:** In grill only. **Alcoholic Beverages:** Used discreetly after park hours only. **Vehicle Maximum Length:** 40 ft. **Other:** No firearms or fireworks.

TO GET THERE

US 1 south from Miami to mile marker 102.5

KEY LARGO
Key Largo Kampground

101551 Overseas Hwy., Key Largo 33037. T: (305) 451-1431; F: (305) 451-8083; www.KeyLargo.org/accommodations.

🚐 ★★★★   ▲ ★★

Beauty: ★★★	Site Privacy: ★★
Spaciousness: ★★★	Quiet: ★★★★
Security: ★★★★★	Cleanliness: ★★★★
Insect Control: ★★★	Facilities: ★★★★

This campground is occupied partly by those who own the sites; rentals are not uncommon but are made available on an individual basis through the office. Travelers can overnight in the tent area—a grassy, shaded park near the entrance. The atmosphere is made even more peaceful with coconut palm trees, mahogany, gumbo limbo, and mangroves lining the park, providing habitat to tiny crabs and raccoons. Manatees sometimes venture into the marina from the surrounding bone flats—shallow waterways dotted with protected mangrove islands. Owner's sites reveal an interesting crowd, with

fragrant flower and tropical-fruit gardens, wind chimes, and colorful flags. The campground employs interpreters during the winter season to accommodate guests from German, French, and Spanish-speaking countries.

BASICS

Operated By: Key Largo Kampground, Inc. **Open:** All year. **Site Assignment:** Reservations requested, 1-night non-refundable deposit. **Registration:** Office. **Fee:** $24.50–$52.50 (waterfront); M,V. **Parking:** Yes.

FACILITIES

Number of RV Sites: 171. **Number of Tent-Only Sites:** 38. **Hookups:** Water, electric (20, 30 50 amps), sewer, cable TV. **Each Site:** Some tables & grills. **Dump Station:** Yes. **Laundry:** Yes. **Pay Phone:** Yes. **Rest Rooms and Showers:** Yes. **Fuel:** No. **Propane:** No. **Internal Roads:** Paved, in good condition. **RV Service:** Referral. **Market:** 2 blocks south. **Restaurant:** 2 blocks south. **General Store:** Yes. **Vending:** Yes. **Swimming Pool:** Yes. **Playground:** Yes. **Other:** Marina, boat dock, beach, volleyball, horseshoe & shuffleboard courts. **Activities:** Bingo, game nights, pot-luck dinners, BBQ nights. **Nearby Attractions:** Coral reef, scuba, snorkeling, deep-sea fishing. **Additional Information:** Key Largo Chamber of Commerce, (800) 822-1088, www.keylargo.org.

RESTRICTIONS

Pets: On leash only. **Fires:** In grill only. **Alcoholic Beverages:** On site only, no offensive behavior. **Vehicle Maximum Length:** 35 ft. **Other:** No firearms or fireworks.

TO GET THERE

US 1 south from Miami to Key Largo (first Key), left on Samson Rd. at mile marker 101.5, 2 blocks to campground.

LAKE BUENA VISTA
Disney's Fort Wilderness Resort and Campground

4510 North Fort Wilderness Trail, Lake Buena Vista 32830. T: (407) 824-2900; F: (407) 824-3508; www.disneyworld.com.

🚐 ★★★★   ▲ ★★★

Beauty: ★★★★	Site Privacy: ★★★
Spaciousness: ★★★★	Quiet: ★★★★
Security: ★★★★★	Cleanliness: ★★★★★
Insect Control: ★★★★★	Facilities: ★★★★★

There's something very different at Disney's Campground. Just as the Magic Kingdom is like no other country and its Main Street like no other town, Disney's Fort Wilderness is a far cry from any other campground we've seen in Florida. For example, you'll be hard-pressed to find a mosquito here, even though the little blood-sucking bugs are a veritable plague throughout most of the rest of the state and beyond. Just as in the Magic Kingdom, the campgrounds are perfectly landscaped and maintained, and plenty of trees and shrubs create a nice sense of seclusion from neighboring campsites. Fort Wilderness offers 20 loops of campsites, plus another 8 for cabins, all spread comfortably across the more than 700-acre campground. Entertainment is also true Disney style, with two video arcades, nightly musical shows around the campfire, two swimming pools, a beach, fitness walks, bike, boat, and ski rentals available. Horseback trails, pony rides and hay rides, canoeing and kayaking add to the fun. But perhaps the best thing about Fort Wilderness is its convenient location close to all of Disney's parks—and early daily admission and free transportation to them all is allowed for campers. Enjoy!

BASICS

Operated By: Walt Disney World. **Open:** All year. **Site Assignment:** Reservations accepted through www.disneyworld.com or (407) 934-7639; 1-night stay deposit, refundable up to 72 hours in advance. **Registration:** Park office. **Fee:** $39; M, V, D, AE, DC, CB. **Parking:** Yes.

FACILITIES

Number of RV Sites: 784. Number of Tent-Only Sites: 83. Hookups: Water, electric (20, 30, 50 amps), sewer, cable TV. **Each Site:** Picnic table, grill. **Dump Station:** No. **Laundry:** Yes. **Pay Phone:** Yes. **Rest Rooms and Showers:** Yes. **Fuel:** No. **Propane:** Yes. **Internal Roads:** Paved, in good condition. **RV Service:** Referral. **Market:** Yes. **Restaurant:** Yes. **General Store:** Yes. **Vending:** Yes. **Swimming Pool:** Yes. **Playground:** Yes. **Other:** Tennis, basketball & volleyball courts, beach, bike paths, fitness trail, marina, shuffleboard, horseshoes, horse stables, petting farm. **Activities:** Fishing, musical campfire shows, boating, biking, horseback riding, sports. **Nearby Attractions:** Disneyworld Magic Kingdom & MGM, Epcot Center & Animal Kingdom theme parks. **Additional Infor-**

mation: Orlando Official Visitor Center, (407) 363-5872, www.orlandoinfo.com.

RESTRICTIONS

Pets: On leash only, proof of rabies, please mention pets when booking reservation. **Fires:** In grill only. **Alcoholic Beverages:** Allowed. **Vehicle Maximum Length:** None. **Other:** No fireworks, firearms must be stored at front desk.

TO GET THERE

Exit I-4 at and follow signs to the Magic Kingdom.

LIVE OAK

Spirit of the Suwannee Music Park

3076 95th Dr., Live Oak 32060. T: (904) 364-1683 or (800) 224-5656; F: (386) 364-2998; www.music liveshere.com; spirit@musicliveshere.com.

🚐 ★★★★	⛺ ★★★★★
Beauty: ★★★★★	Site Privacy: ★★★
Spaciousness: ★★★★★	Quiet: ★★★★
Security: ★★★★★	Cleanliness: ★★★★
Insect Control: ★★★★	Facilities: ★★★★★

Music is a mainstay of the local activities—bring your own and join in or come for the frequent concerts, which include nationally known musicians of a variety of genres, from bluegrass and country to Christian and rock. Campers can choose from full-hookup RV sites to rentable trailers called cabins to a tree house overlooking the outdoor amphitheater.

BASICS

Operated By: The Cornett family. **Open:** All year. **Site Assignment:** Reservations accepted, deposit 20%, refundable up to 15 days in advance. **Registration:** Park office. **Fee:** $25; M, V, D. **Parking:** Yes.

FACILITIES

Number of RV Sites: 1100. Number of Tent-Only Sites: 600 acres of primitive camping. **Hookups:** Water, electric (20, 30, 50 amps), sewer, cable. **Each Site:** Picnic table. **Dump Station:** Yes. **Laundry:** Yes. **Pay Phone:** Yes. **Rest Rooms and Showers:** Yes. **Fuel:** No. **Propane:** No. **Internal Roads:** Paved & gravel in good condition. **RV Service:** Referral. **Market:** 4.5 mi. south on Hwy. 129 to I-10. **Restaurant:** 4.5 mi. north on Hwy. 129 to I-75. **General Store:** Yes. **Vending:** Yes. **Swimming Pool:** Yes. **Playground:** Yes. **Other:** Paddleboat & canoe rentals, amphitheater, restaurant, pickin' shed, horse stables, 15 mi. of trails, 3 stages, gamefield for up to 20,000 people. **Activities:** Playing and/or listening to music, canoeing, fishing, hiking, horseback riding. **Nearby Attractions:** Inquire at campground. **Additional Information:** Suwannee County Tourist Development Council, (386) 362-3071, www.suwanneechamber.com.

RESTRICTIONS

Pets: On leash only. **Fires:** Must be attended. **Alcoholic Beverages:** Allowed. **Vehicle Maximum Length:** None. **Other:** No firearms.

TO GET THERE

4.5 mi. south of I-75 at Hwy. 129/Live Oak; 4.5 mi. north of I-10 at Hwy. 129/Live Oak.

MADISON

Yogi Bear's Jellystone Park Camp/ Resort

Rte. 1 Box 3199J, Ragans Lake Rd., Madison 32340. T: (850) 97308269; F: (850) 973-4114; www.madisonfl.com/jellystone; yogibear@madisonfl.com.

🚐 ★★★★★	🏕 ★★★★
Beauty: ★★★	Site Privacy: ★★★
Spaciousness: ★★★★	Quiet: ★★★★
Security: ★★★★	Cleanliness: ★★★★★
Insect Control: ★★★★	Facilities: ★★★★★

Although this campground is conveniently situated right off the highway in north-central Florida, it's much more than a parking lot for overnight travelers. This campground offers plenty of opportunities for play—it is quickly becoming a destination in itself. It is the only Yogi Bear Jellystone campground in Florida, and Yogi himself often visits to cheer the children in a wide variety of activities, from mini-golf to a water slide. Regular tram rides take visitors to the back lot to see the frontier village, often the site of paint-ball showdowns. Some of the largest and most scenic sites are located on the lakeshore. Others are opposite a small pine forest, giving the campground a very spacious and comfortable feel with grass underfoot. Rest rooms are private, individual shower/toilet rooms. About half the sites are pull-throughs, but most people want to stay awhile to relax and enjoy the activities. Kids are entertained throughout the days, and karaoke and even an "opry" hall features occasional performances for older travelers.

BASICS

Operated By: Jim & Latrelle Ragans. **Open:** All year. **Site Assignment:** Reservations accepted w/ credit card, deposit $25, refundable if cancelled 48 hours in advance. **Registration:** Park office. **Fee:** $25; MC, V, D, AE. **Parking:** Yes.

FACILITIES

Number of RV Sites: 92. **Number of Tent-Only Sites:** 8. **Hookups:** Water, electric (20, 30, 50 amps), sewer. **Each Site:** Picnic table, grill, fire ring, lantern. **Dump Station:** Yes. **Laundry:** Yes. **Pay Phone:** Yes. **Rest Rooms and Showers:** Yes. **Fuel:** No. **Propane:** No. **Internal Roads:** Gravel, in good condition. **RV Service:** Referral. **Market:** 4 mi. north on Hwy. 53. **Restaurant:** 2 mi. north on Hwy. 53. **General Store:** Yes. **Vending:** Yes. **Swimming Pool:** Yes. **Playground:** Yes. **Other:** Lake, waterslide, frontier town, tram tours, minigolf, rec hall, movie room. **Activities:** Holiday parties, volleyball tournaments (June), kids weekends (July), bingo, paintball. **Nearby Attractions:** Capitol city, Tallahassee. **Additional Information:** Madison County Tourism Development Council, (850) 973-2788, www.madisonfl.org.

RESTRICTIONS

Pets: On leash only, in designated areas. **Fires:** In grill & fire rings only. **Alcoholic Beverages:** At site only. **Vehicle Maximum Length:** None. **Other:** Don't feed the alligators.

TO GET THERE

Exit I-10 east of Tallahassee at Madison, Exit 37, take Hwy. 53 south to Ragans Lake Rd. (first road to right), turn right and follow 0.75 mi. to campground.

MALABAR

Camelot RV Park

1600 US Hwy. 1, Malabar 32950. T: (321) 724-5396; F: (321) 724-9022; www.camelotrvpark.com; Camelot@camelotrvpark.com.

🚐 ★★★★★	🏕 n/a
Beauty: ★★★	Site Privacy: ★★★
Spaciousness: ★★★	Quiet: ★★★
Security: ★★★★★	Cleanliness: ★★★★★
Insect Control: ★★★★★	Facilities: ★★★★★

More like a small village than a typical RV park, this 15-acre complex seems a comfortable location for travelers with time to stay awhile in this quiet and peaceful section of Florida's central east coast. Owners help visitors get to know their neighbors by organizing frequent leisure events such as pitch-in dinners and dances. If the office happens to be closed when you arrive, you may self-select from among many large, grassy sites dotted with oak and palm trees, then register at your convenience. The campground offers a nice view of the Intracoastal Waterway/Indian River across the road, where a private fishing dock is available for guests. Dolphins and manatees can often be spotted passing by in the river. Snowbirds will appreciate that this park offers RV storage, too.

BASICS

Operated By: Owners Bob Sr., Bobby, Liz & John Ritter. **Open:** All year. **Site Assignment:** Reservations accepted, deposit recommended. **Registration:** Office. **Fee:** $23 May–Nov., $27 Nov.–May; M, V. **Parking:** Yes.

FACILITIES

Number of RV Sites: 130. **Number of Tent-Only Sites:** 0. **Hookups:** Water, electric (30, 50 amps), sewer, cable TV, phone, modem. **Each Site:** Picnic table, grill, patio. **Dump Station:** Yes. **Laundry:** Yes. **Pay Phone:** Yes. **Rest Rooms and Showers:** Yes. **Fuel:** No. **Propane:** Yes. **Internal Roads:** Paved, in good condition. **RV Service:** Referral. **Market:** 2 mi. south on US 1. **Restaurant:** Walking distance south. **General Store:** No. **Vending:** Yes. **Swimming Pool:** No. **Playground:** No. **Other:** Basketball, shuffleboard, & bocci courts, rec hall, fishing dock. **Activities:** Bingo, musical performances & dances, BBQ dinners, craft groups, boating, fishing. **Nearby Attractions:** Intracoastal Waterway (Indian River), Beach. **Additional Information:** Melbourne/Palm Bay Area Chamber of Commerce, (800) 771-9922, www.melpb-chamber.org.

RESTRICTIONS

Pets: On leash only. **Fires:** In grill only. **Alcoholic Beverages:** Allowed. **Vehicle Maximum Length:** Big rigs welcome. **Other:** Quiet time 10 p.m.–8 a.m.

TO GET THERE

I-95 Exit 70 east on Hwy. 514, 4.5 mi. to US 1, south 2 blocks to park.

MARIANNA
Arrowhead RV Park

4820 US Hwy. 90 East, Marianna 32446. T: (850) 482-5583 or (800) 643-9166; www.arrowheadcamp.com.

🚐 ★★★★   ⛺ ★★★

Beauty: ★★★	Site Privacy: ★★
Spaciousness: ★★	Quiet: ★★★★
Security: ★★★★★	Cleanliness: ★★★★
Insect Control: ★★★★	Facilities: ★★★★

This large, friendly campground offers a comfortable place to stay for those visiting the Marianna area not far from Tallahassee. Although it. is on the main highway of the small town, the adjacent lake and plenty of tall trees give the camp a rural atmosphere. The half of the campground north of the pool and pavilion and running along the water's edge is more desirable, with curving roads and more wooded sites, although even the less private sites are still pleasant, with grass underfoot and a few trees. There's plenty to do here, too, with boat rentals and fishing docks on Merritt's Mill Pond, a spring-fed lake that boasts the world-record red-eye fish (called a shell cracker in these parts) ever caught. Kids like the mini-golf and game room, and families appreciate the security of the gated entrance adjacent to the office.

BASICS

Operated By: Bill Reddoch. **Open:** All year. **Site Assignment:** Reservations. **Registration:** Park office. **Fee:** $16; MC, V, D, AE. **Parking:** Yes.

FACILITIES

Number of RV Sites: 200. **Number of Tent-Only Sites:** 45. **Hookups:** Water, electric (20, 30 amps), sewer, cable TV. **Each Site:** Picnic table, trash can. **Dump Station:** Yes. **Laundry:** Yes. **Pay Phone:** Yes. **Rest Rooms and Showers:** Yes. **Fuel:** Yes. **Propane:** Yes. **Internal Roads:** Hard-packed dirt, in good condition. **RV Service:** Referral. **Market:** 0.5 mi. **Restaurant:** 0.5 mi. west on US 90. **General Store:** Yes. **Vending:** Yes. **Swimming Pool:** Yes. **Playground:** Yes. **Other:** Lake, boat launch, fishing docks, recreation pavilion, game room. **Activities:** Swimming, fishing, boating. **Nearby Attractions:** Florida Caverns State Park, Falling Waters State Park, 3 golf courses. **Additional Information:** Jackson County Tourist Development Council, (850) 482-8061.

RESTRICTIONS

Pets: On leash only. **Fires:** In fire rings only. **Alcoholic Beverages:** Allowed. **Vehicle Maximum Length:** None.

TO GET THERE

1.5 mi. from I-10 Exit 21 (Marianna), 1 mi. north on Hwy. 71 to US 90, 0.5 mi. west to campground.

MARIANNA

Florida Caverns State Park

3345 Caverns Rd. (SR 166), Marianna 32446. T: (850) 482-1228; www.dep.state.fl.us/parks.

🚐 ★★★★★   ⛺ ★★★★★

Beauty: ★★★★★   Site Privacy: ★★★★
Spaciousness: ★★★★   Quiet: ★★★★★
Security: ★★★★★   Cleanliness: ★★★★★
Insect Control: ★★★★   Facilities: ★★★★★

Who knew there were caves in Florida? Sure enough when the land rises just a bit above sea level, caverns are revealed beneath the surface of the earth. Left behind by the retreating sea millions of years ago, a dozen caves have been discovered in this state park (but only one is open for public exploration). The park also features a beautiful blue swimming hole. This is one of the nicest parks we've visited in Florida.

BASICS

Operated By: Florida Dept. of Environmental Protection, Division of Recreation & Parks. **Open:** All year. **Site Assignment:** Reservations accepted. **Registration:** Park office. **Fee:** $14; MC, V. **Parking:** Yes.

FACILITIES

Number of RV Sites: 32. **Number of Tent-Only Sites:** 0. **Hookups:** Water, electric. **Each Site:** Picnic table, fire ring, clothes poles. **Dump Station:** Yes. **Laundry:** No. **Pay Phone:** Yes. **Rest Rooms and Showers:** Yes. **Fuel:** No. **Propane:** No. **Internal Roads:** Paved, in good condition & somewhat bumpy dirt roads. **RV Service:** No. **Market:** 3 mi. south on SR 166 to US 90, 2 mi. east to town. **Restaurant:** 3 mi. south on SR 166 to US 90, 2 mi. east to town. **General Store:** Yes. **Vending:** Yes. **Swimming Pool:** Blue Hole spring-fed pond & beach. **Playground:** No. **Other:** Cave, visitors center features geologic & historic exhibits, golf course, boat launch. **Activities:** Guided cave

tours, swimming, canoeing, hiking, fishing, golf. **Additional Information:** Jackson County Chamber of Commerce, (850) 482-8061.

RESTRICTIONS

Pets: On leash only. **Fires:** Fire ring only. **Alcoholic Beverages:** Not allowed. **Vehicle Maximum Length:** 30 ft. **Other:** No firearms, no fireworks.

TO GET THERE

On SR 166 (Caverns Rd), 3 mi. north of US 90.

MELBOURNE BEACH

Sebastian Inlet State Recreation Area

9700 S. A1A, Melbourne Beach 32951. T: (407) 984-4852 or (561) 589-9659 or (321) 984-4852; www.myflorida.com.

🚐 ★★★★   ⛺ ★★★★

Beauty: ★★★★   Site Privacy: ★★
Spaciousness: ★★★   Quiet: ★★★★
Security: ★★★★★   Cleanliness: ★★★★★
Insect Control: ★★★★   Facilities: ★★★★★

Although there aren't a lot of trees to shade the campsites at Sebastian Inlet State Recreation Area, neither are there many obstructions to the view. This is one of the few campgrounds we found that allows campers overnight positions on the waterfront. In this case, sites 1–14 look across the road and directly over Sebastian Inlet, and sites 35–50 on the other side of the campground sit on a tidal lagoon, although the view may be somewhat obscured by brush and sea grape trees, a few strangler figs, sabal palm, and gumbo limbo trees. Wood storks and mocking birds can be seen foraging along the shoreline and among the plants. This state park also offers an unusual bonus, the waterfront restaurant that serves lunch and breakfast. Finally, this beach is known as one of the best surfing areas in the world and hosts several international surfing competitions.

BASICS

Operated By: Florida Dept. of Environmental Protection, Division of Recreation & Parks. **Open:** All year. **Site Assignment:** Reservations accepted up to 11 months in advance, 1-night stay refundable up to 24 hours in advance. **Registration:** Ranger's office or park entrance gate. **Fee:** $15 May–Nov., $19 Dec.–Apr.; M,V, D,AE. **Parking:** Yes.

FACILITIES

Number of RV Sites: 51. **Number of Tent-Only Sites:** 0. **Hookups:** Water, electric (30 amps). **Each Site:** Picnic table, fire ring. **Dump Station:** Yes. **Laundry:** Yes. **Pay Phone:** Yes. **Rest Rooms and Showers:** Yes. **Fuel:** No. **Propane:** No. **Internal Roads:** Paved, in good condition. **RV Service:** Referral. **Market:** About 6 mi. north on Hwy. A1A in Melbourne Beach. **Restaurant:** Park offers ocean-side café serving breakfast & lunch, or 6 mi. north on A1A. **General Store:** Yes. **Vending:** Yes. **Swimming Pool:** No (Indian River & Ocean). **Playground:** No. **Other:** Boat dock, ramp & marina w/ boat, canoe, kayak, & pontoon rentals; Fishing museum & Treasure museum. **Activities:** Fishing, boating, swimming, surfing. **Nearby Attractions:** Pelican Island National Wildlife Refuge, immediately south of Sebastian Inlet State Recreation Area on A1A. **Additional Information:** Melbourne/Palm Bay Area Chamber of Commerce, (800) 771-9922, www.melpb-chamber.org.

RESTRICTIONS

Pets: On leash only. **Fires:** In grill or fire ring only. **Alcoholic Beverages:** Not allowed. **Vehicle Maximum Length:** None. **Other:** Quiet time 11 p.m.–8 a.m., no firearms or fireworks.

TO GET THERE

US 1 to Wabasso, CR 510 east 5 mi. through "Town of Orchid" to A1A, north 7 mi. to Sebastian State Recreation Area.

MEXICO BEACH/PANAMA CITY
Rustic Sands RV Resort

800 N 15th St., Mexico Beach 32456. T: (850) 648-5229; F: (850) 648-4349; rentacabin@aol.com.

🚐 ★★★   ▲ ★★

Beauty: ★★	Site Privacy: ★★
Spaciousness: ★★	Quiet: ★★
Security: ★★★	Cleanliness: ★★★★
Insect Control: ★★★	Facilities: ★★★

This campground is near, but not on, the busy strip near Panama City Beach. It's less than a mile away from the ocean and has a boat ramp and all the joys that come with both. The campground

itself offers a small fishing pond for those content with the more restful atmosphere under tall pine trees. Bird houses have been erected to provide habitat for the feathered snow birds known to pass through on annual treks. A pool was under construction so should be available by time of publication, and kids will enjoy the playground and basketball courts. Pleasantly grassy campsites are 20 feet wide and laid out in circles. Some have bushy buffers, but they're not very private. Some have pull-through capability. Tiny cabins and mobile-home sites are available for rental, but traveling RVers and tenters are welcome.

BASICS

Operated By: Manager. **Open:** All year. **Site Assignment:** First come, first served. **Registration:** Office. **Fee:** $18; MC, D,V. **Parking:** Yes.

FACILITIES

Number of RV Sites: 32. **Number of Tent-Only Sites:** 16. **Hookups:** Water, electric (30 amps.), sewer, cable TV, phone. **Each Site:** Picnic table. **Dump Station:** Yes. **Laundry:** Yes. **Pay Phone:** Yes. **Rest Rooms and Showers:** Yes. **Fuel:** No. **Propane:** Yes. **Internal Roads:** Crushed shell in good condition. **RV Service:** Referral. **Market:** 0.75 mi. to US 98. **Restaurant:** 0.75 mi. to US 98. **General Store:** Yes. **Vending:** Yes. **Swimming Pool:** Yes. **Playground:** Yes. **Other:** Fishing pond, rec hall. **Activities:** Fishing, swimming, boating. **Nearby Attractions:** Beach, marina w/ boat ramp & boat charters. **Additional Information:** Panama City Beaches Chamber of Commerce, (850) 235-1159, www.pcbeach.org.

RESTRICTIONS

Pets: On leash only. **Fires:** Yes. **Alcoholic Beverages:** Allowed. **Vehicle Maximum Length:** None.

TO GET THERE

US 98 to N. 15th St., 0.75 mi. north to entrance on left.

MIAMI

Miami/Everglades KOA Kampground

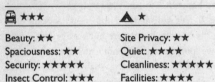

20675 SW 162nd Ave., Miami 33187. T: (305) 233-5300 or (800) 562-7732; www.miamicamp.com; admin@koamiami.com.

🚐 ★★★   ▲ ★

Beauty: ★★	Site Privacy: ★★
Spaciousness: ★★	Quiet: ★★★★
Security: ★★★★★	Cleanliness: ★★★★★
Insect Control: ★★★	Facilities: ★★★★

Miami/Everglades KOA Kampground provides the standards ensured by KOA, so while crowds can be expected, travelers can also rely on cleanliness and comfort. Set amid Miami-Dade County farms—which feed the nation during the winter months—this quiet and peaceful yet somewhat lonely campground was once a grove and still boasts mature avocado and mango trees throughout the grounds and even on several sites. Fruit is free for those who wish to pluck it from the branches. Coconut trees and cascading fuchsia bouganvillea complete the subtropical atmosphere. The park is 25 miles south of Miami and 6 miles east of Everglades National Park, providing easy access to the best attractions South Florida has to offer. Sites are side-by-side, most are pull-through, almost giving the less-than-pleasant effect of a parking lot. The best sites are on the outer edges, the west side of the campground offers more shade trees. Tent sites offer no privacy and no ambience. A fine place to park while visiting the area, but not a destination in itself.

BASICS

Operated By: Managers Jim & Julia Champion. **Open:** All year. **Site Assignment:** Reservations recommended, $25 deposit, refunds up to 4 p.m. day prior. **Registration:** Camp office. **Fee:** $34; MC, V, D, AE. **Parking:** Yes.

FACILITIES

Number of RV Sites: 257. **Number of Tent-Only Sites:** 13. **Hookups:** Water, electric (30, 50 amps), sewer. **Each Site:** Picnic table, tree. **Dump Station:** Yes. **Laundry:** Yes. **Pay Phone:** Yes. **Rest Rooms and Showers:** Yes. **Fuel:** No. **Propane:** Yes. **Internal Roads:** Paved, in good condition. **RV**

Service: Mobile RV service available. **Market:** Farmers markets open Dec.–May, 1.5 mi. west on Krome Ave., or go about 5 mi. south on Krome to find a grocery in Homestead. **Restaurant:** 5 mi. east on Quail Roost to Miami or 5 mi. southwest in Homestead. **General Store:** Yes. **Vending:** Yes. **Swimming Pool:** Yes. **Playground:** Yes. **Other:** Soccer field. **Activities:** Soccer, shuffleboard, volleyball. **Nearby Attractions:** Monkey Jungle, Everglades National Park, city of Miami, Florida Keys, Indian Casino. **Additional Information:** Greater Miami CVB, (888) 76-MIAMI, www.tropicoolmiami.com.

RESTRICTIONS

Pets: On leash only. **Fires:** In grills only. **Alcoholic Beverages:** Allowed. **Vehicle Maximum Length:** None.

TO GET THERE

Exit Florida Turnpike 13, Eureka Dr. (SW 184 St.), west to SW 117 Ave., south 1 mi. to Quail Roost Dr., west 5 mi. to campground.

MICANOPY

Paynes Prairie State Preserve

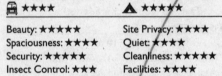

100 Savannah Blvd., Micanopy 32667. T: (352) 466-3397; F: (352) 466-4297; www.AFN.org/`prairie; Prairie@AFN.org.

🚐 ★★★★   ▲ ★★★★★

Beauty: ★★★★★	Site Privacy: ★★★★
Spaciousness: ★★★★	Quiet: ★★★★
Security: ★★★★★	Cleanliness: ★★★★★
Insect Control: ★★★	Facilities: ★★★★

This 21,000-acre wildlife preserve is quite unique, as it provides a safe home for free roaming wild horses, herds of bison, and "cracker" cattle brought to the state by Spanish pioneers. Visitors are quite likely to encounter deer and perhaps even these more unusual animals during a camp stay. An observation tower provides a panoramic view of the prairie—take binoculars so you'll be sure to capture images when you see the buffalo roam across the prairie. The two small campground loops of the Puc Puggy Campground (named for the nickname of the prairie's founder, William Bartram) provide a quiet hideaway, with wooded terrain and sand and dirt underfoot. None of the sites are pull-through, but there is some vegetation separating each from the next. The camping area is a short hike from the lake.

BASICS

Operated By: Florida Dept. of Environmental Protection, Division of Recreation & Parks. **Open:** All year. **Site Assignment:** First come, first served, reservations accepted up to 11 months in advance by credit card, cancellations refundable up to 24 hours in advance. **Registration:** Park office. **Fee:** $13; MC, V. **Parking:** Yes.

FACILITIES

Number of RV Sites: 35. **Number of Tent-Only Sites:** 15. **Hookups:** Electric, water. **Each Site:** Picnic table, grill. **Dump Station:** Yes. **Laundry:** No. **Pay Phone:** Yes. **Rest Rooms and Showers:** Yes. **Fuel:** No. **Propane:** No. **Internal Roads:** Paved, in good condition. **RV Service:** No. **Market:** US 441 south 1 mi. to small grocery store. **Restaurant:** US 441 north 8 mi. to Gainesville. **General Store:** No. **Vending:** No. **Swimming Pool:** No. **Playground:** Yes. **Other:** Wildlife preserve, hiking, biking, horse trails, observation tower, visitors center. **Activities:** Fishing, boating, hiking, horseback riding, educational programs, guided trail hikes. **Nearby Attractions:** Antique stores in historic Old Micanopy, Historic home of Marjorie Kinnan Rawlings in nearby Cross Creek. **Additional Information:** Alachua County CVB, (352) 374-5260.

RESTRICTIONS

Pets: On leash & on paved roads only, not allowed in campground. **Fires:** In grills unless restrictions in effect. **Alcoholic Beverages:** Not allowed. **Vehicle Maximum Length:** None. **Other:** No firearms, no fireworks, no feeding wildlife, no collecting firewood, stay on established trails. Quiet time 11 p.m.–6 a.m.

TO GET THERE

I-75 to Exit 75/Micanopy, 2 mi. east to US 441 north 1 mi. to park entrance on right.

OHIO KEY
Sunshine Key Fun Resort

38801 Overseas Hwy., Big Pine Key 33043.
T: (305) 872-2217; F: (305) 872-3801; www.RVON THEGO.com; NHCFLSK@Terranova.net.

 ★★★   ★★★

Beauty: ★★   Site Privacy: ★
Spaciousness: ★   Quiet: ★★
Security: ★★★★★   Cleanliness: ★★★★★
Insect Control: ★★★★   Facilities: ★★★★★

A great campground for RVers who love to boat and fish—this Encore property offers a boat dock as well as a few waterfront sites under the perpetual sunshine of the Florida Keys. Book early, especially for winter visits. Gravel and white sand underfoot and scattered small trees and bushes give a stark appearance. There are virtually no buffers between sites: this location is here for recreation, not the wilderness experience, although registered campers can visit a bird sanctuary across the highway. Tennis and basketball courts at the campground add to the fun, and a pool-side snack bar provides refreshment.

BASICS

Operated By: National Homes Community/ Encore. **Open:** All year. **Site Assignment:** By request on site or by phone in advance, 1-night rental deposit by credit card, refundable up to 7 days prior. **Registration:** Office. **Fee:** $25; MC, V, D, AE. **Parking:** Yes.

FACILITIES

Number of RV Sites: 397. **Number of Tent-Only Sites:** 0. **Hookups:** Electric (30, 50 amps), water, sewer, cable TV. **Each Site:** Tables. **Dump Station:** Yes. **Laundry:** Yes. **Pay Phone:** Yes. **Rest Rooms and Showers:** Yes. **Fuel:** Yes. **Propane:** Yes. **Internal Roads:** Paved & gravel, in good condition. **RV Service:** Referral. **Market:** 8 mi. south to Big Pine Key. **Restaurant:** 8 mi. south to Big Pine Key (plus pool side café for breakfast & lunch). **General Store:** Yes. **Vending:** Yes. **Swimming Pool:** Yes. **Playground:** No. **Other:** Game room, basketball, volleyball, horseshoes, tennis court, shuffleboard, boat marina. **Activities:** Boating, fishing, kayaking, scuba, snorkeling (rentals available), winter recreation program includes bingo, shows, & dinners. **Nearby Attractions:** Beach, Key West is 61 mi. away. **Additional Information:** Florida Keys & Key West Tourist Council, (800) 648-5510, www.fla-keys.com.

RESTRICTIONS

Pets: On leash only. **Fires:** In grill only (not provided). **Alcoholic Beverages:** Allowed. **Vehicle Maximum Length:** 45 ft. **Other:** Max. 6 campers per site.

To Get There

US 1 south from Miami 61 mi. to mile marker 39, campground on west (Gulfside).

OKEECHOBEE
Zachary Taylor Camping Resort

2995 Hwy. 441 S.E., Okeechobee 34974. T: (863) 763-3377 or (reservations only): 888-282-6523; www.campfloridarv.com; ZTResort@ictransnet.com.

🚐 ★★★★   ⛺ ★★★

Beauty: ★★★★	Site Privacy: ★★
Spaciousness: ★★★	Quiet: ★★★★
Security: ★★★★★	Cleanliness: ★★★★★
Insect Control: ★★★★	Facilities: ★★★★★

This rural campground has been run by Chuck Freed for a quarter century. A haven for fisherpeople, the most scenic campsites abut Taylor creek, which flows into Lake Okeechobee, the state's largest lake and well known for its premium bass fishing. In times of drought the connection to the lake is blocked by manmade dike. Nonetheless, proximity to the lake makes this campground a favorite for those who love to fish. Supplies are only a short distance away in the town of Okeechobee, too. Tall moss-draped cypress trees shade many sites and lean out over the river, narrow wooden docks lead out from the waterfront sites for boaters access, and alligators, turtles, and herons share the river while gray squirrels scamper along the banks. Bird calls and the whistling of a nearby train provide a nighttime lullaby. Paved circular roads shared by about 100 permanent renters and 150 sites for travelers (each with concrete pads surrounded by grass and trees) wind through the camp. Cabins, a rec hall, and screened pool are provided as well as small separate toilet and shower stalls—be sure to ask for the key to the always-locked facilities reserved for overnight guests. Late arrivals can call ahead, and instructions will be posted at the entrance gate or on-site security guard will greet and guide you after hours.

Basics

Operated By: Owners Chuck & Fran Freed. **Open:** All year. **Site Assignment:** Reservations welcome, non-refundable deposit required. **Registration:** Office. **Fee:** $29; MC, V. **Parking:** Yes.

Facilities

Number of RV Sites: 250. **Number of Tent-Only Sites:** 0. **Hookups:** Electric (30 amps), water, sewage. **Each Site:** Picnic table, fire rings on waterfront sites. **Dump Station:** Yes. **Laundry:** Yes. **Pay Phone:** Yes. **Rest Rooms and Showers:** Yes ($2 key deposit). **Fuel:** No. **Propane:** No. **Internal Roads:** Paved, in good condition. **RV Service:** Referral. **Market:** 3 mi. north on US 441 in Okeechobee. **Restaurant:** 3 mi. north on US 441 in Okeechobee. **General Store:** Yes. **Vending:** Yes. **Swimming Pool:** Yes. **Playground:** No. **Other:** Boat Ramp, open grassy field for play. **Activities:** Fishing, boating (rental available), shuffleboard, horseshoes, group crafts in winter, holiday parties, fishing tournaments. **Nearby Attractions:** Lake Okeechobee, Brighton Indian gaming casino. **Additional Information:** Okeechobee County Tourist Development Council, (863) 763-3959, (800) 871-4403.

Restrictions

Pets: On leash only. **Fires:** In grill or fire ring only. **Alcoholic Beverages:** Allowed. **Vehicle Maximum Length:** 40 ft.—call for availability. **Other:** 1 car per site, 1 family per site.

To Get There

From US 441 south from Okeechobee 2 mi. to US 441 east 1 mi. to SE 30th Terrace, left (north) to campground entrance.

OUTDOOR RESORTS OF CHOKOLUSKEE
Outdoor Resorts of Chokoluskee

P.O. Box 39, Chokoluskee 34138. F: (941) 695-3338; www.outdoor-resorts.com.

🚐 ★★★★★   ⛺ ★★★★

Beauty: ★★★	Site Privacy: ★★★
Spaciousness: ★★★	Quiet: ★★★
Security: ★★★★	Cleanliness: ★★★★★
Insect Control: ★★★	Facilities: ★★★★

This owner-occupied park offers rental units as well as sites for travelers. Sites are large, with concrete pads and grass, some on the waterfront. On the Turner River, which runs from the Everglades and out to the Gulf of Mexico after passing through the intricate Ten Thousand Islands, the park offers a marina and boat, canoe and kayak rentals as well as fishing gear. But with many other amenities, such as three swimming pools and tennis courts, there's plenty to do for those who aren't interested in fishing, too.

BASICS

Operated By: Manager Kenny Brown. **Open:** All year. **Site Assignment:** Reservations accepted, 1-night deposit required, refunded w/ at least 7-day notice cancellation. **Registration:** Office. **Fee:** $40. **Parking:** Yes.

FACILITIES

Number of RV Sites: 283. **Number of Tent-Only Sites:** 0. **Hookups:** Water, electric (30, 50 amps), sewer, cable TV, phone. **Each Site:** None. **Dump Station:** Yes. **Laundry:** Yes. **Pay Phone:** No. **Rest Rooms and Showers:** Yes. **Fuel:** Yes. **Propane:** No. **Internal Roads:** Paved, in good condition. **RV Service:** Referral. **Market:** 2 mi. north in Everglades City. **Restaurant:** 2 mi. north in Everglades City. **General Store:** Yes. **Vending:** No. **Swimming Pool:** Yes (3 pools). **Playground:** No. **Other:** Tennis courts, shuffleboard, rec hall, weight room, marina. **Activities:** Winter activities include dinners, bingo, ice cream socials, craft exhibits, etc. **Nearby Attractions:** Ten Thousand Islands, Everglades National Park. **Additional Information:** Everglades Chamber of Commerce.

RESTRICTIONS

Pets: Yes. **Fires:** In grill only. **Alcoholic Beverages:** Yes, in moderation. **Vehicle Maximum Length:** 45 ft. plus.

TO GET THERE

US 41 from Miami (60 mi.) or Naples (40 mi.) to CR 29, south through Everglades City across 3 mi. causeway to Chokoluskee, to campground on left.

PALM BAY
Lazy K RV Park

5150 Dixie Hwy., N.E., Palm Bay 32905. T: (321) 724-1639.

🚐 ★★★   ▲ n/a

Beauty: ★★   Site Privacy: ★
Spaciousness: ★   Quiet: ★★★
Security: ★★★★★   Cleanliness: ★★★★
Insect Control: ★★★   Facilities: ★★

This small, private RV park is one of only a few along this central eastern segment of Florida's coastline. Clean and well maintained by owners, who live on the premises, sites are large and grassy, with a concrete pad, with a few trees and bushes scattered among them, and a backdrop of trees surrounding the U-shaped park. A dog walk runs along the adjacent railroad track, but one of the nicest features at this small mom-and-pop park is the view. Across the street from the park is the Intracoastal Waterway (known here as the Indian River), providing a lovely scene.

BASICS

Operated By: Owners Terry & Pat. **Open:** All year. **Site Assignment:** First come, first served. **Registration:** Park office. **Fee:** $18; M, V. **Parking:** Limited.

FACILITIES

Number of RV Sites: 63. **Number of Tent-Only Sites:** 0. **Hookups:** Water, electric (30, 50 amps), sewer, cable TV, phone. **Each Site:** Picnic table. **Dump Station:** Yes. **Laundry:** Yes. **Pay Phone:** Yes. **Rest Rooms and Showers:** Yes. **Fuel:** No. **Propane:** No. **Internal Roads:** Paved, in good condition. **RV Service:** Referral. **Market:** 3 mi. north to Palm Bay Rd., 2 mi. west. **Restaurant:** 3 mi. north to Palm Bay Rd., 2 mi. west. **General Store:** No. **Vending:** No. **Swimming Pool:** No. **Playground:** No. **Other:** Intracoastal Waterway across the street. **Activities:** Fishing, swimming, boating. **Nearby Attractions:** Beach. **Additional Information:** Palm Bay Area Chamber of Commerce, (800) 276-9130, www.palmbaychamber.com.

RESTRICTIONS

Pets: On leash only. **Fires:** In grill only. **Alcoholic Beverages:** Allowed. **Vehicle Maximum Length:** Big rigs welcome. **Other:** No tents.

TO GET THERE

I-95 Exit 70, east on Hwy. 514 4 mi. to US 1, north 0.5 mi.

PANAMA CITY BEACH
Emerald Coast RV Beach Resort

1957 Allison Ave., Panama City Beach 32407. T: (850)235-0924 or (800) BEACH-RV; F: (850) 235-9609; www.RVResort.com; ECRVBR@aol.com.

🚐 ★★★★★   ▲ ★★

Beauty: ★★★   Site Privacy: ★★
Spaciousness: ★★★   Quiet: ★★★
Security: ★★★★★   Cleanliness: ★★★★★
Insect Control: ★★★★★   Facilities: ★★★★★

Given top designations by industry campground rating services, the Emerald Coast RV Beach Resort bills itself as "the highest-rated resort in North America." The four-year-old resort has earned the compliment by creating a clean, well-manicured park with comfortable clubhouse and amenities—including big-screen TV—all kept in top condition. Premium cable channels are available on-site as well. For those who find concrete roads, pads, and patios plus two trees too ascetic, a pair of stocked fishing lakes and recreational area abut the camper lots, providing a taste of nature. Colorful lilies and oleander bloom throughout the park, lending the tropical flair of Florida to the easy living provided at Emerald Coast. Even mosquitoes aren't too bad, thanks to an underground drainage system that eliminates bug-breeding grounds. Daily trash pickup at each site is another big plus that helps keep the park spotless and vermin-free. Many sites are pull-through, and "super sites" can accommodate the largest vehicles with triple slideouts.

BASICS

Operated By: Owners Mr. & Mrs. Hartka. **Open:** All year. **Site Assignment:** Reservations accepted by phone w/ 1-day deposit, $50 for week, or $100 for month; cancellations w/ 14-day notice, less $10 administrative fee. **Registration:** Office. **Fee:** $32; MC, V. **Parking:** Yes.

FACILITIES

Number of RV Sites: 143. **Number of Tent-Only Sites:** No tents or pop-ups allowed. **Hookups:** Water, electric (30, 50 amps), sewer, cable TV, phone. **Each Site:** Table. **Dump Station:** Yes. **Laundry:** Yes. **Pay Phone:** Yes. **Rest Rooms and Showers:** Yes. **Fuel:** No. **Propane:** Yes. **Internal Roads:** Paved, in good condition. **RV Service:** Referral. **Market:** 0.75 mi. west on US 98 to supermarket. **Restaurant:** 0.75 mi. west on US 98. **General Store:** Yes. **Vending:** Yes. **Swimming Pool:** Yes. **Playground:** Yes. **Other:** Rec room w/ computer & free e-mail, free coffee, putting green, shuffleboard, sand volleyball, fishing lake, bike rentals, horseshoes, sandbox. **Activities:** Free shuttle to the beach, family cookouts, breakfasts, bingo, card games, movies, organized outings to area restaurants & attractions. **Nearby Attractions:** Zoo next door, beach, pier & boat charters, outlet shopping mall, 18-hole golf course, amusement park.

Additional Information: Panama City Beach CVB, (800) PC-BEACH, www.800pcbeach.com.

RESTRICTIONS

Pets: Gentle breeds only, leash required. **Fires:** In grill only. **Alcoholic Beverages:** Allowed. **Vehicle Maximum Length:** None. **Other:** No tents or pop-ups.

TO GET THERE

Park is on Allison Ave. between US 98 and Alt. 98, 1.5 mi. west of Hathaway Bridge (SR 231).

PENSACOLA

Bayside Pensacola—Perdido Bay Kampground Resort

33951 Spinnaker Dr., Lillian 36549. T: (334) 961-1717 or (800) 562-3471; F: (334) 961-1717; www.koa.com/where/fl/01102.htm; perdidokoa@gulftel.com.

🚐 ★★★★	🏕 ★★★
Beauty: ★★★	Site Privacy: ★★
Spaciousness: ★★★★	Quiet: ★★★★
Security: ★★★★★	Cleanliness: ★★★★★
Insect Control: ★★★	Facilities: ★★★★★

We planned to end our day on Perdido Key outside Pensacola so we could spend the evening at the legendary rock/country pub and club, the Florabama on the state line. Alas, each campground we found on the island appeared to be nothing more than a beach-side or near-beach parking lot, wall-to-wall with metal traveling vehicles. We kept on going, right across the Florida line into Alabama, where suddenly rolling green hills and a herd of frolicking deer in the twilight convinced us that we had found the best place around. We settled in at the KOA on Perdido Bay. With 80 pull-through sites and a dock that runs down to the bay, this campground looked like paradise.

BASICS

Operated By: Owner Denise Valentyne. **Open:** All year. **Site Assignment:** Reservations accepted, 1-night deposit, refundable 24 hours. **Registration:** Park office. **Fee:** $23. **Parking:** Yes.

FACILITIES

Number of RV Sites: 100. **Number of Tent-Only Sites:** 10. **Hookups:** Water, electric (30, 50 amps), sewer, cable TV. **Each Site:** Picnic table. **Dump Station:** Yes. **Laundry:** Yes. **Pay Phone:**

Yes. **Rest Rooms and Showers:** Yes. **Fuel:** No. **Propane:** No. **Internal Roads:** Paved, in good condition. **RV Service:** Referral. **Market:** 4 mi. east. **Restaurant:** 3 mi. east or west. **General Store:** Yes. **Vending:** Yes. **Swimming Pool:** Yes. **Playground:** Yes. **Other:** Basketball court, boat ramp & pier, rec room, shuffleboard, horseshoes, RV wash station. **Activities:** Saturday wagon rides & ice-cream socials. **Nearby Attractions:** Gulf Shores National Seashore. **Additional Information:** Pensacola Convention & Visitor Center, (800) 874-1234, www.visitpensacola.com; Perdido Key Area Chamber of Commerce, (800) 328-0107, www.perdidochamber.com.

RESTRICTIONS

Pets: On leash only. **Fires:** In grills & designated areas only. **Alcoholic Beverages:** Allowed. **Vehicle Maximum Length:** None. **Other:** No fireworks, no generators, no clotheslines, quiet hours 10 p.m.–8 a.m.

TO GET THERE

From I-10 or Alt 90 in Pensacola, west to Hwy. 297 south to Blue Angel Rd., south to Bauer Rd./US 98, 3 mi. west across Perdido Bay into Alabama, first left after bridge is Hwy. 99, south to campground.

PORT ST. JOE (APALACHICOLA, PANAMA CITY)

Indian Pass Campground

2817 Indian Pass Rd., Port St. Joe 32456. T: (850) 227-7203; www.indianpasscharters.com/campground; daniel2@gtcom.net.

🚐 ★★★	⛺ ★★★★
Beauty: ★★★★	Site Privacy: ★★★
Spaciousness: ★★★	Quiet: ★★★★
Security: ★★★	Cleanliness: ★★★
Insect Control: ★★	Facilities: ★★★★

Bugs! A pod of dolphin has been seen playing in adjacent Indian Pass Sound, alligators live there and swim past the campground occasionally, a 12-foot shark sighted recently, swimming the off-shore waters. St. Vincent Island, visible from the campground, is a national wildlife refuge and home to a red wolf–breeding and reintroduction program as well as to 500–600 pound sambar deer, exotic animals from southeast Asia, introduced by the island's previous private owners in

the early 1900s along with other non-native game for hunters. The campground itself is beautiful and scenic, with honeysuckle-scented air, although just as rustic as you might guess for a fisherman's hideout.

BASICS

Operated By: Owners, the Captains of Indian Pass Charters. **Open:** All year. **Site Assignment:** First come, first served; reservations accepted, no deposit required. **Registration:** Office. **Fee:** Call ahead for details. **Parking:** Yes.

FACILITIES

Number of RV Sites: 38. **Number of Tent-Only Sites:** 0. **Hookups:** Water, electric (30, 50 amps.). **Each Site:** Picnic table. **Dump Station:** Yes. **Laundry:** Yes. **Pay Phone:** Yes. **Rest Rooms and Showers:** Yes. **Fuel:** Yes. **Propane:** No. **Internal Roads:** Gravel. **RV Service:** Referral. **Market:** 3.5 mi. west to Indian Pass. **Restaurant:** 3.5 mi. west to Indian Pass. **General Store:** Yes. **Vending:** Yes. **Swimming Pool:** Yes. **Playground:** No. **Other:** Boat ramp. **Activities:** Fishing, charters available. **Nearby Attractions:** National Wildlife Habitat. **Additional Information:** Apalachicola Bay Chamber of Commerce, (850) 653-9419, www.baynavigator.com.

RESTRICTIONS

Pets: Welcome, leashed if necessary. **Fires:** Fire rings only. **Alcoholic Beverages:** Allowed. **Vehicle Maximum Length:** 45 ft.

TO GET THERE

From Apalachicola, travel west on Hwy. 98 approximately 6 mi., follow left fork on C30, 9 mi. west/left, to C30B/Indian Pass Rd. south/left 3.5 mi.

SANTA ROSA BEACH

Grayton Beach State Recreation Area

357 Main Park Rd., Santa Rosa Beach 32549. T: (850) 231-4210; www.myflorida.com.

🚐 ★★★★	⛺ ★★★★★
Beauty: ★★★★★	Site Privacy: ★★★★
Spaciousness: ★★★	Quiet: ★★★★★
Security: ★★★★★	Cleanliness: ★★★★★
Insect Control: ★★★	Facilities: ★★★★★

Sandwiched between the tourist meccas of Seaside—an urban demonstration project touted as an ecologically-sound pedestrian community but looking more like a lot of tightly packed tourist dwellings—and Sandestin, a resort hotel community that similarly packs in huge numbers of vacationers, Grayton Beach State Recreation Area offers a glimpse of the world's best beaches without being marred by rows of rooftops or other burdens of civilization. Here is a place where citizens can really appreciate the preservation of land via government park systems. The broad, white-sand beaches and turquoise waters clearly deserve the recurring annual recognitions they receive, and thousands upon thousands of people (and birds) flock to this haven of American beauty. Park rangers distribute a guide to area birds visitors might watch for, from grosbeaks to grebes, herons to hawks, with a cuckoo or two, loons, and starlings. Though small, Grayton Beach provides a perfect, quiet respite from the booming cities surrounding it, perhaps one of the last bastions of safety for passing birds and snowbirds alike.

BASICS

Operated By: Florida Dept. of Environmental Protection, Division of Recreation & Parks. **Open:** All year. **Site Assignment:** Reservations accepted up to 11 months in advance, 1-night deposit required. **Registration:** Office. **Fee:** $10 Oct.–Feb., $16 Mar.–Sept.; AE, MC, V, D. **Parking:** Yes.

FACILITIES

Number of RV Sites: 37. **Number of Tent-Only Sites:** 0. **Hookups:** Water, electric. **Each Site:** Picnic table, fire ring, clothesline poles. **Dump Station:** Yes. **Laundry:** No. **Pay Phone:** Yes. **Rest Rooms and Showers:** Yes. **Fuel:** No. **Propane:** No. **Internal Roads:** Paved & shell, in good condition. **RV Service:** Referral. **Market:** 12 mi. west on Hwy. 98. **Restaurant:** 12 mi. west on Hwy. 98. **General Store:** No. **Vending:** Yes. **Swimming Pool:** No. **Playground:** No. **Other:** One of the best beaches in the nation, hiking trails, boat ramp. **Activities:** Swimming, fishing, boating, hiking, birding. **Nearby Attractions:** Eglin Air Force Base. **Additional Information:** South Walton Tourist Development Council, (800) 822-6877, www.beachesofsouthwalton.com.

RESTRICTIONS

Pets: Not allowed in campground. **Fires:** In grill only. **Alcoholic Beverages:** Not allowed. **Vehicle Maximum Length:** None.

TO GET THERE

US 98 west from Panama City Beach to CR 30A—scenic coastal route—to park, just west of Seaside.

SANTA ROSA BEACH

Top Sail Hill Preserve State Park: Gregory E. Moore RV Resort

7525 W. County Hwy. 30A, Santa Rosa Beach 32459. T: (850) 267-0299; (877) BEACH-RV; F: (850) 267-9014; www.topsailhill.com; topsailhill@gnt.net.

🚍 ★★★★★   ▲ n/a

Beauty: ★★★   Site Privacy: ★★★★
Spaciousness: ★★★★   Quiet: ★★★★
Security: ★★★★★   Cleanliness: ★★★★★
Insect Control: ★★★★★   Facilities: ★★★★★

Proud recipient of top ratings from two RV industry watchdogs, the Gregory E. Moore RV Resort at Topsail Hill Preserve State Park is the crown of camper habitats. Well-manicured and trimmed, the RV parking areas offer bushy buffers amid scattered tall pines lining concrete drives, pads, and patios. Twenty pull-through sites are available for the largest rigs around.

BASICS

Operated By: Florida Dept. of Environmental Protection, Division of Recreation & Parks. **Open:** All year. **Site Assignment:** First come, first served or reservations accepted w/ deposit, refundable up to 24 hours in advance. **Registration:** Office. **Fee:** $32; MC, V, D. **Parking:** Yes.

FACILITIES

Number of RV Sites: 156. **Number of Tent-Only Sites:** 0. **Hookups:** Water, electric (30, 50 amps), sewer, cable TV. **Each Site:** Picnic table, grills at pull-through sites. **Dump Station:** No. **Laundry:** Yes. **Pay Phone:** Yes. **Rest Rooms and Showers:** Yes. **Fuel:** No. **Propane:** Yes. **Internal Roads:** Paved. **RV Service:** Referral. **Market:** 2 mi. east on Hwy. 98. **Restaurant:** 0.25 mi. south on Hwy. 30A. **General Store:** Yes. **Vending:** Yes. **Swimming Pool:** Yes. **Playground:** No. **Other:** 1,650-acre preserve w/ hiking trails & bike path, tennis courts, shuffleboard, basketball, 3 lakes, clubhouse w/ library. **Activities:** Fishing, biking, hiking,. **Nearby Attractions:** 1 mi. walking trail to top-rated beach. **Additional Information:** South Walton Tourist Development Council, (800) 822-6877, www.beachesofsouthwalton.com.

RESTRICTIONS

Pets: On leash only, proof of vaccinations required. **Fires:** In grill only. **Alcoholic Beverages:** After hours only. **Vehicle Maximum Length:** None. **Other:** No tents (pop-ups okay), quiet hours 11 p.m.–7 a.m.

TO GET THERE

From US 98 and Hwy. 30A near Sandestin, south 0.25 mi. on 30A to park entrance.

SARASOTA
Myaka River State Park

13207 SR 72, Sarasota 34241. T: (941) 361-6511; F: (941) 361-6501; www.myaka.sarasota.fl.us.

🚐 ★★★   ▲ ★★★★

Beauty: ★★★★★   Site Privacy: ★★★
Spaciousness: ★★★   Quiet: ★★★★★
Security: ★★★★★   Cleanliness: ★★★★
Insect Control: ★★★   Facilities: ★★★★

Scenic and swampy, this alligator habitat is well known as home to a number of incredible birds, including bald eagles, great blue herons, great horned owls, sandhill cranes, wild turkeys, and ruby-throated hummingbirds, and as rest stop for passers-by, such as the roseate spoonbill, loons, Canadian geese, mallards, and peregrine falcons. Local volunteers even built a bridge that lifts observers seven flights of stairs into the tree tops to gain perspective on life among their feathered friends. Other creatures include fox, bobcat, deer, wild hogs, and the occasional black bear. Campers can enjoy the campgrounds, which can get a bit swampy during rainy season, usually Aug. and Sept., when the mosquitoes are out in full force. Many visitors bring their boats along to explore the lakes and the wild and scenic Myaka River, so named as part of a government preservation program that will protect it from scientific "engineering," a common practice designed to improve conditions but which ultimately is often discovered to bring negative results for tampering with nature. Myaka was one of Florida's first state parks, so it has been well preserved. Cabins here are very nice, built by the Civilian Conservation Corps in the 1930s and still sturdy—much larger and nicer than modern campground 'cabins'.

BASICS

Operated By: Florida Dept. of Environmental Protection, Division of Recreation & Parks. **Open:** All year. **Site Assignment:** Reservations accepted up to 11 months in advance, 1-night deposit, refundable if cancelled by 5 p.m. the day before. **Registration:** Office. **Fee:** $15 May–Nov., $18 Dec.–Apr.; M, V, D, AE. **Parking:** Yes.

FACILITIES

Number of RV Sites: 48. **Number of Tent-Only Sites:** 28. **Hookups:** Water, electric (20, 30 amps). **Each Site:** Picnic table, grill or fire ring. **Dump Station:** Yes. **Laundry:** No. **Pay Phone:** Yes. **Rest Rooms and Showers:** Yes. **Fuel:** No. **Propane:** No. **Internal Roads:** Paved & dirt, in good condition. **RV Service:** Referral. **Market:** A little less than 10 mi. west to Sarasota. **Restaurant:** A little less than 10 mi. west to Sarasota. **General Store:** Yes. **Vending:** Yes. **Swimming Pool:** No. **Playground:** Yes. **Other:** Canopy walkway for tree-top-level bird-watching, boat ramp, tram & airboat rides, nature trails. **Activities:** Fishing, birding (a favorite Audubon Society bird habitat), hiking, horseback riding, biking. **Nearby Attractions:** Selby Botanical Gardens & Ringling Museum in Sarasota. **Additional Information:** Sarasota CVB, (800) 522-9799, www.sarasotafl.org.

RESTRICTIONS

Pets: Not allowed in camping areas because of alligators. **Fires:** Contained only, provided there is no burn ban. **Alcoholic Beverages:** Not allowed. **Vehicle Maximum Length:** 34 ft. **Other:** No firearms or fireworks.

TO GET THERE

I-75 Exit 37/ SR 72, east 9 mi. to park on left.

SEBRING
Highlands Hammock State Park

5931 Hammock Rd., Sebring 33872. T: (863) 386-6094; www.myflorida.com.

🚐 ★★★★   ▲ ★★★★★

Beauty: ★★★★★   Site Privacy: ★★★
Spaciousness: ★★★   Quiet: ★★★★
Security: ★★★★★   Cleanliness: ★★★★★
Insect Control: ★★★★   Facilities: ★★★★

This beautiful central Florida state park boasts a pristine hardwood hammock featuring tall pines and oak trees alongside cypress and native palms. Nature trails wind through samples of ancient hardwoods as well as swampy marshlands. A wide variety of native fauna has been found in the decades-old protected area, including the rare Florida panthers, black bears, river otters, raccoons, and foxes. Dual camping rings offer quiet sites under cover of the trees with easy access to shower and laundry facilities. Back-in only, dirt-ground sites are about 20 ξ 30 to 50 feet, with slight wooded buffer between each. A community campfire circle is available for evening activities. Although Florida summers are known for their heat, humidity, and mosquitoes, this forested atmosphere in the central state offers the promise of cooler, less humid nights than some. Park gates are locked at night, with security lock codes distributed to campers for access.

BASICS

Operated By: State Dept. of Environmental Protection. **Open:** All year. **Site Assignment:** Reservations up to 11 months in advance, no deposit but credit card number to guarantee, cancel by 5 p.m. day before. **Registration:** Park Ranger office. **Fee:** $8 May–Oct., $13 Nov.–Apr.; MC, V. **Parking:** Yes.

FACILITIES

Number of RV Sites: 138. **Number of Tent-Only Sites:** 24. **Hookups:** Electric, water. **Each Site:** Picnic tables. **Dump Station:** Yes. **Laundry:** Yes. **Pay Phone:** Yes. **Rest Rooms and Showers:** Yes. **Fuel:** No. **Propane:** No. **Internal Roads:** Paved & smooth dirt roads, good condition. **RV Service:** Referral. **Market:** 6 mi. south on US 27. **Restaurant:** Yes. **General Store:** Yes. **Vending:** Yes. **Swimming Pool:** No. **Playground:** Yes. **Other:** Horseshoes, shuffleboard, checkers. **Activities:** Horse trails (bring your own horse), nature trails, bike trails, guided ranger walks & tram tours. **Nearby Attractions:** Prestigious annual auto race & year-round activities at nearby Sebring Raceway. **Additional Information:** Highlands County CVB, (863) 385-1316, (800) 255-1711.

RESTRICTIONS

Pets: On leash only. **Fires:** In grill only. **Alcoholic Beverages:** Not allowed. **Vehicle Maximum Length:** 45 ft. **Other:** No firearms, no fireworks, no intoxicants.

TO GET THERE

Four mi. west of Sebring on SR 634

ST. AUGUSTINE
Anastasia State Park

NA ?

1340A A1A South, St. Augustine 32080. T: (904) 461-2033; F: (904) 461-2006; www.myflorida.com.

🚐 ★★★★   ⛺ ★★★★★

Beauty: ★★★★★   Site Privacy: ★★★
Spaciousness: ★★   Quiet: ★★★
Security: ★★★★★   Cleanliness: ★★★★
Insect Control: ★★★   Facilities: ★★★★★

Crowded and very popular, this ocean-side park provides a beautiful example of Florida's coastal dunes undisturbed by development. Although all sites are back-in in the seven U-shaped camping areas, some are more crowded than others, and none are actually on the water. The Sea Bean circle seemed to offer the most privacy, and the Coquina circle, where we stayed, was most crowded. Nonetheless, the park was quiet by 11 p.m., and the dense trees and bush buffer provided a sense of seclusion. In addition to preserved and protected sand dunes and sea oats, endangered sea turtles are common to the shoreline here during nesting season, May to Sept. If you should happen to be lucky enough to spot a turtle laying eggs, or her hatchlings making their way from nest back to the ocean, be careful not to interfere with the process with sound or lights.

BASICS

Operated By: Florida Dept. of Environmental Protection, Division of Recreation & Parks. **Open:** All year. **Site Assignment:** Reservations accepted up to 11 months in advance, 1-night deposit, refundable up to 24 hours in advance. **Registration:** Park office. **Fee:** $18; M, V, D. **Parking:** Yes.

FACILITIES

Number of RV Sites: 104. **Number of Tent-Only Sites:** 35. **Hookups:** Water, electric. **Each Site:** Picnic table, fire ring. **Dump Station:** Yes. **Laundry:** Yes. **Pay Phone:** Yes. **Rest Rooms and Showers:** Yes. **Fuel:** No. **Propane:** No. **Internal Roads:** Paved & dirt, in good condition. **RV Service:** Referral. **Market:** 3 mi. south from park entrance. **Restaurant:** 1 mi. north or south from park entrance. **General Store:** Yes. **Vending:** Yes. **Swimming Pool:** No (beach). **Playground:** Yes. **Other:** Windsurf, kayak & canoe rentals; beach, fishing pier, hiking trails. **Activities:** Summer evening programs at the campfire circle, surfing, kayaking, canoeing, sailing, swimming, fishing, hiking. **Nearby Attractions:** Historic Fort Castillo de San Marcos; Lighthouse Museum; historic St. Augustine, Florida's oldest city; farmer's market (south from park on A1A about 3 mi. at public fishing pier & information center), dog-friendly beach 3 mi. south of the city fishing pier. **Additional Information:** St. Augustine, Ponte Vedra & the Beaches CVB, (800) OLD-CITY, www.visitoldcity.com.

RESTRICTIONS

Pets: In designated areas (not on beach), on leash only, proof of vaccination. **Fires:** In grills & designated areas only. **Alcoholic Beverages:** Not during park hours. **Vehicle Maximum Length:** 35 ft.—call ahead for up to 40 ft. **Other:** No driving on beach, do not damage or disturb dunes, nature, or wildlife.

TO GET THERE

Exit I-95 at Rte. 207, north approximately 5 mi. to SR 312, east 3 mi. to Anastasia Island, left on A1A 1.5 mi. north to park on right.

ST. GEORGE ISLAND
Dr. Julian G. Bruce St. George Island State Park

1900 E. Gulf Beach Dr., St. George Island 32328. T: (850) 927-2111; www.myflorida.com.

🚐 ★★★★	⛺ ★★★★
Beauty: ★★★★★	Site Privacy: ★★★★
Spaciousness: ★★★★	Quiet: ★★★★★
Security: ★★★★★	Cleanliness: ★★★★★
Insect Control: ★★★★	Facilities: ★★★★★

St. George Island Park is a beautifully preserved example of Florida's famous Emerald Coast beaches—the park has nine miles of pristine beach front, half accessible only by boat or foot. The rather stark park is largely made up of drifts of snow-white sands covered with small, wind-bent pines and sea oats, pink and purple flower vines crawling across them. The smooth, soft slopes may call upon your instincts to climb, but you must resist the urge—this weather-shaped landscape is fragile, and the island depends on the dunes to protect against erosion. A number of interesting creatures make their home in the park and on the island. There were eight eagles nests when we visited, and we saw several eagles,

standing proudly atop pine trees, light poles, and cellular towers, living comfortably amid civilization. Strangely, a coyote has been detected on the island, and there are alligators, nesting sea turtles, cardinals, pelicans, and osprey. Campers will appreciate the nicely wooded camping areas, with nice bushy buffers around the rather smallish sites. The full-facility campground offers 60 back-in sites, but no pull-throughs. A primitive camping area is available for tenters willing to hike two-and-a-half miles.

BASICS

Operated By: Florida Dept. of Environmental Protection, Division of Recreation & Parks. **Open:** All year. **Site Assignment:** Reservations accepted up to 11 months in advance, 1-night deposit, refundable up to 24 hours in advance. **Registration:** Park office. **Fee:** $10 Sept.–Jan., $16 Feb.–Aug. **Parking:** Yes.

FACILITIES

Number of RV Sites: 60. **Number of Tent-Only Sites:** Primitive camping area. **Hookups:** Water, electric. **Each Site:** Picnic table, fire ring. **Dump Station:** Yes. **Laundry:** No. **Pay Phone:** Yes. **Rest Rooms and Showers:** Yes. **Fuel:** No. **Propane:** No. **Internal Roads:** Paved & crushed shell, in good condition. **RV Service:** Referral. **Market:** Approx. 4 mi. west on Gulf Beach Dr. to St. George. **Restaurant:** Approx. 4 mi. west on Gulf Beach Dr. to St. George. **General Store:** No. **Vending:** Yes. **Swimming Pool:** No (beach). **Playground:** Yes. **Other:** Boat ramp, nature trails. **Activities:** Swimming, fishing, hiking. **Nearby Attractions: Nearby Attractions:. Additional Information:** Apalachicola Bay Chamber of Commerce, (850) 653-9419, www.baynavigator.com.

RESTRICTIONS

Pets: On leash only, not allowed on beaches, boardwalks, or dunes. **Fires:** In grill only. **Alcoholic Beverages:** Not during park hours. **Vehicle Maximum Length:** 35 ft. **Other:** No firearms or fireworks, no vehicles off roadways, do not walk over dunes or vegetation, do not feed wildlife, quiet hours starting 11 p.m.

TO GET THERE

From US 98 at Eastpoint (just east of Apalachicola), cross Eastpoint Bridge/Hwy. 300 to St. George Island, then turn left on Gulf Beach Blvd. (still Hwy. 300) to park, about 5 mi.

ST. JAMES CITY
Fort Myers Pine Island KOA

5120 Stringfellow, St. James City 33956. T: (941) 283-2415 or (800) KOA-8505; F: (941) 283-2415; www.pineislandkoa.com; pineislkoa@aol.com.

🚐 ★★★★   ▲ ★★

Beauty: ★★	Site Privacy: ★★
Spaciousness: ★★★★	Quiet: ★★★★
Security: ★★★★★	Cleanliness: ★★★★★
Insect Control: ★★	Facilities: ★★★★★

To say that this RV park is out of the way would be a great understatement—and that is exactly why so many campers love it. Pine Island is one of the last remaining rural outposts on Florida's southwest coast, offering a down-home feeling, farmers markets, and fishing villages. Although there are no pull-through sites, most are very large. The campground is on the waterfront, but views are completely obscured by mangrove trees. Most sites have a palm tree, and there is a nice expanse of green grass, but little shade. If you plan to visit in July, be sure to ask about Mango-Mania, an island festival that celebrates the many varieties of mangoes and avocados that grow on the island, and features live music and entertainment plus foods from area restaurants.

BASICS

Operated By: Manager John Streeter. **Open:** All year. **Site Assignment:** Reservations accepted, $20 deposit required, refundable up to 24 hours in advance. **Registration:** Office. **Fee:** $27 May–Nov., $45 Dec.–Apr. **Parking:** Yes.

FACILITIES

Number of RV Sites: 368. **Number of Tent-Only Sites:** 0. **Hookups:** Water, electric (30 amps), sewer, cable TV. **Each Site:** Picnic table. **Dump Station:** Yes. **Laundry:** Yes. **Pay Phone:** No. **Rest Rooms and Showers:** Yes. **Fuel:** No. **Propane:** Yes. **Internal Roads:** Paved, in good condition. **RV Service:** Maintenance on-site & referral. **Market:** 5 mi. north or convenience mart 2 mi. south. **Restaurant:** 2–4 mi. south. **General Store:** Yes. **Vending:** Yes. **Swimming Pool:** Yes. **Playground:** Yes. **Other:** Clubhouse, exercise room, hot tub, game room w/ computers & Internet access, library, big-screen TV. **Activities:** Shuttle to beach, cultural activities, flea market, etc. **Nearby Attractions:** Island is surrounded by the Gulf of

Mexico. **Additional Information:** Greater Pine Island Chamber of Commerce, 941-283-0888, www.pineislandchamber.org/.

RESTRICTIONS

Pets: On leash only, max. 2 pets. **Fires:** In grill only. **Alcoholic Beverages:** Allowed. **Vehicle Maximum Length:** None. **Other:** Quiet time 10 p.m., no swimming in lakes.

TO GET THERE

I-75 Exit 26 at Hwy. 78/Bayshore Rd. (becomes Pine Island Rd.) west 21 mi. to Stringfellow, south 6 mi. to KOA.

SUGARLOAF KEY
Sunburst RV Park

P.O. Box 440179, Sugarloaf Key 33044. T: (305) 745-1079 or (800) 354-5524; F: (305) 745-1680; www.RVONTHEGO.com; NHCFLLL@Terranova.net.

🚐 ★★★   ▲ ★★★

Beauty: ★★★	Site Privacy: ★★
Spaciousness: ★★★	Quiet: ★★★★
Security: ★★★★	Cleanliness: ★★★★
Insect Control: ★★★	Facilities: ★★★★

Several campers have discovered that Lazy Lake—now called Sunburst since being bought by National Homes Communities in 1999—can provide an affordable stay in the Florida Keys, an increasingly rare circumstance. This small campground recalls the truly rustic atmosphere that made the Keys famous but which is quickly being replaced by all things shiny and new, big and corporate. Permanent guests have added on sun rooms and wooden decks, large potted palms and hanging parrot lights. Built around a man-made lake and surrounded by mud flats, Lazy Lake offers several waterfront sites plus free kayaks and paddle boats for exploring the turquoise waters. Mangrove trees lines the edges of the campground, a plus for their erosion prevention benefits, but they can get a little smelly, as their roots are in constant state of decay from standing in water. Mangroves are protected thanks to their role as foundation for ecosystems around the world, so they are revered and there is no getting rid of them without special compensation. There's nothing fancy about Sunburst, but some will find that the rural atmosphere is a welcome reprieve from busy city life as well as from the heavily commercialized atmosphere found in Key West and increasingly throughout the Keys. For those who prefer a more modern, standardized environment, there are plenty of campgrounds nearby that will fit the bill.

BASICS

Operated By: National Home Communities. **Open:** All year. **Site Assignment:** Length of stay. **Registration:** Office. **Fee:** $35; MC, V, D, AE. **Parking:** Yes.

FACILITIES

Number of RV Sites: 94. **Number of Tent-Only Sites:** 6. **Hookups:** Electric (30, 50 amps), water, sewage, cable TV. **Each Site:** Picnic table, some w/ grill. **Dump Station:** Yes. **Laundry:** Yes. **Pay Phone:** Yes. **Rest Rooms and Showers:** Yes. **Fuel:** No. **Propane:** No. **Internal Roads:** Paved, in good condition. **RV Service:** Referral. **Market:** Convenience mart 1.5 mi. west to US 1 (Overseas Hwy.), supermarket 8 mi. north on US 1. **Restaurant:** 1.5 mi. west to US 1. **General Store:** Yes. **Vending:** Yes. **Swimming Pool:** Yes. **Playground:** No. **Other:** Paddleboat & kayak rentals, rec room. **Activities:** Boating, fishing, winter recreation activities include bingo & group dinners. **Nearby Attractions:** Beach, Key West. **Additional Information:** Florida Keys & Key West Tourist Council, (800) 648-5510, www.fla-keys.com.

RESTRICTIONS

Pets: On leash only. **Fires:** In grill only. **Alcoholic Beverages:** Allowed. **Vehicle Maximum Length:** 42 ft.—call ahead.

TO GET THERE

US 1 south from Miami 81 mi. to mile marker 19, less than a mile further south to Johnson Rd., left 1 mile to campground on right, sign says Lazy Lake.

SUNRISE

Markham Park

16001 W. SR 84, Sunrise 33326. T: (954) 389-2000; www.broward.org/parks.

🚐 ★★★   ⛺ ★★★★

Beauty: ★★★	Site Privacy: ★★★
Spaciousness: ★★★	Quiet: ★★★★
Security: ★★★★	Cleanliness: ★★★★★
Insect Control: ★★★	Facilities: ★★★★★

Markham Park may be smaller than other nearby RV campgrounds like C.B. Smith Park, but its proximity to the Everglades gives this park an edge than can't be matched in the area. An abundance of alligators fill the waterways, canals, and lakes of the park, so keep dogs leashed and away from water. Other fauna include raccoons, foxes, and deer, and there have even been sightings of Florida's endangered panther on the outskirts of the park. Hike through the woods in the southwest corner of the park to a land bridge over the canal and to the dike, which provides a rare hilltop hike along the edge of the Everglades. It's a great place to enjoy the sunset—but don't stay too late, the walk back through darkened woodlands can be eerie! Ample trees give a wilderness feel that is largely missing in most of South Florida. Cul-de-sacs provided for camping create small, private enclaves for small groups.

BASICS

Operated By: Broward County. **Open:** All year. **Site Assignment:** First come, first served; weekends fill up fast so reservations suggested, deposit full amount or arrangement by agreement. **Registration:** At park office. **Fee:** $19 plus $4 for non-Florida residents Dec. 1–Mar. 31; MC, V, D. **Parking:** Yes.

FACILITIES

Number of RV Sites: 88. **Number of Tent-Only Sites:** 10. **Hookups:** Water, electric (20, 50 amps), sewer. **Each Site:** Grills or fire ring, picnic table. **Dump Station:** Yes. **Laundry:** No. **Pay Phone:** Yes. **Rest Rooms and Showers:** Yes. **Fuel:** No. **Propane:** No. **Internal Roads:** Paved, in good condition. **RV Service:** No. **Market:** Grocery & pharmacy across the street from entrance to the park. **Restaurant:** Snack bar at pool Feb.–Labor Day, restaurants across the street from the park entrance. **General Store:** No. **Vending:** No. **Swimming Pool:** Yes. **Playground:** Yes. **Other:** Boat ramp. **Activities:** Bike rentals, bike & jogging paths, canoe, paddleboat & johnboat rentals, fishing permitted, model airplane field, tennis, racquetball & target range. **Nearby Attractions:** Sawgrass Mills Mall (the world's largest outlet mall) is 5 mi. northwest, beaches are 15 mi. east in Fort Lauderdale & Hollywood. **Additional Information:** Greater Fort Lauderdale CVB, (800) 231-SUNNY, www.sunny.org.

RESTRICTIONS

Pets: On leash only. **Fires:** Ground fires in fire pits w/ park ranger permission only. **Alcoholic Beverages:** In designated areas only, no glass containers. **Vehicle Maximum Length:** None.

TO GET THERE

I-595 west from Fort Lauderdale, about 15 mi. to Exit at SW 136th Ave., continue west on SR 84 about 1 mi. to park entrance on right.

TALLAHASSEE

Tallahassee RV Park

6504 Mahan Dr., Tallahassee 32308. T: (850) 878-7641; F: (850) 878-7082.

🚐 ★★★   ▲ ★★

Beauty: ★	Site Privacy: ★
Spaciousness: ★★	Quiet: ★★★
Security: ★★★★★	Cleanliness: ★★★★★
Insect Control: ★★★	Facilities: ★★★

Made for you if you're just passing through, the Tallahassee RV Park is the long, grassy backyard of the Schlinger family home. Surrounded by pine trees, pretty oleanders, crepe myrtle, and honeysuckle, the park provides a clean, quiet, and restful spot for relaxing the road-weary. A bird house provides a similar way-station for feathered friends. Grassy, mostly pull-through sites are neat with a little extra greenery—each has a bush and a tree—if not as private as longer-term visitors might prefer. A central modem connection is provided in the office, along with basic supplies. A few extra sites are available in front when needed, which should keep the back lot from getting too crowded. This is a nice, rural residential location in spite of its easy access to the adjacent intersection of I-10 and US 90.

BASICS

Operated By: Don Schlinger. **Open:** All year. **Site Assignment:** Reservations accepted w/ credit card number, refunds w/ 24 hour cancellation. **Registration:** Office, late registrants self-register. **Fee:** $22.75; MC, V, D. **Parking:** Yes.

FACILITIES

Number of RV Sites: 66. **Number of Tent-Only Sites:** 0. **Hookups:** Water, electric (20, 30, 50 amps) Sewer. **Each Site:** Picnic table, pine tree, & a bush. **Dump Station:** No. **Laundry:** No. **Pay Phone:** No. **Rest Rooms and Showers:** Yes.

Fuel: No. **Propane:** No. **Internal Roads:** Paved, in good condition. **RV Service:** Referral. **Market:** 3 mi. west on US 90 to Publix. **Restaurant:** 2 mi. west on US 90. **General Store:** Yes. **Vending:** No. **Swimming Pool:** No. **Playground:** No. **Activities:** Inquire at campground. **Nearby Attractions:** Capitol city of Tallahassee, Florida State University. **Additional Information:** Tallahassee Area CVB, (800) 628-2866.

RESTRICTIONS

Pets: On leash only. **Fires:** In grill only. **Alcoholic Beverages:** Allowed. **Vehicle Maximum Length:** None.

TO GET THERE

I-10 Exit 31A at US 90, west 0.5 mi. to campground on right.

TENNILLE

Steinhatchee RV Refuge

P.O. Box 48, Perry 32348. T: (352) 498-5192 or (800) 589-1541; www.steinhatcheeoutpost.com; steinhatchee@perry.gulfnet.com.

🚐 ★★★   ▲ ★★

Beauty: ★★	Site Privacy: ★★
Spaciousness: ★★★	Quiet: ★★★★★
Security: ★★★	Cleanliness: ★★★
Insect Control: ★★	Facilities: ★★★★

Lonely but not forgotten, this hunters' haven is one of the last vestiges of natural Florida. How long it will last, sandwiched between high-tourist traffic areas of the Gulf Coast and Panama Beach, isn't likely to be long. Not to mention the fact that ammunition is offered for sale at area convenient stores—perhaps wildlife is as at risk now as it will be in the near future when development comes to town. RVers may enjoy the extreme quiet and laid-back atmosphere of the park, especially if they're here to enjoy the adjacent nature opportunities along Steinhatchee River and the Gulf of Mexico. Wide, grassy sites provide an easy backdrop and parking spot, but don't expect the polished shine of some other RV resorts. This rustic piece of Old Florida is for hearty Florida crackers (our slang for natives).

BASICS

Operated By: Private operator. **Open:** All year. **Site Assignment:** Reservations available. **Registration:** Camp store. **Fee:** $18. **Parking:** Yes.

FACILITIES

Number of RV Sites: 100. **Number of Tent-Only Sites:** 0. **Hookups:** Water, electric, sewer. **Each Site:** Picnic table, grill, some w/ patio. **Dump Station:** Yes. **Laundry:** Yes. **Pay Phone:** Yes. **Rest Rooms and Showers:** Yes. **Fuel:** Yes. **Propane:** Yes. **Internal Roads:** Grass. **RV Service:** Referral. **Market:** On site. **Restaurant:** If livers, gizzards, & okra work for you, restaurant on site at the camp store. **General Store:** Yes. **Vending:** Yes. **Swimming Pool:** No. **Playground:** Yes. **Other:** Volleyball, basketball courts. **Activities:** Fishing, volleyball, basketball, boating. **Nearby Attractions:** Beaver Spring Creek, Cooper Spring Creek, Steinhatchee Falls.

RESTRICTIONS

Pets: On leash only. **Fires:** In grill only. **Alcoholic Beverages:** Allowed. **Vehicle Maximum Length:** None.

TO GET THERE

US 19 to Tennille at Hwy. 51, camp to the left/southwest.

THONOTOSASSA (TAMPA)
Hillsborough River State Park

15402 US 301 North, Thonotosassa 33592. T: (813) 987-6771; www.myFlorida.com.

🚐 ★★★★   ⛺ ★★★★★

Beauty: ★★★★★   Site Privacy: ★★★
Spaciousness: ★★★★   Quiet: ★★★★★
Security: ★★★★★   Cleanliness: ★★★
Insect Control: ★★★   Facilities: ★★★★

Designated a park in 1936, this 2,994-acre plot of land boasts oak, hickory, magnolia, and native sabal palm trees, with an undergrowth of palms that ensures you'll remember you're in Florida. Wild deer, bobcat, foxes, alligators, raccoons, grey squirrels, armadillos, and snakes take cover in the brush and along the scenic Hillsborough River, which runs through the park and features a unique set of rapids for canoeists and kayakers. A suspension bridge carries hikers across the river to hike a section of the Florida Trail.

BASICS

Operated By: Florida Dept. of Environmental Protection, Division of Recreation & Parks. **Open:** All year. **Site Assignment:** First come, first served; reservations accepted by phone w/ credit card up to 11 months in advance, full refund if cancelled by 5 p.m. the day prior. **Registration:** Park office. **Fee:** $16.70; MC, V. **Parking:** Yes.

FACILITIES

Number of RV Sites: 64. **Number of Tent-Only Sites:** 30. **Hookups:** Water, electric (30 amps). **Each Site:** Picnic table, fire ring. **Dump Station:** Yes. **Laundry:** Yes. **Pay Phone:** Yes. **Rest Rooms and Showers:** Yes. **Fuel:** No. **Propane:** No. **Internal Roads:** Paved & crushed shell, in good condition. **RV Service:** No. **Market:** 9 mi. south to Tampa. **Restaurant:** 9 mi. south to Tampa. **General Store:** Yes. **Vending:** Yes. **Swimming Pool:** Yes. **Playground:** Yes. **Other:** Boat ramp, hiking trails, bridges over river, Historic Fort Foster. **Activities:** Hiking, canoeing, kayaking, fishing, guided tours of fort on weekends, special events. **Nearby Attractions:** Busch Gardens, Adventure Island Water Park, Museum of Science & Industry. **Additional Information:** Tampa Bay CVB, (800) 44-TAMPA, www.visittampabay.com.

RESTRICTIONS

Pets: On leash only and in designated areas only, proof of rabies vaccination. **Fires:** In grills or fire rings only. **Alcoholic Beverages:** Not allowed. **Vehicle Maximum Length:** None. **Other:** No firearms, no fireworks, no collecting of firewood or any other flora or fauna, no feeding of wildlife.

TO GET THERE

I-75 Exit at Fowler Ave., east 5 mi. to US 301, north 9 mi. to park on left.

WEST PALM BEACH
Lion Country Safari KOA

2000 Lion Country Safari Rd., Loxahatchee 33470. T: (561) 793-9797 or (800) 562-9115; F: (561) 793-9603; www.lioncountrysafari.com; koa@lioncountrysafari.com.

🚐 ★★★★★   ⛺ ★★★★

Beauty: ★★★   Site Privacy: ★★
Spaciousness: ★★★   Quiet: ★★★
Security: ★★★★★   Cleanliness: ★★★★★
Insect Control: ★★★★   Facilities: ★★★★★

Through the village of Royal Palm Beach and past the interesting city of Wellington where many residents are aviators and share runways for driveways, finally you'll find a very unique attraction—Lion Country Safari, home to hundreds of African animals for more than 30 years.

BASICS

Operated By: Managers. **Open:** All year. **Site Assignment:** Reservations accepted, 1-night deposit required, refundable up to 48 hours in advance, less a $4 administrative fee. **Registration:** Park office. **Fee:** $27.50; M, V, D, AE. **Parking:** Yes.

FACILITIES

Number of RV Sites: 203. **Number of Tent-Only Sites:** 22. **Hookups:** Water, electric (30, 50 amps), sewer. **Each Site:** Picnic table, concrete pad. **Dump Station:** Yes. **Laundry:** Yes. **Pay Phone:** Yes. **Rest Rooms and Showers:** Yes. **Fuel:** No. **Propane:** Yes. **Internal Roads:** Paved, in good condition. **RV Service:** Referral. **Market:** Approx. 10 mi. east on Southern Blvd. **Restaurant:** Approx. 4 mi. east on Southern Blvd. **General Store:** Yes. **Vending:** Yes. **Swimming Pool:** Yes. **Playground:** Yes. **Other:** Horseshoes, shuffleboard, volleyball, basketball & petanque (similar to bocci) courts. **Activities:** Swimming, horseshoes, shuffleboard, basketball, petanque, visiting the adjacent Lion Country Safari. **Nearby Attractions:** Lion Country Safari, a 500-acre wildlife preserve park where African animals such as rhinoceroses, elephants, lions, tigers are among the more than 1,000 animals who roam free throughout the preserve. Visitors may observe the animals from the safety of enclosed vehicles as they drive through the preserve. An amusement park offers rides, mini-golf, paddle boats, petting zoo. **Additional Information:** Palm Beach County CVB, (800) 554-PALM, www.palmbeachfl.com.

RESTRICTIONS

Pets: On leash only. **Fires:** In grill only. **Alcoholic Beverages:** Allowed. **Vehicle Maximum Length:** Big rigs welcome. **Other:** Quiet hours 10 p.m.–8 a.m., no bike riding after dusk, children must wear helmets when riding.

TO GET THERE

Exit I-95 at Southern Blvd., west 20 mi. to campground.

Georgia

It is with her high Appalachian views; her rich history memorialized in stately mansions and great plantations; her primordial swamps crawling with creatures and draped in moss; her golden coast graced with wide beaches and magical islands; and with her great winding rivers feeding the land and imagination that Georgia beckons. Likely, after you journey through the state and experience firsthand her richness, the memory of your stay will be slow to fade. Begin your camping expedition in north Georgia's mountainous region, where you'll find yourself atop **Brasstown Bald,** Georgia's highest peak at 4,700 feet above sea level. The days are cool, even when summer swelters below, and thundering waterfalls, miles of hiking trails, and lazy floats down the **Chattahoochee River** occupy visitors. Just around the corner, you might be surprised by **Helen,** a Bavarian town seemingly transplanted from the Alps to America's Deep South.

Move on to the **Atlanta** metro region. While it may seem strange to choose a campsite near this bustling metropolis, the number of recreational opportunities in this area will surprise you. The Chattahoochee River meanders through Atlanta, where river recreation opportunities await. Enjoy rafting and boating, or visit the **Chattahoochee Nature Center** to stroll along a scenic boardwalk. Be sure to visit **Stone Mountain,** a monolith of granite displaying one of the world's largest relief sculptures. Venture on foot up the side of the mountain or take a sky lift to the top to enjoy a breathtaking view. Below, visit the **Antebellum Plantation,** where you can wander through both an 1800's mansion and slave quarters. After exploring, brush yourself off and visit some of Atlanta's cultural treasures including the **Civil War Museum, High Museum of Art,** and the **Margaret Mitchell House,** where the author penned *Gone With the Wind.*

As you travel southward, you can't help but be mesmerized by the scenic expanse of 90 miles of Georgian coastline. Feel the warm salt air hug you as you adventure to one of the state's many islands. **Cumberland Island** admits only 300 visitors each day to enjoy and explore its untamed wilderness, but camping is allowed. Enjoy the **Okefenokee National Wildlife Refuge** from a boat, or dare yourself to paddle a canoe through the blackwater swamp as you watch the surface bubble with the teeming life below. Visit sweet **Savannah,** whose curious inhabitants and beautiful scenery were recently popularized by the book and film *Midnight in the Garden of Good and Evil.* You'll soon learn that Savannah didn't need Hollywood's endorsement; she is a star of her own making. Savannah makes a nice transition to Georgia's Historic South, where campers can hike the trails of **Oconee National Forest** or fish on **Oconee Lake.** Canoeing and camping along the **Altamaha River,** lined by swamps and sandbars, provides campers and nature lovers a grand adventure. With so much to do, Georgia and her charm will likely entice you to a second visit.

The following facilities accept payment in checks or cash only:

Bar Harbor Campground, Bar Harbor

Camden Rockport Camping, Rockport

Cupsuptic Campground, Oquossoc

Gray Homestead Campground, Southport

Hermit Island Campground, Small Point

Honey Run Beach & Campground, Peru

Sherwood Forest Campsite, New Harbor

Shore Hills Campground, Boothbay Harbor

Somes Sound Campground, Mt. Desert Island

South Arm Campground, Andover

The Moorings, Searsport

Whispering Pines, East Orland

Wolfeboro Campground, Wolfeboro

Campground Profiles

ALBANY
The Parks at Chehaw

Philema Rd. (Hwy. 91N), Albany 31701. T: (229) 430-5275; www.parsatchehaw.org.

🚐 ★★★★   ⛺ ★★★★

Beauty: ★★★★	Site Privacy: ★★
Spaciousness: ★★★★	Quiet: ★★★★
Security: ★★★★	Cleanliness: ★★★★
Insect Control: ★★★	Facilities: ★★★★★

Located just outside of Albany, this 800-acre park is a great destination for families. Fairly suburban in nature, the park has 52 RV sites that are moderately spaced but offer little privacy. Each site has water and electrical hookups and all back-in parking. The camping is not remarkable, but the activities nearby are. Within short walking distance is an amazing contemporary playground with slides, rungs, and other fun activities. Fishing, cycling, mountain biking, and hiking are all recreation possibilities, and those wishing to see cheetahs, beers, bison or elk in the Georgia piney woods only need walk a short distance to the Wild Animal Park.

BASICS

Operated By: John Fowler. **Open:** All year. **Site Assignment:** First come, first served. **Registration:** At ticket booth prior to set up. **Fee:** $14 RV, $8 tent. **Parking:** 2 vehicles per site.

FACILITIES

Number of Multipurpose Sites: 52. **Hookups:** Water, electric (30 amps). **Each Site:** Water, electricity. **Dump Station:** Yes. **Laundry:** Yes. **Pay Phone:** No. **Rest Rooms and Showers:** Yes. **Fuel:** 5 min. on Philema Rd. **Propane:** No. **Internal Roads:** Dirt. **RV Service:** No. **Market:** 5 min. on Philema Rd. **Restaurant:** Savanna Café. **General Store:** Gift shop. **Vending:** Yes. **Swimming Pool:** No. **Playground:** Yes. **Other:** Covered picnic shelters by reservation. **Activities:** BMX riding, hiking, fishing, mountain biking, train rides, playground. **Nearby Attractions:** Public boat ramp (1 mi.), Wild Animal Park, Mt. Zion Albany Civil Rights Movement Museum, Albany Museum of Art.

RESTRICTIONS

Pets: On leash only. **Fires:** Allowed. **Alcoholic Beverages:** Not allowed. **Vehicle Maximum Length:** None. **Other:** 14-day max. stay limit.

TO GET THERE

From Atlanta, take I-75S to Exit 32 (Hwy. 300). Go south on Hwy. 300, then turn right on Hwy. 32. Follow Hwy. 32 and turn left on Hwy. 91 (Philema Rd.); go 9 mi. to the park, which is on the right.

APPLING
Mistletoe State Park

Rte. 1 Box 335, Appling 30802. T: (706) 541-0321; www.gastateparks.org.

🚐 ★★★★   ⛺ ★★★★

Beauty: ★★★★★   Site Privacy: ★★★★
Spaciousness: ★★★★   Quiet: ★★★
Security: ★★★★★   Cleanliness: ★★★★
Insect Control: ★★★★   Facilities: ★★★

Located immediately northwest of Augusta, Mistletoe State Park is known as one of the best bass fishing destinations in the United States. Camping is relegated to the northern part of the 1,900 acre park, but comes with great views of the lake. Primitive camping is limited to four walk-in sites. For RVs, back-in sites dominate, but there are a few pull-throughs. All have water and electric hook-ups. Site size and privacy vary quite a bit; look around, and try to get sites 20 or 79—these are the creme of the crop. Shuffleboard, volleyball, and hiking are available, if you didn't come her to fish. Two trails leave from the campground to connect with the rest of the park.

BASICS

Operated By: Georgia Dept. of Natural Resources. **Open:** All year. **Site Assignment:** Reservations or first come, first served. **Registration:** At camp office. **Fee:** $13–$15. **Parking:** Yes.

FACILITIES

Number of Multipurpose Sites: 92. **Hookups:** Water, electric (30 amps). **Each Site:** Grill, fire ring, picnic table, lantern pole. **Dump Station:** Yes. **Laundry:** Yes. **Pay Phone:** Yes. **Rest Rooms and Showers:** Yes. **Fuel:** No. **Propane:** No. **Internal Roads:** Gravel. **RV Service:** 15 mi. in Thompson. **Market:** In Thompson. **Restaurant:** In Thompson. **General Store:** No. **Vending:** Yes. **Swimming Pool:** No. **Playground:** Yes. **Activities:** Shuffleboard, volleyball, canoe rental, hiking, biking. **Nearby Attractions:** Augusta, Fun City, Golf Museum, Riverwalk.

RESTRICTIONS

Pets: On leash only. **Fires:** Allowed. **Alcoholic Beverages:** Not allowed. **Vehicle Maximum Length:** 50 ft. **Other:** 14-day max. stay limit.

TO GET THERE

From I-20, take Exit 175 (Hwy. 150). Go north 7.9 mi. to the park.

BISHOP
Pine Lake RV Campground 21

5540 High Shoals Rd., Hwy. 186, Bishop 30621.
T: (706) 769-5486; F: (706) 769-6553; members.aol.com/pinelakerv/index.html; pinelakerv@aol.com.

🚐 ★★★★   ⛺ ★★★

Beauty: ★★★★   Site Privacy: ★★★★
Spaciousness: ★★   Quiet: ★★★★
Security: ★★★   Cleanliness: ★★★★
Insect Control: ★★★   Facilities: ★★★

If you can get past the kitschy "Happy Campers are Our Business" slogan, this is a surprisingly nice, nature-oriented private campground. The pretty setting and the people (a mostly older crowd when we visited) together make this a pleasant place to be, picturesque and heavily wooded. It is a rural spot in north-central Georgia, with good security in part due to its remoteness. There are both back-in and pull-through sites, and although they are smallish, they have foliage between them for better privacy than is offered at a lot of commercial campgrounds. Also, despite the lovely hilly surroundings, the campsites themselves are flat, with gravel ground cover. We recommend sites 3, 15, and 16 in particular. The ponds here are stocked with catfish, bass, and bluegill, but they do have a bit of an algae problem. For its privacy, beauty, friendliness, and character, this campground is a delight.

BASICS

Operated By: Britt, Linda, & John Chandler. **Open:** All year. **Site Assignment:** Revervations preferred. **Registration:** At camp office. **Fee:** $21. **Parking:** On site.

FACILITIES

Number of RV Sites: 23. **Number of Tent-Only Sites:** 7. **Hookups:** Water, electric (30 amps), sewer. **Each Site:** Gravel site. **Dump Station:** Yes. **Laundry:** Yes. **Pay Phone:** Yes. **Rest Rooms and Showers:** Yes. **Fuel:** No. **Propane:** No. **Internal Roads:** Gravel. **RV Service:** In Athens. **Market:** In Athens or Watkinsville. **Restaurant:** In Athens or Watkinsville. **General Store:** Yes. **Vending:** Yes. **Swimming Pool:** No. **Playground:** Yes. **Activities:** Bird-watching, nature trails. **Nearby Attractions:** State Botanical Gardens, antebellum homes, University of Georgia.

RESTRICTIONS

Pets: On leash only. **Fires:** Not allowed. **Alcoholic Beverages:** Not allowed. **Vehicle Maximum Length:** None.

TO GET THERE

From I-20, go north on Hwy. 441-129 to Bishop. Turn west on Hwy. 186 and go 1.4 mi. to entrance.

BLAIRSVILLE

Vogel State Park

7485 Vogel State Park Rd., Blairsville 30512. T: (706) 745-2628; www.gastateparks.org.

🚐 ★★★★   ⛺ ★★★★

Beauty: ★★★★★	Site Privacy: ★★★★
Spaciousness: ★★★★	Quiet: ★★★
Security: ★★★★	Cleanliness: ★★★★
Insect Control: ★★★★	Facilities: ★★★

Many of today's state parks wouldn't exist, at least not as we reocognize them, if not for the work of the Civilian Conservation Corps—Vogel State Park is one such park. The CCC's handiwork is easily seen here, and a small museum honors their work. When the heat of the summer hits the rest of the state, Vogel is a great place to visit. The 85 sites have electric and water hookups (there are 18 walk-in sites without these amenities). The sites are all large, but some of them are practically on top of one another. This place is very woody, hence quite shady, but the ground cover is minimal, reducing privacy in some areas. Recommended sites are toward the back of the campground. In addition to hiking, visitors can take a boat out on beautiful Lake Trahlyta.

BASICS

Operated By: Georgia Dept. of Natural Resources. **Open:** All year. **Site Assignment:** Reservations or first come, first served. **Registration:** At Visitors Center. **Fee:** $10–$25. **Parking:** Yes.

FACILITIES

Number of RV Sites: 84. **Number of Tent-Only Sites:** 18. **Hookups:** Water, electric (50 amps). **Each Site:** Grassy, gravel pads. **Dump Station:** Yes. **Laundry:** Yes. **Pay Phone:** Yes. **Rest Rooms and Showers:** Yes. **Fuel:** No. **Propane:** No. **Internal Roads:** Paved. **RV Service:** No.

Market: In Blairsville. **Restaurant:** In Owltown or Hiawasee. **General Store:** Yes. **Vending:** Yes. **Swimming Pool:** No. **Playground:** Yes. **Activities:** Swimming, fishing, hiking, paddle boating, mini golf. **Nearby Attractions:** CCC Museum, Appalachian Trail, Walasi-Yi Center, Dahlonega Gold Museum, numerous waterfalls.

RESTRICTIONS

Pets: Yes. **Fires:** In fire rings only. **Alcoholic Beverages:** Restricted. **Vehicle Maximum Length:** 50 ft.

TO GET THERE

11 mi. south of Blairsville via US Hwy. 19-129.

BLUE RIDGE

Lake Blue Ridge Campground

6050 Appalachian Hwy, Blue Ridge 30513. T: (706) 632-3031.

🚐 ★★★★   ⛺ ★★★★★

Beauty: ★★★★★	Site Privacy: ★★★★★
Spaciousness: ★★★★★	Quiet: ★★★★★
Security: ★★★★★	Cleanliness: ★★★
Insect Control: ★★★★★	Facilities: ★★★

Pretty much everything is secondary to the lake at Lake Blue Ridge, including campsite amenities. The surrounding North Georgia mountains and Chattahoochee National Forest lend the place a pristine air. This is not a great place for RVers though, as there are no hookups and no pull-throughs and few of the sites are level. However, if you're a camper who doesn't mind roughing it a bit (including a long walk to the outhouse), this is otherwise a really beautiful place to camp. Campsites are palatial in size and completely wooded, and the sites located in the lake loop (sites 49–56) are absolutely gorgeous. The lake offers the typical roster of water sports, and anglers can fish for bass, bream, catfish, perch, and crappie. A six-tenths-mile loop trail follows the lakeshore, providing good views of the water.

BASICS

Operated By: USDA Forest Service. **Open:** Apr. 1–Oct. 31. **Site Assignment:** Inquire at campground. **Registration:** At campsite or w/ host. **Fee:** $8–$10. **Parking:** On site.

FACILITIES

Number of RV Sites: 0. **Number of Tent-Only Sites:** 58. **Hookups:** None. **Each Site:** Picnic table, grill, tent pads. **Dump Station:** No. **Laundry:** No. **Pay Phone:** No. **Rest Rooms and Showers:** Yes. **Fuel:** No. **Propane:** No. **Internal Roads:** Paved. **RV Service:** No. **Market:** In Blue Ridge. **Restaurant:** In Blue Ridge. **General Store:** Nearby on Old US 76. **Vending:** No. **Swimming Pool:** No. **Playground:** No. **Activities:** Hiking, boating, fishing, water skiing, swimming. **Nearby Attractions:** Blue Ridge Lake, scenic railway, fish hatchery, Chattahoochee National Forest. **Additional Information:** Fannin County Chamber of Commerce, (800) 899-6867 or www.blueridgemountains.com.

RESTRICTIONS

Pets: On leash only. **Fires:** In fire rings only. **Alcoholic Beverages:** Allowed. **Vehicle Maximum Length:** None. **Other:** 14-day max. stay limit.

TO GET THERE

Take Old US 76 east for 1.5 mi. to Dry Branch Road. Turn right and go 3 mi. to entrance sign.

BRUNSWICK
Blythe Island Regional Park

6616 Blythe Island Hwy., Brunswick 31523. T: (800) 343-7855 or (912) 261-3805.

🚐 ★★★★   ⛺ ★★★★

Beauty: ★★★★★	Site Privacy: ★★★★
Spaciousness: ★★★★★	Quiet: ★★★★★
Security: ★★★★	Cleanliness: ★★★★
Insect Control: ★★★	Facilities: ★★★

This campground is a great place to use as a base for touring the Jekyll Island area and nearby beaches. Pretty and well-maintained, Blythe Island's sites are surprisingly large. Lovely shade trees and a variety of native scrub brush provide some privacy between sites. Sites 54, 56, 57, 60, 61, 63, 65, and 67 are the largest, most secluded, and most attractive in the campground. The small lake is stocked with fish for anglers, and a nice swimming beach serves one section. None of the sites are actually lakeside, though none are very far from the water; the closest sites to the swimming beach are 1–13. The wide variety of on-site activities include hiking and biking trails, boat and kayak rentals, tournament horseshoes, and a field archery range. Campers can also make use of the nearby Blythe Island Marina to arrange for fishing or touring excursions or to dock their own boats.

BASICS

Operated By: County Glynn. **Open:** All year. **Site Assignment:** Reservations or first come, first served. **Registration:** At camp office. **Fee:** $20–$23. **Parking:** Yes.

FACILITIES

Number of RV Sites: 97. **Number of Tent-Only Sites:** 26. **Hookups:** Water, electric (30 amps), sewer. **Each Site:** Shell covering. **Dump Station:** Yes. **Laundry:** Yes. **Pay Phone:** Yes. **Rest Rooms and Showers:** Yes. **Fuel:** No. **Propane:** Yes. **Internal Roads:** Gravel. **RV Service:** In Brunswick. **Market:** In Brunswick or Dock Junction. **Restaurant:** In Fancy Bluff or Brunswick. **General Store:** No. **Vending:** Yes. **Swimming Pool:** No. **Playground:** Yes. **Activities:** Swimming, fishing, boating, horseshoes, archery. **Nearby Attractions:** Saint Simons, Sea Island, & Jekyll Islands, Cumberland Island.

RESTRICTIONS

Pets: On leash only. **Fires:** Allowed. **Alcoholic Beverages:** Not allowed. **Vehicle Maximum Length:** 40 ft.

TO GET THERE

From I-95, take Exit 29 (US 17 S.). Go 1 mi. to GA 303 N., then 3 mi. to campground.

BUFORD
Shoal Creek

6300 Shadburn Ferry Rd., Buford 30518. T: (877) 444-6777.

🚐 ★★★★★   ⛺ ★★★★★

Beauty: ★★★★★	Site Privacy: ★★★★★
Spaciousness: ★★★★★	Quiet: ★★★★★
Security: ★★★★★	Cleanliness: ★★★★★
Insect Control: ★★★	Facilities: ★★★

This pretty, well-run campground is one of the finest in Georgia. Set on the shores of Lake Lanier in a ritzy, suburban neighborhood and overseen by the U.S. Army Corps of Engineers, Shoal Creek is a popular place that can get packed with campers. In addition, the lakeside setting means that boat noise is a fact of life for visitors; ask attendants for recommendations on quieter campsites. All sites here are quite large, with lovely shade trees above and screening foliage in between. Sites 55–57 are particularly shady and private; nearby, sites 36–39 and

51–54 are also particularly sizable and secluded, site 40 even more so. The half-loop that makes up sites 31–35 has breathtaking lake views. Lake Lanier features ten other campgrounds (see profiles for Lake Lanier Islands and Chestnut Ridge in Flowery Branch), 43 day-use parks, ten marinas, and nine state, county, and city parks.

BASICS

Operated By: Army Corps of Engineers. **Open:** Mar. 30–Sept. 23. **Site Assignment:** Reservations accepted. **Registration:** Entrance station. **Fee:** $12–$22, plus day use fees. **Parking:** limited.

FACILITIES

Number of Multipurpose Sites: 107. **Hookups:** Some water, some electric (30 amps). **Each Site:** Table, grill, lantern posts, fire pit. **Dump Station:** Yes. **Laundry:** Yes. **Pay Phone:** Yes. **Rest Rooms and Showers:** Yes. **Fuel:** No. **Propane:** No. **Internal Roads:** Paved. **RV Service:** No. **Market:** In Buford. **Restaurant:** In Buford. **General Store:** Less than 10 mi. **Vending:** Drinks only. **Swimming Pool:** No. **Playground:** Yes. **Other:** Swim area, boat ramp. **Activities:** Baseball, horseshoes. **Nearby Attractions:** Lake Lanier Island water park & golf course, concerts. **Additional Information:** Visitor Center, (770) 945-9531.

RESTRICTIONS

Pets: On leash only. **Fires:** In fire rings only. **Alcoholic Beverages:** Not allowed. **Vehicle Maximum Length:** None. **Other:** 14-day max. stay limit.

TO GET THERE

From Atlanta, take I-85N to I-985 take Exit 8 and turn left onto Hwy. 347. Turn left onto McEver Rd. then right on Shadburn Ferry Rd., which ends at the campground.

CARTERSVILLE
Allatoona Landing Campground

24 Allatoona Landing Rd., Cartersville 30121. T: (770) 974-6068.

🚐 ★★★   ⛺ ★★★

Beauty: ★★★★	Site Privacy: ★★★
Spaciousness: ★★	Quiet: ★★★
Security: ★★★★	Cleanliness: ★★★★
Insect Control: ★★★★	Facilities: ★★★

This large campground is very popular, which means it's often crowded. Combine that with small- to mid-size campsites, and you lose a little when it comes to spaciousness and privacy. The owners of Allatoona Landing do run a tight ship, so the property is well-maintained and reasonably clean. Be aware that railroad tracks pass very near the campground, so some train noise is inevitable (especially for those sites nearest the campground office). Allatoona Lake offers plenty of options for water sports enthusiasts, including elaborate boating facilities, and an extensive swimming beach. Sites 85, 86, 93, 95–101, and 103 are shaded and pretty, while 87 and 89–92 are the nicest waterfront sites. Sites 60–73 and 75, 77, 79, 81, 83, and 88 are closest to the swimming beach.

BASICS

Operated By: Private operator. **Open:** All year. **Site Assignment:** By reservation. **Registration:** At camp office. **Fee:** $20–$25. **Parking:** 2 vehicles per site.

FACILITIES

Number of RV Sites: 120. **Number of Tent-Only Sites:** 20. **Hookups:** Water, electric (30, 50 amps), sewer. **Each Site:** Picnic table. **Dump Station:** Yes. **Laundry:** Yes. **Pay Phone:** Yes. **Rest Rooms and Showers:** Yes. **Fuel:** Yes. **Propane:** Yes. **Internal Roads:** Paved. **RV Service:** Yes. **Market:** In Bartow or Acworth. **Restaurant:** In Cartersville or Acworth. **General Store:** Yes. **Vending:** Yes. **Swimming Pool:** Yes. **Playground:** Yes. **Activities:** Fishing, boating. **Nearby Attractions:** Barnsly Gardens, Coopers Iron Works, Dellinger Park Complex, Etowah Arts Gallery, Etowah Indian Mounds, Lake Allatoona, Red Top State Park, Royal Oaks Golf Course. **Additional Information:** Cartersville-Barton County Welcome Center, (770) 387-1357.

RESTRICTIONS

Pets: On leash, some restrictions. **Fires:** In designated areas only. **Alcoholic Beverages:** Allowed. **Vehicle Maximum Length:** 25 ft.

TO GET THERE

From I-75, take Exit 283. Go 2 mi. to campground entrance (in front of 2nd set of RR tracks).

CARTERSVILLE
Red Top Mountain State Park

50 Lodge Rd., Cartersville 30120. T: (770) 975-4226; www.gastateparks.org.

🚐 ★★★★   ⛺ ★★★★

Beauty: ★★★★   Site Privacy: ★★★
Spaciousness: ★★★   Quiet: ★★★★
Security: ★★★★★   Cleanliness: ★★★★
Insect Control: ★★★★   Facilities: ★★★

Red Top Mountain was once an important mining area for iron—the red-colored soil gives this
away. Located a short distance from I-75 and
near the town of Acworth, this park offers great
camping opportunities on Allatoona Lake. Tent
campers have a section all to themselves (sites
37–60), but water and power hookups are only
available in the 63 other sites. Sites 1–12 are
pull-throughs; the rest are back-ins. The area is
nicely wooded, offering shade to small but picturesque sites. Every Saturday from May until
early September, the park has a bluegrass and
storytelling program. In addition to tennis, mini
golf, and boating, the park has 11.5 miles of
trails to explore.

BASICS

Operated By: Georgia Dept. of Natural
Resources. **Open:** All year. **Site Assignment:**
Reservations or first come, first served. **Registra-
tion:** At visitor center or lodge. **Fee:** $12–$18.
Parking: 2 vehicles per site.

FACILITIES

Number of RV Sites: 63. **Number of Tent-
Only Sites:** 29. **Hookups:** Water, electric (50
amps). **Each Site:** Wooded w/ tent pad, grill, fire
ring. **Dump Station:** Yes. **Laundry:** No. **Pay
Phone:** Yes. **Rest Rooms and Showers:** Yes.
Fuel: No. **Propane:** No. **Internal Roads:** Paved.
RV Service: In Acworth. **Market:** In Acworth.
Restaurant: In Cartersville or Acworth. **General
Store:** In visitor center. **Vending:** Yes. **Swimming
Pool:** Yes. **Playground:** Yes. **Other:** Gated park.
Activities: Tennis, mini golf, hiking, boating, swim-
ming, game room. **Nearby Attractions:** Etowah
Indian Mounds State Historic Site, Kennesaw
Mountain National Battlefield Park, Weinman Min-
eral Museum. **Additional Information:**
Cartersville-Barton County Welcome Center, (770)
387-1357.

RESTRICTIONS

Pets: On leash only. **Fires:** In fire rings only. **Alcoholic Beverages:** At sites only. **Vehicle Maximum Length:** 40 ft. **Other:** No bicycles allowed
on trails.

TO GET THERE

From Atlanta, go north on I-75 to Exit 285. Go
right on Red Top Mountain Rd. across Lake
Allatoona to the state park.

CHATSWORTH

Woodring Branch Campground

5026 Woodring Branch Rd., Oakman 30732. T: (706)
334-2248; www.reserveusa.com or
www.sam.usace.army.mil/op/rec/carters.

🚐 ★★★★★   ⛺ ★★★★★

Beauty: ★★★★★   Site Privacy: ★★★★★
Spaciousness: ★★★★★   Quiet: ★★★★★
Security: ★★★★★   Cleanliness: ★★★★
Insect Control: ★★★★   Facilities: ★★★

This Corps of Engineers Campground is exceptionally beautiful and quiet, with most sites very
close to the shores of Carters Lake. A very rural
spot in the northwest corner of the state, this
campground boasts huge wooded sites, with
some foliage in between. All of the sites are back-
ins, with paved RV and car spaces, fine (pea-
sized) gravel pads for tents, picnic tables, and so
on. Almost every site has a gorgeous lake view,
and the most amazing is from site 35. Site 31 is
especially secluded, although its view is not as
stunning, and 17 is the most impressively huge.
Don't let the spacious, peaceful atmosphere fool
you, however. There is plenty of recreation to
choose from, including water sports. The beauty
and privacy make this a great spot for couples,
but families will also enjoy the space and activities immensely.

BASICS

Operated By: Army Corps of Engineers. **Open:**
Apr.–Oct. **Site Assignment:** Reservations
accepted. **Registration:** At camp office. **Fee:**
$8–$18. **Parking:** Yes.

FACILITIES

Number of RV Sites: 31. **Number of Tent-
Only Sites:** 11. **Hookups:** Water, electric (20, 30
amps). **Each Site:** Tent pad, picnic table. **Dump
Station:** Yes. **Laundry:** Yes. **Pay Phone:** Yes. **Rest
Rooms and Showers:** Yes. **Fuel:** No. **Propane:**
No. **Internal Roads:** Paved. **RV Service:** No.
Market: In Chatsworth. **Restaurant:** In
Chatsworth. **General Store:** No. **Vending:** Soft
drinks. **Swimming Pool:** Yes. **Playground:** Yes.

Activities: Boating, hiking trails, water skiing.
Nearby Attractions: Antique shopping, outlet mall, Cherokee Indian Museum, Fort Mountain State Park.

RESTRICTIONS

Pets: On leash only. **Fires:** In designated areas. **Alcoholic Beverages:** At sites only. **Vehicle Maximum Length:** None.

TO GET THERE

From Ellijay, travel west on Hwy. 282. Follow signs approximately 4 mi. to the campground

CLARKESVILLE
Moccasin Creek State Park

3655 Hwy. 197, Clarkesville 30523. T: (706) 947-3194.

🚐 ★★★★	⛺ ★★★★
Beauty: ★★★★	Site Privacy: ★★★★
Spaciousness: ★★★★	Quiet: ★★★★
Security: ★★★★	Cleanliness: ★★★★
Insect Control: ★★★★	Facilities: ★★★

High in the Blue Ridge Mountains and surrounded on three sides by the enormous Lake Burton, Moccasin Creek State Park offers a unique opportunity for campers with disabilities. The majority of the property is wheelchair-accessible, including a fishing pier reserved exclusively for handicapped visitors, seniors, and children. Despite its mountainous location, the campground is relatively flat. This makes it easy to maneuver around in large RVs, bicycles, and wheelchairs. Canoeing on the lake is a treat, though the high elevation and terrain mean that sudden winds can blow up (some strong enough to tip canoes over in the lake's center). Several trails wind through the mountains around the lake, including an easy walk to Hemlock Falls and a more rugged trek to Moccasin Creek Falls. The fall colors are especially beautiful here, making it very difficult to score a vacancy during Oct.

BASICS

Operated By: Georgia Dept. of Natural Resources. **Open:** All year. **Site Assignment:** First come, first served. **Registration:** Office. **Fee:** $18–$22. **Parking:** On site.

FACILITIES

Number of RV Sites: 54. **Number of Tent-Only Sites:.** **Hookups:** Water, electric. **Dump Station:** Yes. **Laundry:** Yes. **Pay Phone:** Yes. **Rest**

Rooms and Showers: Yes. **Fuel:** No. **Propane:** No. **Internal Roads:** Yes. **RV Service:** No. **Market:** In Clarkesville. **Restaurant:** In Clarkesville. **General Store:** On Hwy. 197. **Vending:** Yes. **Swimming Pool:** No. **Playground:** Yes. **Other:** Observation tower. **Activities:** Hiking, fishing, canoeing (seasonal). **Nearby Attractions:** Appalachian Trail, Chattahoochee National Forest.

RESTRICTIONS

Pets: On leash only. **Fires:** In fire rings only. **Alcoholic Beverages:** Not allowed. **Vehicle Maximum Length:** 40 ft.

TO GET THERE

20 mi. north of Clarkesville on GA Hwy 197 or 15 mi. west of Clayton on GA Hwy 76 & GA Hwy 197

CLAYTON
Rabun Beach Campground

5100 Lake Rabun Rd., Lakemont 30552. T: (706) 782-3320; F: (706) 782-3320.

🚐 ★★★★	⛺ ★★★★★
Beauty: ★★★★★	Site Privacy: ★★★★★
Spaciousness: ★★★★★	Quiet: ★★★★★
Security: ★★★★	Cleanliness: ★★★★
Insect Control: ★★★★★	Facilities: ★★

Those wanting a beautiful and secluded camping experience in rural Georgia will do well to visit Rabun Beach. A gravel road leads campers to 80 sites (5 of which are tent-only). Most of the RV-friendly sites, with water and electric hookups, are back-ins, but a few are pull-throughs. Though the entire area is attractive, sites 49 and 53 are truly gorgeous. No sites are situated directly on Lake Rabun, but all are within easy walking distance. Visitors have their pick of sites during the week, but even on busy weekends visitors will have little problem finding one of the many spacious and well-shaded sites unoccupied. Not far from this extraordinary campground is Tallulah Gorge State Park, sometimes referred to as the Grand Canyon of the southeast, and a 1.3 mile trail leads to 50-foot Angel Falls.

BASICS

Operated By: US Forest Service. **Open:** May–Nov. **Site Assignment:** First come, first served. **Registration:** At camp office; no reservations; cash or check only. **Fee:** $10–$18. **Parking:** In campground.

FACILITIES

Number of RV Sites: 75. **Number of Tent-Only Sites:** 5. **Hookups:** Water, electric (20 amps). **Each Site:** Grill, picnic table, tent pad. **Dump Station:** Yes. **Laundry:** No. **Pay Phone:** Yes. **Rest Rooms and Showers:** Yes. **Fuel:** No. **Propane:** No. **Internal Roads:** Gravel. **RV Service:** No. **Market:** 6 mi. **Restaurant:** 2 mi. **General Store:** No. **Vending:** No. **Swimming Pool:** No. **Playground:** No. **Other:** Lake on site. **Activities:** Hiking, swimming, boating, fishing. **Nearby Attractions:** Angel Falls, Tallulah Gorge overlook. **Additional Information:** Rabun County Civic Center, (706) 212-2149.

RESTRICTIONS

Pets: On leash only. **Fires:** In fire rings only. **Alcoholic Beverages:** Allowed. **Vehicle Maximum Length:** 35 ft.

TO GET THERE

From Hwy. 441 in Clayton, go 2 mi. and turn right on the Wiley Connector. Go 0.1 mi. and turn left on Old Hwy. 441. Go 2 mi. and turn right on Lake Rabun Rd. The campground is 4 mi. ahead on the right.

COMMERCE

The Pottery Campgrounds

Exit 53, I-85, Commerce 30529. T: (800) 223-0667; www.cravenpottery.com.

🚐 ★★★   ⛺ n/a

Beauty: ★★★   Site Privacy: ★★★
Spaciousness: ★★★   Quiet: ★★★
Security: ★★★★   Cleanliness: ★★★
Insect Control: ★★★   Facilities: ★

A relatively new campground associated with The Pottery home and garden outlet store, The Pottery Plant greenhouse and gardens, and Stringers Fish Camp and Oyster Bar, the Pottery Campground is a no-frills way station for campers visiting area attractions. There are no activities or facilities of note—just hookups and a bathhouse. That said, the sites are of good size and mostly shady. Campsite 13 is long and shady, while site 48 is new and nicely set into the hillside; both are pull-throughs. If pottery-related shopping doesn't thrill you, both Lake Hartwell and Lake Lanier are nearby, along with a plethora of recreational options.

BASICS

Operated By: Craven, Inc. **Open:** All year. **Site**

Assignment: First come, first served, 24-hours cancellation policy. **Registration:** At back house office, w/ security guard, or by envelope. **Fee:** $20. **Parking:** On site.

FACILITIES

Number of RV Sites: 52. **Number of Tent-Only Sites:** 0. **Hookups:** Water, electric (30 amps), sewer. **Each Site:** Brick oven, picnic table. **Dump Station:** Yes. **Laundry:** No. **Pay Phone:** Yes. **Rest Rooms and Showers:** Yes. **Fuel:** No. **Propane:** No. **Internal Roads:** Paved. **RV Service:** 10 mi. **Market:** 0.5 mi. **Restaurant:** Stringer's Fish Camp, 0.5 mi. **General Store:** 0.5 mi. **Vending:** Yes. **Swimming Pool:** No. **Playground:** No. **Activities:** Outlet shopping, watersports at nearby lakes. **Nearby Attractions:** Steven Tanger outlet stores, The Pottery store, The Pottery Plant greenhouse & gardens.

RESTRICTIONS

Pets: On leash only. **Fires:** In grills only. **Alcoholic Beverages:** Not allowed. **Vehicle Maximum Length:** None.

TO GET THERE

From I-85 N., take exit 149. Turn right onto Hwy. 441. The campground is on the right behind The Pottery store.

CORDELE

Georgia Veterans Memorial State Park

2459-A US Hwy 280 West, Cordele 31015. T: (229) 276-2371.

🚐 ★★★★   ⛺ ★★★★

Beauty: ★★★★★   Site Privacy: ★★★★
Spaciousness: ★★★★★   Quiet: ★★★★
Security: ★★★★   Cleanliness: ★★★★
Insect Control: ★★★   Facilities: ★★★★★

This popular campground, only a few miles from Cordele, has ample sites with moderate hardwood shade. The generally flat landscape is very picturesque and tranquil. RV Camping Areas 1 and 2 (sites 1–53) are arranged by Lake Blackshear, with campsites 1–27 set on the lakefront itself. These are the best sites in the campground, especially sites 25–27 (all are pretty, but site 27 is especially huge and gorgeous). Sites 52 and 53 are particularly large pull-throughs. Camping Area 3 (sites 54–76) is a separate loop set back in the woods; its sites are not as nice as the others. Across the lake are the park's main facilities (the visitor center, a museum, military exhibits, nature trails, etc.); that's also where you'll find tent camping areas and cottages. This campground has plenty of options for groups, from a fully equipped conference center to a separately-reserved, secluded area for group primitive camping.

BASICS

Operated By: Georgia Dept. of Natural Resources. **Open:** All year. **Site Assignment:** Can reserve waterfront or non-waterfront. **Registration:** At visitor center. **Fee:** RV $10.35–$20, tent $9.15–$18, cottages $75–$90. **Parking:** At site or in park.

FACILITIES

Number of RV Sites: 77. **Number of Tent-Only Sites:.** **Hookups:** Water, electric (30, 50 amps), cable. **Each Site:** Grills. **Dump Station:** Yes. **Laundry:** Yes. **Pay Phone:** Yes. **Rest Rooms and Showers:** Yes. **Fuel:** Nearby. **Propane:** Nearby. **Internal Roads:** Paved. **RV Service:** No. **Market:** In Codele. **Restaurant:** In Cordele. **General Store:** Yes. **Vending:** Yes. **Swimming Pool:** Yes. **Playground:** Yes. **Other:** 10 Cottages. **Activities:** Nature trail, golf, boating, water skiing, fishing model airplane flying. **Nearby Attractions:** Warner Robins Air Museum, Chehaw Wild Animal Park. **Additional Information:** Cordele Chamber of Commerce, (229) 273-1668 or www.cordele-crisp-chamber.com.

RESTRICTIONS

Pets: On leash only. **Fires:** In fire rings only. **Alcoholic Beverages:** At sites only. **Vehicle Maximum Length:** 50 ft.

TO GET THERE

The park is 9 mi. west of I-75 (Exit 101) near Cordele on US Hwy 280

CUMMING

Bald Ridge

4100 Bald Ridge Rd., Cumming 30040. T: (770) 889-1591.

🚐 ★★★★	⛺ ★★★★
Beauty: ★★★★★	Site Privacy: ★★★★
Spaciousness: ★★★★★	Quiet: ★★★★
Security: ★★★★★	Cleanliness: ★★★★★
Insect Control: ★★★	Facilities: ★★★

This extraordinarily well-manicured campground is situated in a nice suburban to rural area about 30 miles northeast of Atlanta. The sites vary from shady to open, with gorgeous views, though not a great deal of privacy, at lakefront sites 39–53. We also recommend lakefront sites 70–72, which offer lovely views and are fairly secluded as well. Avoid sites 81 and 82 if possible, as they are adjacent to the sewer, and keep in mind noisy boats when choosing a site near the water. Lake Sidney Lanier is host to several Army Corps of Engineers campgrounds, and Bald Ridge is the flagship, with facilities to accommodate RVs and tents quite well (although the restrooms are nicer at a couple of the other campgrounds). Some back-ins and some pull-throughs, the extremely large, paved sites also include a sizeable gravel picnic and tent area. Between the gates and the general seclusion, security here is excellent, and it is a wonderful spot for families.

BASICS

Operated By: Army Corps of Engineers. **Open:** Feb. 22–Nov. 19. **Site Assignment:** Reservations accepted. **Registration:** Park entry station. **Fee:** $12–$22. **Parking:** On site.

FACILITIES

Number of RV Sites: 82. **Number of Tent-Only Sites:** 0. **Hookups:** Water, electric (30, 50 amps),sewer. **Each Site:** Picnic table, grill, fire pits. **Dump Station:** Yes. **Laundry:** Yes. **Pay Phone:** No. **Rest Rooms and Showers:** Yes. **Fuel:** Nearby. **Propane:** Nearby. **Internal Roads:** Paved. **RV Service:** No. **Market:** In Cumming. **Restaurant:** In Cumming. **General Store:** Nearby. **Vending:** Yes. **Swimming Pool:** No. **Playground:** Yes. **Activities:** Boating, fishing, swimming. **Nearby Attractions:** Lake Lanier Island water park & golf course. **Additional Information:** Cumming-Forsyth County Chamber of Commerce, (770) 887-6461 or www.forsythchamber.org,.

RESTRICTIONS

Pets: On leash only. **Fires:** In fire rings only. **Alcoholic Beverages:** Not allowed. **Vehicle Maximum Length:** None. **Other:** 14-day max. stay limit.

TO GET THERE

Take 400N to Exit 16. Turn right on Pilgrim Mill Rd., then turn right on Sincllair Shores Rd. Turn left on Bald Rich Rd, which ends at the campground.

DARIEN
Inland Harbor RV Park

Hwy. 251 E, Darien 31305. T: (912) 437-6172.

🚐 ★★   ▲ n/a

Beauty: ★★★   Site Privacy: ★★
Spaciousness: ★★★   Quiet: ★★
Security: ★★   Cleanliness: ★★★
Insect Control: ★★★   Facilities: ★

The sites, all pull-throughs, at Inland Harbor RV Park are of medium size overall, though they're still large for a private campground. Strictly a stopover on the way up or down the coast on I-95, this campground caters to big rigs and through-travelers. Sites are relatively well shaded, but there is not much screening between you and your neighbor. You probably wouldn't stick around the property to do anything but relax between road trips. That said, the campground is perfectly fine as a practical base for exploring coastal attractions. The proximity of the highway creates significant road noise, so ask for quieter sites away from the road.

BASICS
Operated By: Lois Truhlar. **Open:** All year. **Site Assignment:** First come, first served. **Registration:** At office. **Fee:** $17. **Parking:** In campground.

FACILITIES
Number of RV Sites: 60. **Number of Tent-Only Sites:** 0. **Hookups:** Water, electric (50 amps), sewer, phone, cable. **Each Site:** Picnic table, grill. **Dump Station:** Yes. **Laundry:** Yes. **Pay Phone:** Yes. **Rest Rooms and Showers:** Yes. **Fuel:** No. **Propane:** No. **Internal Roads:** Paved. **RV Service:** No. **Market:** 1 mi. **Restaurant:** Less than 1 mi. **General Store:** No. **Vending:** No. **Swimming Pool:** No. **Playground:** No. **Activities:** Visiting the coast. **Nearby Attractions:** Rice Plantation, Sapalo Island.

RESTRICTIONS
Pets: Yes. **Fires:** In grills only. **Alcoholic Beverages:** Allowed. **Vehicle Maximum Length:** 70 ft.

TO GET THERE
From I-95, go 2.5 mi. east on Hwy. 251 to the campground.

ELBERTON
Bobby Brown State Park

2509 Bobby Brown State Park Rd., Elberton 30635. T: (706) 213-2046; www.gastateparks.org.

🚐 ★★★★   ▲ ★★★

Beauty: ★★★★   Site Privacy: ★★
Spaciousness: ★★★   Quiet: ★★★★
Security: ★★★★★   Cleanliness: ★★★★
Insect Control: ★★★★   Facilities: ★★★

One of several camping areas located on the Georgia–South Carolina border, Bobby Brown State Park is situated on what was once the historic boomtown of Petersburg, established in 1798. Now campers come to the 665-acre park to relax and take part in the many activities available here, including fishing, boating, swimming, and hiking. Water and electric hookups are available at the park's 61 sites, which are a mix of pull-throughs and back-ins. When compared to other state parks, these sites are a bit small, but they still are larger than many private campgrounds. If you want premium access to the Broad River, pay $1 more and stay at sites 3–13, but look to see if site 60 is open—it's arguably one of the best in the park. Visitors who get the itch to explore will want to check out Pioneer Nancy Hart's Cabin or the Granite Museum.

BASICS
Operated By: Georgia Dept. of Natural Resources. **Open:** All year. **Site Assignment:** Reservations or first come, first served. **Registration:** At main office. **Fee:** $13–$16. **Parking:** 2 vehicles per site.

FACILITIES
Number of RV Sites: 61. **Number of Tent-Only Sites:** 2 primitive areas. **Hookups:** Water, electric (30, 50 amps). **Each Site:** Picnic table, grill, fire ring, lantern pole. **Dump Station:** Yes. **Laundry:** Yes. **Pay Phone:** Yes. **Rest Rooms and Showers:** Yes. **Fuel:** No. **Propane:** No. **Internal Roads:** Paved. **RV Service:** 22 mi. **Market:** 22 mi. **Restaurant:** 10 mi. **General Store:** No. **Vending:** Soft drinks. **Swimming Pool:** Yes. **Playground:** Yes. **Activities:** Hiking trails, boat launch, 72,000-acre lake, fishing pier, canoes, pedal boats. **Nearby Attractions:** Pioneer Nancy Hart's Cabin, Granite Museum.

RESTRICTIONS

Pets: On leash (6 ft. or less) only. **Fires:** In fire rings only. **Alcoholic Beverages:** At sites only. **Vehicle Maximum Length:** 40 ft. **Other:** 14-day max. stay limit.

TO GET THERE

From I-85, exit at Hwy. 175 and go to Elberton. Then take Hwy. 72 east for 15 mi. Turn right on Bobby Brown State Park Rd. Go 7 mi. to the park entrance.

ELLIJAY

Doll Mountain Campground

P.O. Box 96, Oakman 30732. T: (706) 276-4413; www.carterslake.com or www.reserveusa.com.

🚐 ★★★★★   ▲ ★★★★★

Beauty: ★★★★★   Site Privacy: ★★★★★
Spaciousness: ★★★★★ Quiet: ★★★★★
Security: ★★★★   Cleanliness: ★★★★
Insect Control: ★★★★★ Facilities: ★★★

Doll Mountain Campground is an excellent property located on the shores of Carter Lake, itself an outdoor activity paradise. There are several camping and recreation areas to choose from on the lake, and Doll Mountain is among the nicest. Most campsites are very spacious, and all are heavily wooded. However, because the sites are strung out along a thin spit of land projecting into the lake, almost all sites have beautiful lake views. Sites 1, 2, 4, 6, and 7 are small, pretty pull-throughs, but they are not as secluded as the other sites. Sites 15, 15A, and 16 are somewhat cramped and distastefully close to the dump station. The best location by far is the loop containing sites 39–46; site 45 is particularly gorgeous. Doll Mountain's sites also vary a bit in terms of overall privacy; some don't have much, but others are some of the most secluded we've seen.

BASICS

Operated By: Army Corps of Engineers. **Open:** Apr.–Oct. **Site Assignment:** Reservations preferred. **Registration:** At camp office. **Fee:** $12–$18. **Parking:** On site.

FACILITIES

Number of RV Sites: 39. **Number of Tent-Only Sites:** 25. **Hookups:** Water, electric (30 amps). **Each Site:** Picnic table, fire pit. **Dump Sta-**

tion: Yes. **Laundry:** Yes. **Pay Phone:** Yes. **Rest Rooms and Showers:** Yes. **Fuel:** Nearby. **Propane:** No. **Internal Roads:** Paved. **RV Service:** Yes. **Market:** In Ellijay. **Restaurant:** In Ellijay. **General Store:** No. **Vending:** Soft drinks. **Swimming Pool:** Yes. **Playground:** Yes. **Activities:** Basketball, boating, ampitheather, hiking, swimming. **Nearby Attractions:** Battle ground, Lake Chattahoochee.

RESTRICTIONS

Pets: On leash only. **Fires:** In designated areas only. **Alcoholic Beverages:** At sites only. **Vehicle Maximum Length:** 35 ft. **Other:** 2-day min. on weekends.

TO GET THERE

From Ellijay, travel 11 mi. southwest on Hwy. 382. Follow signs to campground.

EULONIA

Lake Harmony RV Park

Rte. 3 Box 3128, Townsend 31331. T: (888) 767-7864; www.lakeharmonypark.com.

🚐 ★★★   ▲ ★★

Beauty: ★★★   Site Privacy: ★★
Spaciousness: ★★   Quiet: ★★★★
Security: ★★★★   Cleanliness: ★★★★
Insect Control: ★★★ Facilities: ★★★

Located south of Savanah and just north of Brunswick, Lake Harmony provides visitors with a place to rest within easy reach of Georgia's coastal attractions. Access to I-95 is convenient, yet the park is quiet and has rural feel. The 50 sites are a mixture of pull-throughs and back ins, with 25 additional sites designated as tent-only. The sites are small, with sand and pine straw ground cover, which is sufficient but could use a little work. With a few exceptions, the sites are shady. Fishing, boating, and swimming are available, but those campers wanting to explore may venture onto nearby Saint Simons for hiking, kayaking, or shopping. Others may wish to visit Cumberland Island National Seashore, which is accessed by ferry only.

BASICS

Operated By: Larry Kosior. **Open:** All year. **Site Assignment:** Reservations preferred. **Registration:** At camp office. **Fee:** $18–$20. **Parking:** In campground.

FACILITIES

Number of RV Sites: 50. **Number of Tent-Only Sites:** 25. **Hookups:** Water, electric (30 amps), sewer, cable. **Each Site:** Picnic tale, grill. **Dump Station:** No. **Laundry:** Yes. **Pay Phone:** Yes. **Rest Rooms and Showers:** Yes. **Fuel:** No. **Propane:** Yes. **Internal Roads:** Packed sand. **RV Service:** No. **Market:** 5 mi. **Restaurant:** 0.5 mi. **General Store:** Limited groceries. **Vending:** No. **Swimming Pool:** No. **Playground:** No. **Other:** Lake w/ swimming beach on site. **Activities:** Fishing, boating, swimming, bird-watching, game room, shuffleboard. **Nearby Attractions:** St. Simons Island, Brunswick, Cumberland Island, Okefenokee Swamp.

RESTRICTIONS

Pets: On leash only. **Fires:** In designated areas only. **Alcoholic Beverages:** Restricted. **Vehicle Maximum Length:** 65 ft.

TO GET THERE

Take I-95 Exit 58 in Townsend. Park is 0.6 mi. from exit.

FARGO
Stephen Foster State Park

Route 1 Box 131, Fargo 31631. T: (912) 637-5274.

🚐 ★★★★★	▲ ★★★★★
Beauty: ★★★★★	Site Privacy: ★★★★★
Spaciousness: ★★★★★	Quiet: ★★★★★
Security: ★★★★★	Cleanliness: ★★★★★
Insect Control: ★★	Facilities: ★★★

The extremely remote location of Stephen C. Foster State Park means that its campground is extraordinarily peaceful and serene. The park is the main Georgia entrance to the Okefenokee Swamp and related Okefenokee National Wildlife Refuge. Campsites are huge, densely shaded, and wooded for offering plenty of privacy. The natural scenery and wildlife are the obvious attractions here, and all that prevents this campground from getting five stars in beauty are the occasional intrusions of telephone lines and unsightly utility buildings. Even so, the quiet blackwater of the swamp, the stately cypress groves, and the hanging curtains of Spanish moss still make this one of the prettiest campgrounds in the region. Families often walk the grounds at night to watch the droves of wild deer that wan-

der placidly by. Be sure to bring insect repellant and mosquito netting, since the swampy conditions are heaven for all manner of bloodsuckers.

BASICS

Operated By: Georgia Dept. of Natural Resources. **Open:** All year. **Site Assignment:** First come, first served except during peak season when sites are assigned. **Registration:** Office. **Fee:** $18–$20. **Parking:** On site.

FACILITIES

Number of RV Sites: 49. **Number of Tent-Only Sites:** 17. **Hookups:** Water, electric (20, 30 amps). **Each Site:** Picnic table, grill. **Dump Station:** Yes. **Laundry:** Yes. **Pay Phone:** Yes. **Rest Rooms and Showers:** Yes. **Fuel:** No. **Propane:** No. **Internal Roads:** Paved. **RV Service:** No. **Market:** In Ernest. **Restaurant:** In Ernest. **General Store:** Yes. **Vending:** Yes. **Swimming Pool:** No. **Playground:** Yes. **Activities:** Fishing, boating, canoeing. **Nearby Attractions:** Okefenokee Swamp, Suwanee Canal Recreational Area, Laura S. Walker State Park.

RESTRICTIONS

Pets: On leash only. **Fires:** Allowed. **Alcoholic Beverages:** At sites only. **Vehicle Maximum Length:** 50 ft.

TO GET THERE

Take US 441 to Fargo. Go 18 mi. on Hwy 177N to the state park.

FLOWERY BRANCH
Chestnut Ridge Campground

6515 Chestnut Ridge Rd., Flowery Branch 30542. T: (770) 967-6710.

🚐 ★★★★★	▲ ★★★★★
Beauty: ★★★★★	Site Privacy: ★★★★★
Spaciousness: ★★★★★	Quiet: ★★★★★
Security: ★★★★★	Cleanliness: ★★★★★
Insect Control: ★★★★	Facilities: ★★★

Another gorgeous campground in the Lake Lanier resort area (see profiles for Shoal Creek in Buford and Lake Lanier Islands), Chestnut Ridge sits on a small peninsula in an upscale residential neighborhood. Campsites are large, shaded, and many have screening foliage between them. Most sites are fairly close together; campsites 1–13 have the most elbow room, while sites 23–29 are the most secluded.

As with other properties in this Army Corps of Engineers–managed area, boat noise is often the only downside; ask attendants for recommendations about the quietest sites. Chestnut Ridge is most often full on weekends. This campground offers little more than nice accommodations, as most visitors come for lake activities and water sports. However, there's plenty to do in the area, since Lake Lanier has 43 day-use parks, ten marinas, and nine state, county, and city parks.

BASICS

Operated By: Army Corps of Engineers. **Open:** Mar. 29–Sept. 8. **Site Assignment:** 60% reservable, 40% first come, first served. **Registration:** Park entry station. **Fee:** $12–$22 plus day use fees. **Parking:** On site.

FACILITIES

Number of RV Sites: 85. **Number of Tent-Only Sites:.** **Hookups:** Water, electric (30,50 amps), sewer. **Each Site:** Grills, fire pits, picnic table. **Dump Station:** Yes. **Laundry:** Yes. **Pay Phone:** No. **Rest Rooms and Showers:** Yes. **Fuel:** No. **Propane:** Nearby. **Internal Roads:** Paved. **RV Service:** No. **Market:** In Flowery Branch. **Restaurant:** In Flowery Branch. **General Store:** Nearby. **Vending:** Drink only. **Swimming Pool:** No. **Playground:** Yes. **Activities:** Boating, lake swimming, fishing. **Nearby Attractions:** Lake Lanier Island water park & golf course. **Additional Information:** City of Flowery Branch, (770) 967-6371 or www.cityoffflowerybranch.org.

RESTRICTIONS

Pets: On leash only. **Fires:** In fire rings only. **Alcoholic Beverages:** Not allowed. **Vehicle Maximum Length:** None. **Other:** 14-day max. stay limit.

TO GET THERE

From Atlanta, take I-85N to I-985. Take Exit 8 and turn left onto Hwy. 347, turn right onto McEver Rd., and turn left on Gaines Ferry Rd. Then turn right onto Chestnut Ridge Rd., which ends at the campground

FORSYTH
Forsyth KOA Campground

414 South Frontage Rd., Forsyth 31029. T: (478) 994-2019; www.koa.com.

 ★★★   ★★

Beauty: ★★★★   Site Privacy: ★★
Spaciousness: ★★★   Quiet: ★★★
Security: ★★★   Cleanliness: ★★★★★
Insect Control: ★★★★   Facilities: ★★★

In some ways a typical private campground, this KOA is recommended on the basis of friendly owners, cleanliness, and the general sweetness of kids feeding ducks and geese at the fishing pond. Privacy and site size are average for a private campground, and the main detractor is certainly the parks proximity to I-75. Forsyth is a lovely small town, but the noise of the interstate warrants seeking out sites as far from the traffic as possible. Most of the sites are pull-throughs, with gravel, gras,s or pine straw ground cover. The plentiful pine trees help make this an attractive campground, but be mindful of limited security. There is no gate, and again—it is very close to the interstate. The combination of activities in Forsyth and several possible day-trips do add up to a good family camping spot. Located in the center of the state, we recommend this as an ideal midway stop for midwesterners en route to Florida.

BASICS

Operated By: KOA Kampgrounds. **Open:** All year. **Site Assignment:** Reservations accepted. **Registration:** At camp office. **Fee:** $17–$23. **Parking:** 2 vehicles per site.

FACILITIES

Number of RV Sites: 130. **Number of Tent-Only Sites:** 10. **Hookups:** Water, electric (30 amps), sewer. **Each Site:** Picnic table, grill. **Dump Station:** Yes. **Laundry:** Yes. **Pay Phone:** Yes. **Rest Rooms and Showers:** Yes. **Fuel:** 1 mi. **Propane:** Yes. **Internal Roads:** Gravel. **RV Service:** Yes. **Market:** In Forsyth. **Restaurant:** In Forsyth. **General Store:** No. **Vending:** No. **Swimming Pool:** Yes. **Playground:** Yes. **Activities:** Volleyball, badminton, fishing, basketball, boating. **Nearby Attractions:** Historic Juliette, driving tours of historic homes, Six Flags.

RESTRICTIONS

Pets: On leash only. **Fires:** In designated areas. **Alcoholic Beverages:** At sites only. **Vehicle Maximum Length:** None.

TO GET THERE

Exit I-75 at Exit 186 and follow the signs.

FORTSON

Blanton Creek Park

1516 Bartletts Ferry Rd., Fortson 31808. T: (706) 643-7737.

🚐 ★★★★   ▲ ★★★

Beauty: ★★★★★	Site Privacy: ★★★★
Spaciousness: ★★★★	Quiet: ★★★★★
Security: ★★★★★	Cleanliness: ★★★
Insect Control: ★★★	Facilities: ★★★

Blanton Creek Park is one of numerous Georgia Power–owned campgrounds scattered across the state. This lakeside property has an unusual layout. The hilly terrain rolls down to the shores of Lake Harding, and the roads and campsites form terraces on the hillside. The overall effect is quite lovely, and the only real aesthetic downside to the campground are the less-than-clean facilities (the bathrooms were particularly gross on our visit). Assuming that gets taken care of, there's little to fault in the large campsites set under gorgeous woods. If you're looking for a good pull-through, there aren't many to choose from; however, site 7 is a nice one, and site 12 is even better. Sites 44–47 have fantastic lake views. The tent area here has a nice views too, but it's really too crowded to recommend.

BASICS

Operated By: Georgia Power Company. **Open:** Apr.–Labor Day. **Site Assignment:** Reservations accepted. **Registration:** Office. **Fee:** $14 per vehicle. **Parking:** In campground.

FACILITIES

Number of RV Sites: 43. **Number of Tent-Only Sites:** 8. **Hookups:** Electric. **Each Site:** Picnic tables, grills. **Dump Station:** Yes. **Laundry:** Yes. **Pay Phone:** Yes. **Rest Rooms and Showers:** Yes. **Fuel:** No. **Propane:** No. **Internal Roads:** Paved & gravel. **RV Service:** In Columbus. **Market:** In Columbus. **Restaurant:** In Columbus. **General Store:** No. **Vending:** Yes. **Swimming Pool:** Yes. **Playground:** Yes. **Other:** Group wilderness camping. **Activities:** Boating, fishing, hiking. **Nearby Attractions:** Calloway Gardens, Pine Mountain, Franklin D. Roosevelt State Park. **Additional Information:** Georgia Power, (888) GPC-LAKE.

RESTRICTIONS

Pets: On leash only; 2 pet max. **Fires:** In grills only. **Alcoholic Beverages:** Not allowed. **Vehicle**

Maximum Length: Call ahead for details. **Other:** big rigs welcome.

TO GET THERE

From I-185, take Exit 21 and go 0.25 mi. west on Hwy. 116, then 3.5 mi. west on Hwy. 103, then 1 mi. south on Lick Skillet Rd.

GREENSBORO

Old Salem

1530 Old Salem Rd., Greensboro 30642. T: (706) 467-2850.

🚐 ★★★   ▲ ★★★

Beauty: ★★★	Site Privacy: ★★★
Spaciousness: ★★★	Quiet: ★★★
Security: ★★★★★	Cleanliness: ★★★★
Insect Control: ★★★★	Facilities: ★★★

The most elaborate of Georgia Power's campgrounds on Lake Oconee (see the following profile for Parks Ferry), Old Salem focuses mostly on lake activities and water sports. This campground is quite popular, and the large number of children and vehicles can make it less than tranquil. Campsites vary in size, but most are acceptably large; all are nicely wooded. The best campsites by far are 85, 87, 89, and 91, with 91 leading the pack. All of these are extremely choice and hard to get due to their lakeside setting and close proximity to the campers-only boat dock. Families might prefer sites 78–80, which are adjacent to the beach house and playground.

BASICS

Operated By: Georgia Power Company. **Open:** Mar.–Oct. **Site Assignment:** First come, first served. **Registration:** Office. **Fee:** $12–$14 plus parking fee. **Parking:** In campground.

FACILITIES

Number of RV Sites: 67. **Number of Tent-Only Sites:** 25. **Hookups:** Water, electric (20, 30 amps). **Each Site:** Picnic areas. **Dump Station:** Yes. **Laundry:** Yes. **Pay Phone:** Yes. **Rest Rooms and Showers:** Yes. **Fuel:**. **Propane:** Yes. **Internal Roads:** Paved. **RV Service:** Yes. **Market:** Nearby. **Restaurant:** Nearby. **General Store:** Inquire at campground. **Vending:** Inquire at campground. **Swimming Pool:** No. **Playground:** Yes. **Activities:** Swimming areas, fishing, boating, volleyball. **Nearby Attractions:** Iron Horse, museum, Green

County Courthouse. **Additional Information:** Chamber of Commerce, (800) 886-5253 www.greeneccoc.org.

RESTRICTIONS

Pets: Yes. **Fires:** Allowed. **Alcoholic Beverages:** Inquire at campground. **Vehicle Maximum Length:** Call ahead for details. **Other:** Big rigs welcome.

TO GET THERE

From Jct. I-20 Exit 130 and Hwy. 44: Go 7 mi. SW on Hwy. 44, then 0.75 mi. SE on Linger Longer Rd. then 1 mi. SW on paved road. Follow signs.

GREENSBORO

Parks Ferry

125 Wallace Dam Rd., Eatonton 31024. T: (706) 453-4308.

🚐 ★★★★	▲ ★★★
Beauty: ★★★★	Site Privacy: ★★
Spaciousness: ★★★	Quiet: ★★★★
Security: ★★★★★	Cleanliness: ★★★★
Insect Control: ★★★★	Facilities: ★★★

One of several Georgia Power campgrounds on Lake Oconee (see the preceeding profile of Old Salem), Parks Ferry is a tight triple loop of campsites set next to the lake and a tiny "wildlife habitat." This property is not as nice as nearby Old Salem, and its long sites are a bit sandwiched together. However, it's also not as crowded as its Oconee sibling, which translates to a bit more quiet and overall privacy. A lovely forest of hardwoods on the grounds also makes the place more attractive than it might otherwise be. A small beach and boat facilities make Parks Ferry a viable alternative when other Lake Oconee campgrounds are overwhelmed with visitors.

BASICS

Operated By: Georgia Power Company. **Open:** Apr. 13–Sept. 4. **Site Assignment:** First come, first served, reservations. **Registration:** Gatehouse. **Fee:** $12–$14. **Parking:** On site.

FACILITIES

Number of RV Sites: 85. **Number of Tent-Only Sites:** 40. **Hookups:** Water, electric. **Each Site:** Grill, picnic, fire pit. **Dump Station:** Yes. **Laundry:** Yes. **Pay Phone:** Yes. **Rest Rooms and Showers:** Yes. **Fuel:** No. **Propane:** No. **Internal**

Roads: Paved. **RV Service:** 10 mi. **Market:** 5 mi. **Restaurant:** 10 mi. **General Store:** 10 mi. **Vending:** Drink only. **Swimming Pool:** No. **Playground:** Yes. **Activities:** Beachfront, boat ramp, volleyball. **Nearby Attractions:** Iron Horse, museum, Green County Courthouse. **Additional Information:** Green County Chamber of Commerce, (800) 886-5253 or www.greeneccoc.org.

RESTRICTIONS

Pets: On leash only. **Fires:** In fire rings only. **Alcoholic Beverages:** Not allowed. **Vehicle Maximum Length:** 40 ft. **Other:** Big rigs welcome.

TO GET THERE

From I-20 Exit 130, go right on Hwy. 44 for 5.5 mi. and turn right on Kerry Station Rd. Continue for 3.5 mi, turn left on Parkshill Rd., and continue for1 mi. to the park on your right

HARTWELL

Hart State Park

330 Hart State Park Rd., Hartwell 30643. T: (706) 376-8756; www.gastateparks.org.

🚐 ★★★★	▲ ★★★★
Beauty: ★★★★	Site Privacy: ★★★★
Spaciousness: ★★★★	Quiet: ★★★
Security: ★★★★	Cleanliness: ★★★★
Insect Control: ★★★	Facilities: ★★★★

The 55,590-acre Hartwell Reservoir is the main attraction at Hart State Park Campground. Anglers can fish for largemouth and hybrid bass, striper, black crappie, bream, rainbow trout, and walleyed pike in the reservoir's waters, and the campground's boat ramp and six docks make water access easy. Both the size and overall privacy of these campsites vary immensely. Sites 28–37 are a bit more spacious than most, and they have decent shade and good lake views. Two big pull-throughs can be found at sites 59 and 60. The adjacent sites 56–58 are not level enough to suit most RVers. A few nature trails lace the edge of the property, and a multi-use trail for hiking and biking offers a good jaunt south of the campground. No visit to the area could possibly be complete with a pilgrimage to nearby Elberton, the "Granite Capital of the World."

BASICS

Operated By: Georgia Dept. of Natural Resources. **Open:** All year. **Site Assignment:** First come, first served. **Registration:** Park entry station. **Fee:** Call ahead for details. **Parking:** On site.

FACILITIES

Number of RV Sites: 76. **Number of Tent-Only Sites:** 25. **Hookups:** Water, electric (20, 30 amps), sewer. **Each Site:** Picnic, fire ring, grill, lantern pole. **Dump Station:** Yes. **Laundry:** Yes. **Pay Phone:** Yes. **Rest Rooms and Showers:** Yes. **Fuel:** No. **Propane:** No. **Internal Roads:** Paved. **RV Service:** 30 mi. **Market:** 5 mi. **Restaurant:** 5 mi. **General Store:** 5 mi. **Vending:** Yes. **Swimming Pool:** No. **Playground:** Yes. **Activities:** Hiking, fishing, biking, swimming beach, picnic shelters, Cricket Theater, boat ramps, canoes, pedal boats. **Nearby Attractions:** Hartwell Golf Club, Tugaloo State Park, Granite Capital of World, Hartwell Lake & Dam. **Additional Information:** Hart County Chamber of Commerce, (706) 376-8590 or www.hart-chamber.org.

RESTRICTIONS

Pets: On leash only. **Fires:** Fire rings only. **Alcoholic Beverages:** At sites only. **Vehicle Maximum Length:** 35 ft. **Other:** No entry after 11 p.m.

TO GET THERE

From Hartwell, drive north on Hwy. 29. Turn left on Ridge Rd. and go 2 mi. to the park.

HARTWELL

Payne's Creek

P.O. Box 248, Hartwell 30645-0298. T: (877) 444-6777; www.reserveusa.com.

🚐 ★★★★★   ⛺ ★★★★★

Beauty: ★★★★★   Site Privacy: ★★★★★
Spaciousness: ★★★★★   Quiet: ★★★★
Security: ★★★★★   Cleanliness: ★★★★
Insect Control: ★★★★   Facilities: ★★★

Situated on the Georgia–South Carolina border, this lakeside campground is in easy striking distance from I-85, yet remains fairly remote. Incredibly large sites lie throughout the grounds. Heavy vegetation between sites offers great privacy, and all but a few are on the water. The best of these sites—20, 21, 23, 27–29, 34, and 35—offer wide, beautiful views of the lake. Both back-ins and pull-throughs are available, though the preferred areas have large, circular pull-throughs. No developed sites are designated

tents-only, though there is a nearby primitive area. A boat-ramp provides great opportunity to access the nearly 56,000-acre Hartwell Lake, and those wishing to see a working power plant can visit the Hartwell Power plant a few miles away.

BASICS

Operated By: Army Corps of Engineers. **Open:** May–Sept. **Site Assignment:** Reservation only. **Registration:** By phone or at the website, at least 2 days in advance. **Fee:** 12. **Parking:** At site or designated areas.

FACILITIES

Number of RV Sites: 0. **Number of Tent-Only Sites:** Unnumbered primitive. **Number of Multipurpose Sites:** 52. **Hookups:** Water, electric (20, 30, 50 amps), sewer. **Each Site:** Water, electricity. **Dump Station:** Yes. **Laundry:** No. **Pay Phone:** Yes. **Rest Rooms and Showers:** Yes. **Fuel:** No. **Propane:** No. **Internal Roads:** Paved. **RV Service:** In Hartwell. **Market:** In Hartwell. **Restaurant:** In Hartwell. **General Store:** No. **Vending:** No. **Swimming Pool:** No. **Playground:** Yes. **Activities:** Boating, swimming. **Nearby Attractions:** Marinas, boat slips, rentals.

RESTRICTIONS

Pets: On leash (6 ft. or less) only. **Fires:** In fire rings or grills; burn only fallen or purchased wood. **Alcoholic Beverages:** Not allowed. **Vehicle Maximum Length:** 60 ft. **Other:** 14-day max. stay limit; campers are to occupy sites overnight; no guns or fireworks.

TO GET THERE

From I-85, take Exit 177. Proceed south on Hwy. 77 for 5 mi. Follow directional signs the last 10 mi. to the campground.

HARTWELL

Watsadler

P.O. Box 278, Hartwell 30643. T: (888) 893-0678; www.reserveusa.com.

🚐 ★★★★   ⛺ ★★★★

Beauty: ★★★★★   Site Privacy: ★★★★
Spaciousness: ★★★   Quiet: ★★★★
Security: ★★★★   Cleanliness: ★★★★
Insect Control: ★★★   Facilities: ★★★

Another U.S. Army Corps of Engineers property, Watsadler is one of several campgrounds resting on the shores of Hartwell Lake (but this is the only one open year-round). You'd expect this remote property to be dead quiet, but the large number of vehicles in the park tends to create a lot of background noise. Site size varies from fair to huge, with shade ranging from slight to heavy. A few campsites are extremely private, but most are not. Lakeside sites 9 and 10 are among the exceptions, boasting not only a good amount of screening foliage, but also a lot of room and fantastic lake views. Site 5 is also quite picturesque. The July Fourth fireworks here are said to be particularly impressive.

BASICS

Operated By: Army Corps of Engineers. **Open:** Mar. 1–Nov. 30. **Site Assignment:** Reservations accepted. **Registration:** Office. **Fee:** $16–40. **Parking:** On site.

FACILITIES

Number of Multipurpose Sites: 51. **Hookups:** Water, electric (50 amps), sewer. **Each Site:** Fire pit. **Dump Station:** Yes. **Laundry:** No. **Pay Phone:** Yes. **Rest Rooms and Showers:** Yes. **Fuel:** No. **Propane:** No. **Internal Roads:** Paved. **RV Service:** In Hartwell. **Market:** In Hartwell. **Restaurant:** In Hartwell. **General Store:** No. **Vending:** No. **Swimming Pool:** No. **Playground:** Yes. **Other:** Boat ramp, courtesy dock. **Activities:** Inquire at campground. **Nearby Attractions:** Clemson University, Hartwell Dam, July 4th fireworks. **Additional Information:** Hart County Chamber of Commerce, (706) 376-8590 or www.hart-chamber.org.

RESTRICTIONS

Pets: On leash only. **Fires:** In fire rings only. **Alcoholic Beverages:** Not allowed. **Vehicle Maximum Length:** Call ahead for details. **Other:** 14-day max. stay limit.

TO GET THERE

From I-85, take Exit 177 onto Hwy. 77 towards Hartwell. In Hartwell, take Hwy. 29N towards Anderson, South Carolina. The campground is 4 mi. outside of Hartwell

HELEN

Cherokee Campground

45 Bethel Rd., Sautee 30571. T: (706) 878-2267.

🚐 ★★★	⛺ ★★
Beauty: ★★★	Site Privacy: ★★★
Spaciousness: ★★★	Quiet: ★★★

Security: ★★★★	Cleanliness: ★★★★
Insect Control: ★★★★	Facilities: ★★

The 48 sites of this private campground are small but sufficient, with some shade provided by young trees. The absence of underbrush allows easy walking between sites but does little for privacy. Tenters will enjoy soft-mulch tent pads, and all visitors can listen to live music performed on weekends during peak season. This private campground may not have astounding views, but it's proximity to the area's cultural and outdoor activities definitely recommends it. Unicoi State Park, the Appalachian Trail, Anna Ruby Falls, and Brasstown Bald provide some of the outdoor fun. Those wanting an Old World experience can drive to nearby Helen, where German crafts and food are readily available in this Alpine-theme town. Reserve far in advance if you intend to camp during the annual Oktoberfest (mid-September through the beginning of November).

BASICS

Operated By: Ed & Julie Digiorgion. **Open:** All year. **Site Assignment:** First come, first served. **Registration:** At camp office. **Fee:** Full hookups $20, no hookups $18, for cable add $2. **Parking:** In campground.

FACILITIES

Number of RV Sites: 48. **Number of Tent-Only Sites:** Tent area. **Hookups:** Water, electric (20, 30 amps), sewer, phone, cable. **Each Site:** Picnic table. **Dump Station:** Yes. **Laundry:** Yes. **Pay Phone:** Yes. **Rest Rooms and Showers:** Yes. **Fuel:** No. **Propane:** No. **Internal Roads:** Half paved, half gravel. **RV Service:** 15 mi. **Market:** 5 mi. **Restaurant:** 1 mi. **General Store:** Yes. **Vending:** No. **Swimming Pool:** No. **Playground:** No. **Other:** Pavilion available. **Activities:** Hiking, trout fishing, horseback riding. **Nearby Attractions:** Anna Ruby Falls, Appalachian Trail, whitewater rafting.

RESTRICTIONS

Pets: On leash only. **Fires:** Allowed. **Alcoholic Beverages:** Allowed. **Vehicle Maximum Length:** 45 ft.

TO GET THERE

Take I-85N to I-985N, which becomes Hwy. 365. At the second light, turn left onto Hwy. 384. When the road ends, turn right onto Hwy. 75. 1 mi. north of Helen, take a left onto Hwy. 356 at mi. marker 5.

HELEN

Unicoi State Park

1788 Hwy. 356, Helen 60543. T: (706) 878-3982; www.gastateparks.org.

🚐 ★★★★   ⛺ ★★★★

Beauty: ★★★★★   Site Privacy: ★★★★
Spaciousness: ★★★★   Quiet: ★★★★
Security: ★★★★   Cleanliness: ★★★★
Insect Control: ★★★★   Facilities: ★★★★

Platform camping and walk-in tent sites are only some of the camping possibilities found in this 1023-acre state park. RVers will find comfort in the 52 back-in sites with water, electric, and sewer hookups. Gorgeous hardwoods and pines tower over most of the sites, and though the camping areas are beautiful throughout, the most notable areas are those near Big Brook Spur. Weekend visitors should plan ahead, as the park often fills up. Even weekday camping here is not be a solitary experience. Though the alpine village of Helen and the Dahlonega Gold Museum lie within easy driving distance, visitors will want to remain in the park and take advantage of its offerings as well. Activities include hiking, biking, fishing, and canoeing, and the on-site restaurant and conference center provide resources for groups of all sizes.

BASICS

Operated By: Georgia Dept. of Natural Resources. **Open:** All year. **Site Assignment:** First come, first served. **Registration:** At camp office. **Fee:** Full hookup $20, RV w/ electric & water hookups $18, tent w/ electric & water hookups $16, walk-in tent $14. **Parking:** On site.

FACILITIES

Number of RV Sites: 52. **Number of Tent-Only Sites:** 48. **Hookups:** Water, electric (30 amps), sewer. **Each Site:** Grill, picnic table, tent pad. **Dump Station:** Yes. **Laundry:** Yes. **Pay Phone:** Yes. **Rest Rooms and Showers:** Yes. **Fuel:** No. **Propane:** No. **Internal Roads:** Paved. **RV Service:** On site. **Market:** 3 mi. **Restaurant:** On site. **General Store:** Yes. **Vending:** Yes. **Swimming Pool:** No. **Playground:** Yes. **Other:** Programs, tours, lake on site, conference center on site. **Activities:** Hiking, mountain biking, fishing, swimming, boating. **Nearby Attractions:** Anna Ruby Falls, Dahlonega Gold Museum, Appalachian Trail.

RESTRICTIONS

Pets: On leash (6 ft. or less) only. **Fires:** Allowed. **Alcoholic Beverages:** Allowed. **Vehicle Maximum Length:** 40 ft. **Other:** 14-day max. stay limit.

TO GET THERE

Take I-85N to I-195 N., which becomes Hwy. 365. At the second light, turn left onto Hwy. 384. At end of the road, turn right onto Hwy. 75. 1 mi. north of Helen, take a right onto Hwy. 356 and follow signs to the campground.

HIAWASSEE

Bald Mountain Park

3540 Fodder Creek Rd., Hiawassee 30546. T: (706) 896-8896; www.baldmountainpark.com.

🚐 ★★★   ⛺ ★★★

Beauty: ★★★★   Site Privacy: ★★
Spaciousness: ★★   Quiet: ★★★
Security: ★★★★   Cleanliness: ★★★
Insect Control: ★★★★   Facilities: ★★★★

In the far north of the state, this extremely rural private resort campground lies in a flat valley with pretty views of the surrounding mountains. Sites with good views are 2–18 on Lakeside Ln., and more open, with even better views, are sites 1–54 between Doe Lane Dr. and Lakeside Ln. For nicely wooded sites with pine straw ground cover, go for 64, 66, 68, 70, 73, 75 and 77. All of the sites are back-in, some open, others beautifully wooded. Most of the sites are grass-covered, though some have gravel or pine straw. The campground is fairly secure in terms of its rural setting, but it is also very crowded, so privacy is not generally the best here. The resort hosts rodeo events and fairs during the summer, so check the schedule. Despite the cigarette butts that cover some areas, the recreational opportunities and the vicinity to the Appalachian Trail and other attractions, make this a family-friendly campground.

BASICS

Operated By: Family owned. **Open:** Apr. 1–Oct. 31. **Site Assignment:** First come, first served. **Registration:** Office or night box. **Fee:** $17–$21. **Parking:** On site.

FACILITIES

Number of RV Sites: 300. **Number of Tent-Only Sites:**. **Hookups:** Electric (20, 30 amps), water sewer. **Each Site:** Picnic table, fire pit. **Dump Station:** Yes. **Laundry:** Yes. **Pay Phone:** Yes. **Rest Rooms and Showers:** Yes. **Fuel:** No. **Propane:** No. **Internal Roads:** Gravel. **RV Service:** Yes. **Market:** In Hiawasee. **Restaurant:** In Hiawasee. **General Store:** Yes. **Vending:** Yes. **Swimming Pool:** Yes. **Playground:** Yes. **Activities:** Fishing, golf, volleyball, boating, gameroom. **Nearby Attractions:** Brasstown Valley Resort, Lake Chatuge, Appalachian Trail, Helen (Bavarian village). **Additional Information:** Towns County Chamber of Commerce, (800) 981-1543 or www.towns-county-chamber.org.

RESTRICTIONS

Pets: Yes. **Fires:** Designated areas only. **Alcoholic Beverages:** At sites only. **Vehicle Maximum Length:** 35 ft. **Other:** Firearms prohibited.

TO GET THERE

From Rt. 288, turn onto Fodder Creek Rd. The entrance is 4 mi. south on the left.

JACKSON
High Falls State Park

76 High Falls Park Dr., Jackson 30233. T: (478) 993-3053; www.gastateparks.org.

🚐 ★★★★　　🅰 ★★★★

Beauty: ★★★★	Site Privacy: ★★★
Spaciousness: ★★★★	Quiet: ★★
Security: ★★★	Cleanliness: ★★★★
Insect Control: ★★★	Facilities: ★★★★

In spite of its proximity to I-75, this park has a real rural feel to it. RVers and tent-campers share all 112 sites, which have full hookups available. Moderately wooded with tall hardwoods, most sites have ample shade, though the limited underbrush reduces privacy. Those wishing to fall asleep to the sound of rushing water should camp in Area 2, situated next to the Towaliga River. Rigs needing lots of space should head for Loop B (sites 82–90). It's more open here, but the new bathhouse is nice. For a more secluded experience, look to Area 1 (sites 109–122). The curious will find trails that wind past ruins in this former industrial town. Canoes and paddleboats are available to explore High Falls Lake. But, if it has been rainy, you may want to just stare at the water rushing over the park's namesake.

BASICS

Operated By: Georgia Dept. of Natural Resources. **Open:** All year. **Site Assignment:** Reservations available. **Registration:** At camp office. **Fee:** $18–$20. **Parking:** In campground.

FACILITIES

Number of RV Sites: 112. **Number of Tent-Only Sites:** 0. **Hookups:** Water, electric (50 amps). **Each Site:** Water, electricity, grill, picnic table. **Dump Station:** Yes. **Laundry:** Yes. **Pay Phone:** Yes. **Rest Rooms and Showers:** Yes. **Fuel:** No. **Propane:** No. **Internal Roads:** Paved. **RV Service:** No. **Market:** Across the street from park. **Restaurant:** Across the street from park. **General Store:** Across the street from park. **Vending:** Soft drinks. **Swimming Pool:** Yes. **Playground:** Yes. **Activities:** Hiking, fishing, paddle boating, boat rental, mini golf. **Nearby Attractions:** Jarrell Plantation State Historic Site, Indian Springs State Park, Piedmont National Wildlife Refuge, Oconee National Forest.

RESTRICTIONS

Pets: On leash only. **Fires:** Allowed. **Alcoholic Beverages:** Not allowed. **Vehicle Maximum Length:** None. **Other:** 2 tents max. per site.

TO GET THERE

The park is 1.8 mi. east of I-75, Exit 198, at High Falls Rd.

JACKSON
Indian Springs State Park

678 Lake Clark Rd., Flovilla 30216. T: (770) 504-2277; www.gastateparks.org.

🚐 ★★★★　　🅰 ★★★★

Beauty: ★★★★	Site Privacy: ★★★★★
Spaciousness: ★★★★★	Quiet: ★★★★
Security: ★★★★	Cleanliness: ★★★★
Insect Control: ★★★	Facilities: ★★★

Campers with a penchant for history will want to visit Indian Springs State Park, believed to be the oldest park in the nation The park has 88 sites for RVs, trailers and tents, as well as 30 more primitive sites for tents only. All the sites are pull-throughs, and include electrical, water, and cable hookups. The area is nicely shaded, with pines and the occasional hardwood. Each sight has ample space in which to relax, but the phone lines running through the park and the well-used outhouses detract from the overall beauty. Those wishing to explore can find a spring house built by the Civilian Conservation Corps. The Creek Native Americans used this spring to heal the ill and impart vigor to the healthy. Today, visitors can participate in a number of activities, including swimming, fishing, and boating. Nearby points of interest include the Jarrell Plantation State Historic Site and the Historic Indian Springs Hotel.

BASICS
Operated By: Georgia Dept. of Natural Resources. **Open:** All year. **Site Assignment:** Sites assigned based on vehicle size. **Registration:** At camp office. **Fee:** $15–$18. **Parking:** In campground.

FACILITIES
Number of RV Sites: 88. **Number of Tent-Only Sites:** 0. **Hookups:** Water, electric (30 amps), cable. **Each Site:** Picnic table, fire pit. **Dump Station:** Yes. **Laundry:** Yes. **Pay Phone:** Yes. **Rest Rooms and Showers:** Yes. **Fuel:** No. **Propane:** No. **Internal Roads:** Paved. **RV Service:** 30 mi. **Market:** 5 mi. in Jackson. **Restaurant:** 5 mi. in Jackson. **General Store:** Outside park. **Vending:** Soft drinks. **Swimming Pool:** No. **Playground:** No. **Activities:** Pedal boats, fishing, swimming, golf. **Nearby Attractions:** Jarrell Plantation State Historic Site, High Falls State Park, Piedmont National Wildlife Refuge, Historic Indian Springs Hotel.

RESTRICTIONS
Pets: On leash only. **Fires:** Allowed but subject to seasonal bans. **Alcoholic Beverages:** Not allowed. **Vehicle Maximum Length:** None.

TO GET THERE
From I-75 S., take Exit 205 to Jackson. Proceed south on Hwy. 42 to the park. From I-75 N., take Exit 188 and proceed north on Hwy. 42. The park is approximately 15 mi. from the interstate.

JEKYLL ISLAND
Jekyll Island Campground

1197 Riverview Dr., Jekyll Island 31527. T: (912) 635-3021; www.jekyllisland.com; campground@jekyllisland.com.

 ★★★★   ★★★★

Beauty: ★★★★   Site Privacy: ★★★
Spaciousness: ★★★★   Quiet: ★★★★
Security: ★★★★   Cleanliness: ★★★★
Insect Control: ★★★   Facilities: ★★★

Located in a historic resort community, Jekyll Island Campground offers spectacular views of the ocean and shoreline. Covered with gorgeous live oak and pine trees, the area has a wonderfully serene and laid back vibe. Since the sites vary greatly in size, we recommend sites J7, J11, H15, and H16, as they are the most spacious and secluded. The back tent areas of the campground are generally much nicer. The facilities on the campground are satisfactory but basic. Georgia's mild winters make the campground a perfect winter destination. The campground is more crowded in the spring and summer, and therefore we recommend that you call in advance for availability during these times. Security at Jekyll Island is mediocre, but the campground does have the advantage of being secluded.

BASICS
Operated By: Private operator. **Open:** All year. **Site Assignment:** Reservations accepted. **Registration:** Office. **Fee:** $12–$20. **Parking:** On site.

FACILITIES
Number of RV Sites: 158. **Number of Tent-Only Sites:** 41. **Hookups:** Water, electric, sewer. **Each Site:** Picnic table. **Dump Station:** Yes. **Laundry:** Yes. **Pay Phone:** No. **Rest Rooms and Showers:** Yes. **Fuel:** No. **Propane:** Yes. **Internal Roads:** Paved. **RV Service:** No. **Market:** In Brunswick. **Restaurant:** In Brunswick. **General Store:** Yes. **Vending:** Yes. **Swimming Pool:** Yes. **Playground:** No. **Activities:** Biking, golfing, fishing, tennis. **Nearby Attractions:** Sea turtle walks, nature center, carriage tours, historic district. **Additional Information:** Jekyll Island CVB, www.jekyllisland.com or (877) 453-5955.

RESTRICTIONS
Pets: On leash only. **Fires:** Allowed. **Alcoholic Beverages:** At sites only. **Vehicle Maximum Length:** None. **Other:** $3 daily parking fee.

TO GET THERE
Take I-95 to Exit 29. Follow the signs on US 17 for 10 mi. and turn right onto Drowning Musgrove Causeway (GA 520). The Jekyll Island Welcome Center is 4 mi. on the left.

KENNESAW

KOA–Atlanta North

2000 Old US 41, Kennesaw 30152. T: (770) 427-2406; F: (770) 429-1014; www.koa.com.

🚐 ★★★   ⛺ ★★

Beauty: ★★★	Site Privacy: ★★
Spaciousness: ★★★	Quiet: ★★★
Security: ★★★	Cleanliness: ★★★★
Insect Control: ★★★★	Facilities: ★★★

Situated 20 miles northwest of Atlanta, this KOA campground provides easy access to the city. Located just off a busy, suburban road, the campground has a pretty fish pond with large koi and a waterfall at the entrance. Though the atmosphere is relaxing, the experience is more residential than rural. Numbered "streets" help orient people in this large facility, creating a sense of home away from home. Both pull-throughs and back-ins are available, all paved, and those who tent camp have a designated area located right at the entrance. The campground is mostly shady, though a few areas have more sunlight than others, and sites 165–170 and 65–67 have more than their share of tree shade. Besides the many attractions found in Atlanta, nearby Kennesaw Mountain offers over 16 miles of trails, and the Big Shanty Museum retells the history of The General, a famous Civil War Locomotive.

BASICS

Operated By: People, Inc. **Open:** All year. **Site Assignment:** First come, first served. **Registration:** At camp office. **Fee:** 30 amp hookups $28, 50 amp hookups $30, 10% AAA, AARP, or KOA discount. **Parking:** 2 vehicles per site.

FACILITIES

Number of RV Sites: 231. **Number of Tent-Only Sites:** 17. **Hookups:** Water, electric (20, 30, 50 amps), sewer. **Each Site:** Picnic table, tent pad. **Dump Station:** Yes. **Laundry:** Yes. **Pay Phone:** Yes. **Rest Rooms and Showers:** Yes. **Fuel:** No. **Propane:** Yes. **Internal Roads:** Paved. **RV Service:** 2 mi. **Market:** 0.5 mi. **Restaurant:** 1 mi. **General Store:** 0.5 mi. **Vending:** Yes. **Swimming Pool:** Yes. **Playground:** Yes. **Activities:** Basketball, TV room, game room. **Nearby Attractions:** Whitewater rafting, Kennesaw Battlefield Park, American Adventures, Six Flags.

RESTRICTIONS

Pets: On leash only. **Fires:** In fire rings only. **Alcoholic Beverages:** At sites only. **Vehicle Maximum Length:** None. **Other:** 14-day max. stay limit.

TO GET THERE

Take I-75N to Exit 269. Turn left and go 3 mi. At Old US 41, turn right. After 0.5 mi., the campground is on the right.

KINGSLAND

Country Oaks Campground

6 Carlton Cemetary Rd., Kingsland 31548. T: (912) 729-6212.

🚐 ★★★   ⛺ n/a

Beauty: ★★★	Site Privacy: ★★
Spaciousness: ★★★	Quiet: ★★★★
Security: ★★★★	Cleanliness: ★★★★
Insect Control: ★★★	Facilities: ★

A middling campground with few frills, Country Oaks does enjoy the benefits of very courteous and helpful owner/managers. Campsites vary significantly in size, and some are quite small (the pull-through sites are largest). All are shaded, with a scattering of nice oaks, but there is not much privacy. The campsites are laid out in three rows, with sites 19–28 being the most secluded (they're also near a small creek). Sites 12–18 and 29–44 are nearest the general store and bathhouse; sites 1–11 are just off the access road and I-95, and these sites may experience significant road noise. Toilet cleanliness left something to be desired on our visit. The owners encourage guests to pet the friendly horses, and buggy rides are available. The mostly older clientele seems to relish the relaxed pace here, often enjoying an afternoon in swinging chairs and rockers on the general store's wraparound porch

BASICS

Operated By: Lonnie & Karen Gay. **Open:** All year. **Site Assignment:** First come, first served. **Registration:** Office. **Fee:** $20–$22. **Parking:** On site.

FACILITIES

Number of RV Sites: 44. **Number of Tent-Only Sites:** 0. **Hookups:** Water, electric (30, 50 amps), sewer. **Each Site:** Picnic table. **Dump Station:** No. **Laundry:** Yes. **Pay Phone:** Yes. **Rest Rooms and Showers:** Yes. **Fuel:** No. **Propane:**

Yes. **Internal Roads:** Paved. **RV Service:** 2.5 mi. **Market:** 2.5 mi. **Restaurant:** 2.5 mi. **General Store:** Yes. **Vending:** Yes. **Swimming Pool:** No. **Playground:** No. **Activities:** Boating, fishing, horseshoe. **Nearby Attractions:** Jacksonville Flea Market, Fernandina, Daytona Jacksonville Beaches, Okefenokee Wetlands, Summer Wars. **Additional Information:** Kingsland CVB, (800) 433-0225 or www.visitkingsland.com.

RESTRICTIONS
Pets: On leash only. **Fires:** In fire rings only. **Alcoholic Beverages:** Allowed. **Vehicle Maximum Length:** None.

TO GET THERE
Take I-95 to Exit 1 in Georgia and go 0.2 mi.

LAKE LANIER ISLANDS
Lake Lanier Islands

6950 Holiday Rd., Lake Lanier Islands 30518. T: (770) 932-7270; www.lakelanierislands.com; wbeavers@llimail.com.

🚐 ★★★★   ⛺ ★★★★

Beauty: ★★★★★   Site Privacy: ★★★
Spaciousness: ★★★★   Quiet: ★★★★
Security: ★★★★★   Cleanliness: ★★★★
Insect Control: ★★★★ Facilities: ★★★★★

This huge property is a complete vacation destination. Lake Lanier Islands is spread over the eponymous clumps of land in Lake Lanier, a U.S. Army Corps of Engineers project which has many recreational options of its own. Like the other ten campgrounds on the lake (see profiles of Shoal Creekin Buford and Chestnut Ridge in Flowery Branch), boat noise is always a factor for campers; ask attendants for recommendations on quieter campsites. Most sites are well shaded, and some have screening foliage; size varies greatly. In contrast to some nearby campgrounds that are entirely lake-focused, Lake Lanier Islands has several other choices for campers—two golf clubs, an equestrian center, mountain bike rentals, a water park, and more. If you want to explore the surrounding area, the region offers 43 day-use parks, ten marinas, and nine state, county, and city parks.

BASICS
Operated By: Winston Beaver-Manager. **Open:** May–Sept. **Site Assignment:** First come, first served, also reservations. **Registration:** Campground office. **Fee:** $20–$30. **Parking:** On site.

FACILITIES
Number of RV Sites: 271. **Number of Tent-Only Sites:** 31. **Hookups:** Water, electric, some sewer. **Each Site:** Picnic areas. **Dump Station:** Yes. **Laundry:** Yes. **Pay Phone:** Yes. **Rest Rooms and Showers:** Yes. **Fuel:** No. **Propane:** Yes. **Internal Roads:** Paved. **RV Service:** 4 mi. **Market:** 7 mi. **Restaurant:** Less than 7 mi. **General Store:** Yes. **Vending:** No. **Swimming Pool:** No. **Playground:** Yes. **Other:** Full golf course. **Activities:** Boating, beach, waterpark, wave pool, equistrian center, mountain biking. **Nearby Attractions:** Lake Lanier Islands Resort.

RESTRICTIONS
Pets: On leash only. **Fires:** In fire rings only. **Alcoholic Beverages:** Not allowed. **Vehicle Maximum Length:** None. **Other:** 2 vehicles per family.

TO GET THERE
From Atlanta, take I-85N to I-985N (Exit 113). Take Exit 8 (Friendship Rd.), and turn left. Continue 4 mi. to the campground

LAKE PARK
Eagles Roost Campground

5465 Mill Store Rd., Lake Park 31636. T: (229) 559-0141; www.eaglesroostcampground.com; camp@eaglesroostcampground.com.

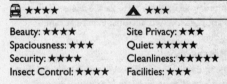

🚐 ★★★★   ⛺ ★★★

Beauty: ★★★★   Site Privacy: ★★★
Spaciousness: ★★★   Quiet: ★★★★★
Security: ★★★★   Cleanliness: ★★★★★
Insect Control: ★★★★ Facilities: ★★★

Located right off I-75, just a few miles from the Florida state line, this park offers convenience as well as all the amenities of a top notch vacation spot. Surrounded by gorgeous hardwoods draped in Spanish moss, the Eagle's Roost offers its guests the tranquility of a rural setting, along with a myriad of activities both inside and outside the park. There is a swimming pool, playground and a rec room for the kids inside the campground itself, while nearby, guests can enjoy Georgia's Wild Adventures , Okefenokee Swamp, or Reed Bingham State Park. Section A, or the Club Deluxe area, is our pick for the best spots at the Eagle's Roost, as the internal roads here are paved and each site is equipped with a concrete pad. Of the 42 available spots in this section, we would have to say that sites 34 through 42 are the most beautiful, surrounded by plenty of those moss-covered hardwoods. For families with children, however, our pick for the best spots would have to be sites 5, 6, and 7, as they are the closest to the pool, playground, and store. The sites in the B and C sections aren't up to par with those in the A section, being closer together, and the roads here are packed sand instead of asphalt. Overall, this is an attractive, well run facility. However, our advice to anyone planning to travel in this area is to do so in the early to mid-spring, as this part of Georgia is nearly unbearable when summer is in full swing.

BASICS

Operated By: Terry Herndon. **Open:** All year. **Site Assignment:** First come, first served. **Registration:** Office. **Fee:** $19–$25. **Parking:** On site.

FACILITIES

Number of RV Sites: 160. **Number of Tent-Only Sites:.** **Hookups:** Water, electric (50 amps). **Each Site:** Picnic table. **Dump Station:** Yes. **Laundry:** Yes. **Pay Phone:** Yes. **Rest Rooms and Showers:** Yes. **Fuel:** No. **Propane:** Yes. **Internal Roads:** Gravel. **RV Service:** Yes. **Market:** Yes. **Restaurant:** Nearby. **General Store:** Yes. **Vending:** No. **Swimming Pool:** Yes. **Playground:** Yes. **Activities:** Okeefenokee Swamp Park, Wild Adventures, Reed Bingham State Park, Stephen C. Foster Park. **Nearby Attractions:** Inquire at campground.

RESTRICTIONS

Pets: On leash only. **Fires:** None. **Alcoholic Beverages:** Allowed. **Vehicle Maximum Length:** None.

TO GET THERE

From I-75 Exit 5, go northbound and take a right at the first light. The campground is 1 mi. on left

LAVONIA

Tugaloo State Park

1763 Tugaloo State Park Rd., Lavonia 30553. T: (706) 356-4362; www.gastateparks.org.

 ★★★   ★★★

Beauty: ★★★★   Site Privacy: ★★★
Spaciousness: ★★★   Quiet: ★★★
Security: ★★★★★   Cleanliness: ★★★
Insect Control: ★★★   Facilities: ★★★

Between the lovely Pine stand and the views of Hartwell Lake, beauty is the major draw of this State Park campground. Located in the northeast corner of the state, the campground feels quite rural despite its proximity to I-85. And it is well-guarded, making this is one of the region's more secure spots for camping. Unfortunately the restrooms are lousy, and the facilities are lacking in general. But the nearby recreation opportunities and the natural setting help make this an attractive spot nonetheless. With roughly equal numbers of back-in and pull-through sites, the campground sits on a peninsula, and the sites closest to the water are recommended, naturally. The sites, all gravel, vary greatly in size, but are all pretty and wooded. Fishing—especially for large-mouth bass—and water sports make this a fun, if noisy, campground that is excellent for families. Keeping in mind the larger crowds in warmer weather, due to the allure of the water, this park offers a pleasant stay in a tent or RV.

BASICS

Operated By: Georgia Dept. of Natural Resources. **Open:** All year. **Site Assignment:** Reservations accepted. **Registration:** At camp office. **Fee:** $16. **Parking:** In campground.

FACILITIES

Number of Multipurpose Sites: 117. **Hookups:** Water, electric (30 amps), sewer. **Each Site:** Picnic shelter. **Dump Station:** Yes. **Laundry:** Yes. **Pay Phone:** Yes. **Rest Rooms and Showers:** Yes. **Fuel:** No. **Propane:** Yes. **Internal Roads:** Paved. **RV Service:** Yes. **Market:** No. **Restaurant:** No. **General Store:** Yes. **Vending:** Yes. **Swimming Pool:** Yes. **Playground:** Yes. **Activities:** Fishing, boating, hiking, volleyball, horseshoes, mini golf. **Nearby Attractions:** Ty Cobb Museum, Victoria Bryant State Park & Golf Course, Tallulah Gorge State Park, Hartwell Dam.

RESTRICTIONS

Pets: On leash only. **Fires:** In fire rings only. **Alcoholic Beverages:** At sites. **Vehicle Maximum Length:** 35 ft.

TO GET THERE

Take I-85 to Exit 173. Follow the signs to Gerrard Rd. Turn right and go 1.5 mi. to Hwy. 328. Turn left and proceed 3.3 mi. to the park.

LINCOLNTON

Elijah Creek State Park

2959 McCormick Hwy., Lincolnton 30817. T: (706) 359-3458 or (800) 864-7275; www.gastateparks.org.

🚐 ★★★★   ▲ ★★★★

Beauty: ★★★★   Site Privacy: ★★★
Spaciousness: ★★★   Quiet: ★★★
Security: ★★★★★   Cleanliness: ★★★★
Insect Control: ★★★   Facilities: ★★★★

Named after the frontiersman and Revolutionary War hero Elijah Clark, this is one of the more popular state parks in the area. Expect lots of running kids, buzzing boats, and other noises associated with large camps. RVers and tent campers have a choice of 165 sites. Most of the sites have some shade but with very little undergrowth. In Campground 1, sites 38 and 53 are gorgeous, 56 is quite secluded, and 23–31 have lovely open views (though all are a bit crowded). Campground 2 has sites that are quite shady (108–115) and some with nice views (116–118). Be sure to avoid all sites near boat ramps, especially during summer weekends. The park offers hiking, swimming and fishing thanks to Clarks Hill Lake, as well as a museum depicting colonial life. Several annual events, including an arts and crafts festival and a bluegrass festival, mean potential visitors should call well in advance.

BASICS

Operated By: Georgia Dept. of Natural Resources. **Open:** All year. **Site Assignment:** Reservations or first come, first served. **Registration:** At camp office. **Fee:** $18–$20. **Parking:** 2 vehicles per site.

FACILITIES

Number of RV Sites: 165. **Number of Tent-Only Sites:** 0. **Hookups:** Water, electric (50 amps), cable. **Each Site:** Picnic table, fire pit. **Dump Station:** Yes. **Laundry:** Yes. **Pay Phone:** Yes. **Rest Rooms and Showers:** Yes. **Fuel:** 2 mi. **Propane:** 2 mi. **Internal Roads:** Paved & gravel. **RV Service:** Housecalls available. **Market:** In Martins Crossroads. **Restaurant:** 7 mi. **General Store:** No. **Vending:** Soft drinks. **Swimming Pool:** No. **Playground:** Yes. **Other:** 3rd weekend in October—Oldtimer's Festival. **Activities:** Boating, water skiing, fishing, museum tours, hiking, miniatue golf, swimming, volleyball. **Nearby Attractions:** Misteltoe State Park, Bobby Brown State Park, historic Washington, Clarks Hill Dam.

RESTRICTIONS

Pets: On leash only. **Fires:** In fire rings only. **Alcoholic Beverages:** Not allowed. **Vehicle Maximum Length:** 40 ft.

TO GET THERE

Go 7 mi. northeast of Lincolnton on US Hwy. 378.

MARIETTA

Brookwood RV Resort Park

1031 Wylie Rd., Marietta 30067. T: (877) 727-5787; F: (770) 427-8410; www.brookwoodrvresort parks.com; info@brookwoodrvresortparks.com.

🚐 ★★★   ▲ n/a

Beauty: ★★★   Site Privacy: ★★
Spaciousness: ★★   Quiet: ★★
Security: ★★   Cleanliness: ★★★★★
Insect Control: ★★★★   Facilities: ★★★

For those desiring a camping experience convenient to exploring Atlanta, Brookwood Resort Park is the place. Just 13 miles from downtown, the campground provides a refreshing oasis amidst the bustle of the metroplitan area. Visitors won't mistake this for a more secluded, mountain experience (a car dealership lies next door), but setting up beneath the tall pine trees beats a musty hotel room. Full hookups along with cable and phones are complemented by a concierge service that will deliver rental cars as needed. Most of the sites are spacious (a few are not), with either gravel, grass or a mixture of the two on the ground.

BASICS

Operated By: The Sullivan family. **Open:** All year. **Site Assignment:** Reservations preferred. **Registration:** At camp office. **Fee:** $37. **Parking:** In campground.

FACILITIES

Number of RV Sites: 70. **Number of Tent-Only Sites:** 0. **Hookups:** Water, electric (20, 30, 50 amps), sewer, phone, cable. **Each Site:** Level, paved, full hookups. **Dump Station:** Yes. **Laundry:** Yes. **Pay Phone:** Yes. **Rest Rooms and Showers:** Yes. **Fuel:** No. **Propane:** Yes. **Internal Roads:** Paved. **RV Service:** Concierge service. **Market:** In Marietta. **Restaurant:** In Marietta. **General Store:** No. **Vending:** Soft drinks. **Swimming**

Pool: Yes. **Playground:** No. **Activities:** Inquire at campground. **Nearby Attractions:** White Water Park, Kennesaw Civil War Museum, Underground Atlanta.

RESTRICTIONS

Pets: Yes. **Fires:** No. **Alcoholic Beverages:** At sites only. **Vehicle Maximum Length:** 45 ft.

TO GET THERE

From downtown Atlanta, go 13 mi. on I-75N to exit 261 and drive west.

McDONOUGH
Atlanta South KOA RV Resort

281 Mt. Olive Rd., McDonough 30253. T: (800) 562-6073; www.koa.com.

🚐 ★★★   ▲ ★

Beauty: ★★★★	Site Privacy: ★★★
Spaciousness: ★★★	Quiet: ★★★
Security: ★★★	Cleanliness: ★★★★
Insect Control: ★★★	Facilities: ★★★

Campers come to Atlanta South KOA for convenience rather than escape, as the area is suburban in nature. Located 30 minutes south of Atlanta, this campground is 15 miles from the Atlanta Speedway, so potential visitors should check far in advance to insure a spot during speedway weekends. Most of the sites are pull-throughs, though back-ins are found along the campground's perimeter. Water, sewer, and electric hookups are available. There is a beautiful tent-only area, but it isn't very level. Each site is mix of pine straw and gravel, and though there are sufficient trees to provide shade, mostly pine and maple, the understory does little to provide privacy.

BASICS

Operated By: Don Goetz. **Open:** All year. **Site Assignment:** Reservations or first come, first served. **Registration:** At camp office. **Fee:** $26–$28. **Parking:** In campground.

FACILITIES

Number of RV Sites: 144. **Number of Tent-Only Sites:** 10. **Hookups:** Water, electric (30, 50 amps), sewer. **Each Site:** Picnic table, grill. **Dump Station:** Yes. **Laundry:** Yes. **Pay Phone:** Yes. **Rest Rooms and Showers:** Yes. **Fuel:** No. **Propane:** Yes. **Internal Roads:** Gravel. **RV Service:** Washing $5. **Market:** In Mcdonough. **Restaurant:** In Mcdo-

nough. **General Store:** No. **Vending:** No. **Swimming Pool:** Yes. **Playground:** Yes. **Other:** Cabins available, $36. **Activities:** Swimming, pond fishing, nature trails. **Nearby Attractions:** Atlanta Motor Speedway.

RESTRICTIONS

Pets: On leash w /restrictions. **Fires:** In fire rings only. **Alcoholic Beverages:** Allowed. **Vehicle Maximum Length:** 70 ft.

TO GET THERE

From I-75 N., take Exit 222 (or Exit 72 from I-75 S.). Go west on Jodeco Rd. Mt. Olive Rd. and the campground are on the left.

McRAE
Little Ocmulgee State Park

P.O. Drawer 149, McRae 31055. T: (229) 868-7474; www.gastateparks.org.

🚐 ★★★★   ▲ ★★★★

Beauty: ★★★★★	Site Privacy: ★★★
Spaciousness: ★★★★	Quiet: ★★★★
Security: ★★★★	Cleanliness: ★★★★
Insect Control: ★★★	Facilities: ★★★★★

A small park created by private land donations and the work of the Civilian Conservation Corps, Little Ocmulgee State Park offers a pleasant retreat from the more popular (and populated) campgrounds in the area. The lodge is the center of activity here, and only lodge and cottage guests can use its swimming pool (though its restaurant is open to everyone, of course). However, you don't need the pool when you can just take a dip in the lake, which has its own pleasant little beach. A fairly low-key place, most campers seem to visit here to stroll along the nature trail or to tee off on the 18-hole golf course. Be sure to keep moving on the trail, though—the path passes near a buzzard rookery, and stationary campers might draw some interested, circling birds above.

BASICS

Operated By: Georgia Dept. of Natural Resources. **Open:** All year. **Site Assignment:** First come, first served. **Registration:** At lodge prior to set up. **Fee:** $15–$19. **Parking:** On site.

FACILITIES

Number of RV Sites: 55. **Number of Tent-Only Sites:** 0. **Hookups:** Water, electric (50 amps), cable. **Each Site:** Fire pit. **Dump Station:** Yes. **Laundry:** Yes. **Pay Phone:** Yes. **Rest Rooms and Showers:** Yes. **Fuel:** No. **Propane:** No. **Internal Roads:** Paved. **RV Service:** No. **Market:** 2 mi. in McRae. **Restaurant:** At lodge. **General Store:** No. **Vending:** Yes. **Swimming Pool:** No. **Playground:** No. **Activities:** Fishing, boating, beach area, tennis, nature trails, mini golf. **Nearby Attractions:** Georgia Veterans State Park & Golf Course, General Coffee State Park & Heritage Farm, Jefferson Davis Memorial State Historic Site.

RESTRICTIONS

Pets: On leash (6 ft. or less) only. **Fires:** In fire rings only. **Alcoholic Beverages:** Allowed, cups only at the beach. **Vehicle Maximum Length:** 40 ft.

TO GET THERE

The park is 2 mi. north of McRae via US Hwys. 319 and 441.

NICHOLLS
General Coffee State Park

46 John Coffee Rd., Nicholls 31554. T: (912) 384-7082.

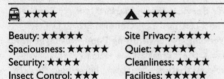

🚐 ★★★★	⛺ ★★★★
Beauty: ★★★★★	Site Privacy: ★★★★
Spaciousness: ★★★★★	Quiet: ★★★★★
Security: ★★★★	Cleanliness: ★★★★
Insect Control: ★★★	Facilities: ★★★★★

Approximately six miles from Douglas, this rural park includes Seventeen Mile River, which creates six small lakes as it winds through a Cypress swamp. The variety of foliage includes pines and hardwoods draped with Spanish moss. The park was donated to the state by a group of Coffee County citizens in 1970 and was named after General John Coffee, a planter, US Congressman and military leader. In addition to camping, it offers several exhibits at Heritage Farm, including a tobacco barn, a cane mill, and, yes, barnyard animals as well. With comfortable, gravel pull-through sites, the campground has a relatively serene, spacious feel. Both multipurpose camping Areas 1 and 2 are loops, and Area 1 includes a grassy field and playground, although the playground at the picnic area is much nicer. There are separate tent areas, but the facilities overall make both tent and RV camping quite pleasant here. This is a secure spot, largely

due to the rural setting and sparse crowds, good for families and privacy.

BASICS

Operated By: Georgia Dept. of Natural Resources. **Open:** All year. **Site Assignment:** First come, first served. **Registration:** Inside main gate. **Fee:** $13–$15. **Parking:** On site.

FACILITIES

Number of Multipurpose Sites: 50. **Hookups:** Electric (30 amps), water, sewer. **Each Site:** Picnic shelters. **Dump Station:** Yes. **Laundry:** Yes. **Pay Phone:** Yes. **Rest Rooms and Showers:** Yes. **Fuel:** No. **Propane:** No. **Internal Roads:** Gravel. **RV Service:** Yes. **Market:** No. **Restaurant:** No. **General Store:** No. **Vending:** Yes. **Swimming Pool:** Yes. **Playground:** Yes. **Other:** Amphitheater. **Activities:** Hiking, nature programs, fishing, boating. **Nearby Attractions:** Historical farm w/ live animals. **Additional Information:** (800) 864-PARK.

RESTRICTIONS

Pets: No. **Fires:** Allowed. **Alcoholic Beverages:** Allowed. **Vehicle Maximum Length:** Must park in 120-ft. pull-through. **Other:** $2 parking pass.

TO GET THERE

From Rt. 221, exit at Rt 32, and turn right at the Keystone Dr. Entrance after the train tracks.

OCHLOCKNEE
Sugar Mill Plantation RV Park

4857 McMillan Rd., Ochlocknee 31773. T: (229) 227-1451 or (888) 375-3246; sugarmillrv@yahoo.com.

🚐 ★★★	⛺ ★★★
Beauty: ★★★	Site Privacy: ★★
Spaciousness: ★★★	Quiet: ★★★★
Security: ★★★	Cleanliness: ★★★★
Insect Control: ★★★	Facilities: ★★★

This is a lovely private campground in a rural area near the Florida panhandle a few miles from the small town of Thomasville. We found very nice folks here and a positive atmosphere all around, with a generally older crowd. The sites are medium in size, both back-ins and pull-throughs, and the quiet is one of the park's more attractive features. The campground is fairly wooded, with about half the sites in some shade, and ground cover is of grass or pine straw. Especially quiet and wooded are sites 15–18. The landscaping includes palmetto bushes and pampas grass. There is a goose pond, and the fishing ponds are stocked with bass and catfish. This is not the most private or spacious campground, but it is quite pleasant, more so than many commercial campgrounds. And, as the name implies, there are plantations and sites of historic interest to be enjoyed nearby.

BASICS

Operated By: Private operator. **Open:** All year. **Site Assignment:** Reservations accepted. **Registration:** At camp office. **Fee:** $19. **Parking:** In campground.

FACILITIES

Number of RV Sites: 120. **Number of Tent-Only Sites:** 0. **Hookups:** Water, electric (20, 30, 50 amps), sewer. **Each Site:** Picnic table. **Dump Station:** Yes. **Laundry:** Yes. **Pay Phone:** Yes. **Rest Rooms and Showers:** Yes. **Fuel:** No. **Propane:** Yes. **Internal Roads:** Paved & gravel. **RV Service:** Yes. **Market:** In Ochlocknee. **Restaurant:** In Ochlocknee. **General Store:** Yes. **Vending:** No. **Swimming Pool:** No. **Playground:** No. **Activities:** Fishing, basketball, potluck dinners, game nights, shuffleboard. **Nearby Attractions:** Thomas County Historical Museum, historic plantation tours, antique shops.

RESTRICTIONS

Pets: On leash only. **Fires:** In designated areas. **Alcoholic Beverages:** At sites only. **Vehicle Maximum Length:** None.

TO GET THERE

The campground is located 8 mi. north of Thomasville on Hwy. 19.

PERRY
Fair Harbor RV Park & Campground

515 Marshallville Rd., Perry 31069. T: (877) 988-8844; www.fairharborrvpark.com.

🚐 ★★★★	🅰 n/a
Beauty: ★★★★	Site Privacy: ★★
Spaciousness: ★★	Quiet: ★★★★
Security: ★★★	Cleanliness: ★★★★
Insect Control: ★★★★	Facilities: ★★★

Not far from the Georgia National Fairgrounds, Fair Harbor provides a nice, under-developed camping experience just two-tenths of a mile from I-75. The 100-acre park has 150 RV sites,

mostly pull-throughs. The 30, densely wooded, tent-only sites are well removed from the rest of the area and have water and electric hookups. Though less shady, the RV sites are quite large, which provides a bit of privacy. For a quieter experience, campers should choose sites closer to the tent-only area. Breakfast is served Tuesday through Saturday. Campers may want to visit during the Georgia National Livestock Show and Rodeo in February as well as the Georgia State Fair in August, but plan ahead as the park fills quickly.

BASICS

Operated By: Tim McCord & Kirk Morris. **Open:** All year. **Site Assignment:** Reservations or first come, first served. **Registration:** At camp office. **Fee:** $11–$22. **Parking:** In campground.

FACILITIES

Number of RV Sites: 150. **Number of Tent-Only Sites:** 30. **Hookups:** Water, electric (20, 30, 50 amps), sewer, cable. **Each Site:** Picnic table, grill. **Dump Station:** Yes. **Laundry:** Yes. **Pay Phone:** Yes. **Rest Rooms and Showers:** Yes. **Fuel:** No. **Propane:** Yes. **Internal Roads:** Paved, sites gravel. **RV Service:** 15 min. **Market:** In. Perry. **Restaurant:** Less than 1 mi. **General Store:** Limited. **Vending:** No. **Swimming Pool:** No. **Playground:** No. **Other:** Breakfast Tue.–Sat.; RV storage available. **Activities:** Pond fishing, horseshoes. **Nearby Attractions:** Georgia Music Hall of Famr, the Hay House, Andersonville National Cemetery, Massee Lane Gardens, Museum of Aviation, Georgia Agricenter, fairgrounds.

RESTRICTIONS

Pets: On leash only. **Fires:** Allowed. **Alcoholic Beverages:** Allowed. **Vehicle Maximum Length:** None.

TO GET THERE

Take I-75 Exit 135. Go 0.1 mi. to campground.

PERRY
Twin Oaks RV Park

Hwy. 26, Perry 31069. T: (478) 987-9361.

🚐 ★★★	🅰 n/a
Beauty: ★★★★	Site Privacy: ★★★
Spaciousness: ★★★	Quiet: ★★★
Security: ★★★	Cleanliness: ★★★★
Insect Control: ★★★★	Facilities: ★★

In the center of the state, this private campground has a rural feel despite its proximity to I-75. The RV park itself boasts huge sites and welcomes big rigs, but not tents. Among its pluses are spanking new restrooms and showers, shade at almost all sites, and RV-friendly facilities. There are both back-in and pull-through sites, with gravel and a nice grassy spot at each site. The whole place is landscaped, pretty, and pleasant, and there is even a little green between some of the sites. Security may be a concern due to the nearby interstate traffic and the lack of a gate, however. Recreation at the RV park is available, and there is plenty in Perry to keep the whole family entertained. With the possible exception of the highway noise, we agree with the park's advertisement: this is a "quiet country" vacation spot, good for families and all ages.

BASICS

Operated By: Harvey Youngblood. **Open:** All year. **Site Assignment:** First come, first served. **Registration:** At camp office. **Fee:** $17. **Parking:** In campground.

FACILITIES

Number of RV Sites: 72. **Number of Tent-Only Sites:** 0. **Hookups:** Water, electric (50 amps), sewer. **Each Site:** Gravel w/ concrete patio, picnic table. **Dump Station:** Yes. **Laundry:** Yes. **Pay Phone:** Yes. **Rest Rooms and Showers:** Yes. **Fuel:** No. **Propane:** Yes. **Internal Roads:** Gravel. **RV Service:** No. **Market:** In Perry. **Restaurant:** 1 mi. **General Store:** Across the street from park. **Vending:** No. **Swimming Pool:** No. **Playground:** No. **Activities:** Horseshoes, volleyball. **Nearby Attractions:** Andersonville, fairground, Civil War Museum.

RESTRICTIONS

Pets: On leash only. **Fires:** Some sites. **Alcoholic Beverages:** At sites only. **Vehicle Maximum Length:** None.

TO GET THERE

Take I-75S from Atlanta to Exit 127. The campground is just below Perry on Hwy. 26.

PINE MOUNTAIN

F. D. Roosevelt State Park

2970 Hwy. 190, Pine Mountain 31822. T: (706) 663-4858; www.gastateparks.org.

 🚐 ★★★★ ▲ ★★★★

Beauty: ★★★★	Site Privacy: ★★★★
Spaciousness: ★★★★	Quiet: ★★★
Security: ★★★★	Cleanliness: ★★★★
Insect Control: ★★★	Facilities: ★★★★★

In west-central Georgia, this state park is—you guessed it—all about Franklin D. Roosevelt. Actually, they also have the nature thing going for them, in the form of hiking and horseback riding amongst hardwoods and pines and fishing on the lovely Lake Delanor. Despite its secluded, rural setting, the campground stays busy on holidays and weekends, and we suggest going during the off-season if you seek quiet. There are both back-in and pull-through sites, mostly gravel. Although most sites are plenty shady, there is little if any foliage between them. We recommend Campground 5 for its privacy and huge pull-throughs, and the great lake views are in Campground 1 at sites 3 and 4. In Campground 2, sites 33–41 are nicely wooded, and the best tent camping is in Campground 3, as it is more wooded and private (although it is not paved). For the natural beauty of the setting and the historical interest of the attractions in the area, this is a well-rounded spot for families and all generations.

BASICS

Operated By: Georgia Dept. of Natural Resources. **Open:** All year. **Site Assignment:** Reservations accepted. **Registration:** At camp office. **Fee:** $15–$17. **Parking:** In campground.

FACILITIES

Number of Multipurpose Sites: 140. **Hookups:** Water, electric (50 amps). **Each Site:** Picnic area. **Dump Station:** Yes. **Laundry:** Yes (on weekends). **Pay Phone:** Yes. **Rest Rooms and Showers:** Yes. **Fuel:** No. **Propane:** No. **Internal Roads:** Paved. **RV Service:** No. **Market:** No. **Restaurant:** No. **General Store:** No. **Vending:** No. **Swimming Pool:** Yes. **Playground:** Yes. **Activities:** Hiking, biking, fishing, boating, horseback riding. **Nearby Attractions:** Little White House State Park, Sprewell Bluff State Park, West Point Lake.

RESTRICTIONS

Pets: Yes. **Fires:** In designated areas. **Alcoholic Beverages:** At sites only. **Vehicle Maximum Length:** 40 ft.

To Get There

The park is located just off I-185 near Callaway Gardens, west of Warm Springs on Hwy. 190, and south of Pine Mountain off US Hwy. 27.

PINE MOUNTAIN

Pine Mountain Campground

8804 Hamilton Rd. (Hwy. 27), Pine Mountain 31822. T: (706) 663-4329; F: (706) 663-9837; www.gocampingamerica.com/pinemountain; jenningspmcg@aol.com.

★★★   ★★

Beauty: ★★★★   Site Privacy: ★★
Spaciousness: ★★★   Quiet: ★★★
Security: ★★   Cleanliness: ★★★★
Insect Control: ★★★   Facilities: ★★★

Located in the foothills of the Appalachian Mountains, this private campground is a rural spot in the vicinity of small town charm and historic tourist attractions such as Callaway Gardens and FDR's Little White House. This is a pretty campground with private, relatively large sites and lots of pine trees. Between kids and highway noise, this is not a terribly quiet campground, but there are extensive facilities and they are well maintained. The pull-through sites in the back are more spacious and are further from the highway noise, but beware the large chunky gravel (the sites in the front have smaller gravel). There are no gates, and the campground is quite visible from the highway, so security is not great. Ideal for families, the campground also offers some adult amenities, including a spa. Bring the kids (or not) and enjoy the trees!

BASICS

Operated By: Private operator. **Open:** Apr.–Oct. **Site Assignment:** Reservations accepted. **Registration:** At camp office. **Fee:** $18–$26. **Parking:** In campground.

FACILITIES

Number of RV Sites: 154. **Number of Tent-Only Sites:** 0, tenters use RV sites. **Hookups:** Water, electric (20, 30, 50 amps), sewer. **Each Site:** Picnic area. **Dump Station:** Yes. **Laundry:** Yes. **Pay Phone:** Yes. **Rest Rooms and Showers:** Yes. **Fuel:** Yes. **Propane:** Yes. **Internal Roads:** Paved & gravel. **RV Service:** No. **Market:** No. **Restaurant:** No. **General Store:** No. **Vending:** No. **Swim-**ming **Pool:** Yes. **Playground:** Yes. **Activities:** Miniature golf, swimming, boating. **Nearby Attractions:** Callaway Gardens, FDR's Little White House, Warm Springs, Wild Animal Safari Park. **Additional Information:** Inquire at campground

RESTRICTIONS

Pets: Yes. **Fires:** Allowed. **Alcoholic Beverages:** Inquire at campground. **Vehicle Maximum Length:** 40 ft. **Other:** No fireworks.

To Get There

Take I-85S to I-185. Take Exit 42, Hwy. 27. Turn left and go 8 mi. to the campground.

RICHMOND HILL

Fort McAllister State Historic Park

3984 Ft. McAllister Rd., Richmond Hill 31324. T: (912) 727-2339; www.ftmcallister.org or www.gastateparks.org; ftmcallr@coastalnow.net.

★★★★   ★★★★

Beauty: ★★★★★   Site Privacy: ★★★★
Spaciousness: ★★★★★   Quiet: ★★★★★
Security: ★★★★   Cleanliness: ★★★★
Insect Control: ★★★   Facilities: ★★★★

Not far from the Georgia coast on the banks of the Great Ogeechee River, campers at Fort McAllister will find a place to rest their heads among civil war history. The 57 RV sites and 12 tent-only sites lie beneath the giant live oaks that grow in this former battlefield. Water and electric hookups are available in this first come, fist served campground. A Civil War Museum and tours of the fort are possible, just call for reservations.

BASICS

Operated By: Georgia Dept. of Natural Resources. **Open:** All year. **Site Assignment:** First come, first served. **Registration:** Museum office. **Fee:** RV $17, tent $5–$15. **Parking:** On site.

FACILITIES

Number of RV Sites: 53. **Number of Tent-Only Sites:** 12. **Hookups:** Water, electric (30 amps). **Each Site:** Grill, picnic table. **Dump Station:** Yes. **Laundry:** Yes. **Pay Phone:** Yes. **Rest Rooms and Showers:** Yes. **Fuel:** Nearby. **Propane:** Nearby. **Internal Roads:** Paved; sites grass & gravel. **RV Service:** In Richmond Hill. **Market:** 10 mi. **Restaurant:** Nearby. **General Store:** 4 mi. **Vending:** Soft drinks. **Swimming Pool:** No.

Playground: Yes. **Activities:** Hiking, picknicking, salt water fishing, canoeing, kayaking. **Nearby Attractions:** Civil War museum, fort tours (call for reservations). **Additional Information:** Richmond Hill CVB, (912) 756-2676 or www.richmondhillcvb.org.

RESTRICTIONS

Pets: On leash & attended. **Fires:** In fire rings only. **Alcoholic Beverages:** At sites only. **Vehicle Maximum Length:** 50 ft.

TO GET THERE

Take I-95 Exit 90. Go 10 mi. east to Georgia Spur 144. Turn left, then go until the road dead-ends at the park (4.4 mi.).

RICHMOND HILL
KOA–Savannah South

P.O. Box 309, Richmond Hill 31324. T: (912) 756-3396.

🚐 ★★★   ▲ ★★★

Beauty: ★★★★	Site Privacy: ★★★
Spaciousness: ★★★	Quiet: ★★★★
Security: ★★★	Cleanliness: ★★★★
Insect Control: ★★★	Facilities: ★★★

Located in a suburban setting, this campground contains sites that are small but attractive. The area is mostly shady with a few open sites scattered throughout the site. For the nature lover, the campground has a 35-acre fishing lake that also contains hundreds of ducks, geese, swans, and egrets. The sites closest to the lakefront are by far the prettiest. However, the sites do not offer much privacy. We recommend visiting Savanna South in the fall or the spring when the weather is most pleasant. Reservations are preferred for this KOA campground. However, the campground's security measures are lacking, so be mindful.

BASICS

Operated By: Private operator. **Open:** All year. **Site Assignment:** First come, first served. **Registration:** Office. **Fee:** $27–$36. **Parking:** On site.

FACILITIES

Number of RV Sites: 130. **Number of Tent-Only Sites:** 15. **Hookups:** Electric (50 amps), water. **Each Site:** Picnic table, fire pit. **Dump Station:** Yes. **Laundry:** Yes. **Pay Phone:** Yes. **Rest Rooms and Showers:** Yes. **Fuel:** No. **Propane:**

Yes. **Internal Roads:** Paved. **RV Service:** No. **Market:** In Richmond Hill. **Restaurant:** In Richmond Hill. **General Store:** Yes. **Vending:** Yes. **Swimming Pool:** Yes. **Playground:** Yes. **Activities:** Fishing, boating, bird-watching, basketball, shuffleboard, game room. **Nearby Attractions:** Savannah, Fort Stewart, Fort McAllister State Historic Park. **Additional Information:** Richmond Hill CVB (912) 756-2676 or www.richmondhillcvb.org.

RESTRICTIONS

Pets: Yes. **Fires:** Designated areas only. **Alcoholic Beverages:** Not allowed. **Vehicle Maximum Length:** None.

TO GET THERE

From I-95 take Exit 87 and turn left onto US 17 South. The campground is 0.5 mi. on left.

RINGGOLD
KOA–Chattanooga South

199 KOA Blvd., Ringgold 30736. T: (706) 937-4166; www.koa.com; koakamp@catt.com.

🚐 ★★★   ▲ ★★

Beauty: ★★★★	Site Privacy: ★★★
Spaciousness: ★★★	Quiet: ★★★★
Security: ★★★	Cleanliness: ★★★
Insect Control: ★★★★	Facilities: ★★★

Whether civil war enthusiasts or just families on vacation, campers will find this KOA park offers a relaxing camp experience within easy reach of Chattanooga. A mix of gravel and paved roads provides access to the sites, some of which have tent pads. The prettiest and shadiest sites are located on the east side, near the pet kennel. A minimal understory limits privacy, but campers have some room to move about, as sites are medium to large in size. Those wishing to remain in the campground will find an outdoor theater, volleyball court, basketball court, and horseshoe pits. Campers venturing beyond the park can visit to civil war battlefields (Chickamauga and Chattanooga National Military Park) or the Tennessee Aquarium, Ruby Falls, or the Tennessee Valley Railroad.

BASICS

Operated By: KOA Kampgrounds. **Open:** All year. **Site Assignment:** Reservations accepted. **Registration:** At camp office. **Fee:** $25. **Parking:** In campground.

FACILITIES

Number of RV Sites: 65. **Number of Tent-Only Sites:** 21. **Hookups:** Water, electric (30, 50 amps). **Each Site:** Picnic table, fire pit. **Dump Station:** Yes. **Laundry:** Yes. **Pay Phone:** Yes. **Rest Rooms and Showers:** Yes. **Fuel:** Yes. **Propane:** Yes. **Internal Roads:** Paved & gravel. **RV Service:** Yes. **Market:** In Chattanooga. **Restaurant:** In Chattanooga. **General Store:** Yes. **Vending:** No. **Swimming Pool:** Yes. **Playground:** Yes. **Activities:** Outdoor theater, volleyball, basketball, horseshoes. **Nearby Attractions:** Tennessee Aquarium, Ruby Falls, outlet malls, Rock City, Lost Sea, area flea markets, Southern Belle riverboat.

RESTRICTIONS

Pets: On leash only. **Fires:** Allowed. **Alcoholic Beverages:** At sites only. **Vehicle Maximum Length:** None.

TO GET THERE

From I-75, take the Battlefield Pkwy./Fort Oglethorpe exit and proceed west on Hwy. 2 for 300 yards to the camp entrance.

RISING FAWN
Cloudland Canyon State Park

122 Cloudland Canyon Park Rd., Rising Fawn 30738. T: (706) 657-4050; www.gastateparks.org.

🚐 ★★★★   ⛺ ★★★★★

Beauty: ★★★★★   Site Privacy: ★★★★★
Spaciousness: ★★★★★   Quiet: ★★★★
Security: ★★★★★   Cleanliness: ★★★★
Insect Control: ★★★★   Facilities: ★★★★

Cloudland is one of the most scenic parks in Georgia. The 2,200-acre park has 75 sites with an additional 30 primitive tent sites. All of the back-in sites are huge, while the size of the pull-throughs varies greatly. Still, the entire area is gorgeous and heavily wooded, providing great privacy between sites, some of which are quite large and secluded. The nearby town of Trenton provides supplies to the forgetful camper. Tennis and swimming are available, but the hiking trails take visitors to the park's centerpiece—the canyon, which varies in depth between 800 and nearly 2000 feet. Those who come to relax at Cloudland may still hear the call of Rock City, a private attraction located close by. Visitors may even want to zip up to Chattanooga, where a myriad of activities, including the Tennessee Aquarium, and the Chattanooga Choo Choo, await

BASICS

Operated By: Georgia Dept. of Natural Resources. **Open:** All year. **Site Assignment:** Reservations preferred. **Registration:** At camp office. **Fee:** $10–$19. **Parking:** 2 vehicles per site.

FACILITIES

Number of RV Sites: 75. **Number of Tent-Only Sites:** 30. **Hookups:** Water, electric (30 amps). **Each Site:** Picnic table, fire pit. **Dump Station:** Yes. **Laundry:** Yes. **Pay Phone:** Yes. **Rest Rooms and Showers:** Yes. **Fuel:** No. **Propane:** No. **Internal Roads:** Paved. **RV Service:** No. **Market:** In Trenton. **Restaurant:** In Trenton. **General Store:** No. **Vending:** Soft drinks. **Swimming Pool:** Yes. **Playground:** Yes. **Other:** Waterfall trails. **Activities:** Hiking, backpacking, tennis, swimming. **Nearby Attractions:** Chief Van House State Historic Site, Ruby Falls, Incline Railroad, Lookout Mountain, Tennessee Aquarium.

RESTRICTIONS

Pets: On leash only. **Fires:** Allowed. **Alcoholic Beverages:** Yes, in a cup. **Vehicle Maximum Length:** None.

TO GET THERE

The campground is located 5 mi. east of Trenton or 18 mi. northwest of Lafayette via GA 136.

RUTLEDGE
Hard Labor Creek State Park

P.O. Box 247, Rutledge 30663. T: (706) 557-3001; www.gastateparks.org.

🚐 ★★★★   ⛺ ★★★★

Beauty: ★★★★★   Site Privacy: ★★★★
Spaciousness: ★★★★   Quiet: ★★★★
Security: ★★★★   Cleanliness: ★★★★
Insect Control: ★★★   Facilities: ★★★★★

Named either by slaves working in nearby fields or by Indians who thought the creek was difficult to ford, Hard Labor Creek State Park conjures up very different associations these days. The park's golf course is known as a good value, offering a pro shop, driving range, and unlimited weekday play packages. Campsite sizes vary, but most are spacious and nicely wooded. The campground abuts a swimming beach on the small but pleasant Lake Brantley. Lakeside sites 50 and 51 have nice water views, and sites 22 and 27 are pleasantly secluded; site 42 is a particularly nice pull-through. Nearby, campers can visit Stone Mountain or the Oconee National Forest. There's also a large on-site horse stable with special campsites for equestrians, as well as access to multi-use trails open to both horses and hikers.

BASICS

Operated By: Georgia Dept. of Natural Resources. **Open:** All year. **Site Assignment:** Reservations only. **Registration:** At camp office. **Fee:** $15–$17. **Parking:** 2 vehicles per site.

FACILITIES

Number of RV Sites: 47. **Number of Tent-Only Sites:** 4. **Hookups:** Water, electric (30 amps). **Each Site:** Picnic table, grill, fire ring. **Dump Station:** Yes. **Laundry:** Yes. **Pay Phone:** Yes. **Rest Rooms and Showers:** Yes. **Fuel:** No. **Propane:** No. **Internal Roads:** Paved. **RV Service:** 20 mi. **Market:** 5 mi. **Restaurant:** 5 mi. **General Store:** 15 mi. **Vending:** Yes. **Swimming Pool:** No. **Playground:** Yes. **Activities:** Beach area, golf, hiking trails, horse stable. **Nearby Attractions:** Stone Mountain, Oconee National Forest, Athens, Panola Mountain & State Conservation Park.

RESTRICTIONS

Pets: On leash only. **Fires:** In fire rings only. **Alcoholic Beverages:** Allowed. **Vehicle Maximum Length:** None. **Other:** 14-day max. stay limit.

TO GET THERE

Take exit 105 on I-20E. Proceed 3 mi. on Fairplay Rd.

SAVANNAH
Skidaway Island State Park NP

52 Diamond Causeway, Savannah 31411-1102. T: (912) 598-2300; www.gastateparks.org.

🚐 ★★★★★   ⛺ ★★★★★

Beauty: ★★★★★   Site Privacy: ★★★★★
Spaciousness: ★★★★★   Quiet: ★★★★★
Security: ★★★★   Cleanliness: ★★★★
Insect Control: ★★★   Facilities: ★★★

Historic Savannah is the cultural anchor of this state park, and the rich, diverse physical environment makes it a stunner for nature lovers as well.

It is a glorious, beautiful place offerig both fresh and salt water, oodles of wildlife viewing, and plenty of natural variety in the forest portions of the park. It is an urban to suburban setting, so we do not recommend sites near the main road, but the sites themselves are indeed quite large and attractive, with spanish moss dripping from the trees above. All of the sites are pull-throughs, and they have pine straw and packed dirt ground cover. Especially huge are sites 1–10, and exceptionally gorgeous are 55, 57, and 59. The only turn-off here are the yucky facilities, but if you can tolerate that, the beauty and privacy more than make up for it. Savannah is a large enough town to provide entertainment for all travelers, and the campground itself is good for families and all ages. For history and/or nature nuts, this is a supreme vacation spot.

BASICS

Operated By: Georgia Dept. of Natural Resources. **Open:** All year. **Site Assignment:** Reservations accepted. **Registration:** At camp office. **Fee:** $16–$18. **Parking:** 2 vehicles per site.

FACILITIES

Number of Multipurpose Sites: 88. **Hookups:** Water, electric (30 amps), cable. **Each Site:** Picnic table. **Dump Station:** Yes. **Laundry:** Yes. **Pay Phone:** Yes. **Rest Rooms and Showers:** Yes. **Fuel:** Nearby. **Propane:** No. **Internal Roads:** Paved. **RV Service:** No. **Market:** In Savannah. **Restaurant:** In Savannah. **General Store:** No. **Vending:** Yes. **Swimming Pool:** Yes. **Playground:** Yes. **Activities:** Hiking, nature trail, bird-watching, swimming, museum & interpretative center. **Nearby Attractions:** Wormsloe State Historic Site, Fort McAllister State Historic Park, Fort Morris State Historic Site, Skidaway Marine Institute, historic Savannah, Tybee Island beaches.

RESTRICTIONS

Pets: On 6-ft leash. **Fires:** Allowed. **Alcoholic Beverages:** Not allowed. **Vehicle Maximum Length:** None.

TO GET THERE

From I-16 in Savannah, exit at I-518 (Exit 164A), which merges with DeReene Ave. Turn right on Waters Ave. and go straight ahead to Diamond Causeway.

ST. MARY'S
Crooked River State Park

6222 Charlie Smith Sr. Hwy., St. Mary's 31558.
T: (912) 882-5256; www.gastateparks.org.

🚐 ★★★★   ▲ ★★★★

Beauty: ★★★★★   Site Privacy: ★★★★
Spaciousness: ★★★★★   Quiet: ★★★★★
Security: ★★★★   Cleanliness: ★★★★
Insect Control: ★★   Facilities: ★★★

Situated in a gorgeous pine stand, this State Park campground also boasts Spanish moss-draped oaks at most campsites. This is a serene campground near the small coastal town of St. Mary's in the southernmost part of the state. Most of the sites are pull-throughs, and they tend to be spacious (some are huge) with pine straw and packed dirt for ground cover. The best views of the intercoastal marshland can be found at sites 10, 11, and 39. Some other sites offer more privacy, such as 44, which is a giant pull-through that would be great for big-rigs. This is a wonderful place for families who want privacy, with plenty of outdoor recreation and water sports available to campers. In addition, the historical intrigue of the nearby McIntosh Sugar Works and the wild horses and mansion ruins at Cumberland Island National Seashore make this a lovely place for a vacation.

BASICS
Operated By: Georgia Dept. of Natural Resources. **Open:** All year. **Site Assignment:** Reservations or first come, first served. **Registration:** At camp office. **Fee:** $18. **Parking:** In campground.

FACILITIES
Number of RV Sites: 62. **Number of Tent-Only Sites:** 0. **Hookups:** Water, electric (30, 50 amps), cable. **Each Site:** Picnic shelter. **Dump Station:** Yes. **Laundry:** Yes. **Pay Phone:** Yes. **Rest Rooms and Showers:** Yes. **Fuel:** In St. Mary's. **Propane:** In St. Mary's. **Internal Roads:** Paved. **RV Service:** In Brunswick or Jacksonville. **Market:** 10 min. **Restaurant:** In St. Mary's. **General Store:** 3 mi. **Vending:** Soft drinks. **Swimming Pool:** Yes. **Playground:** Inquire at campground. **Activities:** Saltwater fishing, boating, kayaking, hiking, mini golf. **Nearby Attractions:** Cumberland Island National Seashore, Jekyll Island, Okefenokee National Wildlife Refuge, Fernandina Beach.

RESTRICTIONS
Pets: On leash (6 ft. or less) only. **Fires:** In fire ring or grill. **Alcoholic Beverages:** Yes, in a cup. **Vehicle Maximum Length:** None.

TO GET THERE
The campground is located 7 mi. north of St. Mary's on GA Spur 40 or 12 mi. east of Kingsland off US Hwy. 17 (8 mi. off I-95).

STONE MOUNTAIN
Stone Mountain Family Campground

Hwy. 78 East, Stone Mountain 30086. T: (800) 385-9807 or (770) 498-5710; F: (770) 413-5082; www.stonemountain.com.

🚐 ★★★   ▲ ★★★

Beauty: ★★★★   Site Privacy: ★★
Spaciousness: ★★★   Quiet: ★★
Security: ★★★   Cleanliness: ★★★★
Insect Control: ★★★★   Facilities: ★★★★★

In spite of touting 441 wooded campsites (43 of these primitive tent sites), Stone Mountain is quite a friendly and relaxing place. Campers expecting a remote experience won't find it, but visitors ready to take advantage of the many activities available at Stone Mountain will have a field day. Nearby activities include a swimming beach with a water slide, Stone Mountain Museum, a train ride, and a hike to the top of Stone Mountain. The famous laser light show occurs on Saturdays in season (everyday between mid-May and mid-August). Keep in mind that camping costs are in addition to the entrance fee. Most sites have water, electric, and sewer hookups in addition to a grill, picnic table and tent pad. Not all sites are on the water, but all are within easy walking distance.

BASICS
Operated By: Silver Dollar City, Inc. **Open:** All year. **Site Assignment:** First come, first served. **Registration:** At camp office. **Fee:** $37 lakeside full, $32 lakeside partial, $28 lakeside tent, $22 primitive tent. **Parking:** 2 vehicles per site.

FACILITIES
Number of RV Sites: 398. **Number of Tent-Only Sites:** 43. **Hookups:** Water, electric (20, 30, 50 amps), sewer. **Each Site:** Grill, picnic table, tent pad, fire ring. **Dump Station:** Yes. **Laundry:** Yes.

Pay Phone: Yes. **Rest Rooms and Showers:** Yes. **Fuel:** No. **Propane:** Yes. **Internal Roads:** Paved. **RV Service:** 6 mi. **Market:** 2 mi. **Restaurant:** In park. **General Store:** 1 mi. **Vending:** Yes. **Swimming Pool:** Yes. **Playground:** Yes. **Other:** Laser show, sky lift. **Activities:** Tennis, golf, fishing, hiking, volleyball, lake, horseshoes, riverboat cruise, antebellum plantation, petting zoo. **Nearby Attractions:** Beach & waterslide complex, Stone Mountain Museum, Children's Barn, Cross Roads attraction.

RESTRICTIONS

Pets: On leash only. **Fires:** In fire rings only. **Alcoholic Beverages:** Not allowed. **Vehicle Maximum Length:** 50 ft. **Other:** 14-day max. stay limit.

TO GET THERE

From Atlanta, take I-285E to Exit 39B, Hwy. 78E Go 7.5 mi. to the park. After entering the park, take first left and go 2 mi. to campground.

Kentucky

The state of Kentucky has a rich historical heritage going back to colonial times and before. Thousands of years before Europeans came to America, regions in western Kentucky along the Ohio and Mississippi rivers were inhabited by bands of ancient mound-building Indians. Later, tribes of Shawnee, Iroquois, Delaware, and Chickasaw lived in the area as well. Many of these fought or were allied with American pioneers during skirmishes and wars before and during the American Revolution. Many frontiersmen established settlements in eastern and central Kentucky. One of these was Boonesborough, on the Kentucky River about 45 miles east of present-day Harrodstown, founded by the famous Daniel Boone.

Following the Revolutionary War, Kentucky became the 15th state of the Union. Native American claims to Kentucky were erased in 1818, when the last Chickasaw lands in the western part of the state were acquired by the US government. In the years leading up the Civil War, large portions of Kentucky were cleared for farming, especially tobacco. As the agricultural industry kicked into high gear and steamboats appeared, the city of Louisville (located on the Ohio River) became the state's principal trade center.

Kentucky was sharply divided at the outbreak of the Civil War, having strong pro-slavery and pro-Union factions. Though Kentucky's government declared itself neutral in the fighting and refused calls for volunteers from both the Union and Confederacy, neither side really respected the state's neutrality. Both moved armies through Kentucky at various times, and several large battles were fought there early in the war. Eventually, both the Confederacy and Union claimed Kentucky as an ally (there was a star for the state on both governments' flags). After suffering repeated Confederate invasion, the state government finally sided with the Union, which spared Kentucky from the Union's harsh Reconstruction policies.

The post-Civil War era saw many outbreaks of local strife and discord (including the infamous Hatfield-McCoy feud on the West Virginia border). However, the state as a whole began to prosper economically. Through the twentieth century, Kentucky has become known for its thriving urban centers (**Louisville, Lexington, Bowling Green**), its rich natural beauty (**Land Between the Lakes, Mammoth Cave National Park, Big South Fork National River & Recreation Area, Daniel Boone National Forest, Cumberland Gap National Historic Park**), fine Kentucky bourbon (**Maker's Mark Distillery** near Loretto), horse racing (the **Kentucky Derby** at Louisville's Churchill Downs), and the Bluegrass region (the Shaker village of Pleasant Hill, Stephen Foster balladry in Bardstown, the historic state capital of **Frankfort**).

In addition to hundreds of private campgrounds of every size and type, Kentucky has a great deal of parkland with its own share of camping choices. Five nationally designated outdoor recreation areas cover close to a million acres of Kentucky soil. In addition there are many more state resort parks, wildlife refuges, and private campgrounds to enjoy nature at its most pristine. Throughout the state, you can find miles of trails, acres of lakes, and uncountable rivers, streams, mountains, and forests that make great places to park an RV or pitch a tent.

Campground Profiles

BARDSTOWN

My Old Kentucky Home State Park

P.O. Box 323, Bardstown 40004-0323. T: (502) 348-3502.

🚐 ★★★★   ▲ ★★★★

Beauty: ★★★★	Site Privacy: ★★★
Spaciousness: ★★★	Quiet: ★★
Security: ★★★	Cleanliness: ★★★★
Insect Control: ★★★★	Facilities: ★★★★

Though it's proper name is Federal Hill Mansion, this parks centerpiece was immortalized in Stephen Foster's ballad "My Old Kentucky Home." Visiting My Old Kentucky Home is a religious pilgrimage for many Kentuckians. For others, it's a fascinating way to learn about lifestyles of the aristocracy in antebellum Kentucky. The campground is just around the corner from the mansion. It's fairly attractive, with ample-sized sites. All sites are paved, with back-in parking. Though the campground would be a lot nicer without the telephone lines, sites are shaded by gorgeous mature trees. Our favorite sites, 19 and 21, enjoy views of the state park golf course. The campground is located in the heart of Bardstown and has no gates, making security fair. For less crowded touring, avoid My Old Kentucky Home on summer and holiday weekends.

BASICS

Operated By: State of Kentucky. **Open:** Apr.–Oct. **Site Assignment:** First come, first served. **Registration:** Office. **Fee:** $16; 10% senior discount. **Parking:** On site.

FACILITIES

Number of RV Sites: 39. **Number of Tent-Only Sites:.** **Hookups:** Water, electric. **Each Site:** None. **Dump Station:** Yes. **Laundry:** Nearby. **Pay Phone:** Yes. **Rest Rooms and Showers:** Yes. **Fuel:** No. **Propane:** No. **Internal Roads:** Paved. **RV Service:** No. **Market:** Nearby. **Restaurant:** Nearby. **General Store:** Nearby. **Vending:** Yes. **Swimming Pool:** No. **Playground:** Yes. **Activities:** picnicking, golfing, tennis. **Nearby Attractions:** Amphitheater, house museum.

RESTRICTIONS

Pets: On leash. **Fires:** Fire ring. **Alcoholic Beverages:** Not allowed. **Vehicle Maximum Length:** No limit. **Other:** Check out at 2 p.m.

TO GET THERE

Located in Bardstown on US Hwy. 150.

BENTON

Sportsman's Anchor Resort & Marina

12800 US Hwy. 68 East, Benton 42025. T: (270) 354-6568 or (800) 326-3625; www.kentuckylake.com/anchor; anchor@vci.net.

🚐 ★★★   ▲ ★★★

Beauty: ★★★★	Site Privacy: ★★★
Spaciousness: ★★	Quiet: ★★★
Security: ★★★	Cleanliness: ★★★★
Insect Control: ★★★	Facilities: ★★★

Sportsman's Anchor is located in a remote though touristy area on Ruff Creek, a branch of Kentucky Lake. The RV sites are a bit small and on top of each other (no understory adds to lack of privacy), but those with boats will appreciate the adjacent full-service marina. The 15 tent-only primitive sites have more elbow room, and they are very attractive, especially for a private campground. The entire campground is shaded by pines and hardwood trees. However, there are no waterside sites, though the creek can be seen through the trees. There are not a lot of activities on the grounds—a pool and playground are located at the entrance—but Land Between the Lakes Recreation Area is only a five-minute car drive away. There, visitors can hike, boat, ride horses, bike, or hunt.

BASICS

Operated By: Raymond & Lynn Meyers. **Open:** Seasonal. **Site Assignment:** Assigned at registration. **Registration:** Office. **Fee:** $16–$23. **Parking:** On site.

FACILITIES

Number of RV Sites: 49. **Number of Tent-Only Sites:**. **Hookups:** Water, electric, sewer, cable TV. **Each Site:** Tent pad, picnic table. **Dump Station:** Yes. **Laundry:** Yes. **Pay Phone:** Emergency use only. **Rest Rooms and Showers:** Yes. **Fuel:** No (Gas dock in progress). **Propane:** Gas dock in progress. **Internal Roads:** Gravel. **RV Service:** 15 mi. north. **Market:** Yes. **Restaurant:** 1 mi. **General Store:** Yes. **Vending:** No. **Swimming Pool:** Yes (seasonal). **Playground:** Yes. **Other:** Gift shop, country store. **Activities:** game room, shuffleboard, fishing, boat rentals. **Nearby Attractions:** Kentucky Dam Village SRP, Land Between the Lakes. **Additional Information:** Park Manager.

RESTRICTIONS

Pets: On leash/not in rental units. **Fires:** Small on site (no fire rings). **Alcoholic Beverages:** In covered container only. **Vehicle Maximum Length:** 40 ft.

TO GET THERE

I-24 Exit 25 A east on Purchase Parkway, turn east on Hwy. 68, 14 mi. on right (large blue/white sign).

BOW

Dale Hollow Lake SP

6371 State Park Rd., Bow 42717-9728. T: (270) 433-7431.

🚐 ★★★★	⛺ ★★★★

Beauty: ★★★★★	Site Privacy: ★★
Spaciousness: ★★★	Quiet: ★★★★
Security: ★★★★★	Cleanliness: ★★★★★
Insect Control: ★★★	Facilities: ★★★★

Known for its clear, clean waters, Dale Hollow Lake attracts scuba divers, water skiers, and anglers. With a former world record for smallmouth bass, the lake is hailed as one of the best fishing spots in the Southeast. Other catches include crappie, bream, muskie, walleye, and four more bass species. The campground is laid out on 18 cul-de-sacs containing 8 sites each. Though sites are small, the campground feels open due to its layout and lack of understory. A few areas enjoy shade, but most lack trees. Parking pads are paved, back-in style. The equestrian camping area is the prettiest. If you left your horse at home, try areas L and N, which offer shady trees. Lucky for campers, there's a swimming pool at the campground. Remote and gated, this campground is very safe. Avoid Dale Hollow Lake on busy holiday weekends.

BASICS

Operated By: State of Kentucky. **Open:** year-round. **Site Assignment:** First come, first served. **Registration:** At camp office. **Fee:** 12. **Parking:** On site.

FACILITIES

Number of RV Sites: 144. **Number of Tent-Only Sites:**. **Number of Multipurpose Sites:** Combined. **Hookups:** Electric, water. **Each Site:** Picnic Shelter. **Dump Station:** Yes. **Laundry:** Yes. **Pay Phone:** Yes. **Rest Rooms and Showers:** Yes. **Fuel:** 9 mi. away. **Propane:** 9 mi. **Internal Roads:** Paved & gravel. **RV Service:** No. **Market:** No. **Restaurant:** Dining, 3 meals. **General Store:** No. **Vending:** Drink only. **Swimming Pool:** Yes. **Playground:** Yes. **Other:** Public swimming lake. **Activities:** Skiing, fishing, boating hiking, scuba diving, biking, amphitheater. **Nearby Attractions:** Nature trails, Tomkind Field, Cordell Hall, Alvin York's Birth place. **Additional Information:** Check out 2 p.m.

RESTRICTIONS

Pets: On leash. **Fires:** Fire ring. **Alcoholic Beverages:** Not allowed. **Vehicle Maximum Length:** No limit.

TO GET THERE

From I-65, exit at Cumberland parkway (Exit No. 43) & take KY 90 east at Glasgow.

BOWLING GREEN
Bowling Green, KY KOA Kampground

1960 Three Springs Rd., Bowling Green 42104.
T: (270) 843-1919; www.bgkoa.com.

🚐 ★★★   ▲ ★★

Beauty: ★★★★   Site Privacy: ★★
Spaciousness: ★★★   Quiet: ★★★★
Security: ★★   Cleanliness: ★★★★
Insect Control: ★★★★   Facilities: ★★★

Convenient to I-65, the Bowling Green KOA offers attractive sites laid out in five rows of pull-through sites with back-in sites along the back of the park. Sites, which tend to be long and narrow, are average sized. Almost every site enjoys the shade of mature trees. Parking pads are gravel. Our favorite site, shady number 60, is an excellent place for a tent or pop-up. RV campers should head for a more spacious pull-through site in the 40s or 76–78. The campground is located in the bustling town of Bowling Green, and has no gates, making security poor. Bowling Green is home to the National Corvette Museum, which displays over 50 rare Corvettes. Plan ahead for a memorable day trip to Mammoth Cave National Park—with so many cave tours offered, you may have trouble choosing. Avoid the area on summer holidays.

BASICS
Operated By: Koa Kampgrounds, Dan & Yvonne Goad. **Open:** Year-round. **Site Assignment:** First come, first served. **Registration:** Office. **Fee:** $20–$30. **Parking:** On site.

FACILITIES
Number of RV Sites: 124. **Number of Tent-Only Sites:** 6. **Hookups:** Water, electric (20, 30, 50 amps), sewer. **Each Site:** Fire ring. **Dump Station:** Yes. **Laundry:** Yes. **Pay Phone:** Yes. **Rest Rooms and Showers:** Yes. **Fuel:** No. **Propane:** Yes. **Internal Roads:** Paved. **RV Service:** No. **Market:** No. **Restaurant:** No. **General Store:** Yes. **Vending:** Yes. **Swimming Pool:** Yes. **Playground:** Yes. **Other:** Lake & duck pond. **Activities:** Fishing, tennis, golf. **Nearby Attractions:** Mammoth Cave National Park, skating rink, Corvette assembly plant tours, Shaker Museum. **Additional Information:** check out at noon.

RESTRICTIONS
Pets: On leash. **Fires:** Only in designated areas. **Alcoholic Beverages:** At site only. **Vehicle Maximum Length:** No limit.

TO GET THERE
From I-65 take Exit 22, then turn north on US 231. Turn left on KY 884 (Three Springs Rd.) and campground is app. 1.5 mi.

BURNSIDE
General Burnside State Park

P.O. Box 488, Burnside 36119-0488. T: (606) (561) 4104.

🚐 ★★★★   ▲ ★★★★

Beauty: ★★★★   Site Privacy: ★★★★
Spaciousness: ★★★★   Quiet: ★★★★
Security: ★★★★   Cleanliness: ★★★★
Insect Control: ★★★   Facilities: ★★★★

General Burnside Island's campground rests on gentle, verdant hills and offers uncommonly tidy sites. Though site size varies, most are larger than average. About a dozen sites are totally open, but the rest are shaded by lovely mature trees. Many enjoy a measure of privacy. Sites offer paved, back-in style parking. Families should head for sites 1–4, right next to the playground. Other RV campers should try sites 30, 31, or 88, which are secluded. Very shady sites include 74 and 76. General Burnside Island is accessible by a bridge across 50, 000-acre Lake Cumberland, and boasts excellent amenities. A well-appointed marina aids fishermen in their quest for crappie and largemouth, smallmouth, and striped bass. The park is incredibly isolated, making security good. Visit any time except summer holidays—there's plenty of elbow room on the island.

BASICS
Operated By: State of Kentucky. **Open:** Apr. 1–Oct. 31. **Site Assignment:** Reservations not accepted, first come, first serve. **Registration:** Control station. **Fee:** $14. **Parking:** Site plus overflow parking.

FACILITIES
Number of RV Sites: 110. **Number of Tent-Only Sites:** Tent area. **Hookups:** Water, electric. **Each Site:** Picnic shelter. **Dump Station:** Yes. **Laundry:** Yes. **Pay Phone:** Yes. **Rest Rooms and**

Showers: Yes. **Fuel:** No (8 mi., Somerset). **Propane:** Yes (8 mi., Somerset). **Internal Roads:** Paved. **RV Service:** No. **Market:** No. **Restaurant:** No. **General Store:** No. **Vending:** Yes. **Swimming Pool:** Yes. **Playground:** Yes. **Activities:** Boating, fishing, golf. **Nearby Attractions:** Cumberland State Resort Park. **Additional Information:** Somerset CVB, (800) 642-6287.

RESTRICTIONS

Pets: On leash, no tying to trees or bushes, clean up after. **Fires:** Fire ring only. **Alcoholic Beverages:** Not allowed. **Vehicle Maximum Length:** No limit. **Other:** Firearms & fireworks.

TO GET THERE

From US 27 south in Somerset go 8 mi.

CADIZ
Lake Barkley State Resort Park

Box 790, Cadiz 42211-0790. T: (270) 924-1131.

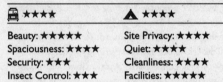

Beauty: ★★★★★	Site Privacy: ★★★★
Spaciousness: ★★★★	Quiet: ★★★★
Security: ★★★	Cleanliness: ★★★★
Insect Control: ★★★	Facilities: ★★★★★

There are an abundance of campgrounds to choose from in western Kentucky. Campers wishing to pamper themselves should visit Lake Barkley. Located close to the Land Between the Lakes Recreation Area, Lake Barkley has 78 RV sites with water and electric hookups. The sites are larger than average, and a gorgeous forest surrounds the campground. What's intriguing is the number of activities available, both on site and off. The heart of the resort is the Fitness Center, where Nautilus machines and fitness cycles await, preceding an inviting sauna and massage. There is also an indoor heated pool for the winter months. Those desiring more outdoors-oriented activities can fish, swim, or water-ski on Lake Barkley, practice their aim at the local trapshoot range, or enjoy over nine miles of hiking trails. This is a popular place; the lodge and cottages book nearly a year in advance—RVs have a distinct advantage as there are no advance reservations.

BASICS

Operated By: State of Kentucky. **Open:** Year round. **Site Assignment:** First come, first served.

Registration: Office. **Fee:** $10–$14. **Parking:** On site.

FACILITIES

Number of RV Sites: 78. **Number of Tent-Only Sites:.** **Hookups:** Water, electric (15 amps). **Each Site:** None. **Dump Station:** Yes. **Laundry:** Yes. **Pay Phone:** Yes. **Rest Rooms and Showers:** Yes. **Fuel:** No. **Propane:** No. **Internal Roads:** Paved. **RV Service:** No. **Market:** Nearby. **Restaurant:** Nearby. **General Store:** No. **Vending:** Yes. **Swimming Pool:** No. **Playground:** Yes. **Other:** Fitness center. **Activities:** Fishing, boating, lake swimming, golf, tennis, hiking. **Nearby Attractions:** Jefferson Davis Monument State Historic Site.

RESTRICTIONS

Pets: On leash. **Fires:** Fire pits. **Alcoholic Beverages:** Not allowed. **Vehicle Maximum Length:** 45 ft.

TO GET THERE

29 mi. west of Hopkinsville. Take US 68 west to KY 1489.

CARROLLTON
General Butler SRP

P.O. Box 325, Carrollton 41008-0325. T: (502) 732-4384.

🚐 ★★★★	🏕 ★★★
Beauty: ★★★★	Site Privacy: ★★★
Spaciousness: ★★★	Quiet: ★★★
Security: ★★★	Cleanliness: ★★★★
Insect Control: ★★★★★	Facilities:

Named for William Orlando Butler, a Carrollton veteran of the War of 1812 and the US-Mexican War, General Butler State Resort Park has a pretty campground just outside of Carrollton. Set in a pleasant stretch of river valley at the confluence of the Kentucky and Ohio Rivers (and on the shores of the 30-acre Butler Lake), the park is well forested with oaks and a variety of other trees. Campsites vary in size, and the parking areas are somewhat small, but the space between sites is usually acceptable. Lakeside campsites 55–59 and 86 are the most secluded and attractive. However, though Butler Lake has a swimming beach accessible to campers, swimming is contingent upon lifeguard availability. Also, the lake was noticeably overgrown with algae when we visited. Regardless, the variety of on-site activities make this campground a popular choice for families.

BASICS

Operated By: Kentucky State Parks. **Open:** Apr. 1–Oct. 31. **Site Assignment:** First come, first served. **Registration:** Camp gate or front desk, no reservations. **Fee:** $18, over 2 adults $1 extra. **Parking:** On site.

FACILITIES

Number of RV Sites: 0. **Number of Tent-Only Sites:** 0. **Number of Multipurpose Sites:** 111. **Hookups:** Electric, water. **Each Site:** Table, grill. **Dump Station:** Yes. **Laundry:** Yes. **Pay Phone:** Yes. **Rest Rooms and Showers:** Yes. **Fuel:** No. **Propane:** No. **Internal Roads:** Paved. **RV Service:** No. **Market:** No. **Restaurant:** Yes. **General Store:** No. **Vending:** Drinks only. **Swimming Pool:** No. **Playground:** Yes. **Activities:** Nature trail, boat dock, golf course for fee. **Nearby Attractions:** Historic Carrollton, Outlet Shopping. **Additional Information:** www.carrolltonky.com.

RESTRICTIONS

Pets: On leash. **Fires:** Fire ring. **Alcoholic Beverages:** Not allowed. **Vehicle Maximum Length:** No limit.

TO GET THERE

44 mi. northeast of Louisville. Take I-71 to Carrollton.

CAVE CITY
Yogi Bear's Jellystone Park

1002 Mammoth Cave Rd., Cave City 42127. T: (270) 773-3840.

🚐 ★★★	⛺ ★★★
Beauty: ★★★★	Site Privacy: ★★
Spaciousness: ★★★	Quiet: ★★★
Security: ★★★	Cleanliness: ★★★★
Insect Control: ★★★★	Facilities: ★★★★

Located three miles from the Entrance to Mammoth Cave National Park, Yogi's is a good choice for families with small children. The marvelous national park includes the world's largest surveyed cave plus vast acres of rolling hills above it. The cave was used by people as early as 2000 BC, when pre-historic Americans mined for minerals. This isn't the most attractive Jellystone Park we've seen, but it has the kind of family-friendly amenities folks expect from Yogi, including a

duck pond. Sites tend to be long and narrow and larger than average. Most sites offer pull-through, gravel parking. Choose from sites in Area A, which is more level, or Area B, which contains more spacious sites. Avoid this touristy area on summer and holiday weekends. And watch your valuables, as there are no gates at this bustling campground.

BASICS

Operated By: Joe & Pat Baffuto. **Open:** Year round. **Site Assignment:** First come, first served except weekends & holidays. **Registration:** ranger station. **Fee:** $25–$30. **Parking:** On site.

FACILITIES

Number of RV Sites: 150. **Number of Tent-Only Sites:** 60. **Hookups:** Water, electric (30 amps); sewer extra. **Each Site:** Picnic table, fire ring. **Dump Station:** Yes. **Laundry:** Yes. **Pay Phone:** Yes. **Rest Rooms and Showers:** Yes. **Fuel:** No. **Propane:** Yes. **Internal Roads:** Paved & gravel. **RV Service:** Yes. **Market:** No. **Restaurant:** Yes. **General Store:** Yes. **Vending:** Yes. **Swimming Pool:** Yes. **Playground:** Yes. **Other:** Water slide, cabins. **Activities:** Planned events, nature hikes, mini-golf. **Nearby Attractions:** Mammoth Cave National Park, wax museum, antique shops, Alpine Slide Fun Park. **Additional Information:** Checks are only accepted 2 weeks or more prior to arrival.

RESTRICTIONS

Pets: On leash. **Fires:** Fire ring. **Alcoholic Beverages:** At site only. **Vehicle Maximum Length:** No limit.

TO GET THERE

Take Cave City Exit No. 53 off I-65 and go 0.5 mi. west on Hwy. 70 to the park.

CINCINNATI
Cincinnati South KOA

P.O. Box 339, Crittendon 41030. T: (859) 428-2000.

🚐 ★★★	⛺ ★★★
Beauty: ★★★★	Site Privacy: ★★★
Spaciousness: ★★	Quiet: ★★
Security: ★★	Cleanliness: ★★★★
Insect Control: ★★★★★	Facilities: ★★★

With friendly new owners, this nice-looking KOA is inviting. The campground is laid out on a gently sloping hillside with a pond at the bottom. Sites are average sized, with plenty of grass and shady trees. Parking is on gravel, and most sites are pull-through style. Unfortunately, this KOA is sandwiched between two noisy roads. For quiet, we recommend sites in the 30s and 40s, in the campground's interior. Sites 85 and 86 are the prettiest, offering views of the small fishing pond. Tent campers should also ask for pond-side sites. The campground is 27 miles south of Cincinnati, making it convenient to Paramount's King's Island theme park and river-boat casinos on the mighty Ohio. Security is passable—there are no gates, but the surrounding suburban neighborhood is very nice.

BASICS

Operated By: Doug Mullins. **Open:** Year round. **Site Assignment:** First come, first served also reservations. **Registration:** Office, self-register after hours. **Fee:** $30 full hookup w/ 50 amps, $25 full hookup, $23 water & electric, $20 primitive; prices for 2 people, $4 per additional adult, $3 child; KOA discounts available (cash, V, MC, D). **Parking:** At sites only.

FACILITIES

Number of RV Sites: 86. **Number of Tent-Only Sites:** 8 primitive. **Number of Multi-purpose Sites:** 10. **Hookups:** Water, electric (15, 30, 50 amps), sewer at 25 sites. **Each Site:** Picnic table, most sites w/ fire ring and/or grill. **Dump Station:** Yes. **Laundry:** Yes. **Pay Phone:** Courtesy. **Rest Rooms and Showers:** Yes. **Fuel:** No. **Propane:** Yes. **Internal Roads:** Paved. **RV Service:** 6 mi. in Walton. **Market:** 6 mi. in Dry Ridge. **Restaurant:** 5 mi. in Dry Ridge. **General Store:** Convenience store on-site, 6 mi. in Dry Ridge. **Vending:** Yes. **Swimming Pool:** Yes. **Playground:** Yes. **Other:** Rec. lodge, dock, game room, picnic areas. **Activities:** Fishing lake, paddle boats, basketball. **Nearby Attractions:** Cincinnati Zoo & Botanical Gardens, casino cruises, Taft Museum of Art, American Classical Music Hall of Fame, Krohn Conservatory, National Underground Railroad Freedom Center. **Additional Information:** Greater Cincinnati CVB, (513) 621-2142.

RESTRICTIONS

Pets: On leash only. **Fires:** Allowed, fire rings only. **Alcoholic Beverages:** Not allowed (dry county). **Vehicle Maximum Length:** 85 ft.

TO GET THERE

From I-75 take Exit 166 (5 mi. south of the junction w/ I-71) and head east to US 25. Drive south 2.5 mi. on Hwy. 25 and the campground is on the right.

CORBIN

Cumberland Falls State Resort/Park

7351 Hwy. 90, Corbin 40701-8857. T: (606) 528-4121 or (800) 325-0063; www.kystateparks.com.

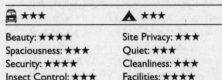

Beauty: ★★★★	Site Privacy: ★★★
Spaciousness: ★★★	Quiet: ★★★
Security: ★★★★	Cleanliness: ★★★
Insect Control: ★★★	Facilities: ★★★★

The campgrounds at Cumberland Falls aren't the tidiest we've ever seen, but they're reasonably attractive. Though site size varies, most are adequate. In the main campground, parking is paved. The nicest sites, 126–137, surround the cul-de-sac at the rear of the campground and offer back-in style parking. Sites 111–155 are downright plain. The smaller campground near the swimming pool is less developed and more attractive. Here, 13 sites with gravel parking line a shady mountain ridge. Known as the "Niagara of the South, " Cumberland Falls measures 125 feet in width and plunges 60 feet into the Cumberland River. Folks flock to the waterfall on full moons, when its mist creates a spectacular moon-bow. Park offerings, including numerous planned activities, are outstanding. To see the sights without hordes of people around you, try to plan a mid-week, full moon visit. Security is good at this remote park.

BASICS

Operated By: Kentucky State Parks. **Open:** Apr.–Oct. **Site Assignment:** First come, first served; no reservations. **Registration:** Camp store, after hours register next morning. **Fee:** $14 RV, $10.50 tent; prices for 2 people, $1 per additional person; 16 & under free; senior discount available (cash, personal check, V, MC, D, AE). **Parking:** At site (2 cars), in parking lot.

FACILITIES

Number of RV Sites: 35. **Number of Tent-Only Sites:** 15. **Number of Multipurpose Sites:** None. **Hookups:** Water, electric (20, 30, 50 amps). **Each Site:** Picnic table, fire ring w/ grill. **Dump Station:** Yes. **Laundry:** Yes. **Pay Phone:** Yes. **Rest Rooms and Showers:** Yes. **Fuel:** No. **Propane:** No. **Internal Roads:** Paved. **RV Service:** 15 mi. in Corbin. **Market:** 15 mi. in Corbin. **Restaurant:** Park restaurant. **General Store:** Camp store, Wal-Mart 15 mi. in Corbin. **Vending:** Yes. **Swimming Pool:** Yes. **Playground:** Yes. **Other:** Lodge, meeting room, Bob Blair Museum, stables, picnic areas & pavilion. **Activities:** Fishing, boating, canoeing, rafting, nature trails, tennis, horseshoes, shuffleboard, bird-watching, guided equestrian trails, naturalist & recreation programs in summer, square dancing. **Nearby Attractions:** Cumberland, Eagle, Yahoo & Dog Slaughter Falls, Daniel Boone National Forest, Berea Crafts Center, White Hall State Historic Site, Fort Boonesborough State Park, Colonel Harland Sanders Café & Museum. **Additional Information:** Corbin Chamber of Commerce, (606) 528-6390.

RESTRICTIONS

Pets: On leash only. **Fires:** Allowed, in fire ring only. **Alcoholic Beverages:** Not allowed. **Vehicle Maximum Length:** 36 ft. (sites vary). **Other:** 14-day stay limit, quiet hours enforced.

TO GET THERE

From I-75, take Exit 15 (from the south) or 25 (from the north) and head west on US Hwy. 25. Drive 7 mi. until merging w/ Hwy. 90. Drive another 7–8 mi. to the park, and the campground is on the left.

DAWSON SPRINGS

Pennyrile Forest State Park Resort

20781 Pennyrile Lodge Rd., Dawson Springs 42408-9212. T: (270) 797-3421.

🚐 ★★★★	🛖 ★★★★
Beauty: ★★★★	Site Privacy: ★★★
Spaciousness: ★★★	Quiet: ★★★★★
Security: ★★★★	Cleanliness: ★★★★
Insect Control: ★★★★	Facilities: ★★★★★

This campground is set in one of the most lush and beautiful forests in western Kentucky.

Despite its relative closeness to the highway, the property has a remote and rural feel. Campsites are of moderate size, and all have at least partial shade. With a huge range of on-site activities, Pennyrile Forest is a big hit with families; expect large crowds of children. There's plenty for everyone to do, including good fishing on Pennyrile Lake for bluegill, channel catfish, crappie, and largemouth bass. If you're done with water sports, seven hiking trails weave their way through the forested hills around the lake, ranging from easy, level rambles to more rugged hikes. Both a nine-hole regulation golf course and a quirky mini-golf course are available for campers' use.

BASICS

Operated By: Kentucky State Parks. **Open:** Mar.–Oct. **Site Assignment:** First come, first served. **Registration:** Office. **Fee:** $14 for adults, $1 additional adults. **Parking:** On site.

FACILITIES

Number of RV Sites: 0. **Number of Tent-Only Sites:** 0. **Number of Multipurpose Sites:** 68. **Hookups:** Electric, water during season. **Each Site:** Table, grill. **Dump Station:** Yes. **Laundry:** Yes. **Pay Phone:** Yes. **Rest Rooms and Showers:** Yes. **Fuel:** No. **Propane:** No. **Internal Roads:** Paved. **RV Service:** No. **Market:** 3 mi. on hwy 109. **Restaurant:** Yes. **General Store:** Yes. **Vending:** Yes. **Swimming Pool:** No. **Playground:** Yes. **Other:** Public beach, nature trails. **Activities:** Golf course for fee, mini-golf for fee, boat dock, fishing. **Nearby Attractions:** Trail of Tears.

RESTRICTIONS

Pets: On leash. **Fires:** Fire ring. **Alcoholic Beverages:** Not allowed. **Vehicle Maximum Length:** No limit.

TO GET THERE

20 mi. northeast of Hopkinsville on KY 109 North from western Kentucky Parkway, exit at Dawson Springs and take KY 103 south.

EDDYVILLE

Indian Point

1136 Indian Hills Trail, Eddyville 42038. T: (270) 388-2730.

🚐 ★★★	🛖 ★
Beauty: ★★★	Site Privacy: ★★

Spaciousness: ★★   Quiet: ★★★
Security: ★★★★   Cleanliness: ★★
Insect Control: ★★★   Facilities: ★★★

This campground on Lake Barkley is not nearly as attractive as nearby Lake Barkley State Resort Park or the beautiful campgrounds at Land Between the Lakes National Recreation Area. It's laid out in three areas with small sites. Sites have back-in, gravel parking. There are shady trees at most sites. Without greenery between sites, there is no privacy. The prettiest sites, 226–237, are situated on a cul-de-sac near the lake and are generally leased seasonally. If you can't get one of these, choose a site based on location in the campground. Incidentally, on our visit this campground's bathrooms left much to be desired in terms of cleanliness. There are no gates, but the campground is a rural location, making security fine. Avoid this place like the plague on holiday weekends.

BASICS

Operated By: Robert & Kathy Murphy. **Open:** Apr. 1–Nov.1. **Site Assignment:** First come, first served. **Registration:** Office. **Fee:** $19–$22. **Parking:** Yes.

FACILITIES

Number of RV Sites: 200. **Number of Tent-Only Sites:** Available. **Hookups:** sewer, electric.water. **Each Site;** None. **Dump Station:** Yes. **Laundry:** Yes. **Pay Phone:** Yes. **Rest Rooms and Showers:** Yes. **Fuel:** No. **Propane:** Yes. **Internal Roads:** Paved. **RV Service:** Yes. **Market:** Nearby. **Restaurant:** Nearby. **General Store:** Yes. **Vending:** Inquire at campground. **Swimming Pool:** Yes. **Playground:** Yes. **Other:** Boat dock & ramp, tennis courts, volleyball courts. **Activities:** Inquire at campground. **Nearby Attractions:** Inquire at campground.

RESTRICTIONS

Pets: On leash. **Fires:** Fire ring. **Alcoholic Beverages:** On Campsites only. **Vehicle Maximum Length:** Call ahead for details.

TO GET THERE

Exit 45 off I-24. Take Hwy. 293 south. Follow signs.

ELKHORN CITY
Breaks Interstate Park

P.O. Box 100, Breaks 24607. T: (540) 865-4413; www.breakspark.com.

🚐 ★★★★   ⛺ ★★★★

Beauty: ★★★★★   Site Privacy: ★★★★
Spaciousness: ★★★   Quiet: ★★★
Security: ★★★★   Cleanliness: ★★★★
Insect Control: ★★★★★   Facilities: ★★★★

Administered jointly by the states of Kentucky and Virginia, Breaks Interstate contains the largest canyon east of the Mississippi. The canyon was formed by the Russell Fork River over a period of 250 million years. Today, the Russell Fork is frequented by whitewater rafters and stocked with trout. Anglers can also head for 12-acre Laurel Lake, which is stocked with bass and bluegill. Equestrian trails meander through the wooded uplands. Twelve miles of hiking trails include a demanding path to the river. The lovely campground features small, but picturesque sites situated on a heavily wooded mountainside. Parking is on gravel, and there are both back-in and pull-through sites, with a little bit of greenery between them. Loop B offers more spacious, yet less private sites than Loop A. Our favorite sites in Loop A are 56, 60, and 61. On Loop B, we like site 34. Section C is our absolute favorite, containing some large pull-through sites on top of the mountain. Security is fine at this remote park. Treat yourself—visit in June when the rhododendrons are in bloom.

BASICS

Operated By: VA & KY state parks. **Open:** Apr.–Oct. **Site Assignment:** First come, first served. **Registration:** Office. **Fee:** $7–$10. **Parking:** On site.

FACILITIES

Number of RV Sites: 122. **Number of Tent-Only Sites:** 0. **Hookups:** Water, electric (50 amps), sewer. **Each Site:** Picnic tables, grill. **Dump Station:** Yes. **Laundry:** Yes. **Pay Phone:** Yes. **Rest Rooms and Showers:** Yes. **Fuel:** No. **Propane:** No. **Internal Roads:** Paved. **RV Service:** Yes. **Market:** Yes. **Restaurant:** Yes. **General Store:** Yes. **Vending:** Yes. **Swimming Pool:** Yes. **Playground:** Yes. **Other:** Horseback riding stable. **Activities:** Boating, fishing, mountain biking, hiking.

Nearby Attractions: Red River Gorge. **Additional Information:** (800) 982-5122.

RESTRICTIONS

Pets: On leash. **Fires:** Only in designated areas. **Alcoholic Beverages:** Not allowed. **Vehicle Maximum Length:** 40 ft.

TO GET THERE

I-64 East to Exit 98 onto Bert T. Combs Mtn. Pkwy. East. Turn right onto US 460. Stay straight onto KY 114. Take US 23 South to US 199 South. Take the US 460/KY 80 ramp. Stay straight to go onto US 460. Turn right onto KY 80 East that goes by the park.

FALLS OF ROUGH

North Fork Park, Rough River Lake

14500 Falls Of Rough Rd., Fall of Rough 95313. T: (270) 257-8139.

🚐 ★★★	▲ ★★★
Beauty: ★★★★	Site Privacy: ★★★
Spaciousness: ★★★	Quiet: ★★★
Security: ★★★★	Cleanliness: ★★★★
Insect Control: ★★★	Facilities: ★★★

North Fork Park lies in the northern area of the Pennyroyal Region of Kentucky, a place where ancient sandstone, shale, and limestone cliffs abound. This is also the land of caves, and Mammoth Cave lies about 40 miles to the south. North Fork Park is rural in the extreme; if you aren't content to enjoy the peepers and birds while camping here, you'll feel quite isolated. You'll have plenty to do if you enjoy hiking, boating and swimming. Be sure to provision yourself well—it is a long drive to pick-up anything forgotten. There are only a few pull-through sites in this 107-site park, with electric and water hookups available at most sites. The best views can be had from sites 6–11, though 86–88 have nice views too.

BASICS

Operated By: Corps of Engineers. **Open:** Apr. 19–Sept. 14. **Site Assignment:** Reservation 2 day advance, (888) 444-6777. **Registration:** Tollhouse. **Fee:** $14–$22 night. **Parking:** In designated areas.

FACILITIES

Number of RV Sites: 107. **Number of Tent-Only Sites:**. **Number of Multipurpose Sites:** Combined. **Hookups:** Electric (some), water. **Each**

Site: Picnic Shelters. **Dump Station:** Yes. **Laundry:** No. **Pay Phone:** Yes. **Rest Rooms and Showers:** Yes. **Fuel:** No. **Propane:** No. **Internal Roads:** Paved. **RV Service:** No. **Market:** No. **Restaurant:** No. **General Store:** No. **Vending:** No. **Swimming Pool:** No. **Playground:** Yes. **Activities:** Boating, hiking. **Nearby Attractions:** Mammoth Caves, Limestone Cliffs. **Additional Information:** (270) 257-8139.

RESTRICTIONS

Pets: On leash. **Fires:** Only in designated areas. **Alcoholic Beverages:** Not allowed. **Vehicle Maximum Length:** 64 ft.

TO GET THERE

The Campground is 70 mi. southwest of Louisville, KY. Take US 60., go 10 mi. to Harred, KY. Go 9 mi. west on Hwy. 79 to the campground entrance.

FALLS OF ROUGH

Rough River Dam State Resort Park

450 Lodge Rd., Falls of Rough 40119-9701. T: (270) 257-2311.

🚐 ★★★	▲ ★★★
Beauty: ★★★★	Site Privacy: ★★★
Spaciousness: ★★★	Quiet: ★★★★
Security: ★★★★★	Cleanliness: ★★★★
Insect Control: ★★★★	Facilities: ★★★★

Situated on 4, 860-acre Rough River Lake, this state resort park runs a marina with 150 rental slips. Fishermen head back to shore with Kentucky bass, bluegill, channel catfish, crappie, and rough fish. Unique park facilities include a 3,200-foot airstrip, air camp, and shuttle service to the lodge. Though the attractive campground lines the Rough River, sites don't enjoy water views. There are both back-in and pull-through sites, with patchy gravel parking. Most sites are well shaded, but there is little undergrowth to provide privacy between sites. Sites are larger than average. RV campers should head for one of the pull-through sites, 32–66. Tent campers should head for site 4 or 5, at the end of a pretty little spur. This park rarely fills to capacity, so it's an excellent destination for all but the busiest holiday weekends. Visit in spring in order to enjoy dogwood and redbud blooms. Security is excellent at this isolated park.

BASICS

Operated By: Kentucky State Parks. **Open:** Apr. 1–Oct. 31. **Site Assignment:** First come, first served. **Registration:** Office. **Fee:** $8.50–$16. **Parking:** Camp Site & Main Lodge.

FACILITIES

Number of RV Sites: 66. **Number of Tent-Only Sites:.** **Hookups:** Electric, water on some. **Each Site:** Fire ring. **Dump Station:** Yes. **Laundry:** Yes. **Pay Phone:** Yes. **Rest Rooms and Showers:** Yes. **Fuel:** No. **Propane:** No. **Internal Roads:** Paved & gravel. **RV Service:** No. **Market:** No. **Restaurant:** Yes. **General Store:** Nearby. **Vending:** Yes. **Swimming Pool:** No. **Playground:** Yes. **Other:** Public beach. **Activities:** Marina fishing, nature trail, golf, mini-golf, recreation courts. **Nearby Attractions:** Manmade Falls antique shops, outdoor theatre. **Additional Information:** (270) 257-2311.

RESTRICTIONS

Pets: On leash. **Fires:** Fire ring. **Alcoholic Beverages:** Not allowed. **Vehicle Maximum Length:** Call ahead for details. **Other:** 14 day max.

TO GET THERE

Located on KY 79. From Western Kentucky Parkway, Exit KY 79 north from Caneyville or exit on KY 259 north at Leithfield and travel to park via KY 54 from Leithfield. Driving south form Hardinsburg and US 60.

FALMOUTH

Kincaid Lake State Park

565 Kincaid Park Rd., Falmouth 41040. T: (859) 654-3531; www.kystateparks.com.

🚐 ★★★	⛺ ★★★
Beauty: ★★★	Site Privacy: ★★
Spaciousness: ★★★	Quiet: ★★★
Security: ★★★★	Cleanliness: ★★★★
Insect Control: ★★★	Facilities: ★★★★★

Located near the historic town of Falmouth, Kincaid Lake is a quaint state park tucked far from any major development and noise. Tent-only sites, which outnumber RV sites, are mainly primitive. The RV sites are fairly close together, but some of them are pretty deep. Phone lines running throughout the campground detract from it's beauty. The shadiest and most tranquil area of the campground can be found at sites 42–52. All of these sites are back-in, and have electric and water hookups during the season. Activities include boating on Kincaid Lake (rentals available), hiking along the parks nature trail, as well as swimming and mini-golf. Those who brig a fishing rod will be pleased with the large population of keeper- and trophy-sized largemouth bass. The Licking River is also nearby; a livery rents boats for interested parties.

BASICS

Operated By: Kentucky State Parks. **Open:** Year round. **Site Assignment:** No reservations, first come first serve. **Registration:** At camp office. **Fee:** $8.50–$16. **Parking:** inquire at registration.

FACILITIES

Number of RV Sites: 84. **Number of Tent-Only Sites:** 125. **Hookups:** Water, electric (seasonal). **Each Site:** Table. **Dump Station:** Yes. **Laundry:** Yes. **Pay Phone:** Yes. **Rest Rooms and Showers:** Yes. **Fuel:** Yes. **Propane:** Yes. **Internal Roads:** Paved. **RV Service:** No. **Market:** Yes. **Restaurant:** No. **General Store:** Yes. **Vending:** Yes. **Swimming Pool:** Yes (fee). **Playground:** Yes. **Other:** Amphitheater. **Activities:** Boat rental, fishing, mini-golf (fee), hiking, tennis, athletic multi-courses. **Nearby Attractions:** Historic Falmouth, Kincaid regional Theatre. **Additional Information:** Park Manager (Jeff P. Auchter).

RESTRICTIONS

Pets: On leash. **Fires:** Fire rings only. **Alcoholic Beverages:** Not allowed. **Vehicle Maximum Length:** No limit. **Other:** 14-day max. stay.

TO GET THERE

48 mi. southeast of Covington. Take I-275 East to US 27 South to Falmouth and KY 159 to the park.

FRANKLIN

Franklin KOA Kampground

2889 Scottsville Rd., Franklin 32135. T: (270) 586-5622; F: (270) 586-9123; www.KOA.com/whereKY; camping@KOA.net.

🚐 ★★★	⛺ ★★
Beauty: ★★★	Site Privacy: ★★
Spaciousness: ★★	Quiet: ★★
Security: ★★★	Cleanliness: ★★★★
Insect Control: ★★★	Facilities: ★★★

Located just east of the historic town of Franklin, this KOA campground is easily accessible from the interstate. However, this means the grounds can be a bit noisy. Those wishing a quieter experience should look for sites toward the back of the campground (sites 34–68), while campers with children may want to choose sites 26–30 because of their proximity to the playground and pool. History buffs will be interested to know that due to a surveyor's error, people with disputes were able to duel here legally until about 1920. Two famous duelists included Sam Houston, the Governor of Tennessee, and Andrew Jackson, the winning general at the Battle of New Orleans and the seventh president of the United States.

BASICS

Operated By: Clyde Dittbenner. **Open:** Year round. **Site Assignment:** Reservations accepted, site assigned a time of registration. **Registration:** Office. **Fee:** Tent $18–$23, Cabins $37–$49, accepted MC, V, D, $2.50 for add'l person. **Parking:** Designated area assigned/no parking on the grass.

FACILITIES

Number of RV Sites: 82. **Number of Tent-Only Sites:** 22. **Hookups:** Water, electric (30, 50 amps), sewer. **Each Site:** Table, fire rings. **Dump Station:** Yes. **Laundry:** Yes. **Pay Phone:** Yes. **Rest Rooms and Showers:** Yes. **Fuel:** Yes. **Propane:** Yes. **Internal Roads:** Paved. **RV Service:** No, storage & supplies. **Market:** Nearby. **Restaurant:** No. **General Store:** Yes. **Vending:** Yes. **Swimming Pool:** Yes. **Playground:** Yes. **Activities:** Game room, horseshoe, volleyball. **Nearby Attractions:** Opryland, Mammoth Caves, Dueling Grounds, Kentucky Downs. **Additional Information:** Franklin KOA, (800) 562-5631.

RESTRICTIONS

Pets: On leash. **Fires:** Fire ring only. **Alcoholic Beverages:** Allowed. **Vehicle Maximum Length:** No limit. **Other:** Check out is noon.

TO GET THERE

From I-65 take Exit 6 onto Hwy. 100, go 100 yards west on Hwy. 100, entrance on the left.

GREENUP

Greenbo Lake State Resort Park

HC 60 Box 52, Greenup 41144-9517. T: (606) 473-7324; F: (606) 473-7741; www.kystateparks.com; bobby.bowe@mail.state.ky.us.

🚐 ★★★　　　　　🔺 ★★★

Beauty: ★★★★　　　Site Privacy: ★★
Spaciousness: ★★★　　Quiet: ★★★
Security: ★★★★　　　Cleanliness: ★★★★
Insect Control: ★★★　　Facilities: ★★★★★

The attractive campground at Greenbo Lake is laid out in three spurs and a loop adjacent to Claylick Creek. There are average sized sites with paved, back-in parking. With woods flanking the campground, some sites enjoy cool shade, while others are totally open. Privacy is minimal. For families we recommend sites 29 and 30 near the wash house and playground. For tent campers, we recommend 16 and 17, tucked into the back of the primitive area. Security is passable; there are no gates, but the park is remote. Visit during the week in the summertime. This park's myriad recreation draws massive crowds. Children love the corkscrew water slide at the swimming pool. The state park is also a hiking haven, with 25 miles of easy to challenging hiking. With two largemouth bass records, fishing in the 225-acre Greenbo Lake is excellent.

BASICS

Operated By: Kentucky State Parks. **Open:** Apr.–Oct. (lodge etc. open all year). **Site Assignment:** First come, first served; no reservations. **Registration:** Check in station. **Fee:** $16 full hookup, $10 primitive; price for 2 people, $1 per additional adult, 16 & under free; senior & disabled discounts available, Kentucky POWs free (cash, personal checks, AE, V, MC, D). **Parking:** At site (2 cars), in parking lot.

FACILITIES

Number of RV Sites: 0. **Number of Tent-Only Sites:** 31 primitive. **Number of Multipurpose Sites:** 63. **Hookups:** Water, electric (30 amps). **Each Site:** Picnic table, grill, fire ring, asphalt pad. **Dump Station:** Yes. **Laundry:** Yes. **Pay Phone:** Yes. **Rest Rooms and Showers:** Yes. **Fuel:** No. **Propane:** Yes. **Internal Roads:** Paved. **RV Service:** 10 mi. in Greenup. **Market:** 5–10 mi. in Greenup. **Restaurant:** Park restaurant. **General Store:** Camp store, 10 mi. in Greenup. **Vending:** Yes. **Swimming Pool:** Yes (Memorial Day–Labor Day). **Playground:** Yes. **Other:** Lodge, marina, picnic area & shelters. **Activities:** Water sports (no jet-ski), canoe, pontoon, paddle boat, rowboat & motorboat rentals, fishing, hiking trails, mini-golf, tennis, basketball, bicycle rentals, summer organized activities. **Nearby Attractions:** Golf course, Jesse Stuart Birthplace, Kentucky Highlands Museum & Discovery Center, Paramount Arts Center, McConnell House, Carter Caves & Grayson Lake state Parks. **Additional Information:** Boyd/ Greenup Counties Chamber of Commerce, (606) 324-5111.

RESTRICTIONS

Pets: On leash only. **Fires:** Allowed in sites, fire rings, only. **Alcoholic Beverages:** Not allowed. **Vehicle Maximum Length:** 45 ft. (sites vary). **Other:** 14-day stay limit, no ATVs.

TO GET THERE

From I-64, take Exit 172 and drive 18 mi. north on KY 1. Turn left onto KY 1711/State Park Rd. and the campground is 3 mi. on the left.

HARDIN

Kenlake State Resort Park

542 Kenlake Rd., Hardin 42048-937. T: (270) 474-2211 or (800) 325-0143; www.state.ky.us.

🚐 ★★★★   ▲ ★★★★

Beauty: ★★★★	Site Privacy: ★★★★
Spaciousness: ★★★★	Quiet: ★★★★
Security: ★★★★	Cleanliness: ★★★★
Insect Control: ★★★	Facilities: ★★★★★

Located minutes from the 170,000-acre Land Between the Lakes National Recreation Area, the campground at Kenlake State Resort Park rests on the western shore of Kentucky Lake. You don't have to be a boat enthusiast to visit, but water activities are a significant reason people come here. The 90 back-in sites (each with water and electric hookups) have small parking areas, but the space in between sites is more than adequate. There are only a few waterfront sites (62–69 and 24–29); they are pretty but the ground is not level. The campground is separated from the rest of the resort by Hwy. 68, so while the resort offers tennis, golfing and some hiking, you might as well visit Land Between the Lakes since you have to get in your car anyway. The resort is host to several festivals throughout the year, including the Hot August Blues Festival and the Aurora County Festival.

BASICS

Operated By: State of Kentucky. **Open:** Year round. **Site Assignment:** Reservations not accepted, first come, first served. **Registration:** Contact station. **Fee:** $14. **Parking:** In designated areas assigned, must have car pass/visitor pass visible.

FACILITIES

Number of RV Sites: 90. **Number of Tent-Only Sites:** Tent area. **Hookups:** Water, electric (30, 50 amps), sewer. **Each Site:** Picnic shelters, fire ring. **Dump Station:** Yes. **Laundry:** Yes. **Pay Phone:** Yes. **Rest Rooms and Showers:** Yes. **Fuel:** 2–3 mi. away. **Propane:** 2.5 mi. **Internal Roads:** Paved. **RV Service:** No. **Market:** No, 0.5 mi. away. **Restaurant:** Yes. **General Store:** No. **Vending:** No. **Swimming Pool:** Yes. **Playground:** Yes. **Other:** Meeting rooms. **Activities:** Fishing, boating, golf, tennis, nature trails. **Nearby Attractions:** Kentucky Dam Village SRP, Hardin Southern Railway, The Homeplace 1850, North-South Trail. **Additional Information:** State of Kentucky, (859) 384-3522.

RESTRICTIONS

Pets: On leash. **Fires:** Fire ring. **Alcoholic Beverages:** Not allowed. **Vehicle Maximum Length:** No limit. **Other:** No firearms or fireworks.

TO GET THERE

40 mi. southeast of Paducah. Going east on I-24 exit to the Purchase Parkway, then exit on US 68 east, going west on I-24, take the Cadiz exit to US 68/KY 80 West.

HENDERSON

John James Audubon State Park

P.O. Box 576, Henderson 42419-0576. T: (270) 826-2247; F: (270) 826-2286; www.kystateparks.com; maryd.miller@mail.state.ky.us.

🚐 ★★★   ▲ ★★★

Beauty: ★★★★	Site Privacy: ★★★
Spaciousness: ★★★	Quiet: ★★
Security: ★★	Cleanliness: ★★★★
Insect Control: ★★★★	Facilities: ★★★★

Audubon State Park, a little green oasis in the city of Henderson, maintains nice sports facilities including a nine-hole golf course and fishing on the park's small lake. Anglers are rewarded with largemouth bass, bluegill, and catfish. Henderson residents are proud to know that John James Audubon lived here. Today, over 20 species of warblers visit the state park every spring. The campground is laid out in one large loop with three partitions. RV sites 1–28 and tent sites 8T–17T abut the highway and are not recommended. Quieter sites include RV sites 40–63 and tent sites 1T–7T. Site size and distance between sites vary, but most are adequate. Parking is paved, back-in style. Almost all sites are well shaded by sycamore, cottonwood and other species. There are no gates at this urban campground, making security iffy. Visit during the week to avoid summer crowds.

BASICS

Operated By: Kentucky State Parks. **Open:** Year round. **Site Assignment:** First come, first served; no reservations; honor system in winter. **Registration:** Entrance kiosk, self-register after hours. **Fee:** $18 RV; $10 winter flat rate; prices for 2 people, $1 per additional person; 16 & under free (cash, personal check, V, MC, D, AE). **Parking:** At site (2 cars), in parking lot.

FACILITIES

Number of RV Sites: 0. **Number of Tent-Only Sites:** 10 primitive. **Number of Multipurpose Sites:** 69. **Hookups:** Water, electric (50 amps). **Each Site:** Picnic table, grill, fire ring. **Dump Station:** Yes. **Laundry:** Yes. **Pay Phone:** Yes. **Rest Rooms and Showers:** Yes. **Fuel:** No. **Propane:** No. **Internal Roads:** Paved. **RV Service:** 8 mi. in Evansville, Indiana. **Market:** 0.25 mi. **Restaurant:** Within 1 mi. in Henderson. **General Store:** 0.5 mi. in Henderson. **Vending:** Yes. **Swimming Pool:** No. **Playground:** Yes. **Other:** John James Audubon Museum & Nature Center, meeting rooms, picnic area & shelters, boat dock (trolling motors only). **Activities:** 9-hole golf course, pro shop, club & cart rentals, fishing, paddle boat, canoe & hydrobike rentals (seasonal), hiking trails, tennis (seasonal), ropes challenge course (w/ facilitator only), interpretive & recreation programs year-round. **Nearby Attractions:** Ellis Park Race Course, Aztar Casino Riverboat, Audubon Mill Park, Wesselman Woods Nature Preserve, Angel Mounds Prehistoric Native American Site. **Additional Information:** Henderson Tourism Commission (270) 826-3128, Evansville CVB (800) 433-3025 www.evansvillecvb.org.

RESTRICTIONS

Pets: On leash only. **Fires:** Allowed, in fire ring only. **Alcoholic Beverages:** Not allowed. **Vehicle Maximum Length:** 45 ft. (sites vary). **Other:** 14-day stay limit, no pets on trails except designated pet trail.

TO GET THERE

From the Pennyrile Parkway, drive north until it merges w/ US 41. The park is 1.5 mi. north on the right.

JAMESTOWN

Lake Cumberland State Resort Park

5465 State Park Rd., Jamestown 42629. T: (270) 343-3111.

🚐 ★★★★   ▲ ★★★★

Beauty: ★★★★	Site Privacy: ★★★★
Spaciousness: ★★★★	Quiet: ★★★
Security: ★★★	Cleanliness: ★★★★
Insect Control: ★★★	Facilities: ★★★★★

Set on a large peninsula protruding into the 50,250-acre Lake Cumberland, this extremely popular state resort park has plenty to do and an upscale feel. Unfortunately, the large crowds make for a hectic atmosphere, and they also somewhat overwhelm the staff's efforts to keep the campground clean. Many families means many children, as well as lots of cars, trucks, and other vehicles. Though campsite size varies, most are large, and some are quite close together. Some sites have both a nice forest canopy as well as screening ground foliage for privacy. The prettiest campsites are sites 19–21, 38, and 72–75. An unsightly telephone wire runs right through the loop of sites 49–52. Generally, the most visually attractive sites are not as level as others. The large lake means that all varieties of boating and water sports take up most campers' time here, but there's also various sports activities and a four-mile loop nature trail.

BASICS

Operated By: State of Kentucky. **Open:** Apr.–Nov. **Site Assignment:** First come, first served. **Registration:** Entrance Gate. **Fee:** $8.50 Tent, $10 RV. **Parking:** On site.

FACILITIES

Number of RV Sites: 113. **Number of Tent-Only Sites:** 34. **Hookups:** Water, electric (20 amps). **Each Site:** Picnic Tables. **Dump Station:** Yes. **Laundry:** Yes. **Pay Phone:** Yes. **Rest Rooms and Showers:** Yes. **Fuel:** 5 mi. **Propane:** 5 mi. **Internal Roads:** Paved. **RV Service:** No. **Market:** No. **Restaurant:** Yes. **General Store:** Yes. **Vending:** Yes. **Swimming Pool:** Yes. **Playground:** Yes.

Activities: Golf, Game Room, Mini-golf, Stables, Hiking, Fishing. **Nearby Attractions:** Wolf Greek Dam & Fish Hatchery. **Additional Information:** Check out 2 p.m.

RESTRICTIONS

Pets: On leash. **Fires:** Fire ring. **Alcoholic Beverages:** Not allowed. **Vehicle Maximum Length:** No limit.

TO GET THERE

Located 45 min. West of Somerset. Take Cumberland Parkway to US 127.

LEXINGTON

Kentucky Horse Park Campground

4089 Iron Works Parkway, Lexington 40511. T: (859) 259-4257 or (800) 370-6416; F: (859) 255-2690; www.kyhorsepark.com; campground@kyhorsepark.com.

🚐 ★★★   ⛺ ★★★

Beauty: ★★★★	Site Privacy: ★★
Spaciousness: ★★★	Quiet: ★★★
Security: ★★	Cleanliness: ★★★★
Insect Control: ★★★★	Facilities: ★★★★

Beautiful Kentucky Horse Park rests on 1, 200 acres of verdant rolling horse pasture enclosed and subdivided by 30 miles of pristine white fence. The park's mission is multi-fold. It's a working horse farm, educational facility (with two superb museums and two theaters), competition venue, and tasteful theme park. Children can pet ponies and enjoy a number of exhibitions and shows. The flat campground is passably attractive, with spruce fir and pine shading the sites. It's laid out in two concentric figure eights, with sites in the rear (160–171 and 29–41) enjoying views of the polo fields. Medium-sized sites feature paved, back-in style parking, with short parking pads. The campground is convenient to restaurants in Lexington and outlet mall shopping in Georgetown. Security is marginal at this giant campground with no gates. Visit during the week for less crowded touring, but avoid weekdays in late spring when armies of school children invade.

BASICS

Operated By: Kentucky Tourism Development Cabinet. **Open:** Year round. **Site Assignment:** First come, first served. **Registration:** Trading post, host makes rounds after hours. **Fee:** $23 developed, $20 seniors, $15 primitive; prices for 6 people, $2 per additional person (cash, personal checks, V, MC, D, AE). **Parking:** At site (2 cars), in parking lot.

FACILITIES

Number of RV Sites: 0. **Number of Tent-Only Sites:** Primitive, undesignated. **Number of Multipurpose Sites:** 260. **Hookups:** Water, electric (20, 30, 50 amps). **Each Site:** Picnic table, fire ring, paved pad. **Dump Station:** Yes. **Laundry:** Yes. **Pay Phone:** Yes. **Rest Rooms and Showers:** Yes. **Fuel:** No. **Propane:** No. **Internal Roads:** Paved. **RV Service:** 5 mi. in Lexington. **Market:** 10 mi. in Georgetown. **Restaurant:** Park Restaurant, within 4 mi. **General Store:** Camp store, 10 mi. in Georgetown (Wal-Mart). **Vending:** Yes. **Swimming Pool:** Yes. **Playground:** Yes. **Other:** Pavilion, museum, gallery, gift shop. **Activities:** Horse drawn tours, riding shows, events, square dancing (occasional), tennis, croquet, volleyball, basketball, horseshoes. **Nearby Attractions:** Aviation Museum of Kentucky, Keeneland Race Course, Lexington Center/ Rupp Arena, Mary Todd Lincoln House, Thoroughbred Center, University of Kentucky. **Additional Information:** Lexington CVB, (800) 845-3959, www.visitlex.com.

RESTRICTIONS

Pets: On leash only. **Fires:** Allowed, fire rings only. **Alcoholic Beverages:** Not allowed. **Vehicle Maximum Length:** 45 ft. **Other:** 14-day stay limit.

TO GET THERE

From I-75 (2 mi. north of the junction w/ I-64), take Exit 120. The Park is immediately on the east and the campground is on the east side of the park.

LONDON

Levi Jackson Wilderness Road State Park Campground

998 Levi Jackson Mill Rd., London 40744-8944. T: (606) 878-8000; F: (606) 864-3825; www.kystateparks.com; william.meadors@mail.state.ky.us.

🚐 ★★★★   ⛺ ★★★★

Beauty: ★★★★	Site Privacy: ★★★
Spaciousness: ★★★	Quiet: ★★★★
Security: ★★★★	Cleanliness: ★★★★
Insect Control: ★★★	Facilities: ★★★★

Levi Jackson Wilderness Road offers diverse family recreation, including a large swimming pool with a water slide and an 18-hole mini-golf course. Traversing the park, the Wilderness Road is believed by many historians to be the most significant trail in the westward flow of English colonists. Lucky hikers can retrace the steps of Daniel Boone. The pretty campground is laid out in many small areas containing both back-in and pull-through sites. Sites have paved parking and are larger than average. Most sites are shady, while a few are open. Many sites are lovely, especially the larger pull-throughs. We particularly fancy sites in Area D, which enjoy a dense tree canopy. Parents, keep your children away from the vexing, ugly, old, and rusty barbed wire fence that runs the length of the campground. Security is passable—there are no gates at this small town campground. Avoid this park on summer weekends and holidays.

BASICS

Operated By: Kentucky State Parks. **Open:** Year round. **Site Assignment:** First come, first served; no reservations; honor system in winter. **Registration:** Camp store, after hours register next day (honor system in winter). **Fee:** $18 developed, $14 tent, pop–up, designated areas; prices for 2 people, $2 per additional person; 16 & under free; $10 winter flat rate; Seniors & KY disabled discounts available (cash, personal check, V, MC, D, AE). **Parking:** At site (2 cars), in parking lot.

FACILITIES

Number of Multipurpose Sites: 146. **Hookups:** Water, electric (20, 30, 50 amps). **Each Site:** Picnic table, fire ring. **Dump Station:** Yes. **Laundry:** Yes. **Pay Phone:** Yes. **Rest Rooms and Showers:** Yes. **Fuel:** No. **Propane:** No. **Internal Roads:** Paved. **RV Service:** 12 mi. in Corbin. **Market:** Within 5 mi. in London. **Restaurant:** Within 5 mi. in London. **General Store:** camp store, Wal-Mart 5 mi. in London. **Vending:** Beverages only. **Swimming Pool:** Yes (& wading pool & waterslides). **Playground:** Yes. **Other:** Rec. room, Mountain Life Museum, McHargue's Grist Mill (operational summertime), picnic areas, gazebo, amphitheater, bird sanctuary. **Activities:** Mini-golf, hiking trails, horseshoes, basketball, summer organized activities. **Nearby Attractions:** Daniel Boone Motocross Park, Renfro Valley Entertainment Center, Berea Crafts Center, White Hall State Historic Site, Fort

Boonesborough State Park, Colonel Harland Sanders Café & Museum. **Additional Information:** London Chamber of Commerce, (606) 864-4789.

RESTRICTIONS

Pets: On leash only. **Fires:** Allowed, fire ring only. **Alcoholic Beverages:** Not allowed. **Vehicle Maximum Length:** 60 ft. (sites vary). **Other:** 14-day stay limit.

TO GET THERE

From I-75, take Exit 38 and drive 3 mi. east on Hwy. 192. Turn south on US Hwy. 25 and drive 2 mi. to the first traffic light. Turn left onto State Rte. 1006. Drive 1.5 mi. into the park.

LUCAS

Barren River Lake State Park

1149 State Park Rd., Lucas 42156-9709. T: (270) 646-2151.

🚐 ★★★★	🏕 ★★★★
Beauty: ★★★★	Site Privacy: ★★★
Spaciousness: ★★★★	Quiet: ★★★★
Security: ★★★★★	Cleanliness: ★★★★
Insect Control: ★★★	Facilities: ★★★★★

The campground at Barren River Lake lies in graceful rolling hills surrounded by woods. The pretty campground contains back-in and pull-through sites with paved parking. Pull through sites are often huge and open. Some, like 79A and 79B, enjoy view s of a green hillside. Back-in sites tend to be average sized and shadier. Our favorite back-in sites numbered in the 80s and 90s. Security is very good, with gates at the campground entrance. Barren River Lake offers outstanding recreational facilities, including a marina with rental slips (100 open and 40 covered). The lake supports bluegill, channel catfish, crappie, rough fish, and largemouth, white, and hybrid striped bass. The park's many planned events climax with the annual Glasgow Highland Games in June. Approximately 35 miles north of the park, Mammoth Cave National Park makes an excellent day trip. Avoid this popular state park on summer holidays and weekends.

BASICS

Operated By: State of Kentucky. **Open:** Apr. 1–Oct. 31. **Site Assignment:** First come, first served. **Registration:** Office. **Fee:** $14. **Parking:** On site.

FACILITIES

Number of RV Sites: 99. **Number of Tent-Only Sites:** Tent area. **Hookups:** Water, electric. **Each Site:** Picnic table. **Dump Station:** Yes. **Laundry:** Yes. **Pay Phone:** Yes. **Rest Rooms and Showers:** Yes. **Fuel:** 3.5 mi. **Propane:** 3.5 mi. **Internal Roads:** Paved. **RV Service:** No. **Market:** No. **Restaurant:** Dining room. **General Store:** Yes. **Vending:** Yes. **Swimming Pool:** Yes (beach). **Playground:** Yes. **Activities:** Basketball, golf, nature trails, horseback riding, boating. **Nearby Attractions:** Dale Hollow Lake, Old Mulkey historic site. **Additional Information:** US Army Corps of Engineers, (606) 642-3308.

RESTRICTIONS

Pets: On leash. **Fires:** Fire rings only. **Alcoholic Beverages:** Not allowed. **Vehicle Maximum Length:** No limit.

TO GET THERE

From Bowling Green, take I-65 south to the Cumberland Parkway and drive east, then go south on US 31 East to the park.

MAMMOTH CAVE
Mammoth Cave National Park

P.O. Box 7, Mammoth Cave 42259. T: (270) 758-2328.

🚐 ★★★★★   ⛺ ★★★★★

Beauty: ★★★★★   Site Privacy: ★★★★
Spaciousness: ★★★★★ Quiet: ★★★★
Security: ★★★★★   Cleanliness: ★★★★★
Insect Control: ★★★ Facilities: ★★★★

Fascinating Mammoth Cave has seen plenty of adventure during its 4000-year relationship with humans. Tour guides are full of anecdotes about the characters who've contributed to the cave's colorful history—of course many of these folks were just trying to make a buck. With over 345 miles of mapped passages, it's the longest cave in the world. Above ground, the rolling woodlands within the park contain 70 miles of multi-use trails. The beautiful Headquarters Campground is laid out in three loops, with paved back-in and pull-through sites. Site size is ample, with pull-through sites tending to be larger than back-in sites. Most sites enjoy a fair amount of seclusion.

Sites 65–83, on the second loop are pretty and quiet. Sites 26–34 are also quite nice-looking, but maybe noisy. Situated near a noisy road, sites 1–10 and 11–21 should be avoided. The campground is remote and gated, making it ultra-safe. Visit during the week in the summer.

BASICS

Operated By: National Park Service. **Open:** Mar.–Oct. **Site Assignment:** First come, first served. **Registration:** Entrance kiosk. **Fee:** $14. **Parking:** In designated areas.

FACILITIES

Number of RV Sites: 106. **Number of Tent-Only Sites:** 0. **Hookups:** None. **Each Site:** Picnic table, fire grate. **Dump Station:** Yes. **Laundry:** Yes. **Pay Phone:** Yes. **Rest Rooms and Showers:** Yes. **Fuel:** Yes. **Propane:** Yes. **Internal Roads:** Paved. **RV Service:** No. **Market:** No. **Restaurant:** No. **General Store:** Yes. **Vending:** No. **Swimming Pool:** No. **Playground:** No. **Activities:** Hiking, horseback riding, fishing. **Nearby Attractions:** Mammoth Cave, water slides, golfing. **Additional Information:** Check out at 11 a.m.

RESTRICTIONS

Pets: On leash. **Fires:** Only in designated areas. **Alcoholic Beverages:** Not allowed. **Vehicle Maximum Length:** 32 ft. **Other:** Mopeds & motorcycles only on improved roads.

TO GET THERE

Exit 53 off I-60.

MIDDLESBORO
Cumberland Gap National Historical Park

US 25 E South, Middlesboro 40965. T: (606) 248-2817.

🚐 ★★★★★   ⛺ ★★★★★

Beauty: ★★★★★   Site Privacy: ★★★★★
Spaciousness: ★★★★★ Quiet: ★★★★★
Security: ★★★★   Cleanliness: ★★★★
Insect Control: ★★★★ Facilities: ★★★★

Millions of years of wind and water carved this natural gap in the Appalachian Mountains. It was first used by migrating animals, then by Native Americans, and more recently by frontiers-people headed to settle the American West. Historians estimate that 12,000 settlers passed through Cumberland Gap by the end of the

American Revolution. Learn about these folks, including Daniel Boone, who shaped the gap's history at the Visitor's Center in Kentucky. The national historic park straddles the Kentucky-Virginia border and dips into Tennessee at its southern tip. The beautiful Wilderness Road campground is actually in Virginia. Sites are commodious. With plenty of space and foliage between them, sites are also secluded. Campsites feature gravel, back-in parking under a canopy of oak, poplar, and hickory. Our favorite sites, E1, E2, E4, and F9, are extremely private. The campground at Cumberland Gap is fairly remote, making it safe. Visit the park during the week for less crowded touring.

BASICS

Operated By: State of Kentucky. **Open:** Year round. **Site Assignment:** First come, first served. **Registration:** Ranger station. **Fee:** $10–$15. **Parking:** On site.

FACILITIES

Number of RV Sites: 41. **Number of Tent-Only Sites:** 119. **Hookups:** Electric (30 amps), sewer. **Each Site:** Picnic shelters. **Dump Station:** Yes. **Laundry:** No. **Pay Phone:** Yes. **Rest Rooms and Showers:** Yes. **Fuel:** Nearby. **Propane:** Nearby. **Internal Roads:** Gravel. **RV Service:** Nearby. **Market:** Nearby. **Restaurant:** Nearby. **General Store:** Nearby. **Vending:** No. **Swimming Pool:** No. **Playground:** No. **Activities:** Hiking, horseback riding. **Nearby Attractions:** Abraham Lincoln Museum, Pine Mountain State Park, Museum of Appalachia, antique shops.

RESTRICTIONS

Pets: On leash. **Fires:** Fire ring. **Alcoholic Beverages:** At site only. **Vehicle Maximum Length:** No limit.

TO GET THERE

From I-75, take Exit 25E on Corbin.

MOREHEAD
Twin Knobs Recreation Area

5195 KY Hwy. 801 South, Morehead 40351. T: (606) 784-8816.

🚐 ★★★★★   ⛺ ★★★★★

Beauty: ★★★★★   Site Privacy: ★★★★★
Spaciousness: ★★★★★   Quiet: ★★★★★
Security: ★★★★★   Cleanliness: ★★★★
Insect Control: ★★★   Facilities: ★★★

Gorgeous Twin Knobs Recreation Area includes quite a few sites with gorgeous views of 8, 270-acre Cave Run Lake. Anglers know the lake for its muskie, but it also supports largemouth bass, bluegill, crappie, and catfish. The lake lies within the northern tip of giant Daniel Boone National Forest, which maintains 115 miles of multi-use trails in this district alone. The campground at Twin Knobs offers incredibly spacious with dense undergrowth providing a lush barrier between sites. Most sites are shaded by various hardwoods. Some parking is on pavement, while other parking is on fine gravel. All sites offer back-in parking. Large groups looking for double sites should head for J9 and J10. Gorgeous lakefront sites include D9, D11, and D13, F22–F28, and I7–I9. Elegant loop B is tucked into the woods and offers the most secluded sites. Security is excellent—the campground is remote and gated. Avoid Twin Knobs on busy summer holidays.

BASICS

Operated By: Recreation Resource Management. **Open:** Mar. 30–Oct. 29. **Site Assignment:** Most sites first come, first served; $8.35 reservation fee for few select sites. **Registration:** Entrance station. **Fee:** $12–$25. **Parking:** On site.

FACILITIES

Number of RV Sites: 216. **Number of Tent-Only Sites:**. **Hookups:** Water, electric (50 amps), sewer. **Each Site:** Picnic table, grill. **Dump Station:** Yes. **Laundry:** No. **Pay Phone:** Yes. **Rest Rooms and Showers:** Yes. **Fuel:** No. **Propane:** No. **Internal Roads:** Paved. **RV Service:** No. **Market:** No. **Restaurant:** No. **General Store:** Yes. **Vending:** No. **Swimming Pool:** No. **Playground:** No. **Other:** Large sandy beach w/ summer concessions. **Activities:** Hiking, volleyball, lake swimming, boating, fishing, weekly amphitheater programs. **Nearby Attractions:** Cave Run Lake, Minor E. Clark Fish Hatchery, Clear Creek Furnace. **Additional Information:** (606) 784-6428.

RESTRICTIONS

Pets: On leash. **Fires:** In grills only. **Alcoholic Beverages:** Not allowed. **Vehicle Maximum Length:** No limit.

TO GET THERE

From I-64 take Exit 133 and go south on KY 801. Campground is 9 mi. on right.

OLIVE HILL
Grayson Lake State Park

314 Grayson Lake Park Rd., Olive Hill 41164-9213.
T: (606) 474-9727.

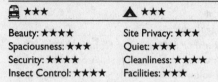

Beauty: ★★★★   Site Privacy: ★★★
Spaciousness: ★★★   Quiet: ★★★
Security: ★★★★   Cleanliness: ★★★★
Insect Control: ★★★★   Facilities: ★★★

Grayson Lake's geology, terrain, and scenery make this a particularly striking place to camp, even though the property is fairly mediocre overall. A walled canyon of sandstone bluffs looms over the lake's waters. Historically, Shawnee and Cherokee Indians camped in the area while hunting, and European frontiersman used the cliffs as a source of flint and saltpeter (an ingredient of gunpowder). A short nature trail allows one to view the distinctive flora and rock formations of the area. Most of the campsites are open, with a few well shaded; all are medium-sized. Sites 13, 14, and 27 are pretty and shaded, while sites 29–32 are completely open. Site 57 is a nice, big pull-through. Lots of children were in evidence when we visited, and it looks like the campground might serve as a sort of local teen hangout.

BASICS
Operated By: Kentucky State Parks. **Open:** Apr. 1–Oct. 31. **Site Assignment:** First come, first served. **Registration:** Check in station. **Fee:** $16. **Parking:** On site.

FACILITIES
Number of RV Sites: 71. **Number of Tent-Only Sites:** 0. **Hookups:** Electric, water. **Each Site:** Table, fire ring. **Dump Station:** Yes. **Laundry:** Yes. **Pay Phone:** Yes. **Rest Rooms and Showers:** Yes. **Fuel:** No. **Propane:** No. **Internal Roads:** Paved. **RV Service:** Ashland, 45 minutes. **Market:** Soft Drinks, ice, fire wood. **Restaurant:** Grayson, 12 mi. **General Store:** No. **Vending:** No. **Swimming Pool:** No. **Playground:** Yes. **Other:** Marina, beach available Memorial Day & Labor Day. **Activities:** Boating, hiking, golf course available summer 2002. **Nearby Attractions:** Carter Caves State Resort Park, Greenbo Lake.

RESTRICTIONS
Pets: On leash. **Fires:** Fire ring. **Alcoholic Beverages:** Not allowed. **Vehicle Maximum Length:** No limit. **Other:** 14 day max.

TO GET THERE
Take I-64 to the Grayson exit, go South on KY 7 through the town of Grayson. Park is 12 mi. from I-64.

PRESTONBURG
Jenny Wiley State Resort Park

75 Theatre Ct., Prestonberg 41653-9799. T: (606) 886-2711 or (800) 325-0142; www.state.ky.us.

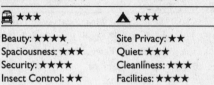

Beauty: ★★★★   Site Privacy: ★★
Spaciousness: ★★★   Quiet: ★★★
Security: ★★★★   Cleanliness: ★★★
Insect Control: ★★   Facilities: ★★★★

Jenny Wiley State Resort Park offers excellent recreational facilities in the hills of eastern Kentucky. The park roads follow the shoreline of Dewey Lake, which supports largemouth and hybrid striped bass, bluegill, catfish, and crappie. There are 10 miles of hiking trails in the park, with 60 more miles in the surrounding countryside. It's a shame the campground isn't as pretty as the rest of the park. Sites are laid out on four spurs. Sites are frighteningly similar. Each square, mid-sized site features paved, back-in parking. Sites are totally open to each other, with woods behind them providing partial shade. Since the sites are all the same, choose your site based on location. Jenny Wiley State Park stages musicals and hosts festivals all summer long, keeping the campground busy. It's best to plan a mid-week trip to avoid the crowds Security is excellent—the park is gated and rural.

BASICS
Operated By: US Army Corps of Engineers. **Open:** Apr. 1–Oct.31. **Site Assignment:** First come, first served. **Registration:** Office lodge. **Fee:** $14. **Parking:** in designated areas.

FACILITIES
Number of RV Sites: 111. **Number of Tent-Only Sites:** 30. **Hookups:** Water, electric. **Each Site:** Picnic shelter. **Dump Station:** Yes. **Laundry:** Yes. **Pay Phone:** Yes. **Rest Rooms and Showers:** Yes. **Fuel:** 5 mi. **Propane:** 5 mi. **Internal Roads:** Paved. **RV Service:** No. **Market:** Yes. **Restaurant:** No. **General Store:** Yes. **Vending:** Yes.

Swimming Pool: Yes. **Playground:** Yes. **Other:** Hiking, nature, mt. Bike trails, fishing, boating, golfing. **Activities:** Inquire at campground. **Nearby Attractions:** Breaks Interstate Park, Grave of Jenny Wiley, Pioneer Village, Tunder Ridge, The Samuel May House. **Additional Information:** US Army Corps of Engineers, (606) 642-3308.

RESTRICTIONS

Pets: On leash. **Fires:** Fire ring. **Alcoholic Beverages:** Not allowed. **Vehicle Maximum Length:** No limit.

TO GET THERE

From I-64 West take the Mtn. Pkwy. Exit. From I-64 East take the US 23 South Exit. From I-75 take the Daniel Boone Pkwy. Exit. From I-75 south, take the I-64 East Exit.

RENFRO VALLEY

Renfro Valley KOA Kampground

P.O. Box 54 Red Foley Rd., Renfro Valley 40473. T: (606) 256-2474 or (800) KOA-2475; F: (606) 256-2474; www.renfrovalley.com.

🚐 ★★★   ▲ ★★

Beauty: ★★★   Site Privacy: ★★
Spaciousness: ★★★   Quiet: ★★★★
Security: ★★★   Cleanliness: ★★★★
Insect Control: ★★★★   Facilities: ★★★

This passably attractive KOA is convenient if you're headed to Renfro Valley Village for a concert or festival. Renfro Valley is Kentucky's country music capitol and home to the Kentucky Country Music Hall of Fame. There's also oodles of outdoor recreation in this area, which lies at the western edge of massive Daniel Boone National Forest. The campground offers long, narrow, average-sized sites. Many enjoy partial shade, but most are totally open. Most parking is on paved pull-through pads, but internal roads are gravel—oh well. If you're looking for full shade, head to one of the handful of back-in sites. Otherwise, choose your site based on location and rig size. There are no gates, but Renfro Valley is a nice little town. In order to score a site, make advance reservations for special events weekends.

BASICS

Operated By: Don & Pat Miller. **Open:** Year round. **Site Assignment:** First come, first served;

reservations accepted w/ first night deposit; 24-hour cancellation notice for full refund. **Registration:** Store, after hours self-register. **Fee:** $28 full (cable), $23 water & electric, $19 tent; prices for 2 adults or family of four, $1.50 per additional adult; KOA discount (cash, V, MC, D, AE). **Parking:** 1 car at site.

FACILITIES

Number of RV Sites: 0. **Number of Tent-Only Sites:** 40. **Number of Multipurpose Sites:** 100. **Hookups:** Water, electric (20, 30, 50 amps), some sewer, some cable. **Each Site:** Picnic table, fire ring, grill. **Dump Station:** Yes. **Laundry:** Yes. **Pay Phone:** Yes. **Rest Rooms and Showers:** Yes. **Fuel:** No. **Propane:** Yes. **Internal Roads:** Paved. **RV Service:** 25 mi. in Somerset. **Market:** On site, plus RV supplies. **Restaurant:** 0.25 mi. **General Store:** 14 mi. in Berea. **Vending:** Yes. **Swimming Pool:** Yes. **Playground:** Yes. **Other:** Game room, pavilion, outdoor kitchen. **Activities:** Basketball, volleyball, shuffleboard, horseshoes. **Nearby Attractions:** Renfro Valley Country Music Center, Great Saltpeter Cave, Daniel Boone National Forest, 14 mi. to Berea College & crafts, 50 mi. to Lexington. **Additional Information:** Renfro Valley information (800) 765-7464 or www.renfro valley.com, Berea Chamber of Commerce, (859) 986-9760.

RESTRICTIONS

Pets: On leash only. **Fires:** Allowed. **Alcoholic Beverages:** Not allowed (dry county). **Vehicle Maximum Length:** No limit.

TO GET THERE

From I-75, take Exit 62 and drive north 1 mi. on US 25. The campground is on the right.

RICHMOND

Fort Boonesborough State Park

4375 Boonesboro Rd., Richmond 40475. T: (859) 527-3131; www.kystateparks.com.

🚐 ★★★   ▲ ★★★

Beauty: ★★★★   Site Privacy: ★★
Spaciousness: ★★★   Quiet: ★★
Security: ★★★   Cleanliness: ★★★★
Insect Control: ★★★   Facilities: ★★★

Here's a rhetorical question: Why build a campground next to a sewage treatment plant? Suffice to say that the campground at Fort Boonesborough would be much more desirable without the aforementioned eyesore. The campground is situated on a gentle hill partially shaded by mature hardwoods. Mid-sized sites offer paved, back-in parking (there is one pull-through), and the campground feels claustrophobic due to its popularity. The shadiest sites, in the back of the campground, include 61–74 and 137–139. Security is okay—there are no gates, but the park is in a rural location. Park facilities are excellent. Fort Boonesborough is a reconstruction based on the fort built here by Daniel Boone and Richard Henderson in the 1770s. Costumed guides and artisans perform demonstrations. Fishing on the Kentucky River is also available. Catches include bluegill, bass, and catfish. Avoid Fort Boonesborough on summer holidays and weekends.

BASICS

Operated By: Kentucky State Parks. **Open:** Year round. **Site Assignment:** First come, first served; no reservations. **Registration:** Entrance booth, night arrival register next morning. **Fee:** $18 RV, $10 primitive; price for 2 people, $1 per additional adult, 16 & under free; senior & disabled discounts available, Kentucky POWs free (cash, local checks, AE, V, MC, D). **Parking:** At site, in parking lot.

FACILITIES

Number of RV Sites: 0. **Number of Tent-Only Sites:** Primitive, undesignated. **Number of Multi-purpose Sites:** 167. **Hookups:** Water, electric (20, 30, 50 amps). **Each Site:** Picnic table, grill, fire rings in primitive area. **Dump Station:** Yes. **Laundry:** Yes. **Pay Phone:** Yes. **Rest Rooms and Showers:** Yes. **Fuel:** No. **Propane:** No. **Internal Roads:** Paved. **RV Service:** 25 mi. in Lexington. **Market:** 8 mi. in Winchester. **Restaurant:** 0.25 mi. **General Store:** Camp store, 8 mi. in Winchester. **Vending:** Yes. **Swimming Pool:** Yes (seasonal, w/ waterslide). **Playground:** Yes. **Other:** Rec building, gift shop, meeting room, picnic shelters, boat ramp. **Activities:** Fishing, mini-golf, nature trails, seasonal organized activities. **Nearby Attractions:** Boone Station State Historic Site, Natural Bridge State Resort Park, Daniel Boone National Forest, 15 mi. to Lexington. **Additional Information:** Lexington CVB (800) 845-3959, www.visitlex.com.

RESTRICTIONS

Pets: On leash only. **Fires:** Allowed, fire ring only. **Alcoholic Beverages:** Not allowed. **Vehicle Maximum Length:** No limit. **Other:** 14-day stay limit.

TO GET THERE

From I-75, take Exit 95 and drive 5.5 mi. northeast on State Rte. 627. Turn right on KY Hwy. 388 and the campground is on the left. From I-64, take Exit 94/Winchester and drive 10 mi. southwest on Rte. 627. Turn left on Hwy. 388.

SASSAFRAS

Carr Creek State Park

P.O. Box 249, Sassafras 41759. T: (606) 642-4050.

🚐 ★★★★	▲ ★★★★
Beauty: ★★★★★	Site Privacy: ★★
Spaciousness: ★★★★	Quiet: ★★★★
Security: ★★★★	Cleanliness: ★★★★
Insect Control: ★★★★	Facilities: ★★★

The flat, pretty campground at Carr Creek State Park rests in an Appalachian Mountain valley. It offers large sites with paved, back-in parking. Each site also has either a gravel or paved picnic area. Most sites are open to each other, with pleasant woods surrounding the campground. The campground is laid out in two loops, with the nicest sites in the back. Sites 14, 16, 18, 20, 22, and 23, are partially shady, with views of the mountains. The state park offers a full-service marina and fishing on a 750-acre lake. Common catches include bass, crappie and walleye. Carr Creek is so isolated, we thought we would never arrive. But it's definitely worth the drive. Though there is no gate, security is fine. Avoid the park on holiday weekends. Otherwise, these cool mountain highlands are a good summer destination.

BASICS

Operated By: US Army Corps of Engineers. **Open:** Apr. 1–Oct. 31. **Site Assignment:** First come, first served. **Registration:** Office. **Fee:** $16. **Parking:** Designated Areas.

FACILITIES

Number of RV Sites: 39. **Number of Tent-Only Sites:**. **Hookups:** Water, electric. **Each Site:** Picnic shelter. **Dump Station:** Yes. **Laundry:** Yes. **Pay Phone:** Yes. **Rest Rooms and Showers:** Yes. **Fuel:** 1 mi. **Propane:** 1 mi. **Internal Roads:** Paved. **RV Service:** No. **Market:** No. **Restaurant:** No. **General Store:** No. **Vending:** Yes. **Swimming Pool:** Beach area. **Playground:** Yes.

Activities: Fishing, boating, hiking, pontoons, theatre. **Nearby Attractions:** Inquire at campground. **Additional Information:** US Army Corps of Engineers, (606) 642-3308.

RESTRICTIONS

Pets: On leash. **Fires:** Fire ring. **Alcoholic Beverages:** Not allowed. **Vehicle Maximum Length:** No limit.

TO GET THERE

From Hazard on KY 15, Carr creek is located 15 mi.

SCOTTSVILLE

Tailwater Recreation Area

11088 Finney Rd., Glasgow 42141-9642. T: (270) 646-2055.

🚐 ★★★★   🏕 ★★★

Beauty: ★★★★   Site Privacy: ★★★
Spaciousness: ★★★★   Quiet: ★★★★
Security: ★★★★   Cleanliness: ★★★★
Insect Control: ★★★   Facilities: ★★★

The campground at the Tailwater Recreation Area was designed with the avid angler in mind. Most of the 49 sites are right on the water, and those that aren't lie nearby. Most of these sites are long and narrow, and while the trees provide ample shade throughout, the minimal ground cover reduces the privacy between sites. If campers can snag it, site 5 is one of the best in the area; it has one of the only pull-throughs, and the huge site has a gorgeous view. Though the campground can get quite crowded on summer weekends, it seldom fills up. At the time of our visit, the showers were under construction, though they should be completed for the 2002 season. Besides fishing, in-camp activities include horseshoes and hiking.

BASICS

Operated By: US Army Corps of Engineers. **Open:** Apr.–Oct. **Site Assignment:** First come, first served. **Registration:** fee station. **Fee:** $14–$50. **Parking:** On site.

FACILITIES

Number of RV Sites: 49. **Number of Tent-Only Sites:.** **Hookups:** Water, electric (30, 50 amps). **Each Site:** Picnic shelter. **Dump Station:** Yes. **Laundry:** Yes. **Pay Phone:** No. **Rest Rooms and Showers:** Yes. **Fuel:** No. **Propane:** Nearby.

Internal Roads: Paved. **RV Service:** No. **Market:** Nearby. **Restaurant:** No. **General Store:** Nearby. **Vending:** Yes. **Swimming Pool:** No. **Playground:** Yes. **Activities:** Fishing, boating, horseshoes, hiking. **Nearby Attractions:** Buckhorn Lake State Resort.

RESTRICTIONS

Pets: On leash. **Fires:** Only in designated areas. **Alcoholic Beverages:** Not allowed. **Vehicle Maximum Length:** 45 ft.

TO GET THERE

From Glasgow, take Hwy. 31E south for 4 mi.; turn right on 252. Go 8 mi. & cross the dam. The Tailwater entrance road is at the south end of the dam.

SCOTTSVILLE

The Narrows, Barren River Lake

11088 Finney Rd., Glasgow 42141-9642. T: (502) 646-3094.

🚐 ★★★★   🏕 ★★★★

Beauty: ★★★★   Site Privacy: ★★★
Spaciousness: ★★★★   Quiet: ★★★★
Security: ★★★★★   Cleanliness: ★★★
Insect Control: ★★★   Facilities: ★★★

This campground is a bit disappointing compared to other superb US Army Corps of Engineers Campgrounds in the Southeast. Though attractive, parts of the campground need maintenance work. There are weeds popping up through the gravel parking pads. Campsites are larger than average, with back-in parking. Some are well shaded, while others are more open. If you have a big rig, your site choices may be limited, as pad length varies. Our favorites are in Area B. Sites 31 and 32 boast lake views and ample shade. For tent campers, sites 1, 2, 43, 45, 47, 49, and 50 have no hookups, but nestle into the woods and offer seclusion. Remote and gated, security is outstanding here. Fishing in Barren River Lake affords shots at bluegill, channel catfish, crappie, rough fish, and largemouth, white, and hybrid striped bass. In the area, many commercial marinas and bait shops cater to fishermen. Avoid Barren River Lake on busy summer holidays and weekends.

BASICS

Operated By: US Army Corps of Engineers. **Open:** Apr.–Sept. **Site Assignment:** First come, first served. **Registration:** fee station. **Fee:** $16–$19. **Parking:** On site.

FACILITIES

Number of RV Sites: 97. **Number of Tent-Only Sites:.** **Hookups:** Water, electric (50 amps). **Each Site:** Picnic table. **Dump Station:** Yes. **Laundry:** Yes. **Pay Phone:** No. **Rest Rooms and Showers:** Yes. **Fuel:** No. **Propane:** No. **Internal Roads:** Paved. **RV Service:** No. **Market:** Nearby. **Restaurant:** Nearby. **General Store:** Nearby. **Vending:** Yes. **Swimming Pool:** No. **Playground:** Yes. **Activities:** Fishing, boating, swimming in lake. **Nearby Attractions:** The Buckhorn Dam Overlook.

RESTRICTIONS

Pets: On leash. **Fires:** Only in designated areas. **Alcoholic Beverages:** Not allowed. **Vehicle Maximum Length:** 45 ft. **Other:** Max 6 person, 2 vehicles per site.

TO GET THERE

From Glasgow, take Hwy. 31 east for 10 mi.; turn right on 1318. Follow the signs.

SHEPHERDSVILLE

KOA–Louisville South

2433 Hwy. 44 East, Shepherdsville 40165. T: (502) 543-2041.

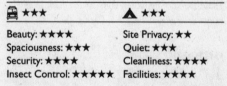

🚐 ★★★	🔺 ★★★
Beauty: ★★★★	Site Privacy: ★★★
Spaciousness: ★★★★	Quiet: ★★★
Security: ★★	Cleanliness: ★★★★
Insect Control: ★★★	Facilities: ★★★

This attractive KOA offers both back-in and pull-through sites laid out in numerous areas. Some sites are wide and as long as 70 feet, while others are pretty dinky. Most sites are shady, though a few are totally open. Parking is on gravel. In the back of the park, the prettiest sites (75–89, 126–130, and 181–191) overlook a cliff leading to the Salt River. The swimming pool and other facilities are in tip-top shape. Security is so-so. The area is densely populated and the campground has no gates. Suburban Shepherdsville is about 20 miles from downtown Louisville. There are plenty of restaurants and shops near the campground. For a pleasant day trip, visit My Old Kentucky Home in Bardstown. Unless you have tickets to an event, avoid the Louisville area

on Kentucky Derby weekend (first Saturday in May) as well as summer holidays.

BASICS

Operated By: Roy J. Tanner & Carol Hylton. **Open:** Year round. **Site Assignment:** First come, first served. **Registration:** Office. **Fee:** $21–$29. **Parking:** On site.

FACILITIES

Number of RV Sites: 108. **Number of Tent-Only Sites:** 37. **Hookups:** Water, electric (50 amps), some sewer, Internet ports. **Each Site:** Fire ring. **Dump Station:** Yes. **Laundry:** Yes. **Pay Phone:** Yes. **Rest Rooms and Showers:** Yes. **Fuel:** No. **Propane:** Yes. **Internal Roads:** Gravel. **RV Service:** No. **Market:** No. **Restaurant:** No. **General Store:** Yes. **Vending:** Yes. **Swimming Pool:** Yes, heated. **Playground:** Yes. **Other:** hot tub. **Activities:** Horse shoes, boating, hiking mini-golf. **Nearby Attractions:** Derby Museum, General Patton Museum, Jim Beam. **Additional Information:** (800) KOA-1880.

RESTRICTIONS

Pets: On leash. **Fires:** Fire ring. **Alcoholic Beverages:** Allowed. **Vehicle Maximum Length:** 100 ft. **Other:** 21 or older in hot tub.

TO GET THERE

I-65 to Exit 117. Go 2 mi. east on Rte. 44.

SLADE

Natural Bridge State Park

2135 Natural Bridge Rd., Slade 40376. T: (606) 663-2214.

🚐 ★★★	🔺 ★★★
Beauty: ★★★★	Site Privacy: ★★
Spaciousness: ★★★	Quiet: ★★★
Security: ★★★★	Cleanliness: ★★★★
Insect Control: ★★★★★	Facilities: ★★★★

It's a shame that the campgrounds at Natural Bridge are so mediocre, given the natural beauty of the land in this part of the Daniel Boone National Forest. With the campgrounds squeezed into tight mountain hollers, sites are on the small side of average. What's more, this park is extremely popular and the campgrounds stay full all summer. Sites offer gravel, back-in parking. Shadiness varies. We recommend shady RV sites in the back of the Whittleton Campground, particularly A33–A35. For tent campers, we like sites in the primitive area, numbered C4–C10. The state park's namesake is a giant sandstone arch. Nearby, the Red River Gorge contains a plethora of rock climbing routes catering to novices and experts. The Red River is known for gorgeous canoeing as well as Class II–III white-water. Security is passable at this isolated state park. Visit in spring or fall if you value solitude.

BASICS

Operated By: State of Kentucky. **Open:** Apr.–Oct. **Site Assignment:** First come, first served. **Registration:** Booth at campground entry. **Fee:** $10–$20. **Parking:** In designated areas.

FACILITIES

Number of RV Sites: 86. **Number of Tent-Only Sites:. Hookups:** Water, electric (20, 30 amps). **Each Site:** Picnic shelters. **Dump Station:** Yes. **Laundry:** Yes. **Pay Phone:** Yes. **Rest Rooms and Showers:** Yes. **Fuel:** Nearby. **Propane:** Nearby. **Internal Roads:** Paved. **RV Service:** No. **Market:** No. **Restaurant:** Yes. **General Store:** No. **Vending:** Yes. **Swimming Pool:** Yes. **Playground:** Yes. **Other:** Nature center. **Activities:** Fishing, mini-golf, hiking. **Nearby Attractions:** Buckhorn Lake State Resort Park. **Additional Information:** check out at 2 p.m.

RESTRICTIONS

Pets: On leash. **Fires:** Fire ring. **Alcoholic Beverages:** Not allowed. **Vehicle Maximum Length:** No limit.

TO GET THERE

I-64 E to Exit 98 onto Bert T. Combs Mtn. Pkwy East. Take KY 11 Exit No. 33 towards Slade/Beattyville. Keep right at the fork in the ramp. Merge onto KY 11. Park is 0.33 mi.

UNION

Big Bone Lick State Park

3380 Beaver Rd., Union 41091-9627. T: (859) 384-3522; www.state.ky.us.

🚃 ★★★★	🔺 ★★★★
Beauty: ★★★★	Site Privacy: ★★
Spaciousness: ★★★	Quiet: ★★★
Security: ★★★★★	Cleanliness: ★★★★
Insect Control: ★★★	Facilities: ★★★★

The institutional-looking campground at Big Bone Lick is not gorgeous, but it's pleasant. Set on a large, gentle hill, the campground features average-sized sites with minimal privacy. Some sites are shady, but the campground is open enough that you can easily see one end from the other. Sites offer paved, back-in parking. Many of the parking pads are short. Our favorite sites, 25–29, are on a cul-de-sac at the end of the campground. Fascinating Big Bone Lick State Park, the birthplace of American vertebrate pale-ontology, was a swamp at the end of the Ice Age. Prehistoric animals, such as giant mammoths, mastodons, ground sloths, and bison, were attracted by the swamp's salt and minerals, became trapped in the quagmire, and died. Their remains fossilized, leaving paleontologists a treasure trove of bones to study. Located near Cincinnati, this park stays busy all summer. Visit during the week, or in spring or fall. Security is excellent.

BASICS

Operated By: State of Kentucky. **Open:** Year round/closed Dec. 23–Dec. 30. **Site Assignment:** reservations not required, first come first serve. **Registration:** Office. **Fee:** $10. **Parking:** On site.

FACILITIES

Number of RV Sites: 62. **Number of Tent-Only Sites:** Tent area. **Hookups:** Water, electric (30, 50 amps), sewer. **Each Site:** Grill, water, picnic table. **Dump Station:** Yes. **Laundry:** Yes. **Pay Phone:** Yes. **Rest Rooms and Showers:** Yes. **Fuel:** 5 mi. **Propane:** 5 mi. **Internal Roads:** Paved. **RV Service:** No. **Market:** Yes. **Restaurant:** No. **General Store:** No. **Vending:** Yes. **Swimming Pool:** Yes. **Playground:** Yes. **Other:** Church services (Apr.–Oct.), observation deck, Museum Store. **Activities:** Miniature golf, fishing, boating, basketball, tennis, softball fields, nature trails. **Nearby Attractions:** Inquire at campground. **Additional Information:** State of Kentucky, (859) 384-3522.

RESTRICTIONS

Pets: On leash. **Fires:** No. **Alcoholic Beverages:** Not allowed. **Vehicle Maximum Length:** No limit. **Other:** No hunting, rappelling, rock climbing, motorized vehicles & bikes, collecting or digging for artifacts.

TO GET THERE

22 mi. southwest of Covington I-75, go south to KY 338, off US 42/127 and I-71/I-75.

Louisiana

Louisiana is one of America's great cultural melting pots. The state's famous festivals are a lively way for visitors to immerse themselves in the local culture. **Mardi Gras** is the crown jewel of Louisiana festivals. From town to town, folks celebrate Mardi Gras in unique ways. Many cities, including **Shreveport-Bossier,** feature family-oriented Mardi-Gras celebrations. Other noteworthy festivals include **Cajun Fun Fest, New Orleans Jazz & Heritage Festival,** and the **Louisiana Folklife Festival.** Call (800) 947-6711 for a statewide calendar of fairs and festivals.

Throughout history, varied peoples have affected Louisiana history and traditions. Native American habitation dates back thousands of years. Learn about these ancient cultures at various mounds and archaeological sights, including **Poverty Point State Historic Site.** Today, the Tunica-Biloxi, Coushatta, and other tribes make rich contributions to the state's economy and culture.

African Americans in Louisiana contribute greatly to the state's fascinating history. Lavish rice and sugarcane plantations in southeastern Louisiana prospered using slave labor. In the twentieth century, New Orleans' African American community gave birth to jazz. The legendary roots of jazz are said to originate at **Congo Square,** where crowds of slaves once sang and danced to African drum beats.

Folks from outside of Louisiana aren't always aware of the state's Hispanic influences. Even before Hernando de Soto arrived in 1541, other Spanish explorers had seen the mouth of the Mississippi. The present day Isleños community of **St. Bernard Parish** preserve their heritage at the **Isleños Museum.** Vestiges of Spanish colonial culture are also evident throughout **New Orleans'** famous historic districts.

Louisiana is famous for its Cajun culture, which arose from the great Acadian Diaspora of 1755. This tragic phase in Cajun history was brought about when the British asked French-speaking colonists in New Brunswick and Nova Scotia to renounce Catholicism. When families refused to renounce their religion, they were forced to flee. Great numbers of Acadians made their way to southern Louisiana, where their culture thrives. Learn about Acadian culture at numerous museums, including **Acadian Village in Lafayette.**

No discussion of Louisiana is complete without mentioning the food—it's fabulous. Even if you're heading to Louisiana for primitive tent camping, make plans to stop at one of the state's fine Cajun or seafood restaurants. A number of excellent guidebooks detail Louisiana cuisine.

Popular tourist attractions in Louisiana include **Mississippi River Steamboat Cruises. Casinos** draw tourists to Shreveport-Bossier City, Marksville, Kinder, Lake Charles, Baton

Rouge, and the New Orleans area. Other worthwhile attractions include: Ark-La-Tex Antique and Classic Vehicle Museum, Sci-Port Discovery Center, Water Town USA, Sports Museum of Champions, Biedenharn Museum and Gardens, **Louisiana Purchase Museum and Gardens,** Northeast Louisiana Children's Museum, Mansfield State Historic Site, Poverty Point State Historic Site, Fort St. Jean Baptiste Historic Site, **Camp Beauregard,** River Oaks Square Arts Center, Frogmore Plantation, Cane River Creole National Historic Park, The Cane River National heritage Area, **Bayou Folk Museum,** Melrose Plantation, World Famous Garden in the Forest, Los Adaes State Historic Site, Lake Charles Carpentier District, DeQuincy Railroad Museum, Chateau des Cocodries, The Zigler Museum, Vermilionville, **Jean Lafitte Acadian Cultural Center,** Children's Museum of Acadiana, Lafayette Natural History Museum, Acadian Memorial, Longfellow-Evangeline State Historic Site, **Louisiana State Arboretum,** Chretien Point Plantation, Shadows-on-the-Teche plantation, Tabasco Factory and Jungle gardens, The Great River Road, Oak Alley Plantation, Laura, Destrehan Plantation, Nottoway Plantation, Houmas House, Tezcuco, Louisiana State Capitol, The Old State Capitol, West Baton Rouge Museum, The USS Kidd, **Port Hudson State Historic Site Civil War Battlefield,** St. Francisville, Rosedown Plantation, and The Myrtles, Audubon State Historic Site.

In the **New Orleans** area, tourist attractions include: The Cabildo, The Presbytere, St. Louis Cathedral, Pontalba Apartments, The Vieux Carré, Top of the Mart, Aquarium of the Americas, Louisiana Superdome, New Orleans Saints, Children's Museum, national D-Day Museum, **Audubon Park, Audubon Zoo,** Warehouse District, cemeteries, Mardi Gras World, German American Museum, Chalmette National Historic Battlefield, Fort Jackson, Rivertown USA, **Abita Brew Pub,** Global Wildlife Center, and Zemurray Gardens.

BASTROP

Chemin-A-Haut State Park

14656 State Park Rd., Bastrop 71220-7078. T: (888) 677-2436; F: (318) 556-7007; www.crt.state.la.us.

🚐 ★★★★ 　　　 ▲ ★★★★

Beauty: ★★★★ 　　　 Site Privacy: ★★★★
Spaciousness: ★★★★ 　 Quiet: ★★★★
Security: ★★★★ 　　　 Cleanliness: ★★★★
Insect Control: ★★★★ 　 Facilities: ★★★

Chemin-A-Haut offers one attractive camping loop. Site size is ample, though privacy varies. The most secluded sites are 11, 12, and 14, in the back of the campground. Though distance between sites varies, all are large and comfortably spaced. Mature trees, including oak, hickory, and pine, shade the campground, and undergrowth provides privacy between sites. Sites feature paved, back-in parking. Chemin-A-Haut is situated on high bluffs overlooking Bayou Bartholomew, and offers a paved walking trail along the water. The large playground and wading pool are a hit with younger children. Older children can cast a line into Big Slough Lake, on the eastern edge of the park. Avoid Chemin-A-Haut on summer and holiday weekends. Summer weather isn't necessarily torturous at this park, so it makes a good mid-week summertime destination. Security is excellent at this very rural park. Gates are locked at night.

BASICS

Operated By: State of Louisiana Dept. of Culture, Recreation & Tourism. **Open:** Year-round. **Site Assignment:** First come, first served, also reservations can be held w/ V or MC (888) 677-1400. If cancelled 15 days or more before the first reserved day then the fee is $10. If cancelled 14 days or less to the first reserved day then the fee is one day's rental of all reserved items. Check-in time is 3 p.m. or later. Check-out time is 11 a.m. or earlier. Stay limit is 15 days. **Registration:** Main office. **Fee:** $12 per night for RV/tent sites, $6 w/ a Golden Access card. **Parking:** 3 car parking at each site/2car & 1 RV.

FACILITIES

Number of Multipurpose Sites: 26. **Hookups:** Electric (30 amps), water. **Each Site:** Tent pad, fire ring, grill, picnic table, lantern hook. **Dump Station:** Yes. **Laundry:** Yes. **Pay Phone:** Yes. **Rest**

Rooms and Showers: Yes. **Fuel:** No. **Propane:** No. **Internal Roads:** Paved. **RV Service:** 15 mi. south in Bastrop. **Market:** 7 mi. south in Log Cabin. **Restaurant:** 15 mi. south in Bastrop. **General Store:** 15 mi. south in Bastrop. **Vending:** Beverage only. **Swimming Pool:** Yes. **Playground:** Yes. **Other:** Hiking trails, Baseball field, boat launch, Group lodging. **Activities:** Boat renting, hiking, fishing, field games. **Nearby Attractions:** Poverty Point State Commemorative Area, Lake D'Arbonne State Park, Handy Brake National Wildlife Refuge, Georgia Pacific Wildlife Management Area, Lake Claiborne State Park, Caney Creek Lake State Park. **Additional Information:** Bastrop-Morehouse Tourism Commission, (318) 281-3794.

RESTRICTIONS

Pets: Leash. **Fires:** Fire ring only. **Alcoholic Beverages:** Allowed. **Vehicle Maximum Length:** 60 ft. **Other:** Be familiar w/ all alligator precautions.

TO GET THERE

From Bastrop take US 425 north approx. 10 mi. Turn right onto LA 2229 (State Park Rd.).

BRAITHWAITE

St. Bernard State Park

P.O. Box 534, Violet 70092. T: (888) 677-7823; F: (504) 682-9960; www.crt.state.la.us; st.bernard@crt.state.la.us.

🚐 ★★★★ 　　　 ▲ ★★★★

Beauty: ★★★★ 　　　 Site Privacy: ★★★
Spaciousness: ★★★★ 　 Quiet: ★★★★
Security: ★★★★ 　　　 Cleanliness: ★★★★
Insect Control: ★★ 　　 Facilities: ★★★

St. Bernard is situated around a series of man-made lagoons and provides a habitat for alligators, turtles, and other wetlands wildlife. The Mississippi River is across Hwy. 39 from the park, and Chalmette National Historic Park is nearby. Less than one hour from downtown New Orleans, St. Bernard is popular with folks from the Crescent City. It should be avoided on holiday and festival weekends, especially Jazz Fest. Visit in early April or in the fall if you value tranquility. St. Bernard offers one camping loop, with sites partially shaded by a variety of trees. We like the shadier sites, including 16, 22, 45, and 46. Site privacy is not exceptional. Site size varies immensely. Some are 90 feet from their neighbors, while others are only 25 feet from neighbors. All sites offer paved, back-in parking. Remote and gated, security at St. Bernard is excellent.

BASICS

Operated By: State of Louisiana, Dept. of Culture, Recreation, & Tourism. **Open:** Year-round. **Site Assignment:** First come, first served, also reservations can be made w/ a V or MC, Deposit is $12 (888) 677-1400. If cancelled the fee is the deposit ($12). Check-in time is 2 p.m. or later. Check-out time is 1 p.m. or earlier. **Registration:** Ranger's station. **Fee:** $12 per night for RV/tent site. $6 w/ Golden Access Card. **Parking:** 2 vehicle parking at site. Overflow parking is available.

FACILITIES

Number of Multipurpose Sites: 51. **Hookups:** Water, Electric (30 amps). **Each Site:** Picnic table, fire ring, concrete patio, grill. **Dump Station:** Yes. **Laundry:** Yes. **Pay Phone:** Yes. **Rest Rooms and Showers:** Yes. **Fuel:** No. **Propane:** No. **Internal Roads:** Paved. **RV Service:** 5 mi. west in Chalmette. **Market:** Convenience store 0.5 mi. north, grocery 2 mi. west. **Restaurant:** 1 mi. west. **General Store:** K-Mart is 7 mi. west in Chalmette. **Vending:** Beverage only. **Swimming Pool:** Yes (open from Memorial Day–Labor Day). **Playground:** Yes. **Other:** Trails, field for athletics, pavilion. **Activities:** Hiking, boating & fishing less than a mi. from the State Park. **Nearby Attractions:** Bayou Sagnette State Park, Fairview Riverside State Park, Louisiana State Museum, New Orleans & the Historic French Quarter, Chalmette Battlefield-Jean Lafitte National Historic Park & Preserve, Isleno Cultural Center-Jean Lafitte National Historic Park & Preserve, San Bernardo Scenic Byway, Bayou Sauvage National Wildlife Refuge. **Additional Information:** St. Bernard Parish Tourist Commission (888) 278-2054.

RESTRICTIONS

Pets: Leash only. **Fires:** Fire ring. **Alcoholic Beverages:** Allowed. **Vehicle Maximum Length:** 50 ft.

TO GET THERE

From I-10 get on 510 (Hwy. 47) towards Chalmette. Go 6 mi. to the intersection of Hwy. 46 and turn left. Go 7 mi. to Hwy. 39 and turn right to go south. Go 0.5 mi. and the entrance is on the left.

CARENCRO
Bayou Wilderness RV Resort

201 St. Clair Rd., Carencro 70520. T: (337) 896-0598; www.bayouwildernessrvresort.com.

🚐 ★★★	▲ n/a
Beauty: ★★★	Site Privacy: ★★
Spaciousness: ★★★	Quiet: ★★★★
Security: ★★★	Cleanliness: ★★★★
Insect Control: ★★★	Facilities: ★★★

This quaint RV park is laid out in rows of pull-through sites with gravel parking. Sites are on the small side, and are mostly open. There are trees on the perimeter of the campground, providing shade for a few of the sites. There are no natural privacy barriers. The nicest sites are 15, 16, 33, 34, 46, 47, 54, and 55. These offer views of a small pond with picturesque cypress trees. The park is located in suburban Lafayette. Nearby, you'll find plenty of restaurants, shopping, and tourist attractions. Notable outings include swamp tours in the mammoth Atchafalaya Basin and Acadian Village, a museum of authentic Acadian houses. Bayou Wilderness is relatively safe; there are no gates, but it's in a quiet area. Visit southern Louisiana in spring or fall for pleasant weather.

BASICS

Operated By: George Cormier & Charlie Montgomery. **Open:** Year-round. **Site Assignment:** Deposit, cancellations must be received one & a half weeks before arrival date. reservations are recommended, pick your own site, check in/check out is at noon, payments can be made w/ V or MC. **Registration:** Main office/grocery store. **Fee:** $29–$23. **Parking:** One RV unit & one vehicle per site. Parking area for additional vehicles.

FACILITIES

Number of RV Sites: 122. **Number of Tent-Only Sites:** 0. **Hookups:** Water, electric (30, 50 amps), some have cable. **Dump Station:** Yes. **Laundry:** Yes. **Pay Phone:** Yes. **Rest Rooms and Showers:** Yes. **Fuel:** No. **Propane:** Yes. **Internal Roads:** Gravel, black top. **RV Service:** Limited (3 mi. in south Lafayette). **Market:** On site. **Restaurant:** 3 mi. in Lafayette. **General Store:** Wal-Mart in Lafayette. **Vending:** No. **Swimming Pool:** Yes. **Playground:** Yes. **Other:** Tennis court, arcade room, volleyball net, Jacuzzi. **Activities:** Tennis arcade games, volleyball, fishing, shuffleboard, horseshoes. **Nearby Attractions:** Tabasco Plant, Acadian Village, Jean Lafitte National Park, Atchafalaya Basin Boat Tour. **Additional Information:** Bayou Teche Visitors Center (888) 565 5939, big rigs welcome.

RESTRICTIONS

Pets: Leash only. **Fires:** Designated areas only. **Alcoholic Beverages:** Allowed. **Vehicle Maximum Length:** 70 ft.

To GET THERE

From I-10, take exit 1033 onto I-49 North. Go 2.5 mi. to Gloria Switch Rd. (exit 2). Turn right, going east, onto Gloria Switch and travel 2.3 mi. (crossing Moss St. at traffic light) until you come to North Wilderness Trail. Turn left, going north, onto North Wilderness Trail. Travel 0.7 mi. to the entrance on the right.

CHATHAM
Caney Creek Lake State Park

State Rd. No. 1209, Chatham 71226. T: (888) 677-2263; F: (318) 249-2671; www.crt.state.la.us.

🚐 ★★★★   ▲ ★★★★

Beauty: ★★★★★	Site Privacy: ★★★★
Spaciousness: ★★★★★	Quiet: ★★★★
Security: ★★★★★	Cleanliness: ★★★★★
Insect Control: ★★★	Facilities: ★★★

Caney Creek features a lovely camping area, with sites laid out along the lakeshore. Sites vary in size-some are very large. Shadiness also varies-though most are shaded by pine and other species, sites 13–17 are more open. All sites offer paved, back-in parking. Few sites offer privacy. The nicest waterfront sites include 38, 40, 42, 43, and 45. However, the crown jewel of Caney Creek is site 54, with its knockout view of the lake. Boasting numerous record catches, Caney Creek is bass fishin' heaven. The park maintains two boat launches and a fishing pier as well as an attractive swimming beach. Even though it's off the beaten path, Caney Creek is very popular and should be avoided on summer holidays and weekends. Security is excellent. Gates are attended during the day and locked at night.

BASICS

Operated By: State of Louisiana Dept. of Culture, Recreation & Tourism (888) 677-1400. **Open:** Year-round. **Site Assignment:** First come, first served,

reservations can be held w/ V or MC (888) 677-1400. If reservations are cancelled then the fee is one day's rent. Check-in time is 2 p.m. or later. Check-out time is 1 p.m. or earlier. Stay limit is 15 days. **Registration:** Main office. **Fee:** $12 a night for RV/tent site rental, $6 w/ Golden Access card. **Parking:** 2 car/1 RV & 1 car at each site, overflow parking available.

FACILITIES

Number of Multipurpose Sites: 73. **Hookups:** Water, electric (30 amps). **Each Site:** Tent pad, grill, fire ring, picnic table. **Dump Station:** Yes. **Laundry:** Yes. **Pay Phone:** Yes. **Rest Rooms and Showers:** Yes. **Fuel:** No. **Propane:** No. **Internal Roads:** Paved. **RV Service:** 35 mi. northeast in West Monroe. **Market:** 6 mi. east in Chatham. **Restaurant:** 6 mi. east in Chatham. **General Store:** 15 mi. west in Jonesboro. **Vending:** No. **Swimming Pool:** No. **Playground:** No. **Other:** Fishing pier, pavilions, boat launch. **Activities:** Picnicking, fishing, boating (bring your own). **Nearby Attractions:** Poverty Point State Commemorative Area, Lake D'Arbonne State Park, Historic Town of Chatham, Lake Claiborne State Park, Jackson Bienville Wildlife Management Area. **Additional Information:** Monroe-West Monroe CVB.

RESTRICTIONS

Pets: Leash. **Fires:** Ring. **Alcoholic Beverages:** Yes (none on beach). **Vehicle Maximum Length:** Approx. 72 ft. **Other:** No 3 or 4 wheelers allowed.

To GET THERE

From Jonesboro go east on LA 4 for 12.8 mi. then turn right onto Lakeshore Dr. State Park Rd. 1209 is on the right, approx. 20 mi. ahead.

COVINGTON
Land-O-Pines

17145 Million Dollar Rd., Covington 70435. T: (985) 892-6023 or (985) 867-8372; F: (985) 898-2072; www.land-o-pines.com; landopines@aol.com.

🚐 ★★★   ▲ ★★★

Beauty: ★★★	Site Privacy: ★★
Spaciousness: ★★★	Quiet: ★★★
Security: ★★★	Cleanliness: ★★★
Insect Control: ★★★	Facilities: ★★★

Land-O-Pines has two things going for it: its location and family-oriented amenities. Here, children enjoy mini-golf, a nice playground, a waterslide and pool, and a duck pond. Adults appreciate the suburban location, with plenty of shopping and restaurants nearby. New Orleans is just across the 26-mile Lake Pontchartrain Causeway. The campground contains residential and overnight sites in two separate areas. The overnight area is laid out in four long rows of back-in campsites. Sites are average sized, with plenty of shady trees. Parking is on grass, and sites are not always well defined. Grassy sites make this park popular with tent campers. The prettiest, quietest sites are on Deer Run Rd., along the back perimeter. Don't visit southern Louisiana in hot, humid late summer. For peachy weather, visit in spring or fall. Security is good–all cars are required to display passes.

BASICS

Operated By: Jim Williamson. **Open:** 7 days, all year. **Site Assignment:** First come, first served also reservations. **Registration:** At store, 7 a.m.–7 p.m. Sunday–Thursday, 10 p.m. Friday, 9 p.m. Saturday. **Fee:** $20 (Monday–Thursday & Winter), $25 (Friday–Sunday), $30 (holidays), rates for 5 people, $5 extra per person, 3 under free, senior discount available; cash, check, money order, V, MC, AE, D. **Parking:** Sites plus parking area.

FACILITIES

Number of Multipurpose Sites: 275 (all sites multi-purpose). **Hookups:** Water, electric (30 amps), some sewer. **Each Site:** Picnic table, fire ring. **Dump Station:** Yes. **Laundry:** Yes. **Pay Phone:** Yes. **Rest Rooms and Showers:** Yes. **Fuel:** Yes. **Propane:** Yes. **Internal Roads:** Gravel. **RV Service:** 10 mi. **Market:** Yes. **Restaurant:** 2 mi. (snack bar on-site). **General Store:** 6 mi. **Vending:** No. **Swimming Pool:** Yes. **Playground:** Yes. **Activities:** Miniature golf, duck pond, water slide, river beach, campground-organized activities weekends, volleyball & basketball courts, game room. **Nearby Attractions:** 17 mi. to New Orleans, Global Wildlife Center, Fontainebleau State Park, Fairview-Riverside State park. **Additional Information:** New Orleans CVB (800) 672-6124, Slidell CVB (504) 646-6426.

RESTRICTIONS

Pets: On leash only. **Fires:** In sites, fire rings only. **Alcoholic Beverages:** Okay. **Vehicle Maximum Length:** 35 ft. **Other:** No 4-wheelers or go-carts.

TO GET THERE

From I-12, take Exit 63B, take Hwy. 25 west to Million Dollar Rd. Turn right, and campground is on the left. From New Orleans, take the Causeway/Hwy. 190 which becomes Hwy. 25, to Million Dollar Rd.

DENHAM SPRINGS
Baton Rouge East KOA

7628 Vincent Rd., Denham Springs 70726. T: (225) 664-7281 or (800) 292-8245.

🚐 ★★★ ▲ ★★

Beauty: ★★★   Site Privacy: ★★
Spaciousness: ★★   Quiet: ★★★
Security: ★★★   Cleanliness: ★★★
Insect Control: ★★★   Facilities: ★★

Located in suburban Baton Rouge, this KOA is convenient for touring the State Capitol, the Old State Capitol, and riverboat casinos. KOA is also near famous historic plantations, including Nottoway Plantation, Houmas House, Tezcuco Plantation, and Oak Alley Plantation. The area offers plenty of shopping and restaurants. The campground is underwhelming, with patchy pavement, dirt, gravel, and grass ground cover. Parking spaces are mostly paved. There are both back-in and pull-through spaces. Sites are small and there is little privacy. Most sites are partially shady. We like the sites in the front of the campground, which are tidier than those in the back. Tent campers will appreciate the private bathrooms. The campground is gated, but not fenced, making security iffy. Avoid southern Louisiana in late summer, when it's steamy enough to cook veggies.

BASICS

Operated By: Bacot Enterprise. **Open:** 7 days, all year. **Site Assignment:** Sites assigned based on unit; reservations w/ credit card deposit; 24-hour cancellation notice required. **Registration:** In store, seasonal hours. **Fee:** $19 tent, $27 (30 amps), $29 (50 amps). (cash, LA check, V, MC, D, AE). **Parking:** Sites plus lot.

FACILITIES

Number of RV Sites: 100. **Number of Tent-Only Sites:** 12. **Number of Multipurpose Sites:** 100 (RV sites). **Hookups:** Water, electric (30, 50 amps), sewage, cable. **Each Site:** Picnic table. **Dump Station:** Yes. **Laundry:** Yes. **Pay Phone:** Yes. **Rest Rooms and Showers:** Yes. **Fuel:** No. **Propane:** Yes. **Internal Roads:** Paved &

gravel. **RV Service:** Within 2 mi. **Market:** Yes. **Restaurant:** 0.5 mi. **General Store:** 1 mi. **Vending:** Beverages only. **Swimming Pool:** Yes. **Playground:** Yes. **Activities:** Game room, pool table, bicycling & hiking trails, City Park adjacent. **Nearby Attractions:** Plantation homes, USS Kidd, Old State Capitol Museum, Louisiana State Capital, Blue Bayou Water Park, Louisiana State University campus. **Additional Information:** Baton Rouge Conventiona nd Visitors Bureau (225) 383-1825.

RESTRICTIONS

Pets: On leash only. **Fires:** In grills, fire rings only (these are not in sites, but scattered around park). **Alcoholic Beverages:** Okay. **Vehicle Maximum Length:** Varies up to 45 ft.

TO GET THERE

Heading West toward Baton Rouge on I-12, take Exit 10 (Denham Springs), turn left at the end of the ramp, and turn right on Vincent Rd. Campground is on the left around the corner. From I-10 (either direction), take the I-12 split, then Exit 10, turn right at the end of the ramp.

DOYLINE
Lake Bistineau State Park

P.O. Box 589, Doyline 71023. T: (888) 677-2478; F: (318) 745-3806; www.la.stateparks.com; lakebistineau@crt.state.la.us.

🚐 ★★★★   ⛺ ★★★★

Beauty: ★★★★★   Site Privacy: ★★★★
Spaciousness: ★★★★★   Quiet: ★★★★★
Security: ★★★★   Cleanliness: ★★★★
Insect Control: ★★★   Facilities: ★★★★

The campground at Lake Bistineau consists of one attractive loop. Many sites have lovely views of the lake with its elegant cypress and tupelo trees. Seven sites offer pull-through parking. The rest offer back-in. Parking is paved. Some sites are huge, including number 26, a pull-through with a lake view. Others are close together and offer little privacy. Lake Bistineau is a 200-year-old man-made lake, first created when a goliath log jam caused the Red River to flood. In 1935, a permanent dam was constructed and the lake was enlarged. It now supports black crappie, largemouth bass, yellow bass, bullheads, blue gill, and red ear sunfish. The state park is divided into two areas, each with its own boat launch

and swimming pool. The campground is in Area 1. Visit Lake Bistineau in late spring or fall for pleasant weather. Avoid the park on summer weekends and holidays.

BASICS

Operated By: Sate Of Louisiana Dept. of Culture, Recreation, & Tourism (888) 677-1400. **Open:** Year-round. **Site Assignment:** First come, first served; V & MC may be used to hold reservations (888) 677-1400. Check-in time is 3 p.m. or later. Check-out time is 11 a.m. or earlier. If cancelled within 48 hours of reserved check-in time then the fee is one day's rent. **Registration:** Main office. **Fee:** $12 for either the tent or RV sites. $6 w/ Golden Access Card. **Parking:** 2 cars or 1 car & 1 RV at each site. Overflow parking is available.

FACILITIES

Number of Multipurpose Sites: 67. **Hookups:** Water & Electricity (20 & 30 amps). **Each Site:** Tent pad, fire ring, picnic table, lantern hook varies. **Dump Station:** Yes. **Laundry:** Yes. **Pay Phone:** Yes. **Rest Rooms and Showers:** Yes. **Fuel:** No. **Propane:** No. **Internal Roads:** Paved. **RV Service:** 30 mi. northwest in Shreveport. **Market:** 6 mi. north in Doyline. **Restaurant:** 10 mi. north in Doyline. **General Store:** 10 mi. north in Doyline. **Vending:** Beverage only. **Swimming Pool:** Yes. **Playground:** Yes. **Other:** Group lodge, boat launch, athletic field, boat rental. **Activities:** Nature trails, boating, swimming. **Nearby Attractions:** **Nearby Attractions:** Lake Claiborne State Park, Historic Town of Minden, Kisatche National Forest-Caney Lakes Recreation Area, Trails End Public Golf Course, Loggy Bayou Wildlife Management Area, Ambrose Mountain, Driskoll Mountain, Mt. Lebanon, Bodcau Wildlife Management Area. **Additional Information:** Shreveport/Bossier Convention & Tourist Bureau (888) 45-VISIT.

RESTRICTIONS

Pets: Leash. **Fires:** Fire ring only. **Alcoholic Beverages:** Allowed. **Vehicle Maximum Length:** Approx. 40 ft. **Other:** No fireworks, acquaint yourself w/ all alligator precautions.

TO GET THERE

From Shreveport, Take I-20 East to Exit 33 (Haughton/Filmore). Go to the right then take an immediate left on Hwy. 3227, which dead-ends into Hwy. 164. Take a right on 164 and go about 4–5 mi. until you reach the town of Doyline. Take a right at the flashing caution light (Hwy. 163). Keep straight about 8 mi. Look for

Lake Bistineau State Park Area sign to the right. Turn left to enter main gate. Stop at park office on right for further instructions.

FARMERVILLE
Lake D'Arbonne State Park

P.O. Box 236, Farmerville 71241. T: (888) 677-5200; F: (318) 368-8207; www.crt.state.la.us.

🚐 ★★★★   🏕 ★★★★

Beauty: ★★★★★   Site Privacy: ★★★★
Spaciousness: ★★★★   Quiet: ★★★★
Security: ★★★★★   Cleanliness: ★★★★★
Insect Control: ★★★   Facilities: ★★★

The beautiful campground at Lake D'Arbonne is situated in two loops with a fishing pier and boat dock at the campground. The campground is shaded by a lovely stand of loblolly pines. And Sites feature paved, back-in parking. Most sites are larger than average, with a little greenery providing privacy barriers between sites. Sites 24, 28, 44, and 45 enjoy lake views, but are less secluded than some others. For elbow room, head to site 20. The lake is home to gorgeous cypress stands as well as record catches of crappie and bass. The park's well-kept fishing facilities augment the fisherman's experience. This park is also popular with road bikers due to its roads winding through shady hills. Avoid Lake D'Arbonne on summer holidays and weekends and during hot July and Aug. This rural park locks its gates at night, making security excellent.

BASICS

Operated By: State of Louisiana Dept. of Culture, Recreation, & Tourism. **Open:** Year-round. **Site Assignment:** First come, first served, Reservations can be held w/ MC or V (888) 677-1400. If cancelled 15 days or more before reserved check-in day the fee is $10. If cancelled 14 days or less before your reserved check-in day then the fee is one day's rental of all reserved items. Check-in time is 2 p.m. or later. Check-out time is 1 p.m. or earlier. 15 day stay limit. **Registration:** Entrance station. **Fee:** $12 a night for RV/tent site, $6 w/ Golden Access card. **Parking:** 2 car/1 RV & 1 car at each site, extra parking available.

FACILITIES

Number of Multipurpose Sites: 65. **Hookups:** Electric (30 amps), water. **Each Site:** Picnic table,

lantern hook, tent pad, grill, fire ring. **Dump Station:** Yes. **Laundry:** Yes. **Pay Phone:** Yes. **Rest Rooms and Showers:** Yes. **Fuel:** No. **Propane:** No. **Internal Roads:** Paved. **RV Service:** 30 mi. southeast in West Monroe. **Market:** 5mi. east in Farmerville. **Restaurant:** 5 mi. east in Farmerville. **General Store:** 5 mi. east in Farmerville. **Vending:** No. **Swimming Pool:** No. **Playground:** Yes. **Other:** Nature trails, tennis courts will be finished in the fall of 2002, fishing piers, volleyball court, horseshoe court. **Activities:** Nature trails, fishing clinic (call for more information), Easter egg hunt, hay rides, tennis starting in the fall of 2002, fishing, picnicking, volleyball, Horseshoe. **Nearby Attractions:** Kisatchie National Forest-Corney Lakes Recreation Area, Lincoln Parish Park, Georgia Pacific Wildlife Management Area, Handy Brake National Wildlife Refuge, Louisiana Purchase Gardens (Berstein Park). **Additional Information:** Union Parish Tourist Commission Bernice (318) 285-9333.

RESTRICTIONS

Pets: Leash. **Fires:** Fire ring only. **Alcoholic Beverages:** Allowed. **Vehicle Maximum Length:** Approx. 72 ft.

TO GET THERE

From Farmerville take LA 2 approx. 5 mi. west on the left side.

GARDNER
Kincaid Lake Recreation Area, Kisatchie National Forest

9912 Hwy. 28 West, Boyce 71409. T: (318) 793-9427; F: (318) 793-9430; www.southernregion.fs.fed.us/kisatchie.

🚐 ★★★★★   🏕 ★★★★★

Beauty: ★★★★★   Site Privacy: ★★★★
Spaciousness: ★★★★★   Quiet: ★★★★★
Security: ★★★★   Cleanliness: ★★★★★
Insect Control: ★★★   Facilities: ★★★★

The campgrounds at Kincaid Lake Recreation Area are gorgeous. Here, large sites are shaded by a variety of lovely southern yellow pine and other upland hardwoods. Dense growth provides privacy between most sites. All sites feature paved, back-in parking. Most of the sites don't have views of the water in summertime, but site 23 has a gorgeous water view in wintertime. We also like site 29, which is gargantuan. Kisatchie National Forest is not one contiguous tract. Rather, the forest consists of five land units in central and northern Louisiana. Kincaid Lake area includes large group and day use facilities. The man-made lake is stocked with sun perch, bass, and catfish. Security is very good here-gates are locked at night during the summer. Summers are extremely hot and humid in southern Louisiana. For the nicest weather, visit in spring or fall.

BASICS

Operated By: USDA Forest Service. **Open:** Year-round. **Site Assignment:** First come, first served, no reservations. **Registration:** Self reservation at fee box. **Fee:** $12 for regular sites, $16 for double sites. **Parking:** At sites, limit 2 vehicles.

FACILITIES

Number of Multipurpose Sites: 41. **Hookups:** Water, electric (30 amps). **Each Site:** Picnic table, lantern post, fire ring. **Dump Station:** Yes. **Laundry:** No. **Pay Phone:** No. **Rest Rooms and Showers:** Yes. **Fuel:** No. **Propane:** No. **Internal Roads:** Paved. **RV Service:** 13 mi. east in Alexandria. **Market:** 13 mi. east in Alexandria. **Restaurant:** 6 mi. east in Tunks. **General Store:** 5 mi. north in Gardner. **Vending:** No. **Swimming Pool:** No. **Playground:** No. **Other:** Picnic pavilions, trails, boat launch, boat dock, fishing pier, swimming beach. **Activities:** Picnicking, road biking, mountain biking, hiking, nature study, swimming, fishing, boating, automobile touring. **Nearby Attractions:** Louisiana Cowboy Town, Frogmore Cotton Plantation & Gins, Tunica-Biloxi Indian Museum, casinos, Hodges Gardens. **Additional Information:** Alexandria/Pineville Area Convention & Visitor's Bureau (800) 551-9546.

RESTRICTIONS

Pets: Leash only. **Fires:** Fire rings only. **Alcoholic Beverages:** Allowed. **Vehicle Maximum Length:** 65 ft.

TO GET THERE

From Alexandria, drive west in LA 28 for 13 mi. Turn left onto LA 121 and drive south for 0.5 mi. Turn right onto Forest Service Rd. 279 and drive south for 6 mi. Turn onto Forest Service Rd. 205, which leads to the campground.

GRAND ISLE
Grand Isle State Park

P.O. Box 741, Grand Isle 70358. T: (225) 787-2559.

🚐 ★★★   ⛺ ★★★★

Beauty: ★★★   Site Privacy: ★
Spaciousness: ★★★   Quiet: ★★★
Security: ★★★★★   Cleanliness: ★★★
Insect Control: ★★   Facilities: ★★★

Grand Isle's 400-foot fishing pier, ponds, and lagoons provide excellent fishing opportunities. Deep-sea fishing off of Grand Isle is extraordinary, and commercial guide services abound. Birdwatchers appreciate the variety of wetland habitats found at Grand Isle. The campgrounds at Grand Isle are smaller than average, with gravel parking for tent campers and grass parking for . All sites feature back-in parking. Sites are totally open, so come equipped with awnings, umbrellas, and sunscreen. Since all sites are bland, choose your site based on proximity to the beach. Tent campers have better choices; primitive camping is allowed on the beautiful beach. Security is excellent at Grand Isle. The park is excruciatingly remote and it's gated. Avoid Grand Isle in late summer, when it's horribly hot. Also, be sure to arm yourself with insect repellent.

BASICS

Operated By: Louisiana State Parks. **Open:** 7 days, all year. **Site Assignment:** No reservations for tent/beach sites. **Registration:** At camp office. **Fee:** $10 per night per vehicle, Golden Access 50% discount (V, MC, cash, money order, LA check). **Parking:** Sites plus overflow.

FACILITIES

Number of RV Sites: 100. **Number of Tent-Only Sites:** 50 (on beach only). **Hookups:** None. **Each Site:** Picnic table. **Dump Station:** Yes. **Laundry:** No. **Pay Phone:** Yes. **Rest Rooms and Showers:** Yes. **Fuel:** No. **Propane:** No. **Internal Roads:** Paved & gravel. **RV Service:** 100 mi. **Market:** 3 mi. **Restaurant:** 3 mi. **General Store:** 3 mi. **Vending:** In the Park. **Swimming Pool:** No. **Playground:** No. **Other:** Fishing piers, fish-cleaning station. **Activities:** Fishing, crabbing, birding, swimming, nature trail, gulf beaches. **Nearby Attractions:** Fishing rodeos in Grand Isle, charter boats, Wisner Wildlife Management Area, Fort Livingston, 2 hours to New Orleans. **Additional Information:** Grand Isle Tourist Commission (985) 787-2997.

RESTRICTIONS

Pets: On leash only. **Fires:** Small okay. **Alcoholic Beverages:** Okay, no glass containers. **Vehicle Maximum Length:** No limit.

TO GET THERE

From US 90 (New Orleans), take LA 1 south to Grand Isle, where Hwy.1 becomes Admiral Craik Dr. The State Park is on the far east end of the island.

HAMMOND

New Orleans/Hammond KOA Kampground

14154 Club Deluxe Rd., Hammond 70403. T: (504) 542-8094.

🚐 ★★★	🏕 ★★
Beauty: ★★★	Site Privacy: ★★
Spaciousness: ★★★	Quiet: ★★★
Security: ★★★	Cleanliness: ★★★★
Insect Control: ★★★	Facilities: ★★★★

KOA Hammond is much less frenetic than nearby Yogi Bear's and is preferable for couples and seniors who value peace and quiet. The pond is stocked with bass for catch and release fishing, and there's a pleasant walking path circling the pond. Either Baton Rouge or New Orleans can be reached in about an hour. The campground features three long rows of pull-through sites, plus a small tent area. Sites feature paved parking. Some are shady while others are totally open. Sites are average sized and none are very private. Sites along the lake, near the cabins, are picturesque and quiet. Stay away from sites 1–23, which are along the main road and tend to be noisy. Southern Louisiana is like a rice steamer in July and August. Visit in the spring or fall for the nicest weather. Security is fair at this suburban campground—there are no gates.

BASICS

Operated By: Surrell Family. **Open:** 7 days, all year. **Site Assignment:** Assigned based on hookups; reservations accepted, especially for holidays & festivals, credit card deposit; 24-hour cancellation for refund (7 days holidays). **Registration:** Camp store, 7 a.m.–7 p.m. **Fee:** $17 tent (dry), $23

electric (30 amps), $25 electric (50 amps), all fees for 2 people, $3 per extra adult, $2 ages 7–17, under 7 free. **Parking:** 1 per site plus overflow.

FACILITIES

Number of RV Sites: 60. **Number of Tent-Only Sites:** 4. **Hookups:** Water, electric (30, 50 amps), sewer. **Each Site:** Picnic table. **Dump Station:** No. **Laundry:** Yes. **Pay Phone:** Yes. **Rest Rooms and Showers:** Yes. **Fuel:** No. **Propane:** Yes. **Internal Roads:** Paved & gravel. **RV Service:** On call, 3 mi. **Market:** Yes. **Restaurant:** Next door. **General Store:** 3 mi. **Vending:** No. **Swimming Pool:** Yes. **Playground:** Yes. **Other:** Hot tub. **Activities:** Game room, pool table, movie rental, horseshoes, volleyball, basketball, paddle-boat rental, mini-golf, fishing, dog park. **Nearby Attractions:** Swamp tours, plantation tours, alligator farm, 45 mi. to New orleans, 40 mi. to Baton Rouge. **Additional Information:** Tangipahoa Parish Tourist Commission (504) 542-7520, New Orleans CVB (800) 672-6124.

RESTRICTIONS

Pets: On leash, except in dog park. **Fires:** Seasonal, limited. **Alcoholic Beverages:** Okay, no glass containers. **Vehicle Maximum Length:** 45 ft.

TO GET THERE

From I-12, take I-55 south to Exit 28, proceed to traffic light, turn left 0.75 mile to the campground.

HOMER

Lake Claiborne State Park

P.O. Box 246, Homer 71040. T: (888) 677-2524; F: (318) 927-2744; www.lastateparks.com; lakeclaiborne@crt.state.la.us.

🚐 ★★★★	🏕 ★★★★
Beauty: ★★★★★	Site Privacy: ★★★★
Spaciousness: ★★★★	Quiet: ★★★★
Security: ★★★★★	Cleanliness: ★★★★
Insect Control: ★★★	Facilities: ★★★★

This gorgeous park is situated on a peninsula jutting into massive Toledo Bend Reservoir. Across the reservoir is Texas' Sabine National Forest. At North Toledo Bend, recreation revolves around fishing for largemouth bass, catfish, and crappie. For landlubbers, there's a nature trail and an Olympic-sized swimming pool. Although the terrain consists of rolling hills, the campground is pretty flat. The beautiful campground is laid out in two loops containing huge sites. Sites are shaded by a variety of tree species dominated by pine. Privacy is provided by greenery between sites. All parking is paved, back-in style. The most private sites are 29–34. We also like sites 13 and 14, which have partial water views. Avoid North Toledo Bend on holiday weekends and during hot late summer. Otherwise, the campground rarely fills up, making it a good destination for an early summer weekend. Security is excellent at this remote park.

BASICS

Operated By: State of Louisiana, Dept. of Culture, Recreation & Tourism (877) 226-7652. **Open:** Year-round. **Site Assignment:** First come, first served, also reservations can be made w/ a V or MC by calling (877) 226-7652. No out of state checks allowed. If reservations are cancelled, the fee is one night's rental. Check-in time is 1 p.m. or later. Check-out time is 1 p.m. or earlier. Stay limit is 15 days. **Registration:** Entrance station. **Fee:** $12 per night for RV/tent sites. $6 w/ a Golden Access card. **Parking:** 2 vehicle parking at each site. Overflow parking is available.

FACILITIES

Number of Multipurpose Sites: 87. **Hookups:** Water, electric (30, 50 amps). **Each Site:** Picnic table, grill, fire ring, some have lantern hook, tent pad. **Dump Station:** Yes. **Laundry:** Yes. **Pay Phone:** Yes. **Rest Rooms and Showers:** Yes. **Fuel:** No. **Propane:** No. **Internal Roads:** Paved. **RV Service:** Approx. 20 mi. northeast in Homer. **Market:** Approx. 15 mi. northwest in Homer. **Restaurant:** Approx. 15 mi. northwest in Homer. **General Store:** Approx. 15 mi. northwest in Homer. **Vending:** No. **Swimming Pool:** No. **Playground:** Yes. **Other:** Group lodging, boat launch, fishing pier, primitive canoe camp sites available, nature trails. **Activities:** Guided/unguided hiking trails, fishing, boating of all kinds, waterskiing, nature-based programs. **Nearby Attractions:** Poverty Point State Historic Site, Lake Bistineau State Park, Lake D'Arbonne State Park, Historic Town of Homer, Lincoln Parish Park, Kisatchie National Forest-Caney Lakes Recreation Area, Caney Creek Lake State Park, Jackson Bienville Wildlife Management Area, Georgia Pacific Wildlife Management Area. **Additional Information:** Homer Chamber of Commerce.

RESTRICTIONS

Pets: Leash only. **Fires:** Ring only. **Alcoholic Beverages:** Allowed. **Vehicle Maximum Length:** 60 ft.

TO GET THERE

From the intersection of Hwy. 79 and Hwy. 146 in Homer, go southeast on Hwy. 146 for 7 mi. and the park entrance will be on the left.

INDEPENDENCE
Indian Creek

53013 West Fontana Rd., Independence 70443. T: (504) 878-6567.

🚐 ★★★	🅰 ★★★
Beauty: ★★★	Site Privacy: ★★★
Spaciousness: ★★★	Quiet: ★★★
Security: ★★★	Cleanliness: ★★★
Insect Control: ★★★	Facilities: ★★★

Indian Creek offers shady sites situated in numerous small sections. Though privacy varies, most sites are on the small side. All sites feature gravel parking. There are both back-in and pull-through sites. Our favorite sites are 86–91, small, wooded, pull-throughs. Families should ask for a site in the front of the park, near the playground, wash house, and other amenities. There's plenty to keep kids busy here, but we don't recommend Indian Creek as a vacation destination. It's better used as a convenient stop over. There are plenty of shops and restaurants nearby. Unfortunately, Indian Creek had an unpleasant smell while we were there. Stay away from southeastern Louisiana in late summer, when the heat and humidity are oppressive. Security is fair. There are no gates, but Indian Creek is in a quiet area.

BASICS

Operated By: Bob & Kathy Albright. **Open:** 7 days, all year. **Site Assignment:** First come, first served also reservations. **Registration:** Office in store, 9 a.m.–8 p.m. Sunday–Thursday, 9 a.m.–10 p.m. Friday & Saturday. **Fee:** Primitive $18.50 ($22 holidays), RV sites $24 ($27 holidays), $5 per extra person, max. 7 people. **Parking:** Sites plus overflow.

FACILITIES

Number of RV Sites: 184. **Number of Tent-Only Sites:** 100 (primitive). **Number of Multipurpose Sites:** 184 (RV sites). **Hookups:** Water, electric (30 amps), some sewer. **Each Site:** Picnic table, grills available. **Dump Station:** Yes. **Laundry:** Yes. **Pay Phone:** Yes. **Rest Rooms and Showers:** Yes. **Fuel:** No. **Propane:** Yes. **Internal Roads:** Gravel. **RV Service:** On call. **Market:** Yes. **Restaurant:** 5 mi. **General Store:** 10 mi. (Wal-Mart), 2 mi. (Piggly Wiggly). **Vending:** Beverages only. **Swimming Pool:** Yes. **Playground:** Yes (2). **Activities:** Fishing pond (catch & release), hiking & biking trails, basketball court, volleyball, horseshoes, paddle-boat & canoe rentals, scheduled activities on weekends. **Nearby Attractions:** Global Wildlife, swamp tours, alligator farm, Aquarium of the Americas, 55 mi. to New Orleans. **Additional Information:** Tangipahoa Parish Tourist Commission (504) 542-7520, New Orleans CVB (800) 672-6124.

RESTRICTIONS

Pets: On leash only. **Fires:** Okay. **Alcoholic Beverages:** Okay. **Vehicle Maximum Length:** 50 ft. **Other:** Quiet hours enforced.

TO GET THERE

From I-55, take Exit 41, go 1,000 feet west on Hwy. 40 to Fontana Rd. Turn left, campground is 1.5 mi. on the right.

KINDER

Grand Casino Coushatta Luxury RV Resort At Red Shoes Park

777 Coushatta Dr. P. O. Box 1510, Kinder 70648. T: (888) 867-8727; F: (337) 738-1201; www.gccoushatta.com; sigc.coushatta.com.

🚐 ★★★★   ⛺ n/a

Beauty: ★★★   Site Privacy: ★★
Spaciousness: ★★★   Quiet: ★★★★
Security: ★★★★   Cleanliness: ★★★★★
Insect Control: ★★★★   Facilities: ★★★★

The Coushatta Tribe of Louisiana run an extremely tidy campground on a flat piece of land behind their Grand Casino. The swimming pool and other facilities are spotless as well. The drawback here is the overly sanitized landscaping. There are no mature trees to break the park's visual monotony. The campground consists of two main areas, which flank a picturesque fishing pond. Sites are larger than average. Sites are neither shady nor private. Each site has paved parking, a paved patio, and a grassy plot. Most sites are pull-through style. Couples seeking solitude should try for lakeside sites 24–39. Families with children should score a site close to the pool. Security is very good. The park is gated 24-hours a day, but there is no fence around the campground. Avoid southern Louisiana in sticky, hot late summer. For the mildest weather, visit in spring or fall.

BASICS

Operated By: Grand Casino Coushatta. **Open:** Year-round. **Site Assignment:** First come, first served, also reservations can be held w/ any major credit card (888) 677-1400. Specific sites may not be reserved. If cancelled 24 hr. or more before the first reserved day then there is no fee. If cancelled within 24 hr. of expected arrival then the fee is the entire cost of using the items that were reserved. Check-in time is 12 p.m. or later. Check-out time is 2 p.m. or earlier. There is no stay limit. **Registration:** Main Lodge. **Fee:** $18.95 plus tax for weekends, $14.95 plus tax for weekdays. **Parking:** 2 vehicle parking at the site. Overflow parking is available.

FACILITIES

Number of RV Sites: 156. **Number of Tent-Only Sites:** 0. **Hookups:** Electric (30, 50 amps), water. **Each Site:** Fire ring, picnic table. **Dump Station:** Yes. **Laundry:** Yes. **Pay Phone:** Yes. **Rest Rooms and Showers:** Yes. **Fuel:** No. **Propane:** No. **Internal Roads:** Paved. **RV Service:** On call. **Market:** 7 mi. south in Kinder. **Restaurant:** 1 mi. **General Store:** 17 mi. north in Oakdale. **Vending:** Beverage & snack. **Swimming Pool:** Yes. **Playground:** Yes. **Other:** Internet hookup in the main lodge, pier, athletic courts, small group chalets. **Activities:** Volleyball, paddle boating, tennis, shuffleboard, Horse shoes, fishing, basketball. **Nearby Attractions:** Grand Casino. **Additional Information:** Avoyelles Commission of Tourism (800) 833-4195.

RESTRICTIONS

Pets: Leash. **Fires:** Fire ring that is located behind the main lodge (not 1 per site). **Alcoholic Beverages:** Allowed. **Vehicle Maximum Length:** No limit.

TO GET THERE

Get off I-10 onto Hwy. 165 (Exit 44) north. The park entrance is approx. 35 mi. north on the left side.

LAFAYETTE
KOA–Lafayette

Rte. 2 Box 261, Scott 70583. T: (337) 235-2739; F: (337) 235-2739; www.koa.com.

🚐 ★★★　　　　　　　Ⓐ ★★

Beauty: ★★★　　　　　Site Privacy: ★★
Spaciousness: ★★★　　Quiet: ★★
Security: ★★★　　　　　Cleanliness: ★★★★
Insect Control: ★★★　　Facilities: ★★★

KOA is a good place to stay while touring Lafayette, the heart of Cajun country. This culturally unique region offers excellent restaurants, gorgeous historic homes, and fabulous outdoor recreation. This KOA offers a nightly 20-minute video and cassette-tape tours about the area. The campground is laid out in rows of long narrow sites. Most sites offer pull-through parking, though some offer back-in. Sites are average sized, with gravel parking and concrete patios. Most sites have no grass. There are shady and open sites. Privacy is minimal. This KOA is next to I-10, making many sites way too noisy for our tastes. Numbers 117–124 and 9–16, quieter sites in the back of the park, enjoy a picturesque view of the fishing pond. Avoid southern Louisiana in muggy July and August. Lafayette is a good winter destination. This suburban park has no gates, but the neighborhood is fine.

BASICS
Operated By: Owned by the Alleman Family. **Open:** Year-round. **Site Assignment:** Reservations recommended (800) 562-0809. D, MC, & V are accepted. To receive refund of deposit, cancellation must be made 24 hours in advance. Check in & check out time is 12 noon. There is no stay limit. **Registration:** Main office. **Fee:** From $26–$28 per night plus tax. **Parking:** There is no parking limit. Overflow parking is available.

FACILITIES
Number of RV Sites: 200. **Number of Tent-Only Sites:** 15. **Hookups:** Electric (30, 50 amps), water, sewer, Internet available but not at each site. **Each Site:** Picnic table, fire ring, grill (some sites), & tent pads (some sites). **Dump Station:** Yes. **Laundry:** Yes. **Pay Phone:** Yes. **Rest Rooms and Showers:** Yes. **Fuel:** No. **Propane:** Yes. **Internal Roads:** Paved. **RV Service:** On call. **Market:** 1 mi. **Restaurant:** 1 mi. **General Store:** 9 mi. east in Lafayette. **Vending:** Beverages only. **Swimming**

Pool: Yes. **Playground:** Yes. **Other:** Group lodging, athletic field, arcade, fishing pier, mini-golf course. **Activities:** Fishing, mini-golf, basketball, volleyball, paddle boats, arcade games. **Nearby Attractions:** Atchafalaya Basin, Acadian Village & Vermillionville, Art Museum, Planetarium, St. John's Cathedral, Evangeline Downs Horse Racing, Jungle Gardens, Saint Martinville. **Additional Information:** Acadia Parish Convention & Visitors Commission.

RESTRICTIONS
Pets: Leash only. **Fires:** Fire ring only. **Alcoholic Beverages:** Allowed. **Vehicle Maximum Length:** 75 ft.

TO GET THERE
From I-10 going west, take Exit 97, go left over the overpass. Turn onto Apollo Rd., the first road on the right.

LAKE CHARLES
Sam Houston Jones

107 Sutherland Rd., Lake Charles 70611. T: (888) 677-7264; www.lastateparks.com; samhouston@crt.state.la.us.

🚐 ★★★★　　　　　　Ⓐ ★★★★

Beauty: ★★★★　　　　Site Privacy: ★★★
Spaciousness: ★★★★　Quiet: ★★★★
Security: ★★★★　　　　Cleanliness: ★★★★
Insect Control: ★★★　　Facilities: ★★★

This suburban park is nestled into the West Fork of the Calcasieu River, where it meets the Houston River. Park boat launches provide access to the Gulf of Mexico as well as the river system. Within the park, a series of lagoons provides refuge for alligators, ducks, and geese. Known as one of the finest bird-watching areas in the state, migratory waterfowl are plentiful here in the spring. There are two camping areas at Sam Houston Jones: Area 1 includes pretty sites lining a lagoon-tent sites 16–19 and RV sites 12–21 are especially attractive. Area 2 may be a better choice for families—sites 35 and 37 are near the playground. All sites are shaded by a variety of trees, including cypress in low-lying areas. There are back-in and pull-through sites. Some sites offer gravel parking, others offer paved. Sites are larger than average, but not very private. Gates lock at night, making security good. Avoid muggy late summer in southern Louisiana.

BASICS

Operated By: State of Louisiana Dept. of Culture, Recreation, & Tourism. **Open:** Year-round. **Site Assignment:** Reservations as well as first come, first served. Reservations can be held w/ V or MC (888) 677-1400. Check in time is 2 p.m. Check out time is 1 p.m. If cancelled 15 or more days in advance, fee is $10. If cancelled 14 or less before the first reserved day, fee is one night's rent of all reserved items; Stay limit is 15 days. **Registration:** Entrance station. **Fee:** $12 for both RV & tent sites, $6 w/ a Gold Access card. **Parking:** 2 car parking at site, overflow parking lot.

FACILITIES

Number of RV Sites: 0. **Number of Tent-Only Sites:** 19. **Number of Multipurpose Sites:** 62. **Hookups:** Electric (20, 30 amps), water; 20 RV sites w/ sewer electric & water. **Each Site:** Fire ring, tent pad, some sites have picnic tables. **Dump Station:** Yes. **Laundry:** No. **Pay Phone:** Yes. **Rest Rooms and Showers:** Yes. **Fuel:** No. **Propane:** No. **Internal Roads:** Paved. **RV Service:** Approx. 15 mi. in West Lake. **Market:** 10 mi. north in Moss Bluff. **Restaurant:** 10 mi. north in Moss Bluff. **General Store:** 10 mi. north in Moss Bluff. **Vending:** No. **Swimming Pool:** No. **Playground:** Yes. **Other:** Group lodge, boat launch, nature trails. **Activities:** Boating, hiking, children's weekend nature activities, picnicking, fishing. **Nearby Attractions:** Creole Nature Trail National Scenic Byway, Sabine National Wildlife Refuge, Cameron Prairie National Wildlife Refuge, Lacassine National Wildlife Refuge, Rockefeller Wildlife Refuge. **Additional Information:** Southwest Louisiana/Lake Charles CVB (800) 456-SWLA.

RESTRICTIONS

Pets: On leash. **Fires:** Fire ring only. **Alcoholic Beverages:** Allowed. **Vehicle Maximum Length:** No limit.

TO GET THERE

From I-10, take Exit No. 33 in Lake Charles. Go north on Hwy. 171. At the first light in Moss bluff take a left onto 378. Take a right onto Sam Houston Jones Pkwy.

MADISONVILLE

Fairview-Riverside State Park

P.O. Box 856, Madisonville 70447. T: (504) 845-3318 or (888) 677-3247; www.crt.state.la.us.

 ★★★   ★★★

Beauty: ★★★★	Site Privacy: ★★★
Spaciousness: ★★★	Quiet: ★★★
Security: ★★★	Cleanliness: ★★★
Insect Control: ★★★	Facilities: ★★★

The nice-looking campground at Fairview-Riverside offers mid-sized sites shaded by moss-laden oaks and other hardwoods. Sites are mid-sized, and there is little foliage to provide privacy between sites. All parking is paved, back-in style. For shade, we like sites near the front of the campground. Popular sites in the back enjoy river views. Fairview-Riverside is an elegant little park nestled into a bend in the Tchefuncte River. Fishing, crabbing, and boating are favorite pastimes here. The historic Otis House (ca. 1880) serves as an elegant reminder of Frank Otis, who, upon his death, donated the park's land to the state in 1961. When we arrived, we were greeted by one of the park's lovely peacocks. Avoid southeastern Louisiana in late summer, when heat and humidity are unbearable. Security is fair at this suburban park; the entrance is gated, but there is no fence around the park.

BASICS

Operated By: Louisiana State Parks. **Open:** 7 days, all year. **Site Assignment:** First come, first served. **Registration:** Park entrance, 6 a.m.–9 p.m. Sunday-Thursday, 6 a.m.–10 p.m. Friday & Saturday. **Fee:** $10 tent, $12 improved; max. 6 people, Golden Access 50% discount. **Parking:** Sites plus parking areas.

FACILITIES

Number of RV Sites: 81. **Number of Tent-Only Sites:** 20. **Number of Multipurpose Sites:** 81 (RV sites). **Hookups:** Water, electric (20, 30, 50 amps). **Each Site:** Picnic table, grill, fire ring, lantern poles on tent sites. **Dump Station:** Yes. **Laundry:** Yes. **Pay Phone:** Yes. **Rest Rooms and Showers:** Yes. **Fuel:** 0.5 mi. **Propane:** No. **Internal Roads:** Paved. **RV Service:** 30 mi. **Market:** 3 mi. **Restaurant:** 1 mi. **General Store:** 10 mi. **Vending:** No. **Swimming Pool:** No. **Playground:** Yes. **Other:** Boat launch. **Activities:** Fishing, skiing, & water sports, rental pavilions, Otis House Museum, walking trail. **Nearby Attractions:** Fontainebleau State Park, Fort Pike State Commemorative Area, Tammany Trace trail for bicycling, hiking, horseback riding, New Orleans. **Additional Information:** New Orleans CVB (800) 672-6124, Slidell CVB (504) 646-6426.

Pets: On leash only. **Fires:** In fire rings, grills only. **Alcoholic Beverages:** Okay. **Vehicle Maximum Length:** No limit. **Other:** 15-day max. stay.

TO GET THERE

From the east, take I-12 Exit 59 at Mandeville (from the west Exit 57). Take Hwy. 190 south to Hwy. 22. Go west 5 mi., the park is on the right. From New Orleans, take the Causeway/ Hwy. 190 north to Hwy. 22.

MANDEVILLE
Fontainebleau State Park

P.O. Box 8925, Mandeville 70470-8925. T: (504) 624-4443 or (888) 677-3668; www.crt.state.la.us.

🚐 ★★★★   ⛺ ★★★★

Beauty: ★★★★	Site Privacy: ★★★★
Spaciousness: ★★★★★	Quiet: ★★★★
Security: ★★★★	Cleanliness: ★★★★
Insect Control: ★★★	Facilities: ★★★

Built on a former sugar plantation, Fountainebleau harbors the ruins of an 1829 sugar mill. The park is situated on Lake Ponchartrain, between Bayou Castine and Cane Bayou. Fishermen may try their luck on the lakeshore or on a two-acre brackish pond. The Tammany Trace, an 18-mile multi-use "rail to trail" conversion, is also near the park. The campgrounds at Fountainebleau feature many attractive sites and a few beautiful sites. There are two main areas, "Improved" and "Unimproved." In the improved area, there are huge pull-through sites with refreshing shade cover, including loblolly pine. Dense foliage provides privacy between some sites. The unimproved area contains more hardwoods, such as sweet gum and live oak, and is preferable for tent campers. When we visited Fountainebleau, they had been awarded $9 million for park renovations over the next three years. The park plans to build additional camping facilities. Security is very good at this suburban park. Gates are locked at night. Avoid southern Louisiana in boiling-hot late summer.

BASICS

Operated By: Louisiana State Parks. **Open:** 7 days, all year. **Site Assignment:** First come, first served. **Registration:** Ranger station, 7 a.m.–9 p.m. Sunday–Thursday, 7 a.m.–10 p.m. Friday & Saturday.

Fee: $10 (no hookups), $12 water & electric; Golden Access $6 (cash, LA check, V, MC). **Parking:** Sites plus lots.

FACILITIES

Number of RV Sites: 132. **Number of Tent-Only Sites:** 200 undesignated primitive sites. **Number of Multipurpose Sites:** 132 (RV sites). **Hookups:** Water, electric (most 30, some 50 amps). **Each Site:** Picnic table (all developed sites, most primitive), grill or fire ring (all developed sites, some primitive). **Dump Station:** Yes. **Laundry:** Yes. **Pay Phone:** Yes. **Rest Rooms and Showers:** Yes. **Fuel:** No. **Propane:** No. **Internal Roads:** Paved. **RV Service:** In Mandeville. **Market:** 2.5 mi. in Mandeville. **Restaurant:** 2.5 mi. in Mandeville. **General Store:** 4 mi. in Mandeville. **Vending:** Beverages only. **Swimming Pool:** Yes. **Playground:** Yes. **Other:** Sailboat launch (shallow). **Activities:** Beach on Lake Ponchartrain, fishing pond, bicycle trail, nature trail, hiking trail, boardwalk, interpretive Ranger programs weekends. **Nearby Attractions:** Swamp tours, antique shopping in Ponchatoula, Tammany Trace bicycling & equestrian trails, Pearl River Wildlife Management Area, New Orleans. **Additional Information:** New Orleans CVB (800) 672-6124.

Pets: On leash only. **Fires:** At sites only. **Alcoholic Beverages:** Okay. **Vehicle Maximum Length:** No limit. **Other:** 15-day max. stay, then 7 days out.

TO GET THERE

From New Orleans, take the Causeway north, across Lake Ponchartrain, then take the first exit onto US 190 East. The park is on the right in 6 mi. From I-12, take Exit 65, then drive 3.5 mi. south to the traffic light at US 190. Turn left and the park is on the right in 2.5 mi.

MARKSVILLE
Paragon RV Resort

124 Earl J. Barbry Sr. Blvd., Marksville 71351. T: (800) 578-7275; www.paragoncasiresort.com.

🚐 ★★★   ⛺ ★★★

Beauty: ★★	Site Privacy: ★★
Spaciousness: ★★★	Quiet: ★★★
Security: ★★★	Cleanliness: ★★★★
Insect Control: ★★★★	Facilities: ★★★

Paragon Casino RV Resort is extremely tidy and just as bland. The minimal landscaping is well manicured. The campground consists of 14 rows of pull-through sites plus a few small back-in areas. There are a few saplings scattered around the campground, but no shade or mature trees. All parking is paved. Sites are all the same, so chose your site based on proximity to the pool and other facilities. Paragon offers the usual casino fare, including nice swimming pools and a 24-hour shuttle to and from the campground. Nearby, you can learn about native Tunica-Biloxi history and culture at the Indian Center and Museum and the Marksville State Pre-Historic Indian Park. Avoid southern Louisiana in steamy late summer. Take care of your valuables; Paragon has no gates.

BASICS

Operated By: Paragon Casino RV Resort. **Open:** Year-round. **Site Assignment:** Reservation recommended, (800) 946-1946. All major credit cards are accepted. If cancelled 48 hrs. in advance there is no penalty. If cancelled within 48 hrs. of the expected arrival date then the penalty is the fee for one night's stay. Check-in time is 11 p.m. Check-out time is 12 noon. There is a 2-week stay limit. **Registration:** RV Lodge. **Fee:** $12.95 per night for full hookups. **Parking:** 2 vehicles at each site, overflow parking is available.

FACILITIES

Number of RV Sites: 185. **Number of Tent-Only Sites:** 0. **Hookups:** Sewer, water cable, & electric (20, 30, 50 amps). **Each Site:** Picnic table. **Dump Station:** Yes. **Laundry:** Yes. **Pay Phone:** Yes. **Rest Rooms and Showers:** Yes. **Fuel:** No. **Propane:** No. **Internal Roads:** Paved. **RV Service:** 30 mi. northwest in Alexandria. **Market:** 1 mi. **Restaurant:** 1 mi. **General Store:** 1 mi. **Vending:** Beverage & snack. **Swimming Pool:** Yes. **Playground:** Yes. **Other:** Pool table, volleyball court, shuffleboard, group lodging, Casino. **Activities:** Pool, shuffleboard, horseshoes, volleyball. **Nearby Attractions:** Paragon Casino. **Additional Information:** Avoyelles Commission of Tourism (800) 833-4195.

RESTRICTIONS

Pets: Leash only. **Fires:** No fire at site unless in a grill (bring your own). **Alcoholic Beverages:** Allowed. **Vehicle Maximum Length:** 75 ft.

TO GET THERE

From 49 exit onto Hwy. 1 going south. Travel approx. 35 mi. and the entrance to the park is on the left behind the casino.

MINDEN

Caney Lakes Recreation Area, Kisatchie National Forest

3288 Hwy. 795, Homer 71040. T: (318) 927-2061; F: (318) 927-6520; www.southernregion.fs.fed.us/kisatchie.

🚐 ★★★★　　　　　▲ ★★★★

Beauty: ★★★★★　　　Site Privacy: ★★★★★
Spaciousness: ★★★★★　Quiet: ★★★★★
Security: ★★★★　　　　Cleanliness: ★★★★
Insect Control: ★★★　　Facilities: ★★★

The beautiful campground at Caney Lakes Recreation Area includes giant sites with paved, back-in parking. Sites are partially shaded by loblolly and short leaf pine and other species. However, growth is not too thick, a blessing which allows campers to enjoy gorgeous water views. On the Turtle Slide tent loop, we especially like waterfront sites 10, 11, 13, and 15. On the Beaver Dam RV loop, we like waterfront sites 10–15. The Caney Lakes area consists of a number of lakes offering excellent fishing for bass, crappie, bluegill, sand bass, and catfish. Boat launches and docks are available at nearby day-use areas. There is also a seven-mile hiking trail. The area is popular in autumn, when its rolling hills are resplendent with color. Visit on weekdays in summer and fall. Security is very good at Caney-the campground is remote and gated.

BASICS

Operated By: Federal Government Caney Ranger District. **Open:** Year-round. **Site Assignment:** First come, first served. **Registration:** Self register at fee box. **Fee:** $10 for RV sites, $5 for tent sites. **Parking:** At sites.

FACILITIES

Number of RV Sites: 26. **Number of Tent-Only Sites:** 21. **Hookups:** Water, electric. **Each Site:** Picnic table, fire ring, grill, tent pads at tent sites. **Dump Station:** Yes. **Laundry:** No. **Pay Phone:** Yes. **Rest Rooms and Showers:** Yes. **Fuel:** No. **Propane:** No. **Internal Roads:** Paved. **RV Service:** 7 mi. south in Minden. **Market:** 7 mi. south in Minden. **Restaurant:** 7 mi. south in Minden. **General Store:** 7 mi. south in Minden. **Vending:** No. **Swimming Pool:** No. **Playground:** No. **Other:** Hiking trails, volleyball net, boat ramp, dock, swimming beach, picnic area. **Activities:** Hiking, fishing, boating, waterskiing, picnicking. **Nearby**

Attractions: Inquire at campground. **Additional Information:** Minden Chamber of Commerce.

RESTRICTIONS

Pets: Leash only. **Fires:** Yes. **Alcoholic Beverages:** Allowed. **Vehicle Maximum Length:** 50 ft.

TO GET THERE

From Shreveport or Monroe take the Minden/ Dubberly Exit. Turn left onto Hwy. 79. Keep straight through the traffic light. Follow the signs.

RIVER RIDGE

KOA–New Orleans West

11129 Jefferson Hwy., River Ridge 70123. T: (504) 467-1792; www.koa.com; nowestkoa@comm.net.

🚐 ★★★   ▲ ★★

Beauty: ★★★   Site Privacy: ★★
Spaciousness: ★★★   Quiet: ★★★★
Security: ★★★   Cleanliness: ★★★★
Insect Control: ★★★   Facilities: ★★

Laid out in three long rows of back-in sites plus another small area, this KOA is not the most attractive one we've seen. The roads consist of patchy black-top, red asphalt, and gravel. Most sites have a wee bit of shade and a wee bit of grass All parking is back-in style. Though RV parking is paved, car parking is gravel. Sites are mid-sized, with little privacy. The shadiest sites, 9–105, line an ugly corrugated metal fence. Avoid sites 46–50, which are unattractive. Three words save this place: location, location, location. The campground is about 15 miles from the French Quarter. There are plenty of restaurants and shops in River Ridge and nearby Kenner. Visit the New Orleans area in spring or fall for the nicest weather. Avoid Mardi Gras and other festival weekends if you value serenity. Always make advance reservations for this KOA.

BASICS

Operated By: The Fedderman Family. **Open:** 7 days a week, all year. **Site Assignment:** Reservations recommended, call (800) 562-5110; first come, first served; must use a credit card to guarantee spot (MC, V, AE, D, or cash accepted); will honor requests for specific sites, if possible. **Registration:** At office, also night registration desk. **Fee:** $22–$32. **Parking:** One vehicle per site.

FACILITIES

Number of RV Sites: 97. **Number of Tent-Only Sites:** 6. **Hookups:** Electric, water, most sewer, most cable. **Each Site:** Picnic table. **Dump Station:** Yes. **Laundry:** Yes. **Pay Phone:** Yes. **Rest Rooms and Showers:** Yes. **Fuel:** No. **Propane:** Yes. **Internal Roads:** Paved. **RV Service:** On call. **Market:** On site. **Restaurant:** 0.25 mi. **General Store:** 1.25 mi. **Vending:** Beverages. **Swimming Pool:** Yes. **Playground:** Yes. **Other:** Shuttle to French Quarter, rental cars. **Activities:** Tour service. **Nearby Attractions:** French Quarter, Audubon Zoo & Botanical Gardens, Aquarium of the Americas, Paddlewheel Boats, Superdome, National D-Day Museum, Destrehon Plantation, Rivertown. **Additional Information:** New Orleans CVB (504) 246-5666.

RESTRICTIONS

Pets: On leash only. **Fires:** Not allowed. **Alcoholic Beverages:** At site only. **Vehicle Maximum Length:** 45 ft.

TO GET THERE

Take I-10 to Exit 223A, Williams Blvd. Go south 3 mi. to the dead end at the levy (3rd St. and Kenner) and turn left. The campground is 0.75 mi. ahead on the left.

ROBERT

Yogi Bear's Jellystone Park

P.O. Box 519, Robert 70455. T: (985) 542-1507; F: (985) 345-6629; yogi121@charter.net.

🚐 ★★★   ▲ ★★★

Beauty: ★★★   Site Privacy: ★★
Spaciousness: ★★★   Quiet: ★★
Security: ★★★   Cleanliness: ★★★
Insect Control: ★★★   Facilities: ★★★★

Families with small children wishing to tour New Orleans should consider Yogi Bear's. Though Yogi's carnival-like atmosphere is demanding, the children will love it here. There are excellent play facilities and non-stop activities, including crafts, hayrides, dance contests, and on and on. The park is reasonably attractive, with camping areas surrounding a long narrow fishing lake. Most sites offer gravel back-in parking, though there are also plenty of pull-throughs. Site size is average and each site has a cement patio. Most sites are partially shady, but there is little foliage to provide privacy between sites. We like area P, which has shady sites and its own pool, wash house, playground, and clubhouse. Back-in sites 80–109 are also shady. Yogi stays busy all summer. Visit during the week in the spring or fall to avoid hot weather and swarms of people. Security is poor at this suburban park-there are no gates.

BASICS

Operated By: Mr. Camper Inc. **Open:** Year-round. **Site Assignment:** Reserve w/ cash, in-state checks, V, MC, D (985) 542-1507; first come first served also. If cancelled 24 hours or more before the first reserved day, fee is $10 & the remaining cost for one night (after $10 is subtracted) is held in the form of a rain check. If cancelled 24 hours or less before the time of expected arrival, the fee is $35. There is no stay limit. **Registration:** Ranger's Station. **Fee:** $39 per night for holidays. Mar.–Nov. weekends, & weekdays Jun.–Aug. are $35 per night. Weekdays Mar.–May, & Sep.–Nov. $28 per night. Dec.–Feb. $22 a night. **Parking:** 2 cars per site plus an overflow parking lot.

FACILITIES

Number of Multipurpose Sites: 374. **Hookups:** Water & electric (20, 30 amps), 320 sites w/ sewer hookup. **Each Site:** Tent pad, picnic table. **Dump Station:** Yes. **Laundry:** Yes. **Pay Phone:** Yes. **Rest Rooms and Showers:** Yes. **Fuel:** No. **Propane:** Yes. **Internal Roads:** Slag. **RV Service:** On call. **Market:** 1 mi. **Restaurant:** 1 mi. **General Store:** 10 mi. in Hammond West. **Vending:** Beverage only. **Swimming Pool:** Yes. **Playground:** Yes. **Other:** Group lodging, basketball courts, volleyball nets, baseball field. **Activities:** Rental Boats, horseshoe, volleyball, nature trails, baseball field, fishing, hay rides, arts & crafts, scavenger hunt, hiking trails, canoe races. **Nearby Attractions:** Swamp & Nature walk in Cypress Swamp, shopping at Prime Outlets Gulfport, Old Mandeville Historic & Shopping District. **Additional Information:** Tangipahoa Parish Tourist Commission, (800) 542-7520.

RESTRICTIONS

Pets: Leash. **Fires:** Not allowed. **Alcoholic Beverages:** Allowed. **Vehicle Maximum Length:** 40 ft. **Other:** No motorboats allowed.

TO GET THERE

From interstate 12, get off on Exit 47 and go 3 mi. north to entrance, which will be on the right.

SHREVEPORT

KOA–Shreveport-Bossier City

6510 West 70th St., Shreveport 71129. T: (318) 678-1010.

🚐 ★★★   ⛺ ★★

Beauty: ★★★   Site Privacy: ★★
Spaciousness: ★★   Quiet: ★★★
Security: ★★   Cleanliness: ★★★
Insect Control: ★★★   Facilities: ★★

This KOA is laid out in six rows of pull-through sites and three rows of back-in sites. Sites are on the small side of average, and are long and narrow. Most parking is on grass, though a few sites have paved pads. Each site has a concrete picnic area. A few sites are by shaded pine trees, but most sites are completely open. Privacy is nil, as there is no greenery between sites. The quietest sites, 61–78, are in the back of the park, away from the I-20 access road. KOA is located in a western suburb of Shreveport, and is convenient to plenty of restaurants, shops, and casinos. Security is fair, as there is no gate. For the nicest weather, visit the Shreveport-Bossier area in the spring or fall.

BASICS

Operated By: Byron Bonewell. **Open:** Year-round. **Site Assignment:** First come, first served also reservations. **Registration:** Reservations (800) 562-1232, office. **Fee:** $26.10–$16.20 (plus tax). **Parking:** 2 vehicle parking per site.

FACILITIES

Number of RV Sites: 78. **Number of Tent-Only Sites:** 3. **Hookups:** Electric (20, 30, 50 amps), cable, sewer, water. **Each Site:** Water, electric, trash pick up, & picnic tables. **Dump Station:** Yes. **Laundry:** Yes. **Pay Phone:** Yes. **Rest Rooms and Showers:** Yes. **Fuel:** No. **Propane:** Yes. **Internal Roads:** Paved & gravel. **RV Service:** No. **Market:** Less than one mi. **Restaurant:** Less than one mi. **General Store:** Less than 1 mi. **Vending:** No. **Swimming Pool:** Yes. **Playground:** Yes. **Other:** Basketball court, volleyball court, adult lounge, rec hall, hot tub. **Activities:** Basketball, volleyball, fishing. **Nearby Attractions:** The American Rose Center, LA Downs Horse Racing, Riverboat Gambling, Cross Lake, Water Town & Hamel's Amusement Park. **Additional Information:** Bossier/Shreveport Convention & Tourist Bureau.

RESTRICTIONS

Pets: Leash only. **Fires:** No. **Alcoholic Beverages:** Not allowed. **Vehicle Maximum Length:** 30 ft.

TO GET THERE

From I-20, take Exit 10 and go south on Pines Rd. Turn right onto West 70th St.

SPRINGFIELD
Tickfaw State Park

27225 Patterson Rd., Springfield 70462-8906. T: (225) 294-5020 or (877) 226-7652 for reservations.

🚐 ★★★★   ⛺ ★★★★

Beauty: ★★★★★   Site Privacy: ★★★★
Spaciousness: ★★★★★   Quiet: ★★★★★
Security: ★★★★★   Cleanliness: ★★★★
Insect Control: ★★★   Facilities: ★★★

Bordered on the southwest side by the Tickfaw River, this state park is popular with canoeists. Lucky visitors spot snowy egrets and great blue herons along the river. Convenient to both Baton Rouge and New Orleans, Tickfaw is extremely popular with Louisiana residents. In the area, folks enjoy pick-your-own strawberry, blackberry, and blueberry farms. The campground features huge, beautiful RV sites with varying degrees of shade. All parking is paved, back-in style, with extremely long pads. Shade and privacy vary from site to site. The tent camping area at Tickfaw is fabulous, with shady woods and a little foliage between most sites. We especially liked tent sites 37, 39, 41, 43, and 47. The wash houses at Tickfaw are also nice–they're spacious and brand new. Avoid southern Louisiana when heat and humidity become oppressive in late summer. Security is excellent at Tickfaw. The park is gated and remote.

BASICS

Operated By: Louisiana State Parks. **Open:** 7 days, all year. **Site Assignment:** First come, first served also reservations. **Registration:** Fee station at park entrance, 7 a.m.–9 p.m. Sunday–Thursday, 7 a.m.–10 p.m. Friday & Saturday. **Fee:** $10 (tent), $12 (electric & water), Golden Access 50% off. **Parking:** Sites plus overflow.

FACILITIES

Number of RV Sites: 30. **Number of Tent-Only Sites:** 20. **Number of Multipurpose Sites:** 30 (RV sites, but no tent pads). **Hookups:** Water, electric (RV only, 20, 30, or 50 amps). **Each Site:** Picnic table, grill/fire ring, lantern post, tent pad (tent sites only). **Dump Station:** Yes. **Laundry:** Yes. **Pay Phone:** Yes. **Rest Rooms and Showers:** Yes. **Fuel:** No. **Propane:** No. **Internal Roads:** Paved. **RV Service:** Yes. **Market:** 4 mi. **Restaurant:** 20 minutes to Hammond. **General Store:** 20 min. to Hammond. **Vending:** Yes. **Swimming Pool:** No. **Playground:** (building one currently). **Activities:** Canoe rentals, fishing, elevated boardwalks, Nature Center w/ guided hikes & childrens' activities, hiking trails. **Nearby Attractions:** Turtle & alligator tours, Ponchatoula Historic District, Fairview-Riverside State Park, Global Wildlife Park, 35 mi. to Baton Rouge, 50 mi. to New Orleans. **Additional Information:** Livingston Parish Tourist Commission, New Orleans CVB (800) 672-6124.

RESTRICTIONS

Pets: No, except in campers. **Fires:** In sites, rings only (firewood from ground only, no cutting). **Alcoholic Beverages:** Okay. **Vehicle Maximum Length:** Varies. **Other:** Speed limit enforced, rangers always on duty.

TO GET THERE

From I-12, take Exit 32 Albany/Springfield, then go south on LA Hwy. 43 for 2 mi., merge w/ LA Hwy. 42, and go one more mile to the center of Springfield. At the only traffic light, turn right (west) on LA Hwy. 1037, and go 6 mi. to Patterson Rd. (from Woodland Baptist Church). Turn left (south) 1.2 mi. to the park entrance.

ST. JOSEPH
Lake Bruin State Park

Rte. 1 Box 183, St. Joseph 71366. T: (318) 766-3530; www.crt.state.la.us.

🚐 ★★★★   ⛺ ★★★★

Beauty: ★★★★★   Site Privacy: ★★★
Spaciousness: ★★★   Quiet: ★★★★
Security: ★★★★   Cleanliness: ★★★★
Insect Control: ★★   Facilities: ★★★★

The pretty campground at this small state park is a real treat. Campers enjoy a view of Lake Bruin, an oxbow lake, formerly part of the Mississippi River. Fishing is excellent here—launches, docks, and three piers support fishermen in their quest for crappie, bluegill, and largemouth bass. The lakeshore is lined with cypress trees, and the sunset over the lake is absolutely gorgeous. The campground is laid out in two areas, each with its own bathhouse. Sites are not outstanding in size or other features. However, the views of Lake Bruin are outstanding. Sumptuous lakefront campsites include numbers 1–20. All sites offer paved back-in style parking. Elegant moss-covered oaks shade campsites, but provide little privacy. Lake Bruin State Park is remote and gated, making it extra secure. Visit in spring or fall for the best weather and the best bass fishin'.

BASICS

Operated By: Louisiana State Parks. **Open:** 7 days, all year. **Site Assignment:** First come, first served. **Registration:** Park entrance, 6 a.m.–9 p.m. Sunday–Thursday, 6 a.m.–10 p.m. Friday & Saturday. **Fee:** $12 any site, Golden Access 50% price (cash, LA check, V, MC). **Parking:** Sites plus overflow.

FACILITIES

Number of RV Sites: 25. **Number of Tent-Only Sites:**. **Number of Multipurpose Sites:** 25 (all sites multipurpose). **Hookups:** Water, electric (5 amps). **Each Site:** Picnic table, grill, fire ring. **Dump Station:** Yes. **Laundry:** Yes. **Pay Phone:** Yes. **Rest Rooms and Showers:** Yes. **Fuel:** No. **Propane:** No. **Internal Roads:** Paved. **RV Service:** 90 mi. in Monroe. **Market:** 3 mi. in St. Joseph. **Restaurant:** 3 mi. in St. Joseph. **General Store:** 45 mi. in Winnsboro. **Vending:** No. **Swimming Pool:** No. **Playground:** Yes. **Other:** Boat launch. **Activities:** Lake swimming, fishing (boat or pier). **Nearby Attractions:** Winter Quarters Commemorative area & Plantation Home, Natchez Trace, Vicksburg casinos, & National Military Park. **Additional Information:** St. Joseph Mayor's Office (318) 766-3713.

RESTRICTIONS

Pets: On leash only. **Fires:** In sites, rings only. **Alcoholic Beverages:** Okay. **Vehicle Maximum Length:** 45 ft.

TO GET THERE

From I-20, take US 65 south to LA 128. Turn left (east), then at LA 606 turn left (north). Turn right on LA 604, campground is on the left. From the south, take US 65 north and turn right (east) on LA 128.

ST. JOSEPH
Shiloh's Lake Bruin

Rte. 1 Box 40, Newellton 71357. T: (318) 766-3334.

🚐 ★★★   ⛺ ★★★

Beauty: ★★★	Site Privacy: ★★
Spaciousness: ★★★	Quiet: ★★★
Security: ★★★	Cleanliness: ★★★
Insect Control: ★★★	Facilities: ★★★

This private campground gives its members first priority, so call for reservations. Shiloh's offers sites right on the shore of Lake Bruin, an oxbow lake known for its lovely cypress-lined shores and populations of crappie, bluegill, and largemouth bass. The campground at Shiloh's is not as spectacular as the lake. Due to the flat terrain, you can see the water from most sites. Nonetheless, we recommend lakefront sites. Sites are average sized, with pull-through gravel parking. Patches of grass and weeds poke up through the gravel at many sites. Most sites enjoy shady pine and oak trees, but there is little growth to provide privacy buffers between sites. Visit Shiloh's in spring and early summer for the best weather and bass fishing. Avoid this area in late summer when heat and humidity are horrendous. Security at Shiloh's is fair; there are no gates, but the park is extremely remote.

BASICS

Operated By: The Pierson Family. **Open:** Year-round. **Site Assignment:** First come, first served; this is a membership park, members receive priority, but it is open to the general public; all credit cards, personal checks, & cash accepted. **Registration:** Main office. **Fee:** $17–$22. **Parking:** At sites & near boat ramp.

FACILITIES

Number of RV Sites: 84. **Number of Tent-Only Sites:** 20. **Hookups:** Electric, water. **Each Site:** Picnic table. **Dump Station:** Yes. **Laundry:** Yes. **Pay Phone:** Yes. **Rest Rooms and Showers:** Yes. **Fuel:** No. **Propane:** No. **Internal Roads:** Gravel & paved. **RV Service:** On call. **Market:** On site. **Restaurant:** 6.5 mi. either direction. **General Store:** 6.5 mi. either direction. **Vending:** Beverages. **Swimming Pool:** Yes. **Playground:** Yes. **Other:** Mini-golf, boat ramp, boat rentals. **Activities:** Water sports, boating, fishing. **Nearby Attractions:** Ulysses S. Grant's winter quarters,

Frogmore Working Plantation, St. Joseph's museums & historical sites, Jerry Lee Lewis Museum. **Additional Information:** St. Joseph City Hall (318) 766-3713.

RESTRICTIONS

Pets: Allowed. **Fires:** In fire rings at sites only. **Alcoholic Beverages:** Allowed. **Vehicle Maximum Length:** 40 ft.

TO GET THERE

Located between Natchez and Vicksburg; from I-20 at Tallulah (Exit 171), take I-65 south 29 mi. to LA 607, take a left and bear right on LA 605. Campground is 2,000 yards on the left

ST. MARTINVILLE

Lake Fausse Pointe State Park

5400 Levee Rd., St. Martinville 70582. T: (888) 677-7200; F: (337) 229-2339; www.crt.state.la.us; lakefaussept@crt.state.la.us.

🚐 ★★★★   🅰 ★★★★

Beauty: ★★★★★   Site Privacy: ★★★★
Spaciousness: ★★★★★   Quiet: ★★★★★
Security: ★★★★★   Cleanliness: ★★★★
Insect Control: ★★★   Facilities: ★★★

At 6,000 acres, Lake Fausse Point is one of Louisiana's larger state parks. The park is situated on a peninsula on Lake Fausse Point. Inside the park is a system of streams, complete with canoe trails. The park also maintains walking and hiking trails with varying difficulty levels. The park is built on former swampland. The park is adjacent to the Atchafalaya Basin, a huge swamp that once covered most of the land between The Mississippi River and Bayou Teche. The flat campground consists of two areas along Barrow Pit Canal. Boat docks at the campgrounds provide convenient access to local waters. Sites are large and lovely. Each site features paved, back-in parking plus a gravel picnic area. A variety of hardwoods shade the campground. Unfortunately, there is little foliage between sites. The nicest sites, 27–33, have gorgeous water views and are closest to the docks. Security is excellent at this ultra remote park. Avoid this area in July and August—the heat and humidity are unbearable.

BASICS

Operated By: State of Louisiana Dept. of Culture, Recreation & Tourism. **Open:** Year-round. **Site Assignment:** First come, first served, also reservation can be held w/ V or MC (888) 677-1400. If cancelled 15 days are more before the first reserved day then the fee is $10. If cancelled 14 days or less before the first reserved day then the fee is one day's rental for all reserved items. Check-in time is 2 p.m. or later. Check-out time is 1 p.m. or earlier. The stay limit is 15 days. **Registration:** Main office. **Fee:** $12 per night for RV/tent site, $6 w/ the Golden Access card. **Parking:** 2 vehicles at each site.

FACILITIES

Number of Multipurpose Sites: 50. **Hookups:** Water, Electric (20, 30, 50 amps). **Each Site:** Tent pad, fire ring, grill, lantern hook, picnic table. **Dump Station:** Yes. **Laundry:** Yes. **Pay Phone:** Yes. **Rest Rooms and Showers:** Yes. **Fuel:** No. **Propane:** No. **Internal Roads:** Paved. **RV Service:** Approx. 60mi. west in Lafayette. **Market:** Approx. 18 mi. west in St. Martinville. **Restaurant:** Approx. 18mi. west in St. Martinville. **General Store:** Approx. 18mi. west in St. Martinville. **Vending:** Beverage only. **Swimming Pool:** No. **Playground:** Yes. **Other:** Volleyball net, athletic fields, nature trails, boat launch. **Activities:** Business retreats, canoe swamp tours, volleyball, basketball, hiking, fishing, backpacking trails where tent camping is available on the trail, overnight canoe rides where tent camping is available, children's activities. **Nearby Attractions:** Cypremort Point State Park, Longfellow-Evangeline State Historic Site, historic Town of St. Martinville, Historic Town of New Iberia, Plantations along Bayou Teche. **Additional Information:** St. Martin Parish Tourist Commission (888) 565-5939.

RESTRICTIONS

Pets: Leash. **Fires:** Fire ring only. **Alcoholic Beverages:** Allowed. **Vehicle Maximum Length:** 62 ft. **Other:** No swimming.

TO GET THERE

From I-10 going south towards Lafayette take Breaux Bridge Town Exit. Turn right onto Hwy. 31 going south and go to St. Martinville. Turn left in St. Martinville onto Hwy. 96 and drive for 3.5 mi. Turn right onto Hwy. 679, drive for 4.3 mi. and then turn left onto Hwy. 3083. Turn right onto Levee Rd. and the park will be 8 mi. south on the right.

VILLE PLATTE
Chicot State Park

3469 Chicot Park Rd., Ville Platte 70586. T: (888) 677-2442; F: (337) 363-2413; www.crt.state.la.us; chicot@crt.state.la.us.

🚐 ★★★★★   ⛺ ★★★★★

Beauty: ★★★★★   Site Privacy: ★★★★★
Spaciousness: ★★★★★   Quiet: ★★★★★
Security: ★★★★★   Cleanliness: ★★★★
Insect Control: ★★★★   Facilities: ★★★

Chicot State Park is adjacent to the Louisiana State Arboretum, which offers educational strolls through 300 acres of mature beech-magnolia forest. The Arboretum is home to diverse plants, showcasing species that usually grow in other parts of the state. Chicot State Park maintains extensive fishing, boating, and swimming facilities along the shore of Lake Chicot. There are two camping areas at Chicot. We fell in love with the beautiful South Landing Campground—it's newer, with bigger sites. All of the sites are shaded by gorgeous trees, and feature paved, back-in parking. Some sites are exceptionally large and many are extremely secluded. In South Landing, the largest sites include 24, 26, and 76. Sites 74 and 75 enjoy a gorgeous view of the lake with its majestic cypress and tupelo. Park gates are locked at night, making Chicot extra secure. This area is unbearably hot and humid in late summer. Visit in spring or fall.

BASICS

Operated By: State of Louisiana Dept. of Culture, Recreation & Tourism. **Open:** Year-round. **Site Assignment:** First come, first served, reservation can be made w/ V or MC (888) 677-1400. If cancelled 15 days or more before the first reserved day the fee is $10. If cancelled 14 days or less before the first reserved day then the fee is one day's rental of all reserved items. Check-in time is 2 p.m. or later. Check-out time is 1 p.m. or earlier. The stay limit is 15 days. **Registration:** Main office at the south entrance. **Fee:** $12 a night for RV/tent site. $6 w/ a Golden Access card. **Parking:** 2 cars/1 RV & 1 car, overflow parking is available.

FACILITIES

Number of RV Sites: 183. **Number of Tent-Only Sites:** 25. **Hookups:** Electric (30 amps), water. **Each Site:** Tent pad at tent sites only, fire ring, grill, picnic table. **Dump Station:** Yes. **Laundry:** Yes. **Pay Phone:** No. **Rest Rooms and Showers:** Yes. **Fuel:** No. **Propane:** No. **Internal Roads:** Paved. **RV Service:** 6 mi. south in Ville Platte. **Market:** 4 mi. south in Ville Platte. **Restaurant:** 4 mi. south in Ville Platte. **General Store:** 8 mi. south in Ville Platte. **Vending:** Beverage only. **Swimming Pool:** Yes. **Playground:** Yes. **Other:** Nature trails, boat launch, group lodge. **Activities:** Fishing (Florida bass), picnicking, hiking, boating. **Nearby Attractions:** Louisiana State Arboretum, Prairie Acadian Cultural Center-Jean Lafitte National Historical Park & Reserve, Acadian Town of Ville Platte, Historic town of Opelousas, Historic Town of Washington, Zydeco Cajun Prairie Scenic Byway, Liberal Theatre/City of Eunice, Thistlethwaite Wildlife Management Area. **Additional Information:** Acadia Parish Convention & Visitors Commission (877) 783-2109.

RESTRICTIONS

Pets: Leash. **Fires:** Fire ring only. **Alcoholic Beverages:** Allowed. **Vehicle Maximum Length:** Approx. 65 ft. **Other:** No gray water on the ground.

TO GET THERE

Coming from the north on I-49, exit on LA 106 south. Turn left off LA 106 onto LA 3042 south. Continue to the main entrance.

WESTWEGO
Bayou Segnette State Park

7777 Westbank Expressway, Westwego 70094. T: (504) 736-7140; bayousegnette@crt.state.la.us.

🚐 ★★★   ⛺ ★★★

Beauty: ★★★★   Site Privacy: ★★★
Spaciousness: ★★★★   Quiet: ★★★
Security: ★★★   Cleanliness: ★★★★
Insect Control: ★★   Facilities: ★★★

Bayou Segnette lies at the conjunction of two kinds of wetland-swamp and marsh. Plentiful bird species include red-winged blackbirds, Mississippi kites, and bald eagles. Located 30 miles from New Orleans, across the Mississippi River, this suburban park is convenient if you're touring the city on a weekend. However, it's not convenient to New Orleans when rush hour traffic climaxes. Avoid the New Orleans area during festivals, when the city is zoo-like, and late summer, when the heat is unbearable. Security is good here—gates are locked at night. The flat, yet attractive campground offers commodious sites. Most sites have at least a little shade and all parking is paved, back-in style. Privacy varies greatly. We recommend sites 13, 15, 62, and 100 for seclusion. Site No. 7 is recommended for families with children—it's next to the playground and wash house. Site No. 81 is extra shady.

BASICS

Operated By: Louisiana State Parks. **Open:** 7 days a week, all year. **Site Assignment:** Reservations accepted w/ a one night deposit; call (888) 677-2296; V, MC, cash, in-state checks; 2 week notice of cancellation for full refund, otherwise $10 fee. **Registration:** Campground office. **Fee:** $12. **Parking:** 2 vehicles per site, also parking lots.

FACILITIES

Number of Multipurpose Sites: 98. **Hookups:** Electric, water. **Each Site:** Picnic table, fire ring w/ grill. **Dump Station:** Yes. **Laundry:** Yes. **Pay Phone:** Yes. **Rest Rooms and Showers:** Yes. **Fuel:** No. **Propane:** No. **Internal Roads:** Paved. **RV Service:** No. **Market:** No. **Restaurant:** 0.5 mi. east. **General Store:** 0.5 mi. east. **Vending:** No. **Swimming Pool:** Yes. **Playground:** Yes. **Other:** Boat landing, wave pool. **Activities:** Hiking, fishing. **Nearby Attractions:** French Quarter, Audubon Zoo & Botanical Gardens, Aquarium of the Americas, Paddlewheel Boats, Superdome, National D-Day Museum. **Additional Information:** New Orleans CVB (504) 246-5666.

RESTRICTIONS

Pets: On leash only. **Fires:** At site only. **Alcoholic Beverages:** Allowed. **Vehicle Maximum Length:** 50 ft. **Other:** Quiet hours enforced.

TO GET THERE

From New Orleans, take US 90 west over the Greater New Orleans Bridge, which turns into the West Bank Expressway. Continue 8 mi. to flashing caution light and take a left on Drake Ave. There is a sign for the park.

ZWOLLE
North Toledo Bend State Park

P.O. Box 56, Zwolle 71486. T: (888) 677-6400; F: (318) 645-4723; www.crt.state.la.us; toledobend@crt.state.la.us.

🚐 ★★★★★	🏕 ★★★★★
Beauty: ★★★★★	Site Privacy: ★★★★★
Spaciousness: ★★★★★	Quiet: ★★★★★
Security: ★★★★	Cleanliness: ★★★★★
Insect Control: ★★★	Facilities: ★★★★

This gorgeous park is situated on a peninsula jutting into massive Toledo Bend Reservoir. Across the reservoir is Texas' Sabine National Forest. At North Toledo Bend, recreation revolves around fishing for largemouth bass, catfish, and crappie. For landlubbers, there's a nature trail and an Olympic-sized swimming pool. Although the terrain consists of rolling hills, the campground is pretty flat. The beautiful campground is laid out in two loops containing huge sites. Sites are shaded by a variety of tree species dominated by pine. Privacy is provided by greenery between sites. All parking is paved, back-in style. The most private sites are 29–34. We also like sites 13 and 14, which have partial water views. Avoid North Toledo Bend on holiday weekends and during hot late summer. Otherwise, the campground rarely fills up, making it a good destination for an early summer weekend. Security is excellent at this remote park.

BASICS

Operated By: State of Louisiana Dept. of Culture, Recreation & Tourism (888) 677-1400. **Open:** Year-round. **Site Assignment:** First come, first served, also reservations can be held w/ V, MC, (888) 677-1400. No out of state checks are accepted. If cancelled the fee is either $10, or the cost of one night's rent (which ever is largest). Check-in time is 3 p.m. or later. Check-out time is 1 p.m. or earlier. Stay limit is 15 days. **Registration:** Park office. **Fee:** $12 per night for RV/tent site. $6 w/ a Golden Access card. **Parking:** 2 vehicle parking at site.

FACILITIES

Number of Multipurpose Sites: 63. **Hookups:** Water, electric (30 amps). **Each Site:** Tent pad, lantern hook, fire ring, picnic table. **Dump Station:** Yes. **Laundry:** Yes. **Pay Phone:** Yes. **Rest Rooms and Showers:** Yes. **Fuel:** No. **Propane:** No. **Internal Roads:** Paved. **RV Service:** 50 mi. east in Natchitoches. **Market:** 8 mi. east in Zwolle. **Restaurant:** 9 mi. east in Zwolle. **General Store:** 20 mi. east in Many. **Vending:** No. **Swimming Pool:** Yes. **Playground:** Yes. **Other:** Boat launch, fishing pier, athletic field, nature trails, group lodging. **Activities:** Field activities, fishing, picnicking, hiking.

Nearby Attractions: Fort Jesup State Commemorative Area, Mansfield State Commemorative Area, Rebel State Commemorative Area, Los Adaes State Commemorative Area, Historic town of Natchitoches, Cane River Country, Kisatchie National Forest-Longleaf Vista National Recreation Trail, Sabine Wildlife Refuge, National Fish Hatchery & Aquarium. **Additional Information:** Sabine Parish Tourist & Recreation Commission/Toledo Bend Country, (800) 358-7802.

RESTRICTIONS

Pets: leash. **Fires:** Fire ring only. **Alcoholic Beverages:** Allowed. **Vehicle Maximum Length:** No limit. **Other:** The office is open from 6 a. m.–9 p.m. so check in & out must happen between those times.

TO GET THERE

From I-49, exit onto Hwy. 6 and go west approx. 30 mi. to Many. Turn right on to Hwy. 171 going north. After passing through the town of Zwolle. Take a left onto Hwy. 482. Turn left onto 3229. The entrance to the park is on the left.

Mississippi

Visitors to Mississippi can explore a rich cultural heritage. As the home of the Delta blues, legend has it that bluesman Robert Johnson sold his soul to the Devil in southern Mississippi. Writers such as Eudora Welty and Nobel laureate William Faulkner immortalized the struggles of fictional Mississippians. Today, much of Mississippi's drama occurs in the casinos that dot the Gulf Coast and the Mississippi River.

Mississippi historical sites span centuries. The **Phau Indian Mounds** in the northeast corner of the state were maintained by ancient nomadic Indians until roughly 1200 AD. Antebellum Mississippi enjoyed a thriving economy based on cotton and slave labor. **Natchez** was at one time purported to have the most millionaires outside of New York City. Many of Natchez's pre-Civil War buildings were spared desecration in the Civil War because of the city's early surrender to the Union forces. Scores of these historic buildings and lavish mansions are open for touring today.

Confederate president Jefferson Davis grew up near **Woodville** in southern Mississippi and retired to **Biloxi** after being acquitted of Federal treason charges.

The fortified port city of **Vicksburg** was the focus of one of the bloodiest and most dramatic campaigns of the Civil War. In the spring and summer of 1863, battles were fought at various sites in west central Mississippi. The campaign culminated in the 47-day siege of Vicksburg, and its capitulation on July 4, 1863. With this victory, the Union gained control of the lower Mississippi River while severing confederate transport and communication with Louisiana, Arkansas and Texas. Learn more at the 1700-acre **Vicksburg National Military Park.**

Think of Mississippi's geography in terms of five regions: the Hills Region lies in the northeast corner of the state and is traced on the eastern side by the Tennessee–Tombigbee Waterway. The flatter-than-a-pancake Delta Region in the northwestern part of the state is bounded by the Mississippi River on its western side. The Capitol/River region in the southwest corner of the state contains the historically and culturally significant cities of Natchez, Vicksburg, and **Jackson.** The central eastern Pines region contains prairies and hills as well as piney forests. Finally, the Coastal region of the southeast is enjoying a tourism boom due to its newly established gaming industry.

The **Natchez Trace Parkway** may have originated as long as 8,000 years ago, as a migratory path for buffalo. Today the historic roadway begins in Natchez and terminates in Nashville, Tennessee. The Trace is designated and maintained as a scenic parkway, with campgrounds and attractions.

Outdoors enthusiasts will find plenty to do in Mississippi, such as freshwater fishing, boating, skiing, and swimming on some of the most surprisingly gorgeous lakes in the southeast. There is also deep-sea fishing, plenty of hunting, hiking, biking, and paddling. Golfers also fare well in Mississippi, where casinos have augmented respected older courses with some exciting new ones.

Popular attractions in Mississippi include: **Bienville National Forest, Beauvoir-Jefferson Davis Home and Presidential Library, DeSoto National Forest,** Native American mounds, plantations and historic buildings, **Gulf Islands National Seashore,** the state capitol in Jackson, **Grand Village of the Natchez Indians, The Old Spanish Fort and Museums,** Elvis Presley's birthplace in **Tupelo** and the **Elvis Presley Center and Museum,** the **Jimmie Rodgers Museum.**

The following facilities accept payment in checks or cash only:

Plantation Park, Natchez

Campground Profiles

ABERDEEN
Blue Bluff

20051 Blue Bluff Rd., Aberdeen 39730. T: (662) 369-2832 or (877) 444-6777; F: (662) 369-0232; www.reserveusa.com.

🚐 ★★★★   ⛺ ★★★★

Beauty: ★★★★	Site Privacy: ★★★★
Spaciousness: ★★★★	Quiet: ★★★
Security: ★★★★★	Cleanliness: ★★★★
Insect Control: ★	Facilities: ★★★

Named for the 80-foot clay and limestone bluffs bordering the park on the eastern side, the campground at Blue Bluff is quite attractive. The campground is laid out in two loops. Most sites are spacious, but sites found in pairs feel small and exposed. Gorgeous tree cover provides shade to all sites. A few sites are secluded, but most are open to their neighbors. The most secluded sites (good honeymoon suites) are 53 and 65. Sites 66–92 include some waterfront sites with nice views. Site 45 wins the beauty pageant with its breathtaking view. Sites 1–32, while nicely wooded, tend to be closer together than the rest. Most sites offers back-in parking; all parking is paved.

BASICS

Operated By: US Army Corps of Engineers. **Open:** Year-round. **Site Assignment:** First come, first served; reservations accepted through the National Recreation Reservation Service (NRRS) at (877) 444-6777 or www.reserveusa.com. Reservations can be made up to 240 days in advance, full payment required upon making reservation; credit card preferred (V, MC, D, AE), or pay by money order if at least 21 days in advance of arrival. $10 fee for cancellation or change of site or dates. Cancellation within three days of arrival charged first night, no-show charged $20 plus first night. **Registration:** Gatehouse or night access lane. **Fee:** $16 for waterfront or sewer, $14 for basic. **Parking:** At site, limit 2 vehicles per site, fee for extra vehicles.

FACILITIES

Number of Multipurpose Sites: 92. **Hookups:** Water, electric (30, 50 amps), 2 w/ sewer. **Each Site:** Picnic table, fire ring, grill, lantern post, impact pad. **Dump Station:** Yes. **Laundry:** Yes. **Pay Phone:** Yes. **Rest Rooms and Showers:** Yes. **Fuel:** No. **Propane:** No. **Internal Roads:** Paved. **RV Service:** 1.5 mi. northwest in Aberdeen. **Market:** 1.5 mi. northwest in Aberdeen. **Restaurant:** 1.5 mi. northwest in Aberdeen. **General Store:** 20 mi. north in Armory. **Vending:** Beverages only. **Swimming Pool:** No. **Playground:** Yes. **Other:** Boat launch, fishing piers, boat ramp, boat docks, fish cleaning station. **Activities:** Swimming beach, hiking trail, volleyball & tennis courts. **Nearby Attractions:** Aberdeen Pilgrimage Antebellum home tours, Blue Bluff River Festival. **Additional Information:** Aberdeen Chamber of Commerce, (662) 369-6488.

RESTRICTIONS

Pets: Leash only. **Fires:** Allowed, fire rings only. **Alcoholic Beverages:** Allowed (no glass bottles). **Vehicle Maximum Length:** 50 ft. **Other:** Title 36 regulations posted.

TO GET THERE

From Columbus, drive 30 mi. north on US 45 to Aberdeen. In downtown Aberdeen, at the intersection of Commerce and Meridian, turn northeast onto Meridian. Cross the railroad tracks and the bridge, then take the first right. The campground is on the left.

BAY ST. LOUIS

Casino Magic RV Park

711 Casino Magic Dr., Bay St. Louis 39520. T: (800) 5-MAGIC-5 or ext. 4802; F: (228) 463-4008; www.casimagic.com.

🚐 ★★★★	▲ n/a
Beauty: ★★★★	Site Privacy: ★★★
Spaciousness: ★★★★	Quiet: ★★★★
Security: ★★★★	Cleanliness: ★★★★
Insect Control: ★★★★	Facilities: ★★★★

Attractive Casino Magic has large sites laid out in two loops that flank the office and washhouse. Few sites are shady. Sites 45, 47, 49, and 50 are shady and roomy, with nice views of the golf course. Sites 4, 5, 7, and 9 enjoy a pleasant view of marshy bayou with ducks and water lilies. All sites feature paved parking, and most have back-in parking. Guests either walk to the casino or take the free 24-hour shuttle. The campground is about one mile from a beach on Bay St. Louis and about 15 miles from beaches on the Gulf of Mexico. Bay St. Louis is an energetic little town with plenty of dining and entertainment. There are no gates at Casino Magic, but the park is patrolled by casino security personnel 24 hours a day. Avoid southern Mississippi in the hot, humid summer months.

BASICS

Operated By: Casino Magic. **Open:** Year-round. **Site Assignment:** Sites assigned; reservations strongly recommended, credit card deposit; 24-hour cancellation notice required for refund; reservations held until 6 p.m. **Registration:** Office (24-hours weekends), late-comers check for instructions at office. **Fee:** $21 for weekdays, $23 for weekends (cash, V, MC, AE, D); Players Club discounts. **Parking:** At sites, not on grass.

FACILITIES

Number of RV Sites: 100. **Number of Tent-Only Sites:** 0. **Number of Multipurpose Sites:** None. **Hookups:** Water, electric (30, 50 amps), sewer, cable TV. **Each Site:** Grill, picnic table. **Dump Station:** No. **Laundry:** Yes. **Pay Phone:** Yes. **Rest Rooms and Showers:** Yes. **Fuel:** No. **Propane:** No. **Internal Roads:** Paved. **RV Service:** On call mechanic. **Market:** 0.5 mi. **Restaurant:** Several at the casiNo. **General Store:** 15 mi. in Gulfport. **Vending:** Yes. **Swimming Pool:** No (hotel access). **Playground:** No. **Other:** Boat launch, pavilion. **Activities:** Free shuttle to casinos (walking distance), The Bridges 18-hole golf course. **Nearby Attractions:** John C. Stennis Space Center, Gulfport boat & bayou tours, Marine Life Oceanarium, Wildlife Management Areas, Bay St. Louis antique shopping. **Additional Information:** Mississippi Gulf Coast CVB, (228) 896-6699.

RESTRICTIONS

Pets: Leash only. **Fires:** Allowed, grills only. **Alcoholic Beverages:** At site only. **Vehicle Maximum Length:** 45 ft. **Other:** One-week stay limit.

TO GET THERE

From I-10, take exit 13 and drive 5 mi. south on State Hwy. 603 to US 90. Turn east and drive on US 90 for 2 mi. Turn left (north) on Blue Meadow Rd. Casino Magic Dr. is 0.5 mi. on the right.

BILOXI

Mazalea Travel Park

8220 West Oaklawn Rd., Biloxi 39532. T: (228) 392-8575; F: (228) 392-4502; wmsentr@aol.com.

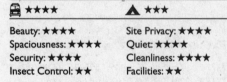

🚐 ★★★★	▲ ★★★
Beauty: ★★★★	Site Privacy: ★★★★
Spaciousness: ★★★★	Quiet: ★★★★
Security: ★★★★	Cleanliness: ★★★★
Insect Control: ★★	Facilities: ★★

Mazalea is 9 miles from the beach and 8 miles from outlet malls. There are over a dozen casinos in Biloxi and scores of restaurants. Tourist attractions include Beauvoir, the retirement home of Jefferson Davis, and art galleries and museums. The campground is adjacent to I-10, making it a cinch to tool around Biloxi. However, this urban locale is cause for security concerns given the park's lack of gates. Snowbirds like to winter at Mazalea, and families flock here in the spring, summer, and fall. Try to visit in spring or fall in order to avoid the heat.

BASICS

Operated By: Williams family. **Open:** Year-round. **Site Assignment:** Sites usually assigned; reservations recommended, no deposit; receive credit toward future stay w/ early departure. **Registration:** Camp store. **Fee:** $20–$22 (cash, check, V, MC, D). **Parking:** At site, in parking lot.

FACILITIES

Number of RV Sites: 134. **Number of Tent-Only Sites:** 5. **Number of Multipurpose Sites:** RV sites can be multipurpose in the off-season only. **Hookups:** Water, electric (30, 50), sewer, cable. **Each Site:** Picnic table. **Dump Station:** Yes. **Laundry:** Yes. **Pay Phone:** Yes. **Rest Rooms and Showers:** Yes. **Fuel:** No. **Propane:** Yes. **Internal Roads:** Paved. **RV Service:** 7 mi. east in D'Iberville. **Market:** Camp store, Wal-Mart 5 mi. east in D'Iberville. **Restaurant:** 3 mi. west in Gulfport. **General Store:** Camp store, Wal-Mart 5 mi. east in D'Iberville. **Vending:** Yes. **Swimming Pool:** No. **Playground:** Yes. **Other:** Activities building. **Activities:** Shuffleboard, horseshoes, winter potluck gatherings. **Nearby Attractions:** Biloxi casinos, museums, outlet shopping, beach within 8 mi. **Additional Information:** Mississippi Gulf Coast CVB, (228) 896-6699.

RESTRICTIONS

Pets: Leash only. **Fires:** Not allowed. **Alcoholic Beverages:** At site only. **Vehicle Maximum Length:** 45 ft.

TO GET THERE

From I-10, take exit 41 (Woolmarket Rd.). The campground is 300 yards south on the right.

BILOXI

Parker's Landing

7577 East Oaklawn Rd., Biloxi 39532. T: (228) 392-7717; F: (228) 392-7717; www.woodalls.com; parkersland@aol.com.

🚐 ★★★★	▲ ★★★
Beauty: ★★★★	Site Privacy: ★★★
Spaciousness: ★★★	Quiet: ★★★
Security: ★★★	Cleanliness: ★★★★
Insect Control: ★★	Facilities: ★★★

Convenient to numerous casinos, restaurants, and tourist attractions, Parker's Landing is located eight miles from the beach in Biloxi. This tidy, urban campground straddles Parker's Creek and maintains a boat ramp. This park doesn't offer the wide assortment of entertainment facilities found at many private campgrounds. There are two camping areas. The older section includes mid-sized sites, which are long, thin, and sandwiched together. Some sites in the older section are open. Others, including sites 64–76 and 50–58, are nicely shaded by pine, cedar, and oak. Newer sites across the creek are completely open and provide parking for two additional vehicles at each site. All parking is paved, and there are pull-through and back-in sites. Parker's Landing is adjacent to I-10 and has no gates, making security marginal. Try to plan a visit for spring or fall.

BASICS

Operated By: Elva & Dennis O'Brian. **Open:** Year-round. **Site Assignment:** Reservations recommended, credit card deposit; 3-day cancellation policy for refund on Holidays. **Registration:** Office. **Fee:** $16–$22 (cash, check, V, MC, AE). **Parking:** At sites, in parking lot.

FACILITIES

Number of RV Sites: 130. **Number of Tent-Only Sites:** 5. **Number of Multipurpose Sites:** 12. **Hookups:** Water, electric (30, 50 amps), sewer, cable. **Each Site:** Picnic table. **Dump Station:** No. **Laundry:** Yes. **Pay Phone:** Yes. **Rest Rooms and Showers:** Yes. **Fuel:** No. **Propane:** Yes. **Internal Roads:** Paved. **RV Service:** 7 mi. east in D'Iberville. **Market:** Camp store, Wal-Mart 5 mi. east in D'Iberville. **Restaurant:** 5 mi. east in D'Iberville. **General Store:** 5 mi. east in D'Iberville. **Vending:** Beverages only. **Swimming Pool:** Yes. **Playground:** No. **Other:** Fire rings by the creek, boat ramp, banquet hall, lodge, gift shop. **Activities:** Creek fishing. **Nearby Attractions:** Biloxi casinos, Beauvoir Jefferson Davis home, museums, outlet shopping, beach within 7 mi. **Additional Information:** Mississippi Gulf Coast CVB, (228) 896-6699.

RESTRICTIONS

Pets: Leash only. **Fires:** Creekside fire-rings only. **Alcoholic Beverages:** Allowed. **Vehicle Maximum Length:** 45 ft.

TO GET THERE

From I-10, take exit 41 (Woolmarket Rd.). The campground is just south of the interstate on the right.

COLUMBUS

DeWayne Hayes Campground

7934 Barton Ferry Rd., Columbus 39701. T: (662) 434-6939 or (877) 444-6777 for reservations; F: (662) 434-9346, Mar. through Oct. only; www.reserveusa.com.

🚐 ★★★★   ⛺ ★★★★

Beauty: ★★★★★   Site Privacy: ★★★
Spaciousness: ★★★★★   Quiet: ★★★★
Security: ★★★★★   Cleanliness: ★★★★
Insect Control: ★   Facilities: ★★★

This area was named after Pfc Loyd DeWayne Hayes, who died at the age of 20 while helping with preparations for the Tennessee-Tombigbee Waterway. Though less wooded, DeWayne Hayes campground has nicer waterfront sites than nearby Town Creek. Sites on the right-hand side of the main road often have water views. The nicest of these are sites 3–36 and 70–92. Site 91 is exceptionally lovely. All sites are large with ample space between neighbors. All are nicely shaded, although there is little privacy between sites. Parking is paved, and most sites are back-ins. Of the pull-throughs, lackluster number 66 is the largest. Day-use facilities are extensive at this rural recreation area. Prepare for monster mosquitoes, and avoid visiting during hot, humid late summer. Excellent destinations when the weather is mild, the campgrounds along the Tennessee-Tombigbee Waterway rarely fill to capacity. Gates lock at night, making this park extremely secure.

BASICS

Operated By: US Army Corps of Engineers. **Open:** Year-round. **Site Assignment:** First come, first served; reservations accepted through the National Recreation Reservation Service (NRRS) at (877) 444-6777 or www.reserveusa.com. Reservations can be made up to 240 days in advance, full payment required upon making reservation; credit card preferred (V, MC, D, AE), or pay by money order if at least 21 days in advance of arrival. $10 fee for cancellation or change of site or dates. Cancellation within three days of arrival charged first night, no-show charged $20 plus first night. **Registration:** Gatehouse. **Fee:** $18 for waterfront & sewer, $16 for waterfront or sewer, $14 for water & electric, $8 for primitive tent site. **Parking:** At site, limit 2 vehicles, fee for extra vehicles.

FACILITIES

Number of RV Sites: 0. **Number of Tent-Only Sites:** 10. **Number of Multipurpose Sites:** 100. **Hookups:** Water, electric (50 amps), 25 w/ sewer. **Each Site:** Picnic table, fire ring, concrete pad, grill, lantern pole. **Dump Station:** Yes. **Laundry:** Yes. **Pay Phone:** Yes. **Rest Rooms and Showers:** Yes. **Fuel:** No. **Propane:** No. **Internal Roads:** Paved. **RV Service:** 5 mi. east in Columbus. **Market:** 7 mi. east in Columbus. **Restaurant:** 5 mi. east in Columbus. **General Store:** 5 mi. east in Columbus. **Vending:** Beverages only. **Swimming Pool:** No. **Playground:** Yes. **Other:** Boat launch, fish cleaning station, picnic shelters, group campfire ring, wildlife viewing area. **Activities:** Cypress Swamp Nature Trail, swimming beach, fishing, volleyball, tennis, hiking. **Nearby Attractions:** Columbus & West Point within 5 mi., Mississippi State University, Tombigbee National Forest, Lake Lowndes State Park. **Additional Information:** Columbus Chamber of Commerce, (662) 327-7796.

RESTRICTIONS

Pets: Leash only. **Fires:** Allowed, fire rings only. **Alcoholic Beverages:** Allowed. **Vehicle Maximum Length:** 50 ft.

TO GET THERE

From Columbus, take US 45 north for 4 mi. to the junction of MS Hwys. 50 and 373. Turn left and follow 373 north for 1.5 mi. to Stenson Creek Rd. and turn left. Drive 2 mi. to Barton's Ferry Rd. Turn left to the entrance.

COLUMBUS

Lake Lowndes State Park

3319 Lake Lowndes Rd., Columbus 39702. T: (662) 328-2110; F: (662) 241-7683; www.mdwfp.com; lowndesl@ayrix.net.

🚐 ★★★   ⛺ ★★★

Beauty: ★★★★   Site Privacy: ★★★
Spaciousness: ★★★   Quiet: ★★★
Security: ★★★   Cleanliness: ★★★★
Insect Control: ★★   Facilities: ★★★★

Situated on 150-acre Lake Lowndes, this state park offers an interesting variety of activities. The small lake is stocked with catfish, crappie, bass, and bream. The campground consists of thee main loops situated in a shady stand of trees dominated by loblolly pine and various oak species. Site size is average, and there is little foliage between sites to provide privacy. All parking is back-in–style and paved. The nicest sites are situated along the lake. There is only one washhouse serving 50 sites, so we anticipate lines for potties on crowded holiday weekends. Located six miles from Columbus, home of Mississippi State University, this campground is busier on fall football weekends. Try visiting in late spring when Mississippi weather is at its best. Security is fair at this rural park, where gates were not locked and night-time patrolling was sporadic when we visited.

BASICS

Operated By: Mississippi Dept. of Wildlife, Fisheries & Parks. **Open:** Year-round. **Site Assignment:** First come, first served; reservations accepted, $15 first night deposit, nonrefundable. **Registration:** Ranger makes rounds in the evening. **Fee:** $14 for full hookup (first night $15 w/ reservation), $13 for water & electric, $9 for tent, seniors, disabled (cash, V, MC, D). **Parking:** At site, in parking lot.

FACILITIES

Number of RV Sites: 0. **Number of Tent-Only Sites:** 12 primitive. **Number of Multipurpose Sites:** 50. **Hookups:** Water, electric (30, 50 amps), some w/ sewer. **Each Site:** Picnic table, grill. **Dump Station:** Yes. **Laundry:** Yes. **Pay Phone:** Yes. **Rest Rooms and Showers:** Yes. **Fuel:** No. **Propane:** No. **Internal Roads:** Paved. **RV Service:** 20 mi. north in Columbus. **Market:** Camp store (in season only), 1 mi. west in Columbus. **Restaurant:** 1 mi. west in Columbus. **General Store:** Camp store (in season only), 2.5 mi. north in Columbus. **Vending:** Yes. **Swimming Pool:** No. **Playground:** Yes. **Other:** Pool table, ping pong table, nature trail, picnic sites, swimming beach, bike trail, equestrian trail, visitor's center, meeting rooms, video games, marina, boat ramp. **Activities:** Disc golf, walking track, boat rentals, tennis, volleyball, basketball, soccer, softball, fishing. **Nearby Attractions:** Over 100 antebellum homes, Historic Downtown Columbus, river ferry, Tennessee-Tombigbee Waterway, art & family festivals. **Additional Information:** Columbus Visitor Information, (662) 329-1191.

RESTRICTIONS

Pets: Leash only. **Fires:** Campsites only. **Alcoholic Beverages:** Not allowed. **Vehicle Maximum Length:** No limit.

TO GET THERE

Take I-82 to Columbus. Take the Least Oaks exit and drive south on State Hwy. 69. Turn east onto Lake Lowndes Rd. The park is 10 mi. southeast of Columbus.

COLUMBUS

Town Creek Campground

3606 West Plymouth Rd., Columbus 39701-9504. T: (662) 327-2142; F: (662) 328-8766; sam.usace.army.mil/op/rec/tenn-tom/camp.html; janalie.m.graham@sam.usacc.army.mil.

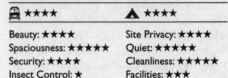

🚐 ★★★★	🛖 ★★★★
Beauty: ★★★★	Site Privacy: ★★★★
Spaciousness: ★★★★★	Quiet: ★★★★★
Security: ★★★★	Cleanliness: ★★★★★
Insect Control: ★	Facilities: ★★★

Yet another lovely impoundment of the Tennessee-Tombigbee River system, Columbus Lake offers excellent fishing, and Town Creek Recreation Area offers excellent amenities for anglers. Within the recreation area, small Kennedy Lake provides additional fishing opportunities, as well as a sandy swimming beach with sundeck. Many campsites boast serene lake views. Site size varies, with lakefront sites often smaller than their upland counterparts. Some sites are totally shady and secluded, while others are only partially shaded and open to neighbors. The campground is laid out in two loops and a spur with paved, back-in parking spaces. There are two attractive pull-through sites, 73 and 78, in the back of the campground. Other beautiful sites include 34, 36, 70, 71, 75, and 83–94. At this very rural campground, security is fine. However, mosquitoes are extremely annoying along the low-lying Tenn-Tom Waterway. Bring plenty of insect repellent. Avoid this area in steamy late summer.

BASICS

Operated By: Army Corps of Engineers. **Open:** Year-round. **Site Assignment:** 60% reserveable, 40% first come, first served. **Registration:** At office. **Fee:** $8–$18. **Parking:** at site, 2 vehicles.

FACILITIES

Number of RV Sites: 100. **Number of Tent-Only Sites:** 110. **Hookups:** Electric (30, 50 amps). **Each Site:** Concrete pads, lantern posts, grills, fire ring, picnic table, access to boat ramp. **Dump**

Station: Yes. **Laundry:** Yes. **Pay Phone:** Yes. **Rest Rooms and Showers:** Yes. **Fuel:** No. **Propane:** No. **Internal Roads:** Paved. **RV Service:** 10 mi. **Market:** Nearby. **Restaurant:** Nearby. **General Store:** Nearby. **Vending:** Yes. **Swimming Pool:** No. **Playground:** Yes. **Other:** Fish-cleaning station, disabled-accessible. **Activities:** Swim beach, multi use park fields, picnic pavilions, nature & hiking trails. **Nearby Attractions:** Inquire at campground.

RESTRICTIONS

Pets: On leash only. **Fires:** Fire ring. **Alcoholic Beverages:** Allowed but not on beach. **Vehicle Maximum Length:** No limit. **Other:** 24 hour attendant.

TO GET THERE

From Columbus, take Hwy. 45 N to junction w/ Hwy. 50 W, turn left, follow Hwy. 50 W past Hwy. 50 Waterway Bridge. Intersection is approximately 2 mi. west of bridge. Turn north, follow signs.

DENNIS

Piney Grove Campground

82 Bay Springs Resource Rd., Dennis 38838. T: (662) 728-1134; www.reserveusa.com.

🚐 ★★★★   ⛺ ★★★★

Beauty: ★★★★★	Site Privacy: ★★★★
Spaciousness: ★★★★★	Quiet: ★★★★
Security: ★★★★★	Cleanliness: ★★★★★
Insect Control: ★	Facilities: ★★★

Piney Grove is typical of the Corps of Engineers campgrounds found along the Tennessee-Tombigbee Waterway; it has incredibly beautiful campsites. All sites are commodious, with ample shade provided by loblolly pine and various hardwoods. Most campsites are afforded plenty of privacy by screening foliage. The peninsular campground contains sites in three main areas. With views of Bay Springs Lake, the area containing sites 55–81 boasts some of the most gorgeous sites in the state. Secluded and picturesque, sites 64 and 75 are absolutely fabulous. All sites have paved parking and a large gravel picnic area. Most sites are back-in. There are 10 pull-throughs sites, the nicest of which is number 113. Situated in the rural, rolling hills of northeast Mississippi, this park locks its gates at night, making it extremely secure. Rarely crowded, it's safe to visit here on summer weekends if you can stand the heat and mosquitoes.

BASICS

Operated By: US Army Corps of Engineers. **Open:** Mid-Mar.–mid-Nov. **Site Assignment:** First come, first served; reservations accepted through the National Recreation Reservation Service (NRRS) at (877) 444-6777 or www.reserveusa.com. Reservations can be made up to 240 days in advance, full payment required upon making reservation; credit card preferred (V, MC, D, AE), or pay by money order if at least 21 days in advance of arrival; $10 fee for cancellation or change of site or dates; cancellation within three days of arrival charged first night; no-show charged $20 & first night. **Registration:** Gatehouse, gate locks at 10 p.m. **Fee:** $18 for waterfront site, $16 for non-waterfront site; 8 people max. **Parking:** At site, limit 3 vehicles, fee for extra vehicles.

FACILITIES

Number of RV Sites: 0. **Number of Tent-Only Sites:** 10 primitive-boat access only (island). **Number of Multipurpose Sites:** 142. **Hookups:** Water, electric (20, 30, 50 amps). **Each Site:** Grill, picnic table, fire ring, lantern pole. **Dump Station:** Yes. **Laundry:** Yes. **Pay Phone:** Yes. **Rest Rooms and Showers:** Yes. **Fuel:** No. **Propane:** No. **Internal Roads:** Paved. **RV Service:** 30 mi. east in Red Bay, AL. **Market:** 25 mi. west in Booneville. **Restaurant:** 25 mi. west in Booneville. **General Store:** 25 mi. west in Booneville. **Vending:** Beverages only. **Swimming Pool:** No. **Playground:** Yes. **Other:** Boat ramp, fishing piers, fish-cleaning station, amphitheater, swimming beach, picnic shelter. **Activities:** Multi-use game courts, nature trails, fishing, swimming, campfire programs in-season. **Nearby Attractions:** Tishomingo State Park, Brices Cross Roads National Battlefield Site, Chickasaw Village, Tupelo, Birthplace of Elvis Presley, Tennessee-Tombigbee Waterway. **Additional Information:** Tupelo CVB, (662) 842-4521.

RESTRICTIONS

Pets: Leash only. **Fires:** Grills, fire rings only. **Alcoholic Beverages:** Not allowed. **Vehicle Maximum Length:** Sites vary (see www.reserveusa.com for site specifications). **Other:** 14-day stay limit.

TO GET THERE

From Tupelo, take the Natchez Trace Parkway northeast 36 mi. to the first exit after crossing the Tennessee-Tombigbee Waterway. Take this exit (Bay Springs Lake) and turn left on Tishomingo CR 1. Drive 0.75 mi. to Mississippi Hwy. 4 and turn left. Drive 1 mi. and turn right on Prentiss CR 3501. Continue 7 mi. to the park. From the intersection of State Hwys. 4 and 30 in Booneville, take State Hwy. 30 east 11 mi. to Burton, and turn right on CR 3501. Follow for 3 mi. and turn left at the sign for Piney Grove Recreation Area.

ENID

Wallace Creek Campground Enid Lake

P.O. Box 10, Enid 38927. T: (662) 563-4571 or (877) 444-6777 for reservations; www.reserveusa.com.

🚐 ★★★★	⛺ ★★★★
Beauty: ★★★★	Site Privacy: ★★★★
Spaciousness: ★★★★	Quiet: ★★★★
Security: ★★★	Cleanliness: ★★★★★
Insect Control: ★★★★	Facilities: ★★★

The Enid Lake area includes verdant rolling hills, blue water, and extensive recreational facilities. Fishing is spectacular here—Enid Lake holds the world's record for largest crappie. With the newest washhouses and largest sites, Wallace Creek is the most appealing campground at Enid Lake. A few choice sites, including 26, 28, 41, 71, 90, 91, and 92, have views of the lake. All campsites at Wallace Creek are spacious and shady, though few are secluded. All parking is paved. Most sites offer back-in parking. Security at Wallace Creek is fair; the campground is very close to I-55, and there are no locked gates at night, although rangers patrol regularly and Enid is in a rural location.

BASICS

Operated By: US Army Corps of Engineers. **Open:** All year, some seasonal. **Site Assignment:** First come, first served; reservations accepted through the National Recreation Reservation Service (NRRS) at (877) 444-6777 or www.reserveusa.com. Reservations can be made up to 240 days in advance, full payment required upon making reservation; credit card preferred (V, MC, D, AE), or pay by money order if at least 21 days in advance of arrival. $10 fee for cancellation or change of site or dates. Cancellation within three days of arrival charged first night, no-show charged

$20 plus first night. **Registration:** Self-registration, booth registration. **Fee:** $10–$15 (cash, V, MC, D, AE). **Parking:** At site, in parking lot.

FACILITIES

Number of RV Sites: 0. **Number of Tent-Only Sites:** 16. **Number of Multipurpose Sites:** 235. **Hookups:** Water, electric (50 amps). **Each Site:** Picnic table, grill, fire ring, lantern pole. **Dump Station:** Yes. **Laundry:** No. **Pay Phone:** Yes. **Rest Rooms and Showers:** Yes. **Fuel:** No. **Propane:** No. **Internal Roads:** Paved. **RV Service:** 21 mi. south in Grenada. **Market:** 13 mi. north Batesville. **Restaurant:** 1 mi. at Enid Dam. **General Store:** 1 mi. at Enid Dam. **Vending:** No. **Swimming Pool:** No (at the State Park). **Playground:** Yes. **Other:** Boat launches, motorcycle trail, picnic shelters, amphitheater, swimming beach, scenic overlook, information center. **Activities:** Fishing, boating (boat rentals at State Park), swimming, hiking, equestrian trail. **Nearby Attractions:** George Payne Cossar State Park, Holly Springs National Forest, attractions in Oxford, Tunica & Memphis. **Additional Information:** Panola Partnership/ Chamber of Commerce, (662) 563-3126.

RESTRICTIONS

Pets: Leash only. **Fires:** Fire rings only. **Alcoholic Beverages:** Allowed (dry county for beer, wet for liquor). **Vehicle Maximum Length:** 40 ft. **Other:** Title 36 regulations posted.

TO GET THERE

From I-55, take exit 233. Proceed 1 mi. east on CR 36. The recreation area is well-marked.

FULTON

Whitten Park Campground (formerly Fulton Campground)

82 Bay Springs Resource Rd., Dennis 38838. T: (662) 862-7070; www.reserveusa.com.

🚐 ★★★★	⛺ ★★★★
Beauty: ★★★★★	Site Privacy: ★★★★
Spaciousness: ★★★★	Quiet: ★★★★★
Security: ★★★★★	Cleanliness: ★★★★★
Insect Control: ★★	Facilities: ★★★

Whitten Park is extremely pretty. The campground is laid out in three loops, each of which has a few waterfront sites. Sites 10, 11, and 12 have pretty water views. Close to the playground, 27 and 28 are excellent choices for families. Sites

42 and 46, the only pull-throughs at Whitten Park, are extremely large. Parking is paved, and sites are shaded by dense woods with foliage providing site privacy. On the property, the Jamie L. Whitten Historical Center features exhibits on the area's economic development. One focus is the Tennessee-Tombigbee Waterway, the largest Corps of Engineers project in history. Built mainly for navigation, the "Ten-Tom" connects the lower Tennessee Valley to the Gulf of Mexico, is five times longer than the Panama Canal, and required moving one third more earth. Security is excellent at this remote, gated campground. This campground rarely fills up, making it a good choice for summer weekend camping.

BASICS

Operated By: US Army Corps of Engineers. **Open:** Year-round. **Site Assignment:** First come, first served; reservations accepted through the National Recreation Reservation Service (NRRS) at (877) 444-6777 or www.reserveusa.com. Reservations can be made up to 240 days in advance, full payment required upon making reservation; credit card preferred (V, MC, D, AE), or pay by money order if at least 21 days in advance of arrival. $10 fee for cancellation or change of site or dates. Cancellation within three days of arrival charged first night, no-show charged $20 plus first night. **Registration:** Gatehouse (gates lock at 10 p.m.). **Fee:** $16 for waterfront, $14 for non-waterfront; fee includes 8 people (cash, personal check, V, MC, D, AE). **Parking:** At sites, in parking lots.

FACILITIES

Number of Multipurpose Sites: 61. **Hookups:** Water, electric (30, 50 amps). **Each Site:** Picnic table, fire ring, grill, lantern pole. **Dump Station:** Yes. **Laundry:** Yes. **Pay Phone:** Yes. **Rest Rooms and Showers:** Yes. **Fuel:** No. **Propane:** No. **Internal Roads:** Paved. **RV Service:** 25 mi. east in Red Bay. **Market:** 2 mi. south in Fulton. **Restaurant:** 2 mi. south in Fulton. **General Store:** Wal-Mart 2 mi. south in Fulton. **Vending:** Beverages only. **Swimming Pool:** No. **Playground:** Yes. **Other:** Boat ramp, fish-cleaning station, fishing piers, boat docks, picnic shelters, information center, Jamie L. Whitten Historical Center. **Activities:** Multi-use courts, swimming (swimming beach for campground use only), fishing, nature trails. **Nearby Attractions:** Bean's Ferry Pottery, Tennessee-Tombigbee Waterway, Elvis Presley Birthplace in Tupelo, Tupelo National Battlefield, Oren Dunn

Museum. **Additional Information:** Tupelo CVB, (800) 533-0611.

RESTRICTIONS

Pets: Leash only. **Fires:** Fire rings only. **Alcoholic Beverages:** Not allowed. **Vehicle Maximum Length:** No limit. **Other:** Title 36 regulations posted.

TO GET THERE

From the intersection of US 78 and MS Hwy. 25 (16 mi. north of Tupelo), take Hwy. 25 north 200 yards. Turn north on Access Rd./Johnny Rankin Memorial Hwy. and drive 4.5 mi. The campground is on the left, inside the Jamie L. Whitten Historical Center and Park.

GRENADA

North Graysport Campground, Grenada Lake

P.O. Box 903, Grenada 38901-0903. T: (662) 226-8963; www.reserveusa.com.

🚐 ★★★★	🏕 ★★★★
Beauty: ★★★★	Site Privacy: ★★★★
Spaciousness: ★★★★	Quiet: ★★★
Security: ★★★	Cleanliness: ★★★★
Insect Control: ★★★	Facilities: ★★★★

The 63,000-acre Grenada Lake is the largest lake in Mississippi, and there is plenty of recreation available here. Stop by the Visitor Center (located on scenic Hwy. 333) to get information on what's available. The North Graysport Campground is one of nine on Grenada Lake. It offers generous sites, with lovely shade provided by mature loblolly pine, short-leaf pine, red cedar, and various oak species. However, there is little privacy between sites. All parking is paved, back-in style. There are no waterfront sites, and many sites are far from the washhouses. So, we recommend choosing a site near the "facilities." Security is fair at this rural campground which doesn't lock its gates at night. Also, the campground gets incredibly crowded in the summer and should be avoided particularly on holiday weekends. Remember that central Mississippi is no place to be when it's hot and humid.

BASICS

Operated By: Us Army Corps of Engineers in conjunction w/ Mississippi Dept. of Wildlife, Fisheries & Parks. **Open:** Year-round. **Site Assignment:** First come, first served; reservations accepted for three night min., w/ $15 nonrefundable first night deposit. **Registration:** Gatehouse. **Fee:** $13 ($15 first night w/ reservation), $10 seniors. **Parking:** At site (preferably not to exceed 3 vehicles).

FACILITIES

Number of RV Sites: 0. **Number of Tent-Only Sites:** 30 (some w/ electric & water in the area). **Number of Multipurpose Sites:** 158. **Hookups:** Water, electric (30, 50 amps). **Each Site:** Picnic table, grill, fire ring, lantern pole, some tent pads. **Dump Station:** Yes. **Laundry:** Yes. **Pay Phone:** Yes. **Rest Rooms and Showers:** Yes. **Fuel:** No. **Propane:** No. **Internal Roads:** Paved. **RV Service:** 5 mi. south in Grenada. **Market:** 7 mi. south in Grenada. **Restaurant:** 7 mi. south in Grenada. **General Store:** 8 mi. south in Grenada (Wal-Mart). **Vending:** Beverages only. **Swimming Pool:** No. **Playground:** Yes. **Other:** Boat launches, picnic area, visitor center, picnic shelters. **Activities:** Several swimming beaches, fishing, boating, amphitheater. **Nearby Attractions:** Historic Grenada, walking & driving tours, Confederate Cemetery, Galloway House Jefferson Davis Civil War Headquarters, Cocchuma Archery Range, Hugh White State Park. **Additional Information:** Grenada Tourism Commission, (800) 373-2571.

RESTRICTIONS

Pets: Leash only. **Fires:** Fire ring only. **Alcoholic Beverages:** Allowed. **Vehicle Maximum Length:** 50 ft.

TO GET THERE

From I-55, take exit 206 and drive east on State Hwy. 8 about 3.5 mi. Turn north on scenic route 333 toward Grenada Dam. Turn left on Toe Rd., next to the dam, and the gatehouse is at the foot of the dam.

GULFPORT

Baywood Campground-RV Park

1100 Cowan Rd., Gulfport 39507. T: (228) 896-4840 or (888) 747-4840; F: (228) 604-1739; www.woodalls.com; wmsentr@aol.com.

🚐 ★★★	🛆 ★★
Beauty: ★★★	Site Privacy: ★★★
Spaciousness: ★★	Quiet: ★★★
Security: ★★	Cleanliness: ★★★
Insect Control: ★★★	Facilities: ★★

One mile from the beach, eight miles from outlet malls, and within easy driving distance of a dozen casinos, Baywood's location is excellent. The campground at Baywood offers mostly back-in parking. Most parking is paved, and the rest is gravel. Sites are on the small side with little privacy. Spanish moss–laden hardwoods provide shade. The campground is laid out in two main areas. Families should look for a site convenient to the pool and playground, such as site 93 or 94. Couples seeking solitude should head to the back and choose a site numbering in the 50's or 60's. This urban campground offers few security measures, as there are no gates. Watch your belongings. We don't recommend Gulf Coast touring in the height of summer, when the heat is unbearable. Winter is also problematic due to the migration of the venerable snowbirds. Visit in the autumn for maximum peace and quiet.

BASICS

Operated By: Marshall J. Williams. **Open:** Year-round. **Site Assignment:** First come, first served; reservations accepted, no deposit required. **Registration:** Office, late-comers register next morning. **Fee:** $24 for pull-through, $23 for back-in; prices for 2 adults & 2 children, $2 per extra person; Good Sam & AAA discounts available (cash, personal check, V, MC). **Parking:** At site, in designated areas (2 vehicles, max.).

FACILITIES

Number of Multipurpose Sites: 114. **Hookups:** Water, electric (30, 50 amps), sewer, cable. **Each Site:** Picnic table. **Dump Station:** Yes. **Laundry:** Yes. **Pay Phone:** Yes. **Rest Rooms and Showers:** Yes. **Fuel:** No. **Propane:** Yes. **Internal Roads:** Paved. **RV Service:** 7 mi. east in Biloxi. **Market:** 0.25 mi. **Restaurant:** 0.25 mi. **General Store:** 0.25 mi. **Vending:** Yes. **Swimming Pool:** Yes. **Playground:** Yes. **Activities:** Fishing pond, recreation center. **Nearby Attractions:** Biloxi, Gulf beaches, Gulf Island national Seashore, Beauvoir Jefferson Davis Home, Barrier Islands, cruises, casinos. **Additional Information:** Mississippi Gulf Coast, CVB (228) 896-6699.

RESTRICTIONS

Pets: Leash only. **Fires:** Allowed, grills only (bring your own). **Alcoholic Beverages:** Allowed, sites only. **Vehicle Maximum Length:** 45 ft. (sites vary). **Other:** No aggressive dogs.

TO GET THERE

From I-10, take exit 38 and drive south 3 mi. on Cowan Lorraine Rd. The park entrance is on the left.

HATTIESBURG
Paul B. Johnson State Park

319 Geiger Lake Rd., Hattiesburg 39401. T: (601) 582-7721; www.mdwfp.com.

🚐 ★★★★   ▲ ★★★★

Beauty: ★★★★   Site Privacy: ★★★
Spaciousness: ★★★   Quiet: ★★★★
Security: ★★★★   Cleanliness: ★★★★
Insect Control: ★★★★   Facilities: ★★★

Paul B. Johnson State Park offers back-in camp-sites situated in one area and 22 pull-through sites in another area. We recommend the back-in area. The pull-through area is crowded and far less attractive. For a nice view of 300-acre Lake Geiger, try back-in sites 15-18 and 65, 67, 69, 71, 77, 78, 80, 85, and 84. These sites are shaded by a variety of tree species, including loblolly, longleaf, and short-leaf pine. All parking is paved. Less than two hours from New Orleans, this park is popular with Crescent City–slickers and should be avoided on summer holidays and weekends. In the summer, this park becomes so hot and humid that you could steam veggies on your car hood. Although the park's surroundings are rural, Hattiesburg businesses are only 15–20 miles away. Park gates are not locked at night, but rangers patrol regularly.

BASICS
Operated By: Mississippi Dept. of Wildlife, Fisheries & Parks. **Open:** All year (office closed Christmas). **Site Assignment:** Some first come, first served; designated sites available for reservation, w/ $15 non-refundable first night deposit. **Registration:** Ranger checks in. **Fee:** $14 for full hookup, $13 for water & electric, $9 for primitive tent sites or seniors. **Parking:** At site, limit 2 vehicles.

FACILITIES
Number of RV Sites: 0. **Number of Tent-Only Sites:** 50 (primitive area, undesignated). **Number of Multipurpose Sites:** 108. **Hookups:** Water, electric (30, 50 amps), sewer in 50 sites. **Each Site:** Picnic table, grill. **Dump Station:** Yes. **Laundry:** Yes. **Pay Phone:** Yes. **Rest Rooms and Showers:** Yes. **Fuel:** No. **Propane:** No. **Internal Roads:** Paved. **RV Service:** 22 mi. north in Hattiesburg. **Market:** 15 mi. north in Hattiesburg. **Restaurant:** 3.5 mi. north in Hattiesburg. **General Store:** 15 mi. north in Hattiesburg. **Vending:** Yes. **Swimming Pool:** No. **Playground:** Yes. **Other:** Boat ramp, lake beach, picnic pavilions, group camp, group camp swim area. **Activities:** Fishing, swimming, paddle boat rentals in-season, fishing boat & canoe rentals year-round, water sports, nature trail. **Nearby Attractions:** Historic Hattiesburg, Camp Shelby Armed Forces Museum, Black Creek, Wildlife Management Areas, University of Southern Mississippi. **Additional Information:** Hattiesburg Chamber of Commerce, (601) 268-3220.

RESTRICTIONS
Pets: 6-ft. leash only. **Fires:** Allowed. **Alcoholic Beverages:** Not allowed. **Vehicle Maximum Length:** 40 ft. **Other:** No metal detectors.

TO GET THERE
From I-59, take exit 59 (Lucedale/Mobile/Hwy. 98 East). Drive 3.5 mi. on Hwy. 98 east to the Hwy. 49/Mississippi Gulf Coast exit. Take Hwy. 49 south 8.5 for mi. The park is on the right.

HERNANDO
South Abutment Campground, Arkabutla Lake

3905 Arkabutla Dam Rd., Coldwater 38618. T: (601) 562-6261 or (877) 444-6777 for reservations; F: (601) 562-8972; www.reserveusa.com.

🚐 ★★★★★   ▲ ★★★★★

Beauty: ★★★★★   Site Privacy: ★★★★★
Spaciousness: ★★★★★   Quiet: ★★★★★
Security: ★★★★★   Cleanliness: ★★★★★
Insect Control: ★★★   Facilities: ★★★

Often less crowded than Enid and Sardis Lakes, Arkabutla Lake also has extensive recreational facilities. Fishermen find catfish, bream, white bass, black bass, and some of the largest crappie in the southeast. All three campgrounds at Arkabutla have nice-looking, commodious sites. We prefer the South Abutment campground; it is the least frequented of the three and has the most spacious washhouse. Sites at south Abutment are shady, and most are secluded. All campsites at Lake Arkabutla have paved parking. There are two pull-throughs at Hernando Point; other sites offer back-in parking. Security at this rural recreation area is fair; gates do not lock, but law enforcement patrols throughout the night.

BASICS
Operated By: US Army Corps of Engineers. **Open:** Year-round. **Site Assignment:** First come, first served; reservations accepted through the

National Recreation Reservation Service (NRRS) at (877) 444-6777 or www.reserveusa.com. Reservations can be made up to 240 days in advance, full payment required upon making reservation; credit card preferred (V, MC, D, AE), or pay by money order if at least 21 days in advance of arrival. $10 fee for cancellation or change of site or dates. Cancellation within three days of arrival charged first night, no-show charged $20 plus first night. **Registration:** Entrance stations. **Fee:** $8–$18 (V, MC, D). **Parking:** At site.

FACILITIES

Number of Multipurpose Sites: 234. **Hookups:** Water, electric (20, 30 amps). **Each Site:** Picnic table, grill, fire ring. **Dump Station:** Yes. **Laundry:** No. **Pay Phone:** Yes. **Rest Rooms and Showers:** Yes. **Fuel:** No. **Propane:** No. **Internal Roads:** Paved. **RV Service:** 40 mi. north in Memphis. **Market:** 15 mi. southeast in Coldwater. **Restaurant:** 5 mi. south in Arkabutla. **General Store:** 15 mi. southeast in Coldwater. **Vending:** No. **Swimming Pool:** No. **Playground:** Yes. **Other:** Boat launch, 36,000 acres, beaches, primitive equestrian trails, picnic areas & shelters, nature trails. **Activities:** Fishing, hunting, swimming, hunting, hiking, wind-sailing, volleyball, fall festival. **Nearby Attractions:** Attractions in Tunica & Memphis; Beale St., Mud Island, Graceland. **Additional Information:** Hernando Chamber of Commerce, (662) 429-9055; or Senatobia Chamber of Commerce, (662) 562-8715.

RESTRICTIONS

Pets: Leash only. **Fires:** Allowed, sites only. **Alcoholic Beverages:** Not allowed. **Vehicle Maximum Length:** No limit.

TO GET THERE

From I-55, take exit 271 (Coldwater) and go west on State Hwy. 306 for 2 mi. Turn left onto US 51 and go south for 1 mi. to Coldwater. At the four-way stop, turn right and go west on Scenic Rte. 304 for 10 mi. to Arkabutla, where 304 turns north. Continue 5 mi. to the Main Dam and office.

JACKSON
LeFleur's Bluff State Park

2140 Riverside Dr., Jackson 39202. T: (601) 987-3923; F: (601) 354-6930; www.mdwfp.com.

 ★★★★   ★★★★

Beauty: ★★★★   Site Privacy: ★★★★
Spaciousness: ★★★★   Quiet: ★★★★
Security: ★★★★   Cleanliness: ★★★★
Insect Control: ★   Facilities: ★★★★★

This family-oriented park is building the state's largest playground. A small fishing lake is stocked with bass, bream, catfish and crappie. The campground is attractive, although you can see suburban neighborhoods from your campsite. Site size is ample, and there are plenty of shady loblolly pines. Parking is on back-in, paved pads. About half of the sites are lakefront. Of these, 6, 7, 12, and 14 are recommended because of their views and proximity to the washhouses. All sites are situated on one loop. Security is very good at this suburban state park; gates are locked at night and attended during the day. When we visited, we were eaten by mosquitoes, and the rangers told us that ants and bees are also problematic. Bring insect repellent.

BASICS

Operated By: Mississippi Dept. of Wildlife, Fisheries & Parks. **Open:** All year (frequent closings in the spring due to flooding). **Site Assignment:** First come, first served; 5 sites available for reservation for 2 night min., $15 nonrefundable first night deposit. **Registration:** Gatehouse, ranger checks in (code required to enter after gate closes-call ahead). **Fee:** $13, $10 seniors. **Parking:** At site, in parking lot, limit 2 vehicles.

FACILITIES

Number of Multipurpose Sites: 30. **Hookups:** Water, electric (50 amps). **Each Site:** Picnic table, grill. **Dump Station:** Yes. **Laundry:** No. **Pay Phone:** Yes. **Rest Rooms and Showers:** Yes. **Fuel:** No. **Propane:** No. **Internal Roads:** Gravel, limestone. **RV Service:** 6 mi. west in Jackson. **Market:** 2 mi. north in Jackson. **Restaurant:** 1 mi. east in Flowood. **General Store:** 3 mi. north in Jackson. **Vending:** Beverages only. **Swimming Pool:** No. **Playground:** Yes. **Other:** Clubhouse, picnic area & pavilion, lodge, meeting rooms. **Activities:** Fishing (trolling motors only), boat rentals year-round, nature trails, 9-hole golf course, driving range, tennis, disc golf. **Nearby Attractions:** Jim Buck Ross Mississippi Agriculture & Forestry Museum, National Agricultural Aviation Museum, Mississippi Governors Mansion, Museum of Art, Natural Science Museum, Mississippi Sports Hall of Fame, Old Capital Museum. **Additional Information:** Jackson CVB,

(800) 354-7695 or (601) 960-1891,
www.visitjackson.com.

RESTRICTIONS

Pets: Leash only. **Fires:** Allowed. **Alcoholic Beverages:** Not allowed. **Vehicle Maximum Length:** 50 ft.

TO GET THERE

From I-55, take exit 98B and drive east on Lakeland Dr. to the second traffic light. Turn right, and the campground is straight ahead.

JACKSON

Timberlake Campground and RV Park

143 Timberlake Dr., Brandon 39047. T: (601) 992-9100; F: (601) 919-0219.

🚐 ★★★   ▲ ★★★

Beauty: ★★★	Site Privacy: ★★
Spaciousness: ★★★★	Quiet: ★★★★
Security: ★★★	Cleanliness: ★★★★
Insect Control: ★★★	Facilities: ★★★

Built on mammoth Ross Barnett Reservoir, Timberlake is enjoyed by anglers. As at Le Fleur State Park, neighboring homes are visible from your campsite. Families will find that the two parks maintain different yet qualitatively comparable recreational facilities. Built on a peninsula, most sites are leased residentially. For overnighters, RV sites N1–N66 are in a shadier, older portion of the park. Sites N1–N8 are popular lakefront sites and cannot be reserved. Sites N67–N108 are newer, completely tree-less, and available for reservations. Sites are large with paved, back-in parking. Even when trees provide shade, there is little privacy. The exceptions are the shadier and more private tent and pop-up areas.

BASICS

Operated By: Pearl River Valley Water Supply District. **Open:** Year-round. **Site Assignment:** First come, first served; designated sites available for reservation, one night deposit, 3 day notice for refund. **Registration:** Office, late-comers register the next day. **Fee:** $17 for full hookups, $15 for water & electric, $12 for tent site, $2 discount for seniors, fee includes 4 people, $1 per extra person (cash, personal check, V, MC, AE, D). **Parking:** At sites.

FACILITIES

Number of RV Sites: 0. **Number of Tent-Only Sites:** 18. **Number of Multipurpose Sites:** 126. **Hookups:** Water, electric (20, 30, 50 amps), sewer in 108 sites. **Each Site:** Picnic table, grill. **Dump Station:** Yes. **Laundry:** Yes. **Pay Phone:** Yes. **Rest Rooms and Showers:** Yes. **Fuel:** No. **Propane:** No. **Internal Roads:** Paved. **RV Service:** 15 mi. north in Gloudtstat. **Market:** 1 mi. in Brandon. **Restaurant:** 1 mi. in Brandon. **General Store:** 0.25 mi. in Brandon. **Vending:** Yes. **Swimming Pool:** Yes. **Playground:** Yes. **Other:** Boat ramp, fishing dock, recreation room. **Activities:** Game room, tennis, boating, skiing, fishing, bicycling & hiking trails. **Nearby Attractions:** Jim Buck Ross Mississippi Agriculture & Forestry Museum/ National Agricultural Aviation Museum, Mississippi Governors Mansion, Museum of Art, Natural Science Museum, Mississippi Sports Hall of Fame, Old Capital Museum. **Additional Information:** Jackson CVB, (800) 354-7695 or (601) 960-1891, www.visitjackson.com.

RESTRICTIONS

Pets: Leash only. **Fires:** Allowed, grills only (need permission for ground fire). **Alcoholic Beverages:** Not allowed. **Vehicle Maximum Length:** 45 ft. (sites vary). **Other:** No mobile homes.

TO GET THERE

From I-55, take exit 98B and drive east 3.2 mi. on Lakeland Dr. East. Turn left on Old Fannin Rd. and go 3 mi. The park is on the left.

MCCOMB

Percy Quinn State Park

1156 Camp Beaver Dr., McComb 39648. T: (601) 684-3938; F: (601) 249-4382; www.mdwfp.com; pqspark@telepak.net.

🚐 ★★★   ▲ ★★★

Beauty: ★★★★	Site Privacy: ★★★
Spaciousness: ★★★★	Quiet: ★★★★
Security: ★★★	Cleanliness: ★★
Insect Control: ★★	Facilities: ★★★★★

With its mild southern climate, Percy Quinn State Park makes a good late fall or early spring destination. Its extensive recreational facilities make it popular with the city folk from "N'awlins"—avoid it like the plague on holiday weekends. The nice-looking campground features various-sized sites shaded by loblolly pine and magnolia. All parking is back-in and paved. Site privacy also varies. Sites 83–91 are recommended if you value elbow room and seclusion. If you prefer a water-view site, make a reservation for site 56 or 58. Site 100 is adjacent to the less-crowded North Swimming Beach, making it a good choice for families.

BASICS

Operated By: Mississippi Dept. of Wildlife, Fisheries & Parks. **Open:** Year-round. **Site Assignment:** Most sites first come, first served; 27 sites (w/ 50 amp hookup) available for reservation, 2 night min. (3-night min. on holidays), $15 non-refundable first night's deposit. **Registration:** Ranger station at entrance gate, late-comers set up & register the next morning. **Fee:** $13 for RV sites, $10 for seniors; $9 for primitive tent sites (cash, personal check, V, MC). **Parking:** At site, in parking lot (2 vehicles, max.).

FACILITIES

Number of RV Sites: 0. **Number of Tent-Only Sites:** 22 (primitive). **Number of Multipurpose Sites:** 100. **Hookups:** Water, electric (30, 50 amps, 50 amps in reserved sites only). **Each Site:** Picnic table, grill, primitive sites include fire ring & lantern pole. **Dump Station:** Yes. **Laundry:** Yes. **Pay Phone:** Yes. **Rest Rooms and Showers:** Yes. **Fuel:** No. **Propane:** No. **Internal Roads:** Paved. **RV Service:** 12 mi. east in McComb. **Market:** Camp store in season, 6 mi. north in McComb. **Restaurant:** 6 mi. north in McComb. **General Store:** Camp store in season, 0.25 mi. **Vending:** Beverages only. **Swimming Pool:** Yes (in day-use area, for a fee). **Playground:** Inquire at campground. **Other:** Marina, boat launch, picnic area & pavilions, lodge & meeting rooms, chapel. **Activities:** Swimming beach, fishing, boat rentals available, nature trail, archery range, 27-hole golf course, tennis, game room, (multipurpose fields at group site only), mini golf. **Nearby Attractions:** Copiah County, Homochitto & Marion County Wildlife Management Areas, Homochitto National Forest. **Additional Information:** Pike County Chamber of Commerce, (601) 684-2291, www.pikeinfo.com.

RESTRICTIONS

Pets: Leash only. **Fires:** Allowed, fire rings & grills only. **Alcoholic Beverages:** Allowed, sites only. **Vehicle Maximum Length:** 40 ft. (sites vary). **Other:** 14-night stay limit.

TO GET THERE

From I-55, take exit 13 and turn west on Fernwood Rd. Follow Fernwood Rd. until it ends and turn right on State Hwy. 48. Look for the park on the left. The park is 1 mi. from the interstate.

MERIDIAN

Meridian East Toomsuba KOA

3953 KOA Campground Rd., Toomsuba 39364. T: (601) 632-1684; F: (601) 632-9493; www.koa.com; koakamp@mississippi.net.

🚐 ★★★   ▲ ★★★

Beauty: ★★★★	Site Privacy: ★★★
Spaciousness: ★★★	Quiet: ★★★★
Security: ★★★	Cleanliness: ★★★★
Insect Control: ★★★	Facilities: ★★★

Situated in a shady grove dominated by loblolly pine, this is an incredibly attractive KOA. Sites at this rural campground are mid-sized and offer gravel parking. Roughly 25% of the sites offer pull-through parking. The prettiest RV campsites (sites 26–29) are the shady back-ins flanking the group tent area. All of the tent sites are nice looking, and some have tent pads. Children will especially like the pool, water slide, and other recreation here. In Meridian, children will enjoy the historic Dentzel Carousel, which has been in operation since 1909. Although there is no gate, this KOA is off the beaten path, making security fair. Avoid visiting Meridian during the hot, humid southern summer. Also avoid this campground on holiday weekends, when its facilities make it popular with families.

BASICS

Operated By: Mike & Shirley Groseclose. **Open:** Year-round. **Site Assignment:** Sites assigned; reservations recommended during summer season & holidays, credit card deposit required for reservation, cancel by 4 p.m. the day before arrival for refund. **Registration:** Store, self-registration at night. **Fee:** $28 for full hookups (50 amps), $25 (30 amps), $23 for water & electric, $20 for tent site, fee includes 2 people, $3 per extra adult, $2 per extra child. **Parking:** At site, in parking lot.

FACILITIES

Number of RV Sites: 0. **Number of Tent-Only Sites:** 6. **Number of Multipurpose Sites:** 43.

Hookups: Water, electric (30, 50 amps), sewer. **Each Site:** Picnic table, fire ring, (tent sites have tent pads). **Dump Station:** Yes. **Laundry:** Yes. **Pay Phone:** Courtesy phones. **Rest Rooms and Showers:** Yes. **Fuel:** No. **Propane:** Yes. **Internal Roads:** Gravel. **RV Service:** 12 mi. southwest in Meridian. **Market:** Grocery on site, supermarket 12 mi. southwest in Meridian. **Restaurant:** Snack bar on site & 12 mi. southwest in Meridian. **General Store:** On site & 12 mi. southwest in Meridian. **Vending:** No. **Swimming Pool:** Yes. **Playground:** Yes. **Other:** Pavilion, snack bar. **Activities:** 550-ft. ground water slide, game room, horseshoes, tetherball, basketball. **Nearby Attractions:** Jimmie Rodgers Museum, Peavey Museum, Antebellum homes, Highland Park, Dentzel Carousel, Dunn's Falls in Enterprise, Hamasa Shrine Temple Theater. **Additional Information:** Meridian Chamber of Commerce, (601) 693-1306.

RESTRICTIONS

Pets: Leash only (clean-up enforced). **Fires:** Allowed, tent sites only. **Alcoholic Beverages:** Allowed, sites only. **Vehicle Maximum Length:** 60 ft. (sites vary). **Other:** Visitors must register at the office.

TO GET THERE

Campground is 12 mi. east of Meridian. From I-59, take exit 165 (Toomsuba). Drive south 1.5 mi. and turn right on KOA Campground Rd. The campground is 1.5 mi. ahead on the right.

MERIDIAN
Twitley Branch Camping Area, Okatibee Lake

9200 Hamrick Rd. North, Collinsville 39325. T: (601) 626-8431; F: (601) 626-8750; www.reserveusa.com.

🚐 ★★★★   ⛺ ★★★★

Beauty: ★★★★★	Site Privacy: ★★★
Spaciousness: ★★★★	Quiet: ★★★★
Security: ★★★★★	Cleanliness: ★★★★
Insect Control: ★★★★	Facilities: ★★★★

Twitley Branch is preferable to nearby Okatibee Water Park campground for both tent and RV campers. There are plenty of activities for all ages at Okatibee Lake, including a water park. About 4,000 acres of forest are available for hunting. The attractive campground features large to huge sites shaded by loblolly pine, black gum, and various oak species. Parking is on gravel and back-in –style. The exceptions are three huge, paved pull-throughs. There is little foliage to provide privacy between sites. Two loops have hookups. Although all lakefront sites are pretty, sites 32–36 on the Black Gum Loop are exceptional for their size and shadiness. The Cypress Loop has no hookups, but it is near a lovely stand of cypress.

BASICS

Operated By: US Army Corps of Engineers. **Open:** Year-round. **Site Assignment:** First come, first served; 38 sites available for reservation through the National Recreation Reservation Service (NRRS) at (877) 444-6777 or www.reserve usa.com. Reservations can be made up to 240 days in advance, full payment required upon making reservation; credit card preferred (V, MC, D, AE), or pay by money order if at least 21 days in advance of arrival. $10 fee for cancellation or change of site or dates. Cancellation within three days of arrival charged first night, no-show charged $20 & first night. **Registration:** Gatehouse, no late registration. **Fee:** $16 for waterfront sites, $14 for non-waterfront sites, $10 for primitive tent sites, fees include 8 people. **Parking:** At site, in parking lot.

FACILITIES

Number of RV Sites: 0. **Number of Tent-Only Sites:** 12 (primitive). **Number of Multipurpose Sites:** 65. **Hookups:** Water, electric (30 amps). **Each Site:** Picnic table, fire ring, grill, lantern pole. **Dump Station:** Yes. **Laundry:** Yes. **Pay Phone:** Yes. **Rest Rooms and Showers:** Yes. **Fuel:** No. **Propane:** No. **Internal Roads:** Paved. **RV Service:** 10 mi. south in Meridian. **Market:** 3 mi. west in Collinsville. **Restaurant:** 10 mi. south in Meridian. **General Store:** 3 mi. west in Collinsville. **Vending:** Beverages. **Swimming Pool:** No. **Playground:** Yes. **Other:** Boat ramps, boat rentals at marina, foot trails, Okatibee Water Park (lodge, playground, water slide, beaches, picnic shelter), beaches, picnic facilities, scenic overlook, amphitheater. **Activities:** Swimming, waterskiing, bank fishing, hunting. **Nearby Attractions:** Mississippi Grand Opera House, Dunn's Falls in Enterprise, Bonita Lakes City Park & golf course, Sam Dale Historic Site. **Additional Information:** Meridian Chamber of Commerce, (601) 693-1306.

RESTRICTIONS

Pets: Leash only (no pets on the beach). **Fires:** Allowed, fire rings only. **Alcoholic Beverages:**

Allowed, at sites only (not allowed on the beach). **Vehicle Maximum Length:** No limit. **Other:** 2 weeks stay limit within 30 days, limit 8 people per campsite.

To Get There

From I-20, take exit 150 and drive north on Hwy. 19 for 8.5 mi. Turn right onto Twitley Branch Rd. and drive 2 mi. to Hamrick Rd. Turn right and drive about 0.75 mi. to the park entrance.

MORTON

Roosevelt State Park

2149 Hwy. 13 South, Morton 38117. T: (601) 732-6316; F: (601) 732-6317; www.mdwfp.com; roosevelt@localink4.com.

🚐 ★★★★★   ⛺ ★★★★★

Beauty: ★★★★★	Site Privacy: ★★★★★
Spaciousness: ★★★★★	Quiet: ★★★★★
Security: ★★★	Cleanliness: ★★★★
Insect Control: ★★	Facilities: ★★★★★

Set in the rolling hills of Bienville National Forest, Roosevelt State Park is one of the most beautiful state parks in Mississippi. The park has plenty of recreation for families. The 160-acre Shadow Lake is stocked with bream, crappie, bass, and catfish. Waterskiing is allowed in summertime, making the park noisier during the day. Commodious sites are shaded by lovely loblolly pine and other species. Plenty of foliage provides privacy between sites. Campsites feature back-in, paved parking. Both camping areas have drop-dead gorgeous lakefront sites. At the old campground, sites 13–15 and 24–28 are choice. At the new campground, snag a site in the 40's, 50's, 80's, or 90's. Security is fair at rural Roosevelt State Park. There are no gates, and the park is close to I-20, but rangers cruise regularly. Folks from Jackson reach the park in under one hour, making it extremely popular. If you're looking for nice weather and solitude, visit in spring or fall.

Basics

Operated By: Mississippi Dept. of Wildlife, Fisheries, & Parks. **Open:** Year-round. **Site Assignment:** Most sites first come, first served; limited sites available for reservation w/ $15 nonrefundable first night deposit. **Registration:** Gate, after-hours

ranger will check in. **Fee:** $14 for full hookups, $13 for water & electric, $9 for primitive tent sites (cash, personal checks, V, MC). **Parking:** At site, in parking lot.

Facilities

Number of RV Sites: 0. **Number of Tent-Only Sites:** 28 (primitive area). **Number of Multipurpose Sites:** 109. **Hookups:** Water, electric (30, 50 amps), 28 sites w/ sewer. **Each Site:** Picnic table, grill, burn-out area. **Dump Station:** Yes. **Laundry:** Yes. **Pay Phone:** Yes. **Rest Rooms and Showers:** Yes. **Fuel:** No. **Propane:** No. **Internal Roads:** Paved. **RV Service:** 32 mi. west in Jackson. **Market:** 2 mi. north in Morton. **Restaurant:** 12 mi. east in Forest. **General Store:** 12 mi. east in Forest. **Vending:** Yes. **Swimming Pool:** Yes (seasonal). **Playground:** Yes. **Other:** Full time catering service for groups, picnic area, pavilions, meeting rooms, group lodge, lodge, picnic facilities, gift shop, amphitheater. **Activities:** Fishing, fishing boat & paddle boat rentals in-season, water slide, swimming, skiing, tennis, softball, nature trail, video games. **Nearby Attractions:** Bienville National Forest, several wildlife management areas, Shockaloe riding trails, Natchez Trace National Scenic Trail. **Additional Information:** Morton Chamber of Commerce, (601) 732-6135.

Restrictions

Pets: Leash only. **Fires:** Allowed, sites only (except under burn ban). **Alcoholic Beverages:** Not allowed. **Vehicle Maximum Length:** 32 ft.

To Get There

The park is located 32 mi. east of Jackson. From I-20, take exit 77 and head north on MS Hwy. 13 for 0.25 mi. The entrance to the park is on the left.

NATCHEZ

Plantation Park

1 Frederick Rd., Natchez 39120. T: (601) 442-5222.

🚐 ★★★   ⛺ n/a

Beauty: ★★★	Site Privacy: ★★★
Spaciousness: ★★★	Quiet: ★★★
Security: ★★★	Cleanliness: ★★★
Insect Control: ★★	Facilities: ★★

This quiet, semi-residential RV park is conveniently located if you plan on to tour historic Natchez. Just before the Civil War, over half of the millionaires in the United States had homes in Natchez. Most of these antebellum mansions survived the war and are open for touring in the spring and fall. Call the Natchez Convention and Visitors Bureau, and plan to visit while the tours are in progress. Plantation Park offers mid-sized sites with plenty of shade, but there is little privacy between sites. All sites offer paved back-in parking. Most of the overnight sights are parallel to Mississippi Hwy. 61. The nicest sites are even numbers 19–31, which are quieter than the other overnight sites. Security at Plantation is fair to good; there is no gate, but the park is in a rural area. Since the swimming pool is the only recreational facility, there's not much here to keep children occupied.

BASICS

Operated By: Plantation Park. **Open:** Year-round. **Site Assignment:** First come, first served; reservations accepted w/ first night deposit (by check, no credit cards), cancel 2 weeks in advance for refund, $5 cancellation fee. **Registration:** Office, late-comers register next morning. **Fee:** $21 for 2 people; $2 per extra person (cash, personal checks only). **Parking:** At site.

FACILITIES

Number of Multipurpose Sites: 45. **Hookups:** Water, electric (30, 50 amps), sewer, cable. **Each Site:** Picnic table, concrete patio. **Dump Station:** No. **Laundry:** Yes. **Pay Phone:** Yes. **Rest Rooms and Showers:** Yes. **Fuel:** No. **Propane:** No. **Internal Roads:** Paved. **RV Service:** 63 mi. east in McComb. **Market:** Camp store, 3 mi. north in Natchez. **Restaurant:** 3 mi. north in Natchez. **General Store:** Camp store, Wal-Mart 5 mi. west in Natchez. **Vending:** Beverages only. **Swimming Pool:** Yes. **Playground:** No. **Activities:** Swimming. **Nearby Attractions:** Historic downtown Natchez, Grand Village of the Natchez Indians, Natchez Trace National Scenic Trail, Jefferson Military College. **Additional Information:** Natchez Visitor Reception Center, (800) 647-6724 or (601) 446-6345, www.natchez.ms.us.

RESTRICTIONS

Pets: Leash only. **Fires:** Allowed, campsites only. **Alcoholic Beverages:** Allowed. **Vehicle Maximum Length:** 70 ft.

TO GET THERE

From the intersection of US 61 and US 84 in Natchez, drive south on US 61 for 3.4 mi. The park entrance is on the left.

OCEAN SPRINGS

Camp Journey's End

7501 Hwy. 57, Ocean Springs 39565. T: (228) 875-2100; www.campjourneys-end.com; info@campjourneys-end.com.

🚐 ★★★★　　　▲ ★★★

Beauty: ★★★★　　　Site Privacy: ★★★
Spaciousness: ★★★★　Quiet: ★★★★
Security: ★★★　　　　Cleanliness: ★★★★
Insect Control: ★★★★　Facilities: ★★★

This is an attractive campground with an uncommonly welcoming staff. On property is "Liberty," a 350-year old live oak tree. Adjacent to the park is Fort Bayou River with its speckled trout. The park maintains a boat ramp and dock. Camp Journey's End is seven miles from the beach and within 35 miles of the casinos, attractions, and restaurants in Biloxi. The campground is one large grid, featuring mid-sized sites and back-in parking. Popular sites 62–73 and 80–91 have paved parking. Other sites may have grass, gravel, or sand parking. Most sites are partially shady, while a few are totally open. Shady sites include 58–61, 74–79, and 99–108. Bathhouses are nicer than average. Camp Journeys End is popular with retirees during the winter and families during the summer and spring. Plan an autumn visit to avoid crowds. The park is right next to I-20 and has no gate; security is not fantastic.

BASICS

Operated By: Craig & Linda Orrison. **Open:** Year-round. **Site Assignment:** First come, first served; reservations accepted, credit card deposit; no charge w/ 24-hour notice of cancellation. **Registration:** Office. **Fee:** $19–$28 for 2 people, $2 for additional children, $3 for adults. **Parking:** At site, in parking lot.

FACILITIES

Number of RV Sites: 118. **Number of Tent-Only Sites:** 15. **Number of Multipurpose Sites:** 10. **Hookups:** Water, electric (30, 50 amps), sewer, cable. **Each Site:** Picnic tables at most sites, grills, fire rings on request. **Dump Station:** Yes. **Laundry:** Yes. **Pay Phone:** Yes. **Rest Rooms and Showers:** Yes. **Fuel:** No. **Propane:** Yes. **Internal**

Roads: Paved. **RV Service:** On call. **Market:** Camp store, 5 mi. south in Ocean Springs. **Restaurant:** Barbecue on site, 1 mi. south in Ocean Springs. **General Store:** Camp store, 5 mi. south in Ocean Springs. **Vending:** Yes. **Swimming Pool:** Yes. **Playground:** Yes. **Other:** Boat launch, 18 mi. of waterway, pier, duck pond. **Activities:** Fishing, boating, horseshoes, basketball, seasonal organized activities. **Nearby Attractions:** Ocean Springs art museums, 11 mi. to Biloxi casinos, Beauvoir Jefferson Davis home, 60 mi. to Mobile, 90 mi. to New Orleans. **Additional Information:** Mississippi Gulf Coast CVB, (228) 896-6699.

RESTRICTIONS

Pets: Leash only. **Fires:** Allowed, fire rings only. **Alcoholic Beverages:** Allowed. **Vehicle Maximum Length:** 40 ft.

TO GET THERE

The campground is 11 mi. east of Biloxi and 20 mi. west of the Alabama state line. From I-10, take exit 57. Drive north on MS Hwy. 57 for 0.25 mi. to the campground.

OCEAN SPRINGS

Davis Bayou Campground, Gulf Islands National Seashore

3500 Park Rd., Ocean Springs 39564. T: (228) 875-3962; F: (228) 872-2954; www.nps.gov.

🚐 ★★★★	🏕 ★★★★
Beauty: ★★★★	Site Privacy: ★★★
Spaciousness: ★★★★	Quiet: ★★★★
Security: ★★★★	Cleanliness: ★★★
Insect Control: ★★	Facilities: ★★★

Gulf Island National seashore consists of 11 geographically distinct units stretching from West Ship Island, MS to Santa Rosa Island, FL. Davis Bayou Recreation Area nestles into the suburban mainland and has no beach. Visitors enjoy the bayou via the boat ramp and fishing pier. The beach is four miles away at Ocean Springs. The small, very pretty campground consists of two loops. The smaller loop (sites 11–19) contains the nicest sites. Sites 12 and 13 are especially gorgeous. These sites are afforded shade and privacy by ample woods, and they include views of the salt marsh. Most sites are wooded with little foliage between them. Site size varies widely, but all are adequate. Parking is paved and back-in–style. Coastal Mississippi can be excruciatingly hot in the summer. Try to plan a visit in spring or fall. Patrolled by rangers all night, security at this national park is good.

BASICS

Operated By: National Park Service. **Open:** Year-round. **Site Assignment:** First come, first served. **Registration:** Office or self-registration. **Fee:** $16 for electric, $14 for water only (cash, personal check, V, MC, D). **Parking:** At sites & parking areas.

FACILITIES

Number of Multipurpose Sites: 51. **Hookups:** Water, electric (50 amps). **Each Site:** Picnic table, grill. **Dump Station:** Yes. **Laundry:** No. **Pay Phone:** Yes. **Rest Rooms and Showers:** Yes. **Fuel:** No. **Propane:** No. **Internal Roads:** Paved. **RV Service:** No. **Market:** No. **Restaurant:** 0.5 mi. west. **General Store:** 1.5 mi. east. **Vending:** No. **Swimming Pool:** No. **Playground:** Yes. **Other:** Boat launches, visitor center, fishing pier, picnic area. **Activities:** Fishing, boating, kayaking, walking trails, bicycle trails; no swimming due to alligators. **Nearby Attractions:** Beaches, museums, boat tours, 4 mi. to Biloxi casinos, 75 mi. to New Orleans. **Additional Information:** Mississippi Gulf Coast CVB, (228) 896-6699.

RESTRICTIONS

Pets: Leash only. **Fires:** Grills only. **Alcoholic Beverages:** Allowed (no glass containers). **Vehicle Maximum Length:** 45 ft. **Other:** No swimming due to alligators.

TO GET THERE

From the west, take I-10 to Ocean Springs and exit at Tucker Rd. Take Tucker Rd. south 5–7 mi. to US 90. Head east (left) on 90 and proceed 5–7 mi. The park is on the right, and the campground is 2 mi. inside the Seashore area on the right. From the east, take I-10 to the Fontainebleau exit. Take State Hwy. 57 south to US 90 west, and the Seashore is on the left.

SARDIS

John W. Kyle State Park

Rte. 1 Box 115, Sardis 38666. T: (662) 487-1345; F: (662) 487-0409; www.mdwfp.com; johnkyle@panola.com.

🚐 ★★★	🏕 ★★★
Beauty: ★★★	Site Privacy: ★★★
Spaciousness: ★★★	Quiet: ★★

Security: ★★★   Cleanliness: ★★★
Insect Control: ★★★   Facilities: ★★★★

John W. Kyle State Park offers some of the best freshwater fishing in the southeast. Best known for prize bass, Sardis Reservoir also has huge crappie. The campground is nice-looking, but families have as many as four vehicles per site, making it crowded and congested. Children, boats, and trucks make the park noisy too. Avoid John W. Kyle on summer weekends and especially on holiday weekends. Situated in a shady stand of mature red oak trees, sites are average-sized. There is little privacy between sites. Both of the camping areas have a few lakefront sites, such as sites 87–90 and 284–287. Of these, site 90 is the top choice for its spaciousness and lovely view.

BASICS

Operated By: Mississippi Dept. of Wildlife, Fisheries & Parks. **Open:** Year-round. **Site Assignment:** First come, first served; 13 sites available for reservation for 3-night min. w/ $15 nonrefundable first night deposit. **Registration:** Gatehouse. **Fee:** $13, $10 for seniors (cash, check, V, MC). **Parking:** At site.

FACILITIES

Number of Multipurpose Sites: 201. **Hookups:** Water, electric (30, 50 amps). **Each Site:** Picnic table, grill, some w/ tent pads, some w/ fire rings. **Dump Station:** Yes. **Laundry:** Yes. **Pay Phone:** Yes. **Rest Rooms and Showers:** Yes. **Fuel:** No. **Propane:** No. **Internal Roads:** Paved. **RV Service:** 8 mi. west in Sardis. **Market:** 8 mi. southwest in Batesville. **Restaurant:** 8 mi. southwest in Batesville. **General Store:** 8 mi. southwest in Batesville. **Vending:** Beverages only. **Swimming Pool:** Yes. **Playground:** Yes. **Other:** Boat launch, snack bar, pavilion, lodge, recreation building, picnic area, 18-hole golf course. **Activities:** Swimming beach, nature trail, playing fields, tennis, water sports, fishing, boat rentals. **Nearby Attractions:** Tunica casinos, Holly Springs National Forest, University of Mississippi in Oxford, 40 mi. to Memphis. **Additional Information:** Sardis Chamber of Commerce, (662) 487-3451.

RESTRICTIONS

Pets: Leash only. **Fires:** Allowed, fire rings only. **Alcoholic Beverages:** Allowed, sites only. **Vehicle Maximum Length:** 32 ft. standard (sites vary).

TO GET THERE

From I-55, take exit 252 onto State Hwy. 315 and drive east for 7 mi. The park entrance is on the right.

TUNICA

Grand Casino RV Resort

111 Resort Village Rd., Robinsonville 38664. T: (800) 946-4946; F: (662) 357-3208; www.grandcasis.com.

🚐 ★★★   ⛺ n/a

Beauty: ★★   Site Privacy: ★★
Spaciousness: ★★★   Quiet: ★★★★
Security: ★★★★   Cleanliness: ★★★★
Insect Control: ★★★   Facilities: ★★★★

The RV resort at Grand Casino Tunica won't win any beauty contests, but it does offer casino patrons a clean, livable place to park their campers. Couples will appreciate the park's attempt to maintain quiet by corralling families with children into a separate area. Families will enjoy the spacious pool and playground. Resort privileges include access to the 18-hole golf course (call for greens fees) and sporting clays. Bus service to and from the casino is provided 24 hours a day. Security (a serious concern at casinos) is good; while not fenced, the campground is gated at all times. The campground is a long walk from the casino and is patrolled by security guards. Tunica is much safer than Las Vegas or Atlantic City—at this rural gaming Mecca, casinos tower over vast acres of flat croplands.

BASICS

Operated By: Grand Casino, Inc. **Open:** Year-round. **Site Assignment:** First come, first served; reservations accepted, no deposit, 24-hour notice for cancellation. **Registration:** Lodge. **Fee:** $19. **Parking:** At site, in parking lot.

FACILITIES

Number of RV Sites: 200. **Number of Tent-Only Sites:** 0. **Number of Multipurpose Sites:** None. **Hookups:** Water, electric (20, 30, 50 amps), sewer, cable. **Each Site:** Picnic table, concrete pads. **Dump Station:** No. **Laundry:** Yes. **Pay Phone:** Yes. **Rest Rooms and Showers:** Yes. **Fuel:** No. **Propane:** Yes. **Internal Roads:** Paved. **RV Service:** 15 mi. north in Southaven. **Market:** 15 mi. north in Southaven. **Restaurant:** In casino. **General Store:** 15 mi. north in Southaven. **Vending:** No. **Swimming Pool:** Yes. **Playground:** Yes. **Other:** Lounge. **Activities:** Casino, volleyball, horseshoes, basketball, shuffleboard, sports green, sporting clays, 18-hole golf course, video arcade, Kids Quest (hands-on activity center). **Nearby Attractions:** Sporting clays, outlet shopping, 15 mi.

to Memphis, Beale St., Mud Island, Graceland. **Additional Information:** Tunica CVB, (888) 4-TUNICA.

RESTRICTIONS

Pets: Allowed. **Fires:** Grills only. **Alcoholic Beverages:** Allowed (no glass bottles). **Vehicle Maximum Length:** No limit.

TO GET THERE

From Memphis, take I-55 to exit 7 (3rd St./ Vicksburg). Take US 61 south 19 mi. to the Tunica Resort on the right. Pass the first entrance, then pass the visitors center and outlet malls and take the next entrance on the right. Pass the golf course, and turn left at the traffic light into the RV park. From Jackson, take I-55 to Hernando, then take State Hwy. 304 west about 17 miles to US 61 North. The resort is 5 mi. on the left (west).

TUPELO

Tombigbee State Park

264 Cabin Dr., Tupelo 38804. T: (662) 842-7669; F: (662) 840-5594; www.mdwfp.com.

🚐 ★★★   ⛺ ★★★

Beauty: ★★★   Site Privacy: ★★
Spaciousness: ★★★   Quiet: ★★★
Security: ★★★   Cleanliness: ★★★
Insect Control: ★★   Facilities: ★★★

This small state park is not as attractive as other Mississippi state parks. We prefer it over private campgrounds in the area for its recreational facilities and seclusion. The campground offers mid-sized sites with paved back-in parking. Most sites enjoy partial shade, but there is no foliage between sites to provide privacy. Trees include a variety of pine and hardwoods. Sites are laid out in a large oval with bathhouses in the middle. Here, each site looks just like its neighbor, so choose yours based on location. Tombigbee State Park maintains extensive facilities for large groups, as well as a fishing lake stocked with bass, bream, and catfish. The park never locks its gates, but it is fairly remote, making security fair. The area around Tupelo tends to be moist and low-lying; mosquitoes and summer heat can be unbearable, so plan accordingly.

BASICS

Operated By: Mississippi Dept. of Wildlife, Fisheries & Parks. **Open:** Year-round. **Site Assignment:** First

come, first served; 3 sites available for reservation, 2 night min., w/ $15 nonrefundable first night deposit. **Registration:** Office, ranger will collect in the evenings. **Fee:** $13 for full hookups ($15 first night if reserved), $12 for water & electric, $8 for primitive tent site, $10 for seniors or disabled. **Parking:** At site.

FACILITIES

Number of RV Sites: 0. **Number of Tent-Only Sites:** 4. **Number of Multipurpose Sites:** 20. **Hookups:** Water, electric (20, 30 amps), 6 sites w/ sewer. **Each Site:** Picnic table, grill, fire ring, some lantern poles. **Dump Station:** Yes. **Laundry:** Yes. **Pay Phone:** Yes. **Rest Rooms and Showers:** Yes. **Fuel:** No. **Propane:** No. **Internal Roads:** Paved. **RV Service:** 35 mi. south in Aberdeen. **Market:** 4 mi. toward Plantersville. **Restaurant:** 4 mi. toward Plantersville. **General Store:** Wal-Mart 10 mi. west in Tupelo. **Vending:** Yes. **Swimming Pool:** No. **Playground:** Yes. **Other:** Picnic area, pavilions, visitor center, group lodge & dining hall, meeting rooms. **Activities:** Fishing, boating (rentals available, paddle boats in-season), nature trail, game room, disc-golf course. **Nearby Attractions:** Natchez Trace National Scenic Trail, Birthplace of Elvis Presley in Tupelo, Tupelo Civil War Battlefield, Tennessee-Tombigbee Waterway, Wildlife Management Areas. **Additional Information:** Tupelo CVB, (800) 533-0611.

RESTRICTIONS

Pets: Leash only, in campground only. **Fires:** Fire rings only. **Alcoholic Beverages:** Not allowed. **Vehicle Maximum Length:** 40 ft.

TO GET THERE

From Tupelo, go south on Main St./State Hwy. 6. Stay on Hwy. 6 south until Plantersville, then turn left and drive east on State Park Rd. The park is 3 mi. east of Plantersville (6 mi. from Tupelo).

VICKSBURG

Magnolia RV Park

211 Miller St., Vicksburg 39180. T: (601) 631-0388; F: (601) 631-0013; magnoliarv@aol.com.

🚐 ★★   ⛺ ★

Beauty: ★★   Site Privacy: ★
Spaciousness: ★★   Quiet: ★★
Security: ★   Cleanliness: ★★★
Insect Control: ★★★   Facilities: ★★

We chose to include this completely treeless RV park because of its location and its tidy rest rooms. Situated in urban Vicksburg, the park is a convenient choice if you're touring Vicksburg National Military Park. There are four rows of pull-through campsites at Magnolia. All sites are completely open. Sites 50–66 are bordered by trees to the north, making them slightly more attractive but not any shadier. All sites are small, and all parking is on gravel. Security is poor, as this park is not gated and is surrounded by urban development. Avoid visiting this historic Mississippi River town in the summer, when heat and humidity become unbearable.

BASICS

Operated By: Dino & Sheryl Ross. **Open:** Year-round. **Site Assignment:** Sites assigned; reservations recommended fall & spring, credit card deposit; cancel by 2 p.m. arrival day for refund. **Registration:** Camp store, after hours registration instructions posted. **Fee:** $20 for 50 amps, $18 for 30 amps, $11 for tent sites; prices for 4 people, $1 per extra person; Good Sam, FMCA, AAA, AARP, Escapees RV Club discounts. **Parking:** At sites, in gravel pads only.

FACILITIES

Number of RV Sites: 66. **Number of Tent-Only Sites:** 4.5 acres of primitive area. **Number of Multipurpose Sites:** None. **Hookups:** Water, electric (20, 30, 50 amps), sewer. **Each Site:** Picnic table. **Dump Station:** No. **Laundry:** Yes. **Pay Phone:** Yes. **Rest Rooms and Showers:** Yes. **Fuel:** No. **Propane:** No. **Internal Roads:** Gravel. **RV Service:** 45 mi. east in Jackson. **Market:** 0.5 mi. in Vicksburg. **Restaurant:** 0.5 mi. in Vicksburg. **General Store:** Camp store (w/ limited RV supplies). **Vending:** Beverages only. **Swimming Pool:** Yes. **Playground:** Yes. **Other:** Meeting room, free casino shuttle. **Activities:** Game room, basketball. **Nearby Attractions:** Casinos, Civil War Battlefield, National Military Cemetery, Biedenharm Coca-Cola Museum, Historic Downtown Vicksburg, Gray & Blue Naval Musem. **Additional Information:** Vicksburg CVB, (601) 636-9421 or (800) 221-3536.

RESTRICTIONS

Pets: Leash only. **Fires:** Not allowed on the ground; bring your own grill. **Alcoholic Beverages:** At site only. **Vehicle Maximum Length:** No limit.

To Get There

From I-20, take exit 1B and drive south on US 61 for 1 mi. Turn right onto Miller St. The park is on the right.

WAVELAND

Buccaneer State Park

1150 South Beach Blvd., Waveland 39576. T: (228) 467-3822; F: (228) 467-1598; www.mdwfp.com; buccaneer@intu.net.

🚐 ★★★   ▲ ★★★

Beauty: ★★★★	Site Privacy: ★★★
Spaciousness: ★★★	Quiet: ★★
Security: ★★★	Cleanliness: ★
Insect Control: ★★★★	Facilities: ★★★★

Children delight in the recreation and folklore here. Legend says that French buccaneer Jean Lafitte buried his loot here in the late 1700s. Lafitte did in fact live in the nearby "Old Pirate House." When we visited, the park and campground both needed a serious cleaning. The campground property includes seven areas. The most spacious and heavily wooded is the loop containing sites 105–149. Even-numbered sites 112–124 have a lovely view of the salt marsh. In other areas, site size and shadiness vary. All sites feature paved, back-in parking.

BASICS

Operated By: Mississippi Dept. of Wildlife, Fisheries & Parks. **Open:** All year (office closed Thanksgiving & Christmas). **Site Assignment:** First come, first served; 25 full hookup sites available for reservation w/ 2-night min. & $15 first night nonrefundable deposit. **Registration:** Office at park entrance, late comers register the next morning. **Fee:** $14 for full hookups, $13 for water & electric, $9 for tent site (cash, personal checks, V, MC). **Parking:** At sites.

FACILITIES

Number of Multipurpose Sites: 386. **Hookups:** Water, electric (20, 30, 50 amps), some w/ sewer. **Each Site:** Grill, picnic table, some w/ tent pad. **Dump Station:** Yes. **Laundry:** Yes. **Pay Phone:** Yes. **Rest Rooms and Showers:** Yes. **Fuel:** No. **Propane:** No. **Internal Roads:** Paved. **RV Service:** 25 mi. east in Gulfport. **Market:** 5 mi. in Waveland. **Restaurant:** 3 mi. in Waveland. **General Store:** Camp store. **Vending:** Beverages only.

Swimming Pool: Yes. **Playground:** Yes. **Other:** Amphitheater, picnic pavilions, multi-purpose court, activity building. **Activities:** Nature trails, disc-golf, tennis, basketball, arcade, beach, fishing, Buccaneer Bay Waterpark (water slide, wave pool, children's pool, snack bar, gift shop, open May–Sept.). **Nearby Attractions:** John C. Stennis Space Center in Bay St. Louis, Marine Life Oceanarium in Gulfport, Bayou & boat tours, Gulf Islands National Seashore. **Additional Information:** Mississippi Gulf Coast CVB, (228) 896-6699.

RESTRICTIONS

Pets: Leash only. **Fires:** Allowed, in designated areas. **Alcoholic Beverages:** Allowed (moderation). **Vehicle Maximum Length:** No limit. **Other:** 14-day stay limit summer season.

TO GET THERE

From I-10, take exit 13 and drive south on State Hwy. 603 about 7 mi. to the coast. Turn right on Beach Blvd. and drive west just over 4 mi. The park is on the right.

North Carolina

With a wide variety of recreational activities to be had from the western mountain region, through the central Heartland, and to the eastern coastal region, North Carolina is a camper's delight. In the Mountains region of North Carolina, you'll find two ranges of the Southern Appalachians, the Blue Ride Mountains, and the Great Smoky Mountains. Here, there are 43 peaks that reach 6,000 feet, and **Mt. Mitchell,** at 6,684 feet, is the highest peak in the eastern United States. Enjoy your camping experience by engaging in the limitless activities available in the mountains: fly-fish for trout in the Great Smoky Mountains on **Kerr** or **Falls Lake;** rock climb or hike at **Table Rock, Looking Glass Rock,** or **Linville Gorge** in Pisgah National Forest; or enjoy exciting white-water rafting on the **Nantahala** and **Pidgeon Rivers.** Along the 252 miles of the **Blue Ridge Parkway** located in North Carolina, you will find five campgrounds, so be sure to stop to enjoy some of the outdoor adventure offered in this area. The **Land of Waterfalls** in the **Pisgah National Forest** offers some breathtaking scenery, and camping in the Great Smoky Mountains might afford you a scenic ride on the railroad to enjoy unsurpassed views of the area.

Also known as the Piedmont and home of America's first gold rush, the Heartland of North Carolina bustles with the state's largest urban areas. Its rolling plains, smooth lakes, meandering rivers, and romantic lagoons provide scenic camping experiences and plenty of water recreation. Be sure to explore the banks and waters of the **Lumber River,** one of North Carolina's four rivers designated as a National Wild and Scenic River. **Lake Norman,** boasting 32,500 acres of water, provides ample opportunity for campers hoping to swim and boat—it's especially nice on those hot, lazy summer days. The **Roanoke Canal Trail** is an excellent stop, with nicely preserved nineteenth-century canal construction and seven miles of unique hiking trails with views of old bridges and steps carved in the earth.

Venture to the Coast where you'll enjoy 300 miles of beach interrupted only by quiet inlets. The history here is rich and inspiration is strong. It was here that Sir Walter Raleigh established the first English Settlement and the Wright Brothers experienced their first flight on the sandy beaches of **Kitty Hawk** in 1903. The city of **New Bern** is known as the birthplace of Pepsi, first marketed as "Brad's Drink." Perhaps you can enjoy a sip of the bubbly drink (does it taste different here?) while enjoying the coastal scenery: historic lighthouses, coasts of islands rising from the water, and graceful seabirds skimming the surface of the sea. Scuba diving proves to be a particularly unusual experience in the "Graveyard of the Atlantic" where you can explore the remains of over 2,000 ships. And it is on the coast where the **Croatan National Forest** offers an excellent stop for campers looking for a wide variety of outdoor activities. Be sure, too, to visit the **Cape Hatteras National Seashore,** where you can enjoy a number of attractions including the Cape Hatteras Lighthouse, which, at 208 feet tall, is the tallest lighthouse in the country.

Campground Profiles

ALBEMARLE
Morrow Mountain State Park

49104 Morrow Mountain Rd., Albemarle 28001. T: (704) 982-4402; F: (704) 982-5323; ncsparks.net; momo@vnet.net.

🚐 ★★★★   ▲ ★★★★

Beauty: ★★★★★	Site Privacy: ★★★
Spaciousness: ★★★★	Quiet: ★★★★
Security: ★★★★	Cleanliness: ★★★★★
Insect Control: ★★★★	Facilities: ★★★★

The campground at Morrow Mountain is situated on gently rolling terrain shaded by pine trees and various hardwoods. Pine straw softens the ground. Many sites enjoy views of pleasant fields, but with little greenery between sites, privacy is minimal. Sites are large, with gravel parking. Most offer back-in parking, though there are couple of pull-through sites. Loop C is recommended for RVs—sites tend to be flatter, with greater maneuverability. Morrow Mountain is the only state park in North Carolina with a swimming pool. For fisherfolk, Lake Tillery supports crappie, largemouth bass, striped bass, white bass, perch, bluegill, and catfish. The park is located in the gentle Uwharrie Mountains and includes 16 miles of hiking trails and 16 miles of equestrian trails. When we visited, we saw neither hide nor hair of rangers or staff, making security a bit iffy. But the park is extremely remote. Visit anytime except summer weekends and holidays.

BASICS

Operated By: North Carolina State Parks. **Open:** All year except Christmas. **Site Assignment:** First come, first served, campers can pick desirable site if the site is vacant. **Registration:** At the campsite. **Fee:** Site w/ no hookups is $12 per night, $10 for senior citizens (62 years of age). **Parking:** 2 vehicle parking at each site.

FACILITIES

Number of Multipurpose Sites: 106. **Hookups:** None. **Each Site:** Picnic table, grill, fire ring, lantern hook, tent pad. **Dump Station:** Yes. **Laundry:** No. **Pay Phone:** Yes. **Rest Rooms and Showers:** Yes. **Fuel:** No. **Propane:** No. **Internal Roads:** Paved. **RV Service:** Approx. 30 mi. in Charlotte. **Market:** 7 mi. west in Albemarle. **Restaurant:** 7 mi. west in Albemarle. **General Store:** 8 mi. west in Albemarle. **Vending:** No (concession stand during the summer months). **Swimming Pool:** Yes (open Jun. 1–Labor Day). **Playground:** No. **Other:** Group lodging, fishing deck, boat launch, amphitheater, primitive camp sites. **Activities:** Boat rental, horseback riding, picnicking, fishing. **Nearby Attractions:** Afro-American Cultural Center, Brem House Artisans Gallery, Charlotte Museum of History, Mint Museum of Art, Paramount's Carowinds Water & Theme Park. **Additional Information:** Charlotte CVB, (704) 334-2282.

RESTRICTIONS

Pets: Leash only. **Fires:** Fire ring & in other designated areas. **Alcoholic Beverages:** Not allowed. **Vehicle Maximum Length:** None.

TO GET THERE

From Albemarle, travel 6 mi. east on NC 740. Follow Morrow Mountain Rd. into the park.

APEX
Crosswinds Campground, Jordan Lake State Recreation Area

280 State Park Rd., Apex 27502. T: (919) 362-0586; F: (919) 362-1621; ncparks.net; jordan.lake@ncmail.net.

🚐 ★★★★   ▲ ★★★★

Beauty: ★★★★	Site Privacy: ★★★★★
Spaciousness: ★★★★★	Quiet: ★★★★
Security: ★★★★★	Cleanliness: ★★★
Insect Control: ★★★★	Facilities: ★★★

Crosswinds has one advantage over nearby Poplar Point: it's smaller. Otherwise, these two campgrounds are comparable. Crosswinds features incredibly large sites amid hills. And double sites (designed for two families to share) are gargantuan. Sites are densely wooded, with plenty of undergrowth providing privacy between sites. Most sites have back-in parking, though there are a handful of pull-through sites. Parking pads are gravel, and each site has a pea gravel picnic area. Our favorite sites in Area A (18, 19, 22, 46, and 47) have pristine lake views. Families should head for sites 36–39 in Area B, which are convenient to the beach. In Area C, we like sites 19 and 21. Recreation revolves around Jordan Lake, which is known for its teeming crappie, catfish, and bass. Crosswinds locks its gates at night. Though it feels extremely rural, it's only about 20 miles from Raleigh. The campground stays busy in the summer. Visit in spring or fall for solitude.

BASICS

Operated By: NC State Parks. **Open:** All year. **Site Assignment:** First come, first served. Reservations can be made if staying 7 nights or more, (919) 362-0586. Cash & checks are accepted. Cancel 2 weeks before the expected arrival date without penalty. Stay limit is 2 weeks. **Registration:** Campground office. **Fee:** Site w/ no hookups is $12 per night, $10 for senior citizens (62 years of age). $17 for sites w/ water & electric, $14 for senior citizens. **Parking:** 2 vehicles at each site, overflow parking available.

FACILITIES

Number of Multipurpose Sites: 177 total, 129 w/ water & electric. **Hookups:** Electric (30 amps), water. **Each Site:** Lantern pole, picnic table, fire ring, grill, trash can. **Dump Station:** Yes. **Laundry:** No. **Pay Phone:** Yes. **Rest Rooms and Showers:** Yes. **Fuel:** No. **Propane:** No. **Internal Roads:** Paved & gravel. **RV Service:** 6 mi. east in Pittsboro. **Market:** 6 mi. east in Pittsboro. **Restaurant:** 6 mi. in Pittsboro. **General Store:** 1 mi. **Vending:** No. **Swimming Pool:** No. **Playground:** No. **Other:** Boat ramps. **Activities:** Fishing, boating, educational activities, hiking. **Nearby Attractions:** African American Cultural Complex, North Carolina Art Museum, Mordecai Historic Park, Exploris, JC Raulston Arboretum. **Additional Information:** Greater Raleigh CVB, (919) 831-2887.

RESTRICTIONS

Pets: Leash only. **Fires:** Allowed. **Alcoholic Beverages:** Not allowed. **Vehicle Maximum Length:** None.

TO GET THERE

From the US1 and US 64 junction, go west on US 64.

APEX

Poplar Point Campground, Jordan Lake State Recreation Area

280 State Park Rd., Apex 27502. T: (919) 362-0586; F: (919) 362-1621; ncparks.net; jordan.lake@ncmail.net.

🚐 ★★★★	🅰 ★★★★
Beauty: ★★★★	Site Privacy: ★★★★★
Spaciousness: ★★★★★	Quiet: ★★★★
Security: ★★★★★	Cleanliness: ★★★
Insect Control: ★★★★	Facilities: ★★★

Mammoth Poplar Point offers sites very much like those at Crosswinds. Both campgrounds feature large sites amongst lovely hills. Most sites are very shady, with plenty of greenery to provide privacy between neighbors. The majority of parking is back-in style, though there are a few sites with pull-through parking. Parking spaces are gravel, with a pea gravel picnic area at each site. Our favorite lake views are at sites C3–C35, F12, F15, F17, F19. Loop E offers picturesque sites near a small pond (E9, E10, E14, and E15 are the nicest). Tent campers should head to E50–E55. RV campers craving a big, gorgeous pull-through should head for E98. Amenities at Poplar Point are also comparable to those at Crosswinds. However, the beach is more likely to be crowded here because there are so many more sites. Security is good—the campground is gated. To avoid throngs of people, visit midweek or in spring or autumn.

BASICS

Operated By: NC State Parks. **Open:** Mar.–Nov. **Site Assignment:** First come, first served. Reservations can be made if staying 7 nights or more, (919) 362-0586. Cash & checks are accepted. If cancelled 2 weeks before expected arrival there is no penalty. Stay limit is 2 weeks. **Registration:** Camp office. **Fee:** Site w/ no hookups is $12 per night, $10 for senior citizens (62 years of age). $17 for sites w/ water & electric, $14 for senior citizens. **Parking:** 2 vehicles at each site, overflow parking available.

FACILITIES

Number of Multipurpose Sites: 580 total, 361 have electric. **Hookups:** Electric (30 amps). **Each Site:** Lantern pole, picnic table, fire ring, grill, trash can. **Dump Station:** Yes. **Laundry:** No. **Pay Phone:** Yes. **Rest Rooms and Showers:** Yes. **Fuel:** No. **Propane:** No. **Internal Roads:** Paved & gravel. **RV Service:** Approx. 6 mi. east in Pittsboro. **Market:** Approx. 6 mi. east in Pittsboro. **Restaurant:** Approx. 6 mi. east in Pittsboro. **General Store:** 1 mi. **Vending:** No. **Swimming Pool:** No. **Playground:** No. **Other:** Boat ramps. **Activities:** Boating, fishing, canoeing, cultural history programs, hiking. **Nearby Attractions:** African American Cultural Complex, North Carolina Art Museum, Mordecai Historic Park, Exploris, JC Raulston Arboretum. **Additional Information:** Greater Raleigh CVB, (919) 831-2887.

RESTRICTIONS

Pets: Leash only. **Fires:** Allowed. **Alcoholic Beverages:** Not allowed. **Vehicle Maximum Length:** None.

TO GET THERE

Go 10 mi. west on US 64 to Wilsonville, then go 2 mi. south on Hwy 1008.

BALSAM

Moonshine Creek Campground

Box 10 Dark Ridge Road 28707. T: (828) 586-6666; www.moonshinecreekcampground.com; moonshinecreek@hotmail.com.

🚐 ★★★★	⛺ ★★★★
Beauty: ★★★★★	Site Privacy: ★★★
Spaciousness: ★★★	Quiet: ★★★★
Security: ★★★★	Cleanliness: ★★★★
Insect Control: ★★★★	Facilities: ★★

Balsam is a sweet little town, with restaurants as close as Waynesville and plenty of mountain recreation nearby. The Blue Ridge Parkway intersects the town, making Balsam a good camping choice for motor tourists. Drive east about ten miles to Richland Balsam, the highest point on the Blue Ridge Parkway (elev. 6,047 feet). The campground offers small, picturesque sites laid out along Moonshine Creek. Tree cover

is lovely. Gravel parking pads overwhelm some sites to the extent that there is little natural ground cover. Our favorite creekside sites, 14, 16, 18, and 20, are nicely situated but have no grass. Other nice sites include 8, which is more spacious than most, and 9–12. Balsam's cool mountain weather is heavenly in the summer. For the least hassled touring, plan a mid-week visit. Security is fine here. There is no gate but the park is extremely remote.

BASICS

Operated By: Mack & Janet McDonald. **Open:** Apr.–Nov. **Site Assignment:** Deposit must be received 7 days prior to reservation; 7-day notice on cancellations for refund; V, MC, check, cash, money order. **Registration:** In office. **Fee:** RV is $24/day, tent is $20/day. **Parking:** At site.

FACILITIES

Number of RV Sites: 59. **Number of Tent-Only Sites:** 30. **Number of Multipurpose Sites:** 0. **Hookups:** Water, sewer, electric (30 amps). **Each Site:** Water, electric, fire ring, picnic table. **Dump Station:** Yes. **Laundry:** Yes. **Pay Phone:** Yes. **Rest Rooms and Showers:** Yes. **Fuel:** No. **Propane:** Yes. **Internal Roads:** Gravel, entrance is asphalt. **RV Service:** 5 mi. toward Waynesville. **Market:** 5 mi. toward Waynesville. **Restaurant:** 5 mi. toward Waynesville. **General Store:** 5 mi. toward Waynesville. **Vending:** No. **Swimming Pool:** No. **Playground:** No. **Other:** Grocery store. **Activities:** Planned cook outs. **Nearby Attractions:** Appalachian Trail, biltmore House, Blowing Rock, Blue Ridge Pkwy., Cherohala Skyway, Cherokee Bear Zoo, Cherokee Corn Maze, Cherokee Indian Museum, Cherokee Indian Reservation, Chimney Rock Park, Deep Creek tubes, Fields of the Wood, Fontana Lake and Dam, Ghost Town in Maggie Valley, Grand Father Mountain, Great Smoky Mountain National Park, Harra's Cherokee Casino, Joyce Kilmer Memorial Forest, Linville Caverns, Mountain Farm & Museum, Moutain Waters Scenic Byway, Nantahala National Forest, Nantahala River Rafting, Oconaluftee Indian Village, Pisgah National Forest, Santa's Land Fun Park & Zoo, Soco Gardens Zoo, Smoky Mountain Country Club, Tribal Bingo, Tsali Trail, Unto These Hills Outdoor Drama.

RESTRICTIONS

Pets: Allowed. **Fires:** Fire rings only. **Alcoholic Beverages:** At site only. **Vehicle Maximum Length:** None.

TO GET THERE

From Cherokee: Drive south on US 441, then northeast on US 74/23. Follow signs to campground.

BUXTON
Cape Woods Campground and Cabins

47649 Buxton Back Rd, Buxton, NC 27920.
T: (252)995-5850; F: (252)995-3732;
www.Capewoods.com.

🚐 ★★★   ⛺ ★★★

Beauty: ★★★★	Site Privacy: ★★
Spaciousness: ★★★	Quiet: ★★★★
Security: ★★★★	Cleanliness: ★★★★
Insect Control: ★★★	Facilities: ★★

Campers who prefer full hookups and wish to tour Cape Hatteras National Seashore are in luck. Attractive Cape Woods is located centrally on Hatteras Island, just a few miles from the Wright Brothers National Memorial, including the first airstrip, site of Orville Wright's historic 1903 flight. The swimming beach at the national seashore is less than five miles from the campground. The park includes back-in sites with grass parking and paved patios at each site. Most sites are average size, though some are long and narrow. Shadiness varies from site to site, though most are partially shady. Since the campground is inland and treed, it stays a little cooler than the national park campgrounds. There is no seclusion. Sites are differentiated by their amenities, so choose your site based on the hookups you need. Security is excellent at Cape Woods. The campground is gated at all times. Avoid Cape Hatteras on summer weekends. Bring bug spray in the summer.

BASICS

Operated By: Kevin & Laurie Morris. **Open:** All year. **Site Assignment:** Encourage reservations. **Registration:** Office. **Fee:** $26–$33. **Parking:** At site.

FACILITIES

Number of RV Sites: 135. **Number of Tent-Only Sites:** 11. **Number of Multipurpose Sites:** 0. **Hookups:** Water, electric (50 amps), septic, cable. **Each Site:** Water, electric (50 amps).

Dump Station: Yes. **Laundry:** Yes. **Pay Phone:** No. **Rest Rooms and Showers:** Yes. **Fuel:** No. **Propane:** Yes. **Internal Roads:** Gravel. **RV Service:** Nearby. **Market:** No. **Restaurant:** No. **General Store:** Yes. **Vending:** Yes. **Swimming Pool:** Yes. **Playground:** Yes. **Activities:** Game room, volleyball, horseshoes, fising. **Nearby Attractions:** NPS Cape Hatteras Lighthouse, Ocracoke Island, 2 mi. from beach.

RESTRICTIONS

Pets: Allowed. **Fires:** Fire pits on some sites. **Alcoholic Beverages:** Allowed. **Vehicle Maximum Length:** None.

TO GET THERE

From Atlanta: I-85 North towards Greenville, take I-40 East toward Raleigh, take Raleigh Chapel Hill Expressway (it becomes Wade Ave.) Turn right onto ramp. Merge onto I-440 North, Take Exit No. 13B toward Rocky Mount/Wilson. In Buxton, bear left at Centura Bank. Buxton Back Rd. is 1 mi. on the left.

CAPE HATTERAS
Cape Point

Route 1 Box 675, Manteo 27954. T: (252) 473-2111; www.nps.gov./caha.

🚐 ★★★   ⛺ ★★★

Beauty: ★★★	Site Privacy: ★★
Spaciousness: ★★★★	Quiet: ★★★★
Security: ★★★	Cleanliness: ★★★★
Insect Control: ★★★	Facilities: ★

This is the least attractive of the Cape Hatteras National Seashore campgrounds. However, this campground is quieter than Oregon inlet because it's further from the main road. Also, sites are larger and more open than at Oregon. Cape Point is completely flat. Sites feature paved, back-in parking and paved picnic table pads. There is no shade or privacy. Vegetation consists of natural marsh grasses that grow on the campground borders. Choose your site based on proximity to beach path or potties. Security is passable; the gates are not locked at night, the area is extremely quiet. Cape Point campers can walk a quarter mile to the beach, through attractive grasses and dunes. Or drive to the Cape Hatteras Lighthouse. At 208 feet, it's the tallest in the United States. There are also hiking trails and fishing piers nearby. Visit Cape Hatteras on weekdays if possible. Prepare to battle insects in the summertime.

BASICS

Operated By: National Park Service. **Open:** May 25–Sept. 2. **Site Assignment:** First come, first served only. Check-out time is noon. Stay limit is 2 weeks. **Registration:** Entrance office. **Fee:** $18, 50% off the price to the holders of a Golden Access/Age card. **Parking:** 2 vehicle parking at each site, overflow parking is available.

FACILITIES

Number of Multipurpose Sites: 202. **Hookups:** None. **Each Site:** Picnic table, grill. **Dump Station:** Yes. **Laundry:** No. **Pay Phone:** Yes. **Rest Rooms and Showers:** Yes. **Fuel:** No. **Propane:** No. **Internal Roads:** Paved. **RV Service:** Approx. 3 mi. north in Buxton. **Market:** Approx. 3 mi. north in Buxton. **Restaurant:** Approx. 3 mi. north in Buxton. **General Store:** Approx. 3 mi. north in Buxton. **Vending:** No. **Swimming Pool:** No. **Playground:** No. **Activities:** Fishing, picnicking, hiking. **Nearby Attractions:** Currituck Beach Lighthouse, Elizabethan Gardens, Engineer Research Development Center, Frisco Native American Museum, Wright Brother's National monument, Lost Colony. **Additional Information:** Outer Banks Visitor's Bureau, (252) 473-2138.

RESTRICTIONS

Pets: Leash only. **Fires:** In grill. **Alcoholic Beverages:** Not allowed. **Vehicle Maximum Length:** 35 ft.

TO GET THERE

From Norfolk, Virginia take 64 going south. Turn onto 168 going south. 168 will turn into 158 and then into NC12. Stay on NC12 going south and the park will be on the Left.

CAPE HATTERAS

Hatteras Sands

BOX 295, Hatteras 27943. T: (252) 986-2422; F: (252) 986-2647; www.hatterassands.com; hatsandscg@aol.com.

🚐 ★★★	⛺ ★★
Beauty: ★★★	Site Privacy: ★★
Spaciousness: ★★	Quiet: ★★★★
Security: ★★★★★	Cleanliness: ★★★★
Insect Control: ★★★	Facilities: ★★★

Hatteras Sands is laid out in two areas surrounded by canals where folks enjoy fishing and crabbing. Each section has its own 24-hour security gate, making the park extremely safe. Other facilities are attractive and clean. The campground's location is excellent—it's in the heart of Hatteras, convenient to restaurants, attractions, and the Ocracoke Ferry. Explore the natural beauty of the coast on a day trip to Ocracoke Island. Hatteras is a popular summer destination and should be avoided on summer holidays and weekends. The campground is totally flat and has no shady trees. Manicured grass and shrubs add some life to the landscape. Campsites are tidy, with paved parking and a paved patio at each site. There are both back-in and pull-though sites. Sites are tiny and offer no privacy. Families should head for sites A1–A9, near the playground and pool area (which includes a children's pool). Couples prefer sites in section B, which is quiet.

BASICS

Operated By: The Williams family. **Open:** Mar. 1–Nov. 31. **Site Assignment:** First come, first served is available but reservations are recommended, (252) 986-2422; V, MC are accepted. If cancelled within 10 days to the expected arrival date, the fee is $10 plus the deposit. Rain checks are available. The check-in & check-out time is 12 noon. **Registration:** Main office. **Fee:** Sites w/ water, sewer, electric, & cable range $35.95–$47.95. Sites w/ water & electric range $32.95–$44.95. Sites w/ no hookups range $28.95–$36.95. (All depending on season.) **Parking:** 2 vehicles at each site, overflow parking is available.

FACILITIES

Number of RV Sites: 100. **Number of Tent-Only Sites:** 20. **Number of Multipurpose Sites:** None. **Hookups:** Water, electric (30, 50 amps), cable, sewer. **Each Site:** Picnic table. **Dump Station:** Yes. **Laundry:** Yes. **Pay Phone:** Yes. **Rest Rooms and Showers:** Yes. **Fuel:** No. **Propane:** No. **Internal Roads:** Paved. **RV Service:** 1 mi. **Market:** 19 mi. north in Avon. **Restaurant:** 1 mi. **General Store:** 75 mi. north in Southern Shores (large chain store). **Vending:** Beverage only. **Swimming Pool:** Yes. **Playground:** Yes. **Other:** Canals, group meeting facilities, club house. **Activities:** Paddle boats, crabbing, fishing, picnicking. **Nearby Attractions:** Ocracoke Island Ferry, Fishing Fleet,

Hatteras Museum, Lost colony, Wright Memorial, Nags Head Dunes. **Additional Information:** Outer Banks Visitor's Bureau, (800) 446-6262.

RESTRICTIONS

Pets: Leash only. **Fires:** No open pit (bring your own grill). **Alcoholic Beverages:** Allowed. **Vehicle Maximum Length:** 36 ft.

TO GET THERE

From Raleigh take Hwy. 64 to the east coast where ts intersects w/ Hwy. 12. Take Hwy. 12 south and go through Cape Hatterasa and the entrance will be on the right.

CAPE HATTERAS
Ocracoke

Route 1 Box 675, Manteo 27954. T: (252) 473-2111; www.nps.gov/caha.

🚐 ★★★★   ▲ ★★★★

Beauty: ★★★★★	Site Privacy: ★★
Spaciousness: ★★★★	Quiet: ★★★★★
Security: ★★★★★	Cleanliness: ★★★★
Insect Control: ★★★	Facilities: ★

Beautiful Ocracoke campground is bounded by gentle natural dunes and native grasses. It is flatter than the campground at Oregon Inlet, allowing for nicer views. We recommend this quiet campground for tent campers. Ocracoke can be reached by ferry only. Once you're on the island, you can explore the beaches once frequented by Blackbeard, or check out the oldest operating lighthouse in North Carolina (built ca. 1823). Many sites on the outside perimeter of the campground are nestled into the dunes. Sites D23, D25, and D27 are especially comfortable for tent campers. RV campers should head for sites B3, D33, D35, and D37, which offer both privacy and long parking pads. If you prefer open sites, there are plenty to choose from. Sites contain back-in parking, paved parking as well as grassy areas. Site size is ample, though spacing between sites varies. Security is excellent; Ocracoke Island is nearly deserted at night. Come prepared to battle insects. Visit midweek for peace and quiet.

BASICS

Operated By: National park service. **Open:** Apr. 13–Oct. 8. **Site Assignment:** First come, first

served only accept between May 15–Sept. 17, reservations can be made at (800) 365-CAMP. V, MC, D are accepted. If cancelled prior to the expected date of arrival the fee is $13.65. If cancelled on the expected day of arrival the fee is $13.65 plus 1 night's stay ($17). Check-out time is 12 noon. Stay limit is 14 days. **Registration:** Main office at campground. **Fee:** $17 per night, 50% off for holders of a Golden Age/Access card. **Parking:** 2 vehicle parking at each site.

FACILITIES

Number of Multipurpose Sites: 136. **Hookups:** None. **Each Site:** Picnic table, grill. **Dump Station:** Yes. **Laundry:** No. **Pay Phone:** Yes. **Rest Rooms and Showers:** Yes (no heated showers). **Fuel:** No. **Propane:** No. **Internal Roads:** Paved. **RV Service:** 1 mi. **Market:** 15 mi. north in Hatteras (must take ferry). **Restaurant:** 15 mi. north in Hatteras (must take ferry). **General Store:** 15 mi. north in Hatteras (must take ferry). **Vending:** No. **Swimming Pool:** No. **Playground:** No. **Activities:** Picnicking, fishing. **Nearby Attractions:** Currituck Beach Lighthouse, Elizabethan Gardens, Engineer Research Development Center, Frisco Native American Museum, Wright Brother's National monument, Lost Colony. **Additional Information:** Outer Banks Visitor's Bureau, (252) 473-2138.

RESTRICTIONS

Pets: Leash only. **Fires:** In grill & on the beach under the high tide line 100 ft. away from vegetation. **Alcoholic Beverages:** Not allowed. **Vehicle Maximum Length:** 35 ft. **Other:** Longer than normal tent stakes are recommended.

TO GET THERE

From Norfolk, Virginia take 64 South. Turn onto 168 South. 168 turns into 158 and then into NC 12. Stay on NC 12 going south and the campground will be on the left.

CAPE HATTERAS
Oregon Inlet    *No Hookups*

Route 1 Box 675, Manteo 27954. T: (252) 473-2111; www.nps.gov/caha.

🚐 ★★★★   ▲ ★★★★

Beauty: ★★★★★	Site Privacy: ★★★
Spaciousness: ★★★★	Quiet: ★★★
Security: ★★★	Cleanliness: ★★★★
Insect Control: ★★★	Facilities: ★

Oregon Inlet is the most attractive of the Cape Hatteras National Seashore campgrounds. It's also the closest to civilization, with quaint private beach houses as little as two miles away. The Wright Brothers National Memorial, including the first flight airstrip, is about 20 miles north. The Bodie Island Lighthouse, built in 1872, is just a few miles north of Oregon Inlet. The campground consists of three loops, built amongst pleasant dunes. Sites are large, with an some privacy provided by the dunes and grasses. Back-in parking spaces may be paved or packed sand. Our favorite sites, 2, 19, 21, and 23, are the most private because they're recessed into the dunes. We also like sites along the back of loops B and C, which are the furthest from Hwy. 12. Oregon Inlet is the most popular of the National Seashore campgrounds, and should be avoided on busy summer weekends. Security is fair—the gates are not closed at night.

BASICS

Operated By: National park service. **Open:** Apr. 13–Oct. 8. **Site Assignment:** First come, first served. Check-out time is 12 noon. Stay limit is 2 weeks. **Registration:** Entrance station. **Fee:** $17 per night, 50% for holders of a Golden Age/Access card. **Parking:** 2 vehicles at each site, overflow parking is available.

FACILITIES

Number of Multipurpose Sites: 120. **Hookups:** None. **Each Site:** Picnic table, grill. **Dump Station:** Yes. **Laundry:** No. **Pay Phone:** Yes. **Rest Rooms and Showers:** Yes. **Fuel:** No. **Propane:** No. **Internal Roads:** Paved. **RV Service:** 5 mi. north in Nags Head. **Market:** 17 mi. north in Manteo. **Restaurant:** 17 mi. north in Manteo. **General Store:** 17 mi. north in Manteo. **Vending:** No. **Swimming Pool:** No. **Playground:** No. **Other:** Group lodging is available for groups w/ 7–30 members. **Activities:** Picnicking, fishing. **Nearby Attractions:** Currituck Beach Lighthouse, Elizabethan Gardens, Engineer Research Development Center, Frisco Native American Museum, Wright Brother's National monument, Lost Colony. **Additional Information:** Outer Banks Visitor's Bureau, (252) 473-2138.

RESTRICTIONS

Pets: Leash only. **Fires:** Grill only. **Alcoholic Beverages:** Not allowed. **Vehicle Maximum Length:** 35 ft.

TO GET THERE

From Norfolk, Virginia take 64 South. Turn onto 168 South. 168 turns into 158 and then into NC 12. Stay on NC 12 going south and the campground will be on the left.

CAROLINA BEACH
Carolina Beach State Park

NO Hookup

P.O. Box 475, Carolina Beach 28428. T: (910) 458-8206; F: (910) 458-6350; www.ncsparks.com; Carolina.Beach@ncmail.net.

🚐 ★★★★   ⛺ ★★★★

Beauty: ★★★★★	Site Privacy: ★★★★★
Spaciousness: ★★★★★	Quiet: ★★★★
Security: ★★★★	Cleanliness: ★★★★
Insect Control: ★★★	Facilities: ★★★

Carolina Beach is a tent camper's dream-come-true. Intrepid RV campers also appreciate the beauty of this campground, even if they must forego hookups for a few days. Sites are commodious and lovely, with a thick understory providing privacy between them. Campsites enjoy the shade of longleaf pine, turkey oak, and live oak. Parking is on gravel and packed sand, and all sites offer back-in parking. The best sites are on the outside of the camping loops. The park is located in a densely developed suburb of Wilmington, at the conjunction of the Cape Fear River and the Intracoastal Waterway. A marina and fishing deck serve anglers and boaters. Swimmers will have to drive a few miles, to the Atlantic Ocean beach at Fort Fisher State Recreation Area. Before you leave Carolina Beach, check out the exhibit on carnivorous plants in the exhibit hall (species found in the park include Venus flytraps, pitcher plants, butterworts, and bladderworts). Security is fair—gates are locked at night, but attended during the day. Avoid visiting on summer weekends.

BASICS

Operated By: NC State Parks. **Open:** All year except Christmas. **Site Assignment:** First come, first served policy, stay limit is 2 weeks. **Registration:** Marina office. **Fee:** $12 per night. **Parking:** 2 vehicle parking at each site.

FACILITIES

Number of RV Sites: 0. **Number of Tent-Only Sites:** 83. **Number of Multipurpose Sites:** 83.

Hookups: None. **Each Site:** Picnic table, grill. **Dump Station:** Yes. **Laundry:** Yes. **Pay Phone:** Yes. **Rest Rooms and Showers:** Yes. **Fuel:** Sold for boats only. **Propane:** No. **Internal Roads:** Paved. **RV Service:** 15 mi. north in Wilmington. **Market:** 2 mi. south in Carolina Beach. **Restaurant:** 2 mi. south in Carolina Beach. **General Store:** 2 mi. south in Carolina Beach. **Vending:** Marina store. **Swimming Pool:** No. **Playground:** No. **Other:** Boat launch, trails. **Activities:** Boat rental, picnicking, hiking, fishing. **Nearby Attractions:** Winter boat cruises. **Additional Information:** Cape Fear Coast CVB, (910) 341-4029.

RESTRICTIONS

Pets: Leash only, not inside buildings. **Fires:** Grill only. **Alcoholic Beverages:** Not allowed. **Vehicle Maximum Length:** Call ahead for details.

TO GET THERE

From Wilmington take NC 421 10 mi. south. Follow signs to entrance.

CHARLOTTE
Carowinds $\cancel{N}$

P.O. Box 410289, Charlotte 28241. T: (800) 888-4386; www.carowinds.com.

🚐 ★★★   ▲ ★★

Beauty: ★★★	Site Privacy: ★★
Spaciousness: ★★★	Quiet: ★★★
Security: ★★★	Cleanliness: ★★
Insect Control: ★★★★	Facilities: ★★★

Near Paramount's Carowinds theme park, this large campground is laid out in four main areas, with average-sized sites. Most are long and narrow, and sandwiched together very tightly. Some sites are partially shady, but many are totally open. There are both back-in and pull-through sites. All have paved parking. The RV area is totally flat and boring. The biggest sites are 201–207. The tent area is slightly more attractive, but not recommended due to poor safety. There are no gates, and suburban Carowinds is full of teenagers. The pool and mini-golf are a minor consolation to the dreariness of the campground. Parents will be glad to know that lifeguards are on duty during pool hours (children under ten must be accompanied by an adult nonetheless). Visit the theme park during the week for less-hassled touring.

BASICS

Operated By: Paramount's Carowinds. **Open:** All year. **Site Assignment:** Reservations recommended. $10 deposit, Cancellation: 48 hours in advance. Payment methods: V, MC, D, AM, & travelers checks, personal checks w/ ID. **Registration:** Office. **Fee:** Call ahead for details. **Parking:** 1 car per site; overflow parking available.

FACILITIES

Number of RV Sites: 150. **Number of Tent-Only Sites:** 50-plus. **Number of Multipurpose Sites:** 0. **Hookups:** Water, sewer, electric (20, 30 amps). **Each Site:** Picnic table, grill. **Dump Station:** Yes. **Laundry:** Yes. **Pay Phone:** Yes. **Rest Rooms and Showers:** Yes. **Fuel:** No. **Propane:** No. **Internal Roads:** Paved. **RV Service:** 5 mi. **Market:** 5 mi. **Restaurant:** 5 mi. **General Store:** 5 mi. **Vending:** No. **Swimming Pool:** Yes. **Playground:** Yes. **Other:** Tram service to & from park. **Activities:** Mini golf, volleyball, set-ups, game room, grocery store, picnic tables, transportation to park, shuffleboard, horseshoes. **Nearby Attractions:** Charlotte Motor Speedway, Charolette coliseum, Cricket Arena, Charolette Convention Center, Ericsson Stadium.

RESTRICTIONS

Pets: Allowed. **Fires:** Not allowed. **Alcoholic Beverages:** At site only. **Vehicle Maximum Length:** None. **Other:** No skateboards or rollerblades.

TO GET THERE

From I-77, take Exit 90. Go west on Carowinds Blvd toward Spartanburg. Turn right on Catawba Trace. The campground is on the left.

CHEROKEE
Cherokee KOA

92 KOA Kampground 12D, Cherokee 28719. T: (828)497-9711.

🚐 ★★★★   ▲ ★★★

Beauty: ★★★	Site Privacy: ★★★
Spaciousness: ★★★	Quiet: ★★★
Security: ★★★★★	Cleanliness: ★★★
Insect Control: ★★★★	Facilities: ★★★★

The KOA in Cherokee is an attractive campground nestled between the Raven Fork River and a narrow trout pond. Sites are on the small side, and this campground is extremely popular. If you value breathing space, KOA Cherokee is not for you. Sites are mostly shady, with paved parking. There are both back-in and pull-through sites. Our favorite sites are those along the river and pond—they have the prettiest views and tend to be the shadiest. The fishing pond is stocked twice a week in season. The recreational facilities here are very good—and very crowded. With 300 campsites, there should be more than one swimming pool and playground. To avoid the vacationing masses, visit during the week in summer and fall. Security is excellent. With gates attended at all times, the park is nearly impenetrable.

BASICS

Operated By: KOA. **Open:** All year. **Site Assignment:** Reservations required 30 days in advance; Pay in full at time of reservation; $50 cancellation fee. **Registration:** Kamping Kottage. **Fee:** RV $25–$50, tent w/ no hookup $20–$40, Kamping Kabins $34–$99. **Parking:** On site.

FACILITIES

Number of RV Sites: 300. **Number of Tent-Only Sites:** 107. **Number of Multipurpose Sites:** 0. **Hookups:** Cable, electric (30 amps). **Each Site:** None. **Dump Station:** No. **Laundry:** Yes. **Pay Phone:** No. **Rest Rooms and Showers:** Yes. **Fuel:** Yes. **Propane:** No. **Internal Roads:** Paved. **RV Service:** Yes. **Market:** on site. **Restaurant:** On site. **General Store:** Yes. **Vending:** Inquire at campground. **Swimming Pool:** Yes. **Playground:** Yes. **Other:** Hot tub. **Activities:** Tennis, basketball, horseshoes, fishing, white-water rafting. **Nearby Attractions:** Inquire at campground.

RESTRICTIONS

Pets: Yes. **Fires:** Only in designated areas. **Alcoholic Beverages:** Allowed. **Vehicle Maximum Length:** Call ahead for details.

TO GET THERE

Take Cherokee North 441 to park boundary then take Big Cove Rd.

CHEROKEE

Great Smoky Mountains National Park Smokemont Campground

Address: 107 Park Headquarters Rd., Gatlinburg 37738. T: (865) 436-1200; F: (865) 436-1204; www.nps.gov/grsm.

 ★★★★   ★★★★

Beauty: ★★★★   Site Privacy: ★★★
Spaciousness: ★★★★   Quiet: ★★★★
Security: ★★★   Cleanliness: ★★★★
Insect Control: ★★★★★ Facilities: ★★★

Situated in a flat river valley, Smokemont is the largest campground in Great Smoky Mountains National Park. It's popular with hikers, who may choose from day or overnight hikes originating at Smokemont. Anglers enjoy the Oconaluftee River, which runs alongside the campground. Automobile touring is another popular pastime—Smokemont is just a few miles from the southern terminus of the Blue Ridge Parkway. Nearby, the town of Cherokee offers casinos, kitsch, and Native American culture and crafts. The long, slender campground includes a large multipurpose camping area as well as an RV-only loop. Sites are on the large side of average, with paved parking. In the RV-only area, sites have back-in parking. In the multipurpose area, there are both back-in and pull-through sites. Though there are some open sites in the RV loop, most sites are deliciously shady and fairly private. For beauty, the nicest sites are 8–18, in the back of the multi-purpose area. Smokemont Campground stays packed on summer and fall weekends. Visit during the week. Security is fair—there are no gates.

BASICS

Operated By: National Park Service. **Open:** All year. **Site Assignment:** First come, first served; reservations accepted for May 15–Oct. 31 up to 5 months in advance, w/ full deposit; $13.25 cancellation fee w/ at least 24-hour notice, otherwise first night plus fee charged; reservations made by calling (800) 365-CAMP or at reservations.nps.gov (personal check, money order, V, D, MC). **Registration:** Self-registration. **Fee:** $14–$17 for up to 6 people, 2 tents or 1 tent & 1 RV (cash only for off-season self-registration). **Parking:** At site (2 vehicles).

FACILITIES

Number of RV Sites: 43. **Number of Tent-Only Sites:** 18. **Number of Multipurpose Sites:** 140. **Hookups:** None. **Each Site:** Picnic table, fire ring, grill, tent pad. **Dump Station:** Yes. **Laundry:** No. **Pay Phone:** Yes. **Rest Rooms and Showers:** Rest rooms, no showers. **Fuel:** No. **Propane:** No. **Internal Roads:** Paved. **RV Service:** No. **Market:** 8 mi. in Cherokee. **Restaurant:** 8 mi. in Cherokee. **General Store:** 20 mi. in Waynesville. **Vending:** No. **Swimming Pool:** No. **Playground:** No. **Other:** Amphitheater, picnic areas, horse trails, interpretive trails. **Activities:** Hiking, fishing, horseback riding, canoeing, backcountry hiking, ranger programs (seasonal). **Nearby Attractions:** Pisgah National Forest, Eastern Cherokee Indian Reservation, Cataloochee Ski Area, Gatlinburg, Pigeon Forge, Dollywood, Asheville. **Additional Information:** Pigeon Forge Visitor Information, (865) 453-5700; Park Information, (865) 436-1200; Asheville Area Chamber of Commerce, (828) 258-6101.

RESTRICTIONS

Pets: On leash only. **Fires:** In fire rings only. **Alcoholic Beverages:** Allowed. **Vehicle Maximum Length:** 35 ft.

TO GET THERE

From US Hwy 441, drive north to Newfound Gap Rd. Smokemont campground is on the right approximately 4 mi. off the highway.

CHEROKEE
Yogi in the Smokies

317 Galamore Bridge Rd., Cherokee, NC 28719. T: (828) 497-9151.

🚐 ★★★   ▲ ★★★

Beauty: ★★★★ Site Privacy: ★★★
Spaciousness: ★★★ Quiet: ★★★
Security: ★★★★ Cleanliness: ★★★
Insect Control: ★★★★ Facilities: ★★★

This Jellystone resort doesn't offer as much recreation as its Gatlinburg counterpart, but it is attractive and kid-oriented. Planned recreation in the summer and fall includes live bands, fishing contests, and costume parties. The playground and pool are aged, but adequate. The campground includes sites in two main areas, which hug a bend in the Raven Fork River. Sites are on the small side. Parking is on packed dirt, grass, and gravel—it's a bit messy. There are both pull-through and back-in sites. Most sites are nicely shaded. Our favorite sites, 114–134E, line the river. Other nice sites include 213–235, which have full hookups and are large and heavily wooded. Security is fair at Yogi's. There are no gates, but the park is very remote. Avoid Cherokee on summer and fall weekends, when hordes of automobiles create gridlock on Cherokee roads.

BASICS

Operated By: Bruce & Sharon Daughters. **Open:** Mar.–Oct. **Site Assignment:** Reservations accepted, 2-day cancellation notice required for deposit refund. **Registration:** Office. **Fee:** RV $22–$31, primitive tent $20. **Parking:** On site.

FACILITIES

Number of RV Sites: 192. **Number of Tent-Only Sites:** 8. **Number of Multipurpose Sites:** 0. **Hookups:** Water, sewer, cable, electric (20, 30 amps). **Each Site:** Picnic table. **Dump Station:** Yes. **Laundry:** Yes. **Pay Phone:** Yes. **Rest Rooms and Showers:** Yes. **Fuel:** No. **Propane:** Yes. **Internal Roads:** Gravel. **RV Service:** No. **Market:** No. **Restaurant:** No. **General Store:** Yes. **Vending:** Yes. **Swimming Pool:** Yes. **Playground:** Yes. **Other:** Arcade. **Activities:** Fishing, tubing, horseshoes, theatre, hiking, mountain biking. **Nearby Attractions:** Great Smoky Mtn. National Park, Dollywood, Ghost Town in the Sky, Pigeon Forge, Mingo Falls, Museum of Cherokee Indians.

RESTRICTIONS

Pets: Yes. **Fires:** Fire rings. **Alcoholic Beverages:** Allowed. **Vehicle Maximum Length:** 46 ft.

TO GET THERE

Take I-40 to Exit No. 27 onto Hwy. 74 West, then to Exit No. 74 onto Hwy. 441 North; 6.5 mi. north of Cherokee. Follow the signs.

DANBURY
Hanging Rock State Park

P.O. Box 278, Danbury 27016. T: (336) 593-8480; F: (336) 593-9166; www.rthcarolinaoutdoors.com; ncs1220@interpath.com.

🚐 ★★★★★   ▲ ★★★★★

Beauty: ★★★★★ Site Privacy: ★★★★★
Spaciousness: ★★★★★ Quiet: ★★★★★
Security: ★★★★★ Cleanliness: ★★★★★
Insect Control: ★★★★ Facilities: ★★★★

Hanging Rock contains 18 miles of easy to strenuous hiking trails, may leading to picturesque waterfalls. There's also a 12-acre lake equipped with a swimming beach for sun-lovers and stocked with bass and bream for fishermen. At the north end of the park, a boat launch provides access to the Dan River for canoeing, tubing, or fishing for small mouth bass and catfish. The campground is laid out in two loops on a gentle mountain ridge. Campsites are lovely; most are extremely large and secluded. Mature trees shade the sites and dense foliage provides a natural barrier between neighbors. Although the park is very popular, the campground is quiet due to adequate spacing between sites. Sites have gravel back-in parking. We especially like sites 8 and 32 for RVs and sites 1 and 4 for tent campers. Security is excellent. Hanging Rock is extra remote and gated. Avoid this park on busy summer and fall weekends.

BASICS

Operated By: NC State Parks. **Open:** All year except Christmas Eve & Christmas Day. **Site Assignment:** First come, first served. Pay w/ in-state check or cash. Check-out time is 3 p.m. **Registration:** At campsite; camp ranger will come by to register. **Fee:** $12–$18 per night. **Parking:** 2 vehicles per site.

FACILITIES

Number of Multipurpose Sites: 73. **Hookups:** None. **Each Site:** Picnic table, tent pad, fire ring, grill. **Dump Station:** No. **Laundry:** No. **Pay Phone:** Yes. **Rest Rooms and Showers:** Yes. **Fuel:** No. **Propane:** No. **Internal Roads:** Paved. **RV Service:** Winston-Salem. **Market:** In Danbury approx. 5 mi. northeast. **Restaurant:** In Danbury approx. 5 mi. northeast. **General Store:** In Danbury approx. 5 mi. northeast. **Vending:** Beverage & Snack from June 1–Labor Day. **Swimming Pool:** Swimming at park lake June 1–Labor Day, extra fee. **Playground:** No. **Other:** Group lodging available, trails. **Activities:** Hiking, rock climbing, picnicking, fishing, Natural & Cultural History Programs, Museum exhibits. **Nearby Attractions:** Diggs Gallery at Winton-Salem State University, Historic Bethabara Park, Old Salem. **Additional Information:** Stokes County EDC, (336) 983-8468.

RESTRICTIONS

Pets: Leash only, attended at all times by responsible adult. **Fires:** Fire ring only. **Alcoholic Beverages:** Not allowed. **Vehicle Maximum Length:** Call ahead for details. **Other:** Max 6 people per site, each site must have at least 1 adult (18 or older), all tent must be on tent pads, visitors out of the park by closing time.

TO GET THERE

From Danbury, take Hwy. 889 going north, go approx. 4 mi. and turn left onto Hanging Rock Rd.

EMERALD ISLE
Holiday Trav-L-Park Resort

9102 Coast Guard Rd., Emerald Isle 28594. T: (252) 354-2250; F: (252) 354-3870; www.htpresort.com; htpresort@mail.clis.co.

🚐 ★★★★	⛺ ★★★
Beauty: ★★★★	Site Privacy: ★★
Spaciousness: ★★	Quiet: ★★★
Security: ★★★★★	Cleanliness: ★★★★★
Insect Control: ★★★	Facilities: ★★★★★

This attractive park is right on the Atlantic Ocean. Holiday Trav-L-Park has extremely nice pools, playgrounds, and other amenities, as well as planned activities in the summer. The most unique amenity is the park's gourmet food and wine shop. Nearby attractions include Fort Macon, a five-sided fort built between 1826 and 1834, and the historic town of Beaufort, including buildings dating back to 1709. The campground is laid out in five long rows of back-in and pull-through sites, terminating at the Atlantic Ocean. Sites in the back, near the ocean, have nice views of the dunes. Landscaping is very tidy, with shady trees in the front of the campground, near the store and pool. Sites are small, with grass parking. Choose your site based on desired location. Security is excellent. Holiday Trav-L-Park is located in an urban resort area, and is conscientious about camper safety. Visit in spring or fall for peace. Avoid the park on crowded summer weekends.

BASICS

Operated By: Watson family. **Open:** Feb. 15–Dec. 5. **Site Assignment:** Reservations recommended, (252) 354-2250. No out-of-state checks allowed, MC, V accepted. If cancelled less than 7 days before the reserved check-in day, the deposit is nonrefundable. There is no check-in time, check-out time is 2 p.m. **Registration:** Check in station. **Fee:** Call ahead for details. **Parking:** 2 vehicles per RV site, 1 vehicle per tent, overflow parking is available.

FACILITIES

Number of RV Sites: 375. **Number of Tent-Only Sites:** 30. **Number of Multipurpose Sites:** 0. **Hookups:** Tent sites have no hookups. 115 of the RV are seasonal, 19 of the RV sites have water, electric (20, 30, 50 amps), cable. The rest of the RV sites have full hookups. **Each Site:** Picnic table. **Dump Station:** Yes. **Laundry:** Yes. **Pay Phone:** Yes. **Rest Rooms and Showers:** Yes. **Fuel:** No. **Propane:** Yes. **Internal Roads:** Paved. **RV Service:** 2 mi. west in Cedarpoint. **Market:** 1 mi. **Restaurant:** 1 mi. **General Store:** 20 mi. north east in Morehead. **Vending:** Beverage & snack. **Swimming Pool:** Yes. **Playground:** Yes. **Other:** Rec. hall, no group lodging. **Activities:** Live entertainment, church service, Bible school, kid's cook-out, bingo, sandcastle competitions, arts & crafts, kite flying. **Nearby Attractions:** Lamb Amphitheater. **Additional Information:** Carteret County Tourism Development, (252) 726-8148.

RESTRICTIONS

Pets: Leash only. **Fires:** No open fires (bring your own grill). **Alcoholic Beverages:** Allowed. **Vehicle Maximum Length:** 45 ft. **Other:** No pets allowed in tenting area, call for more information, (252) 354-2250.

TO GET THERE

Take Hwy. 58 going east through Emerald Isle. Go over the high-rise bridge and at the first stop light after the bridge take a right. The park will be on the left.

FLAT ROCK
Lakewood RV Resort

495 Ballenger Rd, Flat Rock 28731. T: (888) 819-4200; lakewood@brinet.com.

🚐 ★★★　　　　▲ ★

Beauty: ★★★　　　　Site Privacy: ★★
Spaciousness: ★★★　　Quiet: ★★★
Security: ★★★　　　　Cleanliness: ★★★★
Insect Control: ★★★★　Facilities: ★★★

Lakewood is just outside of Hendersonville, convenient to shopping and restaurants. Hendersonville is a good place to stay if you would like to tour Asheville and the mountain towns beyond Brevard. Many shops and buildings in historic downtown Hendersonville are on the National Register of Historic Places. The park is about 50 percent residential, and offers mid-sized campsites with gravel parking and concrete patios. Most sites are open, although a few sites contain young trees. There is little privacy. The campground is laid out in five blocks of back-in sites plus a few rows of pull-through sites. Sites 1–9 in section C are the flattest and most spacious.

Security is fair—there is no gate at this small-town campground. To avoid crowds, visit Hendersonville during the week in the summer and autumn.

BASICS

Operated By: Phil De Masso. **Open:** All year. **Site Assignment:** Reservations one week in advance. **Registration:** Office. **Fee:** RV, starting at $25, tent, starting at $20. **Parking:** At site.

FACILITIES

Number of RV Sites: 100. **Number of Tent-Only Sites:** Use field. **Number of Multipurpose Sites:** 0. **Hookups:** Electric (30, 100 amps). **Each Site:** Concrete pad for table. **Dump Station:** Yes. **Laundry:** Yes. **Pay Phone:** Yes. **Rest Rooms and Showers:** Yes. **Fuel:** No. **Propane:** Yes. **Internal Roads:** Paved. **RV Service:** On site. **Market:** on site. **Restaurant:** On site. **General Store:** On site. **Vending:** Inquire at campground. **Swimming Pool:** Yes. **Playground:** No. **Other:** TV lounge, pool table, club house. **Activities:** Shuffleboard, ping pong, horseshoes, fishing pond. **Nearby Attractions:** Inquire at campground.

RESTRICTIONS

Pets: Allowed. **Fires:** Allowed. **Alcoholic Beverages:** Only at picnic areas & lakeside. **Vehicle Maximum Length:** None.

TO GET THERE

Take I-26 to Exit 22 (Upward Rd), Proceed 0.2 mi. to Ballenger Rd. and turn left. Entrance is 0.3 mi. on the right.

FRANKLIN
Country Woods

60 Country Woods Drive, Franklin 28734. T: (828) 524-4339; F: (828) 524-4339; www.kiz.com/country woods; cwoodsrv@dnet.net.

🚐 ★★★★　　　　▲ n/a

Beauty: ★★★★　　　Site Privacy: ★★★
Spaciousness: ★★★　　Quiet: ★★★★
Security: ★★★★　　　Cleanliness: ★★★★★
Insect Control: ★★★★　Facilities: ★★★

The friendly owners of Country Woods operate an attractive and extremely tidy sites on a terraced mountainside. Sites are small, but picturesque. Sites are nicely wooded. Many have wooden decks or concrete patios. Parking is gravel. Most sites feature back-in parking, but there are a few pull-through sites. Our favorite sites are 18, a large pull-through, and 57, a picturesque wooded campsite in the back of the park. Many sites offer views of the surrounding Black Mountains. Though Country Woods' amenities aren't extensive, they are well maintained and inviting. Franklin is a lovely town, with numerous boutiques and fishing and tubing on the Little Tennessee River. Security is fine here—there are no gates, but Franklin is a very nice town. Avoid the mountains on summer and fall weekends. Instead, visit during the week.

BASICS

Operated By: Darold & Marilyn Long. **Open:** Call ahead for details. **Site Assignment:** May cancel on day of arrival except during Oct. or July. **Registration:** Office. **Fee:** $20/day. **Parking:** 1 car at site, additional parking if necessary.

FACILITIES

Number of RV Sites: 72. **Number of Tent-Only Sites:** 0. **Number of Multipurpose Sites:** 0. **Hookups:** Water, 30 amps electric, sewer, cable. **Each Site:** Picnic table, fire ring. **Dump Station:** Yes. **Laundry:** Yes. **Pay Phone:** Yes. **Rest Rooms and Showers:** Yes. **Fuel:** No. **Propane:** No. **Internal Roads:** Gravel & paved. **RV Service:** 1.5 mi. northwest in Aberdeen. **Market:** 1.5 into city. **Restaurant:** 1.5 into city. **General Store:** 1.5 into city. **Vending:** No. **Swimming Pool:** No. **Playground:** No. **Other:** Gathering room, library, club house, waling trails. **Activities:** Horseshoes, park ket togethers. **Nearby Attractions:** Antique shops, gem mining, hiking rails, waterfalls, Scottish Tartan Museum, Granklin Gem Show, Wayah Bald, Craft fairs, Great Smoky Mountain National Park, Blue Ridge Pkwy., the town of Cherokee, Harrah's Casino, Biltmore House, Smoky Mountain Train Ride & Dillsboro shops.

RESTRICTIONS

Pets: Allowed. **Fires:** Fire rings only. **Alcoholic Beverages:** At site only. **Vehicle Maximum Length:** 40 ft. **Other:** Motorized bikes may be used for transportaion into & out of park only.

TO GET THERE

Located on US 441/23, 2 mi. south of the intersection of 441/23 and Hwy. 64.

FRANKLIN
Standing Indian

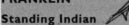

90 Sloan Rd., Franklin 28734. T: (828) 524-6441; www.cs.unca.edu/nfsnc.

🚐 ★★★★   ⛺ ★★★★

Beauty: ★★★★★   Site Privacy: ★★★★
Spaciousness: ★★★★★   Quiet: ★★★★
Security: ★★★★   Cleanliness: ★★★★
Insect Control: ★★★★★   Facilities: ★★★

This beautiful campground is laid out in five loops, with sites offering varying levels of shade and privacy. Some sites are set in areas densely wooded by yellow birch and sugar maple, while others are flatter and more open. Almost all sites are very large. Most of the multipurpose sites have paved parking, while others, recommended for tent campers only, have gravel parking. Four sites offer pull-through parking. The rest are back-in style. RV campers should choose from sites 1–54. Tent campers should head for sites 55–84. Recreation in the area is outstanding. Several hiking trails are accessible from the park, including one that connects with a portion of the Appalachian Trail. Folks also like to fish for native brook trout (rainbow and brown) in the Nantahala River and Kimsey Creek. For a real treat, visit in late May or June, when the rhododendrons are blooming. Security is fine at this remote campground.

BASICS

Operated By: USDA Forest Service. **Open:** Call ahead for details. **Site Assignment:** First come, first served. **Registration:** Office. **Fee:** Call ahead for details. **Parking:** Yes.

FACILITIES

Number of RV Sites: 65. **Number of Tent-Only Sites:** 16. **Number of Multipurpose Sites:** 0. **Hookups:** None. **Each Site:** Picnic table, fire grate, lantern post, tent pad. **Dump Station:** No. **Laundry:** No. **Pay Phone:** Yes. **Rest Rooms and Showers:** Yes. **Fuel:** No. **Propane:** No. **Internal Roads:** Paved. **RV Service:** No. **Market:** No. **Restaurant:** No. **General Store:** Yes. **Vending:** No. **Swimming Pool:** No. **Playground:** No. **Activities:** Hiking, fishing, river swimming. **Nearby Attractions:** Inquire at campground.

RESTRICTIONS

Pets: Allowed. **Fires:** Allowed. **Alcoholic Beverages:** Inquire at campground. **Vehicle Maximum Length:** Call ahead for details.

TO GET THERE

From Franklin, drive on 64 West approx. 13 mi. to West Old Murphy Rd. Turn left and travel approx. 3 mi. to Standing Indian.

HENDERSON

Hibernia

269 Glass House Rd., Henderson 27356. T: (252) 438-7791; F: (252) 438-7582; www.unc.edu/parkproject/kelahi; kerr.lake@ncmail.net.

🚐 ★★★★★   ⛺ ★★★★★

Beauty: ★★★★★   Site Privacy: ★★★★★
Spaciousness: ★★★★★   Quiet: ★★★★★
Security: ★★★★   Cleanliness: ★★★★★
Insect Control: ★★★   Facilities: ★★★

Hibernia is a gorgeous campground with numerous lakefront sites. Sites are huge, with your choice open sites or heavily wooded sites. Often the open sites provide stunning views of Kerr Lake, the banks of which are fortified with either concrete walls, rocks, or other materials to prevent erosion. Parking is on aged gravel, and the campground includes mostly back-in sites. For RVs we recommend Area 2, which has hookups and a newer washhouse. Other recommendations are amazingly lovely sites 43 and 44 in Area 1. Recreation at mammoth Kerr Lake revolves around lake swimming, sailing, boating, and fishing for crappie, channel catfish, and various bass species. There are limited foot paths for walkers and hikers. Hibernia is extremely remote, with gates locked at night, making security very good. Visit anytime except for summer holidays and weekends. Also avoid special-event weekends, such as the Governor's Cup Invitational Regatta and various bass tournaments.

BASICS

Operated By: NC Division of Parks & Recreation. **Open:** All year except Christmas. **Site Assignment:** First come, first served; reservations can be made at (252) 438-7791. Cash & checks are accepted. If cancelled 2 weeks before expected arrival there is no penalty. Stay limit is 2 weeks. **Registration:** Main office at campground. **Fee:**

Site w/ no hookups is $12 per night, $10 for senior citizens (62 years of age). $17 for sites w/ electric, $14 for senior citizens. **Parking:** 2 vehicle parking at each site.

FACILITIES

Number of Multipurpose Sites: 141. **Hookups:** Electric (30 amps). **Each Site:** Some have picnic table, fire ring, grill. **Dump Station:** Yes. **Laundry:** No. **Pay Phone:** Yes. **Rest Rooms and Showers:** Yes. **Fuel:** No. **Propane:** No. **Internal Roads:** Paved. **RV Service:** 15 mi. south in Henderson. **Market:** 15 mi. south in Henderson. **Restaurant:** 15 mi. south in Henderson. **General Store:** 2 mi. from park entrance in Henderson. **Vending:** Beverage only. **Swimming Pool:** No. **Playground:** Yes. **Other:** Group camping available, boat ramp, trails. **Activities:** Fishing, picnicking, boating, hiking, canoeing, natural & cultural history programs. **Nearby Attractions:** Steele Creek & Satterwhite Point. **Additional Information:** Vance County Tourism, (252) 438-5873.

RESTRICTIONS

Pets: Leash only. **Fires:** Designated areas only. **Alcoholic Beverages:** Not allowed. **Vehicle Maximum Length:** 40 ft.

TO GET THERE

From I-85 take Exit 214 and get onto NC 39. Travel approx. 12.5 mi. north on NC 39 and turn right onto Hibernia Rd.

HIGHLANDS

Sassafras Gap

5920 Walhalla Road, Highlands 28741. T: (800) 815-2259; F: (828) 526-3032; www.kiz.com/sassafrasgap; sassa@direcpc.com.

🚐 ★★★   ⛺ ★★★

Beauty: ★★★   Site Privacy: ★★★
Spaciousness: ★★★   Quiet: ★★★★
Security: ★★★   Cleanliness: ★★★
Insect Control: ★★★★   Facilities: ★★★

This funky little campground is something of an anomaly in tony Highlands, a town known for its annual Chamber Music Festival. Down-home Sassafras Gap hosts live bluegrass and folk music events. Adventurous souls should consider a trip down the Chattooga Wild and Scenic River. The campground offers RV campsites laid out in eight rows descending a hillside. Most sites feature gravel pull-through parking and enjoy a little shade. RV sites at the top of the hill, including 19, 33, 34, 48, and 59, are the prettiest. There are two tent areas in the back of the campground, both of which are shady, secluded, and nice-looking. Although the bathrooms are notably spacious and clean, the landscaping is very untidy, with long grass and patchy gravel. Security is fair—there are no gates, but the campground is in the middle of nowhere. Visit during the week in summer and fall.

BASICS

Operated By: Steve Potts. **Open:** Apr.–Oct. **Site Assignment:** $20 deposit or reserve w/ credit card; MC, V, D, AE, cash, check. Must cancel 5 days in advance for refund. **Registration:** In office. **Fee:** $15–$26. **Parking:** At site.

FACILITIES

Number of RV Sites: 77. **Number of Tent-Only Sites:** 21. **Number of Multipurpose Sites:** 0. **Hookups:** Water, sewer, electric (30, 50 amps), cable. **Each Site:** Tables, fire rings, trash pickup. **Dump Station:** No. **Laundry:** Yes. **Pay Phone:** Yes. **Rest Rooms and Showers:** Yes. **Fuel:** No. **Propane:** Yes. **Internal Roads:** Paved & gravel. **RV Service:** 4 mi. toward Highlands. **Market:** on site. **Restaurant:** 5 mi. toward Highlands. **General Store:** 5 mi. toward Highlands. **Vending:** Yes. **Swimming Pool:** No. **Playground:** Yes. **Activities:** 2 ponds & pavilion, gameroom, horseshoes. **Nearby Attractions:** Highland Playhouse, National Wild & Scenic Chattooga River, Highlands Botanical Gardens & Nature Center, whitewater rafting, Whiteside Mountain & Yellow Mountain, tubing, Dry Falls, canoeing, Whitewater Falls, kayaking, Glen Falls, fishing, Foothills Trail, horseback riding, Bartram Trail, golf.

RESTRICTIONS

Pets: Allowed. **Fires:** Fire rings only. **Alcoholic Beverages:** At site only. **Vehicle Maximum Length:** 45 ft.

TO GET THERE

Located 5 mi. south of Highlands, near wild and scenic Chattooga River.

JACKSON SPRINGS
Travel Resorts of America

1059 Sycamore Ln., Jackson Springs, NC 27281.
T: (910) 652-5559; F: (910) 652-2411;
services@travelresorts.com.

🚐 ★★★★   🅰 n/a

Beauty: ★★★★★   Site Privacy: ★★
Spaciousness: ★★★   Quiet: ★★★★★
Security: ★★★★   Cleanliness: ★★★★★
Insect Control: ★★★★   Facilities: ★★★★

Travel Resorts of America is a lovely flat campground situated in a stand of towering pine trees with pine straw ground cover. Picturesque Lake Sycamore is stocked with bass. Manicured landscaping adds to the natural beauty of the setting, and recreational amenities are excellent. This park is preferred over the Heritage for couples who seek solitude. It's also closer to most of the golf courses than the Heritage. The campground is laid out in rows of back-in sites, with large chunky gravel parking pads. Sites are average sized, with little privacy. The quietest sites, 1–12, are the furthest from Sycamore Lane and the closest to the bath house. Security is fine. There is no gate, but the neighborhood is spotless. Avoid this area during golf tournaments. For the best deals on greens fees and the least crowds, visit in the winter—but prepare for cold weather.

BASICS

Operated By: Travel Resorts of America. **Open:** All year. **Site Assignment:** Reservations required. **Registration:** Office. **Fee:** Call ahead for details. **Parking:** Yes.

FACILITIES

Number of RV Sites: 136. **Number of Tent-Only Sites:**. **Number of Multipurpose Sites:** 0. **Hookups:** Water, electric (30, 50 amps). **Each Site:** Water. **Dump Station:** Yes. **Laundry:** No. **Pay Phone:**. **Rest Rooms and Showers:** Yes. **Fuel:** Yes. **Propane:** Yes. **Internal Roads:** Paved & gravel. **RV Service:** Yes. **Market:** Nearby. **Restaurant:** Nearby. **General Store:** Yes. **Vending:** Inquire at campground. **Swimming Pool:** Yes. **Playground:** Yes. **Activities:** Boating, basketball, fishing. **Nearby Attractions:** Rockingham Speedway, Stoneybrook Steeplechase.

RESTRICTIONS

Pets: Allowed. **Fires:** Only in designated areas. **Alcoholic Beverages:** Inquire at campground. **Vehicle Maximum Length:** None.

TO GET THERE

From south US I-95, take Hwy. 501 north to Aberdeen, NC. Turn right onto Roseland Rd. Continue until it ends, turn right onto Sycamore Ln., 3 mi. to entrance.

LINVILLE FALLS
Linville Falls Campground

Mile Post 316.4, Linville 28646. T: (828) 298-0398.

🚐 ★★★★   ▲ ★★★★

Beauty: ★★★   Site Privacy: ★★★
Spaciousness: ★★★★   Quiet: ★★★
Security: ★★★★★   Cleanliness: ★★★★★
Insect Control: ★★★★★   Facilities: ★★★

Linville falls is an excellent choice for nature nuts. Nearby Linville Gorge Wilderness Area is beloved for its fantastic rock formations and dramatic waterfalls. Grandfather Mountain, a privately owned park that was designed by the United Nations as an International Biosphere Reserve, is about 15 miles north of the campground. Like other Blue Ridge Parkway campgrounds, Linville Falls offers separate tent and RV sites interspersed on two loops. Situated in a flat river valley, most sites are shaded by white pine and a variety of hardwoods. Parking is paved, back-in style. The nicest sites are on Loop A, next to picturesque Linville River. Security is good—there are no gates, but the campground is in a remote location. The Blue Ridge Parkway experiences outrageous traffic on summer and fall weekends. If you can't live without gorgeous fall foliage, tour the parkway mid-week.

BASICS
Operated By: National Park Service. **Open:** Call ahead for details. **Site Assignment:** First come, first served. **Registration:** Office. **Fee:** $12. **Parking:** Yes.

FACILITIES
Number of RV Sites: 20. **Number of Tent-Only Sites:** 50. **Number of Multipurpose Sites:** 0. **Hookups:** None. **Each Site:** Picnic table, fireplace. **Dump Station:** Yes. **Laundry:** No. **Pay Phone:** Yes. **Rest Rooms and Showers:** Yes. **Fuel:** No. **Propane:** No. **Internal Roads:** Paved. **RV Service:** No. **Market:** No. **Restaurant:** No. **General Store:** Yes. **Vending:** Inquire at campground. **Swimming Pool:** No. **Playground:** No. **Activities:** Hiking, fishing. **Nearby Attractions:** Linville Gorge, Linville Caverns, Gem Mountain.

RESTRICTIONS
Pets: Allowed. **Fires:** Allowed. **Alcoholic Beverages:** Inquire at campground. **Vehicle Maximum Length:** Call ahead for details.

TO GET THERE
Follow the Blueridge Pkwy. to mile post 316.4. Follow signs to campground.

MARION
Hidden Valley Campground and Waterpark

1210 Deacon Dr., Marion 28752. T: (828)652-7208.

🚐 ★★★★   ▲ ★★★★

Beauty: ★★★★   Site Privacy: ★★★
Spaciousness: ★★★★   Quiet: ★★★
Security: ★★★★   Cleanliness: ★★★
Insect Control: ★★★★   Facilities: ★★★★

Hidden Valley is built into a gorgeous mountainside, leading down to a pond. The campground would be exceptionally beautiful, if not for obtrusive telephone lines and poor road conditions. The water park and playground are appreciated by children, and the park is convenient to the quaint towns of Black Mountain and Chimney Rock. Hidden Valley has uncommonly large campsites for a private campground. Some sites are totally open, including our favorite pull-through sites, B9–B13. Others are nicely shaded, including our favorite back-in sites, B1–B8. These back-in sites enjoy a pretty view across the valley. Tent sites T5–T8 are wooded and private. The rest of the tent sites should be avoided. Hidden Valley is extremely popular on summer and fall weekends. For fewer crowds, visit mid-week. The campground is only about three miles from I-40, but it has a rural feel. There are no gates, making security fair.

BASICS
Operated By: Private operator. **Open:** Apr. 1–Nov. 1. **Site Assignment:** Reservations accepted, w/ a nonrefundable deposit. **Registration:** Office. **Fee:** $18 Tent, $20–$22 RV. **Parking:** At site.

FACILITIES
Number of RV Sites: 62. **Number of Tent-Only Sites:** 9. **Number of Multipurpose Sites:** 0. **Hookups:** Water, sewer, electric (20, 30 amps). **Each Site:** Picnic table, grill on the tent sites. **Dump Station:** Yes. **Laundry:** Yes. **Pay Phone:** Yes. **Rest Rooms and Showers:** Yes. **Fuel:** No. **Propane:** No. **Internal Roads:** Gravel. **RV Service:** Nearby. **Market:** Nearby. **Restaurant:**

Nearby. **General Store:** Yes. **Vending:** Yes. **Swimming Pool:** Yes. **Playground:** Yes. **Other:** Snack bar. **Activities:** Waterslide, mini-golf, paddle boats, game room, fishing, volleyball, basketball, horseshoes, shuffleboard. **Nearby Attractions:** Black Mountain, Chimney Rock.

RESTRICTIONS

Pets: Allowed. **Fires:** Fire rings only. **Alcoholic Beverages:** Not in public areas. **Vehicle Maximum Length:** None.

TO GET THERE

Take I-40 to Exit 86, then north on Hwy 226, follow the signs for 2.5 mi.

MOCKSVILLE
Lake Myers RV Resort

150 Fred Lanier Rd., Mocksville 27028. T: (336) 492-7736.

🚐 ★★★	🅰 ★★★
Beauty: ★★★★	Site Privacy: ★★
Spaciousness: ★★	Quiet: ★★★
Security: ★★★★	Cleanliness: ★★★
Insect Control: ★★★	Facilities: ★★

This attractive campground is set on gentle hills with lovely trees. Though the crowd is older and more residential on weekdays, Lake Myers is inundated by families on the weekends. Why not? Extensive recreation includes two 400-foot water boggans, two Olympic-sized pools, and numerous playgrounds throughout the park. Campsites are small and feel crowded when they're full. Most are shaded by gorgeous hardwoods. Ground cover is gravel. There isn't any grass or pine straw, just gravel. Most sites offer back-in parking, though there are some pull-through sites. Tent campers enjoy their own playground and washhouse, but tent sites are sandwiched between two busy roads. Mocksville is convenient to attractions in Winston-Salem and Lexington. Security is excellent at this rural park. The front gate is attended on weekends and closed at night.

BASICS

Operated By: Private operator. **Open:** Mar.–Nov. (Some sites are opened all year, ask about discounts.) **Site Assignment:** Deposit must be made within 1 week from date of reservation. Deposit will be returned if reservation is cancelled 1 week in advance. **Registration:** Office. **Fee:** $25–$27 per night (Nov.–Feb.). **Parking:** At site.

FACILITIES

Number of RV Sites: 425. **Hookups:** Electric (30 amps), sewer, cable (free), water. **Pay Phone:** Yes. **Rest Rooms and Showers:** Yes. **Fuel:** No. **Propane:** LP Gas. **Internal Roads:** Paved & gravel. **RV Service:** I-40 Exit 150 (15 min. from Lake Myers). **Market:** Nearby. **Restaurant:** Nearby. **General Store:** On site. **Vending:** Inquire at campground. **Swimming Pool:** Yes. **Playground:** Yes. **Other:** Sidewalk café, rec hall, recreation building, pool tables. **Activities:** Paddle boating, canoeing, firewood, fishing, skating, mini-golf, game room, horseshoes, shuffleboard. **Nearby Attractions:** Old Salem, R. J. Reynolds Tobacco Co., Joseph Schitz Brewery, Tanglewood Park.

RESTRICTIONS

Pets: Leash. **Fires:** Allowed. **Alcoholic Beverages:** Keep alcohol concealed. **Vehicle Maximum Length:** Call ahead for details. **Other:** Cars should not be used for transportation within the park. No lake swimming. No motor bikes.

TO GET THERE

Exit I-40 at US Hwy. 64 (Exit 168) (Mocksville Junction) and turn north.

MORGANTON
Steel Creek Park

7081 NC 181, Morganton 28655. T: (828) 433-5660.

🚐 ★★★★	🅰 ★★★★
Beauty: ★★★★	Site Privacy: ★★
Spaciousness: ★★★	Quiet: ★★★★
Security: ★★★★	Cleanliness: ★★★★
Insect Control: ★★★★	Facilities: ★★★★

Steel Creek is a lovely campground situated in a flat mountain valley. Sites fan out from a huge grassy field, and many have lovely views of the surrounding southernmost portion of the Blue Ridge Mountains. Most sites are partially shady. RV sites generally have gravel parking, while tent and pop-up sites usually have grass parking. There are both pull-through and back-in sites. Sites are on the small side, but the setting is so open that we didn't feel penned in. Choose your site based on location and amenities. Families will want to camp closer to the beach, while couples may want to seek a quieter site away from the recreation. Steel Creek has very nice recreational facilities, especially for children. The Blue Ridge Parkway is about 15 miles north, and other tourist attractions are within 30 miles. There is no gate, but it's very remote. So, security is good.

BASICS

Operated By: The Loven family. **Open:** Apr. 1–Nov. 1. **Site Assignment:** First come, first served; reservations for groups only. **Registration:** Main building. **Fee:** $25 per night for up to 4 people, $5 for each additional person. **Parking:** On site.

FACILITIES

Number of RV Sites: 168. **Number of Tent-Only Sites:** 65. **Number of Multipurpose Sites:** 0. **Hookups:** Water, electric (30, 50 amps), sewer. **Each Site:** None. **Dump Station:** Yes. **Laundry:** Yes. **Pay Phone:** Yes. **Rest Rooms and Showers:** Yes. **Fuel:** No. **Propane:** Yes. **Internal Roads:** Paved. **RV Service:** Morganton. **Market:** Morganon. **Restaurant:** Morganton. **General Store:** Morganton. **Vending:** Yes. **Swimming Pool:** No. **Playground:** Yes. **Other:** Beach by creek w/ swimming area. **Activities:** Fishing, game room, horseshoes, mini-golf, waterslide, hiking. **Nearby Attractions:** Mt. Mitchell, Grandfather Mountain, Linville Falls, Linville Cavern, Table Rock.

RESTRICTIONS

Pets: Allowed. **Fires:** Allowed. **Alcoholic Beverages:** Not allowed. **Vehicle Maximum Length:** 45 ft.

TO GET THERE

13 mi. north of Morganton, south on 181 from Linville.

MURPHY
Hanging Dog

201 Woodland Dr., Murphy 28906. T: (828) 837-5152; www.cs.unca.edu/nfsnc.

🚐 ★★★★   ⛺ ★★★★

Beauty: ★★★★   Site Privacy: ★★★★
Spaciousness: ★★★★   Quiet: ★★★★
Security: ★★★★   Cleanliness: ★★★★
Insect Control: ★★★★   Facilities: ★★★

This attractive campground is laid out in four loops, with grass and gravel back-in parking. Site size is ample but not huge. Many sites offer plenty of shade, compliments of pine and vari-

ous oak species. Privacy varies, with wooded sites at the end of loop A tending to be the most private. Our favorite sites are on loop B, which offers views of 6,120-acre Hiwassee Lake. The lake is known for catches including northern pike, bass, and musky. There are also trout streams in the area. Murphy, a charming town, is home to the worthwhile Cherokee County Historical Museum. Security is good at this extremely remote campground. Visit in late spring to enjoy the blooming rhododendrons. Or visit on weekdays in the fall for leaf peeping.

BASICS

Operated By: USDA Forest Service. **Open:** May–Oct. **Site Assignment:** First come, first served. **Registration:** Self-registration on site. **Fee:** $8. **Parking:** At site.

FACILITIES

Number of RV Sites: 60. **Number of Tent-Only Sites:** 9. **Number of Multipurpose Sites:** 0. **Hookups:** None. **Each Site:** Picnic table, fire ring, tent pad, lantern post. **Dump Station:** No. **Laundry:** No. **Pay Phone:** Yes. **Rest Rooms and Showers:** Yes. **Fuel:** No. **Propane:** No. **Internal Roads:** Paved. **RV Service:** No. **Market:** No. **Restaurant:** No. **General Store:** No. **Vending:** No. **Swimming Pool:** No. **Playground:** No. **Activities:** Boating, hiking, fishing. **Nearby Attractions:** Inquire at campground.

RESTRICTIONS

Pets: Allowed. **Fires:** In fire ring. **Alcoholic Beverages:** At site. **Vehicle Maximum Length:** Call ahead for details. **Other:** 14-day stay limit.

TO GET THERE

From Murphy, take Brown Rd. (NC 1326) northwest for 5 mi. Turn left at campground sign. The campground is straight ahead.

NEWPORT
Water's Edge RV Park

1463 Hwy. 24, Newport 28570. T: (252) 247-0494; F: (252) 247-0494; www.watersedge-rvpark.com; rvpark@mail.clis.com.

🚐 ★★★   ⛺ ★★

Beauty: ★★★   Site Privacy: ★★
Spaciousness: ★★   Quiet: ★★★★
Security: ★★★   Cleanliness: ★★★★
Insect Control: ★★   Facilities: ★★

Attractive Water's Edge is located in a suburban area just outside of Morehead City. The park lies along the Bogue Sound and maintains a fishing pier and a laid-back community atmosphere. The park is convenient to area beaches and other attractions. Take a day trip to the historic town of Beaufort, with buildings pre-dating the town's incorporation in 1723. The long, narrow campground consists of mainly back-in sites. Site size varies from small to average. Parking is on a messy mixture of gravel and grass, and shade and privacy vary from site to site. The shadiest sites are along the park boundaries, on both sides. But our favorite sites are in section C, and have views of Bogue sound. Long-term and short-term campers share the same areas. The land and landscaping, with marsh grasses and cattails, are gorgeous. Unfortunately, there are quite a few junky buildings in view. There are no gates, making security at Water's Edge fair. Visit in late spring or fall for peace and quiet.

BASICS

Operated By: Singleton Family. **Open:** All year. **Site Assignment:** Reservations recommended (252) 247-5709. MC, V, AE are accepted. There is no penalty for a cancellation more than 24 hrs. in advance. If cancelled within 24 hrs. of expected arrival date then the deposit is non refundable. Check-in time is 12 noon. Check-out time is 11 a.m. For tent sites the stay limit is 2 weeks. **Registration:** Main office. **Fee:** Full hookup per night is $25, water & electric hookup is $20 per night. The weekly rate is stay six nights & get the seventh night free. $250 monthly rate for RV site plus the bill for the water & electric hookup. **Parking:** 2 vehicles per site, overflow parking is available.

FACILITIES

Number of RV Sites: 72. **Number of Tent-Only Sites:** 14. **Number of Multipurpose Sites:** None. **Hookups:** RV sites have water, electric (20, 30 amps), sewer; tent sites have water & electric (20, 30 amps); some sites w/ no hookups. **Each Site:** Picnic table. **Dump Station:** No. **Laundry:** No. **Pay Phone:** No. **Rest Rooms and Showers:** Yes. **Fuel:** No. **Propane:** No. **Internal Roads:** Paved. **RV Service:** On call. **Market:** 1 mi. **Restaurant:** 3 mi. west in Newport. **General Store:** approx. 3.5 mi. east in Newport. **Vending:** No. **Swimming Pool:** No. **Playground:** No. **Other:** Fishing pier, athletic field, no group lodging. **Activities:** Picnicking, boat rentals. **Nearby**

Attractions: Maritime Museum, NC Aquarium, 19th cent. Fort Macon, Beaufort Historic Site, Blackbeard's stomping grounds. **Additional Information:** Carteret County Tourism Development Bureau, (252) 726-8148.

RESTRICTIONS

Pets: Leash only. **Fires:** In designated area, not on site. **Alcoholic Beverages:** Allowed. **Vehicle Maximum Length:** None.

TO GET THERE

Go east on US 70 for 3 mi. after the city of Havelock. Go 3 stop lights and then turn right onto Hibbs Rd. Go 3 mi. and take a left onto Hwy. 24. Go 1 mi. and turn right into the entrance of the park.

ROARING GAP

Stone Mountain State Park

3042 Frank Parkway, Roaring Gap 28668. T: (336) 957-8185; stonemtn@infoave.net.

🚐 ★★★★   ⛺ ★★★★

Beauty: ★★★★	Site Privacy: ★★★★
Spaciousness: ★★★★	Quiet: ★★★★
Security: ★★★★★	Cleanliness: ★★★★★
Insect Control: ★★★★	Facilities: ★★★★

Stone Mountain State Park is beloved by nature enthusiasts, though it offers a wide range of activities. For the adventurous, there's rock climbing on the park's namesake, a 600-foot gray granite inselberg. Mellower folks can reach the top of Stone Mountain by a short but strenuous hiking trail. Other park activities include trout fishing in mountain streams. The campground consists of two loops, with gravel parking. Sites are shaded by white pine, red ample, and various oak species. A thick understory provides privacy between most sites. Site size is moderate, but there is plenty of space between sites. For tent campers, we recommend sites on the first loop, which tend to be more wooded. For RV campers, we recommend sites 20, 26, and 27, on the second loop. Stone Mountain is extremely secure—it's remote and gates are locked at night. This park stays cool in late summer, making it a great mid-week summer destination.

BASICS

Operated By: State of North Carolina. **Open:** All year. **Site Assignment:** First come, first served

Reservations for groups only. **Registration:** Office. **Fee:** $8–$12 per night. **Parking:** On site.

FACILITIES

Number of RV Sites: 37. **Number of Tent-Only Sites:** 6. **Number of Multipurpose Sites:** 0. **Hookups:** None. **Each Site:** Picnic table, grill, tent pad. **Dump Station:** Yes. **Laundry:** No. **Pay Phone:** Yes. **Rest Rooms and Showers:** Yes. **Fuel:** No. **Propane:** No. **Internal Roads:** Paved & gravel. **RV Service:** Yes. **Market:** Nearby. **Restaurant:** Nearby. **General Store:** Inquire at campground. **Vending:** Inquire at campground. **Swimming Pool:** No. **Playground:** Inquire at campground. **Other:** Waterfalls, mountain cultural exhibit, Hutchingson Homestead. **Activities:** Trout fishing, rock climbing, hiking. **Nearby Attractions:** Inquire at campground.

RESTRICTIONS

Pets: Allowed. **Fires:** Allowed. **Alcoholic Beverages:** Inquire at campground. **Vehicle Maximum Length:** None.

TO GET THERE

From the south: Take US Hwy. 21 to SR 1002, go 4.5 mi. to John P. Frank Pkwy. From the west: Take NC 18 north and turn right on SR 1002, follow SR 1002 to the John P. Frank Pkwy.

RODANTHE
Cape Hatteras KOA Kampgound

Cape Hatteras National Seashore on Hwy. 12 Box 100, Rodanthe 27968. T: (252) 987-2307; F: (252) 987-2535; www.koa.com; capehkoa@pinn.net.

 ★★★   ▲ ★★★

Beauty: ★★★	Site Privacy: ★★
Spaciousness: ★★★	Quiet: ★★
Security: ★★★	Cleanliness: ★★★★
Insect Control: ★★★	Facilities: ★★★

KOA and nearby Camp Hatteras are comparable in most respects. The KOA has nicer washrooms, but Camp Hatteras has a nicer tent-only area. The flat campground is laid out in a giant grid, comprised of both back-in and pull-through sites. Sites are small, and there are no natural privacy barriers. There's also no shade. Although some sites are near the beach, tall dunes obscure views of the Atlantic Ocean. Since there is little resolution between sites, we recommend choosing a site based on proximity to the beach (back of the park), or proximity to pool (front of the park). Cape Hatteras KOA offers planned children's activities and nice recreational facilities. The small town of Rodanthe is adjacent to Pea Island National Wildlife Refuge, a birdwatcher's Mecca. Other popular outings include taking the ferry to Ocracoke Island. Security is fair—there are no gates, but Rodanthe is a safe little town. Don't visit on busy summer weekends.

BASICS

Operated By: KOA, Inc. **Open:** Mar. 1–Dec 1. **Site Assignment:** Reservations recommended (800) 562-5268. All major credit cards are accepted. If cancelled 24 hrs. in advance then there is no penalty. If cancelled after 4 p.m. of the day before expected arrival the penalty is no refund on the deposit. Check-in time is 1 p.m. Check-out time is 12 p.m. Out-of-state checks can be used to make reservations only. There is no stay limit. **Registration:** Main office. **Fee:** Call ahead for details. **Parking:** 2 vehicles at each site, overflow parking is available.

FACILITIES

Number of RV Sites: 324. **Number of Tent-Only Sites:** 36. **Number of Multipurpose Sites:** Some of the RV sites can be used as tent sites. **Hookups:** Water, electric (30, 50 amps), sewer (some). **Each Site:** Picnic table, some have shelters. **Dump Station:** Yes. **Laundry:** Yes. **Pay Phone:** Yes. **Rest Rooms and Showers:** Yes. **Fuel:** No. **Propane:** Yes. **Internal Roads:** Paved. **RV Service:** On call. **Market:** 17 mi. south in Avon. **Restaurant:** 1 mi. **General Store:** 40 mi. north in Kitty Hawk. **Vending:** Beverage only. **Swimming Pool:** Yes. **Playground:** Yes. **Other:** Fishing pier, bike rental, water wars, volleyball court, basketball court, group lodging, horseshoe game area. **Activities:** Picnicking, fishing, volleyball, & basketball. **Nearby Attractions:** Cape Hatteras Lighthouse, Wright Brothers Monument, Elizabethan Gardens, free ferry from Cape Hatteras to Ocracoke Island. **Additional Information:** Outer Banks Visitors Bureau, (252) 473-2138.

RESTRICTIONS

Pets: Leash only. **Fires:** Only below high tide line on the beach. **Alcoholic Beverages:** Allowed. **Vehicle Maximum Length:** None. **Other:** No golf carts allowed.

TO GET THERE

From Virginia Beach take I-64 to Hwy. 168 south. From Hwy. 168 turn onto 158 south. Go through Nagshead NC and turn onto Hwy. 12 going south. The park is 0.25 mi. down the road on the ocean side.

SOUTHMONT

High Rock Lake Marina and Campground

P.O. Box 815, Southmont 27351-0346. T: (336) 798-1196; F: (336) 798-2026; www.gocampingamerica.com/highroads/; highrock@gocampingamerica.com.

🚐 ★★★★   ▲ ★★★★

Beauty: ★★★★★   Site Privacy: ★★★★
Spaciousness: ★★★   Quiet: ★★★
Security: ★★★★   Cleanliness: ★★★★
Insect Control: ★★★   Facilities: ★★★★

This attractive campground is situated on a peninsula on High Rock Lake. Most sites are rented on a seasonal/long term basis, but there are usually a few short-term sites available. Site size is ample, but not huge. Most sites are very shady, and there are often a few trees between sites. Parking is on gravel. There are both pull-through and back-in spaces, and sites are often misrepresented on the park map. Nice looking pull-through sites 77–82, are more likely to be available for short-term campers. Tent sites have a lovely view of the lake, but they are preposterously small. We don't recommend the tent sites. The campground offers boat dockage (fees apply), and other excellent amenities for anglers. Fishing in High Rock Lake is excellent, and usually not too crowded. Avoid this campground on summer holidays. Security is fine here—there are no gates, but the campground is rurally located.

BASICS

Operated By: Lynn & Stephany Farguhar, Owners. **Open:** All year. **Site Assignment:** Reservations reccomended, 2 week cancellation. **Registration:** Office. **Fee:** RV $22–$25 (daily), $154–$175 (weekly); tent $20 (daily), $125 (weekly). **Parking:** 1 vehicle per site, extra overflow area.

FACILITIES

Number of RV Sites: 101. **Number of Tent-Only Sites:** 5. **Number of Multipurpose Sites:** 0. **Hookups:** Water, electric (30, 50 amps). **Each Site:** Cable TV, trash pickup, picnic table, fire ring. **Dump Station:** Yes. **Laundry:** Yes. **Pay Phone:**
Yes. **Rest Rooms and Showers:** Yes. **Fuel:** Yes. **Propane:** Yes. **Internal Roads:** Main paved, some gravel. **RV Service:** 7 mi., Lexington. **Market:** 7 mi. Lexington. **Restaurant:** 7 mi., Lexington. **General Store:** 7 mi., Lexington. **Vending:** Yes. **Swimming Pool:** Yes. **Playground:** Yes. **Other:** Snack bar, game room. **Activities:** Fishing pier, boat rental, waterskiing. **Nearby Attractions:** "RCR Promotions," Welcome Center, Nascar Racing, NC Zoo at Asheboro, Furniture Discovery Center, Furniture Capitol of the World, Lexington BBQ festival (October), Historic Old Salem, Southeast Old Thresher's Reunion (July), Carowinds, Emerald Pointe Water Park.

RESTRICTIONS

Pets: Allowed. **Fires:** Fire rings only. **Alcoholic Beverages:** Yes, only covered containers. **Vehicle Maximum Length:** 50 ft. **Other:** No bike riding after dark, no skateboards or rollerblades allowed. Disorderly behavior, profanity, any firearms (including liscensed concealed weapons), illegal drugs, fireworks, & intoxication are strictly prohibited. No swimming in the lake.

TO GET THERE

From Salisbury take I-85 (US 52) 15 mi. to Exit 91. Exit onto SR 8. Head south on SR 8 for 8 mi.

SPRUCE PINE

Bear Den Campground

600 Bear Den Mountain Rd., Spruce Pine 28777. T: (828) 765-2888; F: (828) 765-2864; www.bear-den.com; bearden@M-Y.net.

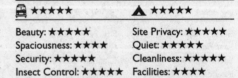

🚐 ★★★★★   ▲ ★★★★★

Beauty: ★★★★★   Site Privacy: ★★★★★
Spaciousness: ★★★★   Quiet: ★★★★★
Security: ★★★★★   Cleanliness: ★★★★★
Insect Control: ★★★★★   Facilities: ★★★★

Bear Den is fabulous. The campground is laid out in four areas nestled into a mountainside right off the Blue Ridge Parkway. Excellent amenities include five playgrounds and a picturesque swimming lake. There's also fishing in the creek bordering the park. Hikers enjoy easy access to miles of trails managed by the National Park Service and US Forest Service. Sites at Bear Den aren't huge, but most feel very private due to the confluence of natural vegetation and thoughtful landscaping; almost all sites are refreshingly wooded with greenery between sites. Parking is on pea gravel and there are back-in and pull-through sites. If your rig fits, go for a pull-through site, as they tend to be more private. Our favorite sites in areas A and B are those on the outside of the loops. In area D, sites 15 and 16 are huge. Security is fine. There are no gates, but the area is pretty remote. The mountain towns that dot the Blue Ridge Parkway in this area are uniformly quaint and worth exploring.

BASICS

Operated By: Moody Family. **Open:** Apr.–Oct. **Site Assignment:** 1-night deposit for reservations; 90% of deposit is refundable if reservation cancelled 7 days in advance; V, MC, D, AE. **Registration:** In office. **Fee:** $27–$58. **Parking:** At site.

FACILITIES

Number of RV Sites: 44. **Number of Tent-Only Sites:** 100. **Number of Multipurpose Sites:** 0. **Hookups:** Water, sewer, electric (30 amps). **Each Site:** Water, electric, fire rings, picnic tables. **Dump Station:** Yes. **Laundry:** Yes. **Pay Phone:** Yes. **Rest Rooms and Showers:** Yes. **Fuel:** No. **Propane:** Yes. **Internal Roads:** Gravel & paved. **RV Service:** 15 mi. toward Spruce Pine. **Market:** on site. **Restaurant:** 15 mi. toward Spruce Pine. **General Store:** 15 mi. toward Spruce Pine. **Vending:** No. **Swimming Pool:** No. **Playground:** Yes. **Other:** Golf cart rentals, store, game room, fire wood, ATM, swimming lake, & nature trails. **Activities:** Pool table, basketball, volleyball, horseshoes, badminton, shuffleboard, ping pong, square dancing, Sunday church services, pinball, video games, canoe & paddleboat rentals. **Nearby Attractions:** Gemstone mining, mini golf, climbing wall, go carts, Mt. Mitchell, golf, Linville Caverns, Linville Gorge, Whitewater rafting, Blue Ridge Pkwy., Grandfather Mtn., Little Switzerland, Museum of NC, Fishing, Blowing Rock, Roan Mtn., Tweetsie Railroad.

RESTRICTIONS

Pets: Allowed. **Fires:** Fire rings only. **Alcoholic Beverages:** Not permitted. **Vehicle Maximum Length:** None.

TO GET THERE

Going north from junction Hwy. 226, it is 6 mi. to mile post 324.8, Bear Den Mtn. Rd. Turn right. Going south from junction Hwy. 221, it is 5.3 mi. to Bear Den Overlook, mile-post 323. Travel another 1.8 mi. to Bear Den Mtn. Rd. (mile post 324.8). Turn left.

STATESVILLE
Midway Campground

Rt. 4 Box 199 B, Statesville 28677. T: (888) 754-4809 (704) 546-7615; F: (704) 546-7615; www.kiz.com/midway; rljenkins@conninc.com.

🚐 ★★★   ⛺ ★★★

Beauty: ★★★★	Site Privacy: ★★★
Spaciousness: ★★★	Quiet: ★★★
Security: ★★★	Cleanliness: ★★★★
Insect Control: ★★★★	Facilities: ★★★

Midway is an attractive campground situated on a hillside sloping down to fishing pond teeming with catfish. Sites are on the small side, but nicely spaced. Most sites are shady, though privacy is not optimal. Parking is on gravel. Most parking pads are back-in, though there are a few very long pull-through sites that can accommodate big rigs. The prettiest sites, 19–24, enjoy views of the pond. The pool is large enough for lap swimmers, and recreation areas are also nicely appointed. Midway has no gates, and is close to I-40 in a rural area, making security fair. South of Statesville is mammoth Lake Norman, offering fishing and boating opportunities. Many buildings in downtown Statesville are on the National Register of Historic Places. For the nicest weather, visit Statesville in late spring or fall.

BASICS

Operated By: Randy & Jocelyn Jenkins. **Open:** All year. **Site Assignment:** Reservations are suggested for holidays & weekends; deposit is based on length of stay; full refund is given on deposit only if cancelled at least 1 week ahead of time; Accepted methods of payment include MC, AE, V. **Registration:** In office. **Fee:** RV is $28–$33/day, tent is $25/day. **Parking:** Yes.

FACILITIES

Number of RV Sites: 60. **Number of Tent-Only Sites:** 13. **Number of Multipurpose Sites:** 0. **Hookups:** Water, sewer, electric (20, 30, 50 amps). **Each Site:** Picnic tables, fire rings. **Dump Station:** Yes. **Laundry:** Yes. **Pay Phone:** Yes. **Rest Rooms and Showers:** Yes. **Fuel:** No. **Propane:** Yes. **Internal Roads:** Paved & gravel. **RV Service:** Exit 170 on I-40. **Market:** On site.

Restaurant: 7 mi. from town. **General Store:** 7 mi. from town. **Vending:** No. **Swimming Pool:** Yes. **Playground:** Yes. **Other:** Game room, ATM machine, modem connection. **Activities:** Basketball, badminton, horseshoes, mini-golf, volleyball, paddleboats, fishing lake, pavillion, Sunday church services. **Nearby Attractions:** Mall.

RESTRICTIONS

Pets: Yes. **Fires:** Fire rings only. **Alcoholic Beverages:** At site only. **Vehicle Maximum Length:** None.

TO GET THERE

Heading east on I-40, take Exit 162. Turn right. Go 0.25 mi. and turn left on Camground Rd. 0.25 mi. to Campground. Heading west on I-40, take Exit 162. Turn left and go 0.5 mi. to Camground Rd. Turn left. Go 0.25 mi. to campground.

SWANNANOA
Asheville East KOA

P.O. Box 485, Swannanoa 28778. T: (800) KOA-5907; F: (704) 686-7758;
www.koakampgrounds.com/where/nc/33116.htm.

🚐 ★★★★	🏕 ★★★★
Beauty: ★★★★	Site Privacy: ★★★★
Spaciousness: ★★★★	Quiet: ★★★
Security: ★★★	Cleanliness: ★★★★
Insect Control: ★★★★	Facilities: ★★★★

The Asheville East KOA is laid out in numerous sections dissected by the Swannanoa River. There are also two ponds adding to the visual appeal of the property. Both the river and the ponds are open for trout fishing (no license required for the ponds). Though site size and privacy vary, most are slightly larger than average. Tree cover ranges from dense to totally open. Parking is on gravel, grass, or dirt, and all sites are back-in style. Our favorite RV sites are found in Section D—these are lakeside, with picturesque views of water lilies. Section G contains shady tent sites. Security is fair; the campground has no gates. Avoid this area on summer and autumn weekends. KOA is a good place to stay if you plan on touring the lovely city of Asheville as well as the wilderness areas east of Black Mountain. A day at the Biltmore Estate, America's largest privately-owned home, is worth inflated admissions prices.

BASICS

Operated By: KOA. **Open:** All year. **Site Assignment:** Reservations recommended. Must cancel 7 days in advance during hohlidays & 2 days in advance during non-holidays to refund deposit. Requested campsites are not guaranteed. Deposit is 1-night rent or can be held w/ a credit card. **Registration:** Payment accepted is V, MC, local checks, travelers checks, or cash. **Fee:** RV site is $24–$28/day. **Parking:** 1 vehicle & camping unit per site. Additional vehicle parking is available.

FACILITIES

Number of RV Sites: 225. **Number of Tent-Only Sites:**. **Number of Multipurpose Sites:** 0. **Hookups:** Water, sewer, electric (20, 30, 50 amps), cable. **Each Site:** Water & electric. **Dump Station:** Yes. **Laundry:** Yes. **Pay Phone:** Yes. **Rest Rooms and Showers:** Yes. **Fuel:** No. **Propane:** Yes. **Internal Roads:** Gravel & dirt. **RV Service:** 10 mi. toward Asheville. **Market:** 2 mi. toward SwannaNoa. **Restaurant:** 10 mi. toward Asheville. **General Store:** 10 mi. toward Asheville. **Vending:** Yes. **Swimming Pool:** Yes. **Playground:** Yes. **Activities:** 2 fishing lakes, trout stream, game room, mini-golf, bicycle rentals, pavilion, basketball, horseshoes, boat rentals, paddle boat rentals, ping pong, walking trail, firewood. **Nearby Attractions:** Maggie Valley, Ridgecrest/Montreat, River Rafting, Horseback Riding, WNC Nature Center.

RESTRICTIONS

Pets: Allowed. **Fires:** Fire rings only. **Alcoholic Beverages:** At site only. **Vehicle Maximum Length:** None.

TO GET THERE

From I-40, take Exit 59. Go north for 1 block to signal (US 70). Turn right and drive tow miles.

TUCKASEGEE
Singing Waters Camping Resort

1006 Trout Creek Rd., Tuckasegee 28783. T: (828) 293-5872; F: (828) 293-3325; www.kiz.com/singingwaters; sngwtrs@dnet.net.

🚐 ★★★★	🏕 ★★★★
Beauty: ★★★★	Site Privacy: ★★★
Spaciousness: ★★★	Quiet: ★★★★
Security: ★★★★	Cleanliness: ★★★★
Insect Control: ★★★★	Facilities: ★★★

This pretty campground is tucked into a wooded mountain valley, with sites alongside bubbling

Trout Creek. With an elevation of 3,000 feet, Singing Waters stays cool, making it an excellent summertime destination—just avoid visiting on busy holidays. Their refreshing natural swimming pond is just the thing to escape summer heat. The campground consists of back-in sites beautifully shaded by mature white pine trees. Parking, on a mixture of pine bark mulch and pine straw, is luxurious. Sites are medium sized, and a little greenery provides privacy. The nicest sites, 28–32, are in the back of the campground along the creek. Two tent sites, 48 and 49, offer raised tent pads and covered picnic tables. More traditional tent camping sites are also available. Security is fine here; there are no gates but the park is off the beaten path. Halfway between Sylva and Cashiers, Singing Waters is in the heart of Pisgah National Forest.

BASICS

Operated By: Cooper family. **Open:** Full hookups are open from Mar.–Dec. Partial hookups are open May–Oct. **Site Assignment:** Reservations recommended, (828) 293-5872. AE, MC, D are accepted. If cancelled within 7 days of the expected arrival date the deposit is nonrefundable. Check-in time is 2 p.m. Check-out time is 12 noon. **Registration:** Registration office. **Fee:** $28–$24 campsites, $26 for full hookups for 2 people. Each additional child (6–17 yrs. old) is $2 more. Each additional adult is $5 more. **Parking:** 2 vehicle parking at each site, overflow parking is available.

FACILITIES

Number of RV Sites: 42. **Number of Tent-Only Sites:** 21. **Number of Multipurpose Sites:** None. **Hookups:** Water, electric (20, 30, 50 amps), 42 sites w/ sewer, water & electric (20, 30, 50 amps). **Each Site:** Picnic table, fire ring, grill. **Dump Station:** No. **Laundry:** Yes. **Pay Phone:** Yes. **Rest Rooms and Showers:** Yes. **Fuel:** No. **Propane:** No. **Internal Roads:** Gravel. **RV Service:** On call. **Market:** 10 mi. south in Cashiers. **Restaurant:** 3 mi. south Cashiers. **General Store:** 17 mi. north in Sylva. **Vending:** Beverage. **Swimming Pool:** No (swimming is OK in pond). **Playground:** Yes. **Other:** Pond, basketball court, volleyball net, trails, rec room, pavilion, no group lodging. **Activities:** Hiking, basketball, volleyball, indoor games. **Nearby Attractions:** Blue Ridge Pkwy., Great Smoky Mountains National Park, Nantahala National Forest, Qualla-Cherokee Indian Reservation, Harrah's Cherokee Casino, Great

Smoky Mountains Railway, Ghost Town in the Sky, Biltmore Estates, white-water rafting, golf, gem mining, boating & fishing, crafts & antique shops. **Additional Information:** Jackson County Chamber of Commerce, (828) 586-2155.

RESTRICTIONS

Pets: Leash only. **Fires:** Fire pit only. **Alcoholic Beverages:** At site only. **Vehicle Maximum Length:** 45 ft.

TO GET THERE

On I-40 from Ashville take Exit 27 onto Smoky Mountain Expressway west. Take Exit 85 and go west. Take a left at the second light and go 17 mi. south on Hwy. 107 to sign for Park. Turn left onto Trout Creek Rd. Go 1 mi. east. The entrance is on the right.

WAKE FOREST

Holly Point State Recreational Area

13304 Creedmoor Rd., Wake Forest 27587. T: (919) 676-1027; F: (919) 676-2954; www.ncsparks.net; Falls.lake@ncmail.net.

🚐 ★★★★★	🏕 ★★★★★
Beauty: ★★★★★	Site Privacy: ★★★★★
Spaciousness: ★★★★★	Quiet: ★★★★★
Security: ★★★★	Cleanliness: ★★★★
Insect Control: ★★★★	Facilities: ★★★

The gorgeous campsites at Holly Point are similar to those at Jordan Lake in terms of size and design. Campers can choose between ultra-private sites set in the woods, or more open sites with fantastic lake views. Sites are gargantuan, with plenty of space between neighbors. Most sites offer pull-through parking, though there are a few back-in spaces. Parking pads are gravel, and need some attention—most had grass growing in them. The prettiest sites are 166 (a huge, gorgeous pull-through), 121–126 (open sites with lake views), and 58, 59, 65, and 66 (on a peninsula, with gorgeous views). Fishing is excellent at Falls Lake. Artificial reefs and underwater fish shelters support bass, crappie, and catfish populations. For hikers, part of the North Carolina Mountains-to-Sea-Trail winds through the park. Though the park feels rural, it's in the Raleigh/Wake Forest suburbs. Security is fine. Gates are not attended during the day, but they are locked at night. Avoid the popular park on summer holidays and weekends.

BASICS

Operated By: NC State Parks. **Open:** All year except Christmas Eve & Christmas Day. **Site Assignment:** Campers may choose their own site. Reservations have to be made 2 weeks in advance for a min. of a 7-night stay. Must give 2-week notice of cancellation. Cash or check payments are accepted. Max. stay is 2 weeks. **Registration:** During peak season at entrance station. Other times the ranger will come to the site. **Fee:** Non-hookup site is $12 per night. A site w/ hookups is $17 per night. Doubles range $24–$34 per night. **Parking:** 2 vehicles per site.

FACILITIES

Number of RV Sites: 87. **Number of Tent-Only Sites:** 62. **Number of Multipurpose Sites:** 7 double w/ electric & water, 2 double w/ water. **Hookups:** Water, electric (20, 30 amps). **Each Site:** Picnic table, fire ring, grill, lantern hook, tent pad. **Dump Station:** Yes. **Laundry:** No. **Pay Phone:** Yes. **Rest Rooms and Showers:** Yes. **Fuel:** No. **Propane:** No. **Internal Roads:** Paved. **RV Service:** Approx. 15 mi. south in Raleigh. **Market:** Approx. 6 mi. north in Wake Forest. **Restaurant:** Appox. 15 mi. south in Raleigh. **General Store:** Approx. 2 mi. north in Wake Forest. **Vending:** No. **Swimming Pool:** No. **Playground:** Yes. **Other:** Group camping, boat ramp, trails. **Activities:** Boating, fishing, hiking. **Nearby Attractions:** Diggs Gallery at Winston-Salem State University, Historic Bethabara Park, Museum of Anthropology, Old Salem. **Additional Information:** Greater Raleigh CVB, (919) 834-2887.

RESTRICTIONS

Pets: Leash only. **Fires:** Designated areas only. **Alcoholic Beverages:** Not allowed. **Vehicle Maximum Length:** 40 ft.

TO GET THERE

From Hwy. 98 turn onto New Light Rd. and go south. Follow the signs.

WAVES

Camp Hatteras

P.O. Box 10, Waves 27968. T: (252) 987-2777; F: (252) 987 2733; www.camphatteras.com; camphatteras7@cs.com.

🚐 ★★★   ⛺ ★★★

Beauty: ★★★   Site Privacy: ★★
Spaciousness: ★★   Quiet: ★★

Security: ★★★★   Cleanliness: ★★★★
Insect Control: ★★★   Facilities: ★★★★

Camp Hatteras is situated on a narrow piece of Hatteras Island and maintains two main camping areas along Hwy. 12, one on each side of the road. The largest area is on the same side as the pool and office, and includes some sites near the Atlantic Ocean. Across the highway, a smaller section includes tent-only sites with pretty views of Pamlico Sound. The recreation and facilities at Camp Hatteras are very nice. Unfortunately, Camp Hatteras offers miserably small campsites, situated in a series of loops. Sites feature paved, back-in parking. There is no shade. Views of the ocean are obscured by dunes. Families should choose their site based on proximity to facilities and the beach. Sites along the perimeter of the park are likely to be a little quieter. Security is very good. The campground is gated and attended at all times. Avoid Hatteras Island on summer holidays and weekends, when masses of people flock here.

BASICS

Operated By: Jett Ferebee. **Open:** All year. **Site Assignment:** Reservations are recommended, (252) 987-2777. MC, AE, D, V are accepted. There in no penalty for cancellation a week in adavance. If cancelled within a week of expected arrival day then the deposit is nonrefundable. Check-in & check-out time is 12 noon. **Registration:** Guardhouse. **Fee:** Winter rates are $29.95 per night for full hookups, $24.95 for tent. Summer rates are $55.95 per night for full hookups, 32.95 per night for tent sites. **Parking:** 2 vehicle at site, overflow parking is available.

FACILITIES

Number of RV Sites: 300. **Number of Tent-Only Sites:** 70. **Number of Multipurpose Sites:** None. **Hookups:** RV sites have cable, sewer, electric (30, 50 amps), water; tent sites have water, electric (30, 50 amps); 60 sites w/ no hookups. **Each Site:** Picnic tables, pads for RV sites. **Dump Station:** No. **Laundry:** Yes. **Pay Phone:** Yes. **Rest Rooms and Showers:** Yes. **Fuel:** No. **Propane:** No. **Internal Roads:** Paved. **RV Service:** On call. **Market:** 18 mi. south in Avon. **Restaurant:** 1 mi. **General Store:** K-Mart 32 mi. north in Kill Devil Hills. **Vending:** Beverage & snack. **Swimming Pool:** Yes. **Playground:** Yes. **Other:** Marina Area, boat ramp (small boats), mini-golf course, arcade. **Activities:** Golfing, wind surfing, sailing, shuffleboard, tennis, arcade games, recreational activities. **Nearby Attractions:** Elizabethan Gardens, Lost colony Drama, Cape Hatteras Lighthouse, Pea Island National Refuge, NC Aquarium, Wright Brothers Memorial. **Additional Information:** Outer Banks Visitors Bureau, (252) 473-2138.

RESTRICTIONS

Pets: Leash only. **Fires:** On beach only. **Alcoholic Beverages:** At sites only. **Vehicle Maximum Length:** 45 ft. **Other:** Family-oriented park.

TO GET THERE

From Virginia beach take Rte. 168 south to Rte. 158 East. Exit onto Rte. 12 South. Turn left into park

WHISPERING PINES
The Heritage

Sadler Family, The Heritage 28387. T: (910) 949-3433; F: (910) 949-5538; www.theheritagenc.com.

🚐 ★★★★　　　　▲ ★★★★

Beauty: ★★★★★　　　Site Privacy: ★★★★
Spaciousness: ★★★★　　Quiet: ★★★★
Security: ★★★★　　　　Cleanliness: ★★★★
Insect Control: ★★★　　 Facilities: ★★★★

The owners of the Heritage are nice folks. Small and inviting, this campground is preferable to nearby Travel Resorts of America if you're traveling with children. The picturesque lake is outfitted with a fun swimming beach and stocked with game fish. Although the park is in a rural location, the golf courses of Pinehurst and its environs are a short drive away. The campground is laid out in five long rows, including both pull-through and back-in sites. Parking is on packed sand and pine straw. Lovely tree cover includes tall southern pines, dogwood, and various oak species. Privacy is good, with a little foliage between most sites. Sites are on the large side of average. Sites 39 and 40 are excellent—secluded and lakefront. Try not to visit the Heritage during a major golf tournament. Security is fine—there are no gates, but the driveway leading to the campground is about a mile long.

BASICS

Operated By: Lee Sadler. **Open:** All year. **Site Assignment:** Reservations accepted. **Registra-**

tion: Office. **Fee:** Call ahead for details. **Parking:** At ofice.

FACILITIES

Number of RV Sites: 56. **Number of Tent-Only Sites:**. **Number of Multipurpose Sites:** 0. **Hookups:** Water, electric (30, 50 amps). **Each Site:** Water, electric, fire rings. **Dump Station:** Yes. **Laundry:** Dryer only. **Pay Phone:** In office. **Rest Rooms and Showers:** Yes. **Fuel:** Nearby. **Propane:** Nearby. **Internal Roads:** Gravel. **RV Service:** Nearby. **Market:** Nearby. **Restaurant:** Nearby. **General Store:** Nearby. **Vending:** Yes. **Swimming Pool:** No. **Playground:** Yes. **Other:** Beach by lake w/ swimming area. **Activities:** Fishing, hiking, boating, horseshoes, volleyball, croquet, shuffleboard, basketball, petting farm. **Nearby Attractions:** Inquire at campground.

RESTRICTIONS

Pets: Yes. **Fires:** In fire ring. **Alcoholic Beverages:** Not in public areas. **Vehicle Maximum Length:** None. **Other:** Children must be attended at all times; check out is at 2 p.m.

TO GET THERE

From Raleigh: Take US Hwy. 1 to Vass, turn right at first stoplight onto Union Church Rd., go 4 mi. and turn onto Heritage Farm Rd., go 1 mi. and turn left into The Heritage. From Southern Pines and Rockingham: Take US Hwy. 1 to Vass, turn left onto Carthage Rd., go 3.5 mi. and turn right onto Heritage Farms Rd., go 0.5 mi. and turn right into The Heritage.

WILKESBORO
Bandits Roost Park, W. Kerr Scott Reservoir

P.O. Box 182, Wilkesboro 28697-0182. T: (336) 921-3390; F: (336) 931-2330; www.saw.usace.army.mil; jory.triplett@usace.army.mil.

🚐 ★★★★　　　　▲ ★★★★★

Beauty: ★★★★★　　　Site Privacy: ★★★
Spaciousness: ★★★★★　Quiet: ★★★★★
Security: ★★★★★　　　Cleanliness: ★★★★★
Insect Control: ★★★★　　Facilities: ★★★

This gorgeous campground features an amazing tent area. Tent campers are treated to stunning views of W. Kerr Scott Reservoir from huge secluded sites. RV campers have good choices too: there are delightfully secluded sites on Loop

B, surrounded by white pine, Virginia pine, and oak trees, or choose an open site with a fabulous view of the lake. We like stunning pull-through sites 24–28, which are situated on a peninsula. Sites 32–35 are also very nice. All sites have gravel parking, with pea gravel picnic areas. Though site size varies, most are large. Bandits Roost is extremely remote, and is gated and guarded, making security outstanding. This area experiences mild summers, making it a good destination in spring, summer, and fall. Just avoid visiting on holiday weekends. Near Bandits Roost are day-use areas and the Skyline Marina, which offers boat launches and other fishing facilities. The reservoir is stocked with crappie, bluegill, catfish, and largemouth and striped hybrid bass.

BASICS

Operated By: US Army Corps of Engineers. **Open:** Apr. 1–Oct. 31. **Site Assignment:** 60% of the site can be reserved (877) 444-6777, MC, V are accepted; the other 40% are first come first served. If cancelled the fee is $10 plus the first nights fee. Check-in time is 4 p.m. The check-out time is 3 p.m. There is a 14-day stay limit. **Registration:** Entrance station. **Fee:** $16 per night for a RV site, $12 for a tent site; $8 & $6 w/ a Golden Age or Golden Access card. **Parking:** 2 vehicle parking at each site, overflow parking is available.

FACILITIES

Number of RV Sites: 42. **Number of Tent-Only Sites:** 42. **Number of Multipurpose Sites:** 0. **Hookups:** Water, electric (30 amps) at RV site, tent sites have no hookups. **Each Site:** Picnic table, fire ring, tent pad, lantern hook. **Dump Station:** Yes. **Laundry:** No. **Pay Phone:** Yes. **Rest Rooms and Showers:** Yes. **Fuel:** No. **Propane:** No. **Internal Roads:** Paved. **RV Service:** 6 mi. north in Wilkesboro. **Market:** 6 mi. south in Wilkesboro. **Restaurant:** 6 mi. south in Wilkesboro. **General Store:** 5 mi. south in Wilkesboro. **Vending:** No. **Swimming Pool:** No. **Playground:** Yes. **Other:** Boating ramp, trails, group lodging. **Activities:** Picnicking, hiking, fishing, basketball, activities in the amphitheater. **Nearby Attractions:** Blue Ridge Pkwy., river rafting. **Additional Information:** Wilkes Chamber of Commerce.

RESTRICTIONS

Pets: Leash only. **Fires:** Fire ring only. **Alcoholic Beverages:** Not allowed. **Vehicle Maximum**

Length: No limit. **Other:** Fishing is state regulated.

TO GET THERE

From I-77, exit onto 421 north, then exit onto Hwy. 268 going west, the park is 6 mi. on the right.

WILKESBORO

Doughton Park Campground

45356 Blue Ridge Parkway 28644. T: (336) 372-4499; www.blueridgeparkway.org.

🚐 ★★★★	🏕 ★★★★
Beauty: ★★★★	Site Privacy: ★★★
Spaciousness: ★★★	Quiet: ★★★
Security: ★★★★	Cleanliness: ★★★★★
Insect Control: ★★★★★	Facilities: ★★★

Doughton Park is the largest recreation area on the Blue Ridge Parkway, and offers plenty of mileage for hikers in the summer and cross-country skiers in the winter. We like the lodge's restaurant for a break from campsite cooking. Nearby, Stone Mountain State Park offers numerous rock climbing routes to the top of the park's namesake. The campground at Doughton is separated into six loops, some for RV campers, others for tent campers. There are both heavily wooded and more open sites, so take your pick. Sites are average sized, with varying levels of privacy. Tent campers seeking private sites should go for walk-in sites 23–33. RV campers looking for solitude should head to the back of the campground. Though there are no gates, security is excellent at this isolated campground. Even though this is a less-trafficked part of the Blue Ridge Parkway, it's best to visit mid-week during summer and fall.

BASICS

Operated By: National Park Service. **Open:** Call ahead for details. **Site Assignment:** First come, first served. **Registration:** Office. **Fee:** Call ahead for details. **Parking:** Yes.

FACILITIES

Number of RV Sites: 25. **Number of Tent-Only Sites:** 110. **Number of Multipurpose Sites:** 0. **Hookups:** None. **Each Site:** Picnic table, fireplace. **Dump Station:** Yes. **Laundry:** No. **Pay Phone:** Yes. **Rest Rooms and Showers:** Yes. **Fuel:** Yes. **Propane:** No. **Internal Roads:** Paved.

RV Service: No. **Market:** No. **Restaurant:** Yes. **General Store:** Yes. **Vending:** Inquire at campground. **Swimming Pool:** No. **Playground:** No. **Activities:** Hiking, fishing. **Nearby Attractions:** Cumberland Knob, Brinegar Cabin.

RESTRICTIONS

Pets: Allowed. **Fires:** Allowed. **Alcoholic Beverages:** Inquire at campground. **Vehicle Maximum Length:** Call ahead for details.

TO GET THERE

From intersection of US 21 and Blue Ridge Pkwy., drive south to mile post 239, or from intersection of NC 18 and Blue Ridge Pkwy., drive north to mile post 239.

WILLIAMSTON

Green Acres Camping Resort

1679 Green Acres Rd., Williamston 27892. T: (252) 792-3939; F: (252) 792-3939; www. martincounty nc.com/mc/greeneacres; bgreene@coastalnet.com.

🚐 ★★★   ▲ n/a

Beauty: ★★★★	Site Privacy: ★★
Spaciousness: ★★★	Quiet: ★★★
Security: ★★★	Cleanliness: ★★★★
Insect Control: ★★★	Facilities: ★★★★

It's a good thing there's plenty to do here—the area around Williamston is completely agricultural. Activities at Green Acres include par-3 golf and fishing in a pretty pond stocked with bream and catfish. Green Acres also offers planned activities. The campground is arranged in two areas. Three rows of sites hug the pond. Sites 1–21 line the pond, and are the most level and picturesque in the park. On the other side of the park, seven rows of sites fan out from the office and other buildings. Looking for shade and quiet? Head for sites 87, 100, 116, 136, and 149. There are both back-in and pull-through sites with packed sand, pine straw, and grass parking. Sites are on the small side of average. Most are partially shady, but none are secluded. Avoid Green Acres on busy summer weekends and holidays; for peace and quiet, plan a mid-week visit. Security is fine at this extremely remote campground.

BASICS

Operated By: The Greene family. **Open:** All year. **Site Assignment:** Reservations are recommended, (888) 792-3939. MC, V, D are accepted. No penalty if cancelled 24 hrs. or more before expected arrival date. If cancelled within the 24 hrs. of the expected arrival date the deposit is nonrefundable. Check-in & check-out time is 2 p.m. **Registration:** Entrance office. **Fee:** $18–$22. **Parking:** 2 vehicle parking at each site, overflow parking is available.

FACILITIES

Number of RV Sites: 100. **Number of Tent-Only Sites:** 75. **Number of Multipurpose Sites:** all. **Hookups:** Water, electric (30 amps), sewer (at 100 sites). **Each Site:** Picnic table, fire ring. **Dump Station:** Yes. **Laundry:** Yes. **Pay Phone:** Yes. **Rest Rooms and Showers:** Yes. **Fuel:** No. **Propane:** Yes. **Internal Roads:** Gravel & dirt. **RV Service:** 25 mi. south in Washington. **Market:** 5 mi. north in Williamston. **Restaurant:** 5 mi. north in Williamston. **General Store:** 5 mi. north in Williamston. **Vending:** Beverage & snack. **Swimming Pool:** Yes. **Playground:** Yes. **Other:** Game room, club house, amphitheater, tennis court, volleyball net, mini & 3-par golf course, no group lodging, live entertainment, church services. **Activities:** Horseshoes, golf, tennis badmitten, bingo, volleyball boat rental. **Nearby Attractions:** The Outer Banks. **Additional Information:** Martin County T&TA, (252) 792-6605.

RESTRICTIONS

Pets: Leash only. **Fires:** Must be contained. **Alcoholic Beverages:** Yes, at sites only. **Vehicle Maximum Length:** 40 ft.

TO GET THERE

US 64 east of Raleigh take Exit 514 onto US 17. Go 4.2 mi. south and turn right onto Roger's Elementary School Rd. going west and travel 1 mi.

South Carolina

South Carolina really packs it in. Visitors encounter a small state rich in history, the arts, and outdoor beauty. Three geographical regions offer diversity not found in many larger states. The coastal low-country is known for its gorgeous live oak and marshes complete with blue heron and other birds. The rolling piedmont offers hunting and freshwater recreation. The highlands lie in the foothills of the Blue Ridge mountains and reach elevations over 3,500 feet.

South Carolina's many native peoples include the Catawba, known for their pottery which has been produced by the same techniques for almost 1,000 years.

European settlers found the South Carolina low-country perfect for rice cultivation, which began in the 1680s. Rice remained essential even as cotton production became more profitable after the invention of the cotton gin in 1793. Rice, cotton, and slave labor brought vast fortunes to Antebellum South Carolina. Many historic homes and plantations stand today and are open for touring. **Charleston's** historic district is the site of urban antebellum buildings as well as **The Dock Street Theater,** the oldest theater building in America. Notable plantations include **Middleton Place,** gathering place for southern strategists in the Revolutionary War, and **Magnolia Plantation,** home of the nation's oldest landscaped garden.

The Civil War began on April 12, 1861 when Confederates attacked Fort Sumter at Charleston Harbor. After this battle, South Carolina saw relatively little fighting, though roughly 13,000 South Carolinians died in the Civil War. In 1864, Charleston was the launch site for the H.L. Hunley, a prototypical submarine that successfully torpedoed and sank the USS Housatonic. A replica of the Hunley is on display at the **South Carolina State Museum** in Columbia.

South Carolina's economy still depends on agriculture (especially soy, tobacco, peaches, and livestock), but textiles, tourism, and numerous other industries also flourish.

Tourists and locals support performing arts in South Carolina. Fine performing arts are appreciated in the state's refurbished opera houses (in **Newberry, Abbeville,** and **Sumter**) and larger venues in **Charleston** and **Greenville**. For casual entertainment, **Myrtle Beach** stages numerous production shows.

Golfers from all over the world pilgrimage to **Hilton Head Island,** site of the Worldcom Classic—The Heritage of Golf (formerly the Heritage Classic). Of the 36 courses in the Hilton Head area, Harbor Town is instantly recognizable with its red-and-white-striped lighthouse visible from many holes. **Myrtle Beach** and the **Grand Strand** now contain over 100 courses, some excellent and others inexpensive. There are few areas in the world that offer so many golfing choices.

Not a golfer? Here are some other recreation opportunities found in South Carolina: **The Greenville County Museum of Art, Bob Jones University Museum & Gallery, Avery Research Center for African American History and Culture, Penn Center, Butterfly Pavilion, Southern Living House at Brookgreen Gardens, South Carolina Foothills Artisans Center, South Beach Adventure Amusement Park, South Carolina Aquarium, Charleston IMAX Theater, Congaree Swamp National Monument, Family Kingdom Amusement Park, Myrtle Beach Pavilion Amusement Park, Paramount's Carowinds, Myrtle Waves Waterpark, Riverbanks Zoo and Botanical Gardens, Greenville Zoo, Emerald Farm.**

The following facility accepts payment in checks or cash only:

Baker Creek State Park, McCormick

Campground Profiles

ANDERSON

Springfield Campground, Hartwell Lake

P.O. Box 278, Hartwell 30643-0278. T: (888) 893-0678; F: (706) 856-0358; www.reserveusa.com.

🚙 ★★★★   ▲ ★★★★

Beauty: ★★★★★	Site Privacy: ★★★★
Spaciousness: ★★★★★	Quiet: ★★★★
Security: ★★★★★	Cleanliness: ★★★★
Insect Control: ★★★	Facilities: ★★★

Springfield Campground at Hartwell Lake boasts some of the most beautiful campsites we've seen. Along the shoreline, most sites have gorgeous water views. Sites 67–79 are especially stunning—huge and private with fabulous views. Sites 32–36 are less private, but have even better views. Sites 25, 26, 47, and 48 are good for families as they are roomy and close to the playground. Sites have gravel parking in pull-throughs and back-ins. There are plenty of shady trees although site privacy varies. One of three reservoirs on the Savannah River, 56,000-acre Lake Hartwell is stocked with crappie, stripers, catfish, and largemouth and hybrid bass. There are a number of other recreation areas within ten miles of the park. Security is outstanding at this rural campground. The gate is guarded by day and locked by night. Avoid Lake Hartwell on holiday weekends and during summer heat.

BASICS

Operated By: US Army Corps of Engineers. **Open:** Apr. 1–Sept. 30. **Site Assignment:** First come, first served; reservations accepted through the National Recreation Reservation Service (NRRS) at (877) 444-6777. Reservations can be made up to 240 days in advance, full payment required upon making reservation; credit card preferred (V, MC, D, AE), or pay by money order if at least 21 days in advance of arrival. $10 fee for cancellation or change of site or dates. Cancellation within 3 days of arrival charged first night, no-show charged $20 plus first night. **Registration:** Gatehouse. **Fee:** $18 peak season, $16 off-season, 10 people max., 1 wheeled camping unit or tents that fit on impact pad. **Parking:** 3 vehicles per site.

FACILITIES

Number of RV Sites: 0. **Number of Tent-Only Sites:** 0 **Number of Multipurpose Sites:** 79. **Hookups:** Water, electric (50 amps). **Each Site:** Picnic table, fire ring or grill, lantern post. **Dump Station:** Yes. **Laundry:** No. **Pay Phone:** Yes. **Rest Rooms and Showers:** Yes. **Fuel:** No. **Propane:** No. **Internal Roads:** Paved. **RV Service:** 30 mi. north in Greenville. **Market:** 7 mi. east in Anderson. **Restaurant:** 4 mi. east in Anderson. **General Store:** 1 mi. east in Anderson. **Vending:** No. **Swimming Pool:** No. **Playground:** Yes. **Other:** Boat ramp, courtesy dock, picnic area. **Activities:** Swimming beaches, fishing, swim access from most campsites. **Nearby Attractions:** Historic Pendleton, Clemson University, Anderson Flea Market,

Anderson County Museum, Arts Center. **Additional Information:** Anderson Chamber of Commerce, (864) 226-3454, www.andersonsc.com.

RESTRICTIONS

Pets: Leash only. **Fires:** Campsites only. **Alcoholic Beverages:** Not allowed. **Vehicle Maximum Length:** No limit. **Other:** 14-day max. stay.

TO GET THERE

From I-85, take Exit 11 onto Hwy. 24 East. Drive 4 mi. to Hwy. 187 South. Turn right onto Hwy. 187 and drive south for 5 miles. Turn right on Providence Church Rd. Follow Providence Church Rd. to the campground.

BLACKSBURG
Kings Mountain State Park   ⅤA

1277 Park Rd., Blacksburg 29702. T: (803) 222-3209; F: (803) 222-6948; www.southcarolinaparks.com; kings_mountain_sp@prt.state.sc.us.

🚐 ★★★★   ⛺ ★★★★

Beauty: ★★★★	Site Privacy: ★★★
Spaciousness: ★★★	Quiet: ★★★★
Security: ★★★★★	Cleanliness: ★★★★
Insect Control: ★★★★	Facilities: ★★★★★

Bordering King's Mountain National Military Park Revolutionary War battle sight, this park is home to the "Living History Farm." This park also offers impressive outdoor activities. Situated in a gorgeous stand of white and red oak and hickory, the hilly campground includes both back-in and pull-through sites. Want a level site? Try 1, 4, 6, 8, 39, or 47 (all back-ins). If you're attached to a pull-through, you may have to deal with sloped parking. All sites are comfortably spaced with some plant growth to provide privacy between sites. Parking is on dirt or gravel. Security is excellent at rural King's Mountain; the park gates are closed at all times and campers are given a combination to open them. The campground was extremely quiet when we visited. In fact, King's Mountain only fills to capacity on holiday weekends, making it an excellent destination on other summer weekends.

BASICS

Operated By: South Carolina State Parks. **Open:** All year. **Site Assignment:** All first come, first served; reservations for handicapped accessible sites only. **Registration:** Camp store, ranger makes rounds off-season. **Fee:** $18 water & electric; $9

tent, South Carolina seniors, & disabled. **Parking:** At sites except tent sites.

FACILITIES

Number of RV Sites: 0. **Number of Tent-Only Sites:** 10 walk-in (with tent pad & fire ring). **Number of Multipurpose Sites:** 116. **Hookups:** Water, electric (20, 30 amps). **Each Site:** Picnic table. **Dump Station:** Yes. **Laundry:** Yes (in-season). **Pay Phone:** Yes. **Rest Rooms and Showers:** Yes. **Fuel:** No. **Propane:** No. **Internal Roads:** Main park roads paved, campground roads gravel. **RV Service:** 8 mi. northwest in Kings Mountain. **Market:** 8 mi. northwest in Kings Mountain. **Restaurant:** 15 mi. north in Gastonia. **General Store:** 10 mi. southeast in Clover, Ace Hardware, or Wal-Mart 16 mi. southeast in York. **Vending:** No. **Swimming Pool:** No. **Playground:** No. **Other:** Living history farm (barn, cotton gin, blacksmith/carpenter shop, gardens, livestock), park store, picnic shelters. **Activities:** Grassy swimming beach, hiking & equestrian trails, equestrian camping, fishing, fishing boat, pedal boat & canoe rentals, mini-golf. **Nearby Attractions:** Kings Mountain National Military Park, Anne Springs Close Greenway nature preserve, Historic Brattonsville, Fort Mill Confederate Park, 30 mi. from Charlotte, North Carolina. **Additional Information:** Clover Chamber of Commerce, (803) 222-3312.

RESTRICTIONS

Pets: Leash (6 ft. max.). **Fires:** Allowed. **Alcoholic Beverages:** Not Allowed. **Vehicle Maximum Length:** 40 ft.

TO GET THERE

From I-85 (NC Exit 2), drive east on State Hwy. 216. 216 turns into Park Rd. and goes through Kings Mountain National Military Park. Headquarters is on the right approx. 9 mi. from I-85.

CALHOUN FALLS
Calhoun Falls State Park

246 Maintenance Shop Rd., Calhoun Falls 29628. T: (864) 447-8267; F: (864) 447-8638; www.southcarolinaparks.com; calhoun_falls_sp@prt.state.sc.us.

🚐 ★★★★★   ⛺ ★★★★★

Beauty: ★★★★★	Site Privacy: ★★★★★
Spaciousness: ★★★★★	Quiet: ★★★★★
Security: ★★★★	Cleanliness: ★★★★★
Insect Control: ★★★★	Facilities: ★★★★

Calhoun Falls SRA was developed jointly by the Corps of Engineers (COE) and South Carolina State Parks. The collaboration is a boon to campers, with recreation typical of state parks and large, gorgeous campsites typical of Corps campgrounds. For fishermen, Lake Russell is home to a variety of bass, bluegill, crappie, and catfish. For the children there are six playgrounds. The campground features extremely spacious sites with paved parking. Each site has a sandy picnic and tent area. Sites are afforded shade and privacy by thick, lovely woods. Campsites with hookups are found in two areas and tent-only sites in a third. Of the lakefront sites, back-ins are often more attractive than pull-throughs. Security is fair at Calhoun Falls; although the park is extremely rural and gates are locked at night, the gates are not always attended during the day. Avoid visiting on busy summer weekends.

BASICS

Operated By: South Carolina State Parks. **Open:** All year. **Site Assignment:** First come, first served; reservations accepted up to 11 months in advance, 2 night min.; full deposit required within 10 days of reservation; 48 hours notice for cancellation refund, $15 cancellation fee. **Registration:** Camp store, rangers collect after hours. **Fee:** $21 for lakefront site w/ reservation, $19 for non–lakefront site w/ reservation, $20 for lakefront sites, $18 for non–lakefront sites, $10 for tent sites, fees include 6 people. **Parking:** Site plus overflow parking.

FACILITIES

Number of RV Sites: 0. **Number of Tent-Only Sites:** 14. **Number of Multipurpose Sites:** 86. **Hookups:** Water, electric (20, 30 amps). **Each Site:** Picnic table, grill, fire ring, lantern holder. **Dump Station:** Yes. **Laundry:** Yes. **Pay Phone:** Yes. **Rest Rooms and Showers:** Yes. **Fuel:** No. **Propane:** No. **Internal Roads:** Paved. **RV Service:** 30 mi. north in Anderson. **Market:** 2 mi. south in Calhoun Falls. **Restaurant:** 2 mi. south in Calhoun Falls. **General Store:** Camp store. **Vending:** Beverages only. **Swimming Pool:** No. **Playground:** Yes. **Other:** Boat ramp. **Activities:** Fishing, skiing, boating, non-motorized boat rentals, swimming when lifeguard on duty, walking trail, basketball, tennis. **Nearby Attractions:** Sumter National Forest, Lake Russell Dam (Information Center in Georgia), Abbeville Historic District,

walking tours. **Additional Information:** Abbeville Chamber of Commerce, (864) 459-4600.

RESTRICTIONS

Pets: Leash. **Fires:** In sites, rings only. **Alcoholic Beverages:** In sites, out of view. **Vehicle Maximum Length:** Varies. **Other:** 14-day max. stay.

To Get There

From Calhoun Falls, at the intersection of SC 81 and SC 72, take SC 81 north 1 mile. The park entrance is on the left.

CHAPIN

Dreher Island State Park

3677 State Park Rd., Prosperity 29127. T: (803) 364-4152; F: (803) 364-0756; www.southcarolinaparks.com; dreher_island_sp@prt.state.sc.us.

🚐 ★★★★ 　　　　🅰 ★★★★

Beauty: ★★★★	Site Privacy: ★★★
Spaciousness: ★★★	Quiet: ★★★★
Security: ★★★★★	Cleanliness: ★★★★
Insect Control: ★★★★	Facilities: ★★★

Recreation includes fishing and boating on Lake Murray. Fisher-folk hook catfish, bream, crappie, yellow perch and largemouth and striped bass. Day-use facilities at this 348-acre park are not extensive, but the campgrounds are lovely. Of the two camping loops, B is nicer. On loop B, we recommend the lakefront sites, which are large and secluded with pretty views. At both loops, site size and privacy vary, but none are small. Gorgeous trees include a variety of oak species, which provide plenty of shade at most sites. All parking is paved. There are a few pull-through sites and plenty of back-in sites. Located in a rural but touristy area, security is good. Gates are attended during the day and locked at night. Close to Columbia, Dreher Island stays full on summer weekends and holidays. We recommend a weekday, spring, or fall visit.

BASICS

Operated By: South Carolina State Parks. **Open:** All year. **Site Assignment:** first come, first served; a few sites available for reservations for $1 extra, 2 night min., full deposit required before arrival, 24 hour cancellation notice for refund less $15 fee. **Registration:** Visitor center, late arrivals may camp in area outside gate. **Fee:** $18 for 6 people (add $1 for reservation). **Parking:** Limit 2 vehicles, overflow parking available.

FACILITIES

Number of RV Sites: 0. **Number of Tent-Only Sites:** 15. **Number of Multipurpose Sites:** 97. **Hookups:** Water, electric (30 amps). **Each Site:** Picnic table, fire ring. **Dump Station:** Yes. **Laundry:** No. **Pay Phone:** Yes. **Rest Rooms and Showers:** Yes. **Fuel:** Yes (automobile & boat). **Propane:** No. **Internal Roads:** Paved. **RV Service:** 30 mi. east in Columbia. **Market:** 10 mi. north in Chapin. **Restaurant:** 10 mi. north in Chapin. **General Store:** Camp store. **Vending:** No. **Swimming Pool:** No. **Playground:** Yes. **Other:** Boat ramps, tackle shop, picnic shelters, screened meeting shelter. **Activities:** Fishing, pontoon boat rentals available, walking trails. **Nearby Attractions:** Columbia historic homes, South Carolina Confederate Relic Room & Museum, Fort Jackson Museum, South Carolina State Museum. **Additional Information:** Capital City Lake Murray Country Visitor Information (803) 781-5940.

RESTRICTIONS

Pets: Leash. **Fires:** In fire rings in sites only. **Alcoholic Beverages:** Not allowed. **Vehicle Maximum Length:** 45 ft. **Other:** 14-day max. stay.

TO GET THERE

From I-26, take Exit 91 at Chapin onto Hwy. 48 west. At Hwy. 76, turn right and look for St. Peters Church Rd. on the left. Turn left and continue until Dreher Island Rd. Turn left and look for State Park Rd. Turn left again. The park is 12 mi. from I-26.

CHARLESTON/MT. PLEASANT

Mt. Pleasant KOA

3157 Hwy. 17 North, Mt. Pleasant 29466. T: (843) 849-5177 or (800) KOA-5796; F: (843) 849-2275; www.koakampgrounds.com.

🚐 ★★★	🅰 ★★★
Beauty: ★★★	Site Privacy: ★★
Spaciousness: ★★	Quiet: ★★★
Security: ★★★	Cleanliness: ★★★★
Insect Control: ★★★★	Facilities: ★★★

Regarding tidiness, we recommend this park over its main competitor, the KOA Charleston. This place is cleaner, though not necessarily prettier. The suburban location of this park is also nice—it's within convenient touring distance of Charleston. And plenty of restaurants and shopping are located in nearby Mount Pleasant. The campground is laid out in 11 rows of pull-throughs plus 4 back-in areas. Sites are on the small side with little privacy. A few sites have shady trees, but most are open. Parking spaces may resemble a crazy quilt—grass, gravel, and packed clay are all present. The nicest sites are B4–B7, which have nice views of the small fishing lake. This suburban campground has no gates, making security fair. Avoid touring Charleston in the humid summertime. Also avoid holiday and summer weekends.

BASICS

Operated By: Gregory family. **Open:** All year. **Site Assignment:** First come, first served; reservations recommended, 2 night min. on holidays, credit card deposit required, 24 hour cancellation notice required for refund. **Registration:** Camp store, night registration available. **Fee:** $30 for sites w/ full hookups, $27 for sites w/ water & electric, $15–$19 for tent sites (cash, personal check, V, MC, D, AE). **Parking:** 2 vehicles per site, plus overflow area.

FACILITIES

Number of RV Sites: 60. **Number of Tent-Only Sites:** 18 (plus primitive overflow area). **Number of Multipurpose Sites:** None. **Hookups:** Water, electric (30, 50 amps), 45 sites w/ sewer, cable. **Each Site:** Picnic table, fire ring. **Dump Station:** Yes. **Laundry:** Yes. **Pay Phone:** Yes. **Rest Rooms and Showers:** Yes. **Fuel:** No. **Propane:** Yes. **Internal Roads:** Gravel. **RV Service:** 20 mi. west in Charleston. **Market:** 1 mi. west in Mt. Pleasant. **Restaurant:** 3 mi. west in Mt. Pleasant. **General Store:** Camp store. **Vending:** Beverages only. **Swimming Pool:** Yes. **Playground:** Yes. **Other:** Rec hall, kamper kitchen, boat dock. **Activities:** Bicycle & boat rentals (paddle, canoe, & kayak), walking trails, mini-golf, horseshoes, volleyball, basketball, ping pong. **Nearby Attractions:** Charleston Historic District, Charles Towne Landing, Patriot's Pointe Naval & Maritime Museum, plantation & garden tours. **Additional Information:** Charleston Area CVB, (843) 853-8000 or (800) 868-8118, www.charlestoncvb.com.

RESTRICTIONS

Pets: Leash. **Fires:** Allowed. **Alcoholic Beverages:** Allowed. **Vehicle Maximum Length:** 40 ft. **Other:** 2-week stay limit.

To Get There

From I-526, take Exit 32. Drive east on US Hwy. 17 for 5 miles. The entrance is on the right.

COLUMBIA

Sesquicentennial State Park

9564 Two Notch Rd., Columbia 29223. T: (803) 788-2706; F: (803) 788-4417; www.southcarolinaparks.com; sesquicentennial_sp@prt.state.sc.us.

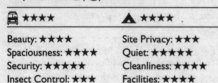

🚐 ★★★★   ▲ ★★★★

Beauty: ★★★★	Site Privacy: ★★★
Spaciousness: ★★★★	Quiet: ★★★★★
Security: ★★★★★	Cleanliness: ★★★★
Insect Control: ★★★	Facilities: ★★★★

This 1,419-acre urban green space includes a 30-acre lake stocked with bass and bream. The log house was built in 1756 in Richland County and moved to Sesquicentennial in 1961. The park's location is excellent if you like to shop and enjoy eating out. The campground consists of two loops, nicely shaded by a gorgeous stand of loblolly and longleaf pine. Campsites are large and most have back-in parking. However, we recommend the larger and more private pull-through sites. Parking is on a mixture of sand, gravel, grass, and pine straw. The campground was quiet when we visited on Labor day weekend. It's often empty in the fall, so it's a great place to stay for University of South Carolina football games or on a holiday weekend.

Basics

Operated By: South Carolina State Parks. **Open:** All year. **Site Assignment:** First come, first served; no reservations. **Registration:** Set-up first, then register at office, ranger makes rounds. **Fee:** $17 includes 6 people. **Parking:** Sites only.

Facilities

Number of Multipurpose Sites: 87. **Hookups:** Water, electric (30 amps). **Each Site:** Picnic table. **Dump Station:** Yes. **Laundry:** No. **Pay Phone:** Yes. **Rest Rooms and Showers:** Yes. **Fuel:** No. **Propane:** No. **Internal Roads:** Paved & dirt. **RV Service:** 20 mi. northeast in Elgin. **Market:** 1 mi. **Restaurant:** 0.25 mi. **General Store:** 1 mi. **Vending:** Beverages. **Swimming Pool:** No. **Playground:** Yes. **Other:** 1756 log house, picnic

shelters, meeting facilities, nature center. **Activities:** Nature programs, nature trail, bicycle trail, fishing, exercise course, (non-motor) boat rentals, swimming, & paddle boat rentals when lifeguard is present. **Nearby Attractions:** Columbia historic homes, South Carolina Confederate Relic Room & Museum, Fort Jackson Museum, South Carolina State Museum. **Additional Information:** Columbia Metropolitan CVB, (803) 254-0479 or (800) 264-4884.

Restrictions

Pets: Leash. **Fires:** In sites only. **Alcoholic Beverages:** Prohibited. **Vehicle Maximum Length:** Varies, up to 40 ft. **Other:** 14-day max. stay.

To Get There

From I-77, take Exit US Hwy. 1/Two Notch Rd. northeast for 13 miles. The park entrance is on the right.

EDISTO ISLAND

Edisto Beach State Park

8377 State Cabin Rd., Edisto Island 29438. T: (843) 869-2156 or (843) 853-8000; F: (843) 869-3023; www.southcarolinaparks.com; edisto_beach_sp@prt.state.sc.us.

🚐 ★★★   ▲ ★★★

Beauty: ★★★★★	Site Privacy: ★★
Spaciousness: ★★★	Quiet: ★★★
Security: ★★★★	Cleanliness: ★★★★
Insect Control: ★	Facilities: ★★★

This is one of the prettiest Oceanside parks we've seen. Sites in the main area are within 100 yards of the beach. Sites in the Live Oak area are within 0.25 mile of the beach. Many sites are shaded by palmetto and live oak, although there is little privacy between them. Site size varies, with most on the small side. Parking is mostly back-in, on a mish-mash of packed sand and oyster shells. Sites 9 and 10 are heavenly—shady and separated from the beach only by gorgeous dunes. Sites 18–20 are also attractive—totally open with ocean views. Recreation at Edisto Beach includes hiking to 4,000-year-old Edisto Indian Mound, "Spanish Mount." Comprised of shells and pottery, it's the second oldest Indian mound in the United States. Security is good—the campground is gated and guarded. Located on a touristy little island, many restaurants are convenient to the park. Avoid this park on summer weekends and holidays.

BASICS

Operated By: South Carolina State Parks. **Open:** All year. **Site Assignment:** First come, first served; no reservations accepted. **Registration:** Registration booth. **Fee:** $22 for sites w/ water & electric, $11 for tent/ walk-in sites; fees include 6 people (cash, personal checks, V, MC). **Parking:** 2 cars per site.

FACILITIES

Number of RV Sites: 0. **Number of Tent-Only Sites:** 5. **Number of Multipurpose Sites:** 91. **Hookups:** Water, electric (20, 30 amps). **Each Site:** Picnic table, fire ring. **Dump Station:** Yes. **Laundry:** No. **Pay Phone:** Yes. **Rest Rooms and Showers:** Yes. **Fuel:** No. **Propane:** No. **Internal Roads:** Gravel. **RV Service:** 20 mi. north toward Charleston. **Market:** 0.25 mi. **Restaurant:** 0.25 mi. **General Store:** Camp store. **Vending:** Beverages. **Swimming Pool:** No. **Playground:** Yes. **Other:** Boat ramp, picnic area. **Activities:** Indian Mound trail to Native American pottery site, fishing, swimming. **Nearby Attractions:** Edisto Island, Historic Beaufort, Charleston plantations, gardens, museums, tours, Charles Towne Landing: first English settlement in South Carolina. **Additional Information:** Charleston Area CVB, (800) 868-8118.

RESTRICTIONS

Pets: Leash, clean-up enforced. **Fires:** Fire rings only. **Alcoholic Beverages:** Not allowed. **Vehicle Maximum Length:** 40 ft. **Other:** 14-day stay limit.

TO GET THERE

From Charleston, drive west on Hwy. 17 for 25 miles. Turn south onto Hwy. 174 and drive for 22 miles. The park entrance is at the end of the highway.

EUTAWVILLE

Rocks Pond Campground and Marina

235 Rocks Pond Rd., Eutawville 29048. T: (803) 492-7711 or (800) 982-0271; F: (803) 492-9469; www.rockspond.com.

Beauty: ★★★	Site Privacy: ★★
Spaciousness: ★★★	Quiet: ★★

Security: ★★★★★	Cleanliness: ★★★★
Insect Control: ★★★★	Facilities: ★★★★

With over 250 tightly-spaced campsites, Rocks Pond has created urban crowding in rural Eutawville. And folks seem to love it, ostensibly because of extensive amenities and recreation, including live bands on the weekends and a children's fishing pond. Avoid this joint on summer weekends and holidays when the crowds are sure to be unbearable. Sites are laid out in a series of monotonous grids except for waterfront sites (numbers 109–127 and 249–268). With boat dockage, sites 128–132 are nearly impossible to obtain. Call well in advance if you'd like one of these. None of the sites are knockout beautiful—choose your site based on location. Most are treeless pull-throughs. Parking is on packed clay or grass. All are level and none have any privacy. Rest rooms are odd; each potty has it's own lavatory, but the lavatory is outside the stall door. Security is excellent—the front entrance is guarded.

BASICS

Operated By: Rutledge Connor. **Open:** All year. **Site Assignment:** First come, first served; reservations accepted for 3-night min., $20 deposit; 7-day cancellation notice for refund less $5 fee. **Registration:** Office, late-comers register next morning. **Fee:** $19–$28 for RV sites based on location relative to water, $16 for tent sites, fees include 4 people, $2 per extra person up to 6 total; designated senior citizens area $10 for 2 people. **Parking:** Site plus overflow parking.

FACILITIES

Number of RV Sites: 226. **Number of Tent-Only Sites:** 30. **Number of Multipurpose Sites:** 226 (RV). **Hookups:** Water, electric (20, 30, 50 amps), sewer. **Each Site:** Picnic table. **Dump Station:** Yes. **Laundry:** Yes. **Pay Phone:** Yes. **Rest Rooms and Showers:** Yes. **Fuel:** Yes. **Propane:** Yes. **Internal Roads:** Paved & gravel. **RV Service:** On call service available. **Market:** 3 mi. in Eutawville. **Restaurant:** 3 mi. in Eutawville, snack bar in-season. **General Store:** Camp store. **Vending:** Beverages. **Swimming Pool:** No. **Playground:** Yes. **Other:** Marina, rec hall, gazebos, meeting rooms, fire rings on request. **Activities:** Boating (rentals available), lake swimming, mini-golf, driving range, skeet range, archery, unique soccer sports, bicycle rentals, fishing guide service (call for rates), Saturday night dances in-season. **Nearby Attractions:** Four golf courses within 25 miles, Lake Marion, Santee community, Palmetto trailhead, 1 hour from Charleston & Columbia. **Additional Information:** Santee Cooper Country Promotions (803) 854-2131.

RESTRICTIONS

Pets: Leash, clean-up enforced. **Fires:** In fire rings only (available on request). **Alcoholic Beverages:** Discouraged. **Vehicle Maximum Length:** No limit.

TO GET THERE

From I-95, take Exit 98. Drive southeast on Hwy. 6 for 9 mi. to Eutawville. At the stop sign, go left following Hwy. 6. Look for the Rocks Pond sign and turn left on Rocks Pond Rd., then right at the dead end. The campground is 18 mi. from I-95.

FAIR PLAY
Lake Hartwell State Park

19138-A South Hwy. 11, Fair Play 29643. T: (864) 972-3352; F: (864) 972-3352; www.southcarolina-parks.com.

🚐 ★★★★   ▲ ★★★★

Beauty: ★★★★★   Site Privacy: ★★★★
Spaciousness: ★★★★★   Quiet: ★★★
Security: ★★★★   Cleanliness: ★★★★
Insect Control: ★★★   Facilities: ★★★

This popular park is located one mile from I-85 on 56,000-acre Lake Hartwell. Activities include fishing for crappie, bream, catfish, stripers, large-mouth, and hybrid bass. There are few land activities at this 680-acre park. Adrenaline lovers should consider a trip down the nearby Chattooga Wild and Scenic River. The campground is laid out in three main loops on two lake peninsulas, with many sites enjoying water views. Site size varies from ample to huge, with shady trees in most areas. Reservable sites, 69–108, are densely wooded. We recommended number 92, which is incredibly secluded (great honeymoon suite!). In the non-reservable sites, 6 and 17 are both large and private with lovely views. All parking is paved. There are both pull-through and back-in sites. Security is not great here; the park is only one mile from the interstate and has no gates. Visit on weekdays or in spring or fall for maximum peace and quiet.

BASICS

Operated By: South Carolina State Parks. **Open:** All year. **Site Assignment:** Most sites first come, first served; 40 sites available for reservation, full payment required in advance; 24-hour notice required for refund, $15 cancellation fee. **Registration:** Store, late comers register next morning. **Fee:** $17 for waterfront sites, $16 for regular sites, $8 for walk-in sites, add $1 for reserved sites, fee includes 10 people (cash, personal checks, V, MC). **Parking:** At sites except walk-in, overflow parking available.

FACILITIES

Number of RV Sites: 0. **Number of Tent-Only Sites:** 13 walk-in. **Number of Multipurpose Sites:** 108. **Hookups:** Water, electric (30 amps). **Each Site:** Picnic table, fire ring. **Dump Station:** Yes. **Laundry:** Yes. **Pay Phone:** Yes. **Rest Rooms and Showers:** Yes. **Fuel:** No. **Propane:** No. **Internal Roads:** Paved. **RV Service:** 13 mi. north toward Seneca. **Market:** 8 mi. south in Lavonia, GA. **Restaurant:** 1.5 mi. **General Store:** 17 mi. north in Seneca (Wal-Mart). **Vending:** Beverages. **Swimming Pool:** No. **Playground:** Yes. **Other:** Boat ramp, picnic shelter, park store. **Activities:** Nature trail, fishing, boating, lake swimming. **Nearby Attractions:** Anderson Historic District, Chattooga National Wild & Scenic River, Cherokee Foothills Scenic Hwy. (11), Sumter National Forest, Walhalla National Fish Hatchery, Issaqueena Falls, Clemson University. **Additional Information:** Anderson Chamber of Commerce, (864) 226-3454.

RESTRICTIONS

Pets: Leash, clean-up enforced. **Fires:** Allowed. **Alcoholic Beverages:** Not allowed. **Vehicle Maximum Length:** 45 ft. **Other:** No fire arms or fire works.

TO GET THERE

From I-85, take Exit 1 onto South Carolina Hwy. 11. Drive about 0.25 mile to the top of the hill. The park is on the left.

HUNTING ISLAND
Hunting Island State Park

2555 Sea Island Parkway, Hunting Island 29920. T: (843) 838-2011; F: (843) 838-4263; www.south-carolinaparks.com; hunting_island_sp@scprt.com.

🚐 ★★★★   ▲ ★★★★

Beauty: ★★★★★   Site Privacy: ★★★
Spaciousness: ★★★   Quiet: ★★★
Security: ★★★★   Cleanliness: ★★★★
Insect Control: ★★★★   Facilities: ★★★★

The atmosphere here is deliciously mellow. The children seem more laid back than at other campgrounds. It could be the gorgeous shade provided by mature pine, palm, and palmetto or the sound of the ocean. Relax in a hammock. Get yourself off the hammock to tour the Hunting Island Lighthouse, in use from 1875 until 1933. Two of the four main loops contain sites near the beach. Site size varies, as does privacy. If you're seeking ample space and privacy, head for sites 166–173 in the back of the campground (farthest from the beach). For the nicest beachfront sites, head for 49–55, 71 and 73. All of these have pretty views of beach dunes. Most parking is back-in on packed sand and pine straw. Mosquitoes and "no-see-ums" are a nuisance, so bring insect repellent. This park is extremely popular—prepare for crowds April through October or try visiting during the week. Security is good, with gates locked at night.

BASICS

Operated By: South Carolina State Parks. **Open:** All year. **Site Assignment:** Most sites first come, first served; 40 sites available for reservation, w/ full deposit; 24-hour cancellation notice for refund less $15 fee. **Registration:** Camp store, late comers register the next morning. **Fee:** $22 for water & electric in-Season, $18 for water & electric off-season, $12 for primitive in-Season, $9 for primitive off-season, add $1 for reservation; prices for 6 people max.; seniors & disabled 50% discount. **Parking:** Limit 2 vehicles per site, overflow parking available.

FACILITIES

Number of RV Sites: 0. **Number of Tent-Only Sites:** 10. **Number of Multipurpose Sites:** 200. **Hookups:** Water, electric (30 amps). **Each Site:** Picnic table, fire ring. **Dump Station:** Yes. **Laundry:** No. **Pay Phone:** Yes. **Rest Rooms and Showers:** Yes. **Fuel:** No. **Propane:** No. **Internal Roads:** Paved, sand, & gravel. **RV Service:** 16 mi. west in Beaufort. **Market:** 12 mi. west on Lady's Island. **Restaurant:** 12 mi. west on Lady's Island. **General Store:** Park store. **Vending:** Yes. **Swimming Pool:** No. **Playground:** No. **Other:** Boat ramp, visitor's center, lighthouse, beach shop, picnic shelters. **Activities:** Lighthouse tours, hiking &

bicycling trail, boardwalk, fishing pier, crabbing, boating, swimming, nature programs. **Nearby Attractions:** Historic Beaufort, boat tours, gardens, walking tours, horse-drawn carriage tours, Port Royal. **Additional Information:** Greater Beaufort Chamber of Commerce, & Visitors Center, (843) 524-3163, www.beaufortsc.org.

RESTRICTIONS

Pets: Leash. **Fires:** Fire rings only. **Alcoholic Beverages:** Not allowed. **Vehicle Maximum Length:** 40 ft. **Other:** 2-week stay limit.

TO GET THERE

From I-95, take Exit 33 and drive south on Hwy. 17, which becomes Hwy. 21. Hwy. 21 ends on Hunting Island. Once on the island, take the first left into the campground. The park is 16 mi. east of Beaufort.

McCORMICK

Baker Creek State Park

Route 3 Box 50, McCormick 29835. T: (864) 443-2457; F: (864) 443-2457; www.southcarolinaparks.com; baker_creek_sp@prt.state.sc.us.

🚐 ★★★★   ▲ ★★★★

Beauty: ★★★★★   Site Privacy: ★★★★
Spaciousness: ★★★★   Quiet: ★★★
Security: ★★★★   Cleanliness: ★★★★
Insect Control: ★★★   Facilities: ★★★

Baker Creek includes 1,300 gorgeous acres of rolling forest. J. Strom Thurmond Reservoir consists of 70,000 acres stocked with crappie, catfish, bream, striper, and several bass species. Despite its rural locale, this popular park should be avoided on summer weekends and holidays. Shaded by a gorgeous stand of loblolly pine trees, campsites at Baker Creek are more spacious than average. Most offer back-in parking. Foliage provides a bit of privacy between sites. Eight sites offer pull-through parking; none are lakefront. Parking is on dirt, gravel, or pine straw. The campgrounds contain two loops forming semi-circles with lake views at many sites. In campground No. 1, the nicest sites are 32–34, 37, 38, 40, 41, and 43. In campground No. 2, the nicer sites, 86–90, are on a small peninsula. Baker Creek locks its gates at night, but the front gate is not attended during the day making security good.

BASICS

Operated By: South Carolina State Parks. **Open:** All year. **Site Assignment:** First come, first served; no reservations. **Registration:** At campsites. **Fee:** $16; South Carolina seniors & disabled 50% discount (cash or check only). **Parking:** At sites only.

FACILITIES

Number of Multipurpose Sites: 100. **Hookups:** Water, electric (20, 30 amps). **Each Site:** Picnic table, 50 sites w/ grill. **Dump Station:** Yes. **Laundry:** No. **Pay Phone:** Yes. **Rest Rooms and Showers:** Yes. **Fuel:** No. **Propane:** No. **Internal Roads:** Gravel, main roads Paved. **RV Service:** 30 mi. north in Greenwood. **Market:** 4 mi. east in McCormick. **Restaurant:** 4 mi. east in McCormick. **General Store:** 4 mi. east in McCormick, 22 mi. to Wal-Mart. **Vending:** Beverages. **Swimming Pool:** No. **Playground:** Yes. **Other:** Boat ramps, picnic shelters, pavilion rental. **Activities:** walking & hiking trails, fishing, basketball, volleyball, horseshoes, seasonal paddle boat rentals. **Nearby Attractions:** Historic McCormick County, Revolutionary War sites, Steven's Creek Heritage Preserve. **Additional Information:** McCormick Chamber of Commerce, (864) 465-2835.

RESTRICTIONS

Pets: Leash only. **Fires:** Ground fires only. **Alcoholic Beverages:** Not allowed. **Vehicle Maximum Length:** 40 ft.

TO GET THERE

From I-20, take Georgia Exit 200 (River Watch Pkwy.). Drive west for approx. 2 mi. and turn right onto Hwy. 28 (Furys Ferry Rd.). Drive north on Hwy. 28 to McCormick and turn left onto US Hwy. 378. Drive west on US Hwy. 378 for 4 miles, then turn right at the park sign. The park is 1 mile ahead on the left.

MODOC

Modoc Campground, J. Strom Thurmond Lake

Route 1 Box 2-D, Modoc 29838. T: (864) 333-2272; F: (864) 333-1150; www.reserveamerica.com; caewx@noaa.gov.

🚐 ★★★★★	🏕 ★★★★★
Beauty: ★★★★★	Site Privacy: ★★★★★
Spaciousness: ★★★★★	Quiet: ★★★★★
Security: ★★★★★	Cleanliness: ★★★★
Insect Control: ★★★★	Facilities: ★★★

Modoc campground on J. Strom Thurmond Lake is one of the most beautiful campgrounds in the Southeast. Sites are incredibly spacious with a large sandy picnic and tent area. Sites are shaded and secluded by lovely loblolly and short-leaf pine and other tree species. All sites have gravel parking. Back-in sites are nice, but many of the pull-throughs are huge. The campground contains four main spurs on two peninsulas. Sites 4–10 are gorgeous, with views of a small inlet. Site 11 is one of the most beautiful we've seen anywhere—unfortunately it has no hookups. Fishermen will find smallmouth, striped, and hybrid bass. Few day-use facilities at the campground keep it blissfully quiet most of the time. Only 40 minutes from Augusta, Modoc's location is extremely rural. Security is excellent as the campground is gated and guarded. Visit Modoc anytime except holiday weekends. It rarely fills to capacity.

BASICS

Operated By: US Army Corps of Engineers. **Open:** Apr. 1–Oct. 31. **Site Assignment:** First come, first served; reservations accepted through the National Recreation Reservation Service (NRRS) at (877) 444-6777. Reservations can be made up to 240 days in advance, full payment required upon making reservation; credit card preferred (V, MC, D, AE), or pay by money order if at least 21 days in advance of arrival. $10 fee for cancellation or change of site or dates. Cancellation within 3 days of arrival charged first night, no-show charged $20 plus first night. *Note:* Due to current construction, Modoc Campground may not accept reservations for the 2002 season, but will resume by 2003. **Registration:** Gatehouse, gates locked at 10 p.m. **Fee:** $18 for up to 12 people. **Parking:** At sites, 4 vehicle limit, $3 per extra vehicle, overflow parking available.

FACILITIES

Number of RV Sites: 0. **Number of Tent-Only Sites:** 0 **Number of Multipurpose Sites:** 49. **Hookups:** Water, electric (50 amps). **Each Site:** Picnic table, grill, fire ring, utility table, lantern holder. **Dump Station:** Yes. **Laundry:** Yes. **Pay Phone:** Yes. **Rest Rooms and Showers:** Yes. **Fuel:** No. **Propane:** No. **Internal Roads:** Most Paved. **RV Service:** 20 mi. south in Augusta. **Market:** 20 mi. south in Augusta. **Restaurant:** 15 mi. north in McCormick. **General Store:** 1 mi. in

Modoc. **Vending:** No. **Swimming Pool:** No. **Playground:** Yes. **Other:** Boat ramp. **Activities:** Hiking trail, beach, swimming, boating, fishing. **Nearby Attractions:** Thurmond Visitor Information Center & Dam; Golf & Gardens in Augusta, Woodrow Wilson's childhood home, Lucy Craft Laney Museum of Black History. **Additional Information:** Augusta Metropolitan CVB, (800) 726-0243.

RESTRICTIONS

Pets: Leash. **Fires:** In grills or rings in sites only. **Alcoholic Beverages:** Not allowed. **Vehicle Maximum Length:** 40 ft. **Other:** 14-day stay limit in 30-day period.

TO GET THERE

From I-20, take Georgia Exit 200 (River Watch Pkwy.), then drive west for 2 mi. to Furys Ferry Rd. (Hwy. 28 West). Turn right and drive north for 13 mi. to Clarks Hill, SC. Continue northwest on Hwy. 221 for 4 miles. The campground entrance is on the left.

MOUNTAIN REST
Oconee State Park

624 State Park Rd., Mountain Rest 29664. T: (864) 638-5353; F: (864) 638-8776; www.southcarolina parks.com; oconee_sp@prt.state.sc.us.

🚐 ★★★★   ⛺ ★★★★

Beauty: ★★★★★   Site Privacy: ★★★★
Spaciousness: ★★★★   Quiet: ★★★★★
Security: ★★★★   Cleanliness: ★★★★
Insect Control: ★★★★   Facilities: ★★★★

Oconee State Park offers large, gorgeous sites in one of the most beautifully forested campgrounds we've seen. Various oak and pine species provide shade and some privacy. A few sites have paved parking and the rest are gravel. There are pull-through and back-in campsites. Our favorite sites are 30, 31, 32, 34 and 36—totally fabulous wooded sites with pull-through, gravel parking and lovely views of the small lake. Other recommendations are 66 and 78. Unfortunately, the bathhouses were grimy during our visit. This remote, peaceful park is cherished by nature lovers. Seeking adventure? Raft the nearby Chattooga National Wild and Scenic River. In season, the gate is attended during the day and locked at night, making security good This off-the-beaten-path park is a good destination on all but the busiest summer weekends. With an elevation of 1,700 feet, the park is usually a few degrees cooler than the South Carolina Piedmont region.

BASICS

Operated By: South Carolina State Parks. **Open:** All year. **Site Assignment:** 125 sites first come, first served; 30 sites available for reservation, 24 hours to 11 months in advance, deposit w/ check 10 days in advance, V or MC within 10 days; $15 cancellation fee. **Registration:** Trading post, park office off-season. **Fee:** $17 water & electric, $9 primitive tent & South Carolina seniors & disabled. **Parking:** At sites except tent sites (walk-in).

FACILITIES

Number of RV Sites: 0. **Number of Tent-Only Sites:** 15 walk-in sites. **Number of Multipurpose Sites:** 140. **Hookups:** Water, electric (30 amps). **Each Site:** Picnic table; walk-in sites have picnic table, grill, fire ring, lantern stand & tent pad. **Dump Station:** Yes. **Laundry:** Yes. **Pay Phone:** Yes. **Rest Rooms and Showers:** Yes. **Fuel:** No. **Propane:** No. **Internal Roads:** some Paved, some gravel. **RV Service:** 30 mi. south in Clemson. **Market:** 15 mi. south in West Union. **Restaurant:** 4 mi. west in Mountain Rest. **General Store:** 4 mi. west in Mountain Rest, Wal-Mart & K-mart 22 mi. south in Seneca. **Vending:** Beverages only. **Swimming Pool:** No. **Playground:** Yes. **Other:** Civilian Conservation Corps Museum, park store in-season, picnic shelters, multi-purpose recreation building, meeting room. **Activities:** Fishing, boating, canoe & fishing boat rentals (check w/ park about bringing your own boat), swimming & paddle boat rentals when lifeguard is present, nature trails, mini-golf, archery range. **Nearby Attractions:** Chattooga National Wildlife & Scenic River, Oconee Station state Historic Site, Cherry Hill National Forest, Devil's Fork State Park, Foothills Trail, Stumphouse Tunnel, golf courses. **Additional Information:** Greater Walhalla Area Chamber of Commerce, (864) 638-2727.

RESTRICTIONS

Pets: 6 ft. leash only. **Fires:** In designated areas only. **Alcoholic Beverages:** Not allowed. **Vehicle Maximum Length:** 35 ft.

TO GET THERE

From I-85, take Exit 1 and drive 23 mi. north on Hwy. 11. At Hwy. 28, turn left and head west for 10 mi. At the fork at Hwy. 107, bear right and drive 2 mi. The park is on the right.

MURRELLS INLET
Huntington Beach State Park

16148 Ocean Hwy., Murrells Inlet 29576. T: (843) 237-4440; F: (843) 237-3387; www.southcarolina-parks.com; huntington_beach_sp@scprt.com.

🚐 ★★★★   ⛺ ★★★★

Beauty: ★★★★   Site Privacy: ★★★★
Spaciousness: ★★★★   Quiet: ★★★
Security: ★★★★★   Cleanliness: ★★★★
Insect Control: ★★★   Facilities: ★★★

Though Huntington Beach is more remote than Myrtle Beach State Park, it's almost as popular, with numerous activities and a pristine beach. Wildlife enthusiasts may see American alligators or loggerhead sea turtles. Bird lovers can spot many species of waterfowl, wading birds, or raptors (including bald eagles). Interpretive programs enrich the experience of low-country ecosystems. Also here is "Atalaya," the 1931 Mediterranean Moorish-style home of the Huntington family. Per Murphy's Law, the nicest campsites are the farthest from the beach. Sites 134–186 are closest to the beach and the least attractive. Walk further to the beach and choose sites 104–130. These are larger, more private and shadier than the rest of the campground and their bath house is brand new. Sites have gravel parking and most are back-in. Size varies. Gated and guarded, security at Huntington Beach is excellent. Avoid this park on summer weekends, when its popularity becomes its downfall.

BASICS

Operated By: South Carolina State Parks. **Open:** All year. **Site Assignment:** First come, first served; reservations accepted for a 2-night min., w/ full deposit 2 weeks prior to reservation, $15 cancellation charge. **Registration:** Camp store, ranger on duty 24-hours. **Fee:** $28 w/ reservation for sites w/ sewer, $25 w/ reservation for sites without sewer, $27 without reservation for sites w/ sewer, $24 without reservation or sewer, $12 for all tent sites, fees include 6 people. **Parking:** Site plus overflow parking.

FACILITIES

Number of RV Sites: 133. **Number of Tent-Only Sites:** 6. **Number of Multipurpose Sites:** 133 (RV). **Hookups:** Water, electric (20, 30 amps), 24 sites w/ sewer. **Each Site:** Picnic table, fire ring.

Dump Station: Yes. **Laundry:** No. **Pay Phone:** Yes. **Rest Rooms and Showers:** Yes. **Fuel:** No. **Propane:** No. **Internal Roads:** Gravel in campground, park is paved. **RV Service:** 25 mi. north in Conway. **Market:** Grocery 3 mi. north or south in Murrells Inlet, Wal-Mart 10 mi. north in Surfside. **Restaurant:** 3 mi. north or south in Murrells Inlet. **General Store:** Camp store. **Vending:** No. **Swimming Pool:** No. **Playground:** No. **Other:** Recreation room, picnic shelters. **Activities:** Beach, swimming, fishing, kayaking, canoeing, hiking trails, coastal exploration program, Atalaya Castle. **Nearby Attractions:** Water Park, Myrtle Beach, Hampton Plantation State Historic Site, Brookgreen Gardens, Pawley's Island. **Additional Information:** Myrtle Beach Area Chamber of Commerce, (843) 626-7444.

RESTRICTIONS

Pets: Leash only. **Fires:** Fire ring only. **Alcoholic Beverages:** Not allowed. **Vehicle Maximum Length:** 50 ft. **Other:** 2 weeks max. stay.

TO GET THERE

From Georgetown, take Hwy. 17 north for 20 miles. The park entrance is on the right. From Myrtle Beach, take Hwy. 17 south for 15 miles. The park entrance is on the left.

MYRTLE BEACH
Barefoot Camping Resort

4825 Hwy. 17 South, N. Myrtle Beach 29582. T: (843) 272-1790; F: (843) 272-4208; www.barefootrvresort.com.

🚐 ★★★   ⛺ ★

Beauty: ★★★   Site Privacy: ★★
Spaciousness: ★★★   Quiet: ★★★★
Security: ★★   Cleanliness: ★★★
Insect Control: ★★★★   Facilities: ★★★★

Barefoot Camping Resort leases most of its sites on a seasonal/residential basis. It's in the heart of the hustle and bustle of Myrtle Beach, convenient to dining, golf, and tourist attractions. You'll experience horrendous traffic if you visit on summer weekends. The campground is laid out in numerous rows of back-in sites, with a few sites near the beach. Sites have dirt, gravel, sand, and grass parking—it's quite a mess. Most sites are shady, though sites near the beach tend to be more open. RV campers should choose sites based on desired distance from the beach. Tent campers should avoid this place altogether—tent sites are wedged into a tight strip next to noisy 48th Ave. South. Security is good at this urban resort. Gates are locked at night.

BASICS

Operated By: Barefoot Resort, Inc. **Open:** All year. **Site Assignment:** First come, first served, but reservations recommended. First nights deposit holds the reservation. Cancellation fee is $5 but if cancelled within 24 hrs. of expected arrival date then the fee is $5 plus the deposit. **Registration:** At camp office. **Fee:** In-Season $36–$40 per night for 4 people (cash, checks, V, MC) $2 extra for each adult up to 8. **Parking:** 2 cars per site.

FACILITIES

Number of RV Sites: 215. **Number of Tent-Only Sites:** 10. **Number of Multipurpose Sites:** 205. **Hookups:** Water, electricity (30, 50 amps), sewer, cable. **Each Site:** Picnic table. **Dump Station:** Yes. **Laundry:** Yes. **Pay Phone:** Yes. **Rest Rooms and Showers:** Yes. **Fuel:** No. **Propane:** Yes. **Internal Roads:** Paved. **RV Service:** On call. **Market:** 1.5 mi. south. **Restaurant:** Cracker Barrel on site. **General Store:** Camp store. **Vending:** Yes. **Swimming Pool:** Yes. **Playground:** Yes. **Other:** Arcade, Lazy River, fitness center, spa. **Activities:** Arcade games, boating, organized activities in-season. **Nearby Attractions:** Dixie Stampede, Alabama Theater, Barefoot Landing, House of Blues. **Additional Information:** North Myrtle Beach Office Chamber of Commerce, (843) 249-3519.

RESTRICTIONS

Pets: Leash only. **Fires:** No. **Alcoholic Beverages:** Allowed. **Vehicle Maximum Length:** 40 ft.

TO GET THERE

From I-95, exit at Florence and take US Hwy. 501 east about 60 mi. to US Hwy. 22. Take US Hwy. 22 north, which merges with US Hwy. 17. The park is 1 mi. north of the intersection of 22 and 17, at 48th Ave. South. 7 mi. north of Myrtle Beach.

MYRTLE BEACH
Lakewood Camping Resort

5901 South Kings Hwy., Myrtle Beach 29575.
T: (877) LAKEWOOD; F: (843) 447-7350;
www.lakewoodcampground.com.

 ★★★★   ▲ ★★★

Beauty: ★★★★	Site Privacy: ★★
Spaciousness: ★★★	Quiet: ★★★
Security: ★★★★★	Cleanliness: ★★★★
Insect Control: ★★★	Facilities: ★★★★★

Gigantic Lakewood is similar to its Myrtle Beach competitors in that it has scads of identical campsites. Tidy and nicely landscaped, Lakewood was awarded National Association of RV Parks and Campgrounds "National RV Park of the Year 2000–2001." Extensive amenities cater to all ages. Choose open sites in the northeastern corner of the park or shadier sites in blocks 1, 2, and 3 south. A variety of trees, including oaks, pines, dogwood, pecan, and cedar provide shade. Parking is on grass, packed sand, or dirt. Laid out in rows with mostly back-in parking, sites are small and there is little privacy. For a quaint view, try sites 2801–2867 which line the small lakes. Families should request sites near the playground. There are restaurants and tourist attractions nearby. Excellent security includes a gated entrance and 24-hour security patrols. Avoid Myrtle Beach during spring break and summer holidays. For quiet, visit in March or October.

BASICS

Operated By: Lakewood Camping Resort, Inc. **Open:** All year. **Site Assignment:** First come, first served, guests may request sites; reservations accepted 48 hours to one year in advance w/ deposit, checks accepted well in advance; in-season oceanfront 7-night min., other sites 4-night min.; 48-hour notice required for refund. **Registration:** Gatehouse, express check-in also available-inquire when making reservations. **Fee:** Peak season oceanfront & prime sites $41 (off-season $22–$31), other sites $36 (off-season $22–$27); prices for 5 people (cash, personal check, V, MC, D). **Parking:** 2 vehicles per site (charge for extras in-season).

FACILITIES

Number of Multipurpose Sites: 1,400. **Hookups:** Water, electric (30, 50 amps), sewer, cable. **Each Site:** Picnic table. **Dump Station:** Yes. **Laundry:** Yes. **Pay Phone:** Yes. **Rest Rooms and Showers:** Yes. **Fuel:** No. **Propane:** No. **Internal Roads:** Paved. **RV Service:** 1 mi. south in Myrtle Beach. **Market:** Camp store, supermarket 0.25 mi. **Restaurant:** 0.25 mi. in Myrtle Beach. **General Store:** Camp store, Wal-Mart 2 mi. south in Myrtle

Beach. **Vending:** Yes. **Swimming Pool:** Yes. **Playground:** Yes. **Other:** Hot tub, RV storage, freshwater fishing, golf-cart rentals, convention services, non-denominational ministry, snack bar. **Activities:** Mini-golf, arcade, pedal boat, kayak, & bicycle rentals, shuffleboard, basketball, horseshoes, volleyball, amphitheater, live entertainment. **Nearby Attractions:** Myrtle Beach historic tours & gardens, Grand Strand, Barefoot Landing, House of Blues, Alabama Theater, Dixie Stampede, Intracoastal Waterway. **Additional Information:** Myrtle Beach Area Chamber of Commerce, (843) 626-7444.

RESTRICTIONS

Pets: Leash (6 ft. max.). **Fires:** Allowed. **Alcoholic Beverages:** Not allowed. **Vehicle Maximum Length:** 40 ft.

TO GET THERE

From the intersection of Hwy. 501 and Hwy. 17, drive south on 17 approx. 5 miles. The entrance is on the left.

MYRTLE BEACH
Myrtle Beach State Park

4401 South Kings Hwy., Myrtle Beach 29575. T: (843) 238-5325; F: (843) 238-9483; www.south-carolinaparks.com.

🚐 ★★★★	⛺ ★★★★
Beauty: ★★★★	Site Privacy: ★★★★
Spaciousness: ★★★★	Quiet: ★★★
Security: ★★★★★	Cleanliness: ★★★
Insect Control: ★★★	Facilities: ★★★

Myrtle Beach State Park maintains a massive campground with large shady sites laid out in a series of semi-circles. Sweet gum, hickory, longleaf pine, and various oak species provide plenty of shade and varying amounts of privacy. Parking is on packed coquina and pine straw. A few sites offer pull-through parking. For privacy and quiet, try Circle 6 (numbers 293–336). Want to be closer to the beach? Try 166–172; these quiet sites are on a dead-end road. With plenty of recreation, Myrtle Beach State Park is popular with locals and tourists. This makes for unbearable crowds on holiday and summer weekends. We urge you to visit in the "off season," preferably autumn to avoid spring-break crowds. This urban park is convenient to restaurants, world-class golf, and other tourist attractions. Security

is excellent; the front gate is attended at all times and locked at night.

BASICS

Operated By: South Carolina State Parks. **Open:** All year. **Site Assignment:** First come, first served; 40 sites available for reservation 24 hours to 11 months in advance, full deposit required, $15 cancellation fee, must cancel before arrival date. **Registration:** Trading post. **Fee:** $26 w/ reservation, $25 without reservation, $20 for overflow tent sites; South Carolina seniors & disabled 50% discount (cash, personal check, V, MC). **Parking:** At sites.

FACILITIES

Number of RV Sites: 0. **Number of Tent-Only Sites:** 45 overflow. **Number of Multipurpose Sites:** 302. **Hookups:** Water, electric (50 amps). **Each Site:** Picnic table. **Dump Station:** Yes. **Laundry:** Yes. **Pay Phone:** Yes. **Rest Rooms and Showers:** Yes. **Fuel:** No. **Propane:** No. **Internal Roads:** Park Paved, campground packed coquina. **RV Service:** 0.25 mi. **Market:** 0.25 mi. **Restaurant:** 0.5 mi. **General Store:** 10 mi. south in Surfside (Wal-Mart). **Vending:** Yes. **Swimming Pool:** No. **Playground:** Yes. **Other:** Fishing pier, boardwalks to beach, snack bar, gift shop, picnic shelters, amphitheater, activity center. **Activities:** Nature center, nature trail, fishing. **Nearby Attractions:** Myrtle Beach historic tours & gardens, Grand Strand, Barefoot Landing, House of Blues, Alabama Theater, Dixie Stampede, Intracoastal Waterway. **Additional Information:** Myrtle Beach Area Chamber of Commerce, (843) 626-7444.

RESTRICTIONS

Pets: Leash. **Fires:** Allowed. **Alcoholic Beverages:** Not allowed. **Vehicle Maximum Length:** 50 ft.

TO GET THERE

From the junction of Hwy. 501 and Hwy. 17, go south for 5 miles. The park is on the left.

MYRTLE BEACH
Myrtle Beach Travel Park

10108 Kings Rd., Myrtle Beach 29572. T: (800) 255-3568 or (843) 449-3714; F: (843) 497-8521; www.myrtlebeachtravelpark.com.

🚐 ★★★★	⛺ ★★★★
Beauty: ★★★★	Site Privacy: ★★
Spaciousness: ★★★	Quiet: ★★★
Security: ★★★★★	Cleanliness: ★★★★
Insect Control: ★★★	Facilities: ★★★★★

This park and its competitors offer frighteningly similar campsites. Resolution between parks is found in activities and amenities offered. This one offers a 17-acre freshwater fishing lake. Most nightly and weekly sites lie between the lake and the ocean. Oceanside sites form 25 identical rows of pull-throughs and 3 identical rows of back-ins. Each treeless site has a covered picnic table. Sites are small and there is no privacy. Parking is on patchy grass and sand. Nicer sites enjoy views of dunes and sea grasses. The shady, nicely landscaped, back-in sites on the other side of the lake are the prettiest. Sites 700–709 and 576–588 are delightful, with pleasant views of the fishing lake.

BASICS

Operated By: Myrtle Beach Travel Park. **Open:** All year. **Site Assignment:** Reservations recommended, w/ $50 deposit, 14 days in advance, 7 night min. Jun. 6–Aug. 15, off-season min. 3 nights, 7 day cancellation notice required for refund. **Registration:** Office. **Fee:** $21–42 for 4 people, $3 per extra person up to 8 total (prices vary seasonally; cash, personal check, V, MC, AE). **Parking:** 1 vehicle per site, $2/day per extra vehicle.

FACILITIES

Number of RV Sites: 0. Number of Tent-Only Sites: 10–15 (tents or pop-ups, water & electric only). **Number of Multipurpose Sites:** 650. **Hookups:** Water, electric (30, 50 amps), sewer, cable. **Each Site:** Picnic table. **Dump Station:** Yes. **Laundry:** Yes. **Pay Phone:** Yes. **Rest Rooms and Showers:** Yes. **Fuel:** No. **Propane:** Yes. **Internal Roads:** Most Paved, some coquina or gravel. **RV Service:** On site. **Market:** 2 mi. in Myrtle Beach. **Restaurant:** On site. **General Store:** On site. **Vending:** Yes. **Swimming Pool:** Yes. **Playground:** Yes. **Other:** Pavilion, recreation room, chapel, RV storage. **Activities:** Freshwater lake, beach front, arcade, paddle boat rental, activities director. **Nearby Attractions:** Myrtle Beach historic plantations, tours, Intracoastal Waterway, amusement parks, Grand Strand, Brookgreen Gardens. **Additional Information:** Myrtle Beach Area Chamber of Commerce, (843) 626-7444.

RESTRICTIONS

Pets: Leash only. **Fires:** Allowed. **Alcoholic Beverages:** At site only. **Vehicle Maximum Length:** No limit. **Other:** No fireworks.

TO GET THERE

From the intersection of US Hwy. 501 and US Hwy. 17, drive north on US 17 approx. 5 miles to Kings Rd. Turn right and the entrance is on the left.

MYRTLE BEACH
Ocean Lakes Family Campground

SMAll no pRivacy

6001 South Kings Hwy., Myrtle Beach 29575.
T: (800) 722-1451 or (843) 238-5636; F: (843) 238-1890; www.oceanlakes.com;
camping@oceanlakes.com.

🚐 ★★★★   ⛺ ★★★

Beauty: ★★★★   Site Privacy: ★★
Spaciousness: ★★★   Quiet: ★★
Security: ★★★★★   Cleanliness: ★★★★
Insect Control: ★★★   Facilities: ★★★★★

Like its competitor (Lakewood Camping Resort), Ocean Lakes has received the "National RV Park of the Year Award" from the National Association of RV Parks and Campgrounds. Campsites are pull-throughs and parking is on grass. Sites are small. Most are completely treeless, so there is no privacy between sites. Short-term sites are laid out in tidy rows on the northeast corner of the park. If you're traveling with children, we recommend a site in the HH area, which is between the pool and the beach. Otherwise choose your site according to proximity to the beach. Ocean Lakes is convenient to all Myrtle Beach attractions, restaurants and shopping. Security is excellent at this urban resort, which is gated and has 24-hour security patrols. Visits during spring break and summer holidays should be avoided completely. If you would like a little peace and quiet visit in March or October.

BASICS

Operated By: Jackson Family. **Open:** All year. **Site Assignment:** Reservations recommended spring, summer, & fall (by site number), 4-night min. Jun. 15–Aug. 15, $50 deposit; 7-day cancellation notice for refund, $10 cancellation fee. **Registration:** Main gate staffed 24 hours, express check-in available—inquire when making reservations. **Fee:** Peak season rates (Memorial Day–Labor Day) ocean front $44.50 (off season $22.50–$30), 3000 section $43.50 (off-season $21.50–$29), 4000 section $42.50 (off-season $20.50–$28); prices for 6 people, subject to 2002 increase (cash, personal check, V, MC, D). **Parking:** 2 cars per site, overflow parking available, $3 per extra car.

FACILITIES

Number of RV Sites: 0. **Number of Tent-Only Sites:** 2. **Number of Multipurpose Sites:** 893. **Hookups:** Water, electric (20, 30, 50 amps), sewer, cable, modem, friendly phone line (free local calls). **Each Site:** Picnic table. **Dump Station:** No. **Laundry:** Yes. **Pay Phone:** Yes. **Rest Rooms and Showers:** Yes. **Fuel:** No. **Propane:** Yes. **Internal Roads:** Paved. **RV Service:** On site. **Market:** 0.25 mi. **Restaurant:** 1 mi. **General Store:** Camp store. **Vending:** Yes. **Swimming Pool:** Yes. **Playground:** Yes. **Other:** Sailboat launch, snack bars, awning sales, golf cart, & automobile rental. **Activities:** Recreation center (full-time staff, year-round), marine life nature center, observation deck, arcade, bank fishing, freshwater lake fishing, mini-golf, golf car & bicycle rentals, basketball, volleyball, shuffleboard, horseshoes, bocci ball, weekly nondenominational church services, special event weekends, live entertainment (ask for schedules). **Nearby Attractions:** Myrtle Beach historic tours & gardens, Grand Strand, Barefoot Landing, House of Blues, Alabama Theater, Dixie Stampede, Intracoastal Waterway. **Additional Information:** Myrtle Beach Area Chamber of Commerce, (843) 626-7444.

RESTRICTIONS

Pets: Leash, clean-up enforced, no vicious breeds. **Fires:** Allowed (not encouraged). **Alcoholic Beverages:** At site only. **Vehicle Maximum Length:** 45 ft.

TO GET THERE

From US Hwy. 501, take Hwy. 544 south until it ends at the coast at Ocean Lakes. The park is 1 mile north of Surfside Beach and 3 mi. south of downtown Myrtle Beach on South Kings Hwy. (17).

NINETY-SIX

Lake Greenwood State Recreation Area

302 State Park Rd., Ninety-Six 29666. T: (864) 543-3535; F: (864) 543-3535;
www.southcarolinaparks.com;
lake_greenwood_sp@prt.state.sc.us.

 ★★★★   ★★★★

Beauty: ★★★★★   Site Privacy: ★★★
Spaciousness: ★★★★   Quiet: ★★★
Security: ★★★★★   Cleanliness: ★★★★
Insect Control: ★★★★   Facilities: ★★★

The lovely campground at Lake Greenwood occupies gently rolling hills with pine straw ground cover. With shadier, prettier sites, campground No. 1 is preferable to campground No. 2. Sites are mostly back-ins with a few pull-throughs. Many have views of Lake Greenwood. Sites are spacious and all parking is paved. Though many sites are shaded by trees, privacy is poor as there is little foliage between sites. Lake Greenwood is stocked with bass, crappie, bream, perch, catfish, and stripers. Visit nearby Greenwood Museum, two-time recipient of "South Carolina Tourist Attraction of the Year" award, or the Ninety-Six National Historical site, which includes ruins of a British Fort used in the American Revolution. Security is excellent at this rural, gated, and guarded state park. This park is extremely popular and should be studiously avoided on summer holidays and weekends. Visit mid-week, in spring or fall.

BASICS

Operated By: South Carolina State Parks. **Open:** All year. **Site Assignment:** Some first come, first served; some sites available for reservation w/ 2 night min., full deposit, 24-hour notice for refund, $15 cancellation fee. **Registration:** Park store, rangers make rounds, late comers register the next morning. **Fee:** $19 for waterfront sites, $18 for non-waterfront sites, fees include 6 people, South Carolina seniors & disabled pay 50%. **Parking:** 2 vehicles per site, overflow parking available.

FACILITIES

Number of RV Sites: 0. **Number of Tent-Only Sites:** 5 (plus primitive group camping). **Number of Multipurpose Sites:** 125. **Hookups:** Water, electric (50 amps). **Each Site:** Picnic table, fire pit. **Dump Station:** Yes. **Laundry:** No. **Pay Phone:** Yes. **Rest Rooms and Showers:** Yes. **Fuel:** No. **Propane:** No. **Internal Roads:** Paved. **RV Service:** On call. **Market:** 5 mi. west in Ninety-Six. **Restaurant:** 5 mi. west toward Greenwood. **General Store:** 1 mi. (also seasonal park store/ tackle shop). **Vending:** No. **Swimming Pool:** No. **Playground:** No. **Other:** Boat ramps, picnic shelters, recreation building, BBQ shelter. **Activities:** Nature trails, fishing wall, boating, swimming, water sports. **Nearby Attractions:** Ninety-Six historic sites, historic Abbeville, Festival of Flowers. **Additional Information:** Greenwood Chamber of Commerce, (864) 223-8431.

RESTRICTIONS

Pets: Leash. **Fires:** Allowed. **Alcoholic Beverages:** Not allowed. **Vehicle Maximum Length:** 45 ft. **Other:** 14 day max. stay in same site, swim at your own risk.

TO GET THERE

From I-26, take Exit 74 and go west on SC Hwy. 34 for 20 miles. Turn right on SC Hwy. 702 and go north for 1 mile. The park is on the right.

PICKENS

Table Rock State Park

158 E. Ellison Ln., Pickens 20671. T: (864) 878-9813; F: (864) 878-9077; www.southcarolinaparks.com; table_rock_sp@prt.state.sc.us.

🚐 ★★★★	⛺ ★★★★
Beauty: ★★★★	Site Privacy: ★★★
Spaciousness: ★★★	Quiet: ★★★★
Security: ★★★★	Cleanliness: ★★★★
Insect Control: ★★	Facilities: ★★★★

Nature lovers enjoy Table Rock and nearby Mountain Bridge Wilderness Area, which includes Caesar's Head State Park and Jones Gap State Park. Caesar's Head boasts dramatic granite cliffs while Jones Gap offers cool valley trails along the Middle Saluda River. A flat granite mountain serves as Table Rock's centerpiece and namesake. The campground includes two loops with mostly back-in parking. Beauty and privacy vary. The nicest section includes sites 25–40 and is heavily wooded. The park does not recommend this area for RVs. But parking spaces are level. If you have a small camper, give them a try. Sites are large, but there is little space between them. All parking is on gravel. Remote and gated, this park has excellent security. Elevations in this area range from 2,000 to 3,500 feet, so summer weather is mild. Visit in spring for solitude or in autumn for beautiful colors.

BASICS

Operated By: South Carolina State Parks. **Open:** All year. **Site Assignment:** First come, first served; 25 sites available for reservation, full payment required within 10 days of reservation; 24-hour cancellation notice for 50% refund. **Registration:**

Camp store or park office. **Fee:** $16 includes 6 people (cash, personal check, V, MC). **Parking:** At site, 2 vehicles max.

FACILITIES

Number of Multipurpose Sites: 100. **Hookups:** Electric (20, 30 amps), water. **Each Site:** Grill, picnic table, fire ring. **Dump Station:** Yes. **Laundry:** Yes. **Pay Phone:** Yes. **Rest Rooms and Showers:** Yes. **Fuel:** No. **Propane:** No. **Internal Roads:** Paved. **RV Service:** 40 mi. west in Greenville. **Market:** 10 mi. south in Pickens. **Restaurant:** On site. **General Store:** 1 mi. **Vending:** No. **Swimming Pool:** Yes. **Playground:** No. **Other:** Boat ramp, fishing pier, park store, meeting facilities, recreation center. **Activities:** Mini-golf, paddle boat, canoe & kayak rentals, nature center, year-round nature programs, hiking trails, fishing, swimming. **Nearby Attractions:** World of Energy at Lake Keowee, Issaqueena & Whitewater Falls, Foothills Trail, Sassafras Mountain. **Additional Information:** Cherokee Foothills Visitors Center/Table Rock State Park Headquarters (864) 878-9813, Pickens Chamber of Commerce (864) 878-3258.

RESTRICTIONS

Pets: Leash only. **Fires:** Allowed. **Alcoholic Beverages:** Not allowed. **Vehicle Maximum Length:** 36 ft.

TO GET THERE

From Pickens, take Hwy. 178 north for 9 miles. Turn right and drive east on Hwy. 11 for 5 miles. The park is on the left.

PLUM BRANCH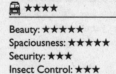

Hamilton Branch State Park, J. Strom Thurmond Reservoir

Route 1 P.O. Box 97, Plum Branch 29845. T: (864) 333-2223; F: (864) 333-2223; www.southcarolina parks.com; hamilton_branch_sp@scprt.com.

🚐 ★★★★	⛺ ★★★★
Beauty: ★★★★★	Site Privacy: ★★★★
Spaciousness: ★★★★★	Quiet: ★★★★
Security: ★★★	Cleanliness: ★★★★
Insect Control: ★★★	Facilities: ★★★

Hamilton Branch is gorgeous. Flatter than others along the Savannah River, this campground features large sites. Loblolly pine and other species provide shade, though there is not much foliage surrounding the sites. With most sites on the waterfront, choosing the prettiest is tough.

We recommend 36–54 and 71–78 for privacy and the nicest views. Most sites are laid out in pairs. Parking is on gravel or packed soil. Ten sites offer pull-through parking. Dock your boat at your campsite when lake levels permit. J. Strom Thurmond is one of the largest lakes in the southeast and is known for bream, crappie, striper, various bass, and catfish. Hamilton Branch doesn't offer many day-use activities, so explore outside the park. Remote, with gates locked at night, security is good at Hamilton Branch. This popular campground is likely to fill up on summer weekends. Plan a visit in the spring or during the week.

BASICS

Operated By: South Carolina State Parks. **Open:** All year. **Site Assignment:** First come, first served; reservations accepted w/ credit card deposit, cancel anytime w/ $15 cancellation fee. **Registration:** In-season at office, off-season at sites. **Fee:** $16 ($17 w/ reservation), $8 disabled & Golden Age discount. **Parking:** At sites.

FACILITIES

Number of RV Sites: 0. **Number of Tent-Only Sites:** 50 (water only). **Number of Multipurpose Sites:** 130. **Hookups:** Water, electric (20, 30, 50 amps). **Each Site:** Picnic table, tent pad, fire ring (some sites), grill (some sites). **Dump Station:** Yes. **Laundry:** No. **Pay Phone:** Yes. **Rest Rooms and Showers:** Yes. **Fuel:** No. **Propane:** No. **Internal Roads:** Paved (most). **RV Service:** 30 mi. south in Augusta. **Market:** 12 mi. north in McCormick. **Restaurant:** 12 mi. north in McCormick. **General Store:** 2 mi. outside park, Wal-Mart 30 mi. south in Augusta. **Vending:** Beverages only. **Swimming Pool:** No. **Playground:** Yes. **Other:** Boat ramps, picnic shelters. **Activities:** Fishing on J. Strom Thurmond Lake, water sports. **Nearby Attractions:** Historic McCormick, Antebellum homes & museums in Edgefield, Parkseed Company & Gardens in Greenwood, 30 mi. to Augusta, Georgia. **Additional Information:** McCormick Chamber of Commerce, (864) 465-2835, Augusta Chamber of Commerce, (706) 821-1300.

RESTRICTIONS

Pets: Leash (6 ft. max.). **Fires:** Allowed. **Alcoholic Beverages:** Allowed. **Vehicle Maximum Length:** 40 ft.

TO GET THERE

From I-20, take Georgia Exit 200 (River Watch Pkwy.), then drive west for 2 mi. to Furys Ferry Rd. (Hwy. 28 West). Turn right and drive north for 13 mi. to Clarks Hill, SC. Continue north on Hwy. 28 for 12 more mi. The park entrance is on the left.

SANTEE
Santee State Park

251 State Park Rd., Santee 29142. T: (803) 854-2408; www.southcarolinaparks.com; santee_sp@prt.state.sc.us.

🚐 ★★★★   ⛺ ★★★★

Beauty: ★★★★★	Site Privacy: ★★★
Spaciousness: ★★★	Quiet: ★★★
Security: ★★★	Cleanliness: ★★★★
Insect Control: ★★★★	Facilities: ★★★★

On Lake Marion, Santee is popular with anglers. Cypress trees and other tree stumps on the lake create a rich habitat for fish. The lake is known for its striped bass, an ocean bass which was trapped during dam construction and has since adapted to freshwater. Two delightful campgrounds offer lakefront sites. Small, quiet "Cypress View" features shady pull-through and back-in sites. "Lakeshore" features rows of mainly back-in sites. Close to the water and shaded by hickory and oak laden with Spanish moss, sites 94, 96, and 98 are especially beautiful. Site size is ample, but there is little privacy between sites. Parking is on sand, dirt, and pine straw. Despite the park's laid-back atmosphere, it's only two miles from I-95. Security is not adequate here. Gates are not attended or locked at night. This extremely popular campground stays busy. We recommend mid-week or off-season touring.

BASICS

Operated By: South Carolina State Parks. **Open:** All year. **Site Assignment:** Mostly first come, first served; limited sites available for reservation for $1 extra, full deposit required within 14 days of reservation; 24-hour notice for refund, $15 cancellation fee. **Registration:** Visitor Center, after-hours registration available. **Fee:** $16 includes 6 people (cash, personal checks, V, MC). **Parking:** 2 vehicles per site, overflow parking available.

FACILITIES

Number of Multipurpose Sites: 163. **Hookups:** Water, electric (20, 30 amps). **Each Site:** Picnic table. **Dump Station:** Yes. **Laundry:** Yes. **Pay**

Phone: Yes. **Rest Rooms and Showers:** Yes. **Fuel:** No. **Propane:** No. **Internal Roads:** Gravel. **RV Service:** On call. **Market:** 4 mi. south in Santee. **Restaurant:** 4 mi. south in Santee. **General Store:** Camp store. **Vending:** Beverages only. **Swimming Pool:** No. **Playground:** Yes. **Other:** Visitor's center, boat ramps, picnic shelters, meeting building. **Activities:** Nature & bicycle trails, fishing pier, seasonal swimming & paddle boat rentals when lifeguard on duty, tennis, nature boat tours. **Nearby Attractions:** Palmetto Trailhead, 3 golf courses, Lake Marion, Santee community, Lonestar Mercantile historic village & restaurant, one hour from Charleston & Columbia. **Additional Information:** Santee Cooper Country, (803) 854-2152, ext. 5; www.santeetourism.com.

RESTRICTIONS

Pets: Leash only. **Fires:** Allowed. **Alcoholic Beverages:** Not allowed. **Vehicle Maximum Length:** 45 ft. **Other:** 14-day max. stay.

TO GET THERE

From I-95, take Exit 98 at Santee. Drive northwest on Hwy. 6 for about 1 mi. Turn right onto State Park Rd. The campground is 2 mi. ahead.

SPARTANBURG

Cunningham RV Park

600 Campground Rd., Spartanburg 29306. T: (864) 576-1973; F: (864) 576-1973; .

🚐 ★★★   ▲ ★★

Beauty: ★★★   Site Privacy: ★★
Spaciousness: ★★   Quiet: ★★★★
Security: ★★   Cleanliness: ★★★★
Insect Control: ★★★★   Facilities: ★★

The campground at Cunningham RV Park is laid out in a grid, with eight rows of pull-through sites. Twelve back-in sites line the eastern perimeter of the property. About half of the sites have a shade tree. Otherwise, the sites are all the same. Choose your site based on tree preference and proximity to facilities. Parking is on grass and all sites are completely level; this park is as flat as Kansas. Sites are small and there is no privacy between sites. Cunningham's playground is fabulous, and potties are super-tidy and spacious. Two miles from the intersections of I-85 and I-26 in urban Spartanburg, Cunningham is convenient to shopping and restaurants. Security

is not great here, as the park is in a developed area and has no gates. Cunningham is a convenient stop-over rather than a vacation destination. Avoid stopping here on summer holidays.

BASICS

Operated By: The Cunningham Family. **Open:** All year. **Site Assignment:** First come, first served; reservations accepted up to 72 hours in advance, no deposit required. **Registration:** Camp store, self-registration after hours. **Fee:** $23 for 2 people; $2 extra for 50 amps or sewage hookup; $4 for additional adults, $2 for additional children. **Parking:** At sites, overflow parking available.

FACILITIES

Number of RV Sites: 0. **Number of Tent-Only Sites: Number of Tent-Only Sites:** 20. **Number of Multipurpose Sites:** 69. **Hookups:** Water, electric (30, 50 amps), some sewer. **Each Site:** Picnic table, fire rings in tent sites only. **Dump Station:** Yes. **Laundry:** Yes. **Pay Phone:** Yes. **Rest Rooms and Showers:** Yes. **Fuel:** No. **Propane:** Yes. **Internal Roads:** Gravel. **RV Service:** Within 4 mi. **Market:** Grocery 3 mi. south in Spartanburg, Wal-Mart 4 mi. south in Spartanburg. **Restaurant:** 1 mi. south in Spartanburg. **General Store:** Camp store, Wal-Mart 4 mi. south in Spartanburg. **Vending:** Beverage only. **Swimming Pool:** Yes. **Playground:** Yes. **Other:** Pool table, foosball. **Activities:** Volleyball, horseshoes, nature area. **Nearby Attractions:** Foothills Trail System, historic homes & plantations, BMW plant tours, Holly Wild Animal Park, Cow Pens National Battlefield. **Additional Information:** Spartanburg CVB, (800) 374-8326.

RESTRICTIONS

Pets: Leash only. **Fires:** Fire rings at tent sites; RV campers bring your own grill. **Alcoholic Beverages:** Allowed. **Vehicle Maximum Length:** No limit.

TO GET THERE

From I-85, take Exit 70 at Spartanburg, then I-26 west 2.5 mi. to Exit 17. Head west on Hwy. 40, then left on Campground Rd. about 1 mi. to the RV park.

SUMMERTON
Santee Lakes Campground

Route 2 Box 542, Summerton 29148. T: (803) 478-2262; F: (803) 478-7197.

🚐 ★★★   ⛺ ★★★

Beauty: ★★★★	Site Privacy: ★★
Spaciousness: ★★	Quiet: ★★★
Security: ★★★★	Cleanliness: ★★★★
Insect Control: ★	Facilities: ★★★

Santee Lakes is a good alternative to Santee State Park when the latter is full. Many of the attractive sites at Santee Lakes have views of adjacent Lake Marion, and most are nicely shaded by lovely mature trees. Sites are laid out in 11 tidy rows. All but 15 sites offer pull-through parking and are deliciously shady. pull-through sites situated closest to the beach have the nicest views of the water. Site size is on the small side of average with little privacy between sites. Santee Lakes is in a touristy area, so there are plenty of nearby restaurants and shops. Security is good; the entrance is guarded during the day and the park is patrolled at night. Lake Marion is extremely popular with fisher folk, so this park stays busy. Try to visit during the week or in spring or fall.

BASICS
Operated By: The Zeiglers. **Open:** All year. **Site Assignment:** First come, first served; reservations recommended (especially holiday weekends), $25 deposit, one week cancellation notice for refund. **Registration:** Camp store, late comers self-register. **Fee:** $23 full hookup, $21 water & electric, $19 tent; fees include 2 adults, $3 per extra person (cash, personal checks, V, MC). **Parking:** 2 vehicles per site, overflow parking available.

FACILITIES
Number of Multipurpose Sites: 170. **Hookups:** Water, electric (30 amps), some sites also w/ sewer & cable. **Each Site:** Picnic tables. **Dump Station:** Yes. **Laundry:** Yes. **Pay Phone:** Yes. **Rest Rooms and Showers:** Yes. **Fuel:** No. **Propane:** No. **Internal Roads:** Dirt. **RV Service:** On call. **Market:** 4 mi. south in Santee. **Restaurant:** 0.5 mi. **General Store:** Camp store. **Vending:** Beverages only. **Swimming Pool:** Yes. **Playground:** Yes. **Other:** Boat ramp, RV storage, recreation building. **Activities:** Beach in-season, game room, swimming, mini-golf, fishing pier, hot tub. **Nearby Attractions:** Santee National Wildlife Refuge, 3 golf courses, Palmetto Trailhead, Lake Marion, Santee community, one hour from Charleston & Columbia. **Additional Information:** Santee Cooper Country Tourism Information, (803) 854-2152, ext. 5; www.santeetourism.com.

RESTRICTIONS
Pets: Leash. **Fires:** Allowed. **Alcoholic Beverages:** Allowed. **Vehicle Maximum Length:** No limit.

TO GET THERE
From I-95, take Exit 102. Drive east on CR 400 for 0.25 miles, then turn right at the stop sign. The campground is on the left.

WINNSBORO
Lake Wateree State Recreation Area

881 State Park Rd., Winnsboro 29180. T: (803) 482-6401; F: (803) 482-6126; www.southcarolinaparks.com; lake_wateree_sp@prt.state.sc.us.

🚐 ★★★★   ⛺ ★★★★

Beauty: ★★★★★	Site Privacy: ★★★★★
Spaciousness: ★★★★	Quiet: ★★★★★
Security: ★★★★★	Cleanliness: ★★★★
Insect Control: ★★★★	Facilities: ★★★

This small state park is situated on 13,700-acre Lake Wateree, one of South Carolina's oldest and best-loved fishing lakes. Waterfowl at Lake Wateree include egrets, blue heron, mallards, and wood ducks. Here, recreation revolves around boating and fishing—there isn't even a swimming beach. But, the lake and the campground are breathtakingly gorgeous. The campground consists of one loop of paved sites. Of these, five offer pull-through parking and the remainder offer back-in parking. Site size varies from average to huge. Tree cover, consisting mainly of pine, is lovely and includes plenty of foliage to provide privacy between sites. Lakefront sites (odd numbers 11–27) and heavily wooded sites in the 50s and 60s are all gorgeous. Security is excellent at this rural state park, as gates are locked at night. For maximum peace and quiet, visit this very pretty little park on weekdays or in the spring or fall.

BASICS
Operated By: South Carolina State Parks. **Open:** All year except Christmas. **Site Assignment:** First

come, first served; 36 sites available for reservations for $1 extra, 24 hours in advance, full deposit within 10 days of reservation; 24 hour cancellation notice for refund. **Registration:** Park store, late comers must have combination to open gate. **Fee:** $18 for waterfront sites (plus $1 w/ reservation), $17 for sites across from water, $16 for all other sites. **Parking:** All wheels on pavement, overflow parking available.

FACILITIES

Number of RV Sites: 72. **Number of Tent-Only Sites:** 0. **Number of Multipurpose Sites:** 72. **Hookups:** Water, electric (20, 30 amps). **Each Site:** Picnic table, fire ring. **Dump Station:** Yes. **Laundry:** No. **Pay Phone:** Yes. **Rest Rooms and Showers:** Yes. **Fuel:** No. **Propane:** No. **Internal Roads:** Paved (excellent condition). **RV Service:** 40 mi. south in Columbia. **Market:** 15 mi. west in Winnsboro. **Restaurant:** 7 mi. west in Winnsboro. **General Store:** Park store. **Vending:** Beverages.

Swimming Pool: No. **Playground:** Yes. **Other:** Boat ramp, fueling dock, tackle shop, picnic area. **Activities:** Nature trail, fishing, boating, swimming area. **Nearby Attractions:** Ridgeway historic village, Columbia historic homes, South Carolina Confederate Relic Room & Museum, Fort Jackson Museum, South Carolina State Museum. **Additional Information:** Columbia Metropolitan CVB, (800) 264-4884 or (803) 254-0479.

RESTRICTIONS

Pets: Leash only. **Fires:** Fire rings only. **Alcoholic Beverages:** Not allowed. **Vehicle Maximum Length:** 40 ft. **Other:** 14 day max. stay.

TO GET THERE

From I-77, take Exit 41 and drive east on SC 20 for 5 mi. to Hwy. 21. Turn left (north) and drive 2 mi. until the first paved road. Turn right on River Rd. and drive 5–7 mi. The park is on the left.

Tennessee

Tennessee was inhabited by Chickasaw, Cherokee, and other Native Americans when Hernando de Soto explored the shore near Memphis in 1541. From that time on, the Spanish maintained a landing site at present-day Memphis. The Spanish brought diseases that killed many Native Americans. As their populations decreased, tribes formed nations. The Cherokee Nation had a particularly strong impact on the culture and history of Tennessee.

In 1682, the French built a temporary post near Memphis under the direction of Rene-Robert Cavalier, Sieur de La Salle. After travelling to the Gulf of Mexico, La Salle claimed all of the land drained by the Mississippi for France. When Britain won the French and Indian War in 1763, it gained control of all territories between the Atlantic Ocean and the Mississippi River.

In spite of a royal proclamation banning white settlement west of the Appalachians, North Carolinians began to settle in Tennessee in the 1760s. These settlers fought against the British in the American Revolution. Though Tennessee has no official nickname, it's often referred to as The Volunteer State to commemorate the valor of native soldiers in wars dating back to the American Revolution.

In the 1770s Daniel Boone blazed the famous **Wilderness Road Trail** through Cumberland Gap to the Kentucky River. Under the leadership of William Blount, John Sevier, and Andrew Jackson, Tennessee attained statehood in 1796.

The young state experienced growth in three distinct economic and cultural regions. The western portion of the state produced cotton and was dependent upon slave labor. Due to its strong cultural and economic ties to the deep south, western Tennessee was loyal to the Confederacy during the Civil War. Central Tennessee saw diversified commercial farming, and also tended to side with the rebels in the Civil War. Hilly Eastern Tennessee was home to small subsistence farms. These independant farmers remained loyal to the Union, and tried to form their own state to avoid secession.

Tennesseans still divide their state into three main regions. Today, the flat Western region, with its fertile soil, is the most heavily farmed. As the home of **W.C. Handy** and **Elvis Presley** among others, **Memphis** has been a major hub for blues and rock 'n' roll music.

The rolling hills of Central Tennessee have an extremely diversified economy, with livestock, including the majestic **Tennessee Walking Horse,** being the most important farm product. The region is also known for automobile and parts manufacturing. In Nashville, the **Grand Ole Opry** has been around since 1925. Today, country music regularly enlivens the pop charts, and **Nashville** is still the heart and home of the industry.

Hilly-to-mountainous Eastern Tennessee is now dependent on manufacturing and tourism. The area is home to the **Cherokee National Forest** and the western half of **Great Smoky Mountains National Park,** an environmentally very important region. Botanists estimate that there are more species of plants in Great Smoky Mountains National Park than in all of Europe.

Tourist attractions in Western Tennessee include: Stax Museum of American Soul Music, **National Civil Rights Museum,** the Shipwreck of the Tennessee River, Tennessee River Folklife Museum, Casey Jones Home & Railroad Museum, Beale Street Historic District, **Graceland: Home of Elvis Presley,** Memphis Motorsports Park, Memphis Pink Palace Museum, Memphis Queen Line Riverboats, Memphis Rock 'n' Soul Museum, Mud Island River Park, The Peabody Hotel (Peabody Ducks), The Pyramid, Sun Studio, Davy Crockett Cabin-Museum, and the **Tennessee River Museum.**

Tourist attractions in Middle Tennessee include: Cumberland Science Museum, Nashville Zoo, Cordell Hull Birthplace Museum & State Park, **Cumberland River Walk in Clarksville,** Fort Donelson National Battlefield & Cemetery, The Homeplace 1850: A Living History Museum, Land Between the Lakes National Recreation Area, The Amish Community in Ethridge, James-Ben Studio and Galleries, Meriwether Lewis National Monument, Nashville Superspeedway, **Jack Daniels Distillery,** Standing Stone Monument, Rattle & Snap Plantation, Belle Meade Plantation, Country Music Hall of Fame, Frist Center for the Visual Arts, General Jackson Showboat, Governor's Executive Residence, Grand Ole Opry & Museum, **The Hermitage,** Music Valley Wax Museum & Sidewalk of the Stars, Nashville Shores, Opryland Hotel, Tennessee State Capitol, Tennessee Titans, Travellers Rest Plantation, Wildhorse Saloon, Historic Shelbyville, Tennessee Walking Horse Museum, Sam Davis Home, Saturn Welcome Center & Plant Tours, and The Arts Center of Cannon County.

Tourist attractions in Eastern Tennessee include: **Dollywood,** Knoxville Zoo, Bristol Motor Speedway, **Chattanooga Choo-Choo,** Battles for Chattanooga Electric Map and Museum, Chickamauga-Chattanooga National Military Park, Lookout Mountain Incline Railway, **Rock City, Ruby Falls, Tennessee Aquarium,** Tennessee Valley Railroad, Cherokee Scenic Loop Tour, Museum Center at 5 Points, Ocoee Whitewater Center, Cumberland Gap National Historic Park, Christus Gardens, Great Smokies Mega Theatre, **Great Smoky Arts & Crafts Community,** Ober Gatlinburg, Ripley's Believe it or Not! Museum, President Andrew Johnson Museum and Library, Andrew Johnson National Historic Site, Rocky Mount Museum, Blount Mansion, Volunteer Landing, The Crockett Tavern Museum, American Museum of Science and Energy, Pigeon Forge/Gatlinburg headline musicians and production shows, Historic Rugby, **NASCAR Speed Park.**

The following facilities accept payment in checks or cash only:

Chilhowee Campground, Cherokee National Forest, Benton

Cosby Campground, Great Smoky Mountains National Park, Cosby

Cove Lake State Park, Caryville

Edgar Evins State Park, Silver Point

Indian Boundary Campground, Cherokee National Forest, Tellico Plains

Montgomery Bell State Park, Burns

Nathan Bedford Forrest State Park, Eva

Old Stone Fort State Archaeological Area, Manchester

Paris Landing State Resort Park, Buchanan

Pin Oak Campground, Natchez Trace State Resort Park, Wildersville

Reelfoot Lake State Park, South Campground, Tiptonville

ASHLAND CITY
Cheatham Lake Lock A Campground

1798 Cheatham Dam Rd., Ashland City 37015.
T: (615) 792-3715 or (877) 444-6777 for reservations; www.reserveusa.com.

🚐 ★★★★   ▲ ★★★★

Beauty: ★★★★★   Site Privacy: ★★★
Spaciousness: ★★★★★   Quiet: ★★★★
Security: ★★★★★   Cleanliness: ★★★★★
Insect Control: ★★★★   Facilities: ★★★

Located on Cheatham Lake, a development intended to improve navigation on the Cumberland River, Lock A campground is popular with fishermen. Catches include crappie, catfish, sauger, bream, and largemouth, striped, and white bass. Adjacent Cheatham State Wildlife Management Area provides hunting opportunities. The campground consists of two RV areas and one tent area. RV parking is paved, back-in style. RV sites are extremely large, while tent sites are a bit smaller. There are some pretty shade trees, but little foliage between sites; privacy is at a minimum while views of Cheatham Lake are optimized. For the loveliest views, head to sites 24–29. Security is excellent at this remote campground; the staff is extremely vigilant and the gates are locked at night. Central Tennessee is very hot and humid in late summer-visit in spring or fall for the nicest weather.

BASICS

Operated By: US Army Corps of Engineers. **Open:** Apr. 12–Oct. 28 (2002). **Site Assignment:** Some first come, first served; most sites available for reservation through the National Recreation Reservation Service (NRRS) at (877) 444-6777 or www.reserveusa.com. Reservations can be made up to 240 days in advance, full payment required upon making reservation; credit card preferred (V, MC, D, AE), or pay by money order if at least 21 days in advance of arrival. $10 fee for cancellation, or change of site or dates. Cancellation within 3 days of arrival charged first night, no-show charged $20 plus first night. Holidays 3-night min., weekends 2-night. **Registration:** Entrance station, gates close at 10 p.m. **Fee:** $23 waterfront, $19 non-waterfront & tent sites (cash, personal check, V, D, MC, AE). **Parking:** At site, on impact area, in parking lot.

FACILITIES

Number of RV Sites: 0. **Number of Tent-Only Sites:** 8 (w/ tent pads). **Number of Multipurpose Sites:** 36. **Hookups:** Water, electric (30 amps). **Each Site:** Picnic table, grill, fire ring, lantern pole. **Dump Station:** Yes. **Laundry:** Yes. **Pay Phone:** No. **Rest Rooms and Showers:** Yes. **Fuel:** No. **Propane:** No. **Internal Roads:** Paved. **RV Service:** 20 mi. in Nashville. **Market:** 11 mi. in Ashland City. **Restaurant:** 11 mi. in Ashland City. **General Store:** 11 mi. in Ashland City. **Vending:** No. **Swimming Pool:** No. **Playground:** Yes. **Other:** Boat launch, fish-cleaning station, amphitheater. **Activities:** Beach swimming, hiking trails, ball field, fishing, water sports, volleyball, basketball, picnic shelter, courtesy dock. **Nearby Attractions:** Nashville, Country Music Hall of Fame, The Parthenon, Belle Meade Plantation, Grand Ole Opry, Opryland Hotel, Hermitage Andrew Jackson Home. **Additional Information:** Nashville Tourism Information, (615) 259-4700.

RESTRICTIONS

Pets: Leash only, not allowed on beach. **Fires:** Allowed, in fire rings & grills only. **Alcoholic Beverages:** Allowed, at sites only. **Vehicle Maximum Length:** Varies (see www.reserveusa.com for site specifications). **Other:** 14-day stay limit.

TO GET THERE

From Nashville, take US Hwy. 12 west 15 mi. to Ashland City. Continue on 12 another 8 mi. to Cheap Hill. Turn left (southwest) on Cheatham Dam Rd. and drive 4 mi. Turn left into the campground.

BENTON
Chilhowee Campground, Cherokee National Forest

Rte. 1 Box 348-D, Benton 37307. T: (423) 338-5201; F: (423) 338-6577; www.southernregion.fs.fed.us/cherokee.

🚐 ★★★★   ▲ ★★★★★

Beauty: ★★★★★   Site Privacy: ★★★★
Spaciousness: ★★★★★   Quiet: ★★★★★
Security: ★★★★★   Cleanliness: ★★★★
Insect Control: ★★★   Facilities: ★★★

Expansive Cherokee National Forest is divided by Great Smoky Mountains National Park and encompasses 620,000 acres of natural and recreation areas. The park includes much of the southern Appalachian Mountains that were razed by poor farming and timbering techniques in the late nineteenth century. In 1911, Congress passed the Weeks Act, establishing National Forests, and Cherokee became one of the first tracts of national forest land. Today, it supports thousands of species of flora and fauna. Breathtaking Chilhowee Campground offers both back-in and pull-through sites on a pristine mountainside. Parking is on pea gravel. Many sites also offer soft pea gravel tent pads. Sites are shaded by a variety of hardwoods and privacy is provided by foliage between most sites. Though site size varies, all are spacious. For space and privacy, we recommend loops A, B, and F. Rest rooms vary; some loops have too few potties. Families should head for the extremely nice rest rooms at loops A and B. Security at Chilhowee is excellent. It's extremely remote and gated. Visit any time except summer holidays.

BASICS

Operated By: US Forest Service. **Open:** Apr.–Oct. **Site Assignment:** First come, first served; no reservations. **Registration:** Self-pay fee station. **Fee:** $15–$18 RV, $12 tent; 5 people max. (cash, personal checks). **Parking:** At site (2 cars), day-use parking lot $3 per day.

FACILITIES

Number of RV Sites: 0. **Number of Tent-Only Sites:** 58. **Number of Multipurpose Sites:** 18 (loops A & B). **Hookups:** Electric (20, 30 amps), loops A & B only. **Each Site:** Picnic table, fire ring, grill, lantern pole, tent pad. **Dump Station:** Yes. **Laundry:** No. **Pay Phone:** No. **Rest Rooms and Showers:** Yes. **Fuel:** No. **Propane:** No. **Internal Roads:** Paved. **RV Service:** 25 mi. in Cleveland. **Market:** 12 mi. in Benton. **Restaurant:** 10 mi. on Hwy. 64 West. **General Store:** 25 mi. in Cleveland. **Vending:** No. **Swimming Pool:** No. **Playground:** No. **Other:** Group picnic area. **Activities:** 7-acre private lake w/ swimming beach, boating (electric trolling motors only), fishing, hiking & mountain-biking trails. **Nearby Attractions:** Benton Falls, kayaking & rafting on the Ocoee & Hiwassee Rivers, Ocoee Whitewater center, Cherohala Skyway National Scenic Byway, Nancy Ward Grave Site, antique shopping. **Additional Information:** Polk county/Copper Basin Chamber of Commerce, (423) 338-5040; Tennessee Overhill Heritage Tourism Assoc., (423) 263-7232.

RESTRICTIONS

Pets: On leash only. **Fires:** In grills, fire rings only. **Alcoholic Beverages:** Not allowed. **Vehicle Maximum Length:** 50 ft. (sites vary).

TO GET THERE

From I-75, take Exit 20 (Cleveland) and go east on the bypass. Drive 5 mi. and take the US Hwy. 64 (Ocoee) Exit. Drive 14 mi. east on 64 to FR 77. Turn left and drive 7 mi. to the campground.

BUCHANAN

Paris Landing State Resort Park

Rte. 1, Buchanan 38222. T: (731) 641-4465 or (800) 250-8614; F: (731) 644-7390; www.tnstateparks.com.

🚙 ★★★★   ▲ ★★★★

Beauty: ★★★★   Site Privacy: ★★★
Spaciousness: ★★★   Quiet: ★★★
Security: ★★★   Cleanliness: ★★★★
Insect Control: ★★★★   Facilities: ★★★★★

Paris Landing offers outstanding recreational amenities, including an 18-hole golf course which has consistently earned four stars from Golf Digest Magazine. On Kentucky Lake, the marina offers 200 rental slips plus other amenities. In the summer, the amphitheater hosts various live performances. The campground is laid out in four loops, among various tree species, including hickory, white and red oak. Most sites are nicely shaded although there is little privacy. Sites with hookups feature paved, back-in parking. Each site has a gravel patio area and sites are mid-sized. For space and privacy, we like sites 21–39 in the back of the campground. There are no gates at Paris Landing, but the park is fairly remote, making security okay. This area sees cold winters and hot summers. Try to visit in late spring or fall.

BASICS

Operated By: Tennessee State Parks. **Open:** Year round. **Site Assignment:** First come, first served; no reservations. **Registration:** At site, host or ranger makes rounds. **Fee:** $17 water & electric, $7 tent; prices for 2 people, $0.50 per additional person (under age 7, free); seniors & disabled discounts available (cash, personal checks). **Parking:** At sites.

FACILITIES

Number of RV Sites: 0. **Number of Tent-Only Sites:** 17 (primitive). **Number of Multipurpose**

Sites: 43. **Hookups:** Water, electric (30 amps). **Each Site:** Picnic table, grill. **Dump Station:** Yes. **Laundry:** Yes (closed in winter). **Pay Phone:** Yes. **Rest Rooms and Showers:** Yes (closed in winter). **Fuel:** No (boat fuel available at marina). **Propane:** No. **Internal Roads:** Paved. **RV Service:** 22 mi. northwest in Murray, KY. **Market:** 18 mi. southwest in Paris. **Restaurant:** Park restaurant, also within 0.25 mi. **General Store:** 1 mi. hardware, 18 mi. southwest in Paris (Wal-Mart). **Vending:** Yes. **Swimming Pool:** Yes. **Playground:** Yes. **Other:** Marina, rental slips, boat launch, picnic grounds w/ pavilions, amphitheater. **Activities:** 18-hole golf course, driving range, practice greens, club & cart rentals, archery range, fishing, water sports, swimming beach, hiking trails, tennis, basketball. **Nearby Attractions:** Natchez Trace, Nathan Bedford Forrest, New Johnsonville, Port Royal & Dunbar Cave State Parks, Fort Donelson National Military Park, Land Between the Lakes National Recreation Area w/ over 100 mi. of mountain-biking trails. **Additional Information:** Paris/Henry County Chamber of Commerce, (731) 642-3431.

RESTRICTIONS

Pets: On leash only. **Fires:** Allowed. **Alcoholic Beverages:** Not allowed. **Vehicle Maximum Length:** 40 ft. (sites vary). **Other:** 14-day stay limit May 1–Aug. 31, no gray water.

TO GET THERE

From Memphis, take US Hwy. 79 east approximately 130 mi. The park is on the left (north) before the bridge across the Tennessee River. From I-24, take Exit 4 (40 mi. northwest of Nashville) and drive west on Hwy. 79 approximately 45 mi. The park entrance is the first right after the bridge. The campground is on the left inside the park.

BURNS
Montgomery Bell State Park

P.O. Box 39, Burns 37029. T: (615) 797-9052; F: (615) 797-3722; www.tnstateparks.com.

🚐 ★★★★ ⛺ ★★★★

Beauty: ★★★★★	Site Privacy: ★★★
Spaciousness: ★★★	Quiet: ★★★★
Security: ★★★★	Cleanliness: ★★★★
Insect Control: ★★★★	Facilities: ★★★★★

Montgomery Bell maintains excellent facilities, including an indoor pool (open all year) and an 18-hole golf course, which *Golf Digest* magazine

has rated as one of the top 100 public courses in the US. Other interesting sites include an 1810 Presbyterian Church and reconstructed minister's home. An ancillary facility, Narrows of the Harpeth State Park, offers canoe access to the Harpeth River. The campground contains small, picturesque sites shaded by a variety of hardwoods including cedar. There is little undergrowth to provide privacy between sites. Some parking spaces are gravel, while others are paved. Most sites offer back-in parking, with the exception of two pull-throughs reserved for handicapped use. The nicest sites line Four Mile Creek, along the back of the campground. Security is fair at this rural park. A ranger is on duty at all times. Don't visit on summer weekends, when the park fills to capacity. Also avoid hot, humid July and August.

BASICS

Operated By: Tennessee State parks. **Open:** All year. **Site Assignment:** First come, first served; no reservations. **Registration:** Attendant or at site. **Fee:** $17 water & electric, $11 tent; prices for 2 people, $0.50 per additional person; senior discounts (cash, personal check). **Parking:** At site.

FACILITIES

Number of RV Sites: 0. **Number of Tent-Only Sites:** 27 (22 primitive). **Number of Multipurpose Sites:** 89. **Hookups:** Water, electric (30, 50 amps). **Each Site:** Picnic table, ground grill. **Dump Station:** Yes. **Laundry:** No. **Pay Phone:** Yes. **Rest Rooms and Showers:** Yes. **Fuel:** No. **Propane:** No. **Internal Roads:** Paved. **RV Service:** 35 mi. in Nashville. **Market:** Within 5 mi. **Restaurant:** Park Restaurant (may close winter), 6 mi. in Dickson. **General Store:** 8 mi. in Dickson or White Bluff. **Vending:** Yes. **Swimming Pool:** No. **Playground:** Yes. **Other:** Boat ramp (electric trolling motors only), conference center, picnic areas & pavilions. **Activities:** Lake swimming, fishing boat & canoe rentals (summer), 18-hole golf course, hiking trails including overnight back-country camping w/ permit, bicycling (on Park roads), tennis, basketball, croquet, shuffleboard, volleyball, ball fields, planned activities (summer). **Nearby Attractions:** Historic Franklin, Harpeth River, Country Music Hall of Fame, Grand Ole Opry, Opryland Hotel, The Parthenon, Hermitage Andrew Jackson Home, Belle Meade Plantation, Vanderbilt University. **Additional Information:** Nashville Tourism information, (615) 259-4700.

RESTRICTIONS

Pets: On leash only. **Fires:** Allowed, ground grills only. **Alcoholic Beverages:** Not allowed. **Vehicle Maximum Length:** 35–40 ft. (sites vary). **Other:** 14-day stay limit, no skateboards or rollerblades, under 13 years of age helmet required on bicycle.

TO GET THERE

From Nashville, take I-40 west 20 mi. to Exit 182. Drive 8 mi. northwest on State Hwy. 96 and turn right on State Hwy. 70. Drive 5 mi. to the park entrance on the right. From the west, take I-40 Exit 172. Drive north on State Hwy. 46 approximately 2 mi. until it intersects with Hwy. 70.

CARYVILLE
Cove Lake State Park

110 Cove Lake Ln., Caryville 37714. T: (423) 566-9701.

🚐 ★★★	▲ ★★★
Beauty: ★★★	Site Privacy: ★★★
Spaciousness: ★★★	Quiet: ★★★
Security: ★★★	Cleanliness: ★★★
Insect Control: ★★★	Facilities: ★★★★

Cove Lake offers nice facilities, including an Olympic-sized swimming pool and separate kiddie pool. Supporting bass, bluegill, and other species, 210-acre Cove Lake is available for bank or row-boat fishing. Hundreds of Canada Geese make Cove Lake their winter home. The campground includes some pretty lake front sites. Unfortunately, these sites have sloped parking spaces and are best for tent campers. Sites are on the small side of average, with little privacy. What's more, this campground is extremely popular. We felt claustrophobic. Sites have gravel, back-in parking. Tree cover ranges from totally shady to totally open. For RVs we recommend the large sites 23, 25, 54, 56, 57, and 59. Security is fine here, with 24-hour patrols. Cold weather aficionados should visit in the winter when hundreds of Canada Geese make Cove Lake their home. Others should visit in spring or fall to avoid the folks that flock here in the summer.

BASICS

Operated By: Tennessee State Parks. **Open:** 7 days a week, all year. **Site Assignment:** No reservations accepted, first come, first served. **Registra-**

tion: Campground office. **Fee:** $14–$17, cash or personal check only. **Parking:** 2 vehicles per site, plus an additional parking lot.

FACILITIES

Number of RV Sites: 0. **Number of Tent-Only Sites:** 4. **Number of Multipurpose Sites:** 100. **Hookups:** Electric (30 amps) & water (except in the winter). **Each Site:** Picnic table, grill. **Dump Station:** Yes. **Laundry:** No. **Pay Phone:** Yes. **Rest Rooms and Showers:** Yes. **Fuel:** No. **Propane:** No. **Internal Roads:** Paved. **RV Service:** 40 mi. south in Knoxville. **Market:** Less than 1 mi. **Restaurant:** At park. **General Store:** Less than 1 mi. **Vending:** Yes. **Swimming Pool:** Yes. **Playground:** Yes. **Other:** Softball field, basketball half-court, tennis courts, paved walking & bicycling trail, indoor pavilion w/ kitchen, picnic tables & pavilions, pool concession stand, pool bathhouse. **Activities:** Ranger programs, bank fishing, volleyball, tennis, basketball, softball, horseshoes, row boat & paddle boat rental, badminton, shuffleboard, ping pong. **Nearby Attractions:** Smoky Mountains, Pigeon Forge, Dollywood, Cumberland Gap National Park. **Additional Information:** Campbell County Chamber of Commerce, (423) 566-0329.

RESTRICTIONS

Pets: On leash only. **Fires:** At sites only. **Alcoholic Beverages:** Not allowed. **Vehicle Maximum Length:** No limit. **Other:** No guns allowed on property.

TO GET THERE

From I-75 take Exit 132, travel east on 25 West, go through the traffic light and the next left is the park's entrance.

CHATTANOOGA
Harrison Bay State Park

8411 Harrison Bay Rd., Harrison 37341. T: (423) 344-2272; F: (423) 344-6061; www.tnstateparks.com.

🚐 ★★★★★	▲ ★★★★★
Beauty: ★★★★★	Site Privacy: ★★★★
Spaciousness: ★★★★★	Quiet: ★★★★
Security: ★★★★	Cleanliness: ★★★★
Insect Control: ★★★★	Facilities: ★★★★★

Attractive Harrison Bay, situated on Chickamauga Lake, offers some of the finest fishing facilities in the state. The Lake supports largemouth bass, crappie, bream, striped bass, and catfish. Other recreation amenities include a swimming pool and separate children's pool. There are four camping areas. We recommend areas A and C, which offer lakefront camping. Although the waterfront sites are gorgeous, they tend to be smaller than inland sites. Luckily, all sites are spacious, but some are huge. The campgrounds are shaded by various tree species, including white oak, maple, hickory, and pine. Privacy varies from site to site. Parking is on gravel and usually back-in style. Area B contains some pull-through sites. Security is excellent at this rural park. Gates close at 10 p.m., and there is a night watchman. Visit in spring or fall for the nicest weather. Avoid the park on holiday weekends.

BASICS

Operated By: Tennessee State Parks. **Open:** All year (closed Monday & Tuesday indefinitely due to budget constraints). **Site Assignment:** First come, first served; no reservations. **Registration:** Camp store in-season, park personnel makes rounds. **Fee:** $10.50–$18 RV, $6.50 tent; prices for 2 people, $0.50 per additional person (cash, personal checks; credit cards accepted at camp store, summer only). **Parking:** At site (2 cars), in parking lot.

FACILITIES

Number of RV Sites: 0. **Number of Tent-Only Sites:** 28. **Number of Multipurpose Sites:** 135. **Hookups:** Water, electric (30 amps). **Each Site:** Picnic table, fire ring. **Dump Station:** Yes. **Laundry:** No. **Pay Phone:** Yes. **Rest Rooms and Showers:** Yes. **Fuel:** No (boat fuel at marina). **Propane:** No. **Internal Roads:** Paved. **RV Service:** 3 mi. south on Hwy. 58. **Market:** 3 mi. north on Hwy. 58. **Restaurant:** Park restaurant (seasonal), 3 mi. on Hwy. 58. **General Store:** Camp store (seasonal), 6 mi. in Chattanooga. **Vending:** Yes. **Swimming Pool:** Inquire at campground. **Playground:** Yes. **Other:** Recreation hall, marina (w/ boat fuel), boat launch, boat slips, children's pool, picnic area & shelters. **Activities:** Golf, fishing, boat rentals, hiking & bicycle trails, nature trail, ball field, badminton, tennis, volleyball, horseshoes, summer programs & entertainment. **Nearby Attractions:** Chattanooga Choo-Choo, Railroad Museum, Tennessee Aquarium, Lookout Mountain, Ruby Falls, Rock City, Incline Railway, Booker T. Washington State Park, Walnut St. Bridge, Chickamauga Battlefield. **Additional Information:** Chattanooga Area CVB, (800) 322-3344 or (423) 756-8687, www.chattanoogafun.com.

RESTRICTIONS

Pets: On leash only. **Fires:** Allowed, fire ring only. **Alcoholic Beverages:** Not allowed. **Vehicle Maximum Length:** No limit. **Other:** 4-week stay limit, firearms, & metal detectors prohibited.

TO GET THERE

From Chattanooga, take Exit 4 off I-75 onto State Rte. 153. Drive north on 153 to the sixth exit and turn north onto State Hwy. 58. Drive 12 mi. to Harrison Bay Rd. and turn left. The park entrance is 1 mi. ahead on the left.

CHATTANOOGA

Holiday Trav-L-Park of Chattanooga

1709 Mack Smith Rd., Chattanooga 37412. T: (706) 891-9766 or (800) 693-2877 for reservations; www.chattacamp.com.

🚐 ★★★	🔺 ★★★
Beauty: ★★★	Site Privacy: ★★
Spaciousness: ★★	Quiet: ★★★★
Security: ★★★	Cleanliness: ★★★★
Insect Control: ★★★★	Facilities: ★★★

Located on a Civil War Battlefield, this park is home to a monument placed here at war's end by the 84th Indiana Volunteer Regiment to commemorate the valor of their slain comrades. The National Park Service provides a free Civil War video, which can be viewed in the campground's lobby. Best Holiday Trav-L-Park is convenient to Chattanooga attractions, restaurants, and shops. The passably attractive campground is laid out in rows of pull-through sites with gravel parking. Though sites are fairly shady, there is no privacy between sites. Sites are on the small side of average. The shadiest sites are 109, 116, 117, 122, and 134. Sites 1–15 are closest to the pool and recreation room. Security is fair at this suburban park. There are no gates, but the neighborhood is fine. Avoid Chattanooga on autumn weekends.

BASICS

Operated By: Green Acres of America, a Limited Partnership. **Open:** All year. **Site Assignment:** First come, first served; reservations accepted w/ credit card deposit; 24-hour cancellation notice required to avoid a charge. **Registration:** Store, night self-registration, or next morning. **Fee:** $23 RV, $21 tent w/ water & electric, $17 tent no hookup; fees for 2 people, $2 charge for each additional person over age 6, cable hookup or 50 amp service (cash, personal check, V, MC). **Parking:** At site, in parking lot.

FACILITIES

Number of RV Sites: 0. **Number of Tent-Only Sites:** 18 primitive. **Number of Multipurpose Sites:** 163. **Hookups:** Water, electric (30, 50 amps), most sites have sewer, cable TV. **Each Site:** Picnic table, fire ring (primitive sites have grill & tent pad). **Dump Station:** Yes. **Laundry:** Yes. **Pay Phone:** Yes. **Rest Rooms and Showers:** Yes. **Fuel:** No. **Propane:** Yes. **Internal Roads:** Paved & gravel. **RV Service:** Chattanooga. **Market:** 2 mi. (also camp store on-site). **Restaurant:** 0.5 mi. **General Store:** 4 mi. to Wal-Mart. **Vending:** Yes. **Swimming Pool:** Yes. **Playground:** Yes. **Other:** Arcade, pavilion. **Activities:** Civil War Battlefield & monument, covered wagon rides, basketball, badminton, horseshoes, summer activities. **Nearby Attractions:** River cruises, Chattanooga Choo-Choo, Tennessee Aquarium, Rock City, Ruby Falls, Incline Railway, Walnut St. Bridge, Chickamauga Battlefield, Booker T. Washington State Park. **Additional Information:** Chattanooga Area CVB, (800) 322-3344 or (423) 756-8687, www.chattanoogafun.com.

RESTRICTIONS

Pets: Leash only. **Fires:** Grills & fire rings only. **Alcoholic Beverages:** At site only. **Vehicle Maximum Length:** 70 ft.

TO GET THERE

From I-75 southbound, take Tennessee Exit 1. From Northbound I-75, take Tennessee Exit 1B. Either way, turn right at the top of the ramp, then left on Mack Smith Rd. The campground is 0.5 mi. from the interstate.

COSBY

Cosby Campground, Great Smoky Mountains National Park

107 Park Headquarters Rd., Gatlinburg 37738. T: (865) 436-1200; F: (865) 436-1204; www.nps.gov/grsm.

🚐 ★★★★	🔺 ★★★★★
Beauty: ★★★★★	Site Privacy: ★★★★
Spaciousness: ★★★★	Quiet: ★★★★
Security: ★★★★	Cleanliness: ★★★
Insect Control: ★★★★	Facilities: ★★★★

Faithful fans laud Cosby as the best kept secret in Great Smoky Mountains National Park. Cosby is rarely crowded, which makes it a fine destination for a summer weekend. The cool mountain air is always refreshing in late summer. Many of the hiking trails emanating from Cosby lead to picturesque waterfalls. The town of Cosby is rich in local lore—it was once considered the "moonshine capitol of the world." This gorgeous campground is designed primarily for tent campers, although many sites accommodate RVs. Site size ranges from large to huge. Sites are found in two sections built into a terraced mountainside. Thick woods shade the sites and provide some privacy between sites. Parking is back-in style, on gravel. Sites at the end of the loops are often more private. Security is fine at Cosby; there are no gates, but the campground is very remote.

BASICS

Operated By: National Park Service. **Open:** Mid-Mar.–Oct. **Site Assignment:** First come, first served; no reservations accepted. **Registration:** Self-register. **Fee:** $14 for 6 people max. per site, 2 tents or 1 RV & 1 tent (cash). **Parking:** At site (2 vehicles).

FACILITIES

Number of Multipurpose Sites: 163. **Hookups:** None. **Each Site:** Picnic table, fire ring, grill, tent pad. **Dump Station:** Yes. **Laundry:** No. **Pay Phone:** Yes. **Rest Rooms and Showers:** Rest rooms, No showers. **Fuel:** No. **Propane:** No. **Internal Roads:** Paved. **RV Service:** 20 mi. in Newport. **Market:** 20 mi. in Newport. **Restaurant:** 3 mi. in Cosby. **General Store:** 20 mi. in Newport. **Vending:** No. **Swimming Pool:** No. **Playground:** No. **Other:** Amphitheater, picnic area, horse trail, interpretive trail. **Activities:** Hiking, fishing, horseback riding, canoeing, backcountry hiking, ranger programs (seasonal). **Nearby Attractions:** Golf courses, Cades Cove, Pigeon Forge, Dollywood, Gatlinburg, whitewater rafting, Cherokee Indian Reservation. **Additional Information:** Gatlinburg Dept. of Tourism, (800) 343-1475; Park Information, (865) 436-1200.

RESTRICTIONS

Pets: 6-ft. leash only. **Fires:** Allowed, fire rings only. **Alcoholic Beverages:** Allowed. **Vehicle Maximum Length:** 25 ft.

TO GET THERE

From US Hwy. 321 at Cosby, drive south 2 mi. and stay southeast on State Hwy. 32 another 2 mi. Stay right and continue approximately 3 mi. to the campground.

COUNCE

TVA Pickwick Dam Campground

Park Rd., Pickwick Dam. T: (256) 386-2228; F: (256) 386-2954; www.tva.gov.

🚐 ★★★★   ▲ ★★★★

Beauty: ★★★★★   Site Privacy: ★★★
Spaciousness: ★★★★   Quiet: ★★★★
Security: ★★★   Cleanliness: ★★★★
Insect Control: ★★★★   Facilities: ★★

When we compare it to the campground at neighboring Pickwick Landing State Park, we prefer the campground at Pickwick Dam because it's enveloped in a gorgeous stand of southern pine. Although the campground is situated parallel to the Tennessee River, sites don't have water views. We recommend the quiet sites in the back of the campground, next to a lovely forest. The campground is completely flat and offers back-in parking on dilapidated gravel. Sites are larger than average. Without undergrowth, there are few privacy barriers between sites. The TVA provides little recreation, but Pickwick Landing State Park offers excellent amenities, including an 18-hole golf course and a restaurant. Pickwick Landing also provides access to mammoth Pickwick Lake and excellent fishing amenities. Fishermen catch bass, bream, catfish, crappie, and sauger. The TVA campground is popular. Avoid visiting on summer weekends. Security is marginal; there is no fence around the campground, but it's in a fairly remote area.

BASICS

Operated By: Tennessee Valley Authority. **Open:** All year. **Site Assignment:** First come, first served; no reservations accepted. **Registration:** Self-registration honor system. **Fee:** $15 hookups, $11 tents; prices for 10 people max., 1 RV; Golden Age & Golden Access discounts honored. **Parking:** At sites (3 vehicles).

FACILITIES

Number of Multipurpose Sites: 88. **Hookups:** 66 sites w/ water, electric (50 amps). **Each Site:** Picnic table, grill, lantern pole, some fire rings. **Dump Station:** Yes. **Laundry:** No. **Pay Phone:** No. **Rest Rooms and Showers:** Yes. **Fuel:** No. **Propane:** No. **Internal Roads:** Paved. **RV Service:** 30 mi. in Burnsville, MS. **Market:** 5 mi. in Counce. **Restaurant:** 2 mi. in Pickwick Landing State Park. **General Store:** Hardware 3 mi. in Counce. **Vending:** No. **Swimming Pool:** No. **Playground:** No. **Activities:** Volleyball, horseshoes, fishing, waterfront walking & biking; water too swift for water sports at campground, 200 yards to activities at Pickwick Landing State Park above the dam. **Nearby Attractions:** Pickwick Landing State Park, Big Hill Pond State Natural Area, Shiloh National Military Park, Corinth National Cemetery & historic district, Tennessee River Museum, historic Savannah, historic Saltillo. **Additional Information:** Savannah/Hardin County CVB, (731) 925-2364.

RESTRICTIONS

Pets: 6-ft. leash max. **Fires:** Allowed. **Alcoholic Beverages:** Not allowed. **Vehicle Maximum Length:** No limit.

TO GET THERE

From Jackson, drive approximately 40 mi. south on US Hwy. 45. Drive 21 mi. east on US Hwy. 64 to Savannah, then 10 mi. south on State Hwy. 128. Turn right at the campground (200 yards before reaching the dam).

CROSSVILLE

Bean Pot Campground

23 Bean Pot Campground Loop, Crossville 38558. T: (931) 484-7671; F: (931) 707-8399; peecehven97 @multipro.com.

🚐 ★★★   ▲ ★★★

Beauty: ★★★★   Site Privacy: ★★★
Spaciousness: ★★★   Quiet: ★★★★
Security: ★★★   Cleanliness: ★★★★
Insect Control: ★★★   Facilities: ★★★

This pleasant campground offers comfortably spaced sites and decent amenities. Bean Pot is convenient to I-40 and Crossville restaurants and shopping. The historic town of Rugby is nearby. Or trek to one of the area's popular waterfalls. Campsites are laid out in five rows of pull-throughs (full hookups), plus one row of back-in sites (water only). Sites are all the same size. Some are more level or shadier than others.

All sites have gravel parking and concrete patios. The nicest sites, 5–8 and 14–18, are shady pull-throughs in the back of the park. However, families may prefer sites closer to the pool and game room in the front of the park. Security is fair. There are no gates, but the campground is not visible from the main road. Make advance reservations if you want to visit on the weekend of the world's largest yard sale (mid-Aug.), when Crossville is very congested.

BASICS

Operated By: Jim & Ghislaine Gallagher. **Open:** All year. **Site Assignment:** First come, first served; reservations accepted w/ first-night deposit; cancellation by noon of arrival date for refund. **Registration:** Office, after-hours registration also. **Fee:** $19 full hookup, $18 water & electric, $15 tent; prices for 2 people, $2 per additional adult, $1 child (cash, personal check, V, MC). **Parking:** At site (2 cars), in parking lot.

FACILITIES

Number of RV Sites: 51. **Number of Tent-Only Sites:** 10. **Number of Multipurpose Sites:** 10. **Hookups:** Water, electric (20, 30, 50 amps). **Each Site:** Picnic table, some grills, some fire rings. **Dump Station:** Yes. **Laundry:** Yes. **Pay Phone:** Yes. **Rest Rooms and Showers:** Yes. **Fuel:** No. **Propane:** Yes. **Internal Roads:** Gravel & paved. **RV Service:** 6 mi. in Crossville. **Market:** 6 mi. in Crossville. **Restaurant:** 1.5 mi. in Crossville. **General Store:** Convenience store on-site, 6 mi. in Crossville. **Vending:** Yes. **Swimming Pool:** Yes. **Playground:** Yes. **Other:** Clubhouse, game room, RV storage. **Activities:** Nature trail, putting green, horseshoes, basketball. **Nearby Attractions:** Golf ("Golf Capital of Tennessee"), antique shopping, Historic Oak Ridge, Ozone, Fall Creek & Burgess Falls, Muddy Pond Mennonite Community, wineries. **Additional Information:** Crossville Chamber of Commerce, (931) 484-8444.

RESTRICTIONS

Pets: On leash only. **Fires:** Allowed in designated areas only. **Alcoholic Beverages:** Allowed at sites only. **Vehicle Maximum Length:** 45 ft.

TO GET THERE

From I-40, take Exit 322. Drive north 1.5 mi. on Peavine Rd./State Hwy. 101. Turn right on Bean Pot Campground Rd. The campground is 0.25 mi. ahead on the left.

CROSSVILLE
Cumberland Mountain State Park

24 Office Dr., Crossville 38555. T: (931) 484-6138 or (800) 250-8618; F: (615) 741-1421; www.tnstateparks.com.

🚐 ★★★★　　　　　🅰 ★★★★

Beauty: ★★★★	Site Privacy: ★★★
Spaciousness: ★★★★	Quiet: ★★★★
Security: ★★★★★	Cleanliness: ★★★★
Insect Control: ★★★★	Facilities: ★★★★★

Cumberland Mountain is home to the largest masonry structure built by the Civilian Conservation Corps, a lovely dam and bridge made of indigenous Crab Orchard stone (a type of sandstone). The park's restaurant offers picturesque lake views. On site, Bear Trace golf course was designed by Jack Nicklaus. Shore fishing on the small lake yields catfish, bass, brim, and bluegill. Unfortunately, the campground is not the most attractive area of the park. It's laid out in a series of loops with some extremely spacious sites. Other sites are average sized. Most sites are nicely shaded, although there is little foliage to provide privacy between sites. Parking is paved, back-in style. For privacy, try sites 11, 30, or 31. The park is in the small town of Crossville. Nonetheless, security is excellent; gates close at night and rangers patrol until midnight. Visit in the spring, early summer, or fall to avoid heat and humidity.

BASICS

Operated By: Tennessee State Parks. **Open:** All year (closed Monday & Tuesday indefinitely). **Site Assignment:** First come, first served; no reservations accepted. **Registration:** Camp store, ranger makes rounds at night. **Fee:** $17 for 2 people, $0.50 per additional person; senior & disabled discounts available (cash, personal checks, V, MC, D, AE). **Parking:** At site (2 vehicles).

FACILITIES

Number of Multipurpose Sites: 142. **Hookups:** Water, electric (30 amps). **Each Site:** Picnic table, grill, some sites w/ lantern pole, fire ring & small gravel pad. **Dump Station:** Yes. **Laundry:** No. **Pay Phone:** Yes. **Rest Rooms and Showers:** Yes. **Fuel:** No. **Propane:** No. **Internal Roads:** Paved. **RV Service:** 4 mi. in Crossville. **Market:** 4 mi. in Crossville. **Restaurant:** Park restaurant (seasonal), several restaurants within 5 mi. **General Store:**

Camp store, 4 mi. in Crossville. **Vending:** Yes. **Swimming Pool:** Yes. **Playground:** Yes. **Other:** Boat house, recreation lodge, picnic area. **Activities:** 18-hole golf course, ball field, tennis, volleyball, rowboat, paddleboat, & canoe rentals (no private boats), hiking & nature trails, basketball, horseshoes, summer naturalist programs. **Nearby Attractions:** Cumberland Homestead Tower Center & Museum, Crossville ("Golf Capitol of Tennessee"), Palace Theater, Chestnut Hill, Highland Manor & Stonehaus Wineries, Bledsoe & Mount Roosevelt State Forests. **Additional Information:** Crossville Chamber of Commerce, (931) 484-8444.

RESTRICTIONS

Pets: On leash & kept quiet. **Fires:** Allowed, in fire ring only. **Alcoholic Beverages:** Not allowed. **Vehicle Maximum Length:** No limit. **Other:** 14-day stay limit (except designated sites), quiet enforced.

TO GET THERE

From I-40 (70 mi. west of Knoxville and 100 mi. east of Nashville), take Exit 317 at Crossville. Drive south 8 mi. on US Hwy. 127. The park entrance is on the right (west).

DOVER

Piney Campground, Land Between the Lakes

100 Van Morgan Dr., Golden Pond 42211. T: (270) 924-2000; F: (270) 924-2087; www.lbl.org.

🚐 ★★★★   ▲ ★★★★

Beauty: ★★★★★	Site Privacy: ★★★
Spaciousness: ★★★★	Quiet: ★★★
Security: ★★★★★	Cleanliness: ★★★★★
Insect Control: ★★★★	Facilities: ★★★★★

Land Between the Lakes, administered by the US Department of Agriculture, offers interesting activities, including hundreds of miles of hiking, canoeing, and mountain biking trails. Other unique facilities include the planetarium and observatory (call for schedule), a nineteenth century Farm, and an elk and bison prairie. There are three multipurpose campgrounds. Piney, located at the south end of the recreation area, offers eight camping loops. Though most sites are larger than average, size varies. Lovely trees, including loblolly and shortleaf pine, shade the campgrounds. There is little foliage between sites. Most sites offer pea gravel, back-in parking. At Black Oak Loop, sites 14, 23–26, 30, and 32 are fabulous, with gorgeous views of Kentucky Lake. Tent campers should head for waterfront sites on the nearly deserted Virginia and Sweet gum loops (non-electric). Extremely remote and gated, Piney is very safe. Avoid this area on summer weekends and holidays. For solitude, plan a late spring or early fall visit.

BASICS

Operated By: USDA Forest Service. **Open:** Mar. 1–Nov. 30. **Site Assignment:** First come, first served; no reservations. **Registration:** Gatehouse, campground entrance. **Fee:** $19 full hookup, $15 water & electric, $12 tent; prices for 8 people; Golden Age & Golden Access discounts available (cash, personal check, V, MC, D, AE). **Parking:** At site (2 vehicles plus camping unit, $4 per additional vehicle).

FACILITIES

Number of RV Sites: 44. **Number of Tent-Only Sites:** 59 primitive. **Number of Multipurpose Sites:** 281. **Hookups:** Water, electric (20, 30 amps). **Each Site:** Picnic table, fire ring, tent pad, lantern pole in primitive area. **Dump Station:** Yes. **Laundry:** Yes. **Pay Phone:** Yes. **Rest Rooms and Showers:** Yes. **Fuel:** No. **Propane:** No. **Internal Roads:** Asphalt gravel. **RV Service:** 25 mi. in Dover. **Market:** 8 mi. in Dover. **Restaurant:** 4 mi. in Dover. **General Store:** camp store, also 8 mi. in Dover. **Vending:** Yes. **Swimming Pool:** No. **Playground:** Yes. **Other:** Elk & Bison prairie, visitor canter, planetarium, The Homeplace-1850, nature center, campfire theater, boat ramps, fishing pier. **Activities:** Swimming beach, fishing, archery range, ball field, bicycle trails, mountain biking trails, equestrian trails, canoeing, hiking trails, softball, volleyball, basketball, summer recreation programs. **Nearby Attractions:** Kentucky Lake, Fort Donelson National Battlefield, Paris Landing State Resort Park, Cross Creek Wildlife Refuge. **Additional Information:** Clarksville Chamber of Commerce, (931) 647-2331; Stewart County Chamber of Commerce, (931) 232-8290; Land Between the Lakes Information, (800) LBL-7077.

RESTRICTIONS

Pets: On leash only. **Fires:** Allowed, fire rings only. **Alcoholic Beverages:** Allowed, sites only. **Vehicle Maximum Length:** No limit. **Other:** 21-day stay limit.

To Get There

From I-24, take TN Exit 4. Drive west on Hwy. 79 for 26 mi. Go through the town of Dover and drive west for 8 more mi. Turn right onto CR 100 and drive north for 4 mi. (When you enter Land between the Lakes, CR 100 turns into The Trace.) Turn left onto Fort Henry Rd. The campground is 8 mi. ahead. From the north, take I-24 to KY Exit 31. Drive south on The Trace 35 mi. to Fort Henry Rd. Turn right and drive west for 8 mi. to Piney Campground.

EVA

Nathan Bedford Forrest State Park

1825 Pilot Knob Rd., Eva 38333. T: (731) 584-1841; F: (731) 584-1841; www.tnstateparks.com.

🚐 ★★★★	▲ ★★★★
Beauty: ★★★★	Site Privacy: ★★★
Spaciousness: ★★★★	Quiet: ★★★★
Security: ★★★	Cleanliness: ★★★★
Insect Control: ★★	Facilities: ★★★★

Located at the southern end of Kentucky Lake, attractive Nathan Bedford Forrest State Park offers limited recreation. Recreation within the park includes a ten-mile hiking trail. Off property, there are marinas and public boat ramps, which provide access to Kentucky Lake, known for its sauger, crappie, bream, catfish, and various bass populations. The Happy Hollow camping loop includes various sized sites under a shady cover of white and red oak, maple, cedar, sycamore, sweetgum and hackberry. However, there is little foliage between sites to provide privacy. Parking is paved, back-in style. The nicest sites, 1, 3, 5, 23, 24, and 31–35, abut the woods in the back of the campground. There are no gates at Nathan Bedford Forrest. However, the park is extremely remote, making security fair. Avoid this part of Tennessee in late summer when the weather tends to extremes of heat and humidity.

Basics

Operated By: Tennessee State Parks. **Open:** All year. **Site Assignment:** First come, first served; no reservations accepted. **Registration:** Park office or ranger makes rounds. **Fee:** $17 RV, $14 developed tent, $10 primitive; prices for 2 people, $0.50 per additional person; senior & disabled discounts available (cash, personal checks). **Parking:** At sites in designated areas only.

Facilities

Number of RV Sites: 0. **Number of Tent-Only Sites:** 13 primitive. **Number of Multipurpose Sites:** 38. **Hookups:** Water, electric (20, 30, 50 amps). **Each Site:** Picnic table, grill, concrete pad. **Dump Station:** Yes. **Laundry:** No. **Pay Phone:** Yes. **Rest Rooms and Showers:** Yes. **Fuel:** No. **Propane:** No. **Internal Roads:** Paved. **RV Service:** Local service. **Market:** 3 mi. in Eva. **Restaurant:** 8 mi. in Camden. **General Store:** 8 mi. in Camden. **Vending:** Beverages only. **Swimming Pool:** No. **Playground:** Yes. **Other:** Boat launch, folk-life museum, picnic areas, & pavilions. **Activities:** Beach swimming in designated areas, fishing, skiing, hiking trails, backpacking, softball, horseshoes, volleyball, ball field, planned programs, managed hunts. **Nearby Attractions:** Paris Landing & Natchez Trace State Parks, Fort Donelson National Historic Site, Lorretta Lynn's Dude Ranch. **Additional Information:** Camden Chamber of Commerce, (731) 584-8395.

Restrictions

Pets: On leash only. **Fires:** Allowed (subject to burn ban). **Alcoholic Beverages:** Not allowed. **Vehicle Maximum Length:** 30 ft. **Other:** No firearms.

To Get There

From Nashville, drive west on I-40 and take Exit 126. Drive north approximately 15 mi. on US Hwy. 641 straight through the by-pass. Continue 2 mi. and turn right onto Main St. Drive through town to Court Square and turn right on Local Rte. 191. This dead-ends in 9 mi. at the park.

GATLINBURG

Elkmont Campground, Great Smoky Mountains National Park

107 Park Headquarters Rd., Gatlinburg 37738. T: (865) 436-1200; F: (865) 436-1204; www.nps.gov.

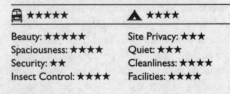

🚐 ★★★★★	▲ ★★★★
Beauty: ★★★★★	Site Privacy: ★★★
Spaciousness: ★★★★	Quiet: ★★★
Security: ★★	Cleanliness: ★★★★
Insect Control: ★★★★	Facilities: ★★★★

Of the Great Smoky Mountains National Park campgrounds, Elkmont is the closest to the tourist attractions at Gatlinburg and Pigeon Forge and the park's Sugarland visitor's center. This campground stays busy all summer, and should be completely avoided on summer holidays. We recommend Elkmont in the spring, when crowds are minimal and wildflowers are blooming. The campground is laid out in a series of loops that are sandwiched together. Though site size is above average, the campground is often so packed with people that you may feel cramped. Shade is provided by a variety of trees, with a little foliage to provide privacy between sites. Sites offer back-in, gravel parking. For peace and quiet, we prefer sections G, H, K, L, M, and N. Security is poor at Elkmont; there are no gates. Safeguard your valuables. Also, mosquitoes can be a nuisance in late summer—bring insect repellent.

BASICS

Operated By: National Park Service. **Open:** Mid-Mar.–Nov. **Site Assignment:** First come, first served; reservations accepted for May 15–Oct. 31 up to 5 months in advance, w/ full deposit; $13.25 cancellation fee w/ at least 24-hour notice, otherwise first night plus fee charged; reservations made by calling (800) 365-CAMP or at reservations.nps.gov (personal check, money order, V, D, MC). **Registration:** Self-registration. **Fee:** $14–$20 for 6 people max. per site, 2 tents or 1 tent & 1 RV; Golden Age & Golden Access discounts available (cash only during self–registration off-Season). **Parking:** At site (2 vehicles).

FACILITIES

Number of RV Sites: 0. **Number of Tent-Only Sites:** 5. **Number of Multipurpose Sites:** 220. **Hookups:** None. **Each Site:** Picnic table, fire ring, grill, gravel tent pad. **Dump Station:** Yes. **Laundry:** No. **Pay Phone:** Yes. **Rest Rooms and Showers:** Rest rooms, no showers. **Fuel:** No. **Propane:** No. **Internal Roads:** Paved. **RV Service:** 10 mi. in Gatlinburg. **Market:** 10 mi. in Gatlinburg. **Restaurant:** 10 mi. in Gatlinburg. **General Store:** 10 mi. in Gatlinburg. **Vending:** No. **Swimming Pool:** No. **Playground:** No. **Other:** Amphitheater, picnic areas, horse trails, interpretive trails. **Activities:** Hiking, fishing, horseback riding, canoeing, backcountry hiking, ranger programs (seasonal). **Nearby Attractions:** Golf courses, Cades Cove, Pigeon Forge, Dollywood, Gatlinburg, white-water rafting, Cherokee Indian Reservation. **Additional Information:** Pigeon Forge Visitor information, (865) 453-5700; Park Information, (865) 436-1200.

RESTRICTIONS

Pets: 6-ft. leash only. **Fires:** Allowed, fire rings only. **Alcoholic Beverages:** Allowed. **Vehicle Maximum Length:** 32 ft.

TO GET THERE

From Gatlinburg drive approximately 6 mi. southwest on Little River Rd. Elkmont Campground is 1 mi. south (left) off Little River Rd.

GATLINBURG

Outdoor Resorts of America

4229 Parkway East, Gatlinburg 37738. T: (865) 436-5861 or (800) 677-5861; www.gocampingamerica.com/orgatlinburg.

🚐 ★★★★★	🏕 n/a
Beauty: ★★★★★	Site Privacy: ★★★
Spaciousness: ★★★★	Quiet: ★★★★★
Security: ★★★★★	Cleanliness: ★★★★★
Insect Control: ★★★★	Facilities: ★★★★

One of the prettiest campgrounds in Gatlinburg, Outdoor Resorts offers extremely well kept recreational facilities. Children enjoy the playground, pool, and mini-golf. Adults appreciate the carefully manicured landscaping, which includes shady weeping willow trees. The campground has two areas separated by the main road. Two creeks flow through the park, lulling campers with their soft bubbling sound. The park would be very quiet in any event—most of the spots are occupied by long-term rentals. RV sites are large, with shrubs and trees providing privacy between many. All parking is paved, back-in style. Each site has a bit of grass and a concrete patio. Ask for a creek-side site. Security is excellent; the gate is locked 24-hours a day. Gatlinburg is extremely pleasant in late summer due to its high elevation. Visit on weekdays for fall "leaf peeping"—weekend crowds are unbearable.

BASICS

Operated By: Outdoor Resorts. **Open:** 7 days, all year. **Site Assignment:** Pick your site; reserve from Jan. 1; $35 deposit holds reservation (pay by check or credit card); cancel 3 days in advance for full refund. **Registration:** At camp office. **Fee:** $30 interior, $35 waterfront, fees include 4 people (cash, check, MC, V). **Parking:** At sites.

FACILITIES

Number of RV Sites: 376. **Number of Tent-Only Sites:** 0. **Hookups:** Water, electric, cable, sewer. **Each Site:** Picnic table, fire ring (most), concrete pad. **Dump Station:** No. **Laundry:** Yes. **Pay Phone:** Yes. **Rest Rooms and Showers:** Yes. **Fuel:** No. **Propane:** Yes. **Internal Roads:** Paved. **RV Service:** Yes. **Market:** 7 mi. west in Gatlinburg. **Restaurant:** On site, in season. **General Store:** 2.5 mi. east. **Vending:** Beverages only. **Swimming Pool:** Yes. **Playground:** Yes. **Other:** Game room & lodge. **Activities:** Fishing lake, trout streams, tennis, shuffleboard, mini-golf, horseshoes, volleyball, church service in-season. **Nearby Attractions:** Gatlinburg attractions, Pigeon Forge attractions, Dollywood, Great Smoky Mountains National Park. **Additional Information:** Pigeon Forge Dept. of Tourism, (800) 251-9100.

RESTRICTIONS

Pets: On leash only. **Fires:** Fire rings only. **Alcoholic Beverages:** Not allowed. **Vehicle Maximum Length:** 40 ft.

TO GET THERE

From I-40, take Exit 440 (Hwy. 321 South). Go south for 7 mi. and turn right before the post office. The entrance is 6.5 mi. ahead on the right.

GATLINBURG

Twin Creek RV Resort

1202 East Parkway, Gatlinburg 37738. T: (865) 436-7081 or (800) 252-8077; F: (865) 430-5742; www.twincreekrvresort.com.

🚐 ★★★★   ▲ n/a

Beauty: ★★★★	Site Privacy: ★★★
Spaciousness: ★★★	Quiet: ★★★
Security: ★★★	Cleanliness: ★★★★★
Insect Control: ★★★★	Facilities: ★★★

Though it's only two miles from downtown Gatlinburg, Twin Creek feels secluded. Built in a picturesque valley, the campground is nicely landscaped and extremely tidy. The pool, whirlpool, and other facilities are in good condition. Beautiful trees shade the campground. Site size is average and there is little privacy. All parking is paved. Some sites offer parallel parking while others offer back-in. Each site has a wooden patio. The prettiest sites, 54–56, are along the creek. Gatlinburg roads become very congested on busy weekends, especially in the fall. We recommend weekday visits. If you visit on a weekend, take advantage of the trolley, which stops inside the park, and can take you all the way to outlet malls in Pigeon Forge. With no gates, security is fair.

BASICS

Operated By: Twin Creek RV Resort. **Open:** Apr.–Nov. **Site Assignment:** Sites assigned; reservations recommended, deposit policy varies. **Registration:** Office, night arrival w/ reservation preferred. **Fee:** $35 peak season, prices vary; AAA, AARP, FMCA, Good Sam discounts available (cash, V, MC). **Parking:** At site (1 car, charge may apply for additional vehicles).

FACILITIES

Number of RV Sites: 75. **Number of Tent-Only Sites:** 0. **Number of Multipurpose Sites:** None. **Hookups:** Water, electric (30, 50 amps), sewer, cable. **Each Site:** Picnic table, fire ring, grill. **Dump Station:** No. **Laundry:** Yes. **Pay Phone:** Yes. **Rest Rooms and Showers:** Yes. **Fuel:** No. **Propane:** No. **Internal Roads:** Paved. **RV Service:** Yes. **Market:** Across the street. **Restaurant:** One block. **General Store:** Camp store, hardware 0.25 mi. **Vending:** Beverages only. **Swimming Pool:** Yes (also whirlpool & wading pool). **Playground:** Yes. **Other:** Arcade, boutique. **Activities:** Jacuzzi, children's pool, Sunday worship service. **Nearby Attractions:** Trolley to Pigeon Forge, Dollywood, Gatlinburg attractions, water park, Dixie Stampede, Elvis Museum, Kids Country, helicopter tours, whitewater rafting, Cherokee Indian Reservation. **Additional Information:** Pigeon Forge Visitor information, (865) 453-5700.

RESTRICTIONS

Pets: On leash only. **Fires:** Allowed, fire rings only. **Alcoholic Beverages:** Allowed, at sites only. **Vehicle Maximum Length:** 45 ft. (sites vary). **Other:** Call ahead about pet restrictions, no motorcycles.

TO GET THERE

From Knoxville, Take I-40 east to Exit 407 and drive approximately 20 mi. south on US Hwy. 441. Turn left on US Hwy. 321 at light No. 3 and the campground is 2 mi. on the right. From

Asheville, take I-40 west to Exit 440 and turn south on Hwy. 321. The campground is approximately 25 mi. on the left.

GATLINBURG
Yogi Bear's Jellystone Park

P.O. Box 282, Gatlinburg 37738. T: (423) 487-5534 or (800) 210-2119 for reservations; gatlyogi@bellsouth.net.

🚐 ★★★★   ⛺ ★★★★

Beauty: ★★★★   Site Privacy: ★★★★
Spaciousness: ★★★   Quiet: ★★★
Security: ★★★★   Cleanliness: ★★★
Insect Control: ★★★★   Facilities: ★★★★★

Seasoned camping families know that Yogi Bear campgrounds offer excellent children's recreation. This park is no exception. Facilities are well maintained and activities are well planned. There are separate tent and RV camping areas. RV site size varies, but none are huge. Parking is on gravel. There are back-in and pull-through sites. Most are shady, and the nicest are along the bubbling creek. Creek-side sites 59–61 are small, but extremely pretty, while creek-side sites 41–50 are more spacious, but not as attractive. The largest site (77, a pull-through) is not creekside. Tent sites are pretty and slightly secluded from the RV sites. There are no gates at this small-town campground, but employees are vigilant (we were questioned twice while on property). Security is good. Visit Gatlinburg in August to enjoy the cool mountain air. Avoid fall weekends, when leaf peepers cause legendary traffic jams in small mountain towns.

BASICS
Operated By: Tim Gordon. **Open:** Mid-Mar.–Nov. 1, limited winter camping. **Site Assignment:** Usually assigned at check-in; reserve one year in advance; $50 deposit, refund w/ 7-day notice for cancellation (less $5 administration fee). **Registration:** At camp office. **Fee:** $25 tent (or AAA, Good Sam, Club Yogi), $31 for 2 people. **Parking:** In sites, except some walk-in tent sites.

FACILITIES
Number of RV Sites: 63. **Number of Tent-Only Sites:** 21. **Hookups:** Water, electric, sewer, cable. **Each Site:** Picnic table, fire ring, gravel. **Dump Station:** Yes. **Laundry:** Yes. **Pay Phone:** Yes. **Rest Rooms and Showers:** Yes. **Fuel:** No. **Propane:** No. **Internal Roads:** Gravel. **RV Service:** 30 mi. west in Sevierville. **Market:** 14 mi. east in Newport. **Restaurant:** 1 mi. west in Cosby. **General Store:** Wal-Mart, 30 mi. west in Sevierville. **Vending:** Yes. **Swimming Pool:** Yes. **Playground:** Yes. **Other:** Movie theater, pavilion. **Activities:** Children's Day Camp (in season), mini-golf, game room, swimming, fishing, hiking, basketball, horseshoes, bingo, live entertainment, wagon rides, church services (in-season). **Nearby Attractions:** Great Smoky Mountains National Park, Pigeon Forge, white-water rafting, outlet shopping, Dollywood, museums, caverns. **Additional Information:** Gatlinburg Dept. of Tourism, (800) 343-1475.

RESTRICTIONS
Pets: Not in tent area, no vicious breeds. **Fires:** Fire rings only. **Alcoholic Beverages:** In sites only. **Vehicle Maximum Length:** 40 ft. **Other:** Max. 6 people per site.

TO GET THERE
From I-40, take Exit 435. Turn right onto Hwy. 321 and go southeast approximately 15 mi. Follow Yogi signs, right at 6 mi., left at 0.25 mi., right at 7 mi., then 2.5 mi. The entrance is on the left.

HENDERSON
Chickasaw State Park

20 Cabin Ln., Henderson 38340. T: (731) 989-5141 or (800) 458-1752; F: (731) 989-5966; www.tnstateparks.com.

🚐 ★★★★   ⛺ ★★★★

Beauty: ★★★★★   Site Privacy: ★★★★
Spaciousness: ★★★★   Quiet: ★★★★
Security: ★★★   Cleanliness: ★★★★
Insect Control: ★★★★   Facilities: ★★★★★

Shady tall pines and hardwoods grace the campgrounds at Chickasaw. There are separate campgrounds for RVs, tents, and equestrian use. The RV campground consists of two loops, each with its own bathhouse. Sites are on the large side of average. All parking is paved and there are pull-through and back-in sites. Foliage between some sites provides seclusion. Our favorite RV sites are the 30s and number 40, which is absolutely gorgeous. The small tent campground is nicely wooded with views of picturesque Lake Placid.

With only six sites, the ratio of potties to camp-sites is unusually high. Lake Placid is stocked with bass and bluegill (no personally owned boats allowed). Adjoining the state park, Chicka-saw State Forest contains 50 miles of roads and multi-use trails. There are no gates, but the park is off the beaten path—security is fair. Visit any time except summer holidays and hot late summer.

BASICS

Operated By: Tennessee State Parks. **Open:** All year (closed Monday & Tuesday indefinitely due to budget constraints). **Site Assignment:** First come, first served; no reservations. **Registration:** At sites, ranger makes rounds. **Fee:** $17 RV & Wran-gler, $11.50 tent; prices for 2 people, $0.50 per additional person; Golden Access, senior discounts (cash, personal check, V, MC, D, AE, DC, CB). **Park-ing:** At sites, in parking lot.

FACILITIES

Number of RV Sites: 0. **Number of Tent-Only Sites:** 29 (water only). **Number of Multipur-pose Sites:** 53 (34 water & electric equestrian sites). **Hookups:** Water, electric (20, 30 amps). **Each Site:** Picnic table, grill. **Dump Station:** Yes. **Laundry:** No. **Pay Phone:** Yes. **Rest Rooms and Showers:** Yes. **Fuel:** No. **Propane:** No. **Internal Roads:** Paved. **RV Service:** 25 mi. in Jackson. **Market:** 3 mi. on Hwy. 100. **Restaurant:** Park restaurant, also 8 mi. in Henderson. **General Store:** 8 mi. in Henderson (hardware), 25 mi. in Jackson (Wal-Mart). **Vending:** Beverages only. **Swimming Pool:** No. **Playground:** Yes. **Other:** Stables, 18-hole golf course, boat dock (electric motors only), picnic shelters, group lodge. **Activi-ties:** Nature trail, equestrian trails, beach, swim-ming (when lifeguard on duty), fishing, rowboat & paddle boat rentals, archery range, tennis, basket-ball, volleyball, ball field, summertime organized activities including square dancing. **Nearby Attractions:** Shiloh Military Park, Pinson Mounds State Park, Casey Jones Museum, Parker's Cross-roads & Britton Lane Civil War Battlefields. **Addi-tional Information:** Jackson Chamber of Commerce, (731) 423-2200.

RESTRICTIONS

Pets: On leash only. **Fires:** In designated areas, grills only. **Alcoholic Beverages:** Not allowed. **Vehicle Maximum Length:** Sites vary. **Other:** 2-week stay limit, no firearms.

TO GET THERE

From US Hwy. 45 (17 mi. south of Jackson), drive west 8 mi. on State Hwy. 100. The park is on the left. From Memphis, drive 80 mi. east on US Hwy. 64, which becomes State Hwy. 100.

HILHAM

Standing Stone State Park

1674 Standing Stone Park Hwy., Hilham 38556. T: (931) 823-6347; F: (931) 823-3984; www.tnstateparks.com.

🚐 ★★★★	🔺 ★★★★
Beauty: ★★★★	Site Privacy: ★★★★
Spaciousness: ★★★★	Quiet: ★★★★★
Security: ★★★★	Cleanliness: ★★★★
Insect Control: ★★★★	Facilities: ★★★★

Located on the Cumberland Plateau, Standing Stone offers sites with gravel, back-in parking. Though most sites are ample, size varies. How-ever, this park is extremely remote and rarely crowded, so you're likely to have plenty of elbow-room. Most sites have some greenery to provide seclusion, and all are nicely shaded by various hardwood species. The largest sites include 1, 24, and 28. Standing Stone maintains nice facilities including an archery range and ten miles of hiking trails. They also host special events such as the Roley Hole Marble Tourna-ment. On property, 69-acre Standing Stone Lake is stocked with bass and bluegill. Nearby, giant Dale Hollow Lake offers some of the best fishing in Tennessee and Kentucky. There are no gates at Standing Stone, making security fair. This pretty park is an excellent destination on summer weekends, though holidays should be avoided.

BASICS

Operated By: Tennessee State Parks Dept. of Environment & Conservation. **Open:** All year (closed Monday & Tuesday indefinitely due to budget constraints). **Site Assignment:** First come, first served; no reservations. **Registration:** Office, or campground host will make rounds, night arrival register next morning. **Fee:** $17 RV, $14 tent; prices for 2 people, $0.50 per additional per-son; Golden Age & Golden Access discounts avail-able (cash, personal check, V, MC, D, AE). **Parking:** At site (2 cars).

FACILITIES

Number of Multipurpose Sites: 36. **Hookups:** Water, electric (30 amps). **Each Site:** Picnic table, grill, fire ring. **Dump Station:** Yes. **Laundry:** Yes. **Pay Phone:** Yes (in park). **Rest Rooms and Showers:** Yes (closed in winter). **Fuel:** No. **Propane:** No. **Internal Roads:** Paved. **RV Service:** 21 mi. in Cookeville. **Market:** 8 mi. on Hwy. 52. **Restaurant:** 12 mi. in Livingston. **General Store:** 12 mi. in Livingston hardware or 21 mi. in Cookeville Wal-Mart. **Vending:** Beverages only. **Swimming Pool:** Yes (seasonal, wading pool also). **Playground:** Yes (3). **Other:** Picnic areas & pavilions, meeting room, rec center w/ ping pong. **Activities:** Jon boat rentals (bring your own trolling motor-electric motors only), bank fishing, hiking trails, basketball, softball field, volleyball, horseshoes, tennis, archery range, Rolley Hole Marble tournament in Sept. **Nearby Attractions:** Dale Hollow Lake, Cordell Hull Birthplace Museum & State Park, Big South Fork National River & Recreation Area, Sgt. Alvin C. York State Historic Site. **Additional Information:** Livingston/Overton County Chamber of Commerce, (931) 823-6421.

RESTRICTIONS

Pets: On leash only. **Fires:** In grills, fire rings only. **Alcoholic Beverages:** Not allowed. **Vehicle Maximum Length:** 30 ft. (sites vary). **Other:** 14-day stay limit.

TO GET THERE

From I-40, take Exit 288 at Cookeville and drive north approximately 10 mi. on State Hwy. 111. Take the bypass to State Hwy. 52 north and drive 12 mi. to the park entrance on the left. This is Rte. 136, and the campground is 1 mi. from Hwy. 52. (This is the only access for RVs, due to a 1-lane bridge on Rte. 136 north of the park.)

HURRICANE MILLS
Loretta Lynn Dude Ranch

General Delivery, Hurricane Mills 37078. T: (931) 296-7700; F: (931) 296-3378; www.lorettalynn.com; campground@lorettalynn.com.

🚐 ★★★★　　　🅰 ★★★★

Beauty: ★★★★　　　Site Privacy: ★★★
Spaciousness: ★★★　Quiet: ★★★
Security: ★★★　　　Cleanliness: ★★★★
Insect Control: ★★★　Facilities: ★★★★

Ms. Lynn's ranch and grounds are enchanting. On property, you'll find her beautifully landscaped massive neo-classical mansion complete with doric columns. The restored gristmill across the river provides idyllic photo opportunities. Inside the gristmill is a museum housing the star's memorabilia and costumes. In season, there are festivals and special events on the grounds (call for schedule). Various outdoor activities are available nearby. The massive campground features some extremely attractive sites, and some downright disappointing sites. Luckily, the less attractive sites are used only on the busiest weekends. In order to choose a pretty site, we recommend arriving a day early if you're visiting on a special event weekend. The nicer portion of the campground has a picturesque creek flowing through the middle and features average sized sites shaded by a variety of hardwoods. Parking is on gravel, and there are both back-in and pull-through sites. Loretta Lynn's Ranch is extremely remote, making gates unnecessary. Security is fine.

BASICS

Operated By: Loretta Lynn Ranch, Inc. **Open:** Apr.–Oct. **Site Assignment:** First come, first served; reservations accepted w/ one-night deposit; 72-hour cancellation notice for refund. **Registration:** Main office, night arrival register next morning. **Fee:** $22 full hookup, $19 water & electric, $17 tent; prices for 2 people, $5 each additional person; seniors 10% discount (cash, personal check, V, MC, D). **Parking:** At sites (2 max.), in parking lot.

FACILITIES

Number of RV Sites: 200. **Number of Tent-Only Sites:** 100s of acres of primitive undesignated tent camping. **Number of Multipurpose Sites:** None. **Hookups:** Water, electric (30, 50 amps), sewer. **Each Site:** Some sites w/ picnic table, grill, fire ring. **Dump Station:** Yes. **Laundry:** Yes. **Pay Phone:** Yes. **Rest Rooms and Showers:** Yes. **Fuel:** No. **Propane:** No. **Internal Roads:** Paved & gravel. **RV Service:** 45 mi. in Dixon. **Market:** 7.5 mi. in Waverly. **Restaurant:** snack bar on-site, 7 mi. in Waverly. **General Store:** Camp store, 7 mi. in Waverly. **Vending:** Yes. **Swimming Pool:** Yes (seasonal). **Playground:** Yes. **Other:** Recreation Hall. **Activities:** Loretta Lynn Home Tour, Western town, Loretta Lynn Museum, fishing, canoeing (seasonal), mountain biking & hiking trails, campfire entertainment (seasonal), hayrides (occasional), horseshoes, softball, volleyball. **Nearby Attractions:** Humphreys County Museum & Civil War Fort, Blue Creek Nature Center, Johnsonville State Historic Park, Tennessee National Wildlife Refuge, Duck River, Nathan Bedford Forrest State Park, 65 mi. to Nashville. **Additional Information:** Waverly Chamber of Commerce, (931) 296-4865.

RESTRICTIONS

Pets: Leash only. **Fires:** Allowed in fire rings only (weather permitting). **Alcoholic Beverages:** Allowed. **Vehicle Maximum Length:** 60 ft. (sites vary). **Other:** No ATVs.

TO GET THERE

From I-40, take Exit 143 and drive north 8 mi. on Loretta Lynn Parkway. The entrance is on the left.

JAMESTOWN
Pickett State Park

4605 Pickett Park Hwy., Jamestown 38556-4141. T: (931) 879-5821; F: (931) 879-4479; www.tnstateparks.com.

🚐 ★★★★   ▲ ★★★★

Beauty: ★★★★   Site Privacy: ★★★
Spaciousness: ★★★★   Quiet: ★★★★★
Security: ★★★★   Cleanliness: ★★★
Insect Control: ★★★★   Facilities: ★★★★

Pickett State Park is adjacent to Daniel Boone National Forest and Big South Fork National River and Recreation Area. The park is known for its surreal rock formations, caves, and natural bridges as well as its botanical diversity. Some scientists believe that Pickett supports the second most diverse flora in the US (Great Smoky Mountains National Park has the most diverse plant life in the US). The campgrounds at Pickett are reasonably attractive, with some open sites and others shaded by white pine trees. Sites are small, but they are spaced far apart, giving campers the feeling of spaciousness. Sites have paved, back-in parking. For space and privacy, we like tent sites 20–30. RVs should head for site 1. Pickett is patrolled by rangers at night and has no gates. Nonetheless, the park's isolation makes it fairly safe. Visit Pickett State Park any time except for summer holidays—it's rarely crowded.

BASICS

Operated By: Tennessee State Parks. **Open:** All year (closed Monday & Tuesday indefinitely). **Site Assignment:** First come, first served; no reservations accepted. **Registration:** Campground host makes rounds (check-in at office in winter). **Fee:** $11 for 2 people, $0.50 per additional person; senior & disabled discounts available (cash, personal checks, V, MC, D, AE). **Parking:** At sites.

FACILITIES

Number of Multipurpose Sites: 40. **Hookups:** Water, electric (20 amps) at most sites. **Each Site:** Picnic table, grill, fire ring. **Dump Station:** Yes. **Laundry:** Yes. **Pay Phone:** Yes. **Rest Rooms and Showers:** Yes. **Fuel:** No. **Propane:** No. **Internal Roads:** Paved. **RV Service:** 60 mi. in Cookeville. **Market:** 13 mi. in Jamestown. **Restaurant:** 13 mi. in Jamestown. **General Store:** 13 mi. in Jamestown. **Vending:** Beverages only. **Swimming Pool:** No. **Playground:** Yes. **Other:** Picnic areas & shelters, nature center, boat dock. **Activities:** Lake swimming, boating, fishing (boat rentals available), tennis, archery, hiking trail, seasonal interpretive programs, seasonal hunts. **Nearby Attractions:** Big South Fork National River & Recreation Area, Rugby, Cordell Hull Birthplace, Alvin C. York Grist Mill. **Additional Information:** Jamestown Chamber of Commerce, (931) 879-9948.

RESTRICTIONS

Pets: On leash only. **Fires:** Allowed, in fire ring only. **Alcoholic Beverages:** Not allowed. **Vehicle Maximum Length:** 25 ft. (sites vary). **Other:** 14-day stay limit.

TO GET THERE

From I-40 Exit 317 (Crossville), drive north 35 mi. on US Hwy. 127. Turn north onto local Rte. 154 and drive another 13 mi. The park entrance is on the left.

KINGSPORT
Warrior's Path State Park

P.O. Box 5026/ Hemlock Rd., Kingsport 37663. T: (423) 239-8531; F: (423) 239-4982; www.tnstateparks.com.

🚐 ★★★★   ▲ ★★★★

Beauty: ★★★★   Site Privacy: ★★★
Spaciousness: ★★★★   Quiet: ★★★
Security: ★★★   Cleanliness: ★★★
Insect Control: ★★   Facilities: ★★★★★

Situated on the Patrick Henry Reservoir on the

Holsten River, Warrior's Path offers great recreation facilities, including an 18-hole golf course and extensive boating and fishing amenities. Fish caught in the reservoir include catfish, crappie, bass, bream, and trout. The Olympic-sized pool is next to the campground. The campground consists of one large loop and one small one. Sites are large, though size varies greatly. Although some sites are open, most are shaded by sugar maple, persimmon, tulip poplars, and various oaks. There are no natural privacy barriers. All sites have paved, back-in parking. We like sites 75–79 for pretty views of the reservoir. Others are too densely wooded to afford views of the water. Warrior's Path is popular with locals and there are no gates, which makes security fair. Insects can be a problem here when it's warm and humid. Avoid popular Warrior's Path on summer weekends.

BASICS

Operated By: Tennessee State Parks. **Open:** All year (closed Monday & Tuesday indefinitely during budget constraints—call ahead). **Site Assignment:** First come, first served; no reservations. **Registration:** Camper check-in station or park office, night arrival register the next day. **Fee:** $17 water & electric, $14 overflow area; fees for 2 people, $0.50 per additional person; seniors 25% discount, disabled 50% w/ proof (cash, personal checks, traveler checks, no credit cards). **Parking:** At sites, in parking lot.

FACILITIES

Number of Multipurpose Sites: 135 (94 developed). **Hookups:** Water, electric (20, 30, 50 amps). **Each Site:** Picnic table, grill, fire ring. **Dump Station:** Yes. **Laundry:** No. **Pay Phone:** Yes. **Rest Rooms and Showers:** Yes. **Fuel:** No. **Propane:** No. **Internal Roads:** Paved. **RV Service:** 5 mi. in Kingsport. **Market:** 1 mi. in Kingsport. **Restaurant:** Snack bars seasonal, 1 mi. in Kingsport. **General Store:** 1.5 mi. to Wal-Mart. **Vending:** Beverages only. **Swimming Pool:** Yes (seasonal). **Playground:** Yes. **Other:** Recreation building w/ table tennis & pool tables, boat ramps, marina, riding stables, picnic area, amphitheater. **Activities:** 18-hole golf course, fishing, boating (boat rentals available, paddle boats seasonal), horseback riding (seasonal), hiking trails, mountain-bike trails, disc-golf, tennis, basketball, volleyball, horseshoes, soccer field. **Nearby Attractions:** Bays Mountain Nature Center, Allandale Mansion, Appalachian Caverns, The Netherland Inn, Steels Creek Park & Nature Cen-

ter. **Additional Information:** Kingsport Chamber of Commerce, (423) 392-8820.

RESTRICTIONS

Pets: Leash only. **Fires:** Allowed, fire rings only. **Alcoholic Beverages:** Not allowed. **Vehicle Maximum Length:** 40 ft. (sites vary). **Other:** 2-week stay limit, no firearms.

TO GET THERE

From I-81, take Exit 59 and turn north on SR 36/Fort Henry Dr. Drive 5 mi. and turn right at the fifth traffic light onto Hemlock Rd. Drive 1.5 mi. to the park entrance on the right.

LAKELAND
KOA–Memphis East

3291 Shoehorn Dr., Lakeland 38002. T: (901) 388-3053.

🚐 ★★★	🅰 ★★
Beauty: ★★★	Site Privacy: ★★
Spaciousness: ★★	Quiet: ★★★
Security: ★★★	Cleanliness: ★★★
Insect Control: ★★★★	Facilities: ★★★

A few miles northeast of Memphis, this KOA is conveniently located for touring the river city. It's also near a large outlet mall and a public golf course. Recreational facilities are average and the park is connected to a residential mobile-home complex. Campsites are small and generally unattractive. The campground contains two rows of pull-throughs and one row of back-ins. Parking is on patchy gravel, and there are a few trees, but little privacy. For convenience, we recommend the pull-through sites closest to the pool and store, including 24F and 26F. For a little shade, we recommend sites 29–33. Security is fair at this suburban to rural park—there is no gate. Visit Memphis in spring or fall for the nicest weather. Avoid the humid summer months.

BASICS

Operated By: Thomas Long. **Open:** 7 days a week, all year. **Site Assignment:** Reservations accepted w/ a credit card deposit (V, MC, or D); 24-hour cancellation required for refund; sites are first come, first served. **Registration:** At office. **Fee:** $17–$25. **Parking:** 2 vehicles per site, plus an additional parking lot.

FACILITIES

Number of RV Sites: 100. **Number of Tent-**

Only Sites: 8. **Hookups:** Electric, water, sewer. **Each Site:** Picnic table. **Dump Station:** Yes. **Laundry:** Yes. **Pay Phone:** Yes. **Rest Rooms and Showers:** Yes. **Fuel:** No. **Propane:** Yes. **Internal Roads:** Paved. **RV Service:** 25 mi. north in Millington. **Market:** In park. **Restaurant:** 0.25 mi. north. **General Store:** In park. **Vending:** No. **Swimming Pool:** Yes. **Playground:** Yes. **Other:** Billiard table, game room. **Activities:** Fishing, pool, ping-pong, video games. **Nearby Attractions:** Graceland, Hunt-Phelan Home, Libertyland, Memphis Queen Line, The Pyramid, Sun Studio, Fire Museum of Memphis, WONDERS: The Memphis International Cultural Series, Memphis Motorsports Park, Lichterman Nature Center, Davies Manor Plantation, Memphis Music Hall of Fame, Slavehaven/Burkle Estate, W.C. Handy Home, Historic Elmwood Cemetery, The Belz Museum, Memphis Pink Palace Museum, Planetarium & IMAX Theater, Mud Island River Park, Ornamental Metal Museum, Beale St., Dixie Gallery & Gardens. **Additional Information:** Lakeland Area Chamber of Commerce, (901) 382-5027; Memphis Area Chamber of Commerce, (901) 575-3500.

<u>RESTRICTIONS</u>

Pets: On leash only. **Fires:** Not allowed. **Alcoholic Beverages:** At site only. **Vehicle Maximum Length:** No limit. **Other:** No swimming in lake; no generators allowed.

<u>TO GET THERE</u>

Take I-40 from Memphis headed northeast. At Exit 20, 0.5 mi. south on Canada Rd., take a left on Monroe and campground is on the left.

LAWRENCEBURG

David Crockett State Park

P.O. Box 398, Lawrenceburg 38464-0398. T: (931) 762-9408; F: (931) 766-0047; www.tnstateparks.com.

 ★★★★   ▲ ★★★★

Beauty: ★★★★★	Site Privacy: ★★★★
Spaciousness: ★★★★	Quiet: ★★★★
Security: ★★★★★	Cleanliness: ★★★★
Insect Control: ★★★★	Facilities: ★★★★

Of the two campgrounds at David Crockett, Campground No. 2 is the prettiest. Flat and shady, with comfortably spaced sites, No. 2 has lovely trees. A little greenery provides barriers between some sites. All sites in No. 2 have back-

in parking. The most private sites in No. 2 are 99–101. Campground No. 1 is more open and includes attractive sites along a creek (15–32). Sites 1, 2, and 3 in Campground No. 1 are the only pull-throughs. Some sites have paved parking while others have gravel. Facilities at David Crockett are very nice and include an Olympic-size swimming pool and a 40-acre fishing lake (no personally owned boats allowed, rentals available). There's a large Amish community in this area, with farm tours available. The James D. Vaughan Museum, memorializing the "Father of Southern Gospel," is also nearby. Security is excellent at remote David Crockett, with gates locked at night. Avoid the park on summer weekends. For the nicest weather, visit in spring or fall.

<u>BASICS</u>

Operated By: Tennessee State Parks. **Open:** All year (closed Monday & Tuesday indefinitely due to budget constraints). **Site Assignment:** First come, first served; no reservations. **Registration:** Office, ranger makes rounds after hours. **Fee:** $17 RV, $14 tent; prices for 2 people, $0.50 per additional person; senior discount available (cash, personal check, V, MC, D, AE). **Parking:** At site.

<u>FACILITIES</u>

Number of RV Sites: 0. **Number of Tent-Only Sites:** 7 primitive (Campground No. 1, closed winter). **Number of Multipurpose Sites:** 107. **Hookups:** Water, electric (30 amps). **Each Site:** Picnic table, grill, fire ring. **Dump Station:** Yes. **Laundry:** No. **Pay Phone:** Yes. **Rest Rooms and Showers:** Yes. **Fuel:** No. **Propane:** No. **Internal Roads:** Paved. **RV Service:** 2 mi. east on Hwy. 64. **Market:** 2 mi. north on Hwy. 43. **Restaurant:** Park restaurant. **General Store:** 3 mi. on Hwy. 43. **Vending:** Beverages only. **Swimming Pool:** Yes. **Playground:** Yes. **Other:** Boat launch, Interpretive Center, wading pool, pool concessions, pool bathhouse. **Activities:** Fishing, paddle boat rentals (seasonal), fishing boat rentals, archery range, hiking & biking trails, tennis, softball, volleyball. **Nearby Attractions:** Historic Downtown Lawrenceburg, Amish Country farm & wagon tours, James D. Vaughan Museum ("The Birthplace of Southern Gospel Music"), Coca Cola Palace, Laurel Hill Lake, Scenic Buffalo River. **Additional Information:** South Central Tennessee Tourism Organization, (931) 762-6944.

<u>RESTRICTIONS</u>

Pets: On leash only. **Fires:** Allowed, grills & Campground No. 1 only. **Alcoholic Beverages:** Not allowed. **Vehicle Maximum Length:** 38 ft. **Other:** 14-day stay limit, fireworks prohibited.

To Get There

From I-65, take Exit 14 onto US Hwy. 64. Drive 30 mi. west to Lawrenceburg. The park is on the right (north) of Hwy. 64, 0.5 mi. west of Lawrenceburg.

LEBANON

Cedars of Lebanon State Park

328 Cedar Forest Rd., Lebanon 37090. T: (615) 443-2769; F: (615) 443-2793; www.tnstateparks.com.

 ★★★★   ▲ ★★★★

Beauty: ★★★★	Site Privacy: ★★★
Spaciousness: ★★★★	Quiet: ★★★★
Security: ★★★★	Cleanliness: ★★★★
Insect Control: ★★★★	Facilities: ★★★★

Named after Biblical references to dense cedar woods in ancient Lebanon, this park maintains nice facilities even though its entrance looks dumpy. There are eight miles of hiking trails, six miles of equestrian trails, and an Olympic-size pool. The park is on flat land without a major body of water; the draw here is the forest. Campgrounds 2 and 3 are the shadiest and prettiest, situated in mature tree stands consisting of about 50% cedar. Sites are large, but there is no greenery between them. There are both back-in and pull-through sites with paved parking. In campground No. 2, we liked site 18. Campground No. 3 contains the largest sites (13–15 were our favorites). There are no gates at this small town park, making security fair. A ranger is on duty at all times. Visit in spring, early summer, or fall. Avoid holiday weekends.

Basics

Operated By: Tennessee State Parks. **Open:** All year (closed Monday & Tuesday indefinitely due to budget constraints). **Site Assignment:** First come, first served; no reservations. **Registration:** Office or camp store, host will check in late comers. **Fee:** $17 RV, $14 tent; prices for 2 people, $0.50 per additional person; senior discount available (cash, personal check, V, MC, AE, D). **Parking:** At site.

Facilities

Number of RV Sites: 0. **Number of Tent-Only Sites:** 30 (tents, pop-ups, 20 amps only). **Number of Multipurpose Sites:** 87. **Hookups:** Water, electric (20, 30, 50 amps). **Each Site:** Picnic table, grill, fire ring, some lantern poles. **Dump Station:** Yes. **Laundry:** Yes. **Pay Phone:** Yes. **Rest Rooms and Showers:** Yes. **Fuel:** No. **Propane:** No. **Internal Roads:** Paved. **RV Service:** 10 mi. in Lebanon. **Market:** In Lebanon. **Restaurant:** 7 mi. in Lebanon. **General Store:** Camp store (seasonal), 8 mi. in Lebanon. **Vending:** Beverages only. **Swimming Pool:** Yes (seasonal). **Playground:** Yes. **Other:** Recreation lodge, assembly hall, nature center, picnic area & shelters, riding stables. **Activities:** Hiking trails, equestrian trails, disc-golf course, ball field, basketball, volleyball, tennis, horseshoes, organized activities in season. **Nearby Attractions:** Lebanon "Antique Capital of the South," Country Music Hall of Fame, Grand Ole Opry, Opryland Hotel, The Parthenon, Hermitage Andrew Jackson Home, Belle Meade Plantation, Vanderbilt University. **Additional Information:** Nashville Tourism information, (615) 259-4700.

Restrictions

Pets: On leash only. **Fires:** Allowed, fire ring only. **Alcoholic Beverages:** Not allowed. **Vehicle Maximum Length:** No limit. **Other:** 14-day stay limit.

To Get There

From I-40, take Exit 238 and drive south 6 mi. on US Hwy. 231. Turn left (east) on Cedar FR and drive into the park. Drive 1 mi. and turn right on WPA Rd. Drive 0.5 mi. to the campground entrance.

MANCHESTER

Old Stone Fort State Archaeological Area

732 Stone Fort Dr., Manchester 37855. T: (931) 723-5073; F: (931) 723-5075; www.tnstateparks.com.

🚐 ★★★★   ▲ ★★★★

Beauty: ★★★★	Site Privacy: ★★★★★
Spaciousness: ★★★★★	Quiet: ★★★★
Security: ★★★	Cleanliness: ★★★★
Insect Control: ★★★★	Facilities: ★★★★

This park's namesake is a 2000-year-old Native American ceremonial site nestled into two forks of the Duck River. The Old Stone Fort consists of 50 acres of flat land enclosed by mounds, walls, and river cliffs, and was actively used for 500 years. The park maintains hiking trails for exploring the ceremonial site and area waterfalls. The campground consists of three loops near the Duck River (no water views). Campsites are commodious and very private due to nice greenery between them. Sites are heavily wooded, with various oak species and other hardwoods. All sites feature paved, back-in parking. The sites in the back of the campground (on the third circle) are the most spacious and private. Old Stone Fort is on the outskirts of Manchester. Gates are locked at night making security good. Old Stone Fort is rarely crowded, so it's a good destination for a summer weekend.

BASICS

Operated By: Tennessee State Parks. **Open:** All year (closed Monday & Tuesday indefinitely). **Site Assignment:** First come, first served; no reservations accepted. **Registration:** Ranger makes rounds. **Fee:** $19 RV, $14 tent; prices for 2 people, $0.50 per additional person; senior & disabled discounts available (cash, personal checks). **Parking:** At sites.

FACILITIES

Number of RV Sites: 0. **Number of Tent-Only Sites:** Primitive area for group camping. **Number of Multipurpose Sites:** 51. **Hookups:** Water, electric (20 amps). **Each Site:** Picnic table, grill, paved pads, most have fire rings. **Dump Station:** Yes (seasonal). **Laundry:** No. **Pay Phone:** Yes. **Rest Rooms and Showers:** Yes. **Fuel:** No. **Propane:** No. **Internal Roads:** Paved. **RV Service:** 1 mi. **Market:** 3 mi. in Manchester. **Restaurant:** Within 2 mi. **General Store:** 3 mi. in Manchester. **Vending:** Beverages only. **Swimming Pool:** No. **Playground:** Yes. **Other:** Picnic areas, museum & visitor center, boat ramp. **Activities:** 9-hole golf course, pro shop (cart & club rentals), nature trails, hiking, fishing (electric trolling motors only), summer organized programs. **Nearby Attractions:** Jack Daniels Distillery, Cumberland Caverns Park, Foothills Craft Shop, Tims Ford Lake, 18-hole golf, Manchester Arts Center. **Additional Information:** Manchester Chamber of Commerce, (931) 723-1486 or (931) 728-7635.

RESTRICTIONS

Pets: On leash only. **Fires:** Allowed, fire rings only. **Alcoholic Beverages:** Not allowed. **Vehicle**

Maximum Length: 30 ft. **Other:** 14-day stay limit.

TO GET THERE

From I-24 (approximately 50 mi. south of Nashville) take Exit 110 and turn southwest on State Rte. 53. Drive 1 mi. and turn right (north) on US Hwy. 41. The park is 0.5 mi. on the left.

MANCHESTER

Manchester KOA

586 Campground Rd., Manchester 37355. T: (931) 728-9777 or (800) 562-7785; F: (931) 728-9750; www.koa.com; manchestertn@mykoa.com.

🚐 ★★★   ⛺ ★★

Beauty: ★★★	Site Privacy: ★★
Spaciousness: ★★★	Quiet: ★★★★
Security: ★★★	Cleanliness: ★★★★
Insect Control: ★★★	Facilities: ★★★

This small urban campground is a good stopover, but if you want to enjoy outdoor recreation near Manchester, we recommend the campground at Old Stone Fort State Archeological Area. Manchester KOA includes five rows of pull-through sites with gravel parking. Sites are average sized and offer no privacy. Most sites are shady. We recommend quiet sites 38–47; these are the furthest from the road. Amenities at this KOA are not extensive, but there are plenty of restaurants, shopping, and attractions nearby, including Old Stone Fort, a 2000-year-old Native American ceremonial site nestled into two forks of the Duck River. Visit Manchester in spring, early summer, or fall for the nicest weather. Security at this KOA is fair—there are no gates, but Manchester is not a dangerous town.

BASICS

Operated By: Dan & Ginny McConaughy. **Open:** All year. **Site Assignment:** Sites assigned; reservations accepted w/ credit card number to hold site, 24-hour cancellation notice required; no-show charged one night. **Registration:** Camp store, self-registration at night. **Fee:** $23–$28 RV, $19–$22 tent; prices for 2 people, $3 per additional adult & $2.50 per child; KOA Value discount available (cash, personal check, V, D, MC, AE). **Parking:** At site (1 vehicle).

FACILITIES

Number of RV Sites: 47. **Number of Tent-Only Sites:** 7. **Number of Multipurpose Sites:** None. **Hookups:** Water, electric (30, 50 amps), sewer, cable, instant, on phone lines. **Each Site:** Picnic table, fire ring, grills at tent sites. **Dump Station:** Yes. **Laundry:** Yes. **Pay Phone:** Yes. **Rest Rooms and Showers:** Yes. **Fuel:** No. **Propane:** Yes. **Internal Roads:** Gravel. **RV Service:** 12 mi. in Tullahoma. **Market:** Within 1 mi. **Restaurant:** Within 1 mi. **General Store:** Camp store, within 1 mi. **Vending:** Beverages only. **Swimming Pool:** Yes. **Playground:** Yes. **Other:** Camping cabins, game room w/ arcade, picnic area. **Activities:** Horseshoes, badminton, volleyball. **Nearby Attractions:** Jack Daniels Distillery, golf courses, Old Stone Fort & Tims Ford State Parks, Arnold Air Force Base, Civil War sites, Staggerwing Museum, Cumberland Caverns, antiquing in & around Manchester. **Additional Information:** Manchester Chamber of Commerce, (931) 723-1486.

RESTRICTIONS

Pets: On leash only. **Fires:** Allowed, fire ring only. **Alcoholic Beverages:** Allowed. **Vehicle Maximum Length:** No limit.

TO GET THERE

From I-24 Exit 114, drive 100 yards southeast on US Hwy. 41. Turn north on Campground Rd. and drive 0.5 mi.

MEMPHIS

Memphis-Graceland KOA

3691 Elvis Presley Blvd., Memphis 38116. T: (901) 396-7125.

🚐 ★★   ▲ ★

Beauty: ★★	Site Privacy: ★★
Spaciousness: ★★	Quiet: ★★
Security: ★★	Cleanliness: ★★
Insect Control: ★★★	Facilities: ★

On our visit, there was an unpleasant smell in the park. It's also a bit expensive—at $35 a night for full hookups, you could just as easily stay in the suburbs and take a taxi to Elvis's mansion. But the location can't be beat—the KOA is catty-corner to Graceland, and the staff will help you arrange shuttle service and tours of Memphis and Tunica, Mississippi. Campsites are extremely small and offer no privacy. There are no trees.

Most sites are pull-thrus with untidy gravel parking. All sites are basically the same. There is no gate at this urban campground, making security poor. We urge all campers to be extremely cautious. Elvis devotees have their own religious holidays, drawing massive crowds. Avoid visits on Elvis's birthday and the anniversary of his death.

BASICS

Operated By: Mary & Jim Parks. **Open:** 7 days a week, all year. **Site Assignment:** Reservations accepted w/ a $25 deposit, payable by V, MC, or D. Checks are acceptable in advance. Full refund w/ a 24-hour notice of cancellation. **Registration:** At office. **Fee:** $22–$34. **Parking:** One vehicle per site, also in the parking lot.

FACILITIES

Number of RV Sites: 72. **Number of Tent-Only Sites:** 50. **Hookups:** Only 13 of the RV sites w/ electric & water hookups. **Each Site:** Picnic tables. **Dump Station:** Yes. **Laundry:** Yes. **Pay Phone:** Yes. **Rest Rooms and Showers:** Yes. **Fuel:** No. **Propane:** Yes. **Internal Roads:** Paved. **RV Service:** Yes. **Market:** Yes. **Restaurant:** Across the street. **General Store:** Yes. **Vending:** Yes. **Swimming Pool:** Yes. **Playground:** Yes. **Activities:** Swimming, walking. **Nearby Attractions:** Graceland, Hunt-Phelan Home, Libertyland, Memphis Queen Line, The Pyramid, Sun Studio, Fire Museum of Memphis, WONDERS: The Memphis International Cultural Series, Memphis Motorsports Park, Lichterman Nature Center, Davies Manor Plantation, Memphis Music Hall of Fame, Slavehaven/Burkle Estate, W.C. Handy Home, Historic Elmwood Cemetery, The Belz Museum, Memphis Pink Palace Museum, Planetarium & IMAX Theater, Mud Island River Park, Ornamental Metal Museum, Beale St., Dixie Gallery & Gardens. **Additional Information:** Memphis Area Chamber of Commerce, (901) 575-3500.

RESTRICTIONS

Pets: On leash only. **Fires:** Not allowed. **Alcoholic Beverages:** Allowed. **Vehicle Maximum Length:** No limit.

TO GET THERE

From Nashville take 40 west to 240 west to I-55 south. Take Exit 5B onto Elvis Presley Blvd. Campground is 1 mi. on the right.

MEMPHIS

T. O. Fuller State Park

1500 Mitchell Rd., Memphis 38109. T: (901) 543-5333; F: (901 785-8485; www.tnstateparks.com.

🚐 ★★★　　　　🅰 ★★★

Beauty: ★★★　　　　Site Privacy: ★★★★
Spaciousness: ★★★　　Quiet: ★★★★
Security: ★★　　　　　Cleanliness: ★★★★
Insect Control: ★★★　　Facilities: ★★★★

Located within Memphis City Limits, T. O. Fuller was designated for African-American usage when it first opened in 1942. The park was later named for Dr. T. O. Fuller, a late-nineteenth-century minister, educator, North Carolina Senator, and committed activist. Interesting recreation and facilities include the reconstructed Chucalissa Indian Village. The campground is contained in one loop, and all sites are at least partially shaded by various hardwoods. Sites are mid-sized and some are fairly private. Sites feature gravel, back-in parking. For shade and privacy, we fancy sites 9, 11, 12, 14, 22, 23, and 24. T. O. Fuller is very popular due to its urban location in Memphis. The campground is likely to fill up for special events. Avoid visiting on "Elvis holidays" such as the King's birthday and the day he died. With no gates, security is poor, so guard your belongings.

BASICS

Operated By: Tennessee State Parks. **Open:** All year (closed Monday & Tuesday indefinitely during budget constraints—call ahead). **Site Assignment:** First come, first served; no reservations accepted (except groups). **Registration:** Visitor Center, night arrival registered by ranger or host. **Fee:** $16 RV, $14 tent plus access fee $0.50 per person, $1 min. **Parking:** At sites.

FACILITIES

Number of Multipurpose Sites: 45. **Hookups:** Water, electric (20, 50 amps). **Each Site:** Picnic table, fire ring, grill, lantern pole. **Dump Station:** Yes. **Laundry:** Yes. **Pay Phone:** Yes. **Rest Rooms and Showers:** Yes. **Fuel:** No. **Propane:** No. **Internal Roads:** Paved. **RV Service:** 10 mi. north in Memphis. **Market:** 5 mi. north in Memphis. **Restaurant:** 5 mi. north in Memphis. **General Store:** 10 mi. north in Memphis (hardware, Wal-Mart). **Vending:** Beverages only. **Swimming Pool:**

Yes (seasonal). **Playground:** Yes. **Other:** Picnic area, pavilions, Chucalissa Indian Museum, pool bathhouse & concessions, archery range. **Activities:** 18-hole golf course (club & cart rentals available, closed Dec. 24 & 25), wildlife viewing wetlands, softball, basketball, tennis, hiking trails. **Nearby Attractions:** Graceland, Beale St., Mud Island, Alex Haley House Museum, National Civil Rights Museum, Peabody Hotel. **Additional Information:** Memphis CVB, (901) 543-5333.

RESTRICTIONS

Pets: Leash only. **Fires:** Fire rings only. **Alcoholic Beverages:** Not allowed. **Vehicle Maximum Length:** No limit. **Other:** 14-day stay limit.

TO GET THERE

From I-55 take Exit 9 and drive 4 mi. east on Mallory Ave. Turn right on Riverport and drive another 4 mi. Turn left on Plant Rd., and the campground is in 0.5 mi.

MILLINGTON

Meeman-Shelby Forest State Park

Rte. 3, Millington 38053. T: (901) 876-5215; F: (901) 876-3217; www.tnstateparks.com.

🚐 ★★★★　　　　🅰 ★★★★

Beauty: ★★★★　　　Site Privacy: ★★★★
Spaciousness: ★★★　　Quiet: ★★★★
Security: ★★★★　　　Cleanliness: ★★★★
Insect Control: ★★★　　Facilities: ★★★★

Meeman-Shelby is bordered on the west by the Chickasaw Bluffs lining the Mississippi River. The park offers lovely wooded campsites, 20 miles of hiking and bridle paths, and an Olympic-sized swimming pool. Boat ramps provide access to the Mississippi and 125-acre Poplar Tree Lake, home to bream, catfish, and largemouth bass. The park is about 15 miles from Memphis so it's a fine place to stay if you're touring the river town. The flat campground is situated in a delightful stand of shady hardwoods, including sweetgum and poplar. In most cases, foliage provides a privacy barrier between sites. Campsites are mid-sized, with paved, back-in parking. For privacy and shade, we like sites 10 and 30. Sites 33–49, which lead out of the campground, are also spacious. Rural Meeman-Shelby closes its gates at night making security good. Western Tennessee is extremely hot and humid in late summer and should be avoided. Also avoid holiday weekends.

BASICS

Operated By: Tennessee State Parks Dept. of Environment & Conservation. **Open:** All year (closed Monday & Tuesday indefinitely due to budget constraints). **Site Assignment:** First come, first served; 5 sites available for reservation w/ $5 nonrefundable deposit. **Registration:** Visitor Center, night arrival register next morning. **Fee:** $16 RV, $14 tent; prices for 2 people, $0.50 per additional person up to 10 max; Golden Age & Golden Access discount, Tennessee seniors $12, out-Of-State seniors $15.50 (cash, personal check, V, MC, D, AE). **Parking:** At site (2 cars), in parking lot.

FACILITIES

Number of Multipurpose Sites: 49. **Hookups:** Water, electric (15, 20, 30 amps). **Each Site:** Picnic table, grill, most sites have fire ring. **Dump Station:** Yes. **Laundry:** No. **Pay Phone:** Yes. **Rest Rooms and Showers:** Yes. **Fuel:** No. **Propane:** No. **Internal Roads:** Paved. **RV Service:** 25 mi. south of Memphis. **Market:** 0.75 mi. or 9 mi. in Millington. **Restaurant:** 9 mi. in Millington. **General Store:** 9 mi. in Millington (Wal-Mart). **Vending:** Yes. **Swimming Pool:** Yes (seasonal). **Playground:** Yes. **Other:** Boat launches (electric motor only), boat dock, fishing pier, visitor center, nature center, recreation lodge, picnic shelters. **Activities:** 2 fishing lakes, fishing boat rentals (seasonal), hiking trails, bicycle trail, disc-golf, horse rentals, bridle paths, volleyball, badminton, horseshoes, softball, managed hunts. **Nearby Attractions:** Graceland, Beale St., Mud Island, Alex Haley House Museum, National Civil Rights Museum, Peabody Hotel. **Additional Information:** Memphis CVB, (901) 543-5333.

RESTRICTIONS

Pets: On leash only. **Fires:** In grills, fire rings only. **Alcoholic Beverages:** Not allowed. **Vehicle Maximum Length:** 45 ft. (sites vary). **Other:** 14-day stay limit, quiet enforced.

TO GET THERE

From I-240, take US Hwy. 51 north 3 mi. to State Rte. 388/North Watkins. Drive north 8 mi. and turn left on Benjestown Rd. Drive 1 mi. to the 4-way stop and turn right. The park entrance is 0.75 mi. on the left. (US Hwy. 55 is accessible from the west from I-40 and I-55 as well.)

NASHVILLE
Nashville KOA Kampground

2626 Music Valley Dr., Nashville 37214. T: (615) 889-0282; F: (615) 883-9113; www.koa.com; nashvillekoa@earthlink.net.

🚐 ★★★★   ▲ ★★

Beauty: ★★★★
Spaciousness: ★★★
Security: ★★
Insect Control: ★★★★
Site Privacy: ★★
Quiet: ★★★★
Cleanliness: ★★★★
Facilities: ★★★★

Nashville KOA campground is fairly attractive and convenient to area attractions, restaurants, and shopping. In the campground, there's a kiddie pool, a playground, and plenty of room for children to run around. Without gates, security at this suburban campground is iffy. Take care of your valuables. Nashville can become unbearably hot and humid in late summer. Visit in spring or fall for optimal weather. Sites are laid out in rows of mostly pull-throughs. All sites are the same passable size and there is no greenery to provide privacy. In other respects, sites vary. Many sites are nicely shaded by mature poplars and other hardwoods. Some sites are completely open. Most parking is paved, though some is gravel. For shade and quiet, head for 50-amp sites Z–Z27, along the back perimeter of the park. Most tent sites are very small and located near the noisy road.

BASICS

Operated By: Kampgrounds of America. **Open:** All year. **Site Assignment:** First come, first served; reservations accepted w/ first-night deposit; 24-hour cancellation notice for full refund. **Registration:** Store/main building, night registration also. **Fee:** $37.95 full hookup, $34.95 water & electric, $24.95 tent; prices for 2 people, $5 per additional adult, $1 child, 6 people max.; KOA discount 10% (cash, V, MC, D). **Parking:** At site (1 car), in parking lot.

FACILITIES

Number of RV Sites: 240. **Number of Tent-Only Sites:** 60. **Number of Multipurpose Sites:** 100 (water & electric only). **Hookups:** Water, electric (30, 50 amps), 240 sites w/ sewer. **Each Site:** Picnic table. **Dump Station:** Yes. **Laundry:** Yes. **Pay Phone:** Yes. **Rest Rooms and Showers:** Yes. **Fuel:** No. **Propane:** Yes. **Internal**

Roads: Paved. **RV Service:** Next door. **Market:** 6 mi. in Nashville. **Restaurant:** At entrance. **General Store:** Convenience store w/ camp supplies on site, K-Mart 6 mi. in Nashville. **Vending:** No. **Swimming Pool:** Yes. **Playground:** Yes. **Other:** Game room, pool tables, outdoor theater, music barn. **Activities:** Basketball, horseshoes, mini-golf, bicycle rental. **Nearby Attractions:** Country Music Hall of Fame, Grand Ole Opry, Opryland Hotel, The Parthenon, Hermitage Andrew Jackson Home, Belle Meade Plantation, Vanderbilt University. **Additional Information:** Nashville Tourism information, (615) 259-4700.

RESTRICTIONS

Pets: Leash only. **Fires:** Not allowed. **Alcoholic Beverages:** Allowed. **Vehicle Maximum Length:** No limit. **Other:** Quiet hours enforced, no generators.

TO GET THERE

Interstates 40, 24, and 65 all intersect with Briley Parkway in Nashville. From Briley Pkwy., take Exit 12 and drive north (the only option) 2 mi. on Music Valley Dr. The campground is on the left.

ONEIDA

Bandy Creek Campground, Big South Fork National River and Recreation Area

4563 Leatherwood Rd., Oneida 37841. T: (931) 879-4869 or (800) 365-CAMP; F: (931) 879-9604; www.nps.gov; biso_information@nps.gov.

🚐 ★★★★	🅰 ★★★★
Beauty: ★★★★	Site Privacy: ★★★★
Spaciousness: ★★★★★	Quiet: ★★★★
Security: ★★★★	Cleanliness: ★★★
Insect Control: ★★★★	Facilities: ★★★★

Straddling the Kentucky-Tennessee border, Big South Fork NRA is far less crowded than nearby Great Smoky Mountains National Park and offers outstanding outdoor recreation. It's known for excellent paddling, with mellow flat water and class I–IV white water. Big South Fork also has 150 miles of hiking trails. Nearby Cumberland Falls is one the most beautiful sights in the US. The campground at Bandy Creek offers attractive and extremely spacious sites. Though most sites are shady, privacy varies greatly, with some very secluded sites and others sandwiched together. There are both back-in and pull-through sites. All have gravel parking. Gorgeous Loop A is for tent campers only. The rest are multipurpose. For seclusion, we like sites 16–19 on loop D. Avoid Big South Fork on holiday weekends and fall leaf peeping weekends. Otherwise, the campground is rarely full. Security is fine at this extremely remote campground.

BASICS

Operated By: National Park Service. **Open:** All year (some areas seasonal). **Site Assignment:** First come, first served; reservations accepted Apr.–Oct. up to 5 months in advance; full deposit, $13.85 cancellation fee w/ 2-day notice or more, same day cancellation one night charged plus fee. **Registration:** Kiosk, after hours register next morning. **Fee:** $18 water & electric, $15 tent; prices for 6 people; Golden Age & Golden Access discounts available (cash, personal checks, V, MC, D). **Parking:** At site (2 cars), in parking lot.

FACILITIES

Number of RV Sites: 0. **Number of Tent-Only Sites:** 50. **Number of Multipurpose Sites:** 100. **Hookups:** Water, electric (20, 30 amps). **Each Site:** Picnic table, fire ring w/ grill, lantern pole, tent pad. **Dump Station:** Yes. **Laundry:** No. **Pay Phone:** Yes. **Rest Rooms and Showers:** Yes. **Fuel:** No. **Propane:** No. **Internal Roads:** Paved. **RV Service:** 80 mi. in Knoxville. **Market:** 12 mi. in Oneida. **Restaurant:** 12 mi. in Oneida. **General Store:** 12 mi. in Oneida. **Vending:** Yes. **Swimming Pool:** Yes (Memorial Day–Labor Day). **Playground:** Yes. **Other:** Visitor Center, stables, picnic area, covered pavilion, Big South Fork Scenic Railway, Blue Heron Outdoor Historical Museum. **Activities:** Hiking & biking trails, horseback riding, fishing, hunting, rafting, canoeing, kayaking, volleyball. **Nearby Attractions:** Highland Manor Winery, Historic Rugby restored Victorian village, Alvin York's Farm & Grist Mill, Cordell Hull Birthplace, Indian Mountain State Park, Pickett State Rustic Park, 80 mi. to Knoxville. **Additional Information:** Oneida Chamber of Commerce, (423) 569-6900; Jamestown Chamber of Commerce, (931) 879-9948.

RESTRICTIONS

Pets: On leash only. **Fires:** Allowed, fire rings only. **Alcoholic Beverages:** Allowed, at sites only. **Vehicle Maximum Length:** 45 ft. (sites vary). **Other:** 13% grade entering campground, 14-day stay limit, quiet hours enforced.

To Get There

From I-75, take Exit 141 (145 from the north) and drive 20 mi. west on State Hwy. 63. At US Hwy. 27, turn right and drive 7 mi. north to Oneida. At the first traffic light, turn left onto local Rte. 297 and drive 15 mi. to the campground on the right.

PIGEON FORGE
Fort Wear RV and Campground

2630 Sequoia Rd., Pigeon Forge 37863. T: (865) 428-1951 or (800) 452-9835 for reservations; www.hometownamerica.net.

🚐 ★★★　　　　　▲ n/a

Beauty: ★★★★　　Site Privacy: ★★★
Spaciousness: ★★★　Quiet: ★★★
Security: ★★　　　Cleanliness: ★★★
Insect Control: ★★★　Facilities: ★★★

Located in Pigeon Forge, Fort Wear is convenient to Dollywood, outlet malls, and restaurants. The triangular campground is nestled into a curve in Walden's Creek. Small children enjoy the kiddie pool, while older children enjoy creek fishing. The Pigeon Forge Trolley stops in front. Sites are laid out in rows of back-ins, plus one small section of pull-throughs (sites 111–116). Site size varies, but most are average-sized. All sites feature gravel parking and plenty of shade trees. For smaller RVs, we recommend 144–154, pretty sites along the creek. Large rigs will need to choose a site close to the pool and store. Security is poor-enveloped by tourist town sprawl, this campground has no gates. Avoid Pigeon Forge on fall weekends. If you can't resist leaf peeping, plan a weekday visit.

Basics

Operated By: Hometown America. **Open:** All year. **Site Assignment:** Sites assigned; reservations recommended, w/ first night deposit, 14-day cancellation notice required for a full refund. **Registration:** Country Store (night registration by pre-arrangement preferred). **Fee:** $27 full hookup, $23.50 water & electric; Good Sam discount available (cash, personal check, V, MC, D). **Parking:** At sites, one car (plus overflow).

Facilities

Number of RV Sites: 160. **Number of Tent-Only Sites:** 0. **Number of Multipurpose Sites:**

None. **Hookups:** Water, electric (30, 50 amps), sewer, cable TV. **Each Site:** Picnic table, fire ring. **Dump Station:** Yes. **Laundry:** Yes. **Pay Phone:** Yes. **Rest Rooms and Showers:** Yes. **Fuel:** No. **Propane:** No (soon to have propane service). **Internal Roads:** Paved. **RV Service:** Pigeon Forge. **Market:** 0.25 mi. **Restaurant:** 0.25 mi. **General Store:** 0.25 mi. hardware, 3 mi. Wal-Mart (also country store on-site). **Vending:** No. **Swimming Pool:** Yes (& wading pool). **Playground:** Yes. **Other:** Game room, trolley service to Pigeon Forge, Country Store, picnic area, RV storage. **Activities:** Fishing creek. **Nearby Attractions:** Pigeon Forge shops & theaters, Dollywood theme park, water park, Dixie Stampede, Elvis Museum, Kids Country, helicopter tours, white-water rafting, Cherokee Indian Reservation. **Additional Information:** Pigeon Forge Visitor Information, (865) 453-5700.

Restrictions

Pets: Leash only. **Fires:** Allowed, fire rings only. **Alcoholic Beverages:** Allowed, at sites only. **Vehicle Maximum Length:** 40 ft. (sites vary).

To Get There

From I-40, take Exit 407 and drive south 13 mi. on US Hwy. 66. Turn right/west at third traffic light onto Wears Valley Rd. Drive 0.5 mi. and turn left/ south onto Sequoia Rd. The campground is straight ahead.

PIGEON FORGE
Riveredge RV Park

4220 Huskey St., Pigeon Forge 37863-3619. T: (800) 477-1205; www.stayriveredge.com.

🚐 ★★★　　　　　▲ n/a

Beauty: ★★★★　　Site Privacy: ★★★
Spaciousness: ★★★　Quiet: ★★★
Security: ★★　　　Cleanliness: ★★★★
Insect Control: ★★★★　Facilities: ★★★

Convenient to Dollywood and outlet mall shopping, Riveredge offers attractive sites under a lovely canopy of trees, including dogwood, maple and various oak species. Though recreation facilities are not extensive, they are in good condition. The Pigeon Forge Trolley stops inside the park—let the trolley driver do the driving on busy weekends when traffic is horrendous. The campground is laid out in rows of back-in sites. The small, picturesque sites have gravel parking and a cement patio. Though the trees provide plenty of shade, there is little privacy between sites. For spaciousness, we prefer sites 41–48 for families and E40–E52 for couples. With a view of a lovely field, site E52 is our top recommendation for adults. Security is marginal—there are no gates and the park is visible from US Hwy. 441. Pigeon Forge is extremely congested on busy weekends, especially in the fall. Try to visit on weekdays.

BASICS

Operated By: Ricky & Ronald Husky. **Open:** All year. **Site Assignment:** Mostly assigned, some first come, first served; $30 credit card deposit required for reservation; 80% refund w/ 7 days notice, 3 day min. on holidays. **Registration:** Store, 8 a.m.–10 p.m. Sunday–Thursday, 8 a.m.–11 p.m. Friday & Saturday. **Fee:** $26.50 includes 2 people, $3 each additional person, children under age 3 free; no discounts. **Parking:** At sites.

FACILITIES

Number of RV Sites: 165. **Number of Tent-Only Sites:.** **Hookups:** Water, electric, sewer, cable. **Each Site:** Picnic table, concrete pad. **Dump Station:** No. **Laundry:** Yes. **Pay Phone:** Yes. **Rest Rooms and Showers:** Yes. **Fuel:** No. **Propane:** No. **Internal Roads:** Paved. **RV Service:** 10 mi. north in Sevierville. **Market:** 0.5 mi. **Restaurant:** 0.25 mi. **General Store:** Wal-Mart 5 mi. in Sevierville. **Vending:** No. **Swimming Pool:** Yes. **Playground:** Yes. **Other:** Trolley service to Pigeon Forge locations. **Activities:** Arcade, game room, fishing. **Nearby Attractions:** Dollywood, Great Smoky Mountains National Park, white water rafting, outlet shopping, museums, caverns. **Additional Information:** Pigeon Forge Dept. of Tourism, (800) 251-9100.

RESTRICTIONS

Pets: On leash only, pet walks. **Fires:** In gravel, or rings only. **Alcoholic Beverages:** Dry county. **Vehicle Maximum Length:** 40 ft. **Other:** No tents; one camping unit per site.

TO GET THERE

From I-40, take Exit 407 (Hwy. 66) and follow signs to Pigeon Forge. Turn left at the crossover between lights 9 and 10. The entrance is on the right.

PIKEVILLE
Fall Creek Falls State Park

Rte. 3 Box 300, Pikeville 37367-9803. T: (423) 881-5298 or (800) 250-8611 for reservations; F: (423) 881-5103; www.tnstateparks.com.

🚐 ★★★★★	▲ ★★★★★
Beauty: ★★★★★	Site Privacy: ★★★★★
Spaciousness: ★★★★★	Quiet: ★★★★★
Security: ★★★★	Cleanliness: ★★★★
Insect Control: ★★★★	Facilities: ★★★★★

This gorgeous park's namesake is the highest waterfall east of the Rocky Mountains. A moderate hike (less than two miles) leads to an area that overlooks the 256-foot waterfall. A short but difficult hike leads to the shady pool at the bottom of the waterfall. In the park are many miles of hiking, walking, road-biking, and mountain-biking trails leading to other beautiful waterfalls and gorges. The campgrounds at Fall Creek Falls are also fabulous, especially the reservation-only area, which is deliciously shaded by indigenous oak-hickory forest. Though sites are spacious and secluded, the campground often feels crowded because it's so large and popular. Most sites offer gravel, back-in parking. A few sites in areas D and E have pull-through parking. Call ahead and obtain a reservation-only site. Security is decent at this very rural park; without gates, rangers patrol nightly. Plan to visit on weekdays, in spring, or in autumn.

BASICS

Operated By: Tennessee State Parks. **Open:** All year. **Site Assignment:** 117 sites first come, first served (plus 10 walk-in sites); 109 sites available for reservation; deposit 2 nights plus $5 fee; 1 week cancellation notice for refund less $5 fee. **Registration:** Camper check-in station or headquarters, night arrivals register next day or ranger makes rounds. **Fee:** $19 full hookup, $17 water & electric, $10 walk-in; prices for 2 people $0.50 per additional person; Golden Access & Golden Age 50% discount, TN seniors 25% discount, out of state seniors $1.50 discount (cash, personal check, V, MC, D, AE). **Parking:** At sites, in parking lot.

FACILITIES

Number of RV Sites: 0. **Number of Tent-Only Sites:** 10 primitive walk-in. **Number of Multipurpose Sites:** 226. **Hookups:** Water, electric (30 amps), 55 sites w/ 50 amps & sewer. **Each Site:** Picnic table, grill, fire ring. **Dump Station:** Yes. **Laundry:** Yes. **Pay Phone:** Yes. **Rest Rooms and Showers:** Yes. **Fuel:** No. **Propane:** Yes (exchange). **Internal Roads:** Paved. **RV Service:** 60 mi. south in Chattanooga. **Market:** 17 mi. east in Pikeville. **Restaurant:** On site. **General Store:** Camp store, 17 mi. east in Pikeville. **Vending:** Yes. **Swimming Pool:** Yes (seasonal). **Playground:** Yes. **Other:** Nature center, recreation hall & arcade, picnic shelters. **Activities:** 18-hole golf course, horseback riding (seasonal), hiking trails, mountain bike trails (seasonal mountain-bike rental), lake fishing, paddle boat & canoe rentals, basketball, softball, tennis, volleyball, horseshoes, shuffleboard, ping pong, pool table, in-season organized activities. **Nearby Attractions:** Pikeville Historic District, Pumpkin Festival, Cumberland Caverns, Ocoee River rafting, 60 mi. to Chattanooga. **Additional Information:** Pikeville Chamber of Commerce, (423) 447-2791.

RESTRICTIONS

Pets: Leash only. **Fires:** Fire rings only. **Alcoholic Beverages:** Not allowed. **Vehicle Maximum Length:** 48 ft. **Other:** 2-week stay limit, except Area D.

To Get There

From Chattanooga, take US Hwy. 27 north for 15 mi. Just past Soddy-Daisy, turn left onto State Hwy. 111. Drive northwest approximately 40 mi. and turn right onto State Hwy. 284. Drive east 8 mi. to the campground. From I-40, take Exit 287 and drive south 30 mi. on State Hwy. 111. Turn left on State Hwy. 284.

PULASKI

Valley KOA Kampground

2289 Hwy. 64, Pulaski 38478. T: (931) 363-4600.

🚐 ★★★   ⛺ ★★★

Beauty: ★★★   Site Privacy: ★★
Spaciousness: ★★★   Quiet: ★★★★
Security: ★★   Cleanliness: ★★★★
Insect Control: ★★★★★   Facilities: ★★★

This park is surprisingly attractive given its location 0.2 miles from I-65 in Pulaski, a small town rich in Civil War history. "Boy Hero" Sam Davis was captured here in November 1863. Today, a Civil War Museum occupies the site of his execution. There are three rows of pull-through sites

plus one row of back-ins. The long, narrow sites are average sized. Parking is on untidy gravel. Landscaping needs some attention. Mature trees provide shade at most sites, but no privacy. Back-in sites 49–60 have nice field views. For full hookups, try pull-through sites 41–48 located in the back of the park; these are quiet and have pleasant views. This park is visible from I-65 and is not fenced or gated. Security is poor. The owner is serious about insect control; he used to be an exterminator. Visit in spring or fall for the nicest weather. Valley KOA Kampground is rarely full.

BASICS

Operated By: Thomas & Rochelle Talmage. **Open:** All year. **Site Assignment:** First come, first served; reservations get preferred sites, $25 deposit; 72-hour cancellation notice required for a full refund (14-day notice for holidays). **Registration:** Store, night self-registration. **Fee:** $25 full hookup, $23 water & electric, $18 tent; fees for 2 people, $2.50 per additional person (cash, personal check, V, MC, AE). **Parking:** At site (one car), in parking lot (charge may apply for extra vehicles).

FACILITIES

Number of RV Sites: 0. **Number of Tent-Only Sites:** 12. **Number of Multipurpose Sites:** 46. **Hookups:** Water, electric (20, 30 amps), some sites w/ sewer. **Each Site:** Picnic table, fire ring. **Dump Station:** Yes. **Laundry:** Yes. **Pay Phone:** Yes. **Rest Rooms and Showers:** Yes. **Fuel:** No. **Propane:** Yes. **Internal Roads:** Gravel. **RV Service:** 10 mi. in Pulaski. **Market:** 12 mi. in Pulaski. **Restaurant:** Next door. **General Store:** 12 mi. in Pulaski (also convenience store on-site w/ some camping supplies). **Vending:** Beverages only. **Swimming Pool:** Yes (plus wading pool). **Playground:** Yes. **Other:** Game room, movie rentals. **Activities:** Nature walks, horseshoes, basketball, volleyball. **Nearby Attractions:** Historic Pulaski, Civil War Museum, Fort Hill, Jack Daniels Distillery, Space Museum (Huntsville, AL). **Additional Information:** Giles County Chamber of Commerce, (931) 363-3789.

RESTRICTIONS

Pets: Leash only. **Fires:** Fire rings only. **Alcoholic Beverages:** Allowed. **Vehicle Maximum Length:** 80 ft. (sites vary).

To Get There

From I-65, take Exit 14. Drive 0.25 mi. east on US Hwy. 64 directly into the campground.

ROCK ISLAND
Rock Island State Park

82 Beach Rd., Rock Island 38581. T: (931) 686-2471 or (800) 713-6065; F: (931) 686-2558; www.tnstateparks.com.

🚐 ★★★★   ⛺ ★★★★

Beauty: ★★★★	Site Privacy: ★★★★★
Spaciousness: ★★★★	Quiet: ★★★★★
Security: ★★★★	Cleanliness: ★★★★
Insect Control: ★★★★	Facilities: ★★★★

This park's centerpiece is the Twin Falls of the Caney Fork River, a dramatic limestone gorge decked out with waterfalls. East of the park is TVA Great Falls Dam and hydroelectric plant. The Blue Hole, one of the best fishing spots in the state of Tennessee, is accessible from the park's boat launch. Nearby, Big Bone Cave offers tours by reservation. The attractive campgrounds at Rock Island include a multipurpose area and a tent-only area. Sites with hookups featured paved, back-in parking spaces. Sites and parking spaces vary greatly in size, though most are ample. The campground is nicely treed, with Virginia pine, tulip poplar, beech and ample of foliage to provide privacy between sites. The nicest sites are 21–23, 41, 43, 45, 47, 48, and 50. Though rangers close the gates nightly, they're not always locked. Rock Island is extremely remote, making security fair. Visit in spring, when heavy rains feed the waterfalls. Avoid holiday weekends.

BASICS

Operated By: Tennessee State Parks. **Open:** All year (closed Monday & Tuesday indefinitely due to budget constraints). **Site Assignment:** First come, first served; reservations available w/ nonrefundable deposit of the first night plus $5. **Registration:** Park office, night arrival register next day. **Fee:** $16 for 2 people, $0.50 per additional person up to 9 max; TN seniors 25% discount, out-of-state seniors 10% (cash, personal checks, V, MC, D, AE). **Parking:** At sites, in parking lots.

FACILITIES

Number of Multipurpose Sites: 60. **Hookups:** Water, electric (30 amps). **Each Site:** Picnic table, grill. **Dump Station:** Yes. **Laundry:** Yes. **Pay Phone:** Yes. **Rest Rooms and Showers:** Yes. **Fuel:** No. **Propane:** No. **Internal Roads:** Paved.

RV Service: 32 mi. in Cookeville. **Market:** 12 mi. southwest in McMinnville. **Restaurant:** Less than 2 mi. **General Store:** 12 mi. southwest in McMinnville. **Vending:** Yes. **Swimming Pool:** No. **Playground:** Yes. **Other:** Boat launch, picnic areas & pavilions. **Activities:** Beach swimming, boating, fishing, water sports, hiking trails, mountain biking, horseshoes, tennis, volleyball, basketball, multi-use fields, interpretive programs, summertime organized activities. **Nearby Attractions:** Cumberland Caverns Park, Virgin Falls Pocket Wilderness, Burgess Falls State Natural Area, Edgar Evins State Park, Fall Creek Falls State Park. **Additional Information:** McMinnville Chamber of Commerce, (931) 473-6611.

RESTRICTIONS

Pets: On leash only. **Fires:** Allowed. **Alcoholic Beverages:** Not allowed. **Vehicle Maximum Length:** No limit. **Other:** 2-week stay limit.

TO GET THERE

From I-24, take the Cookeville Exit onto State Rte. 111 South. Drive south approximately 30 mi. and turn north on State Rte. 136. Drive 2 mi. and turn left onto State Rte. 287. Drive 2 mi. to the park entrance on the right. From I-40, take the Manchester Exit and drive northeast on State Hwy. 55/70 approximately 35 mi. to Rte. 136.

SEVIERVILLE
River Plantation RV Park

1004 Parkway, Sevierville 37862. T: (865) 429-5267 or (800) 758-5267; F: (865) 774-9174; www.riverplantationrv.com; riverrv@aol.com.

🚐 ★★★   ⛺ ★

Beauty: ★★★	Site Privacy: ★★
Spaciousness: ★★★	Quiet: ★★★
Security: ★★★	Cleanliness: ★★★★
Insect Control: ★★★	Facilities: ★★★

River Plantation is not as attractive as many of the older campgrounds in the area. However, sites are easily maneuvered by big rigs. Some sites are shady, though many of the birch and other trees are immature. Most sites feature back-in parking, though there are a few pull-throughs. Parking is on gravel and each site has a concrete patio. Sites along the Little Pigeon River, 201–227, are the nicest, but cost extra. Featureless tent sites are not recommended. As the campground is located in nouveau urban sprawl, restaurants and outlet mall shopping are nearby. Tourist attractions, including Dollywood, charming Gatlinburg, and Great Smoky Mountains National Park are within easy driving distance. Without gates, security is fair at River Plantation. Weekend traffic can be horrendous. Avoid summer holidays and fall leaf-peeping weekends. Do yourself a favor and visit on weekdays.

BASICS

Operated By: Jim & Jack Connor. **Open:** All year. **Site Assignment:** Sites assigned; reservations accepted w/ first-night deposit; 3-day cancellation notice for refund. **Registration:** Office, after-hours self-registration. **Fee:** $26 riverfront, $24 full hookup 50 amps, $22 full hookup 30 amps, $18 water & electric, $14 tent; prices for 2 people, $2.50 per additional person; Good Sam discount honored (cash, personal check, V, MC, D, AE). **Parking:** At site (2 cars).

FACILITIES

Number of RV Sites: 201. **Number of Tent-Only Sites:** 31. **Number of Multipurpose Sites:** None. **Hookups:** Water, electric (30, 50 amps), sewer, cable. **Each Site:** Picnic table, fire ring, concrete pad (RV sites). **Dump Station:** Yes. **Laundry:** Yes. **Pay Phone:** Yes. **Rest Rooms and Showers:** Yes. **Fuel:** No. **Propane:** Yes. **Internal Roads:** Gravel. **RV Service:** 0.25 mi. in Pigeon Forge. **Market:** 0.25 mi. in Pigeon Forge. **Restaurant:** 0.25 mi. in Pigeon Forge. **General Store:** Within 1 mi. in Pigeon Forge. **Vending:** Beverages. **Swimming Pool:** Yes (& hot tub). **Playground:** Yes. **Other:** Arcade, pavilion, hot tub, RV storage. **Activities:** Fishing in Little Pigeon River, horseshoes, basketball, badminton, volleyball. **Nearby Attractions:** Pigeon Forge shops & theaters, Dollywood theme park, water park, Dixie Stampede, Elvis Museum, Kids Country, helicopter tours, whitewater rafting, Cherokee Indian Reservation. **Additional Information:** Pigeon Forge Visitor Information, (865) 453-5700.

RESTRICTIONS

Pets: On leash only. **Fires:** Allowed, fire rings only. **Alcoholic Beverages:** Allowed. **Vehicle Maximum Length:** No limit. **Other:** 7 mph speed limit enforced.

TO GET THERE

From I-40, take Exit 407 and drive south 12 mi. on State Rte. 66. When Rte. 66 becomes US Hwy. 441, continue another 2 mi. to the park on the left/east.

SILVER POINT
Edgar Evins State Park

1630 Edgar Evins State Park Rd., Silver Point 38582-7917. T: (800) 250-8619 or (931) 858-2446; F: (931) 858-3121; www.tnstateparks.com.

🚐 ★★★　　　　　▲ ★★★

Beauty: ★★★★	Site Privacy: ★★★★
Spaciousness: ★★	Quiet: ★★★
Security: ★★★	Cleanliness: ★★★★
Insect Control: ★★★	Facilities: ★★★★

The lovely campground at Edgar Evins offers unique sites, which are built into a terraced hillside and have views of Center Hill Reservoir. Campsites consist of large wooden decks, which accommodate 36-foot campers, depending on availability. Fire rings are beside the camping deck. Although the decks confine your living space to a small area, sites are nicely spaced and buffered by foliage, so you'll have ample privacy. Most sites are plenty shady. Waterfront sites, 43–60, are worth the extra fees—views from these sites are gorgeous. Activities and facilities at Edgar Evins revolve around fishing and boating in the reservoir. Catches include largemouth bass, smallmouth bass, and walleye. The marina is open all year. Security is fair at this rural park; there are no gates, but the park is off the beaten path. This campground only fills on holiday weekends, so it's a good destination for early summer weekends.

BASICS

Operated By: Tennessee State Parks. **Open:** All year (closed Monday & Tuesday indefinitely). **Site Assignment:** First come, first served; no reservations accepted. **Registration:** Campground host makes rounds. **Fee:** $19 waterfront, $17 off-water; prices for 2 people, $0.50 per additional person; senior & disabled discounts available (cash, personal checks, traveler checks). **Parking:** at site (2 vehicles).

FACILITIES

Number of Multipurpose Sites: 60. **Hookups:** Water, electric (30, 50 amps). **Each Site:** Picnic table, grill, fire ring. **Dump Station:** Yes. **Laundry:** No. **Pay Phone:** Yes. **Rest Rooms and Showers:** Yes. **Fuel:** No. **Propane:** No. **Internal Roads:**

Paved. **RV Service:** 60 mi. in Nashville. **Market:** 20 mi. in Cookeville. **Restaurant:** Park restaurant at marina (seasonal), 7 mi. in Silver Point. **General Store:** 20 mi. in Cookeville. **Vending:** Beverages only. **Swimming Pool:** No. **Playground:** Yes. **Other:** Marina w/ rental slips, boat ramps, visitor center, picnic areas & shelters. **Activities:** Nature trails, fishing, boating, lake swimming, horseshoes, badminton, hiking. **Nearby Attractions:** Burgess Falls State Natural Area, Rock Island State Rustic Park, Cumberland Caverns Park, Cedars of Lebanon, 60 mi. to Nashville. **Additional Information:** Cookeville/Putnam County Chamber of Commerce, (931) 520-7727; Nashville Tourism Information, (615) 259-4700.

RESTRICTIONS

Pets: On leash only (no pit bulls). **Fires:** Allowed, in fire ring only (subject to burn ban). **Alcoholic Beverages:** Not allowed. **Vehicle Maximum Length:** 38 ft. (sites vary). **Other:** 14-day stay limit, quiet hours enforced, no gray water dumping, pet policy strictly enforced.

TO GET THERE

From I-40, take Exit 268 and drive south 4.5 mi. on State Hwy. 96. At the stop sign, the park entrance is straight ahead.

SWEETWATER

Sweetwater Valley KOA

269 Murray's Chapel Rd., Sweetwater 37874.
T: (865) 213-3900; F: (865) 213-3900;
www.koa.com; sweetwaterkoa@hotmail.com.

🚐 ★★★	⛺ ★★★
Beauty: ★★★★	Site Privacy: ★★
Spaciousness: ★★★	Quiet: ★★★★
Security: ★★★	Cleanliness: ★★★
Insect Control: ★★★	Facilities: ★★★

Located off of I-75 between Chattanooga and Knoxville, Sweetwater is a convenient stop-over. Alternately, if you want to take mountain drives along the Cherohola Skyway at the height of autumn tourist season, you could use Sweetwater as a less crowded home base. Nearby are shopping and restaurants. The campground is laid out in rows with pull-through parking. Sites are on the small side of average. Although the internal roads are gravel, most RV parking is paved. Some sites are completely shady, while others are completely open. The prettiest sites, 30–34, are located in the back corner of the park, and have gravel parking. Families should head for sites 55–65, which are near the pool and playground. Security is fair-there are no gates, but this is a quiet area. Because it stays relatively cool, eastern Tennessee is lovely in late summer. Avoid visits on holiday weekends.

BASICS

Operated By: Dave & Kathy Wakeham. **Open:** All year. **Site Assignment:** Sites assigned based on RV specifics; reservations available w/ full deposit; 3-day notice for refund less $5. **Registration:** Office in store, self-registration at night. **Fee:** $26 full hookup, $23 water & electric, $19 tent; prices for 2 people, $2.50 per additional adult, $2 per additional child; KOA discount 10%. **Parking:** At site (one car max.), in parking lot.

FACILITIES

Number of RV Sites: 63. **Number of Tent-Only Sites:** 9. **Number of Multipurpose Sites:** None. **Hookups:** Water, electric (30, 50 amps), some sewer. **Each Site:** Picnic table, most sites have grill &/or fire ring. **Dump Station:** Yes. **Laundry:** Yes. **Pay Phone:** Yes. **Rest Rooms and Showers:** Yes. **Fuel:** No. **Propane:** Yes. **Internal Roads:** Gravel (sites paved). **RV Service:** 2 mi. in Sweetwater. **Market:** 3.5 mi. in Sweetwater. **Restaurant:** 1 mi. at interstate. **General Store:** Convenience store w/ camp supplies on site, also 3.5 mi. in Sweetwater. **Vending:** No. **Swimming Pool:** Yes. **Playground:** Yes. **Other:** Pavilion, recreation hall w/ game room, camper kitchen. **Activities:** Volleyball, horseshoes, multipurpose recreation field, fitness room. **Nearby Attractions:** Dollywood, Pigeon Forge, The Lost Sea, Mayfield Dairy, Fort Loudon State Historic Area, 65 mi. to Chattanooga. **Additional Information:** Madisonville Chamber of Commerce, (423) 442-4588.

RESTRICTIONS

Pets: 6 ft. leash only. **Fires:** Fire rings only. **Alcoholic Beverages:** Allowed at sites only. **Vehicle Maximum Length:** No limit. **Other:** Firearms not allowed.

TO GET THERE

From I-75, take Exit 62 and drive 0.75 mi. west on Oakland/State Hwy. 322. Turn south on Murray's Chapel Rd. The campground is 0.25 mi. on the left.

TELLICO PLAINS
Indian Boundary Campground, Cherokee National Forest

250 Ranger Station Rd., Tellico Plains 37385. T: (423) 253-2520; F: (423) 253-2804; www.reserveusa.com.

🚐 ★★★★　　　　▲ ★★★★★

Beauty: ★★★★★　　Site Privacy: ★★★★★
Spaciousness: ★★★★★　Quiet: ★★★★
Security: ★★★★★　　Cleanliness: ★★★★
Insect Control: ★★★★　Facilities: ★★★

Located in Cherokee National Forest, Indian Boundary is an excellent choice for those who savor solitude. The campground is gorgeous and the sites are huge—possibly the largest in the state. Most sites are shaded by thick woods, and afforded privacy by lush foliage. If you prefer a more open site, they're also available. Parking is back-in style, on pea gravel. The nicest sites, 17–20, feature views of the 70-acre lake. Recreation includes driving along the Cherohola Skyway National Scenic Hwy., which stretches from Tellico Plains, Tennessee to Robbinsville, North Carolina. Outdoor recreation abounds: world class whitewater on a number of rivers; 650 miles of trails designated for various uses, including portions of the Appalachian Trail and the John Muir National Recreation Trail; and fishing on the charming Hiwassee River. Security is excellent at remote, gated Indian Boundary campground. Avoid visiting on holiday and autumn weekends.

BASICS

Operated By: US Forest Service. **Open:** Apr.–Oct. **Site Assignment:** 20 sites available first come, first served; reservations accepted through the National Recreation Reservation Service (NRRS) at (877) 444-6777 or www.reserveusa.com. Reservations can be made up to 240 days in advance, full payment required upon making reservation; credit card preferred (V, MC, D, AE), or pay by money order if at least 21 days in advance, $10 fee cancellation fee, cancellation within three days of arrival charged first night, no-show charged $20 plus first night. **Registration:** Self-service fee station. **Fee:** $15 B & C loops, $10 A & D loops; fees include 5 people, 1 sleeping unit; Golden Age & Golden Access discounts available (cash, personal checks). **Parking:** At site, 2 vehicles max.

FACILITIES

Number of Multipurpose Sites: 92. **Hookups:** Some sites w/ electric (20, 30 amps). **Each Site:** Picnic table, grill, lantern pole, tent pad. **Dump Station:** Yes. **Laundry:** No. **Pay Phone:** No. **Rest Rooms and Showers:** Yes. **Fuel:** No. **Propane:** No. **Internal Roads:** Paved. **RV Service:** Athens or Maryville. **Market:** 17 mi. in Tellico Plains. **Restaurant:** 17 mi. in Tellico Plains. **General Store:** Camp store, also 17 mi. in Tellico Plains or 30 mi. in Madisonville. **Vending:** Beverages only. **Swimming Pool:** No. **Playground:** No. **Other:** Boat ramp. **Activities:** Lake sports, swimming, boating (electric trolling motor only), canoe rentals, fishing, hiking, bicycling. **Nearby Attractions:** Bald River Falls, Cherohala Scenic Skyway National Scenic Byway, Fort Loudon State Historic Area, Sequoyah Birthplace Museum, The Lost Sea, Orr Mountain Winery, Coker Creek Village. **Additional Information:** Madisonville Chamber of Commerce, (423) 442-4588.

RESTRICTIONS

Pets: Leash only. **Fires:** Fire rings only. **Alcoholic Beverages:** Allowed, at sites only. **Vehicle Maximum Length:** 25 ft. (sites vary—see www.reserveusa.com for site specifications). **Other:** 14-day stay limit, must stay first night, must not leave site unattended for more than 24 hours.

TO GET THERE

From I-75 at Sweetwater, take Exit 60 onto State Rte. 68. Drive 30 mi. southeast on 68 to Tellico Plains. Take State Rte. 165 east 17 mi. to the Indian Boundary Campground sign at Forest Rte. 345. Turn left and drive 2 mi. on 345 to the stop sign. Turn right and the campground entrance is 0.25 mi. on the right.

TIPTONVILLE
Reelfoot Lake State Park, South Campground

Rte. 1, Tiptonville 38079. T: (731) 253-7756 or (800) 250-8617; F: (731) 253-9652; www.tnstateparks.com.

🚐 ★★★★　　　　▲ ★★★★

Beauty: ★★★★★　　Site Privacy: ★★★
Spaciousness: ★★★★　Quiet: ★★★
Security: ★★★　　　Cleanliness: ★★★★★
Insect Control: ★★　　Facilities: ★★★★

Reelfoot Lake State Park is extremely remote, but it's worth the drive. This beautiful campground features cypress trees along the water and shady hardwoods in the rest of the campground. Sites are mid-sized, but feel a little cramped because the campground is often full. Most sites offer paved parking, though a few in the back have gravel parking. Five sites include pull-through parking and the rest offer back-in parking. With little undergrowth, sites are not very private. The nicest sites, 1–21, are right on the water. The most productive natural fish hatchery in the US, Reelfoot Lake supports over 50 fish species. There are no limits on crappie or bluegill. A large population of Bald Eagles winter on Reelfoot Lake. Naturalists conduct boat tours for viewing the dignified birds. This is one of the most popular parks in Tennessee, and should be avoided on summer weekends and holidays. Instead, visit in the winter or spring (when aquatic flowers bloom). Security is fine.

BASICS

Operated By: Tennessee State Parks. **Open:** All year (closed Monday & Tuesday indefinitely). **Site Assignment:** First come, first served; no reservations accepted. **Registration:** Entrance station. **Fee:** $19 RV lakefront, $17 RV off lake, $16 tent lakefront, $14 tent off lake; prices for 2 people, $0.50 per additional person; senior & disabled discounts (cash, personal check). **Parking:** At site.

FACILITIES

Number of RV Sites: 0. **Number of Tent-Only Sites:** 20 primitive. **Number of Multipurpose Sites:** 86. **Hookups:** Water, electric (30, 50 amps). **Each Site:** Picnic table, grill, some fire rings. **Dump Station:** Yes. **Laundry:** Yes. **Pay Phone:** Yes. **Rest Rooms and Showers:** Yes. **Fuel:** No. **Propane:** No. **Internal Roads:** Paved. **RV Service:** 50 mi. in Mayfield. **Market:** 5 mi. in Tiptonville. **Restaurant:** Park restaurant, several within 5 mi. **General Store:** 5 mi. in Tiptonville, Wal-Mart 20 mi. in Union City. **Vending:** Yes. **Swimming Pool:** Yes (& wading pool). **Playground:** Yes. **Other:** Boat dock, fish-cleaning station, boat launches, picnic areas & pavilions, visitor center & auditorium. **Activities:** Fishing, boating (boat rentals available), seasonal cruise boats, swimming beach, tennis, horseshoes, ping pong, badminton, basketball, nature trails, year-round nature programs. **Nearby Attractions:** Mississippi River, Reelfoot National Wildlife Refuge & Visitor Center, Big Cypress Tree State Natural Area, golf in Union City, Dixie Gunworks Museum, Casino Aztar. **Additional Information:** Reelfoot Lake Tourism Council, (731) 253-2007, www.reelfoottourism.com.

RESTRICTIONS

Pets: On leash only. **Fires:** Allowed. **Alcoholic Beverages:** Not allowed. **Vehicle Maximum Length:** No limit.

TO GET THERE

From Union City (the junction of US Hwy. 51 with US Hwy. 45), drive west 15 mi. on State Hwy. 22. The park is on the right.

TOWNSEND

Cades Cove Campground, Great Smoky Mountains National Park

107 Park Headquarters Rd., Gatlinburg 37738. T: (865) 436-1200; F: (865) 436-1204; www.nps.gov/grsm.

🚐 ★★★★　　🏕 ★★★★

Beauty: ★★★★	Site Privacy: ★★★
Spaciousness: ★★★★	Quiet: ★★★
Security: ★★	Cleanliness: ★★★★
Insect Control: ★★★	Facilities: ★★★★

Cades Cove, the flattest campground in the national park, offers the best RV maneuverability. Located in a mountain valley, this area was once heavily settled and farmed, and evidence of previous human habitation is abundant on area walks and drives. There are plenty of activities at Cades Cove, including bicycle rental and fishing in lovely mountain creeks. Cades Cove is the most popular campground in the national park. Bears are drawn here, so protect your food. With high attendance and no security precautions, you should also protect your valuables. Since the campground stays full all summer, you won't enjoy the solitude offered at Cosby. Circumvent this problem by visiting mid-week in the spring, when wildflowers bloom. The campground is laid out in rows of back-in sites with gravel parking. Pine and various oak species provide shade. Campsites are large, but not very private.

BASICS

Operated By: National Park Service. **Open:** All year. **Site Assignment:** First come, first served;

reservations accepted for May 15–Oct. 31 up to 5 months in advance, w/ full deposit; $13.25 cancellation fee w/ at least 24-hour notice, otherwise first night plus fee charged; reservations made by calling (800) 365-CAMP or at reservations.nps.gov (personal check, money order, V, D, MC). **Registration:** Self-registration. **Fee:** $14–$20 for 6 people max. per site, 2 tents or 1 tent & 1 RV; Golden Age & Golden Access discounts available (cash only during self–registration off-Season). **Parking:** At site (2 vehicles).

FACILITIES

Number of RV Sites: 0. **Number of Tent-Only Sites:** 22. **Number of Multipurpose Sites:** 139. **Hookups:** None. **Each Site:** Picnic table, fire ring, grill, pea gravel tent pad. **Dump Station:** Yes. **Laundry:** No. **Pay Phone:** Yes. **Rest Rooms and Showers:** Yes. **Fuel:** No. **Propane:** No. **Internal Roads:** Paved. **RV Service:** 23 mi. in Maryville. **Market:** 8 mi. in Townsend. **Restaurant:** 8 mi. in Townsend. **General Store:** 23 mi. in Maryville. **Vending:** Yes. **Swimming Pool:** No. **Playground:** No. **Other:** Amphitheater, picnic area, horse trail, interpretive trail. **Activities:** Hiking, fishing, horseback riding, canoeing, backcountry hiking, ranger programs (seasonal). **Nearby Attractions:** Golf courses, Cades Cove, Pigeon Forge, Dollywood, Gatlinburg, whitewater rafting, Cherokee Indian Reservation. **Additional Information:** Pigeon Forge Visitor information, (865) 453-5700; Park Information, (865) 436-1200.

RESTRICTIONS

Pets: 6-ft. leash only. **Fires:** Allowed, fire rings only. **Alcoholic Beverages:** Allowed. **Vehicle Maximum Length:** 35 ft. **Other:** Be aware of bear precautions.

TO GET THERE

From US Hwy. 321 on the east side of Townsend, turn south on State Hwy. 73. Drive 2 mi. and turn right on Laurel Creek Rd. Continue approximately 5 mi. to the campground on the right.

TOWNSEND

Lazy Daze Campground

8429 Scenic Tennessee Hwy. 73, Townsend 37882. T: (865) 448-6061; F: (865) 448-9060; www.Lazy-Dazecampground.com; lazydazetn@aol.com.

 ★★★   ★★★

Beauty: ★★★★	Site Privacy: ★★★
Spaciousness: ★★★	Quiet: ★★★
Security: ★★★	Cleanliness: ★★★
Insect Control: ★★★	Facilities: ★★★★

Conveniently located within one mile of the Townsend entrance to Great Smoky Mountains National Park, Lazy Daze offers small, clean sites with plenty of shade provided by sweet gum and tulip poplar. The rectangular campground offers three types of sites: those with gravel parking only, sites with gravel parking and a concrete patio, and riverside sites. Sites on the Little River are well worth the extra fees—each site has gravel parking, a concrete patio, and a charming view. All sites offer back-in parking and little privacy. Visitors can take inner tubes down the Little River, with access from the campground. Or, take a bike ride along Hwy. 73 (also known as Foothills Parkway). Townsend is an excellent home base for outdoor exploration on summer and fall weekends when the Gatlinburg area becomes unbearably crowded. Nonetheless, reservations are recommended. Holiday visits are not recommended.

BASICS

Operated By: Lissa & Rodney Porter. **Open:** All year. **Site Assignment:** First come, first served; reservations accepted w/ one night deposit; 10-day notice required for cancellation refund. **Registration:** Camp store. **Fee:** $20–$29 for 2 adults & 2 children; $2 per additional adult, $1 per child; Good Sam, Family Campers, senior & group discounts available (cash, personal checks, V, MC, D). **Parking:** At site (1 vehicle), plus limited overflow.

FACILITIES

Number of RV Sites: 45. **Number of Tent-Only Sites:** 7. **Number of Multipurpose Sites:** 21. **Hookups:** Water, electric (20, 30 amps), sewer, cable. **Each Site:** Picnic table, fire ring, concrete pads at RV sites. **Dump Station:** Yes. **Laundry:** Yes. **Pay Phone:** Yes. **Rest Rooms and Showers:** Yes. **Fuel:** No. **Propane:** Yes. **Internal Roads:** Gravel. **RV Service:** 35 mi. in Chilhowee. **Market:** 0.5 mi. **Restaurant:** Within 1 mi. (several). **General Store:** Camp store, hardware 3.5 mi. in Townsend, Wal-Mart 30 mi. **Vending:** No. **Swimming Pool:** Yes. **Playground:** Yes. **Other:** Pavilion, game room, souvenir shop, cabins. **Activities:** River access, tubing, swimming, fishing (fishing supplies at camp store), shuffleboard, badminton, volleyball, horseshoes, basketball. **Nearby Attractions:** Golf courses, Cades Cove, Pigeon Forge, Dollywood, Gatlinburg, whitewater rafting, Cherokee Indian Reservation. **Additional Information:** Pigeon Forge Visitor information, (865) 453-5700.

RESTRICTIONS

Pets: On leash only. **Fires:** Allowed, in fire ring only. **Alcoholic Beverages:** Allowed, in site only. **Vehicle Maximum Length:** 40 ft. **Other:** No diving in the pool, family-oriented campground, quiet enforced.

TO GET THERE

Driving north on US Hwy. 321 into Townsend, continue straight at the traffic light. This becomes State Hwy. 73 and the campground is 1 mi. on the left.

TOWNSEND

Little River Village

8533 State Hwy. 73, Townsend 37882. T: (865) 448-2241 or (800) 261-6370.

🚐 ★★★★   🏕 ★★★★

Beauty: ★★★★   Site Privacy: ★★★
Spaciousness: ★★★   Quiet: ★★★
Security: ★★★   Cleanliness: ★★★★
Insect Control: ★★★★   Facilities: ★★★★

Convenient for entering Great Smoky Mountains National Park at Cades Cove, Little River Village offers nice facilities in a reasonably attractive campground. The playground is excellent for small children, while older children enjoy swimming and tubing in the Little River. The campground contains both back-in and pull-through sites, as well as an unusually large number of tent sites. Site size varies greatly, but most are long, narrow, and sandwiched together. Most are shady, but few enjoy any privacy. Parking is on gravel. Sites along the river are the prettiest. Pop-ups and small rigs should ask for sites 77–84. Tent campers should ask for sites 121–126. Big rigs should ask for sites 11–15. Security is fair—there are no gates, but the location is extremely rural. Visit in late summer to enjoy the cool mountain air. Visit on weekdays in the fall, when leaf peepers descend in droves.

BASICS

Operated By: Chipperfield Family. **Open:** All year. **Site Assignment:** Assigned by number, drop-ins

choose; reserve up to one year in advance w/ credit card, $25 deposit; partial refund if you cancel 7 days ahead. **Registration:** At camp office. **Fee:** Off river: $20 primitive tent, $26 water & electricity, $28 full hookups. On river: $25 primitive tent, $31 water & electricity, $33 full hookups. $2 each extra person over 5. **Parking:** Yes.

FACILITIES

Number of RV Sites: 67. **Number of Tent-Only Sites:** 27 primitive. **Number of Multipurpose Sites:** 27 water & electric. **Hookups:** Water, electric, sewer, cable. **Each Site:** Picnic table, fire ring, lantern post, full hookup sites have paved patio. **Dump Station:** Yes. **Laundry:** Yes. **Pay Phone:** Yes. **Rest Rooms and Showers:** Yes. **Fuel:** Yes. **Propane:** Yes. **Internal Roads:** Paved & gravel. **RV Service:** 22 mi. west in Maryville. **Market:** On property or 3 mi. west in Townsend. **Restaurant:** Fast food on property, 2 mi. to more restaurants. **General Store:** 3.5 mi. west in Townsend. **Vending:** Yes. **Swimming Pool:** Yes. **Playground:** Yes. **Other:** Pavilion. **Activities:** Fishing, swimming, tubing (rentals), walking & bicycle trail, arcade, pool table, horseshoes, volleyball, basketball. **Nearby Attractions:** Great Smoky Mountains National Park, Pigeon Forge, Gatlinburg, Cades Cove pioneer area. **Additional Information:** Townsend Visitors Center, (865) 448-6134; Pigeon Forge Dept. of Tourism, (800) 251-9100.

RESTRICTIONS

Pets: On leash only. **Fires:** Fire rings only. **Alcoholic Beverages:** At sites only. **Vehicle Maximum Length:** 40 ft. **Other:** Max. 6 people, 2 tents.

TO GET THERE

From I-40, take Exit 386 and go south on Hwy. 129 to Maryville. After the Maryville Hospital, bear left onto 321 North and drive 18 mi. into Townsend. In Townsend, go through the stoplight. The campground is 1 mi. ahead on the left.

TOWNSEND

Tremont Hills Campground

P.O. Box 5 Hwy. 73, Townsend 37882. T: (865) 448-6363; F: (865) 448-6459; www.tremontcamp.com; tremontcamp@webtv.net.

 🚐 ★★★★   🏕 ★★★★

Beauty: ★★★★   Site Privacy: ★★★★
Spaciousness: ★★★★   Quiet: ★★★
Security: ★★★   Cleanliness: ★★★★
Insect Control: ★★★★   Facilities: ★★★

This pretty campground offers unusually large sites and is convenient to the Cades Cove entrance to Great Smoky Mountains National Park. In addition to the usual amenities, Tremont Hills offers river inner tubing. The campground consists of three areas. The tent-only and RV-only sections are adjacent to the Little River. While the riverside sites have the prettiest views, they are also the noisiest—Hwy. 73 follows the river on the park's boundary. All sites have gravel, back-in parking. Tremont Hills is nicely shaded and there is some foliage to provide privacy between sites. Like other Smoky Mountain tourist towns, Townsend becomes unbearably crowded on fall weekends. If you can't resist seeing the autumn leaves, visit on a weekday. Security is passable. There are no gates, but Townsend is a safe little town.

BASICS

Operated By: Rob & Sherry Hill. **Open:** Mar.–Nov. (cabins & self-contained rigs remain open in winter). **Site Assignment:** First come, first served; specific sites can be guaranteed w/ 6 days or more; nonrefundable deposit, varies w/ length of stay. **Registration:** Camp store, after hours register next day. **Fee:** $32 Full hookup waterfront, $28 full hookup off water, $23 water & electric, $21 tent waterfront, $18 tent off-water; prices for 2 people, $2 per additional person; FMCA discount available (cash, TN checks, V, MC, D). **Parking:** At site (one car plus camping unit), in parking lot.

FACILITIES

Number of RV Sites: 50. **Number of Tent-Only Sites:** 35. **Number of Multipurpose Sites:** 21. **Hookups:** Water, electric (30 amps), sewer, cable. **Each Site:** Picnic table, fire ring. **Dump Station:** Yes. **Laundry:** Yes. **Pay Phone:** Yes. **Rest Rooms and Showers:** Yes. **Fuel:** No. **Propane:** No. **Internal Roads:** Paved & gravel. **RV Service:** 18 mi. in Pigeon Forge. **Market:** 3 mi. in Townsend. **Restaurant:** 3 mi. in Townsend. **General Store:** Camp store, hardware 3 mi. in Townsend, Wal-Mart 18 mi. in Pigeon Forge. **Vending:** Beverages only. **Swimming Pool:** Yes. **Playground:** Yes. **Other:** Pavilion, game room. **Activities:** Fishing, river tubing, basketball, summer day-camp for children. **Nearby Attractions:** Golf courses, Cades Cove, Great Smoky Mountains National Park, Pigeon Forge, Dollywood, Gatlinburg, whitewater rafting, Cherokee Indian Reservation. **Additional Information:** Pigeon Forge Visitor Information, (865) 453-5700.

RESTRICTIONS

Pets: On leash only. **Fires:** Fire ring only. **Alcoholic Beverages:** Allowed, at sites only. **Vehicle Maximum Length:** 40 ft. (sites vary). **Other:** No parking on the grass, visitors must be registered.

TO GET THERE

From I-40, take Exit 407 and drive 13 mi. south on US Hwy. 441. At Pine Grove, turn southwest on US Hwy. 321/ Scenic Hwy. 73 and drive 16 mi. to Townsend. The campground is on the right.

UNICOI

Little Oak Campground, Cherokee National Forest

P.O. Box 400, Unicoi 37692. T: (423) 735-1500; F: (423) 735-7306; www.r8web.com/cherokee.

🚐 ★★★★   ⛺ ★★★★★

Beauty: ★★★★★   Site Privacy: ★★★★★
Spaciousness: ★★★★★   Quiet: ★★★★★
Security: ★★★★★   Cleanliness: ★★★★★
Insect Control: ★★★★   Facilities: ★★★

With few recreational amenities, the draw at this beautiful campground is the solitude. The campground is laid out on four narrow peninsulas, so almost every site has a view of South Holsten Lake. Sites are large and amply shaded by various oak species, poplar, white pine, and hemlock. Greenery provides privacy between sites. Sites have gravel, back-in parking. Although all sites here are nice, the loveliest views are found on Big Oak Loop. Huge Cherokee National Forest includes hundreds of miles of hiking, mountain biking, and equestrian trails, including the Appalachian Trail, only a few miles from the campground. A popular hike from the campground leads to the Holsten Mountain Fire tower. Security is excellent at Little Oak; the campground is extremely remote. When we visited on a May weekend, the campground was nearly deserted. This is an excellent choice for any summer weekend except for holidays.

BASICS

Operated By: USDA Forest Service. **Open:** Mid-Apr.–mid-Oct. **Site Assignment:** First come, first served; no reservations. **Registration:** Self-registration at fee box. **Fee:** $12, limit 5 people per site. **Parking:** At site.

FACILITIES

Number of Multipurpose Sites: 72. **Hookups:** None. **Each Site:** Picnic table, fire ring, lantern pole. **Dump Station:** Yes. **Laundry:** No. **Pay Phone:** Yes. **Rest Rooms and Showers:** Yes. **Fuel:** No. **Propane:** No. **Internal Roads:** Gravel. **RV Service:** 22 mi. north in Bristol. **Market:** 22 mi. north in Bristol. **Restaurant:** 22 mi. north in Bristol. **General Store:** 22 mi. north in Bristol. **Vending:** No. **Swimming Pool:** No. **Playground:** No. **Other:** Boat ramp, amphitheater, interpretive trails. **Activities:** Hiking, boating, fishing. **Nearby Attractions:** Bristol Caverns, Bristol Motor Speedway. **Additional Information:** Bristol CVB, (423) 989-4850.

RESTRICTIONS

Pets: Leash only. **Fires:** Fire rings only. **Alcoholic Beverages:** Not allowed. **Vehicle Maximum Length:** 30 ft.

TO GET THERE

From Bristol drive south on US Hwy. 421 for 12 mi. Turn right onto Camp Tom Howard Rd. After 0.5 mi., the road becomes gravel FR 87. Continue on 87 for 6 mi. and then turn right onto FR 87G. The campground is 1.5 mi. ahead.

WILDERSVILLE

Pin Oak Campground, Natchez Trace State Resort Park

24845 Natchez Trace Rd., Wildersville 38388. T: (731) 968-3742 or (800) 250-8616 for Pin Oak Lodge; F: (731) 967-9863; www.tnstateparks.com.

🚐 ★★★★   ▲ ★★★

Beauty: ★★★★	Site Privacy: ★★★
Spaciousness: ★★★★	Quiet: ★★★★
Security: ★★★	Cleanliness: ★★★★
Insect Control: ★★★★	Facilities: ★★★★★

Natchez Trace offers top-notch recreational facilities built into rolling hills and woodlands including white oak, pin oak, loblolly pine, and other species. Unique facilities include four small lakes and 250 miles of equestrian trails. The park is also the proud home of the third largest pecan tree in North America. Tidy Pin Oak Campground consists of three loops, each with views of Pin Oak Lake. Landscaping consists of meticulous grass patches and a few young hardwoods planted throughout. There is no shade or privacy. However, the campground's openness makes views of Pin Oak Lake all the more stunning. All sites are larger than average and have gravel parking. Most sites are back-in, although one loop has long narrow pull-thrus. We recommend any of the waterfront sites. Security at Pin Oak is mediocre. There are no gates, but the campground is extremely remote. Avoid western Tennessee in hot, humid late summer.

BASICS

Operated By: Tennessee State Parks. **Open:** All year (closed Monday & Tuesday indefinitely). **Site Assignment:** First come, first served; no reservations accepted. **Registration:** Attendant makes rounds, self-register at night. **Fee:** $19 waterfront, $17 off water; prices for 2 people, $0.50 per additional person; senior & disabled discounts available (cash, personal checks). **Parking:** at site (2 vehicles).

FACILITIES

Number of Multipurpose Sites: 74. **Hookups:** Water, electric (50 amps), sewer. **Each Site:** Picnic table, grill, fire ring w/ grill, lantern pole, gravel pad. **Dump Station:** No. **Laundry:** Yes. **Pay Phone:** Yes. **Rest Rooms and Showers:** Yes. **Fuel:** Yes. **Propane:** No. **Internal Roads:** Paved. **RV Service:** 100 mi. in Nashville. **Market:** 10 mi. in Lexington. **Restaurant:** Park restaurant (seasonal), 10 mi. in Lexington. **General Store:** Park store, hardware 7 mi., Wal-Mart 10 mi. in Lexington. **Vending:** Yes. **Swimming Pool:** No. **Playground:** Yes. **Other:** Picnic shelter, boat dock, camping cabins. **Activities:** Swimming beach, fishing, hunting, hiking trails (including overnight backpacking w/ permit), roads for motorcycles & off-road vehicles, equestrian trails & horse rentals, firing range, ball field, paddle boat rentals, archery range, summer naturalist programs. **Nearby Attractions:** Nathan Bedford Forrest State Historic Area, Mousetail Landing State Rustic park, Tennessee national Wildlife Refuge, Tennessee river, Hurricane Mills Loretta Lynn Dude Ranch. **Additional Information:** Lexington Chamber of Commerce, (731) 968-2126.

RESTRICTIONS

Pets: On leash only. **Fires:** Allowed, in fire ring only. **Alcoholic Beverages:** Not allowed. **Vehicle Maximum Length:** No limit. **Other:** 14-day stay limit, quiet enforced, no parking on the grass.

TO GET THERE

From I-40 Exit 116, drive 10 mi. south on Local Rte. 114 to Pin Oak Lodge Rd. Turn left to get to the campground.

WINCHESTER
Tims Ford State Park

570 Tims Ford. Dr., Winchester 37390-4136. T: (931) 962-1183; F: (931) 962-2704; www.tnstateparks.com.

🚐 ★★★★   ▲ ★★★

Beauty: ★★★	Site Privacy: ★★★★
Spaciousness: ★★★	Quiet: ★★★★
Security: ★★★	Cleanliness: ★★★
Insect Control: ★★★	Facilities: ★★★★★

Tim's Ford State Park has a passably attractive campground, w/ sites nicely shaded by red and white oak, maple, and hickory. Most sites also have a little greenery providing privacy between them. Site size varies-some are among the smallest in the Tennessee State Parks system. Others are livable. A few sites, including 34 and 35, have views of the lake. Many of the sites have very small parking pads. Sites feature paved, back-in parking. 10,700-acre Tims Ford Lake is known for excellent bass fishing, and the park provides ample fishing facilities. In addition to a large swimming pool, the park maintains a diving pool and a children's pool. The 18-hole bent grass golf course was designed by Jack Nicklaus. There are also paved multi-use trails available for exploring the rolling countryside. This park is extremely remote and has no gates. So security is fair. It's extremely popular with families and should be avoided on summer weekends.

BASICS

Operated By: Tennessee State Parks. **Open:** All year. **Site Assignment:** First come, first served; no reservations accepted. **Registration:** Attendant

makes rounds in-season (winter check-in at Visitor Center). **Fee:** $14–$17 RV, $14 tent; prices for 2 people, $0.50 per additional person up to 10 max.; senior & disabled discounts available (cash, personal checks, V, MC, D, AE). **Parking:** At sites, in overflow lot (not on grass).

FACILITIES

Number of Multipurpose Sites: 50. **Hookups:** Water, electric (20, 30 amps). **Each Site:** Picnic table, grill, fire pit, tent pad. **Dump Station:** Yes. **Laundry:** Yes. **Pay Phone:** Yes. **Rest Rooms and Showers:** Yes. **Fuel:** No. **Propane:** No. **Internal Roads:** Paved. **RV Service:** 12 mi. in Winchester. **Market:** 5 mi. **Restaurant:** Park restaurant (seasonal), 12 mi. in Winchester. **General Store:** 12 mi. in Winchester. **Vending:** Beverages only. **Swimming Pool:** Yes (Memorial Day–Mid-Aug.). **Playground:** Yes. **Other:** Picnic areas & shelters, marina w/ snack bar, bait shop & fish-cleaning station, boat dock & launch, recreation complex, visitor center. **Activities:** 18-hole golf course, bicycle trails (bicycle rentals), hiking, fishing (boat rentals), badminton, table tennis, basketball, summer interpretive programs. **Nearby Attractions:** Jack Daniels Distillery, Old Stone Fort State Archaeological Area, Falls Mill, Railroad Museum, Franklin State Forest, South Cumberland State Recreation Area, University of the South. **Additional Information:** Winchester Chamber of Commerce, (931) 967-6788.

RESTRICTIONS

Pets: On leash only. **Fires:** Allowed, fire pits & grills only. **Alcoholic Beverages:** Not allowed. **Vehicle Maximum Length:** Sites vary. **Other:** 14-day stay limit, no parking on the grass.

TO GET THERE

From I-24 Exit 111, turn southwest on State Hwy. 55. Drive approximately 15 mi. into Tullahoma to the second traffic light (US 41A). Drive straight onto State Hwy. 130. Continue south on 130 for 0.75 mi. to Westside Dr. and turn left onto 130 and Westside Dr. Drive 3.5 mi. to the Awalt Rd. fork on the left. Drive 5.5 mi. on Awalt and turn left at Mansford Rd. Drive 1.6 mi. to the Park entrance on the right.

Supplemental Directory of Campgrounds

ALABAMA

Alberta
Chilatchee Creek Park, off CR 29, 36720. T: (334) 573-2562. www.sam.usace.army.mil/op/rec/al_lakes/camp.htm. RV/tent: 53. $8–$14. Hookups: water, electric (30 amps).

Aliceville
Cochrane Campground, 707 Tenntom Park Rd., 35442. T: (205) 373-8806. RV/tent: 59. $8–$12. Hookups: water, electric (50 amps).

Alpine
Logan Landing RV Resort & Campground, 1036 Bear Bryant Rd., 35014. T: (256) 268-0045. RV/tent: 140. $15–$18. Hookups: sewer, electric (30, 50 amps), water, phone.

Andalusia
Conecuh National Forest (Open Pond Campground), Rte. 5 Box 157, 36420. T: (334) 222-2555. RV/tent: 66. $5–$12. Hookups: water, electric.

Ariton
Camp Bama RV Resort & Campgrounds, Hwy. 231, 36311. T: (800) 435-8259. RV/tent: 16. $10. Hookups: water, electric (20, 30 amps), sewer.

Athens
Lucy's Branch Resort & Marina, 5381 Bay Village Dr., 35611. T: (256) 729-6443. RV/tent: 204. $20. Hookups: water, electric (20, 30, 50 amps), sewer.

Atmore
Claude D. Kelley State Park, 580 H. Kyle, 36502. T: (251) 862-2511. www.alapark.com. RV/tent: 25. $11. Hookups: water, electric, sewer.

Auburn
Chewacla State Park, 124 Shell Toomer Pkwy., 36830. T: (334) 887-5621. www.alapark.com. RV/tent: 36. $15. Hookups: water, electric (20, 30 amps), sewer.

Birmingham
Leisure Time Campgrounds, 2670 South College St., 36830. T: (334) 821-2267. RV/tent: 60. $18–$20. Hookups: water, electric (20, 30, 50 amps), sewer, phone.

Birmingham
M & J RV Park, 556 Bessemer Super Hwy., 35228. T: (205) 788-2605. RV/tent: 72. $12–$20. Hookups: water, electric (50 amps), sewer, phone.

Boaz
Barclay RV Parking, 104 South Main St., 35957. T: (256) 593-8769. RV/tent: 22. $12–$15. Hookups: water, electric (30, 50 amps), sewer.

Castleberry
Country Sunshine RV Park, Rte. 2 Box 290, 36432. T: (251) 966-5540. RV/tent: 11. $15. Hookups: water, electric (30, 50 amps), sewer.

Centre
John's Campground & Grocery, 6480 CR 22, 35960. T: (256) 475-3234. RV/tent: 58. $25. Hookups: water, electric (30, 50 amps), sewer, cable.

Centreville
Talladega National Forest (Payne Lake West Side), Oakmulgee Ranger District, US 82/AL 5 North, 35042. T: (205) 926-9765. RV/tent: 77. $4. Hookups: none.

Citronelle
Citronelle Lakeview RV Park, 17850 Municipal Park Dr., 36522. T: (251) 866-9647. RV/tent: 32. $15. Hookups: water, electric (30, 50 amps), sewer.

Clio
Blue Springs State Park, 2595 Hwy. 10, 36017. T: (334) 397-4875. www.alapark.com. RV/tent: 50. $11. Hookups: water, electric (30 amps), sewer.

ALABAMA (continued)

Coaling

Candy Mountain RV Park, 11742 Hagler Coaling Rd., 35449. T: (205) 553-5428. RV/tent: 40. $17. Hookups: water, electric (30, 50 amps), sewer.

Cottondale

Sunset II Travel Park, 5001 JVC Rd., 35453. T: (205) 553-9233. RV/tent: 36. $20. Hookups: water, electric (20, 30, 50 amps), sewer.

Creola

I-65 RV Campground, 730 Jackson Rd., 36525. T: (800) 287-3208. www.i65campground.com. RV/tent: 76. $17–$19. Hookups: electric (20, 30, 50 amps), sewer, phone.

KOA–Mobile North/River Delta, 2350 Dead Lake Marina Rd., 36525. T: (800) KOA-0362. www.koa.com. RV/tent: 42. $18–$20. Hookups: water, electric (20, 30, 50 amps), sewer.

Cullman

Cullman Campground, 215 CR 1185, 35056. T: (256) 734-9794. RV/tent: 75. $13–$15. Hookups: water, electric (20, 30, 50 amps), sewer, phone.

Good Hope Campground, 330 Super Saver Rd., 35055. T: (256) 739-1319. RV/tent: 50. $13–$16. Hookups: water, electric (15, 30 amps), sewer, phone.

Hames Marina & RV Park, 850 CR 248, 35057. T: (256) 287-9785. RV/tent: 48. $10–$15. Hookups: water, electric (30, 50 amps), sewer.

Dauphin Island

Dauphin Island Campground, 109 Bienville Blvd., 36528. T: (251) 861-2742. RV/tent: 150. $15–$22. Hookups: water, electric (30, 50 amps), sewer.

Decatur

Point Mallard Campground, 1800 Point Mallard Dr., 35601. T: (256) 351-7772. RV/tent: 210. $12–$15. Hookups: water, electric (20, 30, 50 amps), sewer.

Demopolis

Forkland Park, Off US 43, 12 miles north of Demopolis, 36732. T: (334) 289-5530. www.sam.usace.army.mil/op/rec. RV/tent: 42. $12–$14. Hookups: water, electric (20, 30 amps).

Foscue Creek Park, 1800 Lockin Dam Rd., 36732. T: (334) 289-5535. www.sam.usace.army.mil/op/rec. RV/tent: 45. $12. Hookups: water, electric (20, 30 amps).

Dothan

Clean Park RV Park, 4100 South Oates St., 36301. T: (334) 792-2000. RV/tent: 150. $15. Hookups: water, electric (30, 50 amps), sewer, cable.

Elberta

Lazy Acres RV Park & Campground, 12160 Wortel Rd., 36530. T: (877) 986-5266. www.lazyacres campground.com. RV/tent: 54. $12. Hookups: water, electric (20, 30, 50 amps), sewer, phone.

Elkmont

Mill Creek RV Park, 28861 Veto Rd., 35620. T: (256) 732-3686. www.millcreekrv.com. RV/tent: 125. $10–$18. Hookups: sewer, electric (30, 50 amps), water, phone.

Equality

Lakeway Pub & Grill and RV Park, P.O. Box 176, 36026. T: (334) 541-2010. RV/tent: 13. $15. Hookups: water, electric (30, 50 amps), sewer.

Eufaula

Lake Eufaula Campground, 151 West Chewalla Creek Dr., 36027. T: (334) 687-4425. RV/tent: 100. $14–$17. Hookups: water, electric (30 amps), sewer.

Fairhope

Driftwood RV Park, 9318 Hwy. 98, 36532. T: (251) 928-8233. RV/tent: 24. $14. Hookups: water, electric (30, 50 amps), sewer.

East Park Plaza, 7625 Parker Rd., 36532. T: (251) 928-7619. RV/tent: 15. $14. Hookups: water, electric (30, 50 amps), sewer.

Safe Harbor RV Resort & Marina, 11401 US Hwy. 98, 36532. T: (800) 928-4544. www.safeharbour resort.com. RV/tent: 105. $20. Hookups: water, electric (30, 50 amps), sewer.

Florala

Florala State Park, P.O. Box 322, 36442-0322. T: (334) 858-6425. RV/tent: 23. $14. Hookups: water, electric (30 amps).

Florence

McFarland Park, South Seminary St., 35630. T: (256) 760-6416. RV/tent: 50. $8–$12. Hookups: water, electric (20, 30 amps).

Veterans Memorial Park, Wilson Dam Rd., 35630. T: (256) 760-6416. RV/tent: 22. $8–$12. Hookups: water, electric (20, 30 amps).

Foley

Helen's RV Park, 10340 South Juniper St., 36535. T: (251) 943-1227. RV/tent: 18. $12. Hookups: sewer, electric (30, 50 amps), water, phone.

Palm Lake RV Court, 15810 Hwy. 59, 36535. T: (251) 970-3773. F: (251) 970-1704. RV/tent: 62. $18. Hookups: water, electric (20, 30, 50 amps), sewer, phone.

Franklin

Isaac Creek Park, Rte. 1 Box 51B, 36444. T: (251) 282-4254. www.sam.usace.army.mil/op/rec/al _lakes/camp.htm. RV/tent: 50. $12–$14. Hookups: water, electric (30, 50 amps).

Gadsden

River Country Campground, 1 River Rd., 35901. T: (256) 543-7111. www.rivercountrycampground. com. RV/tent: 112. $16–$22. Hookups: sewer, electric (30, 50 amps), water, phone.

ALABAMA (continued)

Gallion
Chickasaw State Park, 26955 US Hwy. 43, 36742.
T: (334) 295-8230. www.alapark.com. RV/tent: 8.
$10. Hookups: water, electric (30 amps).

Gardendale
Gardendale Kampground, 2128 Moncrief Rd.,
35071. T: (205) 631-7364. RV/tent: 30. $19.
Hookups: water, electric (20, 30 amps), sewer.

Gulf Shores
Luxury RV Resort, 590 Gulf Shores Pkwy., 36542.
T: (800) 982-3510. RV/tent: 89. $22–$25. Hook-
ups: sewer, electric (30, 50 amps), water, phone.

Southport Campgrounds, 108 West 28th Ave.,
36542. T: (251) 968-6220. RV/tent: 116. $13–$17.
Hookups: water, electric (20, 30 amps), sewer,
phone.

Sun Runners RV Park, 19436 CR 8, 36542. T: (251)
955-5257. RV/tent: 60. $14. Hookups: water, elec-
tric (20, 30 amps), sewer.

Guntersville
Seibold Campground, 54 Seibold Creek Rd., 35976.
T: (256) 582-0040. RV/tent: 102. $17–$20.
Hookups: water, electric (20, 30, 50 amps).

Hamilton
US 78 Campgrounds, 3194 CR 55, 35570. T: (205)
921-2718. RV/tent: 14. $10. Hookups: water, elec-
tric (20, 30, 50 amps), sewer.

Hanceville
Country RV Park, 15959 Hwy. 91, 35077. T: (256)
352-4678. RV/tent: 40. $15–$20. Hookups: sewer,
electric (30, 50 amps), water, phone, cable.

Heflin
Talladega National Forest (Coleman Lake), Shoal
Creek Ranger District, 2309 Hwy. 46, 36264.
T: (256) 463-2272. RV/tent: 39. $12. Hookups:
water, electric (30, 50 amps).

Talladega National Forest (Pine Glen), Shoal Creek
Ranger District, 2309 Hwy. 46, 36264. T: (256)
463-2272. RV/tent: 31. $3. Hookups: none.

Helena
Cherokee Beach Kamper Village, 2800 Hwy. 93,
35080. T: (205) 428-8339. RV/tent: 80. $14.
Hookups: water, electric (30 amps), sewer.

Hope Hull
KOA–Montgomery, 250 Fischer Rd., 36043. T: (800)
KOA-5032. F: (334) 286-1133. www.koa.com.
RV/tent: 125. $19–$35. Hookups: water, electric
(20, 30, 50 amps), sewer, phone.

Huntsville
Ditto Landing Marina Campground, 293 Ditto Landing Rd., 35815. T: (256) 883-9420. www.nservice.

com/ditto_landing. RV/tent: 26. $14. Hookups:
water, electric (30 amps).

Ider
Thunder Canyon Campground, 583 Thunder
Canyon Rd., 35981. T: (256) 632-2103. RV/tent: 50.
$12–$14. Hookups: water, electric (20, 30, 50
amps), sewer.

Jemison
Peach Queen Campground, 12986 CR 42, 35085.
T: (205) 688-2573. RV/tent: 92. $20–$24.
Hookups: water, electric (20, 30, 50 amps), sewer,
phone.

Langston
South Sauty Creek Resort, 6845 South Sauty Rd.,
35755. T: (256) 582-3367. RV/tent: 85. $18.
Hookups: water, electric (20, 30, 50 amps).

Leeds
Holiday Trav-L-Park, 900 Old Ashville Rd., 35094.
T: (205) 640-5300. RV/tent: 137. $17–$20.
Hookups: water, electric (20, 30 amps), sewer.

Leroy
Double R Campground, HC 63 Box 247, 36548.
T: (251) 246-9175. RV/tent: 40. $15. Hookups:
water, electric (20, 30, 50 amps), sewer.

Magnolia Springs
Southwind RV Park, 12821 CR 9N, 36555. T: (251)
988-1216. RV/tent: 120. $18. Hookups: water, elec-
tric (20, 30, 50 amps), sewer.

McCalla
KOA–McCalla/Tannehill, 22191 Hwy. 216, 35111.
T: (800) KOA-9505. www.koa.com. RV/tent: 62.
$17–$24. Hookups: sewer, electric (30, 50 amps),
water, phone.

Millbrook
K & K RV Park, 1810 I-65 Service Rd. East, 36054.
T: (334) 285-5251. RV/tent: 46. $19. Hookups:
water, electric (20, 30, 50 amps), sewer, phone.

Mobile
Brown's RV Park, 1619 Jasper Rd., 36618. T: (251)
342-3383. www.brownsrvpark.com. RV/tent: 34.
$17. Hookups: sewer, electric (30, 50 amps), water,
phone, cable.

Pala Verde RV Park, 3525 Demetropolis Rd., 36693.
T: (251) 660-7148. RV/tent: 19. $15. Hookups:
water, electric (30, 50 amps), sewer.

Montgomery
Gunter Hill Park, 561 Booth Rd., 36108. T: (334)
269-1053. www.sam.usace.army.mil/op/rec/al_
lakes/camp.htm. RV/tent: 146. $8–$14. Hookups:
water, electric (30, 50 amps).

ALABAMA (continued)

Moundville

Moundville Archaeological Park, 13075 Moundville Arch Park, 35474. T: (205) 371-2572. www.ua.edu/ mndville.htm. RV/tent: 34. $10. Hookups: water, electric (20, 30 amps), sewer.

Muscle Shoals

Mallard Creek, P.O. Box 1010 SB1H, 35662. T: (256) 386-2221. RV/tent: 56. $15. Hookups: water, electric (30 amps).

Ohatchee

Coosa Willow Point Campground & Marina, 138 Willow Point Dr., Hwy. 77 North, 36271. T: (800) 566-9906. RV/tent: 74. $15. Hookups: water, electric (20, 30, 50 amps).

Opelika

Lakeside RV Park, 5664 US Hwy. 280 East, 36801. T: (334) 745-5414. RV/tent: 20. $20. Hookups: water, electric (30, 50 amps), sewer.

Opp

Frank Jackson State Park, Rte. 3 Box 73-C, 36467. T: (334) 493-6988. www.dcnr.state.al.us/parks/ frank_jackson_1a.html. RV/tent: 26. $15. Hookups: water, electric (30 amps).

Orange Beach

Beech Camping, 4224 Orange Beach Blvd., #50, 36561. T: (251) 981-4136. RV/tent: 90. $20. Hookups: water, electric (20, 30, 50 amps), sewer.

Ozark

Ozark Trav-L-Park, 4000 US 231 North, 36360. T: (800) 359-3218. www.trav-l-park.com. RV/tent: 45. $21. Hookups: sewer, electric (30, 50 amps), water, phone, cable.

Pelham

KOA–Birmingham South, 222 Hwy. 33, 35124. T: (205) 664-8832. F: (205) 620-1103. www.koa. com. RV/tent: 113. $25–$45. Hookups: water, electric (20, 30, 50 amps), sewer, phone.

Pittsview

Bluff Creek Park, 144 Bluff Creek Rd., 36871. T: (334) 855-2746. RV/tent: 88. $14. Hookups: water, electric (20, 30 amps).

Robertsdale

Hilltop RV Park, 23420 CR 64, 36567. T: (251) 960-1129. RV/tent: 72. $16. Hookups: water, electric (20, 30, 50 amps), sewer, phone.

Russellville

Bear Creek Development Authority, 111 CR 88, 35653. T: (256) 332-4392. F: (256) 332-4372. www.bearcreeklakes.com. RV/tent: 160. $7.50–$12. Hookups: water, electric (30 amps), sewer.

Scottsboro

Crawford RV Park, 4320 South Broad St., 35759-7421. T: (256) 574-5366. www.crawfordrv.com. RV/tent: 12. $18. Hookups: water, electric (30, 50 amps), sewer, cable.

Goose Pond Colony, 417 Ed Hembree Dr., 35769. T: (256) 259-1808. F: (256) 259-3127. www.goose pond.org. RV/tent: 117. $15–$17. Hookups: water, electric (20, 30 amps), sewer, phone.

Selma

Lake Lanier Travel Park, 655 Lake Lanier Rd., 36701. T: (334) 875-1618. RV/tent: 55. $12–$18. Hookups: water, electric (20, 30, 50 amps), sewer.

Paul M. Grist State Park, 1546 Grist Rd., 36701. T: (334) 872-5846. www.dcnr.state.al.us/parks/paul_ m_grist_1a.html. RV/tent: 6. $8–$16. Hookups: water, electric (30 amps), sewer.

Shorter

Wind Drift Campground, At Jct. of I-85 & US 80, 36075. T: (334) 724-9428. RV/tent: 33. $17. Hookups: water, electric (20, 30, 50 amps), sewer, phone.

Siles

Service Park Campground, US Hwy. 84, 36919. T: (251) 754-9658. RV/tent: 32. $12. Hookups: water, electric (20, 30 amps).

Theodore

I-10 Kampground, 6430 Theodore Dawes Rd., 36582. T: (800) 272-1263. RV/tent: 193. $21. Hookups: sewer, electric (30, 50 amps), water, phone.

Town Creek

Doublehead Resort, 145 CR 314, 35672. T: (800) 685-9267. www.doublehead.com. RV/tent: 30. $15. Hookups: water, electric (30, 50 amps).

Troy

Deer Run RV Park, 3736 Hwy. 231 North, 36081. T: (800) 552-3036. F: (334) 670-6759. www.deer runrvpark.com. RV/tent: 74. $19. Hookups: sewer, electric (30, 50 amps), water, phone.

Swindall's Campground, 251 Swindall Rd., CR 14, 36081. T: (334) 566-9980. RV/tent: 350. $15–$16. Hookups: water, electric (20, 30, 50 amps), sewer.

Tuscaloosa

Deerlick Creek, 12421 Deerlick Rd., 35406. T: (205) 553-9373. www.sam.usace.army.mil/op/rec/ war-tom/holt/Default.htm#camp. RV/tent: 46. $8–$12. Hookups: water, electric (30 amps).

Sunset I Travel Park, 3801 11th Ave., 35401. T: (205) 759-2691. RV/tent: 35. $20. Hookups: water, electric (20, 30, 50 amps), sewer.

ALABAMA (continued)

Warrior

Rickwood Caverns State Park, 370 Rickwood Park Rd., 35180-9803. T: (205) 647-9692. www.alapark.com. RV/tent: 13. $14. Hookups: water, electric (30 amps), sewer.

Wetumpka

Fort Toulouse/Jackson Park, 2521 West Ft. Toulouse Rd., 36093. T: (334) 567-3002. RV/tent: 39. $8–$10. Hookups: water, electric (30, 50 amps).

FLORIDA

Alligator Point

KOA–Alligator Point Kampground Resort, 1320 Alligator Dr., 32346. T: (850) 349-2525. F: (850) 349-2067. www.alligatorpointkoa.com. RV/tent: 148. $18–$25. Hookups: water, electric (30, 50 amps), sewer.

Arcadia

Lettuce Lake Travel Resort, 8644 SW Reese St., 34269. T: (863-494-6057. F: (863) 494-4254. RV/tent: 50. $24. Hookups: water, electric (30, 50 amps), sewer, phone.

Riverside RV Resort and Campground, 9770 SW CR 769 (Kings Hwy.), 34269. T: (863) 993-2111 or (800) 795-9733. F: (863) 993-2021. www.river sidervresort.com. RV/tent: 250. $27–$35. Hookups: water, electric (30, 50 amps), sewer, phone.

Astor

St. Johns River Campground, 1520 SR 40, 32102. T: (904) 749-3995. F: (352) 759-3419. www.stjohns rivercampground.com. RV/tent: 85. $20. Hookups: water, electric (20, 30, 50 amps), sewer.

Big Pine Key

Bahia Honda State Park, 36850 Overseas Hwy., 33043. T: (305) 872-2353 or (800) 326-3521. www.reserveamerica.com or www.myflorida.com. RV/tent: 80. $29. Hookups: water, electric.

Big Pine Key Fishing Lodge, Box 430513, 33043. T: (305) 872-2351. RV/tent: 156. $37. Hookups: water, electric (30 amps), solar, cable.

Bokeelia

Tropic Isle RV Park, 15175 Stringfellow Rd. (CR 767), 33922. T: (941) 283-4456. F: (941) 283-7262. RV/tent: 145. $30–$35. Hookups: water, electric (30 amps), sewer.

Bradenton

Encore RV Resort–Sarasota North, 800 Kay Rd. Northeast, 34202. T: (941) 745-2600 or (800) 678-2131. F: (941) 748-8964. www.rvonthego. com. RV/tent: 415. $23–$40. Hookups: water, electric (30, 50 amps), sewer, cable TV, phone.

Pleasant Lake RV Resort, 6653 53rd. Ave. East, 34203. T: (941) 756-5076. F: (941) 727-8520. RV/tent: 343. $34. Hookups: water, electric (30, 50 amps), sewer, cable TV, phone.

Cape Canaveral

Mango Manor, 190 Oak Manor Dr., 32920. T: (321) 799-0741. F: (321) 783-8671. RV/tent: 51. $22. Hookups: water, electric (20, 30, 50 amps), sewer, cable TV, phone.

Cape San Blas

Cape San Blas Camping Resort, 1342 Cape San Blas Rd., 32457. T/F: (850) 229-6800. www.cape sanblas.com/capecamp. RV/tent: 44. $14–$16. Hookups: water, electric (20, 30 amps), sewer.

Carrabelle

Ho-Hum RV Park, 2132 Hwy. 98E, 32322. T: (850) 697-3926. www.hohorvpark.com. RV/tent: 50. $19–$21. Hookups: water, electric, sewer.

Chattahoochee

KOA–Chattachoochee, 2309 Flat Creek Rd., 32324. T: (850) 442-6657. F: (850) 442-6653. RV/tent: 46. $21–$24. Hookups: water, electric (30, 50 amps), sewer.

Clearwater

Travel World RV Park, 12400 US 19 North, 33764. T: (727) 536-1765. F: (727) 532-9385. RV/tent: 200. $20. Hookups: water, electric (50 amps), sewer, cable TV, phone.

Clewiston

Clewiston/Lake Okeechobee Holiday Trav-L Park, Rte. 2 Box 242, 33440. T: (863) 983-7078. F: (863) 983-9108. RV/tent: 124. $15–$26. Hookups: water, electric (30 amps), sewer, phone.

Crooked Hook RV Resort, 51700 US Hwy. 27, 33440. T: (941) 983-7112. F: (941) 983-3022. RV/tent: 180. $25. Hookups: water, electric (30 amps), sewer.

Cocoa Beach

Oceanus Mobile Village Campground, 152 Crescent Beach Dr. (23rd), 32931. T: (321) 783-3871. F: (321) 799-0818. RV/tent: 38. $28. Hookups: water, electric, sewer.

Dade City

Traveler's Rest Resort, 29129 Johnston Rd., 33525. T: (352) 588-2013. F: (352) 588-3462. www.travelers restresort.com. RV/tent: 537. $23. Hookups: water, electric (30, 50 amps), sewer, cable TV.

FLORIDA (continued)

Davenport

Fort Summit Camping Resort, 4200 US 27 North, 33837. T: (863) 424-1880. F: (863) 424-3336. www.koa.com. RV/tent: 300. $29–$33. Hookups: water, electric (50 amps), cable TV, phone.

Daytona Beach

Daytona Beach Campground, 4601 Clyde Morris Blvd., 32129. T: (386) 761-2663. F: (386) 761-2663. RV/tent: 285. $24. Hookups: water, electric (30, 50 amps), sewer, cable TV.

International RV Park and Campground, 3175 West International Speedway, 32124. T: (386) 239-0249. F: (386) 253-7073. RV/tent: 137. $20–$50. Hookups: water, electric (30, 50 amps), sewer.

Nova Family Campground, 1190 Herbert, 32129. T: (386) 767-0095. F: (386) 767-1666. www.go campingamerica.com/novafamilycampground. RV/ tent: 200. $22. Hookups: water, electric, cable TV.

DeBary

High Banks Marina & Campresort, 488 West High Banks Rd., 32713. T: (386) 668-4491. F: (386) 668-5072. RV/tent: 227. $22–$25. Hookups: water, electric (30, 50 amps), sewer.

Delray Beach

Del-Raton Travel Trailer Park, 2998 South Federal Hwy., 33483. T: (561) 278-4633. RV/tent: 60. $33. Hookups: water, electric (20, 30, 50 amps), sewer, phone.

Destin

Camping on the Gulf Holiday Travel Park, 10005 West Emerald Coast Pkwy., 32541. T: (850) 837-6334. F: (850) 654-5048. www.campgulf.com. RV/tent: 192. $29–$62. Hookups: water, electric (20, 30, 50 amps), sewer.

Dover

Citrus Hills RV Park, 5311 ST 60 East, 33527. T: (813) 737-4770. F: (813) 681-8310. RV/tent: 183. $20. Hookups: water, electric (30, 50 amps), sewer.

Dunedin

Dunedin Beach Campground, 2920 Alternate 19 North, 34698. T: (727) 784-3719. F: (727) 787-9821. RV/tent: 233. $29. Hookups: water, electric (50 amps), sewer, cable TV, phone.

Flagler Beach

Bulow Resort, 345 Old Kings Rd. South, 32136. T: (386) 439-9200. F: (386) 439-6757. www.bulow. com. RV/tent: 350. $22. Hookups: water, electric, cable TV.

Picnickers Campground/Shelltown, 2455 North Oceanshore Blvd., 32136. T: (386) 439-5337. F: (386) 439-0853. RV/tent: 56. $20–$23. Hookups: water, electric, sewer.

Fort Lauderdale

Yacht Haven Park & Marina, 2323 State Rd. 84, 33312-4889. T: (954) 583-2322. RV/tent: 250. $24–$35. Hookups: water, electric (20, 30, 50 amps), sewer.

Fort Myers

Shady Acres RV Travel Park, 19370 South Tamiami Trail, 33908. T: (941) 267-8448. F: (941) 267-7016. www.shadyacresfl.com. RV/tent: 316. $28. Hookups: water, electric (20, 30, 50 amps), sewer, cable TV, phone.

The Groves RV Resort, 16175 John Morris Rd., 33908. T: (941) 466-4300. F: (941) 466-6310. RV/tent: 150. $15–$32. Hookups: water, electric (50 amps), sewer, cab le TV, phone.

Fort Myers Beach

Red Coconut RV Resort on the Beach, 3001 Estero Blvd., 33931. T: (941) 463-7200. F: (941) 463-2609. www.redcoconut.com. RV/tent: 250. $25–$52. Hookups: water, electric (50 amps), sewer, cable TV, phone.

Fort Pierce

Road Runner Travel Resort, 5500 St. Lucie Blvd., 34946. T: (561) 464-0969. F: (561) 464-0987. www.roadrunnertravelresort.com. RV/tent: 450. $25. Hookups: water, electric (50 amps), sewer, cable TV, phone.

Fort Walton Beach

Playground RV Park, 777 North Beal Pkwy., 32547. T: (850) 862-3513. F: (850) 864-2468. RV/tent: 56. $22. Hookups: water, electric (50 amps), sewer, cable TV.

Fountain

Pine Lake RV Park, 21036 US Hwy. 231, 32428. T: (850) 722-1401. F: (850) 722-1403. RV/tent: 75. $16. Hookups: water, electric (30 amps), sewer, cable TV.

Freeport

Lazy Days RV Park, 18655 US Hwy. 331 South, 32439. T: (850) 835-4606. F: (850) 835-4605. www.lazydaysrv.net. RV/tent: 27. $20. Hookups: water, electric, sewer, cable TV, phone.

Georgetown

Riverwood RV Village, 1389 CR 309, 32139. T: (386) 467-7144. F: (386) 467-7143. RV/tent: 25. $18. Hookups: water, electric (30, 50 amps), sewer.

Gulf Islands National Seashore

Fort Pickens Area Campground, 1400 Fort Pickens Rd., 32561. T: (850) 934-2622. F: (850) 934-2653. www.nps.gov/guis/pphtml/camping.html. RV/tent: 200. $20. Hookups: water, electric.

FLORIDA (continued)

Haines City

Paradise Island RV Park, 2900 South Hwy. 27, 33844. T: (863) 439-1350. RV/tent: 62. $20. Hookups: water, electric (50 amps), sewer, cable TV, phone.

High Springs

Ginnie Springs Resort, 7300 Northeast Ginnie Springs Rd., 32643. T: (386) 454-2202. F: (386) 454-3201. www.ginniesprings.com. RV/tent: 252. $16. Hookups: water, electric (20, 30, 50 amps).

O'Leno State Park, Rte. 2 Box 1010, 32643. T: (386) 454-1853 or (800) 326-3521. F: (386) 454-2565. www.reserveamerica.com or www.myflorida.com. RV/tent: 59. $10. Hookups: water, electric.

Holiday

Holiday Travel Park, 1622 Aires Dr., 34690. T: (727) 934-6782. F: (727) 939-0278. www.campgulf.com. RV/tent: 703. $28.19–$62. Hookups: water, electric (50 amps), sewer, cable TV, phone.

Holt

River's Edge RV Campground, 4001 Log Lake Rd., 32564. T: (850) 537-2267. RV/tent: 114. $15. Hookups: water, electric, sewer, phone.

Homosassa

Camp 'N' Water Outdoor Resort, 11465 West Priest Ln., 34448. T: (352) 628-2000. F: (352) 628-0066. RV/tent: 95. $21. Hookups: water, electric (50 amps), sewer, cable TV, phone.

Chassahowitzka River Campground, 8600 Miss Maggie Dr., 32623. T: (352) 382-2200. F: (352) 382-2200. www.cclib.org/cccs/parks/facilities/campground/campground.html. RV/tent: 85. $18. Hookups: water, electric, sewer.

Indian Rocks Beach

Indian Rocks Beach RV Resort, 601 Gulf Blvd., 33785. T: (727) 596-7743. F: (727) 593-2896. RV/tent: 55. $30–$50. Hookups: water, electric (30, 50 amps), sewer, cable TV, phone.

Jacksonville

Flamingo Lake RV Resort Park, 3640 Newcomb Rd., 32218. T: (904) 766-0672 or (800) 326-3521. F: (904) 766-8909. www.flamingolake.com. RV/tent: 157. $26. Hookups: water, electric (20, 30, 50 amps), sewer, cable TV, phone.

Huguenot Memorial Park, 10980 Heckscher Dr., 32226. T: (904) 251-3335. F: (904) 251-3019. RV/tent: 71. $6–$8. Hookups: none.

Little Talbot Island State Park, 12157 Heckscher Dr., 32226. T: (904) 251-2320. www.myflorida.com. RV/tent: 40. $10–$14. Hookups: water, electric.

Jennings

Jennings Outdoor Resort, Rte. 1 Box 221, 32053. T: (386) 938-3321. F: (386) 938-3322. RV/tent: 112. $19. Hookups: water, electric (20, 30, 50 amps), sewer, cable TV, phone.

Juno Beach

Juno Beach RV Park, 900 Juno Ocean Walk, 33408. T: (561) 622-7500. RV/tent: 246. $26–$39. Hookups: water, electric (30, 50 amps), sewer.

Jupiter

West Jupiter Camping Resort, 17801 130th Ave. North, 33478. T: (888) 746-6073. F: (561) 743-3738. www.westjupitercampingresort.com. RV/tent: 103. $25–$32. Hookups: water, electric (20, 30, 50 amps), sewer, cable TV, phone.

Key West

Boyd's Key West Campground, 6401 Maloney Ave., 33040. T: (305) 294-1465. F: (305) 293-9301. RV/tent: 124. $56–$70. Hookups: water, electric (30, 50 amps), sewer, cable TV, phone.

Jabours Trailer Court, 223 Elizabeth St., 33040. T: (305) 294-5723. F: (305) 296-7965. www.kwcamp.com. RV/tent: 90. $40–$74. Hookups: water, electric (30 amps), sewer.

Kissimmee

Cypress Cove Nudist Resort, 4425 South Pleasant Hill Rd., 34746. T: (407) 933-5870. F: (407) 933-3559. www.gocampingamerica.com. RV/tent: 100. $54. Hookups: water, electric, sewer.

Mill Creek RV Resort, 2775 Michigan Ave., 34744. T: (407) 847-6288. F: (407) 847-6683. RV/tent: 183. $22. Hookups: water, electric (30 amps), sewer, phone.

Raccoon Lake Camp Resorts, 8555 West Irlo Bronson Hwy., 34747. T: (407) 239-4148. F: (407) 239-0223. RV/tent: 587. $25–$32. Hookups: water, electric (20, 30, 50 amps), sewer.

Southport Campground and Marina, 2001 East Southport Rd., 34746. T: (407) 933-5822. F: (407) 847-4010. www.southportpark.com. RV/tent: 61. $17. Hookups: water, electric (30, 50 amps), sewer.

Tropical Palms Resort, 2650 Holiday Trail, 34746. T: (407) 396-4595. F: (407) 396-8938. RV/tent: 500. $39. Hookups: water, electric (50 amps), sewer, cable TV, phone.

LaBelle

Whisper Creek RV Resort, 1980 Hickory Dr., 33935. T: (863) 675-6888. F: (863) 675-2323. www.whispercreek.com. RV/tent: 396. $21. Hookups: water, electric (30, 50 amps), sewer, cable TV, phone.

Lake City

Waynes RV Resort, Inc., Rte. 21 Box 501, 32024. T: (386) 752-5721. F: (386) 752-5721. RV/tent: 102. $14–$17. Hookups: water, electric, sewer.

Lake Placid

Camp Florida Resort/Lake Placid, 1525 US Hwy. 27 South, 33852. T: (863) 699-1991. F: (863) 699-1995. www.campfla.com. RV/tent: 396. $28. Hookups: water, electric (30, 50 amps) sewer, phone.

FLORIDA (continued)

Lake Worth

Camping Resort of the Palm Beaches, 5332 Lake Worth Rd., 33463. T: (561) 965-1653. F: (561) 965-9095. RV/tent: 150. $35. Hookups: water, electric (30 amps), sewer, cable TV, phone.

Lakeland

Sanlan Ranch Campground, 3929 US 98 South, 33813. T: (863) 665-1726. F: (863) 665-0604. www.sanlan.com. RV/tent: 315. $22–$32. Hookups: water, electric (50 amps), sewer, phone.

Lakeport

Aruba RV Resort, 1825 Old Lakeport Rd., 33471. T: (863) 946-1324. F: (863) 946-1270. www.okee direct.com/arubarv. RV/tent: 156. $20. Hookups: water, electric (30, 50 amps), sewer, cable TV, phone.

Lamont

A Camper's World Campground, Rte. 1 Box 164B, 32336. T: (850) 997-3300. RV/tent: 38. $19. Hookups: water, electric (20, 30, 50 amps), sewer, phone.

Largo

Indian Rocks Travel Park, 12121 Vonn Rd., 33774. T: (727) 595-2228. RV/tent: 30. $19–$22. Hookups: water, electric (30 amps), sewer, cable TV, phone.

Yankee Traveler RV Park, 8500 Ulmerton Rd. (Hwy. 688), 33771. T/F: (727) 531-7998. RV/tent: 210. $20–$22. Hookups: water, electric (30, 50 amps), sewer.

Leesburg

Holiday Travel Resort, 28229 CR 33, 34748. T: (352) 787-5151. F: (352) 787-1052. www.holidaytravel resort.com. RV/tent: 935. $26. Hookups: water, electric (30 amps), sewer, cable TV, phone.

Long Key

KOA–Fiesta Key Kampground, Mile Marker 70, 33001. T: (305) 664-4922 or (800) 562-7730. F: (305) 664-8741. www.koa.com/where/fl/09250. html. RV/tent: 341. $63–$88. Hookups: water, electric, sewer, cable TV, phone.

Marathon

Jolly Roger Travel Park, 59275 Overseas Hwy., 33050-9756. T: (305) 289-0404. F: (305) 743-6913. RV/tent: 131. $31–$48. Hookups: water, electric (20, 30, 50 amps), sewer.

Mexico Beach

Islander RV Park, 2600 US 98, 32410. T: (850) 648-4006. RV/tent: 40. $20. Hookups: water, electric (30 amps), sewer, phone, cable TV.

Miami

Larry and Penny Thompson Park and Campground, 12451 SW 184th St., 33177. T: (305) 232-1049. F: (305) 235-8667. www.co.miamidade.fl.us/parks/ mparks2.htm. RV/tent: 264. $19. Hookups: water, electric (20, 30, 50 amps), sewer.

Milton

Adventures Unlimited, Rte. 6 Box 283, 32570. T: (850) 623-6197. F: (850) 626-3124. www. adventuresunlimited.com. RV/tent: 30. $20. Hookups: water, electric (30 amps).

Mims

KOA–Cape Kennedy, 4513 West Main St., 32754. T: (352) 269-7361. F: (321) 269-1123. www.koa.com. RV/tent: 100. $19–$23. Hookups: water, electric (50 amps), sewer, cable TV, phone.

Naples

Club Naples RV Resort, 3180 Beck Blvd., 34114. T: (941) 455-7275. F: (941) 455-7271. www.club napleserv.com. RV/tent: 309. $24–$38. Hookups: water, electric, cable TV, phone.

Greystone Park, 13300 East Tamiami Trail, 34104. T: (941) 774-4044. RV/tent: 40. $28. Hookups: water, electric, sewer.

Kountree Kampinn RV Resort, 8230 Collier Blvd., 34114. T: (941) 775-4340. F: (941) 775-2269. RV/tent: 161. $27–$35. Hookups: water, electric (30 amps), sewer.

KOA–Naples/Marco Island, 1700 Barefoot Wiliams Rd., 34113. T: (941) 774-5455. F: (941) 774-0788. RV/tent: 186. $29–$47. Hookups: water, electric (20, 30 amps), sewer.

Port of the Islands RV Resort, 12425 Union Rd., 34114. T: (941) 642-5343. F: (941) 642-5343. www. portoftheislands.com/rvresort/. RV/tent: 99. $30. Hookups: water, electric (30 amps), sewer, phone.

Navarre

Navarre Beach Campground, 9201 Navarre Parkway, 32566. T: (850) 939-2188. F: (850) 939-4712. www.navarrebeachcampground.com. RV/tent: 160. $33. Hookups: water, electric (20, 30, 50 amps), sewer, cable TV.

Nokomis

Encore SuperPark–Sarasota, 1070 Laurel Rd., 34275. T: (800) 548-8678. F: (941) 485-5678. www.rvon thego.com. RV/tent: 558. $25–$46. Hookups: water, electric (30, 50 amps), cable TV, phone.

Stay-N-Play RV Resort, 899 Knights Trail, 34275. T: (941) 485-1800. F: (941) 488-1813. www.stay– play.com. RV/tent: 398. $30–$52. Hookups: water, electric (50 amps), cable TV, phone.

O'Brien

Ichetucknee Family Campground, RR 1 Box 1576, 32071. T: (386) 497-2150. F: (386) 497-2150. www. ichetuckneeriver.com. RV/tent: 50. $18–$21.50. Hookups: water, electric (30, 50 amps), sewer.

FLORIDA (continued)

Ocala
KOA–Silver Springs, 3200 SW 38th Ave., 34474.
T: (352) 237-2138. F: (352) 237-9894. RV/tent: 205.
$33–$37. Hookups: water, electric (20, 30 amps),
sewer.

Okeechobee
Bob's Big Bass RV Park, 12766 Southeast Hwy. 441,
34974. T: (863) 763-2638. RV/tent: 43. $15. Hook-
ups: water, electric (20, 30, 50 amps), sewer.

Buckhead Ridge Marina, 670 Hwy. 78B, 34974.
T: (863) 763-2826. F: (863) 467-5555. RV/tent: 112.
$15–$25. Hookups: water, electric (20, 30 amps),
sewer.

KOA–Okeechobee Kampground and Golf Course,
4276 Hwy. 441 South, 34974. T: (863) 763-0231.
F: (863) 763-0531. www.koa.com. RV/tent: 465.
$29–$65. Hookups: water, electric (30, 50 amps)
sewer, cable TV, phone.

Ormond Beach
Encore Superpark Daytona Beach North, 1701
North US 1, 32174. T: (386) 672-3045. F: (386)
672-3026. www.encorerv.com/superparks/florida/
daytonabeachnorth/. RV/tent: 336. $30. Hookups:
water, electric, sewer, cable TV, phone.

Ormond-by-the-Sea
Ocean Village Camper Resort, 2162 Ocean Shore
Blvd., 32176. T: (386) 441-1808. RV/tent: 80. $25.
Hookups: water, electric (30 amps), sewer, cable TV.

Osprey
Oscar Scherer State Recreation Area, 1843 North
Tamiami Trail, 34229. T: (941) 483-5956 or (800)
326-3521. F: (941) 480-3007. www.reserveameri
ca.com or www.myflorida.com. RV/tent: 104. $25.
Hookups: water, electric, sewer.

Palm Harbor
Caladesi RV Park, 205 Dempsey Rd., 34683. T: (727)
784-3622. F: (727) 784-3622. RV/tent: 46. $27.
Hookups: water, electric (20, 30 amps), sewer.

Palmetto
Frog Creek Campground, 8515 Bayshore Rd.,
34221. T: (941) 722-6154. F: (941) 723-5820. www.
frogcreekrv.com. RV/tent: 190. $22. Hookups:
water, electric (30 amps), sewer, phone.

Panacea
Holiday Campground, 14 Coastal Hwy., 32346.
T: (850) 984-5757. F: (850) 984-5757. RV/tent: 80.
$24. Hookups: water, electric (30, 50 amps), sewer.

Panama City Beach
Ocean Park RV Resort, 23026 Panama City Beach
Pkwy., 32413. T: (850) 235-0306. RV/tent: 160. $30.
Hookups: water, electric (30 amps), sewer, cable
TV.

Pensacola
Playa del Rio Park and Yacht Club, Perdido Key,
32507. T: (850) 492-0904. F: (850) 492-4471. www.
playadelrio.com. RV/tent: 30. $19–$35. Hookups:
water, electric (20, 30 50 amps), sewer, cable TV,
phone.

Perdido Key
All Star Campground / Perdido Key, 13621 Perdido
Key Dr., 32507. T: (850) 492-0041. www.allstar-rv.
com. RV/tent: 182. $24–$70. Hookups: water, electric (20, 30, 50 amps), sewer, cable TV, phone.

Perry
Southern Oaks RV Campground and Resort, 3641
Hwy. 19 South, 32347. T: (850) 584-3221. F: (850)
584-3224. RV/tent: 100. $23. Hookups: water, elec-
tric (15, 30, 50 amps), sewer, cable TV, phone.

Port Richey
Suncoast RV Resort, 9029 US 19, 34668. T: (727)
842-9324. RV/tent: 142. $22. Hookups: water, elec-
tric (20, 30, 50 amps), sewer, cable TV, phone.

Port St. Joe
Presnell's Bayside Marina and RV Resort, 2115 Hwy.
C30, 32456. T: (850) 229-2710. RV/tent: 27. $12.
Hookups: water, electric (50 amps).

Punta Gorda
Waters Edge RV of Punta Gorda, 6800 Golf Course
Blvd., 33982. T: (941) 637-4677. F: (941) 637-9543.
RV/tent: 131. $20–$29. Hookups: water, electric
(20, 30, 50 amps), sewer.

Waters Edge RV Resort, Punta Gorda, 33982.
T: (941) 637-4677. F: (941) 637-9543. www.waters
edgervresort.com. RV/tent: 176. $25. Hookups:
water, electric (30, 50 amps), sewer, phone.

Riverview
Alafia River RV Resort, 9812 Gibsonton Dr., 33569-
5399. T: (813) 677-1997. F: (813) 677-1997. RV/
tent: 203. $21. Hookups: water, electric (20, 30
amps), sewer.

Hidden River Travel Resort, 12500 McMullen Loop,
33569. T: (813) 677-1515. RV/tent: 340. $21. Hook-
ups: water, electric (20, 30, 50 amps), sewer.

Rockledge
Space Coast RV Resort, 820 Barnes Blvd., 32955.
T: (321) 636-2873. F: (321) 636-0275. www.usa
star.com/spacecoast/. RV/tent: 240. $35. Hookups:
water, electric (50 amps), sewer.

Ruskin
Hide-A-Way RV Resort, 2206 Chaney Dr., 33570.
T: (813) 645-6037. F: (813) 645-6037. RV/tent: 292.
$22. Hookups: water, electric (30, 50 amps), sewer,
cable TV, phone.

FLORIDA (continued)

Ruskin (continued)

River Oaks RV Resort, 201 Stephens Rd., 33570.
T: (813) 645-2439. RV/tent: 97. $13–$20.
Hookups: water, electric (20, 30, 50 amps), sewer.

Salt Springs

Elite Resorts at Salt Springs, 25250 East Hwy. 316,
32134. T: (352) 685-1900. F: (352) 685-0557. www.
eliteresorts.com. RV/tent: 470. $20. Hookups:
water, electric (20, 30 amps), sewer.

Sanford

Twelve Oaks RV Resort, 6300 State Rte. 46 West,
32771-9290. T: (407) 323-0880. RV/tent: 281. $22.
Hookups: water, electric (30, 50 amps), sewer.

Sarastoa/Siesta Key

Gulf Beach Campground, 8862 Midnight Pass Rd.,
34242. T: (941) 349-3839. RV/tent: 48. $19–$57.
Hookups: water, electric (20, 30, 50 amps), sewer,
cable TV, phone.

Sopchoppy

Ochlockonee River State Park, P.O. Box 5, 32358.
T: (850) 962-2771 or (800) 326-3521. F: (850)
962-2403. www.reserveamerica.com or
www.myflorida.com. RV/tent: 30. $20. Hookups:
water, electric, sewer.

South Bay

South Bay RV Park, 100 Levee Rd., 33493. T: (561)
992-9045. F: (561) 992-9277. RV/tent: 96. $16.50–
$17.60. Hookups: water, electric (30 amps), cable
TV.

St. Augustine

North Beach Camp Resort, 4125 Coastal Hwy.
(A1A), 32084. T: (904) 824-1806. F: (904) 826-
0897. RV/tent: 121. $35. Hookups: water, electric
(30, 50 amps), sewer, cable TV, phone.

St. Augustine Beach

Bryn Mawr Ocean Resort, 4850 A1A South, 32800.
T: (904) 471-3353. F: (904) 471-8730. www.bryn
mawroceanresort.com. RV/tent: 130. $34–$42.
Hookups: water, electric (20, 30, 50 amps), sewer,
cable TV, phone.

Cooksey's Camping Resort, 2795 A1A South, 32080.
T: (904) 471-3171. RV/tent: 244. $30. Hookups:
water, electric (15, 30, 50 amps), sewer, phone.

Ocean Grove Camp Resort, 4225 Hwy. A1A South,
32084. T: (904) 471-3414. F: (904) 461-8403.
www.oceangroveresort.com. RV/tent: 198. $35.
Hookups: water, electric (20, 30, 50 amps), sewer,
cable TV, phone.

KOA–St. Augustine Beach Kampground Resort, 525
West Pope Rd., 32080. T: (904) 471-3113. F: (904)
471-1715. www.koa.com. RV/tent: 71. $36. Hook-
ups: water, electric (30, 50 amps), sewer, cable TV.

St. Petersburg

Robert's Mobile Home and RV Resort, 3390 Gandy
Blvd., 33702. T: (727) 577-6820. F: (727) 577-2621.
RV/tent: 430. $20. Hookups: water, electric (30, 50
amps), sewer, cable TV, phone.

KOA–St. Petersburg/Madeira Beach Kampground,
5400 95th St. North, 33708. T: (727) 392-2233.
F: (727) 398-6081. www.koa.com. RV/tent: 390.
$37–$65. Hookups: water, electric (20, 30, 50
amps), phone.

Thonotassa

Happy Traveler RV Park, 9401 Fowler Ave., 33592. T:
(813) 986-3094. F: (813) 986-9077. RV/tent: 224.
$21. Hookups: water, electric (20, 30, 50 amps),
sewer, phone.

Titusville

The Great Outdoors RV and Golf Resort, 135 Plantation Dr., 32780. T: (800) 621-2267 or 321-269-
5004. F: (321) 269-5004. www.tgoresort.com.
RV/tent: 200. $35. Hookups: water, electric (30, 50
amps), sewer, cable TV.

Venice

Venice Campground and RV Park, 4085 East Venice
Ave., 34292. T: (941) 488-0850. F: (941) 485-1666.
www.campvenice.com/index.shtml. RV/tent: 133.
$28–$36. Hookups: water, electric (30 amps),
sewer.

Wabasso

Vero Beach Kamp RV Resort, 8850 North US Hwy.
1, 32970. T: (561) 589-5665. F: (561) 388-5722.
RV/tent: 120. $20. Hookups: water, electric (30, 50
amps), cable TV.

West Palm Beach

Pine Lake Camp Resort, 7000 Okeechobee Blvd.,
33411. T: (561) 686-0714. RV/tent: 194. $20. Hook-
ups: water, electric (20, 30 amps), sewer, phone.

White Springs

Kelly's RV Park, Rte. 1 Box 370, Rte. 41 South,
32096. T: (386) 397-2616. F: (386) 397-1261. RV/
tent: 76. $16. Hookups: water, electric (30, 50
amps), sewer, phone.

Yulee

Hance's First in Florida RV Park, 3111 Hance Pkwy.
(US 17), 32097. T: (904) 225-2080. F: (904) 225-
2080. RV/tent: 73. $27. Hookups: water, electric
(30, 50 amps), sewer, cable TV, phone.

Zephyrhills

Jim's RV Park, 35120 Hwy. 54 West, 33541-1400. T:
(813) 782-5610. RV/tent: 156. $17. Hookups:
water, electric (20, 30 amps), sewer.

GEORGIA

Acworth

Holiday Marina Harbor & Campground, 5989 Groover's landing, 30102. T: (770) 974-2575. RV/tent: 47. $16–$19. Hookups: water, electric (20, 30 amps), sewer, phone.

Lakemont Campground, 5134 North Shores Rd., 30101. T/F: (770) 966-0302. lakemontjc@aol.com. RV/tent: 100. $16–$21. Hookups: water, electric (20, 30, 50 amps), sewer, phone (modem).

Adel

Reed Bingham State Park, P.O. Box 394, B-1, Rte. 2, 31620. T: (912) 896-3551. reedpark@surfsouth. com. RV/tent: 46. $18–$21. Hookups: water, electric (20, 30 amps), sewer, cable TV, phone.

Albany

Albany RV Resort, 1218 Liberty Expressway Southeast, 31705. T: (800) 424-6301. atrv@surfsouth. com. RV/tent: 31. $17–$19. Hookups: water, electric (20, 30, 50 amps), sewer, cable TV, phone (modem).

Creekside Plantation RV Campground, 2700 Liberty Expressway Southeast, 31705. T: (912) 883-7996. RV/tent: 60. $16. Hookups: water, electric (30, 50 amps), sewer, cable TV, phone (modem).

Devencrest Travel Park, 1833 Liberty Expressway Southeast, 31705. T: (912) 432-2641. RV/tent: 100. $16–$18. Hookups: water, electric (15, 20, 30, 50 amps), sewer, laundry.

Americus

Brickyard Plantation RV & Tent Campground, 1619 US Hwy. 280 East, 31709. T: (912) 874-1234. www. brickyardgolfclub.com. RV/tent: 12. $16. Hookups: water, electric (20, 30 amps), sewer.

Andersonville

City Campground, Rte. 1 Box 800, 31711. T: (912) 924-2558. RV/tent: 40. $14–$16. Hookups: water, electric (15, 20 amps), sewer.

Arabi

Southen Gates RV Park & Campground, 138 Campsite Rd., 31712. T: (912) 273-6464. RV/tent: 55. $19–$21. Hookups: water, electric (20, 30, 50 amps), sewer, phone (modem).

Ashburn

Knights Inn & RV Park, 1971 North St., 31714. T: (229) 567-3334. RV/tent: 77. $10–$12. Hookups: water, electric (20, 30 amps), sewer.

Augusta

Flynn's Inn Camping Village, 3746 Peach Orchard Rd., 30906. T: (706) 798-6912. RV/tent: 61. $12–$14. Hookups: water, electric (30, 50 amps), sewer, phone (modem).

Austell

Arrowhead Campground, 7400 Six Flags Dr. SW, 30001. T: (800) 631-8956. F: (770) 745-8752.
acg@arrowheadcampground.com. RV/tent: 200. $28. Hookups: water, electric (20, 30, 50 amps), sewer, phone (modem).

Barnesville

High Falls Campground, 1046 High Falls Park Rd., 30204. T: (770) 358-2205. RV/tent: 122. $21–$24. Hookups: water, electric (20, 30, 50 amps), sewer, phone, laundry.

Blairsville

Goose Creek Campgrounds, 7061 Goose Creek, 30512. T: (706) 745-5111. RV/tent: 24. $16–$18. Hookups: water, electric (20 amps), sewer.

Lake Nottely RV Park, 350 Haley Cir., 30512. T: (706) 745-8899. F: (706) 745-8806. www.lakenot telyrv.com. RV/tent: 80. $16. Hookups: water, electric (20, 30, 50 amps), sewer, phone (modem).

Mountain Oak Cabins & Campgrouds, 2388 Mulky Gap Rd., 30512. T: (888) 781-6867. www.moun tainoak.com. mofcc@alltel.net. RV/tent: 35. $15–$21. Hookups: water, electric (20, 30, 50 amps), sewer, phone (modem).

Trackrock Campgrounds & Cabins, 4887 Trackrock Campground Rd., 30512. T: (706) 745-2420. www.trackrock.com. trackroc@alltel.net. RV/tent: 90. $16–$18. Hookups: water, electric (20, 30 amps), sewer, phone (modem), laundry.

Blakely

Kolomoki Mounds State Park, Temple Mound Rd., 31723. T: (229) 724-2150. kolomoki@alltel.net. RV/tent: 43. $15. Hookups: water, electric (30 amps), sewer, phone.

Blue Ridge

Cooper Creek Campground, US Forest Service, 650 Appalachian Hwy., 30513. T: (706) 632-3031. RV/tent: 27. $8–$12. Hookups: water, picnic table, restrooms, showers, tent pads.

Deep Hole Campground, US Forest Service, 650 Appalachian Hwy., 30513. T: (706) 632-3031. RV/tent: 12. $8–$12. Hookups: water, picnic table, restrooms, showers, tent pads.

Frank Gross Campground, US Forest Service, 650 Appalachian Hwy., 30513. T: (706) 632-3031. RV/tent: 9. $8–$12. Hookups: water, picnic table, restrooms, showers, tent pads.

Morganton Point, US Forest Service, 650 Appalachian Hwy., 30513. T: (706) 632-3031. RV/tent: 43. $8–$12. Hookups: water, picnic table, restrooms, showers, tent pads.

Mulky Campground, US Forest Service, 650 Appalachian Hwy., 30513. T: (706) 632-3031. RV/tent: 21. $8–$12. Hookups: water, picnic table, restrooms, showers, tent pads.

Whispering Pines Campground, 290 Whipering Pines Rd., 30513. T: (706) 374-6494. RV/tent: 30. $16. Hookups: water, electric (15, 20 amps), sewer, phone.

GEORGIA (continued)

Brunswick

Golden Isles Vacation Park, 7445 Blythe Hwy., 31523. T: (912) 261-1025. RV/tent: 110. $19–$21. Hookups: water, electric (20, 30, 50 amps), sewer, cable TV.

Ocean Breeze Campround, Dover Bluff Rd., 31523. T: (912) 264-6692. RV/tent: 37. $17. Hookups: water, electric (20, 30 amps), sewer, phone.

Buena Vista

Country Vista Campground, Rte. 1 Box 14, 31803. T: (229) 649-2267. RV/tent: 44. $17–$19. Hookups: water, electric (20, 30, 50 amps), sewer, phone (modem), cable TV.

Buford

Bolding Mill Campground, P.O. Box 567, 30515-0567. T: (404) 532-3650. RV/tent: 97. $14–$22. Hookups: water, electric (20 amps), sewer, laundry.

Byron

Interstate Camping, 305 Chapman Rd., 31008. T: (229) 956-5511. www.interstatervcenter. irvcenter@aol.com. RV/tent: 104. $20–$22. Hookups: water, electric (30, 50 amps), sewer, phone (modem).

Calhoun

KOA–Calhoun, 2523 Redbud Rd. Northeast, 30701. T: (800) 562-7512. RV/tent: 87. $21–$24. Hookups: water, electric (15, 20, 30 amps), sewer, laundry.

Carrollton

John Tanner State Park, 354 Tanners Beach Rd., 30117. T: (770) 830-2222. RV/tent: 32. $16–$20. Hookups: water, electric (30, 50 amps), sewer, cable TV.

Cartersville

Clark Creek South, P.O. Box 487, 30120-0487. T: (770) 382-4700. RV/tent: 40. $14–$20. Hookups: water, electric (30 amps), sewer.

KOA–Cartersville, 800 Cassville-White Rd., 30121. T: (404) 382-7333. RV/tent: 117. $20–$22. Hookups: water, electric (20, 30, 50 amps), sewer, laundry.

McKinney Campground, P.O. Box 487, 30120. T: (770) 382-4700. RV/tent: 150. $18–$20. Hookups: water, electric (30, 50 amps), sewer.

Payne Campground, P.O. Box 487, 30120. T: (770) 382-4700. RV/tent: 60. $20. Hookups: water, electric (30 amps), sewer.

Cave Spring

Cedar Creek Park, 6770 Cave Springs Rd., 30124. T: (706) 777-3030. cdrcrkpark@aol.com. RV/tent: 60. $15. Hookups: water, electric (30, 50 amps), sewer.

Cecil

Cecil Bay RV Park, Old Coffee Rd., 31627. T: (229) 794-1484. RV/tent: 100. $14–$16. Hookups: water, electric (20, 30, 50 amps), sewer.

Chatsworth

Fort Mountain State Park, 181 Ft. Mountain Park Rd., 30705. T: (706) 695-2621. fortmtpk@aol.com. RV/tent: 79. $14. Hookups: water, electric (30 amps), sewer, cable TV.

Lake Conasauga Campground, Chattahoochee National Forest, 1755 Cleveland Hwy., 30501. T: (706) 695-6736. www.fs.fed.u/conf/consauga_host.htm. madavis@fs.fed.us. RV/tent: 35. $12–$16. Hookups: water sources, bathhouse, firewood, grill, sewer, table, tent pad.

Chauncey

Jaybird Springs Resort, 1221 Jaybird Springs Rd., 31011. T: (229) 868-2728. RV/tent: 22. $14–$16. Hookups: water, electric (15, 30 amps), sewer, phone.

Clarkesville

Moccasin Creek State Park, Rte. 1 Box 1634, 30523. T: (706) 947-3194. www.georgia.com/parks/moccasin.html. mocccrkpk@stc.net. RV/tent: 54. $12–$16. Hookups: water, electric (30 amps), sewer, firewood, grill.

Clayton

Black Rock Mountain State Park, 3085 Black Rock Mountain Pkwy., 30562. T: (706) 746-2141. brmp@stc.net. RV/tent: 59. $12–$14. Hookups: water, electric (30 amps), sewer, cable TV, laundry, phone.

Cleveland

Crystal Springs Campground, 4542 Hwy. 129 North, 30528. T: (706) 865-6955. RV/tent: 62. $12–$16. Hookups: water, sewer, laundry, pet friendly.

Gold 'n' Gem Grubbin, 75 Gold Nugget Ln., 30528. T: (800) 942-4436. www.goldngem.com. RV/tent: 50. $10–$22. Hookups: water, electric (20, 30, 50 amps), sewer, bathhouse.

Jenny's Creek Family Campground, 4542 Hwy. 129 North, 30528. T: (706) 865-6955. www.jennys creek.com. RV/tent: 70. $14–$18. Hookups: water, electric (15, 20, 30 amps), sewer, laundry.

Leisure Acres Campground, 3840 Westmoreland Rd., 30528. T: (706) 865-4114. F: (706) 865-9544. leisure@aol.com. RV/tent: 92. $18–$20. Hookups: water, electric (30, 50 amps), sewer, phone (modem).

Mountain Creek Grove, 258 Grove Ln., 30528. T: (706) 865-6930. F: (706) 865-5521. www.cyber nude.com/resorts/mtncreek. mtncreek@stc.net. RV/tent: 17. $18–$24. Hookups: water, electric (20, 30, 50 amps), sewer.

GEORGIA (continued)

Mountain Creek Grove Campgrounds, 338 Mountain Creek Cir., 30528. T: (706) 865-6930. www.mountaincreekgrove.com. mtncreek@alltel.net. RV/tent: 110. $7–$15. Hookups: water, electric (30 amps), sewer, shower, bathhouse.

Serendipity Nudist Resort, 95 Cedar Hollow Rd., 30528. T: (706) 219-3993. office@serendipity -park.com. RV/tent: 42. $18–$21. Hookups: water, electric (50 amps), sewer, phone (modem).

Turner Campsite, 142 Turner Campsite Rd., 30528. T: (706) 865-4757. RV/tent: 126. $16–$20. Hookups: water, electric 30 amps), sewer, laundry.

Colquitt

Emerald Lake RV Park & Music Showcase, 698 Enterprise Rd., 31737. T: (229) 758-2929. RV/tent: 20. $16. Hookups: water, electric (30, 50 amps), sewer, laundry.

Lake Pines RV Park & Campground, 6404 Garrett Rd., 31820. T: (706) 561-9675. www.lakepines.net. RV/tent: 68. $18–$20. Hookups: water, electric (20, 30, 50 amps), sewer, phone (modem).

Comer

Watson Mill Bridge State Park, 650 Watson Mill Rd., 30629. T: (706) 783-5349. www.negia.net/~watson/. watson@negia.net. RV/tent: 24. $15. Hookups: water, electric (30 amps), sewer, laundry.

Commerce

KOA–Commerce/Athens Campground, CR 466, 30529. T: (706) 335-5535. RV/tent: 71. $18–$24. Hookups: water, electric (20, 30, 50 amps), sewer, phone (modem).

Cordele

KOA–Cordele, 373 Rockhouse Rd., 31015. T: (800) 562-0275. RV/tent: 73. $22–$24. Hookups: water, electric (20, 30 amps), sewer.

Cornelia

Lake Russell Campground, 1756 Cleveland Hwy., 30501. T: (706) 754-6221. RV/tent: 42. $10–$12. Hookups: water, sewer, table, grill.

Covington

Riverside Estates RV & Camping, 1891-2 Access Rd., 30014. T: (770) 787-3707. RV/tent: 172. $18–$20. Hookups: water, electric (20, 30, 50 amps), sewer, phone (modem), cable TV.

Crawfordsville

Alexander H. Stephens State Historic Park, Hwy. 22 & US 278, 30631. T: (706) 456-2602. ahssp@ g-net.net. RV/tent: 25. $12–$16. Hookups: water, electric (20, 30 amps), sewer, laundry.

Cumming

Sawnee Campground, P.O. Box 567, 30515-0567. T: (770) 887-0592. RV/tent: 56. $16–$22. Hookups: water, electric (20 amps), sewer, laundry.

Shady Grove Campground, P.O. Box 567, 30515-0567. T: (770) 887-2067. RV/tent: 115. $14–$22. Hookups: water, electric (20 amps), sewer, laundry.

Twin Lakes RV Park, 3300 Shore Dr., 30040. T: (770) 887-4400. RV/tent: 90. $16–$18. Hookups: water, electric (30, 50 amps), sewer.

Darien

Tall Pines Campground, Hwy. 251, 31305. T: (912) 437-3966. RV/tent: 45. $16–$18. Hookups: water, electric (30, 50 amps), sewer, laundry.

Dawsonville

Amicalola Falls State Park & Lodge, 418 Amicalola Falls Lodge Rd., 30534. T: (706) 265-4703. www. ngeorgia.com/parks/amicalola.html. RV/tent: 20. $12–$16. Hookups: water, electric (20, 30 amps), sewer, laundry.

Dillard

River Vista Mountain Village, 960 Hwy. 246, 30537. T: (888) 850-7275. www.rvmountainvillage.com. relax@rvmountainvillage.com. RV/tent: 127. $25. Hookups: water, electric (30, 50 amps), sewer, cable TV, laundry.

Donalsonville

Seminole Sportsman Lodge, Marina & Campground, 7966 Marina Rd., 31745. T: (229) 861-3862. F: (229) 861-3501. www.seminolesportsmanlodge. com. brandimist2000@yahoo.com. RV/tent: 24. $16. Hookups: water, electric (20, 30 amps), gas, sewer, modem.

Seminole State Park, Rte. 2 & Hwy. 39, 31745. T: (229) 861-3137. RV/tent: 50. $12–$16. Hookups: water, electric (30 amps), sewer, firewood, grill, laundry.

Eatonton

Lawrence Shoals Park, Junction US 129 & Hwy. 16, 31024. T: (706) 485-5494. RV/tent: 49. $14–$16. Hookups: water, electric (20, 30 amps), sewer, firewood, grill, laundry.

Oconee Springs Park at Lake Sinclair, US 129 & Hwy. 16, 31024. T: (706) 485-8423. www.lakesin clair.org. RV/tent: 52. $12–$25. Hookups: water, electric (20, 30 amps), sewer, firewood, grill, laundry (No Pets).

Old Federal Rd. Park, Junction Hwy. 369 & Hwy. 53, 31024. T: (770) 967-6757. RV/tent: 84. $16. Hookups: water, electric (30, 50 amps), sewer, laundry.

Ellijay

Camp Cherry Log, Littlle Rock Creek Rd., 30540. T: (706) 635-5006. RV/tent: 43. $18–$22. Hookups: water, electric (30, 50 amps), sewer.

Plum Nelly Campground, 15828 South Hwy. 515, 30540. T: (404) 317-2458. RV/tent: 32. $16–$18. Hookups: water, electric (30, 50 amps), sewer.

GEORGIA (continued)

Fitzgerald

Colony City Campground, Perry House Rd., 31750. T: (229) 423-5050. RV/tent: 36. $12–$16. Hook-ups: water, electric (30 amps), sewer, firewood, grill, laundry (No Showers).

Florence

Florence Marina State Park, Junction 39 C & Hwy. 39, 31821. T: (229) 838-6870. flmarina@sowega. net. RV/tent: 44. $16. Hookups: water, electric (30, 50 amps), sewer.

Folkston

Okefenokee Pastimes, Rte. 2 Box 3090, 31537. T: (229) 496-4472. www.okefenokee.com. overnight@okefenokee.com. RV/tent: 22. $18–$22. Hookups: water, electric (30 amps), sewer, firewood, grill, laundry.

Forsyth

L & D RV Park & Campgrounds, Rte. 3 Box 62A, 31029. T: (921) 994-5401. RV/tent: 29. $16–$18. Hookups: water, electric (20, 30, 50 amps), sewer, laundry.

Fort Benning

Uche Creek Campground/Fort Benning Manor, Miller Hall Bldg. 241, 31905. T: (706) 545-4053. F: (706) 545-3057. RV/tent: 85. $18–$22. Hookups: water, electric (30, 50 amps), sewer, cable TV, phone (modem).

Gainesville

Duckett Mill Campground, Hwy. 400 & Duckett Mill Rd., 30506. T: (770) 532-9802. RV/tent: 54. $12–$14. Hookups: table, tent pad, grill, sewer.

Lake Blue Ridge Campground, 1755 Cleveland Hwy., 30501. T: (770) 257-3000. www.fs.fed.us. spayne@fs.fed.us. RV/tent: 58. $10–$12. Hookups: water, rest rooms, showers, tent pads.

Hephzibah

Fox Hollow Campgrounds, 4032 Peach Orchard Rd., 30815. T: (706) 592-4563. RV/tent: 21. $14. Hookups: water, electric (30 amps), phone (modem).

Hiawassee

Enota Campground & Resort, 1000 Hwy. 180, 30546. T: (706) 896-9966. RV/tent: 92. $22–$28. Hookups: water, electric (30, 50 amps), laundry, sewer, phone.

Georgia Mountain Campground, P.O. Box 444, 30546. T: (706) 896-4191. RV/tent: 96. $14–$18. Hookups: water, electric (20, 30 amps), sewer, cable TV, phone (modem).

La Grange

Three Creeks Campground, 305 Old Roanoke Rd., 30241. T: (706) 884-0899. alltel.net. RV/tent: 34. $19–$21. Hookups: water, electric (30, 50 amps), sewer, phone, laundry.

Metter

Beaver Run RV Park & Campground, Rte. 3 Box 168, 30439. T: (912) 685-2594. www.turnstone cabins.com/beaverrun.html. bvrunpk@pineland. net. RV/tent: 71. $20. Hookups: water, electric (30, 50 amps), sewer, phone (modem).

Perry

Boland's Perry Overnight Park, 800 Perimeter Rd., 31069. T: (770) 987-3371. RV/tent: 65. $18. Hookups: water, electric (20, 30 amps), laundry, sewer, cable TV, phone (modem).

Crossroads Travel Park, 1513 Sam Nunn Blvd., 31069. T: (912) 987-3141. RV/tent: 56. $20–$22. Hookups: water, electric (20, 30 amps), sewer, phone (modem).

Rincon

Green Peace RV Park, 155 Caroni Dr., 31326. T: (912) 826-5540. pkavali@aol.com. RV/tent: 50. $11–$14. Hookups: water, electric (30 amps), sewer, phone (modem).

Whispering Pines RV Park, 1755 Hodgeville Rd., 31326. T: (912) 728-7562. F: (912) 728-5519. RV/tent: 53. $23–$25. Hookups: water, electric (20, 30, 50 amps), sewer, phone (modem).

Rome

Coosa River Campground, 181 Lock & Dam Rd., 30161. T: (706) 234-5001. RV/tent: 31. $16–$18. Hookups: water, electric (30, 50 amps), sewer, phone (modem), laundry.

Sautee

Cherokee Campground of White County, 45 Bethel Rd., 30571. T: (706) 878-2267. F: (706) 878-1880. www.mindlessdrivel.org. RV/tent: 48. $18–$20. Hookups: water, electric (20, 30 amps), sewer, cable TV, phone (modem).

Creekwood Cabins & Campground, 5730 Hwy. 356, 30571. T: (706) 878-2164. db.cornerpost.com. creekwoodcamp@yahoo.com. RV/tent: 168. $12–$25. Hookups: water, ellectric (30, 50 amps), sewer, cable TV, bathhouse.

Sleepy Hollow Campground, 307 Sleepy Hollow Rd., 30571. T: (706) 878-2618. RV/tent: 73. $17–$20. Hookups: water, electric (20, 30 amps), sewer, hot showers, playground.

St. George

Hidden River Ranch, 885 Reynolds Bridge Road St., 31646. T: (912) 843-2603. web.infoave.net/~ hiddenriver/index.html. hiddenriver@planettel. net. RV/tent: 30. $10–$17. Hookups: water, electric (30, 50 amps), sewer, phone (modem), laundry.

Statesboro

Parkwood Motel & RV Park, 12188 Hwy. 301 South, 30458. T: (912) 681-3105. parkwood@frontier net.net. RV/tent: 37. $15–$19. Hookups: water, electric (30, 50 amps), sewer, cable TV, phone.

GEORGIA (continued)

Tifton

Amy's South Georgia RV Park, 4632 Union Rd., 31794. T: (912) 386-8441. amysrvpark@ planttel.com. RV/tent: 86. $18–$20. Hookups: water, electric (20, 30, 50 amps), sewer, phone.

Townsend

Lake Harmony RV Park, Rte. 3 Box 3128, 31331. T: (912) 832-4338. www.lakeharmonypark.com. RV/tent: 50. $18–$21. Hookups: water, electric (30 amps), sewer, cable TV, phone (modem).

McIntosh Lake Campgrounds, Rte. 3 Box 3112, 31331. T: (229) 832-6215. RV/tent: 39. $12. Hookups: water, electric (15, 30 amps), sewer, cable TV, phone (modem).

Tybee Island

River's End Campground & RV Park, 915 Polk St., 31328-0988. T: (912) 786-5518. F: (706) 786-4126.

riversendga@gocampingamerica.com. RV/tent: 127. $25–$35. Hookups: water, electric (20, 30, 50 amps), sewer, phone (modem).

Unadilla

South Prong Creek Campground, 627 Hwy. 230, 31091. T: (912) 783-2551. www.southprong.com. tom@southprong.com. RV/tent: 150. $11–$16. Hookups: water, electric (30, 50 amps), sewer, laundry.

Yatesville

Heart of Georgia RV Park, 6722 Hwy. 74, 31097. T: (706) 472-3437. RV/tent: 33. $17–$19. Hookups: water, electric (30, 50 amps), sewer, laundry

KENTUCKY

Aurora

Aurora Oaks Campground, 55 KOA Ln., 42048. T: (888) 886-8704. RV/tent: 60. $15–$18. Hookups: water, electric.

Lakeside Campground & Marina, 12363 US Hwy. 68 East, 42025. T: (270) 354-8157. RV/tent: 140. $19–$21. Hookups: water, electric.

Bardstown

Holt's Campground, 2351 Templin Ave., 40004. T: (502) 348-6717. RV/tent: 60. $16. Hookups: water, electric.

White Acres Campground, 3022 Boston Rd., 62 West, 40004. T: (502) 348-9677. RV/tent: 82. $10–$14. Hookups: water, electric.

Benton

Big Bear Resort, 30 Big Bear Resort Rd., 42025. T: (800) 922-BEAR. RV/tent: 75. $17.29. Hookups: water, electric.

Berea

Oh Kentucky Campground, 1142 Hwy. 21 West, 40403. T: (606) 986-1150. RV/tent: 152. $10–$12. Hookups: water, electric.

Walnut Meadow Campground, 1201 Paint Lick Rd., 40403. T: (606) 986-6180. RV/tent: 123. $8–$12. Hookups: water, electric.

Bowling Green

Beech Bend Family Campground, 798 Beech Bend Rd., 42101. T: (270) 781-7634. RV/tent: 439. $20. Hookups: water, electric.

Buckhorn

Buckhorn Dam Recreation Area (Corps of Engineers–Buckhorn Lake), 104 Tailwater Camp Rd., 41721. T: (606) 398-7251. RV/tent: 31. $16. Hookups: water, electric.

Burkesville

Sulphur Creek Resort, 3498 Sulphur Creek Rd., 42717. T: (270) 433-7200. RV/tent: 22. $20. Hookups: water, electric.

Burnside

Lake Cumberland RV Park, P.O. Box 394 499 Gibson Ln., 42518. T: (606) 561-8222. RV/tent: 40. $15–$20. Hookups: water, electric.

Cadiz

Hurricane Creek Recreational Area (Corps of Engineers–Lake Barkle), Box 218, 42045. T: (270) 362-4236. RV/tent: 45. $10–$20. Hookups: water, electric.

Prizer Point Marina & Resort, 1777 Prizer Point Rd., 42211. T: (270) 522-3762. RV/tent: 102. $18. Hookups: water, electric.

Rockcastle RV Resort & Campground, 1049 Goose Hollow Rd., 42211. T: (270) 522-5530. RV/tent: 57. $8–$15. Hookups: water, electric.

Calvert City

Cypress Lakes RV Park, 54 Scillion Dr., 42029. T: (270) 395-4267. RV/tent: 130. $14–$16. Hookups: water, electric.

KOA–KY Lake Dam/Paducah, 4793 US Hwy. 62, 42029. T: (270) 395-5841. RV/tent: 85. $18.50–$24.50. Hookups: water, electric.

KENTUCKY (continued)

Campbellsville

Green River Lake State Park, Green River Lake State Park, 42718. T: (270) 465-8255. RV/tent: 156. $18. Hookups: water, electric.

Smith Ridge (Corps of Engineers–Green River Lake), 2882 Smith Ridge Rd., 42718. T: (270) 789-2743. RV/tent: 80. $16–$19. Hookups: water, electric.

Canton

Devil's Elbow Campground (Corps of Engineers–Trigg), 100 Devil's Elbow Rd., 42211. T: (270) 924-5878. RV/tent: 22. $10–$13. Hookups: water, electric.

Corbin

Grove Campground, Daniel Boone National Forest, 1700 Bypass Rd., 40391. T: (800) 280-CAMP. RV/tent: 56. $15–$25. Hookups: water, electric.

Danville

Pioneer Playhouse Trailer Park, 840 Stanford Rd./US Hwy. 150, 40422. T: (606) 236-2747. RV/tent: 70. $13. Hookups: water, electric.

Dry Ridge

75 Camper Village, 940 Curry Ln., 41035. T: (606) 824-5836. RV/tent: 70. $15–$20. Hookups: water, electric.

Dunmor

Dogwood Lake & Campground, Box 150, 42339. T: (270) 657-8380. RV/tent: 95. $10–$14. Hookups: water, electric.

Eddyville

Holiday Hills Resort, 5631 KY 93 South, 42038. T: (800) 337-8550. RV/tent: 150. $18–$20. Hookups: water, electric.

Lake Barkley RV Resort, 4481 State Rte. 93 South, 42038. T: (800) 910-PARK. RV/tent: 114. $14–$17. Hookups: water, electric.

Elizabethtown

Glendale Campground, 4566 Sportsman Lake Rd., 42701. T: (270) 369-7755. RV/tent: 100. $16–$20. Hookups: water, electric.

KOA–Elizabethtown, 209 Tunnel Hill Rd., 42701. T: (270) 737-7600. RV/tent: 68. $16–$24.50. Hookups: water, electric.

Falls of Rough

Cave Creek (Corps of Engineers–Rough River Lake), 14500 Falls of Rough R, 40119-6313. T: (270) 257-2061. RV/tent: 86. $8–$12. Hookups: water, electric.

Frankfort

Elkhorn Campground, 165 Scruggs Ln., 40601. T: (502) 695-9154. RV/tent: 125. $17–$21. Hookups: water, electric.

Franklin

KOA–Franklin, P.O. Box 346, 42135. T: (800) 562-5631. RV/tent: 104. $16.50–$22. Hookups: water, electric.

Golden Pond

Energy Lake (LBL) National Recreation Area, 100 Van Morgan Dr., 42211. T: (270) 924-2270. RV/tent: 48. $12–$15. Hookups: water, electric.

Fenton (LBL) National Recreation Area, 100 Van Morgan Dr., 42211. T: (270) 924-2000. RV/tent: 29. $8–$11. Hookups: water, electric.

Rushing Creek (LBL) National Recreation Area, 100 Van Morgan Dr., 42211. T: (270) 924-2000. RV/tent: 40. $9. Hookups: water, electric.

Wrangler (LBL) National Recreation Area, 100 Van Morgan Dr., 42211. T: (270) 924-2000. RV/tent: 163. $11–$18. Hookups: water, electric.

Grand Rivers

Birmingham Ferry (LBL) National Recreation Area, 100 Van Morgan Dr., 42211. T: (270) 924-2000. RV/tent: 46. $8. Hookups: water, electric.

Cravens Bay (LBL) National Recreation Area, 100 Van Morgan Dr., 42211. T: (270) 924-2000. RV/tent: 31. $8. Hookups: water, electric.

Hillman Ferry (LBL) National Recreation Area, 100 Van Morgan Dr., 42211. T: (270) 362-8230. RV/tent: 379. $12–$19. Hookups: water, electric.

Harrodsburg

Chimney Rock Campground, 160 Chimney Rock Rd., 40330. T: (606) 748-5252. RV/tent: 70. $15. Hookups: water, electric.

Cummins Ferry Campground & Marina, 2528 Cummins Ferry Rd., 40372. T: (859) 748-6243. RV/tent: 120. $15–$20. Hookups: water, electric.

Hartford

Ohio County Park, 1802 Country Club Ln., 42347. T: (270) 298-4466. RV/tent: 50. $10–$14. Hookups: water, electric.

Hodgenville

Cruise Inn Campground & Motel, 2784 Lincoln Farm Rd., 42748. T: (270) 358-9998. RV/tent: 20. $14. Hookups: water, electric.

KENTUCKY (continued)

Horse Cave
KOA–Horse Cave, Box 87, 42749. T: (270) 786-2819. RV/tent: 100. $16–$20. Hookups: water, electric.

Hyden
Trace Branch (Corps of Engineers–Buckhorn Lake), 1325 Buckham Dam Rd., 41721. T: (606) 398-7251. RV/tent: 30. free. Hookups: none.

Jamestown
Kendall Recreation Area (Corps of Engineers–Lake Cumberland), 855 Boat Dock Rd., 42501-0450. T: (270) 343-4660. RV/tent: 77. $14–$24. Hookups: water, electric.

Kuttawa
Boyds Landing Campground (Corps of Engineers), P.O. Box 218, 42045-0218. T: (270) 388-2721. RV/tent: 14. $12–$15. Hookups: water, electric.

Leitchfield
Dog Creek (Corps of Engineers–Nolin River Lake), 2150 Nolin Dam Rd., 42207. T: (270) 524-5454. RV/tent: 70. $11–$17. Hookups: water, electric.

Wax Site (Corps of Engineers–Nolin River Lake), 14008 Peonia Rd., 42726. T: (270) 242-7205. RV/tent: 110. $13–$20. Hookups: water, electric.

London
Daniel Boone National Forest (Holly Bay Rec. Area), London Ranger District, 40744. T: (800) 280-CAMP. RV/tent: 94. $5–$10. Hookups: water, electric.

Westgate RV Camping, 254 West Daniel Boone Pkwy, 40741. T: (606) 878-7330. RV/tent: 14. $19.95. Hookups: full.

White Oak Boat-In Campground, Daniel Boone National Forest, Stearns Ranger District Office, P.O. Box 429, Whitley, 42653. T: (606) 864-4163. RV/tent: 51. $6–$9. Hookups: none.

Louisa
The Falls Campground, P.O. Box 643, SR 3, 41230. T: (606) 686-3398. RV/tent: 111. $10.50–$21. Hookups: water, electric.

McDaniels
Axtel Campground (Corps of Engineers–Rough River Lake), Hwy. 79, 40152. T: (270) 257-2584. RV/tent: 158. $15–$22. Hookups: water, electric.

Laurel Branch Campground (Corps of Engineers–Rough River Lake), Hwy. 110, 40152. T: (270) 257-8839. RV/tent: 77. $11–$24. Hookups: water, electric.

Monticello
Conley Bottom Resort, Rte. 5 Box 5360, 42633. T: (606) 348-6351. RV/tent: 170. $15–$25. Hookups: water, electric.

Morehead
Buckskin Run Campground, 1750 801 South, 40351. T: (606) 784-7476. RV/tent: 30. $12–$16. Hookups: water, electric.

Mortons Gap
Pennyrile Campground, P.O. Box 612, 42440. T: (270) 258-5201. RV/tent: 15. $15. Hookups: water, electric.

Mount Olivet
Blue Licks Battlefield State Park, P.O. Box 66, 41064-0066. T: (606) 289-5507. RV/tent: 51. $8.50–$16. Hookups: water, electric.

Mount Vernon
Nicely's Campground, Rte. 2 Box 38, 40456. T: (606) 256-5637. RV/tent: 99. $13.95–$16.95. Hookups: water, electric.

Muldraugh
Military Park (Camp Carlson Army Travel Camp), 9186 US Hwy. 60, 40155. T: (502) 624-4836. RV/tent: 25. $9.50. Hookups: water, electric.

Murray
Wildcat Creek Rec Area, 28 Wildcat Beach Rd., 42071. T: (270) 436-5628. RV/tent: 50. $19. Hookups: water, electric.

Owensboro
Diamond Lake Resort Campground, P.O. Box 211, 42377. T: (270) 229-4961. RV/tent: 440. $19.50. Hookups: water, electric.

Windy Hollow Campground & Recreation Area, 5141 Windy Hollow Rd., 42301. T: (270) 785-4150. RV/tent: 300. $18. Hookups: water, electric.

Paducah
Fern Lake Campground, 5535 Cairo Rd., 42001. T: (270) 444-7939. RV/tent: 70. $20. Hookups: water, electric.

Park City
Cedar Hill Campground, P.O. Box 305, 42160. T: (270) 749-3114. RV/tent: 117. $14.25–$19. Hookups: water, electric.

Pineville
Pine Mountain State Resort Park, 1050 State Park Rd., 40977-0610. T: (606) 337-3066. RV/tent: 32. $10. Hookups: none.

Renfro Valley
Renfro Valley RV Park, US Hwy. 25, 40473. T: (800) 765-7464. RV/tent: 199. $21.20–$23.32. Hookups: water, electric.

Salt Lick
The Outpost RV Park, 340 Cave Run Lake Rd., 40371. T: (606) 683-2311. RV/tent: 89. $15. Hookups: water, electric.

KENTUCKY (continued)

Salt Lick (continued)

Zilpo Recreation Area, Daniel Boone National Forest, P.O. Box 218, 40371. T: (606) 784-7788. RV/tent: 172. $12–$20. Hookups: water, electric.

Sanders

Eagle Valley Camping Resort, 1100 Eagle Valley Rd., 41083. T: (502) 347-9361. RV/tent: 225. $15. Hookups: water, electric.

Scottsville

Bailey's Point Campground (Corps of Engineers–Barren River Lake), 3147 Baileys Point Rd., 42164. T: (270) 622-6959. RV/tent: 215. $16–$19. Hookups: water, electric.

Shelbyville

Guist Creek Marina & Campground, 11990 Boat Dock Rd., 40065. T: (502) 633-1934. RV/tent: 50. $15–$16.50. Hookups: water, electric.

Slade

Koomer Ridge Campground, Daniel Boone National Forest, 705 West College Ave., 40380. T: (606) 663-2852. RV/tent: 54. $10–$15. Hookups: none.

Somerset

Cumberland Point Public Use Area (Corps of Engineers–Lake Cumberland), Rte. 8 Box 173T, 42501. T: (606) 871-7886. RV/tent: 30. $17–$23. Hookups: water, electric.

Fishing Creek Public Use Area (Corps of Engineers–Lake Cumberland), 1611 Hwy. 1248, 42501-0450. T: (606) 679-5174. RV/tent: 44. $17–$24. Hookups: water, electric.

Waitsboro Rec Area (Corps of Engineers–Lake Cumberland), 500 Waitsboro Rd., 42501. T: (606) 561-5513. RV/tent: 26. $14–$24. Hookups: water, electric.

Stearns

Big South Forks Nat'l. River & Rec. Area (Blue Heron), Park Headquarters, 4564 Leatherwood Rd., 37841. T: (423) 569-9778. RV/tent: 45. $15–$18. Hookups: water, electric.

Walton

Oak Creek Campground, P.O. Box 161, 41094. T: (859) 485-9131. RV/tent: 105. $17.50–$21. Hookups: water, electric.

Williamsburg

Williamsburg Travel Trailer Park, 50 Balltown Rd., 40769. T: (800) 426-3267. RV/tent: 56. $12. Hookups: water, electric.

LOUISIANA

Abbeville

Abbeville RV Park, 1004 Jacqulyn St., 70510. T: (337) 898-4042. www.abbevillervpark.com. abbrv@ abbevillervpark.com. RV/tent: 55. $14–$17. Hookups: water, electric (30, 50 amps), sewer.

Betty's RV Park, 2118 South State St., 70510. T: (337) 893-7057. www.bettysrvpark.com. bettybernard@ cox-internet.com. RV/tent: 68. $12–$14. Hookups: water, electric (30, 50 amps), sewer, cable TV.

Herbert's Cajun Haven RV Park, South State & Trahan St., 70510. T: (337) 893-3504. RV/tent: 110. $8–$12. Hookups: water, electric (30, 50 amps), sewer, laundry.

Abita Springs

Family Time Resorts, 24150 Hwy. 435, 70420. T: (504) 892-3565. RV/tent: 68. $12–$14. Hookups: water, electric (30, 50 amps)sewer, phone (modem), laundry.

Alexandria

Fish'n Heav'n RV Park, Robinson Bridge Rd., 71303. T: (318) 448-9269. RV/tent: 31. $18. Hookups: water, electric (30, 50 amps), sewer, laundry, row boat rentals.

KOA–Kincaid Lake Campground, South Kisatchie Ln., 71303. T: (318) 445-5227. RV/tent: 57. $18–$24. Hookups: water, electric (20, 30, 50 amps), sewer, laundry.

Angie

Great Southern RC & Bluegrass Park, Hwy. 21 & Main St., 70426. T: (504) 986-8411. RV/tent: 100. $12–$14. Hookups: water, electric (30, 50 amps), sewer, phone (modem).

Arcadia

Bonnie & Clyde Trade Days & Campground, South Hwy. 9, 71001. T: (318) 263-2437. RV/tent: 97. $15–$20. Hookups: water, electric (30, 50 amps), sewer, phone (modem).

Avoyselles

Grand Avoyelles RV Resort, Southeast & Hwy. 1, 70648. T: (800) 578-7275. RV/tent: 186. $14–$18. Hookups: water, electric (20, 30, 50 amps), sewer, cable TV, phone (modem), playground.

LOUISIANA (continued)

Baker

Azalea Mobile Home and RV Park, 3300 Baker Blvd., 70714. T: (504) 775-1123. RV/tent: 52. $12–$18. Hookups: water, electric (20, 30 amps), sewer, laundry.

Baton Rouge

Farr Park Campground, 6400 River Rd., 70820. T: (225) 769-7805. www.brec.org. RV/tent: 150. $12–$16. Hookups: water, electric (30 amps), sewer, phone (modem), laundry, playground.

Greenwood Park, 13350 Louisiana Hwy. 19, 70821. T: (225) 775-9166. www.brec.org. RV/tent: 75. $10–$12. Hookups: water, electric (30, 50 amps), sewer, phone (modem), laundry.

Knight's RV and Mobile Home Park, 14740 Florida Blvd., 70819. T: (504) 275-0679. RV/tent: 78. $11–$15. Hookups: water, electric (20, 30, 50 amps), sewer.

Beauregard

Longville Lake Park, Hwy. 110, 70652. T: (337) 725-3395. RV/tent: 175. $16. Hookups: water, electric (30, 50 amps).

Benton

Cypress–Black Bayou Recreation, 135 Cypress Park Dr., 71006. T: (318) 965-0007. www.cypressblackbayou.com. RV/tent: 73. $8–$13. Hookups: water, electric (20, 30, 50 amps), sewer.

Bogalusa

Clear Water Creek Resort Inc., 60407 Spring Valley Rd., 70427. T: (504) 732-5555. RV/tent: 55. $10–$16. Hookups: water, electric (20, 30 amps), sewer, bathhouse, showers.

Bossier

Maplewood RV Park, 452 Maplewood Dr., 71111. T: (800) 569-2264. RV/tent: 42. $17. Hookups: water, electric (30, 50 amps), sewer, phone.

Bourg

Grand Bois Campsite, 470 Hwy. 24, 70343. T: (504) 594-7410. RV/tent: 41. $9–$12. Hookups: water, electric.

Boyce

KOA–Alexandria West, 64 Kisatchie Ln., 71409. T: (800) 401-6450. RV/tent: 52. $15–$27. Hookups: water, electric, sewer.

Broussard

Maxie's Campground, P.O. Box, 70518. T: (337) 837-6200. www.maxiescampground.com. maxiescamp@aol.com. RV/tent: 70. $18. Hookups: water, electric (20, 30, 50 amps)sewer, phone (modem), laundry.

De Ridder

Sadler RV Park and Mobile Home, 7196 Main St., 70634. T: (318) 463-5561. RV/tent: 72. $12–$18. Hookups: water, electric (30, 50 amps), sewer, laundry.

Evangeline

Crooked Creek Campground, Hwy. 3187/Parish Police Jury, 70537. T: (337) 599-2661. RV/tent: 100. $12–$16. Hookups: water, electric (30 amps), sewer, laundry.

Florien

Hodges Wilderness Campground, P.O. Box 340, 71429. T: (318) 586-3523. www.hodgespark.com. Hodges@cp.tel.net. RV/tent: 19. $16–$18. Hookups: water, electric (30, 50 amps), sewer, boat rentals.

Greenwood

Kelly's RV Park, 8560 Greenwood Rd., 71033. T: (318) 938-6360. RV/tent: 45. $18. Hookups: water, electric, sewer.

Hammond

Punkin Park Campground, 43037 North Billville Rd., 70404. T: (888) 585 5519. RV/tent: 52. $20. Hookups: water, electric, sewer.

Haughton

Pine Hill Mobile Home and RV, 2 Pine Hill Cir., 71037. T: (318) 949-3916. RV/tent: 28. $10–$14. Hookups: water, electric (20, 30 amps), sewer, bathhouse, showers.

Kinder

Grand Casino Coushatta Luxury RV Resort, 1240 711 Pow Wow Pkwy., 70648. T: (888) 867-8727. RV/tent: 156. $15–$19. Hookups: water, electric, sewer.

Quiet Oaks RV Park, 18159 TV Tower Rd., 70648. T: (318) 756-2230. www.quietoaks.com. RV/tent: 40. $12–$16. Hookups: water, electric (30, 50 amps), sewer, boat rentals.

Leesville

Shady Lake RV Park, 168 Sapphire Ln., 71446. T: (337) 239-4674. RV/tent: 25. $16. Hookups: water, electric (30, 50 amps), sewer, phone (modem).

Many

Cypress Bend Park (Toledo Bend Lake), 3462 Cypress Bend Dr., 71449. T: (318) 256-4118. F: (318) 256-4179. www.toledo-bend.com. srala@toledo-bend.com. RV/tent: 63. $14–$18. Hookups: water, electric (20, 30 amps), sewer, playground.

LOUISIANA (continued)

Marthaville

Country Livin' RV Park, 1115 Hwy. 174, 71450.
T: (318) 796-2543. F: (318) 796-2543. RV/tent: 18.
$15. Hookups: water, electric (30, 50 amps), sewer,
laundry.

Monroe

Monroe Shilo RV and Travel, 7300 Frontage Rd.,
71202. T: (318) 343-6098. RV/tent: 92. $18.
Hookups: water, electric (30 amps), sewer.

Morgan City

Morgan City RV Park, 5428 Hwy. 6, 70380. T: (504)
385-4813. RV/tent: 99. $15–$16. Hookups: water,
electric (30, 50 amps), sewer.

Natchitoches

Nakatosh RV Park, 5428 Hwy. 6, 71457. T: (318)
352-0911. RV/tent: 41. $12–$15. Hookups: water,
electric, sewer.

New Orleans

Parc D'Orleans Campground, 7676 Chef Menteur
Hwy., 70126. T: (504) 244-7434. RV/tent: 71. $16.
Hookups: water, electric (20, 30 amps), sewer.

River Boat Travel Park, 6232 Chef Menteur Hwy.,
70126. T: (504) 246-2628. RV/tent: 111. $10–$16.
Hookups: water, electric (20 amps), sewer, laundry.

Port Allen

Cajun Country Campground, 4667 Rebelle Ln.,
71001. T: (800) 264-8554. RV/tent: 77. $20–$22.
Hookups: water, electric (30, 50 amps), sewer,
phone (modem), laundry.

Ruston

Lincoln Parish Park, 198 Parish Park Rd., 71270.
T: (318) 251-5156. RV/tent: 33. $12. Hookups:
water, electric, sewer.

Shreveport

Campers RV Center, 7700 West 70th St., 71129.
T: (318) 687-4567. RV/tent: 58. $17. Hookups:
water, electric, sewer.

Tallulah

Roudaway RV Park, Hwy. 602, 71282. T: (318) 574-
9026. RV/tent: 48. $10–$12. Hookups: water, electric (20 amps), sewer, laundry.

West Monroe

Cheniere Lake Park–Area 1, 337 Well Rd., 71292.
T: (318) 387-2383. RV/tent: 10. $12–$10.
Hookups: water, electric.

Pavilion RV Park, 309 Well Rd., 71292. T: (318) 322-
4216. RV/tent: 60. $20. Hookups: water, electric
(30, 50 amps), sewer.

MISSISSIPPI

Bay St. Louis

Bay Marina & RV Park & Lodging, 100 Bay Marina
Dr., 39520. T: (228) 466-4970. RV/tent: 33. $20.
Hookups: electric (20, 30, 50 amps).

KOA–Bay St. Louis/Gulfport, 814 Hwy. 90, 39520.
T: (800) 562-2790. RV/tent: 78. $24. Hookups:
electric (20, 30, 50 amps).

McLeod Water Park (Pearl River Basin Dev. Dist.),
Texas Flat Rd., 39520. T: (228) 467-1894. RV/tent:
58. $6–$11. Hookups: water, electric.

Biloxi

Biloxi RV Park & Biloxi Travel Inn, 2010 Beach Blvd.,
39531. T: (228) 388-5531. RV/tent: 36. $22.
Hookups: electric (20, 30, 50 amps).

Cajun RV Park, 1860 Beach Blvd., 39531. T: (228)
388-5590. RV/tent: 126. $24.50–$26.64. Hookups:
electric (20, 30, 50 amps).

Fox's RV Park & Complex, 190 Beauvoir Rd., 39531.
T: (800) 736-7275. RV/tent: 144. $20. Hookups:
electric (30, 50 amps).

Southern Comfort Camping Resort, 1766 Beach
Blvd., 39531. T: (877) 302-1700. RV/tent: 123.
$18–$24. Hookups: water, electric (20, 30, 50
amps).

Clinton

Springridge RV Park, 499 Springridge Rd., 39056.
T: (601) 924-0947. RV/tent: 42. $18. Hookups:
electric (20, 30, 50 amps).

Coldwater

Dub Patton Campground (Corps of Engineers–
Arkabutla Lake), 3905 Arkabutla Dam Rd., 38668.
T: (662) 562-6261. RV/tent: 66. $12–$18.
Hookups: water, electric.

MISSISSIPPI (continued)

Hernando Point (Corps of Engineers–Arkabutla Lake), 3905 Arkabutla Dam Rd., 38668. T: (662) 562-6261. RV/tent: 83. $12–$18. Hookups: water, electric.

Columbia

Whispering Pines RV Park, 7836 Hwy. 49 South, 39402-9169. T: (601) 943-6290. RV/tent: 10. $20. Hookups: water, electric (20, 50 amps).

Columbus

Brown's RV Trailer Park, 2002 Bluecutt Rd., 39705. T: (662) 328-1976. RV/tent: 24. $14. Hookups: electric (20, 30 amps).

Decatur

Turkey Creek Water Park (Pat Harrison Waterway District), 142 Parkway Dr., 39327. T: (601) 635-3314. RV/tent: 22. $8. Hookups: electric (20 amps).

Durant

Holmes County State Park, Old Holmes Park Rd., 39063. T: (662) 653-3351. RV/tent: 28. $10–$13. Hookups: electric (50 amps).

Edwards

Askew's Landing Campground, 3412 Askew Ferry Rd., 39066. T: (601) 852-2331. RV/tent: 89. $14–$16. Hookups: electric (20, 30, 50 amps).

Enid

Chickasaw Hill Campground, 931 CR 36, 38606. T: (662) 563-4571. RV/tent: 51. $12. Hookups: water, electric (30 amps).

Persimmon Hill–South Abutment, 931 CR 36, 38606. T: (662) 563-4571. RV/tent: 72. $12. Hookups: water, electric (30 amps).

Water Valley Landing Campground, 931 CR 36, 38606. T: (662) 563-4571. RV/tent: 29. $12. Hookups: water, electric (30 amps).

Enterprise

Dunn's Falls Water Park (Pat Harrison Waterway District), 6890 Dunn's Falls Rd., 39330. T: (601) 655-9511. RV/tent: 15. $8. Hookups: none.

Escatawpa

Riverbend RV Resort, 10707 Hwy. 613, 39552. T: (228) 475-2429. RV/tent: 77. $16. Hookups: electric (20, 30, 50 amps).

Flora

Mississippi Petrified Forest Campground, 124 Forest Park Rd., 39071. T: (601) 879-8189. RV/tent: 37. $12–$15. Hookups: water, electric (20 amps).

Forest

Bienville National Forest, 246 Mimosa Dr., 39153. T: (601) 469-3811. RV/tent: 35. $7–$13. Hookups: water, electric (20, 30 amps).

Greenville

Delta Village Park, 3836 Hwy. 82 West, 38701. T: (662) 378-3655. RV/tent: 16. $11. Hookups: electric (20, 30, 50 amps).

Grenada

Hugh White State Park, 3170 Hugh White State Park Rd., 38901. T: (662) 226-4934. RV/tent: 200. $13. Hookups: water, electric 30, 50 amps).

Oxbow RV Park, 601 Hwy. 7 North, 38901-8656. T: (662) 226-0751. RV/tent: 49. $17.75. Hookups: electric (20, 30, 50 amps).

Gulfport

Campground of the South, 10406 Three Rivers Rd., 39503. T: (228) 539-2922. RV/tent: 90. $20. Hookups: electric (20, 30, 50 amps).

Country Side RV Park & Tradin' Post, 20278 Hwy. 49, 39574. T: (228) 539-0807. RV/tent: 32. $16. Hookups: electric (20, 30, 50 amps).

San Beach RV Park, 1020 Beach Dr., 39507. T: (228) 896-7551. RV/tent: 102. $22.47. Hookups: electric (20, 30, 50 amps).

Hattiesburg

Military Park, 1001 Lee Ave., 39407-5500. T: (601) 558-2540. RV/tent: 25. $10. Hookups: full.

Quilla's RV Park, 558 South Gate Rd., 39401-9410. T: (601) 544-6837. RV/tent: 28. $15. Hookups: water, electric (20, 30, 50 amps).

Shady Cove RV Park, 7836 Hwy. 49 North, 39405. T: (877) 251-8169. RV/tent: 53. $16. Hookups: water, electric (20, 30, 50 amps).

Hernando

Memphis South Campground & RV Park, 1250 Mt Pleasant Rd. Northeast, 38632. T: (662) 622-0056. RV/tent: 47. $18. Hookups: water, electric (20, 30 amps).

Hollandale

Leroy Percy State Park, Hwy. 12 West, 38748. T: (662) 827-5436. RV/tent: 16. $9–$13. Hookups: water, electric (20, 30 amps).

Holly Springs

Wall Doxey State Park, 3946 Hwy. 7 South, 38635. T: (662) 252-4231. RV/tent: 64. $9–$13. Hookups: water, electric (20, 30 amps).

Houston

Tombigbee National Forest, Hwy. 15 South, 39735. T: (662) 285-3264. RV/tent: 28. $13. Hookups: water, electric (30, 50 amps).

Iuka

JP Coleman State Park, 607 CR 321, 38852. T: (662) 423-6515. RV/tent: 57. $14. Hookups: water, electric.

MISSISSIPPI (continued)

Jackson

Goshen Springs Campground (Pearl River Valley Water Supply District), 1684 Hwy. 43 North, 39042. T: (601) 829-2751. RV/tent: 68. $16. Hookups: water, electric (30 amps).

Swinging Bridge RV Park, 5750 I-55, 39211. T: (601) 502-1101. RV/tent: 35. $22. Hookups: water, electric.

Laurel

KOA–Laurel, 2920 Hwy. 11 North, 39440. T: (800) 562-0378. RV/tent: 88. $24–$27. Hookups: full.

Long Beach

Plantation Pines Campground and RV Park, 19391 28 St., 39560. T: (228) 863-6550. RV/tent: 70. $20. Hookups: full.

Louisville

Legion State Park, Old Hwy. 25 North, 39339. T: (662) 773-8323. RV/tent: 10. $6. Hookups: water, electric.

Ludlow

Coal Bluff Park (Pearl River Valley Water Supply District), 1319 Coal Bluff Rd., 39200. T: (601) 654-7726. RV/tent: 68. $10–$13. Hookups: water, electric (20, 30 amps).

Lumberton

Little Black Creek Water Park (Pat Harrison Waterway District), 2159 Little Black Creek Rd., 39475. T: (601) 794-2957. RV/tent: 125. $14–$17.50. Hookups: water, electric (30 amps).

Mendenhall

D'Lo Water Park, P.O. Box 278, 39062. T: (601) 847-4310. RV/tent: 12. $10. Hookups: water, electric.

Meridian

Campground RV and Trailer Park, Hwy. 45 North, 39301. T: (601) 485-4549. RV/tent: 58. $15–$17. Hookups: full.

Nanabe Creek Campground, 1933 Russell–Mt. Gilead Rd., 39301. T: (601) 485-4711. RV/tent: 95. $14–$18. Hookups: water, electric (20, 30, 50 amps).

Mount Olive

Dry Creek Water Park (Pat Harrison Waterway District), Hwy. 35, 39119. T: (601) 797-4619. RV/tent: 28. $8–$14. Hookups: water, electric (20 amps).

Natchez

Natchez State Park, 40 Wickcliff Rd., 39120. T: (601) 442-2658. RV/tent: 21. $10–$13. Hookups: water, electric (20, 30 amps).

Traceway Campground, 1113 Hwy. 61 North, 39120. T: (601) 445-8278. RV/tent: 40. $14–$17.12. Hookups: water, electric (15, 20, 30, 50 amps).

Ocean Springs

RV-Tel, 2302 Beinville Blvd., 39565-9340. T: (228) 875-2772. RV/tent: 20. $22.50. Hookups: electric (20, 30, 50 amps).

Philadelphia

Frog Level RV Park, 1532 Hwy. 16 West, 39350. T: (601) 650-9621. RV/tent: 52. $18. Hookups: full.

Port Gibson

Grand Gulf Military Park Campground (State), 12006 Grand Gulf Rd., 39150. T: (601) 437-5911. RV/tent: 42. $5–$15. Hookups: electric (20, 30, 50 amps).

Quitman

Clarkco State Park, Hwy. 45 North, 39355. T: (601) 776-6651. RV/tent: 43. $13. Hookups: water, electric (20, 30 amps).

Rosedale

Great River Road State Park, Hwy. 1 South, 38769. T: (662) 759-6762. RV/tent: 61. $13. Hookups: water, electric (30 amps).

Tishomingo

Tishomingo State Park, 105 CR 90, 38873. T: (662) 438-6914. RV/tent: 62. $9–$13. Hookups: water, electric (20, 30, 50 amps).

Tunica

Hollywood Casino RV Resort, P.O. Box 28, 38676. T: (800) 871-0711. RV/tent: 123. $16.20. Hookups: full.

Sam's Town RV Park, 1477 Casino Strip Resorts Blvd., 38664. T: (800) 456-0711. RV/tent: 100. $8. Hookups: full.

Tupelo

Natchez Trace RV Park, P.O. Box 2564, 38803. T: (601) 769-8609. RV/tent: 72. $15.45. Hookups: water, electric (20, 30, 50 amps).

RV Campground at Barnes Crossing, 125 Rd. 1698, 38801. T: (662) 844-6063 or (662) 767-8609. RV/tent: 40. $15. Hookups: full.

Trace State Park, Rte. 1 P.O. Box 254, 39200. T: (662) 489-2958. RV/tent: 25. $10–$13. Hookups: water, electric (20, 30 amps).

Vaiden

Vaiden Campground, P.O. Box 227, 39176. T: (662) 464-9336. RV/tent: 90. $14–$17. Hookups: water, electric (20, 30, 50 amps).

Vicksburg

Vicksburg Battlefield Kampground, 4407 I-20 Frontage Rd., 39183. T: (601) 636-2025. RV/tent: 81. $15–$17. Hookups: water, electric (20, 30 amps).

Wesson

Lake Lincoln State Park, 2573 Sunset Rd. Northeast, 39191. T: (601) 643-9044 or (601) 735-4365. RV/tent: 61. $13. Hookups: water, electric (30 amps).

Wiggins

Flint Creek Water Park (Pat Harrison Waterway District), 1216 Parkway Dr., 39577. T: (601) 928-3051. RV/tent: 170. $18. Hookups: water, electric (30 amps).

NORTH CAROLINA

Advance

Thousand Trails–Forest Lake, 192 Thousand Trails Dr., 27006. T: (800) 722-6411. RV/tent: 265. $20. Hookups: water, electric (20, 30, 50 amps).

Almond

Turkey Creek Campground, P.O. Box 93, 28702-0093. T: (828) 488-8966. RV/tent: 60. $15–$17. Hookups: water, electric (20 amps).

Apex

Jordan Lake State Recreation Area (Parkers Creek), 280 State Park Rd., 27502. T: (919) 362-0586. ils.unc.edu/parkproject/ncparks.html. RV/tent: 250. $12–$17. Hookups: water, electric (20, 30 amps).

Jordan Lake State Recreation Area (Vista Point), 280 State Park Rd., 27502. T: (919) 362-0586. ils.unc.edu/parkproject/ncparks.html. RV/tent: 55. $12–$17. Hookups: water, electric (20, 30 amps).

Ararat

Homeplace Recreational Park, 136 Homeplace Park Rd., 27007. T: (336) 374-5173. www.homeplace recreationpark.com. RV/tent: 152. $18–$20. Hookups: water, electric (30, 50 amps).

Asheboro

Deep River Campground & RV Park, 814 McDowell Country Trail, 27203. T: (336) 629-4069. www. kiz.com/deepriver. RV/tent: 62. $16–$18. Hookups: water, electric (20, 30, 50 amps).

Holly Bluff Family Campground, 4846 NC Hwy. 49 South, 27203. T: (336) 857-2761. RV/tent: 85. $18. Hookups: water, electric 15, 20, 30, 50 amps).

Zooland Family Campground, 3671 Pisgah–Covered Bridge Rd., 27203. T: (336) 381-3422. RV/tent: 100. $14.50–$17. Hookups: water, electric (20, 30 amps).

Asheville

Asheville–Bear Creek RV Park, 81 South Bear Creek Rd., 28806. T: (828) 253-0798. RV/tent: 106. $26–$27. Hookups: water, electric (15, 20, 30, 50 amps).

Campfire Lodgings, 7 Appalachian Village Rd., 28804. T: (800) 933-8012. www.campfirelodgings.com. RV/tent: 21. $23–$35. Hookups: water, electric (20, 30, 50 amps).

Taps RV Park, P.O. Box 865, 28711. T: (828) 299-8277. RV/tent: 52. $23.50. Hookups: water, electric (15, 20, 30, 50 amps).

The French Broad River Campground, 1030 Old Marshall Hwy., 28804. T: (828) 658-0772. RV/tent: 53. $20–$21. Hookups: water, electric.

Avon

Sands of Time Campground, 125 North End Rd., 27915. T: (252) 995-5596. www.sandsoftimecamp-ground.com. RV/tent: 36. $16–$24. Hookups: water, electric (20, 30, 50 amps), sewer.

Balsam

Moonshine Creek Campground, P.O. Box 10, 28707. T: (828) 586-6666. RV/tent: 92. $24. Hookups: water, electric (15, 20, 30 amps).

Boone

Appalachian Campground, 150 Hires Dr., 28607. T: (828) 264-4505. RV/tent: 75. $22. Hookups: water, electric (20, 30 amps).

Flintlock Family Campground, 171 Flintlock Camp-ground Dr., 28607. T: (828) 963-5325. RV/tent: 100. $22. Hookups: water, electric (15, 20, 30, 50 amps).

KOA–Boone, 123 Harmony Mtn Ln., 28607. T: (828) 264-7250. RV/tent: 118. $24–$29. Hookups: water, electric (15, 20, 30, 50 amps).

Waterwheel RV Park, 1655 Hwy. 194 North, 28607. T: (828) 264-5165. RV/tent: 24. $17. Hookups: water, electric (15, 30 amps).

Boonville

Holly Ridge Family Campground, 5140 River Rd., 27011. T: (336) 367-7756. RV/tent: 62. $17.50–$21. Hookups: water, electric (20, 30, 50 amps).

Bryson City

Deep Creek Tube Center & Campground, P.O. Box 105, 28713. T: (828) 488-6055. RV/tent: 37. $18–$21.50. Hookups: water, electric (20, 30 amps).

Smoky Mountain Meadows Family Campground, 755 East Alarka Rd., 28713. T: (828) 488-3672. RV/tent: 53. $14–$15. Hookups: water, electric (15, 30 amps), sewer.

Burnsville

Black Mountain Campground, Pisgah National For-est, Appalachian Ranger District, Toecane Ranger Station, P.O. Box 128, 28714. T: (828) 682-6146. www.cs.unca.edu/nfsnc. RV/tent: 46. $13. Hook-ups: none.

Carolina Hemlock Park, Pisgah National Forest, Appalachian Ranger District, Toecane Ranger Sta-tion, P.O. Box 128, 28714. T: (828) 682-6146. www.cs.unca.edu/nfsnc. RV/tent: 32. $13. Hookups: none.

Candler

KOA–Asheville West, 309 Wiggins Rd., 28715. T: (828) 665-7015. RV/tent: 78. $22–$25. Hookups: water, electric (20, 30, 50 amps).

Cedar Island

Driftwood Campground, Hwy. 12 North, 28520. T: (252) 225-4861. RV/tent: 65. $14–$16. Hookups: water, electric (15, 20, 30 amps).

Cedar Mountain

Black Forest Family Camping Resort, P.O. Box 709, 28718. T: (828) 884-2267. RV/tent: 90. $22. Hookups: water, electric (20, 30, 50 amps).

NORTH CAROLINA (continued)

Charlotte

Elmore Mobile Home Park, 4826 North Tryon St., 28213.T: (704) 597-1323. RV/tent: 25. $20. Hookups: water, electric (15, 20, 30, 50 amps).

Fleetwood RV Racing Camping Resort, 6550 Speedway Blvd., 28027.T: (704) 455-4445. www.gospeedway.com. RV/tent: 254. $15–$25. Hookups: water, electric.

Cherokee

Adventure Trail Campground, P.O. Box 1673, 28719. T: (828) 497-3651. RV/tent: 90. $22. Hookups: water, electric (15, 20, 30 amps).

Bradley's Campground, P.O. Box 88, 28719.T: (828) 497-6051. RV/tent: 42. $14–$15. Hookups: water, electric (15, 20, 30 amps).

Cherokee Campground, P.O. Box 516, 28719. T: (828) 497-9838. RV/tent: 70. $22. Hookups: water, electric (15, 20, 30 amps).

Flaming Arrow Campground, P.O. Box 533, 28719. T: (877) 497-6161. RV/tent: 85. $22.50–$27. Hookups: water, electric (20, 30, 50 amps).

Fort Wilderness Campground and RV Resort, P.O. Box 1657, 28719.T: (828) 497-9331. RV/tent: 120. $23. Hookups: water, electric (15, 30, 50 amps).

Great Smoky Mountain RV Camping Resort, 17 Old Soco Rd., 28789.T: (828) 497-2470. RV/tent: 251. $19. Hookups: water, electric (20, 30 amps).

Indian Creek Campground, 1367 Bunches Creek Rd., 28719.T: (828) 497-4361. RV/tent: 69. $16–$17. Hookups: water, electric (15 amps).

River Valley Campground, P.O. Box 471, 28719. T: (828) 497-3540. RV/tent: 200. $18.50–$21. Hookups: water, electric (20, 30, 50 amps).

Riverside Campground, P.O. Box 58, 28719.T: (828) 497-9311. RV/tent: 30. $18. Hookups: water, electric (15, 30 amps).

Chimney Rock

Creekside Mountain Camping, P.O. Box 251, 28710. T: (800) 248-8118. www.creeksidecamping.com. RV/tent: 90. $21–$23. Hookups: water, electric (15, 20, 30 amps).

Lake Lure RV Park & Campground, 176 Boys Camp Rd., 28746.T: (828) 625-9160. RV/tent: 70. $26–$35. Hookups: water, electric (15, 30 amps).

Coinjock

Hampton Lodge Camping Resort, 1631 Waterlily Rd., 27923.T: (252) 453-2732. RV/tent: 268. $18–$20. Hookups: water, electric (20, 30 amps).

Columbus

Silver Creek Campground, 410 Silver Creek Rd., 28756.T: (800) 510-1603. RV/tent: 62. $19–$21. Hookups: water, electric (20, 30 amps).

Denver

Wildlife Woods Campground, 4582 Beaver Blvd., 28673.T: (704) 483-5611. RV/tent: 305. $22–$27. Hookups: water, electric (15, 20, 30, 50 amps).

Elizabethtown

Jones Lake State Park, 113 Jones Lake Dr., 28337. T: (910) 588-4550. ils.unc.edu/parkproject/nc parks.html. RV/tent: 20. $12. Hookups: none.

Enfield

KOA–Enfield/Rocky Mtn., 101 Bell Acres, 27823. T: (252) 445-5925. RV/tent: 78. $17–$24. Hookups: water, electric (15, 20, 30 amps).

Fayetteville

Fayetteville Spring Valley Park, 4504 US Hwy. 301 South, 28348.T: (910) 425-1505. RV/tent: 36. $18.95–$23.75. Hookups: water, electric (20, 30 amps).

Fletcher

Rutledge Lake Travel Park, 170 Rutledge Rd., 28732. T: (828) 654-7873. www.campingnorthcarolina. com. RV/tent: 75. $20–$30. Hookups: water, electric (20, 30, 50 amps).

Fontana Village

Cable Cove Campground, Nantahala National Forest, Cheoah Ranger District, Rte. 1 Box 16-A, 28721.T: (828) 479-6431. www.cs.unca.edu/nfsnc. RV/tent: 26. $8. Hookups: none.

Fort Mill

KOA–Charlotte/Fort Mill, 940 Gold Hill Rd., 29715. T: (803) 548-1148. RV/tent: 209. $22–$26. Hookups: water, electric (20, 30, 50 amps).

Foscoe

Grandfather Mountain Campground, P.O. Box 2060, 28607.T: (800) 788-2582. RV/tent: 149. $18.50–$22. Hookups: water, electric (20, 30, 50 amps).

Franklin

Carolina Village RV Resort, 20 Carolina Village Cir., 28734.T: (828) 369-5858 or (888) 818-5228. RV/tent: 16. $25. Hookups: water, electric (20, 30, 50 amps).

Cartoogechaye Creek Campground, 91 No Name Rd., 28734.T: (828) 524-8553. RV/tent: 103. $14–$16. Hookups: water, electric (30 amps).

Franklin RV Park, 145 Addington Bridge Rd., 28734. T: (828) 369-5841. RV/tent: 25. $14. Hookups: water, electric (20, 30 amps).

Mi Mountain Campground, 151 Mi Mountain Rd., 28734.T: (828) 524-6155. RV/tent: 48. $19.50. Hookups: water, electric (15, 30 amps).

Old Corundum Mill Campground, 80-33 Nickajack Rd., 28734.T: (828) 524-4663. www.travel.to/old corundum. RV/tent: 86. $18. Hookups: water, electric (20, 30 amps).

NORTH CAROLINA (continued)

Rainbow Springs Campground, 7984 West Old Murphy Rd., 28734. T: (828) 524-6376. RV/tent: 51. $17. Hookups: water, electric (15, 30 amps).

Standing Indian Campground, Nantahala National Forest, Wayah Ranger District, 90 Sloan Rd., 28734. T: (828) 524-6441. www.cs.unca.edu/nfsnc. RV/tent: 84. $12. Hookups: none.

Frisco

Frisco Woods Campground, Cape Hatteras National Seashore, Hwy. 12, P.O. Box 159, 27936. T: (252) 995-5208. www.nps.gov/caha. RV/tent: 225. $22–$37. Hookups: water, electric (15, 20, 30 amps), sewer.

Hatteras Sands Camping Resort, P.O. Box 295, 27943. T: (252) 986-2422. hatsandscg@aol.com. RV/tent: 124. $31.20–$42.95. Hookups: water, electric (15, 20, 30, 50 amps).

Gatesville

Merchants Millpond State Park, 71 US Hwy. 158 East, 27938. T: (252) 357-1191. ils.unc.edu/park project/ncparks.html. RV/tent: 20. $12. Hookups: none.

Gatlinburg

Balsam Mountain (Cherokee, NC), Great Smoky Mountains National Park, 107 Park Headquarters Rd., 37738. T: (423) 436-1200. www.nps.gov/grsm. RV/tent: 46. $14. Hookups: none.

Deep Creek Camp (Bryson City, NC), Great Smoky Mountains National Park, 107 Park Headquarters Rd., 37738. T: (423) 436-1200. www.nps.gov/grsm. RV/tent: 92. $14. Hookups: none.

Glendale Springs

Raccoon Holler, P.O. Box 16, 28629. T: (336) 982-2706. RV/tent: 189. $16–$18. Hookups: water, electric (20, 30 amps).

Goldsboro

Cliffs of the Neuse State Park, 345-A Park Entrance Rd., 28578. T: (919) 778-6234. ils.unc.edu/park project/ncparks.html. RV/tent: 35. $12. Hookups: none.

Eastern Carolina Athletic Park, P.O. Box 160, 27863. T: (919) 580-1100. RV/tent: 22. $20. Hookups: water, electric (20, 30, 50 amps).

Grandy

Yogi Bear Jellystone/Currituck Resort Shores, 6671 Caratoke Hwy., 27939. T: (252) 453-226. RV/tent: 138. $26.50. Hookups: water, electric (20, 30, 50 amps).

Greensboro

Fields RV Campground, 2317 Campground Rd., 27406. T: (336) 292-1381. RV/tent: 29. $13. Hookups: water, electric (20, 30 amps).

Greensboro Campground, 1896 Trox St., 27406. T: (336) 274-4143. RV/tent: 117. $16–$21.50. Hookups: water, electric (20, 30, 50 amps).

Hayesville

Ho Hum Campground, 47 Ho Hum Loop, 28904. T: (828) 389-6740. RV/tent: 88. $20. Hookups: water, electric (15, 20, 30 amps).

Tusquittee Campground & Cabins, 9594 Tusquittee Rd., 28904. T: (828) 389-8520. RV/tent: 18. $15. Hookups: water, electric (15, 20, 30 amps).

Henderson

Bullocksville, Kerr State Recreation Area, 269 Glasshouse Rd., 27536. T: (252) 438-7791. ils.unc.edu/parkproject/ncparks.html. RV/tent: 69. $17. Hookups: water, electric (30 amps).

Henderson Point, Kerr State Recreation Area, 6254 Satterwhite Point Rd., 27536. T: (252) 438-7791. ils.unc.edu/parkproject/ncparks.html. RV/tent: 79. $17. Hookups: water, electric (30 amps).

Nutbush Bridge, Kerr State Recreation Area, 6254 Satterwhite Point Rd., 27536. T: (252) 438-7791. ils.unc.edu/parkproject/ncparks.html. RV/tent: 103. $17. Hookups: water, electric (30 amps).

Satterwhite Point, Kerr State Recreation Area, 269 Glasshouse Rd., 27536. T: (252) 438-7791. ils.unc. edu/parkproject/ncparks.html. RV/tent: 118. $17. Hookups: water, electric (30 amps).

Apple Valley Travel Park, 1 Apple Orchard Rd., 28792. T: (828) 685-8000. RV/tent: 93. $20. Hookups: water, electric (30 amps).

Lazy Boy Travel Park, 110 Old Sunset Hill Rd., 28792. T: (828) 697-7165. RV/tent: 83. $15. Hookups: water, electric (20, 30 amps).

Park Place RV Park, Rte. 2 Box 152B, 28731. T: (828) 693-3831. RV/tent: 48. $16. Hookups: water, electric (20, 30, 50 amps).

Phil & Ann's RV, 818 Tracy Grove Rd., 28731-9618. T: (800) 753-8373. RV/tent: 31. $11.99. Hookups: water, electric (15, 30 amps).

Red Gates RV Park, Rte. 19 Box 89, 28792. T: (828) 685-8787. RV/tent: 18. $14–$15. Hookups: water, electric (20, 30 amps).

Town Mountain Travel Park, 2030 Old Spartanburg Rd., 28792. T: (828) 697-6692. RV/tent: 26. $17. Hookups: water, electric (20, 30, 50 amps).

Highlands

Highlands RV Park, 651 Chestnut St., 28741. T: (828) 526-5985. RV/tent: 6. $40. Hookups: water, electric (20, 30, 50 amps).

Hot Springs

Hot Springs RV Park & Campground, P.O. Box 428, 28743. T: (828) 622-7676. RV/tent: 110. $20. Hookups: water, electric (15, 20, 30 amps).

NORTH CAROLINA (continued)

Hot Springs (continued)

Rocky Bluff Campground, Pisgah National Forest, Appalachian Ranger District, French Broad Ranger Station, P.O. Box 128, 28743. T: (828) 622-3202. www.cs.unca.edu/nfsnc. RV/tent: 30. $8. Hookups: none.

Jacksonville

Cabin Creek Campground & Mobile Home Park, 3200 Wilmington Hwy., 28540. T: (910) 346-4808. RV/tent: 81. $24. Hookups: water, electric (15, 30, 50 amps).

Kitty Hawk

Adventure Bound Campground, 1004 West Kitty Hawk Rd., 27949. T: (252) 255-1130. RV/tent: 20. $12. Hookups: none.

Colington Park Campground, 1608 Colington Rd., 27948. T: (252) 441-6128. RV/tent: 90. $18. Hookups: water, electric (15, 20, 30 amps).

Lake Toxaway

Outdoor Resorts–Blue Ridge, 1 Resorts Blvd., 28747. T: (828) 966-9350. RV/tent: 82. $48. Hookups: water, electric (20, 30, 50 amps).

Laurel Springs

Doughton Park Camp, Blue Ridge National Parkway, Blue Ridge Pkwy., Milepost 239.2, 28644. T: (336) 372-8568. www.nps.gov/blri. RV/tent: 135. $12. Hookups: none.

Linville Falls

Linville Falls Camp, Blue Ridge National Parkway, Blue Ridge Pkwy., Milepost 316.5, 28647. T: (828) 298-0398. www.nps.gov/blri. RV/tent: 70. $12. Hookups: none.

Linville Falls Trailer Lodge & Campground, P.O. Box 205, 28647. T: (828) 765-2681. RV/tent: 46. $20. Hookups: water, electric (15, 20, 30 amps).

Little Switzerland

Crabtree Meadows Camp, Blue Ridge National Parkway, Blue Ridge Pkwy., Milepost 339.5, 28749. T: (828) 298-0398. www.nps.gov/blri. RV/tent: 93. $12. Hookups: none.

Littleton

Outdoor World–Lake Gaston Campground, Rte. 6 Box 236, 27850. T: (252) 586-4121. RV/tent: 191. $25. Hookups: water, electric (30, 50 amps).

Lumberton

Sleepy Bear's Family Campground, 465 Kenric Rd., 28360. T: (910) 739-4372. RV/tent: 80. $19. Hookups: water, electric (20, 30, 50 amps).

Maggie Valley

Meadowbrook Resort, 102 Meadowbrook Loop, 28751. T: (828) 926-1821. RV/tent: 28. $16. Hookups: water, electric (15, 20, 30 amps).

Stone Bridge RV Park, 1786 Soco Rd. US Hwy. 19, 28751. T: (828) 926-1904. RV/tent: 308. $20–$25. Hookups: water, electric (20, 30 amps).

Manteo

Cypress Cove Campground, 818 US 64, 27954. T: (252) 473-5231. www.outerbankscamping.com. RV/tent: 58. $17–$24. Hookups: water, electric (15, 20, 30 amps).

Marion

Buck Creek Campground, 1020 Tom's Creek Rd., 28752. T: (828) 724-4888. RV/tent: 64. $20. Hookups: water, electric (15, 20, 30, 50 amps).

Hidden Valley Campground and Waterpark, Rte. 1 Box 377, 28752. T: (828) 652-7208. RV/tent: 75. $21. Hookups: water, electric (20, 30 amps).

Mocksville

Lake Myers RV Resort, 150 Fred Lanier Rd., 27028. T: (336) 492-7736. RV/tent: 425. $26. Hookups: water, electric (20, 30 amps).

Morehead City

Waters Edge RV Park, 1463 Hwy. 24, 28570. T: (252) 247-0494. RV/tent: 86. $20–$25. Hookups: water, electric (20, 30, 50 amps).

Whispering Pines Family Campground, 25 Whispering Pines, 28570. T: (252) 726-4902. www.ncpines.com. RV/tent: 135. $22–$26. Hookups: water, electric (15, 20, 30, 50 amps).

Murphy

Creekside RV Park, 68 Old Peachtree Rd., 28905. T: (828) 837-4123. RV/tent: 23. $22. Hookups: water, electric (15, 20, 30, 50 amps).

Hanging Dog Campground, Nantahala National Forest, Tusquitee Ranger District, 123 Woodland Dr., 28906. T: (828) 837-5152. www.cs.unca.edu/nfsnc. RV/tent: 67. $8. Hookups: none.

Jackrabbit Mountain Camp, Nantahala National Forest, Tusquitee Ranger District, 123 Woodland Dr., 28906. T: (828) 837-5152. www.cs.unca.edu/nfsnc. RV/tent: 101. $12. Hookups: none.

Peace Valley Campground, P.O. Box 606, 28906. T: (828) 837-6223. RV/tent: 87. $18–$20. Hookups: water, electric (15, 30 amps).

Nebo

Lake James State Park, Rte. 2 Lake James Rd., Hwy. 126, 28761. T: (828) 652-5047. ils.unc.edu/park project/ncparks.html. RV/tent: 20. $12. Hookups: none.

New Bern

Neuse River Campground, 1565 B St., 28560. T: (252) 638-2556. RV/tent: 93. $17–$19. Hookups: water, electric (20, 30 amps), sewer.

NORTH CAROLINA (continued)

Norlina

County Line Park, Kerr State Recreation Area, 6254 Satterwhite Point Rd., 27536. T: (252) 438-7791. ils.unc.edu/parkproject/ncparks.html. RV/tent: 82. $17. Hookups: water, electric (30 amps).

Kimball Point Park, Kerr State Recreation Area, 6254 Satterwhite Point Rd., 27536. T: (252) 438-7791. ils.unc.edu/parkproject/ncparks.html. RV/tent: 91. $17. Hookups: water, electric (30 amps).

Oak Island

Long Beach Campground, 5011 East Oak Island Dr., 28465. T: (910) 278-5737. RV/tent: 184. $18–$25. Hookups: water, electric (15, 20, 30 amps).

Ocracoke

Beachcomber Campground, P.O. Box 203, 27960. T: (252) 928-4031. RV/tent: 29. $20. Hookups: water, electric (30 amps).

Old Fort

Catawaba Falls Campground, Rte. 3 Box 230, 28762. T: (828) 668-4831. RV/tent: 41. $12.50–$15.50. Hookups: water, electric (20, 30 amps).

Pinehurst

Village of Pinehurst RV Park, P.O. Box 5170, 28374. T: (910) 295-5452. RV/tent: 80. $21. Hookups: water, electric (20, 30, 50 amps).

Piney Creek

RiverCamp USA, P.O. Box 9, 28663-0009. T: (336) 359-2267. www.rivercamp.net. RV/tent: 74. $20. Hookups: water, electric (20, 30 amps).

Pink Hill

Maxwell's Mill Campground, 142 Maxwell's Mill Campground Rd., 28572. T: (252) 568-2022. RV/tent: 56. $20. Hookups: water, electric (20, 30, 50 amps).

Pinnacle

Pilot Mountain State Park, 1792 Pilot Knob Park Rd., 27043. T: (336) 325-2355. ils.unc.edu/parkproject/ncparks.html. RV/tent: 49. $12. Hookups: none.

Raleigh

William B. Umstead State Park, 8801 Glenwood Ave., 27612. T: (919) 571-4170. ils.unc.edu/parkproject/ncparks.html. RV/tent: 28. $12. Hookups: none.

Roaring Gap

Stone Mountain State Park, 3042 Frank Pkwy., 28668. T: (336) 957-8185. ils.unc.edu/parkproject/ncparks.html. RV/tent: 37. $12. Hookups: none.

Robbinsville

Cheoah Point Recreation Area, Nantahala National Forest, Cheoah Ranger District, Rte. 1 Box 16A, 28721. T: (828) 479-6431. www.cs.unca.edu/nfsnc. RV/tent: 26. $8. Hookups: none.

Hidden Waters RV Park & Campground, Rte. 3 Box 81, 28771. T: (828) 479-3509. RV/tent: 12. $15. Hookups: water, electric (30 amps).

Tsali Recreational Area, Nantahala National Forest, Cheoah Ranger District, Rte. 1 Box 16A, 28721. T: (828) 479-6431. www.cs.unca.edu/nfsnc. RV/tent: 42. $15. Hookups: none.

Rodanthe

Camp Hatteras, P.O. Box 10, 27968. T: (252) 987-2777. RV/tent: 336. $25.95–$45. Hookups: water, electric (30, 50 amps).

Ocean Waves Campground, P.O. Box 3576, 27982. T: (252) 987-2556. RV/tent: 68. $20–$22. Hookups: water, electric (20, 30, 50 amps).

Rodanthe Shoreline Campground, P.O. Box 272, 27968. T: (252) 987-1431. RV/tent: 10. $14.50–$18.25. Hookups: water, electric (30 amps).

Salisbury

Dan Nicholas Park (Rowan County Park), 6800 Bringle Ferry Rd., 28146. T: (704) 636-0154. RV/tent: 80. $15. Hookups: water, electric (20, 30 amps).

Salter Path

Arrowhead Campground, 1550 Salter Path Rd., 28512. T: (252) 247-3838. RV/tent: 171. $19. Hookups: water, electric (20, 30 amps).

Salter Path Family Campground, P.O. Box 2323, 28512-2323. T: (252) 247-3525. www.salterpath-camping.com. RV/tent: 205. $26–$38. Hookups: water, electric (20, 30 amps).

Sealevel

Cedar Creek Campground & Marina, 111 Canal Dr., 28577. T: (252) 225-9571. RV/tent: 70. $18. Hookups: water, electric (20, 30 amps).

Selma

KOA–Selma/Smithfield, 428 Campground Rd., 27576. T: (919) 965-5923 or (800) 562-5897. RV/tent: 93. $18.50–$24.50. Hookups: water, electric (20, 30, 50 amps).

Shallotte

S & W RV Park, 532 Holden Beach Rd., 28470-1713. T: (910) 754-8576. RV/tent: 22. $16. Hookups: water, electric (30 amps).

Sea Mist Camping Resort, P.O. Box 1481, 28459. T: (910) 754-8916. RV/tent: 250. $18–$27. Hookups: water, electric (15, 30 amps).

Smithfield

Holiday Trav-L-Park Smithfield, 497 US Hwy. 701, 27524. T: (919) 934-3181. RV/tent: 104. $19.25–$20.75. Hookups: water, electric (20, 30 amps).

Spruce Pine

Bear Den Campground, R.F.D. 3 Box 284, 28777. T: (828) 765-2888. RV/tent: 144. $25–$31. Hookups: water, electric (15, 20, 30, 50 amps).

NORTH CAROLINA (continued)

Spruce Pine (continued)

Buck Hill Campground, P.O. Box 238, 28664. T: (800) 387-5224. RV/tent: 59. $21. Hookups: water, electric (15, 20, 30 amps).

Secluded Valley Campground, 8551 19E South, 28657. T: (828) 765-4810. RV/tent: 58. $14. Hookups: water, electric (20, 30 amps).

Statesville

KOA–Statesville, 162 KOA Ln., 28677. T: (704) 873-556 or (800) KOA-5705. RV/tent: 88. $23–$27. Hookups: water, electric (20, 30, 50 amps).

Midway Campground & RV Resort, 114 Midway Dr., 28625. T: (704) 546-7615. RV/tent: 83. $27–$37. Hookups: water, electric (20, 30, 50 amps).

Stoneville

Dan River Campground, 724 Webster Rd., 27048. T: (336) 427-8530. RV/tent: 40. $15. Hookups: water, electric (20, 30, 50 amps).

Sunset Beach

Wishing Well Campground, 520 Seaside Rd. SW, 28468. T: (910) 579-7982. RV/tent: 39. $15. Hookups: water, electric (20, 30 amps).

Swannanoa

Mama Gertie's Hideaway Campground, 620 Patton Cove Rd., 28778. T: (828) 686-4258. RV/tent: 28. $18.50–$22.50. Hookups: water, electric (15, 20, 30, 50 amps).

Miles Motors RV Center & Campground, 15 Patton Cove Rd., 28778. T: (828) 686-3414. RV/tent: 61. $20. Hookups: water, electric (20, 30, 50 amps).

Swansboro

Waterway RV Park, P.O. Box 4847, 28594. T: (252) 393-8715. RV/tent: 334. $25. Hookups: water, electric (15, 20, 30, 50 amps).

Topton

Brookside Campground & Rafting, P.O. Box 93, 28781. T: (828) 321-5209. RV/tent: 46. $14. Hookups: water, electric (15, 20 amps).

Union Grove

Fiddlers Grove Campground, P.O. Box 11, 28689. T: (704) 539-4417. RV/tent: 40. $17–$20. Hookups: water, electric (15, 20, 30, 50 amps).

Van Hoy Farms Family Campground, P.O. Box 38, 28689. T: (704) 539-5493. RV/tent: 147. $21. Hookups: water, electric (15, 30, 50 amps).

Vilas

Vanderpool Campground, 1173 Charlie Thompson Rd., 28692. T: (828) 297-3486. RV/tent: 44. $18. Hookups: water, electric (30 amps).

Wade

KOA–Fayetteville, P.O. Box 67, 28395. T: (910) 484-5500 or (800) KOA-5350. RV/tent: 90. $24–$26. Hookups: water, electric (20, 30, 50 amps).

Washington

Twin Lakes Camping Resort & Yacht Basin, 1618 Memory Ln., 27817. T: (252) 946-5700. www.twinlakesnc.com. RV/tent: 379. $20–$28. Hookups: water, electric (20, 30, 50 amps).

Whichard's Beach Campground, P.O. Box 746, 27889. T: (252) 946-0011. www.whichardsbeach.com. RV/tent: 118. $20–$23. Hookups: water, electric (20, 30, 50 amps).

Waxhaw

Cane Creek Park (Union County Park), 5213 Harkey Rd., 28173. T: (704) 843-3919. RV/tent: 120. $14–$24. Hookups: water, electric (20, 30 amps), sewer.

Waynesville

Winngray Family Campground, 26 Winngray Ln., 28785. T: (828) 926-3170. RV/tent: 150. $20. Hookups: water, electric (15, 20, 30, 50 amps).

White Lake

Camp Clearwater Family Campground, 2038 White Lake Dr., 28337. T: (336) 862-3365. www.camp clearwater.com. RV/tent: 910. $25–$35. Hookups: water, electric (20, 30, 50 amps), sewer.

Whittier

Holly Cove Campground & RV Resort, 341 Holly Cove Rd., 28789. T: (828) 631-0692. RV/tent: 49. $20. Hookups: water, electric (15, 30 amps).

Timberlake Campground, 3270 Conleys Creek Rd., 28789. T: (828) 497-7320. RV/tent: 54. $16.50–$20.50. Hookups: water, electric (15, 20, 30 amps).

Wilkesboro

Warrior Creek Park (Corps of Engineers–West Kerr Scott Reservoir), 499 Reservoir Rd., 28697. T: (336) 921-2177. www.reserveusa.com. RV/tent: 88. $12–$16. Hookups: water, electric (30 amps).

Wilmington

Camelot RV Park, 7415 Market St., 28411. T: (910) 686-7705. RV/tent: 107. $24–$28. Hookups: water, electric (15, 20, 30 amps).

SOUTH CAROLINA

Aiken

Aiken State Natural Area, 1145 State Park Rd., 29856. T: (803) 649-2857. RV/tent: 25. $12. Hookups: water, electric (20, 30 amps).

Crossroads RV Park & Mobile Home Community, 569 Crossreads Park Dr., 29803. T: (803) 642-5702. RV/tent: 22. $18. Hookups: water, electric (20, 30, 50 amps).

Pine Acres Campground, 213 Duke Dr., 29801. T: (803) 648-5715. RV/tent: 30. $18. Hookups: water, electric (20, 30, 50 amps).

Anderson

KOA–Anderson/Lake Hartwell, 200 Wham Rd., 29625. T: (864) 287-3161. www.koa.com. alhkon@carol.net. RV/tent: 70. $21–$29. Hookups: water, electric (30, 50 amps).

Hartwell Four Seasons Campground, 400 Ponderosa Point Rd., 29689. T: (864) 287-3223. RV/tent: 108. $17–$21. Hookups: water, electric (20, 30 amps).

Sadlers Creek State Recreation Park, 940 Sadlers Creek Park Rd., 29626. T: (864) 226-8950. RV/tent: 37. $13.40–$17.15. Hookups: water, electric (30 amps).

Beaufort

Tuck in the Wood Campground, 22 Tuc in de Wood Ln., 29920. T: (843) 838-2267. RV/tent: 75. $21–$23. Hookups: water, electric (30, 50 amps).

Bishopville

Lee State Natural Area, 487 Loop Rd., 29101. T: (803) 428-5307. RV/tent: 25. $11. Hookups: water, electric (30 amps).

Blackville

Barnwell State Park, 223 State Park Rd., 29817. T: (803) 284-2212. RV/tent: 25. $13. Hookups: water, electric (30 amps).

Bluffton

Stoney Crest Plantation Campground, 419 May River Rd., 29910. T: (843) 757-3249. RV/tent: 30. $17. Hookups: water, electric (20, 30 amps).

Camden

Columbia/Camden RV Park, Box 1210, 29301. T: (803) 438-8774 (call collect). RVColaCamden@earthlink.net. RV/tent: 34. $19. Hookups: water, electric (30, 50 amps).

Canadys

Colleton State Park, 147 Wayside Ln., 29433. T: (843) 538-8206. RV/tent: 25. $13. Hookups: water, electric (20 amps).

Shuman's RV Trailer Park, Hwy. 15 North, 29433. T: (843) 538-8731. RV/tent: 15. $10. Hookups: water, electric (20, 30, 50 amps).

Charleston

Campground at James Island County Park, 871 Riverland Dr., 29412. T: (843) 795-7275. www.ccprc.com. RV/tent: 125. $22–$26. Hookups: water, electric (30, 50 amps).

Fain's RV Park, 6309 Fain Blvd., 29406-4986. T: (843) 744-1005. RV/tent: 34. $22. Hookups: water, electric (30, 50 amps).

Lake Aire RV Park and Campground, 4375 Hwy. 162, 29449. T: (843) 571-1271. www.lakeairerv.com. lakeairerv@juno.com. RV/tent: 117. $12–$24.50. Hookups: water, electric (20, 30, 50 amps).

Oak Plantation Campground, 3540 Savannah Hwy., 29455. T: (843) 766-5936. RV/tent: 304. $13.50–$20. Hookups: water, electric (30, 50 amps).

Cheraw

Cheraw State Recreation Area, 100 State Park Rd., 29520. T: (800) 868-9630. RV/tent: 17. $13. Hookups: water, electric (20, 30 amps).

Chester

Chester State Park, 759 State Park Dr., 29706. T: (803) 385-2680. RV/tent: 25. $11. Hookups: water, electric (30 amps).

Clemson

Twin Lakes Campground, US Hwy. 76, 5 miles west of Pendleton, 29670. T: (888) 893-0678 or (706) 856-0300. RV/tent: 102. $12–18. Hookups: water, electric (20, 30 amps).

Columbia

Barnyard RV Park, 4414 Augusta Rd., 29073-7345. T: (803) 957-1238. RV/tent: 97. $17–$18. Hookups: water, electric (20, 30, 50 amps).

Wood Smoke Family Campground, 11302 Broad River Rd., 29063. T: (803) 781-9921. RV/tent: 37. $11–$18. Hookups: water, electric (15, 20, 30 amps).

Conway

Big Cypress Lake RV Park & Fishing Retreat, Cates Bay Hwy., 29527. T: (843) 397-1800. RV/tent: 23. $20–$35. Hookups: water, electric (20, 30, 50 amps).

Dillon

Bass Lake RV Campground, 1149 Bass Lake Pl., 29536. T: (843) 774-2690. RV/tent: 68. $16. Hookups: water, electric (20, 30 amps).

Little Pee Dee State Park, 1298 State Park Rd., 29436. T: (843) 774-8872. RV/tent: 50. $7–$12. Hookups: water, electric (30 amps).

Ehrhardt

Rivers Bridge State Historic Site, Rte. 1, Boox 190, 29801. T: (803) 267-3675. RV/tent: 25. $12. Hookups: water, electric (20, 30 amps).

SOUTH CAROLINA (continued)

Fair Play

Lakeshore Campground, 231 Lakeshore Dr., 29543-2747. T: (864) 972-3330. RV/tent: 50. $22. Hookups: water, electric (20, 30 amps).

Thousand Trails–Carolina Landing, 120 Carolina Landing Dr., 29643-2703. T: (864) 972-3717. RV/tent: 250. $24. Hookups: water, electric (30 amps).

Florence

KOA–Florence, 1115 East Campground Rd., 29506. T: (843) 665-7007. RV/tent: 135. $17–$25. Hookups: water, electric (20, 30, 50 amps).

Swamp Fox Camping, 1600 Gateway Rd., 29501-8123. T: (877) 251-2251 or (843) 665-7007. RV/tent: 61. $15–$16.69. Hookups: water, electric (20, 30, 50 amps).

Fort Mill

KOA–Charlotte/Fort Mill, 940 Gold Hill Rd., 29708. T: (803) 548-1148. RV/tent: 209. $22–$26. Hookups: water, electric (20, 30, 50 amps).

SPM Defender Lakeside Lodges & Campground, 9600 Regent Parkway, 29715. T: (803) 547-3500. RV/tent: 127. $18. Hookups: water, electric (30 amps).

Gaffney

Pine Cone Campground, 160 Sarrett School Rd., 29341. T: (864) 489-2022. pineconerv@aol.com. RV/tent: 91. $20–$23. Hookups: water, electric (20, 30, 50 amps).

Green Pond

Wood Brothers Campground, 8446 Ace Basin Parkway, 29446. T: (843) 844-2208. RV/tent: 42. $15. Hookups: water, electric (20, 30 amps).

Greenville

Flowermill RV Park, 31 Stallings Rd., 29687. T: (864) 877-5079. RV/tent: 30. $14. Hookups: water, electric (20, 30 amps).

Paris Mountain State Park, 2401 State Park Rd., 29609. T: (864) 244-5565. RV/tent: 50. $12. Hookups: water, electric (20, 30 amps).

Rainbow RV Park, 3553 Rutherford Rd., 29687. T: (864) 244-1271. RV/tent: 50. $20. Hookups: water, electric (30, 50 amps).

Scuffletown USA, 603 Scuffle Town Rd., 29681. T: (864) 967-2276. RV/tent: 55. $21. Hookups: water, electric (30, 50 amps).

Springwood RV Park, 800 Donaldson Rd., 29605. T: (864) 277-9789. RV/tent: 55. $18. Hookups: water, electric (30, 50 amps).

Hilton Head Island

Outdoor Resorts/Hilton Head Island Motor Coach Resort, 19 Arrow Rd., 29928-3245. T: (800) 722-2365 or (843) 785-7699. RV/tent: 401. $28–$34. Hookups: water, electric (20, 30, 50 amps).

Outdoor RV Resort & Yacht Club, 43 Jenkins Rd., 29925. T: (843) 681-3256 or (800) 845-9560. www.outdoor-rv.com. outdoorresort@aol.com. RV/tent: 200. $32–$38. Hookups: water, electric (30, 50 amps).

Lancaster

Andrew Jackson State Park, 196 Andrew Jackson Park Rd., 29720. T: (803) 285-3344. RV/tent: 25. $13. Hookups: water, electric (30 amps).

Leesville

Cedar Pond Campground, 4721 Fairview Rd., 29070. T: (803) 657-5993. RV/tent: 32. $16. Hookups: water, electric (30, 50 amps).

Lexington

Edmund RV Park & Campground, 5920 Edmund Hwy., 29073. T: (800) 955-7957. RV/tent: 260. $10–$13. Hookups: water, electric (20, 30, 50 amps).

Liberty Hill

Wateree Lake Campground, P.O. Box 242, 29074. T: (803) 273-3013. RV/tent: 38. $17. Hookups: water, electric (30 amps).

Manning

Campers Paradise, Rte. 6 Box 870, 29102. T: (803) 473-3550. RV/tent: 60. $14–$15. Hookups: water, electric (30 amps).

McCormick

Hickory Knob State Resort Park, Rte. 1 Box 199B, 29835. T: (800) 491-1764. RV/tent: 75. $18. Hookups: water, electric (20, 30 amps).

Myrtle Beach

Apache Family Campground, 900 Kings Rd., 29572. T: (800) 553-1749. RV/tent: 268. $19–$36. Hookups: water, electric (20, 30 amps).

Orangeburg

Sweetwater Lake Campground, Rte. 5, 29135. T: (803) 874-3547 or (800) 553-1749. RV/tent: 50. $15. Hookups: water, electric (15, 20, 50 amps).

Pelion

River Bottom Farms RV Park & Campground, 357 Cedar Creek Rd., 29160. T: (803) 568-4182. riverbottomfarmsr.v.park@myexcel.com. RV/tent: 60. $22. Hookups: water, electric (30 amps).

Pickens

Keowee–Toxaway State Natural Area, 108 Residence Dr., 29685. T: (864) 868-2605. RV/tent: 24. $7–$12. Hookups: water, electric (30 amps).

Point South

KOA–Point South, P.O. Box 1760, 29945. T: (843) 726-5733 or (800) KOA-2948. pointsouthkoa@gocampingamerica.com. RV/tent: 54. $18.90–45. Hookups: water, electric (50 amps).

SOUTH CAROLINA (continued)

The Oaks at Point South RV Resort, Rte. 1, 29945. T: (843) 726-5728. RV/tent: 83. $20.95. Hookups: water, electric (30, 50 amps).

Ridgeway

Ridgeway Campground, P.O. Box 472, 29130. T: (803) 337-8585. RV/tent: 24. $14. Hookups: water, electric (20, 30 amps).

Roebuck

Pine Ridge Campground, 199 Pine Ridge Campground Rd., 29367. T: (864) 576-0302. RV/tent: 45. $16–$22.50. Hookups: water, electric (30, 50 amps).

Santee

Lake Marion Resort & Marina, 510 Rag Time Trail, 29142. T: (803) 854-2136. RV/tent: 65. $16. Hookups: water, electric (20, 30 amps).

Seneca

Crooked Creek RV Park, 777 Arve Ln., 29696. T: (864) 882-5040. RV/tent: 110. $32. Hookups: water, electric (20, 30, 50 amps).

South Of The Border

Camp Pedro, P.O. Box 8, 29547. T: (843) 774-2411 or (800) 845-6011. RV/tent: 100. $17.50. Hookups: water, electric (20, 30, 50 amps).

Spartanburg

Pine Cone Campground, Rte. 4, 29302. T: (864) 585-1283. RV/tent: 12. $12. Hookups: water, electric (30 amps).

Summerton

Taw Caw Campground & Marina, Rte. 4 Box 1740, Summerton, 29148. T: (803) 478-2171. tawcaw@ftc-I.net. RV/tent: 63. $18. Hookups: water, electric (20, 30 amps).

Summerville

Givhans Ferry State Park, 746 Givhans Ferry Rd., 29472. T: (843) 873-0692. RV/tent: 25. $13. Hookups: water, electric (30 amps).

Sumter

Military Park, 314 Lance Ave., 29152. T: (803) 432-7976. RV/tent: 13. $11. Hookups: water electric (20, 30 amps).

Timmonsville

Lake Honey Dew Campground, 2028 Cale Yarborough Hwy., 29161-8223. T: (843) 346-0700. RV/tent: 16. $15. Hookups: water, electric (20, 30, 50 amps).

Townville

Coneross Campground, P.O. Box 278, 30643-0278. T: (888) 893-0678 or (706) 856-0300. RV/tent: 106. $10–18. Hookups: water, electric (20, 30 amps).

Travelers Rest

Holly Hill RV Park, 219 Stamey Valley Rd., 29690. T: (864) 834-0776. RV/tent: 18. $18.50. Hookups: water, electric (20, 30, 50 amps).

Walhalla

Devils Fork State Park, 161 Holcombe Cir., 29676. T: (864) 944-2639. RV/tent: 59. $18. Hookups: water, electric (30 amps).

Walterboro

Green Acres Family Campground, 396 Campground Rd., 29488. T: (800) 474-3450 or (843) 538-3450. RV/tent: 135. $14–$15. Hookups: water, electric (15, 30, 50 amps).

Wedgefield

Poinsett State Park, 6660 Poionsett Park Rd., 29168. T: (803) 494-8177. RV/tent: 50. $8–$$11. Hookups: water, electric (20, 30 amps).

Whitmire

Brickhouse Campground, US Forest Service, 20 Work Center Rd., 29178. T: (864) 427-9858. RV/tent: 23. $5. Hookups: none.

TENNESSEE

Allons

Deep Valley Park & Trout Farm, 755 Hunters Cove Rd., 38541. T: (931) 823-6053. RV/tent: 29. $10–$12. Hookups: water, electric (20, 30 amps), sewer.

Lillydale Campground, 5199 Lillydale Rd., 38541. T: (931) 823-4155. www.reserveusa.com. RV/tent: 114. $13–$22. Hookups: water, electric (20, 30 amps).

Williow Grove, 9997 Willow Grove Rd., 38541. T: (931) 823-4285. www.reserveusa.com. RV/tent: 83. $10–$22. Hookups: water, electric (30, 50 amps).

Athens

Athens I-75 Campground, 2509 Decatur Pike, Hwy. 30, 37303. T: (423) 745-9199. RV/tent: 63. $16–$20. Hookups: water, electric (20, 30 amps), sewer.

TENNESSEE (continued)

Athens (continued)

Over-Niter RV Park, 316 Mt Verd Rd., Hwy. 305, 37303. T: (423) 507-0069. RV/tent: 16. $14–$16. Hookups: water, electric (20, 30, 50 amps), sewer.

Baileyton

Baileyton Camp Inn, 7485 Horton Hwy., 37745. T: (423) 234-4992. RV/tent: 44. $16–$19. Hookups: water, electric (20, 30, 50 amps), sewer, modem.

Blountville

KOA–Bristol/Kingsport, 425 Rocky Branch Rd., 37617. T: (423) 323-7790. F: (423) 323-7790. www. koa.com. RV/tent: 73. $19–$28. Hookups: water, electric (20, 30, 50 amps), sewer, modem.

Rocky Top Campground, 496 Pearl Ln., 37617. T: (800) 452-6456. F: (423) 323-9965. RV/tent: 35. $15–$20. Hookups: water, electric (20, 30, 50 amps), sewer.

Buchanan

Paris Landing State Park, 16055 Hwy. 79 North, 38222. T: (731) 644-7359. www.tnstateparks.com. RV/tent: 44. $14–$17. Hookups: water, electric (30 amps).

Bumpus Mills

Bumpus Mills Recreational Area, 764 Forest Trace, 37028. T: (931) 232-8831. www.reserveusa.com. RV/tent: 33. $10–$18. Hookups: water, electric (30 amps).

Carthage

Defeated Creek Park (Corps of Engineers), State Rte. 85, 37030. T: (615) 774-3141. www.reserve usa.com. RV/tent: 155. $13–$23. Hookups: water, electric (20, 30 amps), sewer.

Indian Creek Park, US 53, north of Chestnut Mound, 37030. T: (615) 897-2233. www.reserve usa.com. RV/tent: 53. $9–$20. Hookups: water, electric (30 amps).

Castalian Springs

Shady Cove Resort & Marina, 1115 Shady Cove Rd., 37031. T: (615) 452-8010. F: (615) 452-4524. RV/tent: 95. $12–$20. Hookups: water, electric (20, 30, 50 amps), sewer, modem.

Celina

Dale Hollow Dam Campground, 5050 Dale Hollow Dam Rd., 38551. T: (931) 243-3554. www.reserve usa.com. RV/tent: 79. $15–$22. Hookups: water, electric.

Chattanooga

Lookout Valley RV Park, 3714 Cummings Hwy., 37419. T: (423) 821-3100. F: (423) 821-5774. RV/tent: 126. $22. Hookups: water, electric (30, 50 amps), sewer, modem.

Raccoon Mountain Campground & RV Park, 319 West Hills Dr., 37419. T: (423) 821-9403. www. raccoonmountain.com. RV/tent: 124. $14–$23. Hookups: water, electric (20, 30, 50 amps), sewer.

Shipp's RV Center & Campground, 3728 Ringgold Rd., 37412. T: (800) 222-4551. www.shippsrv.com. RV/tent: 120. $20–$23. Hookups: water, electric (20, 30, 50 amps), sewer.

Clarksville

Clarksville RV Park & Campground, 1270 Tylertown Rd., 37040. T: (931) 648-8638. RV/tent: 59. $19–$21. Hookups: water, electric (20, 30, 50 amps), sewer, modem.

Clinton

Fox Inn Campground, 2423 Andersonville Hwy., 37716. T: (865) 494-9386. F: (865) 494-6794. www.foxinncampground.com. RV/tent: 93. $15–$24. Hookups: water, electric (20, 30, 50 amps), sewer, modem.

Cornersville

Texas T Campground, 2499 Lynnville Hwy., 37047. T: (931) 293-2500. RV/tent: 40. $14–$16. Hookups: water, electric (30, 50 amps), sewer.

Cosby

Fox Den Campground, 311 South Hwy. 32, 37722. T: (888) 369-3661. RV/tent: 74. $12–$20. Hookups: water, electric (15, 30, 50 amps), sewer.

Crossville

Ballyhoo Family Campground, 256 Werthwyle, 38555. T: (888) 336-3703. RV/tent: 74. $15–$20. Hookups: water, electric (20, 30, 50 amps), sewer.

Roam & Roost RV Campground, 255 Fairview Dr., 38558. T: (877) 707-1414. RV/tent: 24. $13–$18. Hookups: water, electric (30, 50 amps), sewer, modem.

Delano

Hiawassee State Scenic River & Ocoee River (Gee Creek Campground), Spring Creek Rd., 37325. T: (423) 263-0050. F: (423) 263-0103. www.tnstate parks.com. RV/tent: 43. $11. Hookups: none.

Dickson

Dickson RV Park, 2340 Hwy. 46 South, 37055. T: (615) 446-9925. RV/tent: 60. $17–$25. Hookups: water, electric (20, 30 amps), sewer, modem.

Tanbark Campground, 125 South Spradlin Rd., 37055. T: (615) 441-1613. RV/tent: 30. $10–$15. Hookups: water, electric (20, 30, 50 amps), sewer.

Gainesboro

Salt Lick Creek Campground, Smith Bend Rd., 38562. T: (931) 678-4718. www.reserveusa.com. RV/tent: 150. $13–$23. Hookups: water, electric (30 amps), sewer.

TENNESSEE (continued)

Gallatin
Cages Bend Campground, 1125 Benders Ferry Rd., 37066. T: (615) 824-4989. www.reserveusa.com. RV/tent: 43. $19–$23. Hookups: water, electric, sewer.

Gatlinburg
Arrow Creek Campground, 4721 East Pkwy., 37738. T: (865) 430-7433. RV/tent: 63. $16–$20. Hookups: water, electric (20, 30 amps), sewer.

Crazy Horse Campground & RV Resort, 4609 East Pkwy., 37738. T: (800) 528-9003. www.crazyhorse-campground.com. RV/tent: 229. $15–$38. Hookups: water, electric (20, 30, 50 amps), sewer.

Great Smoky Mountains National Park (Cataloochee Camp, Cove Creek, NC), 107 Park Headquarters Rd., 37738. T: (423) 436-1200. www.nps.gov/grsm. RV/tent: 27. $12. Hookups: none.

Greenbrier Island Campground, 2353 East Pkwy., 37738. T: (865) 436-4243. RV/tent: 116. $15–$16. Hookups: water, electric (20, 30 amps), sewer.

Le Conte Vista Campground Resort, 1739 East Pkwy., 37738. T: (865) 436-5437. RV/tent: 75. $19–$23. Hookups: water, electric (15, 30 amps), sewer.

Greenback
Lotterdale Cove, P.O. Box 61, 37742. T: (865) 856-3832. RV/tent: 90. $15. Hookups: electric (20, 30, 50 amps).

Heiskell
Jellystone Camping Resort, 9514 Diggs Gap Rd., 37754. T: (865) 938-6600. RV/tent: 100. $15–$22. Hookups: water, electric (30, 50 amps), sewer.

Henning
Fort Pillow State Park, 3122 Park Rd., 38041. T: (731) 738-5581. F: (731) 738-9117. www.tnstateparks.com. RV/tent: 38. $7. Hookups: none.

Hermitage
Seven Points Campground, Stewarts Ferry Pike, 37076. T: (615) 889-5198. www.reserveusa.com. RV/tent: 60. $17–$25. Hookups: water, electric (30, 50 amps).

Hixson
Chester Frost County Park, 2318 Gold Point Cir. North, 37343. T: (423) 842-0177. RV/tent: 188. $12. Hookups: water, electric (20 amps).

Hohenwald
Thousand Trails–Natchez Trace, 1363 Napier Rd., 38462. T: (931) 796-3212. www.thousandtrails.com. RV/tent: 494. $20. Hookups: water, electric (30 amps), sewer.

Hurricane Mills
KOA–Buffalo, 473 Barren Hollow Rd., 37078. T: (931) 296-1306. www.koa.com. RV/tent: 62. $17–$27. Hookups: water, electric (20, 30, 50 amps), sewer, modem.

Jackson
Jackson Mobile Village & RV Park, 2223 Hollywood Dr., 38305. T: (731) 668-1147. RV/tent: 14. $14. Hookups: water, electric (15, 30 amps), sewer.

Whispering Pines RV Park, 129 McKenzie Rd., 38301. T: (731) 422-3682. RV/tent: 30. $15. Hookups: water, electric (30, 50 amps), sewer.

Jamestown
Maple Hill RV Park, 1386 North York Hwy., US 127, 38556. T: (931) 879-3025. RV/tent: 22. $18–$23. Hookups: water, electric (20, 30, 50 amps), sewer.

Kingston
Four Seasons Campground, 120 Farmer Rd., 37763. T: (800) 990-CAMP. RV/tent: 50. $16–$18. Hookups: water, electric (20, 30 amps), sewer.

Knoxville
Southlake RV Park, 3730 Maryville Pike, 37920. T: (865) 573-1837. RV/tent: 125. $19–$23. Hookups: water, electric (30, 50 amps), sewer, modem.

Kodak
KOA–Knoxville East, 241 KOA Dr., 37764. T: (865) 933-6393. www.koa.com. RV/tent: 153. $19–$27. Hookups: water, electric (20, 30, 50 amps), sewer.

Smoky Mountain Campground, 194 Foretravel Dr., 37764. T: (800) 864-2267. RV/tent: 280. $16. Hookups: water, electric (30, 50 amps), sewer.

Lancaster
Long Branch Campground, 478 Lancaster Rd., 38569. T: (615) 548-8002. www.reserveusa.com. RV/tent: 57. $16–$20. Hookups: water, electric (20, 30 amps).

Lebanon
Countryside Resort, 2100 Safari Camp Rd., 37090. T: (615) 449-5527. www.gocampingamerica.com/countrysidetn. RV/tent: 120. $17–$21. Hookups: water, electric (20, 30, 50 amps), sewer.

Lenoir City
The Crosseyed Cricket, 751 Country Ln., 37771. T: (865) 986-5435. RV/tent: 50. $16–$18. Hookups: water, electric (30, 50 amps), sewer.

Limestone
Davy Crockett Birthplace State Park, 1245 Davy Crockett Park Rd., 37681. T: (423) 257-2167. www.tnstateparks.com. RV/tent: 73. $14–$17. Hookups: water, electric (30 amps), sewer.

Linden
Mousetail Landing State Park, Rte. 3 Box 280B, 37096. T: (731) 847-0841. F: (731) 847-0771. www.tnstateparks.com. RV/tent: 45. $13. Hookups: water, electric (30, 50 amps), sewer.

TENNESSEE (continued)

Manchester

KOA–Manchester, 586 Kampground Rd., 37355. T: (931) 728-9777. F: (931) 728-9750. www.koa.com. RV/tent: 43. $19–$27. Hookups: water, electric (20, 30, 50 amps), sewer, modem.

Whispering Oaks Campground, 812 16th Model Rd., 37355. T: (931) 728-0225. RV/tent: 49. $14–$17. Hookups: water, electric (20, 30 amps), sewer, modem.

Memphis

Camp Memphis/Agricenter International, 7777 Walnut Grove Rd., 38120. T: (901) 757-7790. www. agricenter.org. RV/tent: 600. $18. Hookups: water, electric (30 amps).

Middleton

Thousand Trails–Cherokee Landing, Cherokee Landing Rd., 38052. T: (731) 376-0935. www.thousand trails.com. RV/tent: 296. $20. Hookups: water, electric (30 amps), sewer.

Monroe

Obey River Campground, 100 Park Rd., 38573. T: (931) 864-6388. www.reserveusa.com. RV/tent: 132. $10–$22. Hookups: water, electric (20, 30 amps).

Mt. Juliet

Cedar Creek Campground, 9264 Saundersville Rd., 37122. T: (615) 754-4947. RV/tent: 60. $19–$23. Hookups: water, electric (30 amps).

Nashville

Anderson Road Campground, Anderson Rd., 37217. T: (615) 361-1980. www.reserveusa.com. RV/tent: 37. $11–$13. Hookups: none.

Holiday Nashville Travel Park, 2572 Music Valley Dr., 37214. T: (800) 547-4480. www.citysearch.com/nas/holidaypark. RV/tent: 238. $20–$34. Hookups: water, electric (20, 30, 50 amps), sewer.

Nashville Shores, 4001 Bell Rd., 37076. T: (615) 889-7050. www.nashvilleshores.com. RV/tent: 100. $20–$35. Hookups: water, electric (20, 30, 50 amps), sewer.

Two Rivers Campground, 2616 Music Valley Dr., 37214. T: (615) 883-8559. RV/tent: 105. $20–$28. Hookups: water, electric (20, 30, 50 amps), sewer.

Newport

KOA–Newport I–40/Smoky Mtns, 240 KOA Ln., 37821. T: (423) 623-9004. www.koa.com. RV/tent: 99. $19–$24. Hookups: water, electric (20, 30, 50 amps), sewer, modem.

Triple Creek Campground, 141 Lower Bogard Rd., 37821. T: (423) 623-2020. RV/tent: 79. $10–$15. Hookups: water, electric (20, 30, 50 amps), sewer.

Old Hickory

Shutes Branch Campground, 501 Weather Station Rd., 37075. T: (615) 754-4847. www.reserve usa.com. RV/tent: 35. $11–$17. Hookups: water, electric (30, 50 amps), sewer.

Pickwick Dam

Pickwick Landing State Park, Park Rd., 38365. T: (731) 689-3129. www.tnstateparks.com. RV/tent: 48. $14–$17. Hookups: water, electric (20, 30, 50 amps).

Pigeon Forge

Alpine Hideaway Campground, 251 Spring Valley Rd., 37863. T: (865) 428-3285. RV/tent: 80. $19. Hookups: water, electric (20, 30, 50 amps), sewer.

Clabough's Campground & Market, 405 Wears Valley Rd., 37863. T: (800) 965-8524. RV/tent: 170. $19–$25. Hookups: water, electric (30, 50 amps), sewer.

Creekside Campground, 2475 Henderson Springs Rd., 37863. T: (800) 498-4801. RV/tent: 75. $20–$24. Hookups: water, electric (30, 50 amps), sewer, modem.

Eagle's Nest Campground, 1111 Wears Valley Rd., 37863. T: (865) 428-5841. RV/tent: 200. $17–$22.50. Hookups: water, electric (20, 30 amps), sewer.

Foothills Campground & Cabins, 4235 Huskey St., 37863. T: (888) 428-3818. RV/tent: 39. $20. Hookups: water, electric (20, 30 amps), sewer.

King's Holly Haven RV Park, 647 Wears Valley Rd., 37863. T: (865) 453-5352. RV/tent: 170. $16–$23.40. Hookups: water, electric (20, 30, 50 amps), sewer.

Riverbend Campground, 2479 Riverbend Loop 1, 37863. T: (865) 453-1224. www.smokymtnmall. com/mall/river.html. RV/tent: 120. $16. Hookups: water, electric (30, 50 amps), sewer.

Z Buda's Smokies Campground, 4020 Pkwy., 37863. T: (865) 453-4129. RV/tent: 308. $18. Hookups: water, electric (15, 20, 30 amps), sewer.

Pocahontas

Big Hill Pond State Park, 984 John Howell Rd., 38061. T: (731) 645-7967. www.tnstateparks.com. RV/tent: 30. $10. Hookups: none.

Roan Mountain

Roan Mountain State Resort Park, 1015 Hwy. 143, 37687. T: (423) 772-4178. www.tnstateparks.com. RV/tent: 107. $14–$17. Hookups: water, electric (30 amps).

Sevierville

Ripplin' Waters Campground, 1930 Winfield Dunn Pkwy., 37876. T: (888) RIPPLIN. RV/tent: 156. $18–$19. Hookups: water, electric (20, 30, 50 amps), sewer.

Riverside RV Park & Resort, 4280 Boyds Creek Hwy., 37876. T: (800) 341-7534. www.riverside-camp.com. RV/tent: 180. $16–$20. Hookups: water, electric (30, 50 amps), sewer, modem.

TENNESSEE (continued)

Silver Point

Floating Mill Park Campground, 430 Floating Mill Ln., 38582. T: (931) 858-4845. www.reserveusa. com. RV/tent: 118. $14–$20. Hookups: water, electric (20, 30 amps).

Smithville

Holmes Creek, 2620 Casey Cove Rd., 37166. T: (615) 597-7191. www.reserveusa.com. RV/tent: 97. $14–$20. Hookups: water, electric (20 amps).

Smyrna

Nashville I-24 Campground, 1130 Rocky Fork Rd., 37167. T: (615) 459-5818. RV/tent: 150. $13–$18. Hookups: water, electric (20, 30, 50 amps), sewer, modem.

Springville

Buchanan Resort, 785 Buchanan Resort Rd., 38256. T: (731) 642-2828. www.buchananresort.com. RV/tent: 38. $20. Hookups: water, electric (20, 30, 50 amps), sewer.

Ten Mile

Fooshee Pass (TVA), Rte. 1 Box 504, 37880. T: (423) 334-4842. RV/tent: 55. $11–$15. Hookups: electric (30 amps).

Hornsby Hollow (TVA-Watts Bar Lake), Rte. 1 Box 61, 37880. T: (423) 334-1709. RV/tent: 99. $11–$15. Hookups: water, electric (30, 50 amps).

Townsend

Big Meadow Family Campground, 8215 Cedar Creek Rd., 37882. T: (888) 497-0625. F: (865) 448-3346. www.bigmeadowcampground.com. RV/tent: 86. $24–$35. Hookups: water, electric (30, 50 amps), sewer, modem.

Lazy Daze Campground, 8429 Hwy. 73, 37882. T: (865) 448-6061. F: (865) 448-9060. www.go campingamerica.com/lazydaze. RV/tent: 74. $18–$25. Hookups: water, electric (20, 30 amps), sewer.

Mountaineer Campground, 8451 Hwy. 73, 37882. T: (865) 448-6421. F: (865) 448-2386. www.go campingamerica.com/mountaineer. RV/tent: 49. $19–$26. Hookups: water, electric (30 amps), sewer.

Tuckaleechee Campground, 7301 Punkin Ln., 37882. T: (865) 448-9608. RV/tent: 134. $12–$20. Hookups: water, electric (20, 30 amps), sewer.

Vonore

Notchy Creek Campground, 1235 Corntassle, 37885. T: (423) 884-6280. RV/tent: 51. $15. Hookups: electric (30, 50 amps).

Toqua Beach Campground, Hwy. 360, 37885. T: (423) 884-2344. RV/tent: 25. $15. Hookups: water, electric (30, 50 amps).

Wildersville

Natchez Trace State Park, 24845 Natchez Trace Rd., 38388. T: (731) 968-8176. www.tnstateparks.com. RV/tent: 210. $14–$19. Hookups: water, electric (20, 30, 50 amps), sewer.

Winchester

Tims Ford State Park, 570 Tims Ford Dr., 37398. T: (931) 962-1181. www.tnstateparks.com. RV/tent: 50. $14–$17. Hookups: water, electric (20, 30 amps).

Yuma

Parker's Crossroads Campground, 22580 Hwy. 22 North, 38390. T: (731) 968-9939. home.aeneas. net/~wksmith/pcamp.htm. RV/tent: 75. $14–$19. Hookups: water, electric (20, 30, 50 amps), sewer

Index

Georgia

Notes

Notes

Notes

Notes

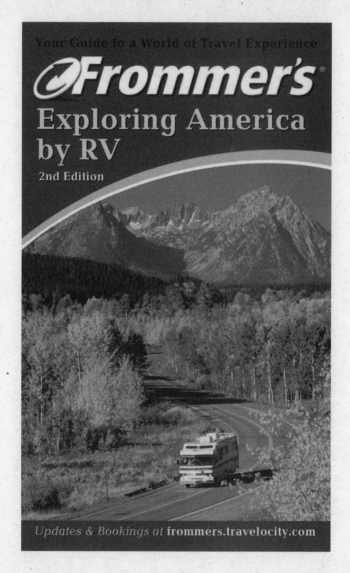